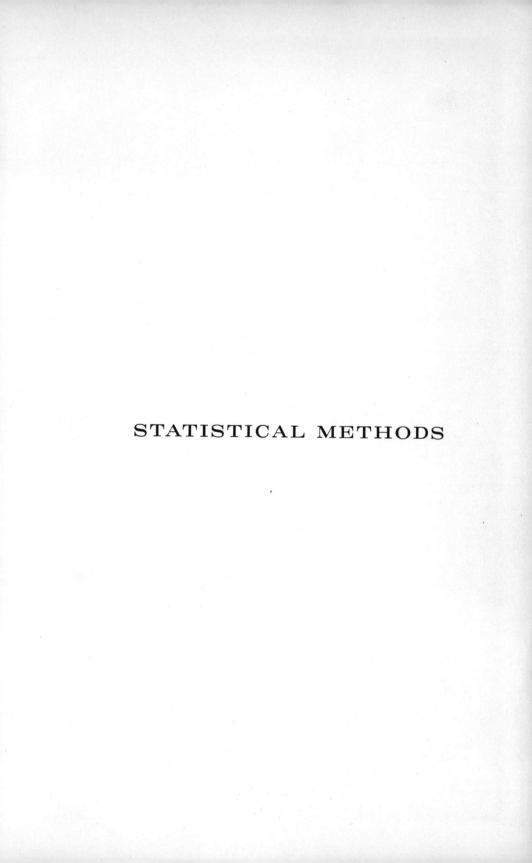

STATISTICAL METHODS

BOOKS BY ALLEN L. EDWARDS

Experimental Design in Psychological Research, Revised Edition
Statistical Methods, Second Edition
Statistical Analysis, Revised Edition
*Workbook to Accompany the Revised Edition
of Statistical Analysis*
*The Social Desirability Variable in Personality
Assessment and Research*
*Expected Values of Discrete Random Variables
and Elementary Statistics*
Techniques of Attitude Scale Construction

ALLEN L. EDWARDS
UNIVERSITY OF WASHINGTON

STATISTICAL
METHODS

Second Edition

HOLT, RINEHART AND WINSTON, INC.

New York · Chicago · San Francisco · Atlanta · Dallas
Montreal · Toronto · London

To Steven

Preface

To say that the behavioral sciences involve a high degree of empiricism is not to deny that theory often plays an important role in these sciences. Rather it is to emphasize that the behavioral sciences are intimately associated with the raw stuff of empiricism—observational data. Theory may be the guide to the choice of observations to be made. Theory may also assist in the integration of conclusions drawn from the data with current knowledge. But the first concern of the behavioral sciences is still with research based upon data and with the conclusions drawn from such data.

Any research worker in the behavioral sciences knows, however, that raw data are seldom in a form such that the conclusions to be drawn from the data are either immediate or obvious. Observations must first be processed, analyzed, or operated upon. In these activities of the behavioral scientist, statistical methods play an important role. It is primarily as a consequence of the application of statistical methods to data that the behavioral scientist decides what conclusions are warranted by the data.

This text illustrates some of the applications of statistical methods in one of the behavioral sciences, psychology. Although the problems and examples are drawn primarily from psychology, students in other behavioral sciences may find the text of interest.

I have assumed that the student reading this text has a working knowledge of algebra. Appendix A provides a brief review of some elementary mathematical rules and principles for those students who may need to revive latent memories. Sets, probability, and the mathematical expectation of a random variable are discussed briefly in Chapter 8. This chapter, like all others in the text, was not written for the student who already has an intimate knowledge of the content of the chapter. It was written for the student who, for one reason or another, needs an introduction to or a brief review of these three important topics. Starting with Chapter 9, I make frequent use of the principles developed in Chapter 8.

In the text itself I have included many proofs. In the early chapters, these proofs are given in sufficient detail that all students should be able to follow them. In later chapters some of the proofs are more concise. The student who has successfully followed the earlier proofs and who understands the text should not have much difficulty in supplying the missing steps. In quite a few cases, I have not given a proof in the text itself, but instead have asked the reader to develop the proof in one of the examples at the end of a chapter. It would be unfair to ask the reader to do something and then not to inform him as to how he performed. I have, therefore, included in Appendix C all of the proofs asked for in the examples.

At the end of each chapter I have included a substantial number of problems and examples. I cannot overemphasize the importance of actually trying to work the examples without referring to the discussion in the text. Doing so provides the reader with an opportunity to find out what he has learned and, equally important, what he has failed to learn and needs to review. Answers to all the examples are given in Appendix C or in the text.

I am indebted to S. Kachigan and Alan J. Klockars for reading the manuscript for errors and for checking all of my calculations.

In addition, I am indebted to the late Sir Ronald A. Fisher and to Messrs. Oliver and Boyd, Ltd., Edinburgh, for permission to reprint Tables IV, V, and VI from their book, *Statistical Methods for Research Workers*. Table I is reproduced by permission of M. G. Kendall and B. B. Smith and the Royal Statistical Society. Portions of Table II have been taken from *Handbook of Statistical Nomographs, Tables and Formulas* by permission of J. W. Dunlap and A. K. Kurtz. Table VIII has been reproduced from G. W. Snedecor's book, *Statistical Methods*, by permission of the author and his publisher, the Iowa State College Press. Table IX is reprinted from *Elementaty Mathematical Tables* by permission of D. E. Smith, W. D. Reeve, and E. L. Morss and their publishers, Ginn & Company. Table X is reprinted by permission of M. D. Davidoff and H. W. Goheen and the Psychometric Society. Table XIII was made possible by permission of E. G. Olds and the Institute of Mathematical Statistics. Table XV is reprinted by permission of Colin White and the Biometric Society.

To the various authors and to the publishers of *Personnel Psychology, Journal of Experimental Education, Journal of Social Psychology, American Psychologist, Journal of Applied Psychology, Journal of Experimental Psychology, Psychological Review, Journal of Abnormal and Social Psychology, American Journal of Psychology, Journal of the Royal Statistical Society, Biometrika, Journal of the American Statistical Association, Annals of Mathematical Statistics, Biometrics,* and *Psychometrika,* I am indebted for permission to quote material and to make use of data published in these journals.

A. L. E.

Seattle, Washington
February 1967

Contents

STATISTICAL METHODS

Measures of Central Tendency and Variability

1.1 Introduction

Statistical methods are tools that can be used in analyzing data and solving problems. The best way to see this is to begin at once by applying statistical methods to a particular problem. The problem we have selected, for purposes of illustration, concerns learning with and without knowledge of results. We present the data obtained in an experiment designed to investigate a certain aspect of this problem and apply statistical methods in analyzing the data. We shall see that statistical methods help us in obtaining answers to questions of interest about the results of the experiment.

In this chapter, we shall not be able to answer all the questions of interest, because the answers to some of these questions require methods of statistical analysis that are more advanced than those that can be presented in an introductory chapter. These methods of statistical analysis will be described in later chapters and, at that time, we shall see how they can be applied to the results of the experiment described here.

1.2 A Problem in Learning

Teaching machines and programed texts are subjects of interest to both teachers and students. In one type of programed text, the student reads a brief passage of one or two sentences called a frame. The sentences in a frame contain one or more blank spaces. For each blank space, the student is required to write a response that will complete the sentence. The answer judged by the author to be correct for a given frame is printed in the text but is concealed from the student until he has made his response. Once the student has responded to the frame, he can then determine immediately whether his response is correct or incorrect by checking it against the printed answer to the frame.

When a reward is administered almost immediately after a response to some stimulus has been made, the response is said to be reinforced. In the case of a programed text, the stimulus is the sentence containing the blank space and the response is the word or term written by the student to complete the sentence. If a student's response to a frame is correct, he receives an almost immediate reward when he checks his answer against the printed answer in the text. Reinforcing a student's response when it is correct is believed to increase the likelihood that it will be elicited by the same stimulus on subsequent occasions and thus to promote learning of the correct response. Of course, if the student responds with the wrong word to a frame, his response is not reinforced. But in a well-written programed text of the kind described, each frame is such that almost all students are able to give the correct answer.

From the viewpoint of learning, there are two basic principles involved in programed texts. The first is that learning requires activity by the student. A programed text forces the student to be active by requiring that he respond to each frame by writing his answer. The second principle is sometimes referred to as "knowledge of results," that is, being told immediately after a response has been made that it is either correct or incorrect. There is considerable evidence to indicate that knowledge of results facilitates learning. Whether this is so because knowledge of results permits the immediate reinforcement of correct responses or because of some other principle need not concern us at this time. Instead, our concern is with a simple experiment that compares the relative effectiveness of learning with and without knowledge of results.

1.3   A Learning Experiment

The subjects for our experiment were 20 pairs of students. The students were paired on the basis of their scores on an academic aptitude test that we have reason to believe is a variable related to learning and retention. One student in each pair is randomly assigned to an *experimental group*, which will study the material with knowledge of results, and the other to a *control group*, which will study the material without knowledge of results. By pairing the students on the basis of their academic aptitude scores we hope to control for any possible difference between the control and experimental groups in learning ability or aptitude.[1]

The experimental group is given a programed text of the kind described earlier in which the correct response to each frame appears on the page fol-

---

[1] This is not the major reason for pairing the subjects in the control and experimental groups, but an adequate explanation of the major reason requires an understanding of material covered in subsequent chapters. See, for example, the discussion of pairing in Chapter 10.

lowing the frame. The student in the experimental group writes his response to a frame, turns the page, and knows immediately whether his response is correct or incorrect. The second frame appears on the same page as the correct response to the first frame. The student answers the second frame, turns the page, and finds the correct answer and also the next frame. He continues in this fashion until he has answered all of the frames in the material he has been given.

The members of the control group receive exactly the same frames as the students in the experimental group except that the correct responses are not given. The student writes his response to each frame, but he cannot then check to determine whether his response is correct or incorrect.

The students in the control and experimental groups attend the same class at the same time for three days each week. At each class session the students study the same section or chapter of the same programed text. At the end of four weeks they are given a criterion test that has been prepared by the author of the programed text to determine their achievement. The numbers given in Table 1.1 are the number of correct responses on the criterion test for each pair of students. We may regard these scores as an index of the degree to which the students have learned the material that they have studied. The scores are the outcome or result of the experiment.[2] We shall use them to illustrate the calculation of various statistics.

1.4   The Range as a Measure of Variability

The scores given in Table 1.1 are values of a *variable*. In this case the variable is the number of correct responses on the criterion test. It is convenient to designate a variable by a capital letter such as X. We have a set of 20 observations of X, one for each of the 20 subjects in the control group. We may represent these 20 observations by $X_1, X_2, X_3, \cdots, X_{20}$. Associated with each observation is a value of the variable and these values are given in Column (2). Thus $X_1 = 14$, $X_2 = 8$, $X_3 = 15, \cdots, X_{20} = 9$. In order to distinguish the scores of the experimental group from those of the control group, we use Y to designate the variable for the experimental group. We also have a set of 20 observations of Y, one for each member of the experimental group, and associated with each of the observations is a value of the variable Y, shown in column (3). Thus $Y_1 = 18$, $Y_2 = 12$, $Y_3 = 10, \cdots, Y_{20} = 8$.

The first thing we may note about the X values in Table 1.1 is that they *vary*, and this is also true for the Y values. One measure of variability is the *range*, which we define as the difference between the largest and the smallest

---

[2] The scores given in Table 1.1 are hypothetical. They are, however, consistent with the outcome of an experiment described by Lublin (1965) in which it was found that the control group obtained a higher mean score on the criterion test than the experimental group.

Table 1.1—Scores on an achievement test for paired subjects in a control and in an experimental group

(1) Pair	(2) Control group X	(3) Experimental group Y
1	14	18
2	8	12
3	15	10
4	16	9
5	8	14
6	15	10
7	15	9
8	17	11
9	18	13
10	13	6
11	10	16
12	19	14
13	20	16
14	17	8
15	14	8
16	10	8
17	14	9
18	15	10
19	13	11
20	9	8
Σ	280	220

observed values of a variable for a given set of measurements. Thus

$$R = X_H - X_L \tag{1.1}$$

where R = the range

X_H = the largest observed value in a given set of measurements

X_L = the smallest observed value is a given set of measurements

For the control group the largest value is $X_{13} = 20$ and the smallest value is $X_2 = X_5 = 8$ and the range is therefore 12. For the experimental group the largest value is $Y_1 = 18$ and the smallest value is $Y_{10} = 6$ and the range for this group is also 12.

If we let n equal the total number of observations in a given set, then we may note that the value of the range is determined only by the two observations with the most extreme values. The range, in other words, does not make use of any of the information about variability that may be provided by the values of the remaining $n - 2$ observations. We shall see later that there are more sensitive measures of variability than the range. These measures of variability are based upon the information provided by all n values of the observations in a given set and not just upon the two most extreme values.

1.5 The Arithmetic Mean and the Difference between Two Means

We paired the subjects in the control and experimental groups on the basis of their academic aptitude test scores. Presumably, then, any difference between the performance of a pair of subjects on the criterion test should not be the result of individual differences in learning ability and retention as measured by the aptitude test. Now, let us assume for the moment, with an understanding that the assumption may be in error, that students will learn just as well without as with knowledge of results. If this assumption is correct, then it also seems reasonable to believe that whether $D = X - Y$ is positive or negative should be a matter of chance. But, if only chance is operating, then it should be just as likely for D to be positive as negative, and this, in turn, means that we would expect 10 values of D to be positive and 10 to be negative.

The values of $D = X - Y$ are given in column (4) of Table 1.2. We note that 16 of the D values are positive and this means that 16 of the subjects in the control group have higher scores on the achievement test than their paired associates in the experimental group. The fact that 16 of the differences favor the member of the control group when by chance only 10 should, would seem to offer some evidence against the belief that knowledge of results necessarily facilitates learning.[3]

Let us consider another possible measure of the difference in performance between the experimental and control groups. This measure is the difference between the means of the two groups. We define the *mean* of a given set of measures as

$$\overline{X} = \frac{\Sigma X}{n} \tag{1.2}$$

where $\overline{X}$ = the arithmetic mean
 n = the number of values of X
 ΣX = the sum of the n values of X

Substituting in (1.2) with the values of X given in Table 1.2, we have

$$\overline{X} = \frac{14 + 8 + 15 + \cdots + 9}{20} = \frac{280}{20} = 14.0$$

---

[3] In Chapter 9 a method is described for determining the probability of 16 or more positive values of D under the hypothesis that negative and positive values are equally likely.

Table 1.2—Achievement test scores of control subjects who studied without and experimental subjects who studied with knowledge of results

Pair	Group		Difference between pairs	Deviations and squared deviations					
	C	E							
(1)	(2)	(3)	(4)	(5)	(6)	(7)	(8)	(9)	(10)
	X	Y	D	x	x^2	y	y^2	d	d^2
1	14	18	−4	0	0	7	49	−7	49
2	8	12	−4	−6	36	1	1	−7	49
3	15	10	5	1	1	−1	1	2	4
4	16	9	7	2	4	−2	4	4	16
5	8	14	−6	−6	36	3	9	−9	81
6	15	10	5	1	1	−1	1	2	4
7	15	9	6	1	1	−2	4	3	9
8	17	11	6	3	9	0	0	3	9
9	18	13	5	4	16	2	4	2	4
10	13	6	7	−1	1	−5	25	4	16
11	10	16	−6	−4	16	5	25	−9	81
12	19	14	5	5	25	3	9	2	4
13	20	16	4	6	36	5	25	1	1
14	17	8	9	3	9	−3	9	6	36
15	14	8	6	0	0	−3	9	3	9
16	10	8	2	−4	16	−3	9	−1	1
17	14	9	5	0	0	−2	4	2	4
18	15	10	5	1	1	−1	1	2	4
19	13	11	2	−1	1	0	0	−1	1
20	9	8	1	−5	25	−3	9	−2	4
Σ	280	220	60	0	234	0	198	0	386

for the mean of the control group. Similarly, we have

$$\bar{Y} = \frac{\sum Y}{n} = \frac{18 + 12 + 10 + \cdots + 8}{20} = \frac{220}{20} = 11.0$$

for the mean of the experimental group. Note that the mean of the differences between the paired values is

$$\bar{D} = \frac{\sum D}{n} = \frac{-4 + (-4) + 5 + \cdots + 1}{20} = \frac{60}{20} = 3.0$$

and that

$$\bar{D} = \bar{X} - \bar{Y} \qquad (1.3)$$

The fact that the mean score of the control group is higher than the mean score for the experimental group provides evidence that, on the average, the control group scores higher on the criterion test than the experimental group. Recall that one member of each pair was assigned at random to the control group and the other to the experimental group. If knowledge of results facilitates learning, then, in general, each member of the experimental group might be expected to score higher on the criterion test than his paired associate in the control group. If this were true, then the mean for the experimental group should be larger than the mean for the control group and $\bar{D}$ should be negative, whereas, it is, in fact, positive.

We have defined the mean as

$$\bar{X} = \frac{\sum X}{n}$$

and multiplying both sides by n, we obtain

$$n\bar{X} = \sum X \tag{1.4}$$

Consequently, we may in any expression involving $\sum X$ substitute $n\bar{X}$ without changing the meaning or value of the expression. The identity given by (1.4) is an important one and we shall have occasion to use it frequently in later developments.

1.6   The Average Deviation as a Measure of Variability

We shall use x to represent the deviation of a given value of X from the mean of a set of measures. Thus, we define

$$x = X - \bar{X} \tag{1.5}$$

Similarly, $y = Y - \bar{Y}$ and $d = D - \bar{D}$. The values of x, y, and d are given in columns (5), (7), and (9), respectively, in Table 1.2. We note that the sums of these columns are all equal to zero.

We can easily prove that the sum of the deviations of the n values of a variable from the mean of the set is always equal to zero. Summing (1.5), we have

$$\sum x = \sum (X - \bar{X}) = \sum X - n\bar{X}$$

But we have shown that $\sum X = n\bar{X}$ and therefore

$$\sum x = \sum (X - \bar{X}) = 0 \tag{1.6}$$

The fact that the sum of the deviations from the mean is always equal to zero is the reason why we cannot simply add the deviations and divide by n to obtain a measure of the average deviation.

We can, however, ignore the signs of the deviations and find the sum of the *absolute* values and divide this sum by n. The resulting value is called the *average deviation*. Thus

$$AD = \frac{\sum |x|}{n} = \frac{\sum |X - \bar{X}|}{n} \tag{1.7}$$

where AD = the average deviation
   $\sum |x|$ = the sum of the absolute values of x
   n = the number of observations in the set

For the control group, we have

$$AD = \frac{\sum |x|}{n} = \frac{54}{20} = 2.7$$

and for the experimental group we have

$$AD = \frac{\sum |y|}{n} = \frac{52}{20} = 2.6$$

The average deviation, because it takes into account the absolute values of all n deviations from the mean, is a somewhat more sensitive measure of variability than the range. In terms of the average deviation, the control group measures are only slightly more variable than those of the experimental group.

The average deviation is one of the easiest measures of variability to understand and had great popularity at one time. It has been found, however, to be of limited utility in statistical theory.

1.7   The Variance and Standard Deviation as Measures of Variability

The most valuable measure of variability is the variance or the square root of the variance, which is called the standard deviation. The variance is based upon the squares of the deviations of the X values from the mean. In calculating the average deviation, the algebraic signs of the deviations were ignored. In doing so we lose valuable algebraic properties of the deviations and of any measure based upon them. Squaring the deviations will maintain the algebraic properties of the deviations. Furthermore, as we shall show later, the sum of squared deviations from the mean is less than the sum of squared deviations from any other value not equal to the mean.[4]

If we square each of the deviations from the mean, sum, and divide by $n-1$, we obtain the *mean square* or *variance* which we designate by s^2. This definition of the variance may be written

---

[4] Minimizing a sum of squared deviations plays an important role in statistical theory and also has practical applications, as we shall see later.

$$s^2 = \frac{\sum (X - \bar{X})^2}{n - 1} = \frac{\sum x^2}{n - 1} \qquad (1.8)$$

The *standard deviation* is the square root of the variance. Thus the standard deviation is equal to $\sqrt{s^2}$ or, as it is more commonly expressed,

$$s = \sqrt{\frac{\sum (X - \bar{X})^2}{n - 1}} = \sqrt{\frac{\sum x^2}{n - 1}} \qquad (1.9)$$

where s = the standard deviation

$\sum x^2$ = the sum of squared deviations from the mean of a set

n = the number of observations in the set

The calculation of the standard deviation may be summarized in the following steps:

1. Find the mean $\qquad\qquad\qquad\qquad\qquad\qquad \bar{X} = \sum X/n$
2. Find the deviation of each value of X from $\qquad x = X - \bar{X}$
   the mean
3. Square each deviation $\qquad\qquad\qquad\qquad\qquad x^2 = (X - \bar{X})^2$
4. Find the sum of the squared deviations $\qquad \sum x^2 = \sum (X - \bar{X})^2$
   (sum of squares)
5. Divide the sum of squares by $n - 1$ to find $\qquad s^2 = \sum x^2/(n - 1)$
   the variance or mean square
6. Extract the square root to find the standard $\qquad s = \sqrt{\sum x^2/(n - 1)}$
   deviation

Extracting the square root (step 6) returns us to our original unit of measurement. For example, if the original values of X were in terms of inches, the standard deviation also would be in terms of inches.

The values of x^2, y^2, and d^2 are given in columns (6), (8), and (10), respectively, in Table 1.2. For the control group, we have

$$s_X{}^2 = \frac{\sum x^2}{n - 1} = \frac{234}{20 - 1} = 12.3158$$

and

$$s_X = \sqrt{\frac{\sum x^2}{n - 1}} = \sqrt{\frac{234}{20 - 1}} = 3.51$$

Similarly, for the experimental group, we have

$$s_Y{}^2 = \frac{\sum y^2}{n - 1} = \frac{198}{20 - 1} = 10.4211$$

and

$$s_Y = \sqrt{\frac{\sum y^2}{n-1}} = \sqrt{\frac{198}{20-1}} = 3.23$$

We note that s_X is only slightly greater than s_Y. Thus the variability in performance of the control and experimental groups, as measured by the standard deviation, is approximately the same for both groups. This finding is consistent with the results obtained when we measured variability in performance of the two groups by means of the average deviation. There also we found that there was only a slight difference between the average deviation for the control group and the average deviation for the experimental group.

We may note the following identity. We have

$$s^2 = \frac{\sum x^2}{n-1}$$

and multiplying both sides by $n - 1$, we obtain

$$(n-1)s^2 = \sum x^2 \tag{1.10}$$

It will be useful in later discussions to know that we may interchange $(n-1)s^2$ and $\sum x^2$ in a given expression without changing the meaning of the expression.

1.8   The Median as a Measure of Central Tendency

The *median* of a set of n values of a variable X may be defined as that value above which and below which 50 percent of the measurements fall. We illustrate the calculation of the median with the scores of the experimental group. Our first step is to arrange the scores given in column (3) of Table 1.2 in order of magnitude from lowest to highest. Column (1) of Table 1.3 gives the values of Y from 18 to 6, the highest and lowest observed values. Column (2) gives the frequency or number of times each value of Y was observed. Measurements arranged in the manner of Table 1.3 are called frequency distributions. A *frequency distribution* shows each possible value of a variable within the range observed and the number of times each value occurred in a set of n observations.

It is customary to regard measurements of *continuous* variables as representing intervals ranging from half a unit below to half a unit above their observed or recorded values. A height recorded in inches, for example, may be regarded as representing an interval ranging from 1/2 inch below up to 1/2 inch above the recorded value. A height of 72 inches, in other words, may indicate a value ranging from 71.5 up to 72.5 inches. If the height were reported to the nearest 1/10 inch, 71.8 inches, for example, it would be regarded

Table 1.3—Frequency distribution of scores on an achievement test for the 20 subjects in the experimental group

(1) Scores	(2) f
18	1
17	
16	2
15	
14	2
13	1
12	1
11	2
10	3
9	3
8	4
7	
6	1
Σ	20

as representing an interval ranging from 71.75 up to 71.85 inches. This is because there are limits to the accuracy of any measuring instrument. Regardless of how fine we may make our units of measurement—that is, how many decimal places we use in reporting them—we still do not know the precise value of the measurement of any continuous variable. Thus although a variable such as length may be continuous, observed or recorded values of the variable are always discrete.

The variable Y, score on the criterion test, is not a continuous variable. The variable is *discrete* because Y can only take the possible values of $0, 1, 2, \cdots, n$, where n is the number of items included in the test. A student may obtain a score of 16 or 17 on the test, but he cannot obtain a score Y such that $16 < Y < 17$. We shall regard measurements of variables which are, in fact, discrete in the same manner as we regard discrete measures of variables which are, in fact, continuous. Thus a score on the criterion test of 20 may be regarded as representing an interval ranging from 19.5 up to 20.5.

To find the median, we first find $n/2$ which, because we have 20 observations in the experimental group, is 10. We wish to find the Y value above which and below which 50 percent or 10 of the measurements fall. If we count upward from the lowest score, we find that $1 + 4 + 3$ will give us 8 of the needed 10 observations. This carries us through the score of 9. There are three values of $Y = 10$ and we need two of these three values. We shall assume that the three observations with $Y = 10$ are distributed uniformly through the interval 9.5 to 10.5. To interpolate into the interval, we merely divide the needed number of observations by the number within the interval and multiply by the width of the interval. Since we need two additional observations to make 10 and since the number within the interval is 3 and since the width of the interval, which we designate by i, is from 9.5 to 10.5 or 1, we have

$$2/3 = .67$$

We add the value obtained above to the lower limit, 9.5, of the interval in which we know the median falls. This gives us the value of the median. Thus we obtain $9.50 + .67 = 10.17$ as the value of the median.

Sometimes in computing the median where we have an even number of observations, we may find that 50 percent of the measurements or scores take us exactly through a given score but that there is a gap between the upper limit of this score and the next score. By a gap, we mean that the possible values between the two scores are missing or do not occur. For example, suppose we had the following measurements: 8, 18, 16, 7, 5, 10, 14, 17. Rearranging these measurements in order of size, we have, from the lowest to the highest:

$$5, 7, 8, 10, 14, 16, 17, 18$$

For this example, n is equal to 8, and 50 percent of n is equal to 4. We need to find the value above which and below which four scores will fall. Counting up from the bottom or lowest score we find that the first four scores take us through 10, the upper limit of which is 10.5. It is true that 50 percent of the scores do fall below 10.5, and that 50 percent fall above this value. But it is also true that 50 percent fall above and below any other value we might choose to select between 10.5 and 13.5. Under these circumstances *we assume that the value that best represents the median is the mid-point of the gap*, 10.5 to 13.5. The range of the gap is equal to $13.5 - 10.5 = 3$. One half of 3 is equal to 1.5, and 1.5 added to the upper limit of 10.5 gives a value of 12 for the median.

If, in the distribution above, there were no gap, that is, if 10 had been followed by 11 rather than by 14, then the median would become *the dividing point between these two scores*. Since the upper limit of 10 is 10.5 and the lower limit of 11 is 10.5, the value arrived at for the median would be 10.5.

The following formula for computing the median will handle all situations except when the median falls in a gap in the distribution of measurements.

$$Mdn = l + \left(\frac{\frac{n}{2} - \sum f_b}{f_w} \right) i \tag{1.11}$$

where Mdn = the median

       l = the lower limit of the interval containing the median

     n = the total number of observations

  Σf_b = the sum of the frequencies or the number of observations below the interval containing the median

   f_w = the frequency or number of observations within the interval containing the median

    i = the size or range of the interval (In the illustrations considered, since i has always equaled 1, it may be ignored; we include it here because this is a more generalized formula which can be used later.)

When the median falls within a gap, its value can readily be determined in the manner described earlier, and no formula is necessary. Formula (1.11) is applicable to measures arranged in a frequency distribution as in Table 1.3 or to measures that have merely been arranged in order of size without a frequency distribution.

We may note, from the definition of the median as that value of X below which and above which 50 percent of the measurements fall, that the median is not influenced by the magnitude or numerical value of the measurements falling on each side of it. The median, for example, would be unchanged if we arbitrarily added 100 to a value of X falling above it. The mean, on the other hand, is the center of balance of the measurements, and changing the value of any single measurement in a distribution would influence the mean. Because the sum of the deviations from the mean is equal to zero, the mean must fall at that point in the distribution of measurements where the sum of the negative deviations balances exactly or is equal to the sum of the positive deviations. Changing any single measurement will move the center of balance and result in a new value for the mean.

1.9   The Semi-Interquartile Range

The measure of variation generally used in connection with the median is the *semi-interquartile range* or Q. To find the value of Q, two other values must be computed: Q_1, the first quartile, and Q_3, the third quartile. Q_1 is the value of X below which 25 percent of the measurements fall and above which 75 percent fall, and Q_3 is the value of X below which 75 percent fall and above which 25 percent fall.[5] To obtain Q_1 we modify formula (1.11) as follows:

---

[5] The median, Q_1, and Q_3 are equivalent to the 50th, 25th, and 75th *centiles*, respectively. The value of X corresponding to any given centile, which we designate by C, is simply that value below which and above which a specified percent of the total number of observations fall. For example, the value of X corresponding to the 90th centile or C_{90} would be that value below which 90 percent of the measurements fall and above which 10 percent fall.

$$Q_1 = l + \left(\frac{\frac{n}{4} - \Sigma f_b}{f_w} \right) i \tag{1.12}$$

where Q_1 = the first quartile

l = the lower limit of the interval containing Q_1

n = the total number of observations

Σf_b = the sum of the frequencies or number of observations *below* the interval containing Q_1

f_w = the frequency or number of observations within the interval containing Q_1

i = the size or range of the interval

It is important to note that the symbols, l, Σf_b, and f_w now refer to Q_1 rather than the median. To find Q_3, we would substitute $3n/4$ or 75 percent of n for $n/2$ in (1.11).[6] The symbols l, Σf_b, and f_w would now refer to Q_3 rather than the median.

The interval $Q_3 - Q_1$ contains the middle 50 percent of the measurements and is known as the *interquartile range*. The semi-interquartile range is one half of the range of the middle 50 percent of the cases and is given by the following formula

$$Q = \frac{Q_3 - Q_1}{2} \tag{1.14}$$

where Q = the semi-interquartile range

Q_3 = the third quartile

Q_1 = the first quartile

1.10   Other Measures of Central Tendency and Variability

There are other kinds of averages than those we have mentioned. One is the *mode*, or measure that occurs most frequently in the distribution of measurements. Another is the *geometric mean*, which is the nth root of the product of the n values of a variable. The geometric mean of 3 and 12, for example, would be $\sqrt{(3)(12)} = \sqrt{36} = 6$, whereas the arithmetic mean would be 7.5. We shall have occasion to refer again briefly to the geometric mean in connection with measures of relationships. Another measure of central tendency is the *harmonic mean*, which is defined as the reciprocal of the arithmetic mean of the reciprocals of the measurements. The harmonic mean is used in problems involving the averaging of rates.

There are also other measures of variability in addition to those we have

---

[6] It is obvious that (1.11) can, with appropriate modifications, be used to find the value of X corresponding to any centile. For example, to find the 90th centile we would have $C_{90} = l + [(.9n - \Sigma f_b)/f_w]i$, where l, Σf_b, and f_w now refer to C_{90}.

described. One such is the *middle 80 percent range*. Another is the *probable deviation* or *probable error*, which was widely used in the past, but which is practically never used now to describe variability. The probable deviation is approximately 2/3 the size (more precisely, .6745) of the standard deviation.

The measures of central tendency and variability that we have treated briefly in this section are used very infrequently in the behavioral sciences and, with the exception of the geometric mean, have little bearing upon the statistical methods developed later. We shall consequently say no more about them. Our basic measure of central tendency will be the mean, and our basic measure of variability will be the standard deviation or its square, the variance. We shall refer to these measures constantly. Be sure that you thoroughly understand their calculation.

1.11   Samples and Statistics

We have more or less avoided the use of the term "sample" up to this point, but to continue to do so would prove awkward. In your own experience you have "sampled" foods and then made judgments or based future reactions on your experience with these samples; that is, you may ask for more or you may refuse more because you assume that the remainder of the food will be very much like the sample you tasted. An observer would probably note that you do two things when you sample: (1) you deal with only a part or portion of some whole, and (2) you assume that this part or portion is in some way representative of the whole. This is very similar to the meaning of a sample in statistics.

The statistical *sample* consists of the particular group of observations that has been selected for investigation, and, generally, the sample being studied is assumed to be representative of some larger group from which the sample was selected. The larger group is called a *population* or *universe*. A measure such as the mean or standard deviation derived from a sample is called a *statistic*. The corresponding mean or standard deviation that would be obtained if the population instead of the sample had been studied is called a *parameter*. Because statistics are based upon only a part of the total population, they may vary from sample to sample.

Statistics, in the absence of any other information, are the best *estimates* we have of the population parameters. Two statistics that we have discussed in this chapter, the mean and the variance, are, as we have emphasized previously, basic. To find them you need to compute only two sums: ΣX and $\Sigma (X - \overline{X})^2$. We need ΣX in order to find the mean and we need $\Sigma (X - \overline{X})^2$ in order to find the variance or the standard deviation. Later we shall find that there are easier ways of computing these statistics when we have to deal with either a large number of observations or when the measures have large numerical values.

1.12   A Proof concerning the Sum of Squared Deviations from the Mean

We stated earlier in the chapter that the sum of squared deviations $\Sigma (X - \overline{X})^2$ for a set of n measurements is less than $\Sigma (X - m)^2$ where m is any arbitrary constant such that $m \neq \overline{X}$. We now prove that this statement is true.[7] Let $X' = X - m$ and $x = X - \overline{X}$. Then

$$X' - x = (X - m) - (X - \overline{X})$$

and

$$X' = x + (\overline{X} - m)$$

Let $d = \overline{X} - m$. Then

$$X' = x + d$$

and

$$X'^2 = x^2 + 2xd + d^2$$

Summing over the n values, we have

$$\sum X'^2 = \sum x^2 + 2d \sum x + nd^2$$

But d is a constant and $\Sigma x = \Sigma (X - \overline{X}) = 0$. Therefore, $2d \Sigma x = 0$ and

$$\sum X'^2 = \sum x^2 + nd^2$$

Then $\Sigma X'^2$ can eqyal Σx^2 only if $d^2 = 0$. But d^2 will be equal to zero, only if $m = \overline{X}$. Thus, if $m \neq \overline{X}$, we have

$$\sum (X - m)^2 > \sum (X - \overline{X})^2$$

1.13   A Note to the Student

At this point, statistical analysis may seem utterly complex and confusing. If so, part of the difficulty is that in this chapter we have introduced, briefly, a number of important concepts and symbols that are new and strange to you. It will require some time, study, and practice in manipulation before these concepts and symbols become familiar and you feel at ease with them. You will then know at sight that x means $X - \overline{X}$ without having to think about its meaning. And so it will be with the other symbols and concepts.

Many of the topics introduced in this chapter had to be treated in very brief fashion. To have discussed them in greater detail would have forced us to digress from our main purpose of *introducing* you to the topics. You may have many questions that have been left unanswered. You may wonder

---

[7] If you have difficulty in following this and other proofs given in the text, then you need to review the material in Appendix A.

whether any conclusions could be drawn from the experiment on studying with and without knowledge of results. There was a mean difference of three points in favor of the control group, but could this have happened just by chance?[8] If the same experiment were repeated, how do we know that the outcome might not favor the experimental group? The fact that in many other studies it has been found that knowledge of results does facilitate learning should make us consider carefully possible explanations of why the control group mean in this study was higher than that of the experimental group mean.[9] You probably have other questions, such as why we divided by $n - 1$ instead of n in finding the variance.[10] To have attempted to answer these and other questions at this time would have resulted in nothing but additional confusion. We shall come back to these questions in later chapters.

EXAMPLES

1.1—A class in applied psychology made the following scores on a weekly quiz. Find the mean of the scores.

30	28	26	25	23	21	20
29	28	26	24	23	21	20
29	27	26	24	22	21	19
29	27	25	24	22	20	19
28	26	25	24	21	20	18

1.2—Find the median for each of the following sets of measurements.

(a)   23, 23, 22, 22, 22, 20, 17, 17, 17, 17, 15, 15, 13, 13, 13, 12, 12
(b)   20, 20, 19, 17, 17, 17, 15, 15, 15
(c)   15, 13, 11, 9, 6, 4, 2
(d)   24, 22, 19, 17, 16, 14, 8, 6
(e)   38, 35, 34, 33, 30, 28, 20, 17
(f)   95, 94, 90, 88, 87, 85, 83, 80, 78, 70
(g)   14, 12, 11, 11, 10, 9, 9, 9, 9, 9, 8, 8, 4
(h)   170, 164, 160, 160, 159, 158, 158, 158, 158, 157, 156, 154, 150, 150
(i)   25, 24, 24, 23, 23, 22, 22, 22, 22, 21, 21, 21, 21, 20, 20, 20, 19, 19, 18, 17
(j)   50, 48, 45, 42, 40, 36, 34, 31, 29, 28
(k)   4, 4, 4, 4, 4, 4, 4, 3, 3, 3, 1, 0
(l)   25, 22, 18, 17, 16, 15, 14, 10, 8, 5, 5, 4, 3
(m)   14, 10, 8, 8, 8, 2, 1, 0, 0, 0

---

[8] Methods for evaluating the difference between two means are described in Chapter 10.

[9] Lublin (1965) discusses some of the possible reasons why the mean for her control group was higher than the mean for her experimental group.

[10] We shall prove in Chapter 10 that dividing the sum of squared deviations from the mean by $n - 1$ results in an unbiased estimate of the population variance σ^2, whereas division by n does not. Because division by $n - 1$ provides a satisfactory measure of the sample variance and also an unbiased estimate of the population variance, there is no reason to have two definitions of the sample variance, one for the case of division by n and another for the case of division by $n - 1$ when we wish to use the sample variance as an estimate of the population variance.

1.3—Find the mean, variance, and standard deviation of the following set of measurements.

25	24	22	21	20	19	18	17	14
25	24	22	21	20	19	18	15	
25	24	22	21	20	18	17	15	
25	23	21	21	19	18	17	14	
24	23	21	20	19	18	17	14	

1.4—Find the median, Q_1, and Q_3 for the measurements in Example 1.3.

1.5—Find the median, 60th centile, and 13th centile for the following set of measurements.

30, 30, 29, 27, 25, 23, 23, 23, 22, 21, 19, 18, 17, 16, 15, 14, 13, 13

1.6—Two sections in psychology were given an academic aptitude test. The scores for each group were as follows:

Section 1				Section 2			
82	84	80	90	74	84	66	68
80	82	80	82	74	80	62	80
76	86	76	88	72	86	68	76
90	78	78	78	70	78	74	76
88	78	84	80	82	78	68	64

(a) Find the mean, average deviation, variance, and standard deviation for each section.
(b) Which group is more homogeneous with respect to intelligence as measured by the test?
(c) Other factors being equal, which group would you predict to have the higher average score on the final examination in the course?
(d) How many scores are more than 3 standard deviations above the mean or 3 standard deviations below the mean in Section 1?

1.7—Write a symbolic equivalent for each of the following. For example, $X - \bar{X}$ could also be written x.

(a) $X - \bar{X}$
(b) ΣX
(c) Σx^2
(d) $\bar{X}$
(e) $(X - \bar{X})^2$
(f) s^2
(g) $(n - 1)s^2$

(h) $\Sigma X/n$
(i) s
(j) $n\bar{X}$
(k) x
(l) $\Sigma x^2/(n - 1)$
(m) $\Sigma (X - \bar{X})$

1.8—Prove that the sum of the deviations from the mean is equal to zero for a set of n measurements.

1.9—Prove that if observations are paired so that if $D = X_1 - X_2$, then the mean of the differences $\bar{D}$ is equal to the difference between the means $\bar{X}_1 - \bar{X}_2$.

1.10—If we know the means, $\bar{X}_1$ and $\bar{X}_2$, of two sets of observations and also the number of observations, n_1 and n_2, in each set, then we can find the mean of the combined sets. Write the formula that would be used in finding this mean. Note that the formula could be extended to any number of sets of observations.

1.11—Translate each of the verbal statements given below so that it is expressed in terms of the statistical symbols used in the chapter. For example, the statement "if every measure in a set of n is squared and the sum of all of these squared measurements is obtained and from this sum there is subtracted n times the square of the mean of the measurements, the result will be $n - 1$ times the variance" could be written as follows:

$$\sum X^2 - n\bar{X}^2 = (n - 1)s^2$$

(a) If the mean is subtracted from each of the measurements in a set of n and the remainder is squared, the sum of all such squares will be $n - 1$ times the variance.

(b) If the mean is subtracted from each of the measurements in a set of n, the sum of the remainders will be zero.

(c) If the number 10 is subtracted from each measurement in a set of n, the mean of these remainders will be 10 less than the mean of the original scores.

(d) If each score in a set of n scores is increased by 1 and the result squared, the sum of these squares will be equal to the sum of three terms, namely, the sum of the squares of the original scores, twice the sum of the original scores, and the number of observations in the distribution.

(e) If we subtract the mean of a distribution from a given score and square this deviation, it will be equal to the original score squared minus 2 times the original score times the mean, plus the mean squared.

(f) If each score in a set of n scores is multiplied by a constant k and the products are summed, the result will be equal to the constant times the sum of the original scores.

1.12—Prove that $\sum (X - \bar{X})^2$ is less than $\sum (X - m)^2$ for any set of n values of X, if $m \neq \bar{X}$.

1.13—For the values of $D = X - Y$, given in Table 1.2, find the median and the variance.

1.14—Give a one-sentence definition of each of the following terms or concepts:

range

variable

mean

absolute value of x

average deviation

variance

standard deviation

median

frequency distribution

continuous variable

discrete variable

semi-interquartile range

first quartile

third quartile

interquartile range

mode

geometric mean

sample

population

statistic

parameter

CHAPTER 2

Simplifying Statistical Computations

2.1 Introduction

The calculation of the mean and standard deviation is fairly simple when we have a relatively small number of observations. However, and this will often be the case, if the mean is a value such as 67.43 or 67.438, then the calculation of $\Sigma (X - \overline{X})^2$ may involve the squaring and adding of four- or five-digit numbers. And if we have a large number of observations, then the calculation of the sum of squares may be quite tedious. In this chapter, we consider some techniques that can be used to simplify our calculations.

2.2 The Approximate Nature of Measurements

In the last chapter we touched briefly upon the meaning of a measurement or score when we considered the calculation of the median. At that time we pointed out that measurements are made and reported to the nearest unit, whatever that unit happens to be. All observed or recorded values of a variable are *discrete*, regardless of whether the variable itself is continuous or discrete. Height, for example, may be reported to the nearest inch despite the fact that there is not a jump from one inch to the next, but an infinite number of possible values between, say, 70 and 71 inches. A height, then, reported as 70 inches is not necessarily the precise value upon close examination that it might at first seem to be. But then neither would a reported value of 70.001 inches be an exact value, for, regardless of how many decimal places are used in reporting the measurement, additional decimal places are always, theoretically at least, possible.

This is true of all measurements of continuous variables. Time may be

21

measured in terms of years, months, weeks, days, hours, minutes, seconds, milliseconds, and so on, each succeeding unit being more precise than the one before, but even milliseconds are not exact, but only approximate, values. What we have said about time applies also to measurements of other continuous variables. Because of the approximate nature of measurement, we customarily regard a height reported as 70 inches as representing an interval ranging from 69.5 up to 70.5 inches. Similarly, we shall regard measurements of discrete variables such as scores on psychological tests or the number of correct responses in a discrimination experiment as representing intervals ranging from half a unit below up to half a unit above the reported or observed value. For example, if a subject makes 10 correct responses in a discrimination experiment, we shall regard this value as representing an interval ranging from 9.5 up to 10.5.

2.3   Significant Figures

A question that students frequently ask is: How many decimal places should I carry in my computations? There is no *exact* answer to this question as it is phrased. More properly, the question should be: How many *significant figures* should I carry? But even here there is no exact answer, but only "good" or established practice and "poor" or not common practice—like "good" and "bad" usage in English. In view of what we have said concerning the approximate nature of measurements, 28, 280, and 2800 each contains only two significant figures. That is because the zeros used in the second and third numbers are merely used to locate decimal points; they are "fillers." The first value, 28, represents a range from 27.5 up to 28.5; the second, 280, a range from 275 up to 285; the third, 2800, a range from 2750 up to 2850. However, if 280 and 2800 had been written as 280. and 2800., with a decimal point, then the zeros would have been considered significant figures and the range of 280. would be from 279.5 up to 280.5 and the range of 2800. from 2799.5 up to 2800.5. In the measurements used throughout this book, we shall follow the common practice of not writing the decimal point after numbers such as 70 or 60 or 210, but assume that it is understood. When a score is reported as 60, for example, it will be assumed that this represents an interval from 59.5 up to 60.5.

There are "rules" governing the number of significant figures in the answers to problems involving multiplication, division, addition, and subtraction, but they would have to be ignored when an involved series of operations must be performed. Following rigidly any single set of rules would involve exaggerations of inaccuracies. The best single principle to follow is to carry along more figures in various computations than you intend to retain in the final answer, and then to round back to a reasonable number of places in reporting your answer. We shall first consider what we mean by a "reasonable" number of places in an answer before turning to the problem of "rounding."

An examination of the research literature in a given field will indicate current practice. In psychology, education, and the behavioral sciences, the following is common practice:

1. The mean is usually reported to two or three decimal places.
2. The median is usually reported to two or three decimal places.
3. The variance is usually reported to three or four decimal places.
4. The standard deviation is usually reported to two or three decimal places.
5. Standard errors, which we have not discussed as yet, are usually reported to two or three decimal places.
6. Correlation coefficients and other measures of association to be discussed later, are usually reported to two or three decimal places.
7. Proportions are seldom reported to more than four decimal places and usually to two or three places.
8. Ratios, used in tests of significance, which we shall discuss later, are usually reported to two or sometimes to three decimal places.

When the number of observations involved in calculating any of the above statistics is large, then they may be reported to an additional decimal place. However, when the number of observations is small, such professed accuracy is not only not necessary but may be misleading in that it implies that the reported values of the statistics are more accurate than they in fact are. If the mean is to be reported to two decimal places, then $\Sigma\ X/n$ should be carried to three places and rounded back to two. This practice may be followed in calculating all other statistics also; carry along two or three extra figures in doing the calculations and then round back in your final answer.

2.4   Rounding Numbers

In rounding numbers to the nearest whole number, we proceed as follows: 8.4 becomes 8; 7.1 becomes 7; 3.2 becomes 3; 7.6 becomes 8; 7.8 becomes 8; and 6.6 becomes 7. What is the rule we have followed? If the decimal fraction was less than .5 we dropped it and let the number stand; if the decimal fraction was greater than .5, we raised the number by one. If we round to one decimal place, we follow the same rule: 8.46 becomes 8.5; 7.32 becomes 7.3; 6.11 becomes 6.1; and 4.654 becomes 4.7.

Difficulties in rounding are apt to arise when we are asked to round numbers such as these: 5.5 and 4.5 to the nearest whole number; 8.550 and 5.650 to one decimal place. In these cases, 5.5 becomes 6; 4.5 becomes 4; 8.550 becomes 8.6; and 5.650 becomes 5.6. All of these numbers involve the dropping of a 5, which is right on the border line. The rule by common practice is this: If the number preceding the 5 that is to be dropped is an even number, then we do not change it, but if the number preceding the 5 is odd, then it is raised by one. This is an arbitrary rule, to be sure, and it could just as well be the other way around. Either one would work and would tend to balance out individual errors in rounding a large number of values.

2.5   Raw Score Formula for the Sum of Squares[1]

Column (1) of Table 2.1 gives the values of a set of $n = 15$ scores on a Thurstone attitude scale. For these scores we have

$$\bar{X} = \frac{\sum X}{n} = \frac{75}{15} = 5$$

In column (2) we have the values of $x = X - \bar{X}$ and column (3) gives the squares of these deviations. Summing, we obtain

$$\sum x^2 = \sum (X - \bar{X})^2 = 122$$

Table 2.1—A set of scores on a Thurstone attitude scale illustrating coding by subtraction

(1) X	(2) x	(3) x^2	(4) X^2	(5) $X - 4$	(6) $(X - 4)^2$
11	6	36	121	7	49
8	3	9	64	4	16
5	0	0	25	1	1
2	−3	9	4	−2	4
4	−1	1	16	0	0
7	2	4	49	3	9
1	−4	16	1	−3	9
2	−3	9	4	−2	4
5	0	0	25	1	1
9	4	16	81	5	25
7	2	4	49	3	9
1	−4	16	1	−3	9
4	−1	1	16	0	0
5	0	0	25	1	1
4	−1	1	16	0	0
$\sum$ 75	0	122	497	15	137

[1] In this and subsequent sections of the chapter, we present a number of proofs. To follow and to understand these proofs requires nothing more than the recognition of an identity and the application of the rules and principles given in Appendix A. If you have difficulty with a given proof, then you need to review the material in Appendix A. In particular, review the section on summation.

We now show that it is not necessary to subtract $\overline{X}$ from each value of X in order to calculate $\Sigma\, x^2$. We have

$$x = X - \overline{X}$$

and

$$x^2 = X^2 - 2X\overline{X} + \overline{X}^2$$

Summing

$$\sum x^2 = \sum X^2 - 2\overline{X}\sum X + n\overline{X}^2$$
$$= \sum X^2 - 2n\overline{X}^2 + n\overline{X}^2$$

or

$$\sum x^2 = \sum X^2 - \frac{(\sum X)^2}{n} \tag{2.1}$$

Column (4) of Table 2.1 gives the values of X^2. We see that $\Sigma\, X^2 = 497$. Then, substituting the appropriate values from Table 2.1 in (2.1) we get

$$\sum x^2 = 497 - \frac{(75)^2}{15} = 122$$

and this is the same value we obtained when we worked with the actual deviations from the mean.

We see from the above that it is possible to calculate $\Sigma\, x^2$ directly from the original values of X without first subtracting the mean. All that is necessary is to square X and then find $\Sigma\, X^2$. We then subtract $(\Sigma\, X)^2/n$ from $\Sigma\, X^2$. The result is $\Sigma\, x^2 = \Sigma\, (X - \overline{X})^2$. The term $(\Sigma\, X)^2/n$ is called the *correction term* for the sum of squares. With a modern electric desk calculator, it is possible to calculate both $\Sigma\, X$ and $\Sigma\, X^2$ in one operation. To do this we enter a value of X in the keyboard and then press a "square" key. One dial of the machine will then register X and the other X^2. By locking these dials and entering the successive values of X in the keyboard, we can cumulate X and X^2 and the final result will be $\Sigma\, X$ and $\Sigma\, X^2$. This method is recommended for all calculations performed with a desk calculator.

2.6   Subtraction of a Constant

Let m be any arbitrary constant and let

$$X' = X - m$$

Then

$$\sum X' = \sum X - nm$$

and dividing by n, we have

$$\overline{X}' = \overline{X} - m$$

or

$$\overline{X} = \overline{X}' + m \qquad (2.2)$$

If we let $m = 4$, then column (5) of Table 2.1 gives the values of $X' = X - 4$ and we see that $\Sigma X' = 15$ and $\overline{X}' = 15/15 = 1$. Substituting in (2.2) with $\overline{X}' = 1$ and $m = 4$, we find that the mean of the X values is

$$\overline{X} = 1 + 4 = 5$$

It is sometimes convenient to subtract some constant from each value of X in order to simplify the calculation of $\overline{X}$. For example, if we had a set of n values of X such that all values were equal to or greater than 100, then we might let $m = 100$, so that $X' = X - 100$. We would then sum the X' values and use (2.2) to calculate $\overline{X}$.

We note that

$$X' - \overline{X}' = (X - m) - (\overline{X} - m)$$
$$= X - \overline{X}$$

Then

$$\sum (X' - \overline{X}')^2 = \sum (X - \overline{X})^2$$

and therefore

$$\sum (X - \overline{X})^2 = \sum X'^2 - \frac{(\sum X')^2}{n} \qquad (2.3)$$

If we have coded a set of X values by subtracting some constant m to obtain $X' = X - m$, then we can square the X' values, find the sum of the squared values, subtract $(\Sigma X')^2/n$ and the result will be $\Sigma x^2 = \Sigma (X - \overline{X})^2$.

Column (6) of Table 2.1 gives the values of X'^2 where $X' = X - 4$. We find that $\Sigma X'^2 = 137$ and that $\Sigma X' = 15$. Then, substituting in (2.3), we have

$$\sum (X - \overline{X})^2 = 137 - \frac{(15)^2}{15} = 122$$

as before.

2.7 Dividing by a Constant

Let i be any arbitrary constant and let

$$X' = X/i$$

Then

$$\sum X' = \sum X/i$$

and dividing by n

$$\bar{X}' = \bar{X}/i$$

or

$$\bar{X} = i\bar{X}' \qquad (2.4)$$

Column (1) of Table 2.2 gives the values of a variable X and we see that $\bar{X} = \Sigma X/n = 100/10 = 10$. We also have in column (3) values of x^2 and $\Sigma x^2 = \Sigma (X - \bar{X})^2 = 96$. Column (4) shows the values of $X' = X/i$ where we have let $i = 2$. We have $\Sigma X' = 50$ and $\bar{X}' = 50/10 = 5$. Then substituting in (2.4) with $\bar{X}' = 5$ and $i = 2$, we have

$$\bar{X} = (2)(5) = 10$$

Table 2.2—Coding scores by division

(1) X	(2) x	(3) x^2	(4) $X' = X/2$	(5) $X'^2 = (X/2)^2$
12	2	4	6	36
10	0	0	5	25
8	−2	4	4	16
10	0	0	5	25
14	4	16	7	49
6	−4	16	3	9
8	−2	4	4	16
16	6	36	8	64
6	−4	16	3	9
10	0	0	5	25
Σ 100	0	96	50	274

We see that if the values of a variable have been divided by some constant i, so that $X' = X/i$, then we can sum the X' values and use (2.4) to find the mean of the values of X.

We note that if $X' = X/i$, then

$$X' - \bar{X}' = \frac{X}{i} - \frac{\bar{X}}{i}$$

$$= \frac{1}{i}(X - \bar{X})$$

and

$$\Sigma (X' - \bar{X}')^2 = \frac{1}{i^2} \Sigma (X - \bar{X})^2$$

or

$$i^2 \sum (X' - \bar{X}')^2 = \sum (X - \bar{X})^2$$

Then

$$\sum (X - \bar{X})^2 = i^2 \left(\sum X'^2 - \frac{(\sum X')^2}{n} \right) \qquad (2.5)$$

We can, therefore, find $\sum (X - \bar{X})^2$ basing our calculations upon the X' values.

Column (5) of Table 2.2 gives the values of X'^2 where $X' = X/2$. We see that $\sum X'^2 = 274$ and that $\sum X' = 50$. Then substituting in (2.5) we have

$$\sum (X - \bar{X})^2 = (2)^2 \left(274 - \frac{(50)^2}{10} \right) = 96$$

2.8 Grouping Measures into Classes or Intervals

The most commonly used method of coding scores or measurements is by grouping them into classes to form a *frequency distribution*. Earlier we discussed precision of measurement. Grouping may be thought of as the equivalent of using a less precise measuring instrument and is most valuable when we have a large number of observations. Instead of dealing with the individual values of a variable X, we group them into a number of equal intervals or classes. We then assign a single value to all of the observations in a given class. If we code these class values by subtracting a constant and then dividing by a constant, we can simplify our calculations considerably.

Table 2.3 gives the values of a set of $n = 100$ scores on a test. We could of course find $\sum X$ and $\sum X^2$ using the values given in the table. With a desk calculator this would not be a difficult task. But, if you do not have a desk

Table 2.3—Scores obtained by 100 students on a test

87	76	73	70	67	66	64	63	61	60
85	75	72	69	67	65	64	62	61	60
82	74	71	69	67	65	63	62	61	60
78	74	71	68	66	65	63	62	61	60
77	74	70	68	66	64	63	62	61	60
60	59	58	57	56	54	52	50	46	43
60	59	58	57	55	54	52	49	46	42
60	59	58	57	55	53	51	49	46	38
60	59	58	56	55	53	51	48	45	35
60	59	57	56	54	53	50	47	44	33

calculator available, it would be worthwhile to group the measures into classes and then do your calculations with the coded values assigned to the classes.

2.9   Number of Classes or Intervals

In making a frequency distribution of the scores shown in Table 2.3, we could use an interval of 1 by placing numbers ranging from 87, the highest observed value in the table, to 33, the lowest observed value in the table, at the left-hand side of a sheet of paper and making a tally mark (/) each time one of these values was found in the table. This, however, would still leave the scores spread out; we would have 55 possible values recorded at the left if the scores are grouped in intervals of 1 or the original unit of measurement. With an interval of 1, we have as many classes as there are possible values of X for a given range.

Fortunately, experience has demonstrated that quite accurate results can be obtained in statistics when, for purposes of computation, we work with a much smaller number of classes or intervals, say from 10 to 20. Our first suggestion for grouping scores, then, will be that we group them so as to have from 10 to 20 classes or groups. The larger the number of intervals or classes, the more precise, but also the more complicated, will be the computations. Consequently, the number of class intervals we decide to work with will be dictated by our desire for accuracy and for convenience.

2.10   Size of the Class Interval

To determine what size interval we should use, we first find the range. In the present problem we have $R = 87 - 33 = 54$. We then divide the range by the number of class intervals we want to use. For example, if we want approximately 10 classes, we have $54/10 = 5.4$ which, rounded, is 5. Then, if we use a class interval of 5, we shall have approximately 10 classes.

If we decide that we want to work with approximately 15 class intervals, we have $54/15 = 3.6$, which, when rounded, indicates that we should use 4 as the size of the class interval. A class interval of 2 would give slightly more than 20 classes and an interval of 3 would give slightly less than 20 classes.

2.11   Limits of the Intervals

It is convenient to start class intervals so that the lower recorded limit of the interval is some multiple of the size of the class interval. For example, if the size of the interval is 3, then intervals are started with some multiple of 3 such as 6, 9, 12, or 15, and so forth. However, if there is any apparent tendency for the original measures to cluster about particular values, then the limits of the intervals might be established in such a way that these clusters will fall toward the mid-points of the various intervals. Because this will not necessarily be the case and because we desire some uniformity in the procedures to be used, we shall always begin class intervals with a multiple of the size of the interval.

For the data of Table 2.3, we shall use a class interval of 5. Because the lowest value in the table falls between 30 and 35, we shall have to begin the first interval with 30 in order to include this score.

Although it is customary to record the limits of the intervals as 30–34, 35–39, 40–44, and so on, for a class interval of 5, we must remember what we have previously said about the meaning of a score; that is, that it represents a range extending half a unit below up to half a unit above the observed values. The same principle applies to class intervals. The interval 30–34 is to be regarded as representing a range from 29.5 up to 34.5.

2.12   Tallying the Scores

The next step in making a frequency distribution, after the size of the class interval and the limits of the intervals have been determined, is to tally the scores. The various class intervals are listed in Table 2.4 according to the accepted practice of placing the highest interval at the top. As the scores are taken, one at a time, a tally mark is placed opposite the interval in which the score falls. When four tally marks (////) have been made in a given interval, the fifth is made by a cross tally, thus (/X//). The sum of the tally marks for each interval gives the frequency of scores within the interval. The sum of all the frequencies gives the total number of measurements or n. In Table 2.4 the frequency for each class interval is given in column (3), headed f.

Table 2.4—Frequency distribution of scores given in Table 2.3

(1) Scores	(2) Tally marks	(3) f
85–89	//	2
80–84	/	1
75–79	////	4
70–74	/X// ////	9
65–69	/X// /X// ///	13
60–64	/X// /X// /X// /X// /X// /	26
55–59	/X// /X// /X// ////	19
50–54	/X// /X// //	12
45–49	/X// ///	8
40–44	///	3
35–39	//	2
30–34	/	1

2.13   Assumptions concerning Grouped Measures

What assumptions can we make concerning the scores as they are now grouped or classified? A convenient assumption is that the *best single value to represent all of the observations within a given interval is the mid-point of that interval*. We shall find that the mean and standard deviation based upon this assumption will not be seriously in error.

The interval 30–34 has as its lower limit 29.5 and the interval 35–39 has 34.5 as its lower limit. We describe the intervals as being *closed* at their lower limits, by which we mean that the interval 30–34 includes the value of its lower limit, 29.5, and the interval 35–39 includes the value of its lower limit, 34.5. The upper limits of the interval are described as *open*, by which is meant that the interval 30–34 does not contain the value 34.5 and the interval 35–39 does not contain the value 39.5. In other words, the upper limit of the first interval is 34.4999 . . . which approaches but does not include 34.5. Similarly, the upper limit of the interval 35–39 is 39.4999 . . . which approaches but does not include the value 39.5.

To find the mid-point of an interval we first find the range of the interval. For the first interval we have 34.49999 . . . − 29.5 Thus the range is approximately equal to 5; one half of the range is approximately 2.5. Then the mid-point of the first interval is approximately 29.5 + 2.5 or 32. In the same manner we can find the approximate mid-points of each of the other class intervals. These are given in column (3) of Table 2.5. We assume that the two observations falling within the interval 85–89 can both be represented by a single value, the mid-point of the interval, or 87. A similar assumption is made concerning the observations in each of the other class intervals.

2.14   Coding the Mid-Points

You will note that by letting the mid-points of the intervals represent all of the observations within a given interval, we have reduced the number of different values that we have to deal with to 12, the number of mid-points. That is, we now have only 12 different values of X and these are 32, 37, 42, . . . , 87. Now, subtract a constant m from each of the 12 values of X. A convenient constant to subtract is the value of the mid-point of the lowest class interval, which, in this case is 32.

The resulting values of $X - m = X - 32$ are given in column (4) of Table 2.5. We now divide each of the $X - m$ values by $i = 5$, the size of the class interval. Then we have

$$X' = (X - m)/i \qquad (2.6)$$

or, for the present example,

$$X' = (X - 32)/5$$

These X' values are given in column (5) of Table 2.5. We shall use the X' values defined in (2.6) to find the mean and standard deviation of the original X values.

Table 2.5—Calculation of the mean and standard deviation from scores coded by grouping

(1) Scores	(2) f	(3) Mid-point	(4) $X - 32$	(5) $X' = (X - 32)/5$	(6) fX'	(7) fX'^2
85–89	2	87	55	11	22	242
80–84	1	82	50	10	10	100
75–79	4	77	45	9	36	324
70–74	9	72	40	8	72	576
65–69	13	67	35	7	91	637
60–64	26	62	30	6	156	936
55–59	19	57	25	5	95	475
50–54	12	52	20	4	48	192
45–49	8	47	15	3	24	72
40–44	3	42	10	2	6	12
35–39	2	37	5	1	2	2
30–34	1	32	0	0	0	0
Σ	100				562	3568

2.15   Calculation of the Mean

To find $\Sigma X'$, we first multiply each of the X' values by its corresponding frequency, f. The products fX' are given in column (6) of Table 2.5. Summing, we have $\Sigma fX' = 562$. We note that

$$\Sigma fX' = \frac{\Sigma f(X - m)}{i}$$

$$= \frac{\Sigma fX - m\Sigma f}{i}$$

and dividing by n

$$\overline{X}' = \frac{\overline{X} - m}{i}$$

or

$$\overline{X} = m + i\overline{X}' \qquad (2.7)$$

Then $\overline{X}' = \Sigma fX'/n = 562/100 = 5.62$. Substituting in (2.7) with $\overline{X}' = 5.62$,

$m = 32$, and $i = 5$, we have

$$\bar{X} = 32 + 5(5.62)$$
$$= 60.10$$

as the mean of the X values.

2.16   Calculation of the Standard Deviation

In column (7) of Table 2.5 we give the products, fX'^2. These products are most easily obtained by multiplying the entries in the column headed fX', column (6), by the entries in the column headed X', column (5); that is, we find the product $X'fX' = fX'^2$. Summing, we have $\Sigma fX'^2 = 3568$.

We note that

$$X' - \bar{X}' = \frac{X - m}{i} - \frac{\bar{X} - m}{i}$$

$$= \frac{X - \bar{X}}{i}$$

and that

$$\Sigma f(X' - \bar{X}')^2 = \frac{1}{i^2} \Sigma f(X - \bar{X})^2$$

or

$$\Sigma f(X - \bar{X})^2 = i^2 \sum f(X' - \bar{X}')^2$$

Then we also have

$$\Sigma f(X - \bar{X})^2 = i^2 \left(\sum fX'^2 - \frac{(\sum fX')^2}{n} \right) \tag{2.8}$$

Substituting in (2.8) with $\Sigma fX'^2 = 3568$, $\Sigma fX' = 562$, and $i = 5$, we have

$$\Sigma f(X - \bar{X})^2 = (5)^2 \left(3568 - \frac{(562)^2}{100} \right) = 10{,}239$$

Then the variance of X will be given by

$$s_X^2 = \frac{\Sigma f(X - \bar{X})^2}{n - 1} \tag{2.9}$$

and the standard deviation by

$$s_X = \sqrt{\frac{\Sigma f(X - \bar{X})^2}{n - 1}} \tag{2.10}$$

For the variance of X, we have

$$s_X{}^2 = \frac{10{,}239}{100 - 1} = 103.42$$

and

$$s_X = \sqrt{\frac{10{,}239}{100 - 1}} = 10.2$$

2.17   Subtracting a Constant Other than the Mid-Point of the Lowest Interval

You may note several things from Table 2.5. First, it is not necessary to go through all the steps we have described in arriving at the X' values shown in column (5). If the same coding procedure that we have described is used, all that is necessary is to number the lowest class interval zero and to assign the values 1, 2, 3, 4, 5, and so on, to the successive class intervals. This will apply to all distributions coded in the manner described. There is no necessity, in other words, to subtract the mid-point of the lowest class interval from the other mid-points and then to divide each of these values by i, the size of the class interval. We have gone through these steps in the table merely to indicate the nature of the coded X' values shown in column (5).

A second thing to observe is that it would have been possible to subtract some mid-point other than that of the lowest class interval. We could have subtracted, for example, the mid-point of some interval toward the center of the distribution from the other mid-points before dividing by i, the size of the interval. If we had subtracted the mid-point of the class interval 60–64, then the X' value for this interval would be zero. The interval directly above would have an X' value of 1, the next interval an X' value of 2, and so on. The interval directly below 60–64 would have an X' value of -1, the next an X' values of -2, and so on. This coding procedure would give us slightly smaller X' values to use in our computations, but would have introduced some negative X' values. Regardless of which mid-point we subtract, the resulting mean and standard deviation will be the same. As a general practice, it is convenient to start the lowest class interval with zero and to number up from there. This procedure makes coding a routine affair.

2.18   The Charlier Checks

There are checks on the accuracy of your computations. They are known as the "Charlier checks" and in the present problem may be made by adding 1 to each X' value in column (3) of Table 2.5. Use these values of $X' + 1$ to find $\Sigma f(X' + 1)$ and $\Sigma f(X' + 1)^2$. If the computations in the first and second instance have both been correctly made, then the following relations will hold:

$$\sum f(X' + 1) = \sum fX' + n$$

and

$$\sum f(X' + 1)^2 = \sum fX'^2 + 2\sum fX' + n$$

Application of the Charlier checks is shown in columns (6), (7), and (8) of Table 2.6. We see that $\sum f(X' + 1) = 65$ and that $\sum f(X' + 1)^2 = 243$. Then our original values of $\sum fX' = 45$ and $\sum fX'^2 = 133$ must be correct because

$$65 = 45 + 20$$

and

$$243 = 133 + (2)(45) + 20$$

Table 2.6—Illustration of the "Charlier checks"

(1) Scores	(2) f	(3) X'	(4) fX'	(5) fX'^2	(6) $X' + 1$	(7) $f(X' + 1)$	(8) $f(X' + 1)^2$
30–32	1	5	5	25	6	6	36
27–29	2	4	8	32	5	10	50
24–26	5	3	15	45	4	20	80
21–23	7	2	14	28	3	21	63
18–20	3	1	3	3	2	6	12
15–17	2	0	0	0	1	2	2
$\sum$	20		45	133		65	243

2.19   Calculation of the Median

In the previous chapter we illustrated the calculation of the median with a frequency distribution in which the size of the class interval was 1. As a formula for calculating the median, we had

$$Mdn = l + \left(\frac{\frac{n}{2} - \sum f_b}{f_w} \right) i$$

where l is the lower limit of the interval in which the median falls, $\sum f_b$ is the sum of the frequencies below this interval, f_w is the frequency within the interval in which the median falls, and i is the size of the interval. Applying this formula to the distribution of scores in Table 2.5, we have

$$Mdn = 59.5 + \left(\frac{50 - 45}{26}\right)5$$

$$= 60.46$$

2.20 Summary of Steps in Coding a Frequency Distribution

Here is a summary of the steps in coding measurements by grouping them in a frequency distribution:

1. Determine the range of the measurements.
2. Divide the range by the number of class intervals you wish to work with, say 15. The quotient, when rounded, gives the size of the class interval to use.
3. Begin the lowest interval with some multiple of the size of the class interval—a multiple that is equal to or just below the smallest value of X in the set of n.
4. Code the lowest class interval zero, the next 1, the next 2, and so forth, until the highest class interval has been coded. These numbers correspond to the values of X'.
5. Apply (2.7) for the mean and (2.8) for the sum of squares. Then use (2.10) to find the standard deviation.

If you are doing your calculations with a desk calculator, you may not want to record the X values in a frequency distribution, but may still wish to transform them into X' values. This is easily accomplished. Follow the procedure above through the third step. Then take the lower limit (recorded limit) of the first interval and divide this by i (the size of the class interval). This will be a whole number because the lower recorded limit of the first interval is a multiple of i. Call the quotient k. Now divide each value of X by i, discarding any remainder. Subtract the value of k and this will give you the X' value for X.

To illustrate the above procedure, consider a few of the X values in Table 2.3. We have decided to use an interval of 5, and the lower recorded limit of the first interval is 30. This limit divided by $i = 5$ gives $k = 6$. Then $X = 33$ divided by 5 gives 6 and a remainder of 3 that we discard. Subtracting $k = 6$, we have $X' = 0$ for $X = 33$. Dividing $X = 56$ by 5 we have 11 and a remainder that we discard. Subtracting $k = 6$, we have $X' = 5$ for $X = 56$. In the same manner we can find the X' values for each value of X in Table 2.3.

If you do not trust your mental arithmetic, write down the recorded limits of the class intervals and assign $X' = 0$ to the lowest interval, $X' = 1$ to the next, and so on. Then, the X' value corresponding to any given value of X can be quickly determined by reference to this table.

EXAMPLES

2.1—Here is a set of $n = 7$ measurements for which calculations are very simple.

$$29 \quad 28 \quad 27 \quad 25 \quad 24 \quad 22 \quad 20$$

(a) Find the mean and sum of squares using deviations from the mean.
(b) Subtract 22 from each score and find the mean and sum of squares of the original values using these coded scores.
(c) Find the sum of squares using $\Sigma X^2 - (\Sigma X)^2/n$.

2.2—Make a frequency distribution of the measurements given below. Let $i = 3$ and begin the first interval with 6.

(a) Find the mean and standard deviation from the frequency distribution.
(b) Check your computations by means of the Charlier checks.

44	40	35	34	32	31	30	29	27
43	40	35	34	31	31	30	29	27
42	37	35	33	31	30	29	29	27
40	36	34	33	31	30	29	28	26
40	35	34	32	31	30	29	28	26
26	25	24	24	23	23	22	22	22
26	25	24	23	23	23	22	22	22
26	25	24	23	23	23	22	22	22
25	25	24	23	23	23	22	22	22
25	25	24	23	23	22	22	22	22
22	21	20	20	20	19	18	18	18
22	21	20	20	19	18	18	18	17
21	21	20	20	19	18	18	18	17
21	21	20	20	19	18	18	18	17
21	20	20	20	19	18	18	18	17
17	17	16	15	14	14	13	12	9
17	17	16	15	14	14	13	12	9
17	16	16	15	14	14	13	12	9
17	16	16	15	14	14	13	11	8
17	16	15	15	14	13	12	11	7

2.3—Find the mean, median, and standard deviation of the following frequency distribution.

Scores	f	X
60–62	1	8
57–59	3	7
54–56	2	6
51–53	7	5
48–50	11	4
45–47	10	3
42–44	9	2
39–41	5	1
36–38	5	0

2.4—Find the mean, median, and standard deviation of the following frequency distribution.

Scores	f
27–29	1
24–26	2
21–23	4
18–20	5
15–17	3
12–14	2
9–11	2
6– 8	1

2.5—Make a frequency distribution of the scores given below. Let $i = 3$ and begin the first interval with 15. Find the mean, median, 30th centile, and standard deviation.

42	16	38	29	33	35	40	32	34
43	19	26	27	33	38	20	37	34
46	36	25	23	30	42	38	20	
40	36	24	22	32	45	22	18	
39	37	28	31	32	22	20	35	
20	18	42	35	35	35	35	31	

2.6—Marks (1943) gave a test, designed to measure attitude toward Negroes, to 2096 Negro youth living in rural sections of the south. A low score on the test indicates a favorable attitude, and a high score indicates an unfavorable attitude. Find the mean and standard deviation of the distribution of scores.

Scores	f
14	12
13	53
12	96
11	152
10	219
9	273
8	255
7	227
6	203
5	172
4	144
3	117
2	86
1	54
0	33

2.7—Kelly and Fiske (1950) gave the Miller Analogies Test to 367 Veterans Administration trainees in clinical psychology. The distribution of scores was as given below. Find the mean and standard deviation.

Scores	f
95–99	2
90–94	20
85–89	36
80–84	55
75–79	59
70–74	59
65–69	56
60–64	23
55–59	27
50–54	12
45–49	3
40–44	10
35–39	3
30–34	1
25–29	1

2.8—If $X' = X - m$, then prove that

$$\overline{X} = m + \frac{\sum X'}{n}$$

2.9—Prove that

$$\sum (X - \overline{X})^2 = \sum X^2 - \frac{(\sum X)^2}{n}$$

2.10—If $X' = X - m$, then prove that

$$\sum (X - \bar{X})^2 = \sum X'^2 - \frac{(\sum X')^2}{n}$$

2.11—If $X' = X/i$, then prove that

$$\sum (X - \bar{X})^2 = \left(\sum X'^2 - \frac{(\sum X')^2}{n}\right)i^2$$

2.12—If $X' = (X - m)/i$, then prove that

$$\bar{X} = m + \left(\frac{\sum X'}{n}\right)i$$

2.13—If $X' = iX$, then prove that

$$\bar{X} = \frac{\sum X'}{ni}$$

2.14—If $X' = iX$, then prove that

$$\sum (X - \bar{X})^2 = \left(\sum X'^2 - \frac{(\sum X')^2}{n}\right)\frac{1}{i^2}$$

2.15—If $\Sigma X = 100$ and $n = 33$, what would you report as the value of the mean?

2.16—What is the difference between a constant and a variable?

2.17—Suppose that $X_H = 145$ and $X_L = 93$.

(a) What size class interval would you use if you wanted approximately 15 classes?

(b) What would be the range of the lowest class interval?

(c) What would be the value of the mid-point of the lowest class interval?

(d) What size interval would you use if you wanted approximately 10 classes?

(e) What would be the range of the lowest class interval?

(f) What should be the value of the mid-point of the lowest class interval?

CHAPTER 3

Graphical Representation of Frequency Distributions

3.1 Introduction

A frequency distribution of scores on the Minnesota Psycho-Analogies Test for 158 students majoring in psychology is shown in Table 3.1. There are two forms of the Psycho-Analogies Test, A and B, and each form consists of 75 items. The scores given in Table 3.1 are on Form A. The following is an example of the type of problem contained in the test, with the correct response given in italics:

Orchestra : Violinist : : Test : (1) Battery; (2) Item Analysis;
(3) *Item;* (4) Validity.

Levine (1950) reports data showing that mean scores on the Psycho-Analogies Test rise successively from 51.7 for graduating seniors to 66.6 for third-year graduate students in psychology. Advanced students in psychology, in other words, actually do perform better on the average on the test than less advanced students in psychology.

The scores in Table 3.1 are grouped in a class interval of 3, and the frequency distribution is based upon a combined group of seniors, and first-, second-, and third-year graduate students. The frequency distribution, with its mean of 59.3 and standard deviation of 8.1, gives a concise description of the 158 scores.

3.2 The Histogram

The frequency distribution of Table 3.1 can also be portrayed by means of a *histogram*. The histogram enables one to obtain a picture of the distribution quite readily. The histogram or column chart of the distribution is shown in Figure 3.1.

Table 3.1—Frequency distribution of scores on Form A of Minnesota Psycho-Analogies Test for 158 students majoring in psychology*

$$(\overline{X} = 59.3; \; s = 8.1)$$

(1) Class interval	(2) Mid-points of intervals	(3) f	(4) p	(5) cf	(6) cp	(7) Upper limits of intervals
72–74	73	4	.03	158	1.00	75
69–71	70	15	.09	154	.97	71
66–68	67	21	.13	139	.88	68
63–65	64	21	.13	118	.75	65
60–62	61	24	.15	97	.61	62
57–59	58	16	.10	73	.46	59
54–56	55	23	.15	57	.36	56
51–53	52	15	.09	34	.22	53
48–50	49	7	.04	19	.12	50
45–47	46	3	.02	12	.08	47
42–44	43	4	.03	9	.06	44
39–41	40	1	.01	5	.03	41
36–38	37	3	.02	4	.03	38
33–35	34	1	.01	1	.01	35
Σ		158	1.00			

* Data from Levine (1950).

In plotting a histogram, it is customary to represent the scores on the horizontal axis and the frequencies on the vertical axis. In graphic work, the horizontal axis is called the X axis or *abscissa*, and the vertical axis is called the Y axis or *ordinate*. The horizontal distance from the Y axis to a point on the graph is called the *abscissa* of the point. The vertical distance from the base line or X axis to a point on the graph is called the *ordinate* of the point. Two values, written in the order (X, Y), representing, respectively, the abscissa and ordinate of a point, are called the *coordinates* of a point. It is customary to write the X value first and the Y value second.

In general, people seem to find most pleasing a rectangular frame in which the vertical axis is somewhere between 60 and 75 percent of the length of the horizontal axis. For this reason, tall, narrow graphs and wide, flat graphs may be avoided. Graph paper, with lines ruled 10 to the inch, which can be obtained from most college book stores, will enable you to arrange a pleasing graph when plotting distributions.

It may be noted that on the horizontal axis of Figure 3.1 we have recorded the mid-points of the class intervals, 34, 37, . . . , and 73, rather than the limits of the intervals. The mid-points are the single scores that we may assume best represent all of the scores falling within a given interval. For each mid-point we have a corresponding frequency, and the paired midpoints and frequencies are the coordinates of the set of points to be plotted. For example, the first three coordinates are (34, 1), (37, 3), and (40, 1). These coordinates are plotted in Figure 3.1 along with the other coordinates obtained from columns (2) and (3) of Table 3.1. It is sometimes said that the Y values are plotted *against* those of X or that Y is plotted *on* X.

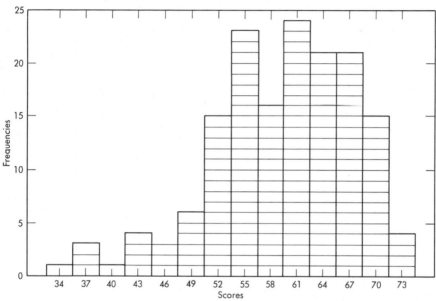

Figure **3.1**—Histogram for the distribution of scores given in Table 3.1. The vertical axis gives the frequency or number of scores in each class interval.

In the histogram, each column represents a frequency corresponding to the number of scores in a given interval. We may think of each column as being subdivided into small rectangles, equal in size, with a single rectangle representing a single score. The columns of the histogram are built up by piling these rectangles one on top of the other. Thus each score in the distribution corresponds to an area given by the dimensions of the small rectangle. The total area under the histogram would simply be the sum of the areas of the individual rectangles. In the histogram of Figure 3.1 we actually show these rectangles for purposes of illustration. We would, however, have no reason for showing them when our interest is in merely the picture of the frequency distribution given by the histogram. For graphical purposes, the columns would either be shaded or left blank.

Because we know that the total area of Figure 3.1 is made up of 158 little rectangles of equal area, one for each of the 158 scores, we can express the ordinate of each column of the histogram as a proportion of the total area. We obtain these proportions by dividing each of the frequencies of the various class intervals by 158. The resulting proportions are shown in column (4) of Table 3.1. This procedure suggests that we could also plot a histogram with proportions rather than frequencies on the vertical axis. We have done this in Figure 3.2. Comparing Figure 3.2 with Figure 3.1, we see that no change

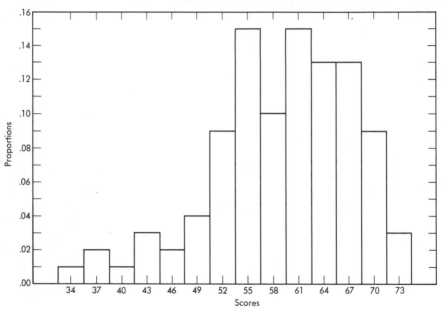

Figure **3.2**—Histogram for the distribution of scores given in Table 3.1. The vertical axis gives the proportion of the total number of scores in each class interval.

has been made in the general form or shape of the histogram through the use of proportions rather than frequencies on the vertical axis.

When we sum the frequencies represented by the ordinates of the histogram of Figure 3.1, we obtain the total number of observations: 158. If we sum the proportions represented by the ordinates of the histogram of Figure 3.2, we would obtain 1.00. The ordinates of Figure 3.2 give the proportion of the total area in each column of the histogram.

3.3   The Frequency Polygon

We may also portray the frequency distribution of Table 3.1 by means of a *frequency polygon*. We again find the mid-points of the various class intervals and the frequencies corresponding to these mid-points. We then plot the frequencies against the corresponding mid-points. The plotted points are then connected by straight lines. It is customary to extend the distribution one class interval below and one class interval above those actually used in order to bring the ends of the frequency polygon down to the base line or horizontal axis. The frequency polygon for the data of Table 3.1 is shown in Figure 3.3.

You may observe that the area under the frequency polygon will be equal to the area under the histogram for the same distribution, if they are drawn on the same scale. We have taken a section, the first few intervals, of the

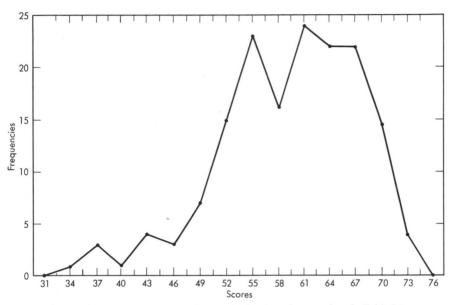

Figure **3.3**—Frequency polygon for the distribution of scores given in Table 3.1.

histogram of Figure 3.1 and magnified it in Figure 3.4. Note that the shaded right triangles or areas are added by the frequency polygon and that these areas correspond to the unshaded right triangles or areas eliminated or cut off when we impose the frequency polygon on the histogram. Thus, for each section or area of the histogram cut off by the frequency polygon, an equal corresponding section or area is added. The areas of the histogram and the corresponding frequency polygon are the same.

You should not get the false notion that it is possible to erect ordinates at any score on the base line of Figure 3.3 and then to read the frequency corresponding to this score at the point where the ordinate intersects the graph of the frequency polygon. We can, from the frequency polygon or histogram, tell only the frequency of scores within a given interval and not the frequencies corresponding to each individual score. Our base line representing the scores is essentially discontinuous. We have frequencies corresponding only to selected points on the X axis, namely, the mid-points of the class intervals.

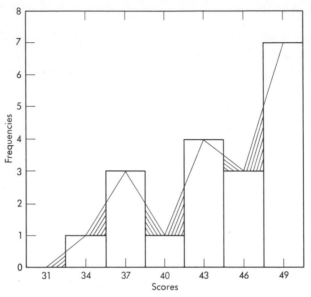

Figure **3.4**—Section of the histogram and frequency polygon for the distribution of scores given in Table 3.1.

3.4   The Cumulative-Proportion Graph

Another useful way of depicting a frequency distribution is in terms of its *cumulative-proportion* or *percentage graph*. Note the entries in column (5) of Table 3.1. These are the cumulative frequencies, and they are obtained by adding to the frequency in each interval the sum of the frequencies falling below the interval. For example, the cumulative frequency corresponding to the interval 45–47 is 12. This entry is obtained by adding the frequencies falling below this interval, $1 + 3 + 1 + 4 = 9$, to the frequency within the interval, 3, which gives us 12. The cumulative frequency for the highest class interval, 72–74, is 158, and represents the sum of all of the frequencies below this interval, 154, plus 4, the frequency within the interval.

If we divide each of the cumulative frequencies by 158, we shall have the cumulative proportions shown in column (6) of Table 3.1. Since multiplication is easier than long division, a simple way of obtaining the cumulative proportions is to find first the reciprocal of the total number of observations.[1]

---

[1] Table II in Appendix B gives the reciprocals of the numbers 1 to 1000.

For the data of Table 3.1, this is $1/158 = .00633$. We can then multiply each of the cumulative frequencies by this reciprocal and obtain the cumulative proportions.[2] Multiplying one number by the reciprocal of another is the same as dividing the first by the second.

In plotting the histogram and frequency polygon, we found the mid-points of the class intervals and then plotted the frequencies against these values. For the cumulative distribution, we find the upper limits (the recorded instead of the theoretical upper limits will do) of the intervals and plot the cumulative frequencies or proportions against these values. The reason for this is that the cumulative frequency or proportion entered for a given interval represents the frequency or proportion of the total number of measures

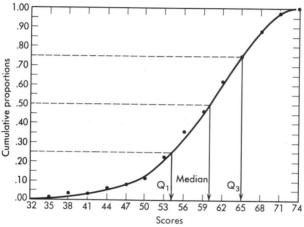

Figure 3.5—Cumulative proportion graph for the distribution of scores given in Table 3.1.

falling below the upper limit of the interval. The upper limits (recorded) of the intervals are shown in column (7) of Table 3.1.

We have plotted the cumulative-proportion distribution for the 158 scores on the Minnesota Psycho-Analogies Test in Figure 3.5. Note that the graph rises most rapidly toward the center of the score distribution and only slightly less rapidly from 68 to 74. The slow acceleration of the graph at the left of the distribution immediately tells the experienced student that there is a tail—a series of intervals with small frequencies—toward the low end of the score distribution. If you will go back and look at either the frequency polygon, Figure 3.3, or the histogram, Figure 3.1, you will see what is meant by a tail to the left or low end of the score distribution.

---

[2] The cumulative proportions in column (6) of Table 3.1 were obtained in this way. You will note that if the proportions given in column (4) are added to obtain the cumulative proportions, some of these values will differ slightly from those shown in column (6) of the table as a result of rounding errors.

3.5   Skewed Distributions

It is customary to describe a distribution with a tail toward the left or low end of the score distribution as *left* or *negatively skewed*. A distribution with a tail toward the right or high end of the score distribution is described as being *right* or *positively skewed*. The relative position of the mean and median in a negatively skewed distribution is shown in Figure 3.6 and in a positively skewed distribution in Figure 3.7.

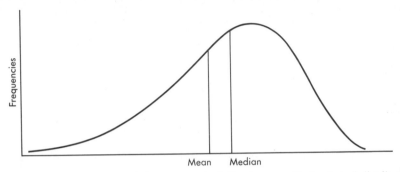

Figure **3.6**—Relative position of the mean and median in a negatively skewed distribution.

Because the sum of the positive deviations from the mean must be equal to the sum of the negative deviations, one or two extremely high values in a set of *n* observations will have the effect of "pulling" the mean toward them and away from the center of the distribution. One or two extremely low scores will tend to pull the mean toward them or toward the low end of the distribution. The median, on the other hand, is not influenced by the values of extreme scores. It is merely the point on each side of which there are an equal number of scores. Consequently, when a distribution is negatively skewed, the median will be larger than the mean, as in Figure 3.6, where values along the horizontal axis, as usual, increase from left to right. When a distribution is positively skewed, the median will be smaller in value than the mean, as in Figure 3.7.

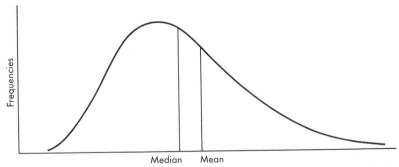

Figure **3.7**—Relative position of the mean and median in a positively skewed distribution.

Can you imagine what the graph of a cumulative distribution that is positively skewed would look like? If your imagination, or reasoning, is not sufficient, turn your book upside down and look at Figure 3.5. A positively skewed distribution would show a rapid and then slow rise or acceleration toward the right or upper end of the score distribution, as Figure 3.5 would look when turned upside down.

Note that in the negatively skewed distribution of Figure 3.5, the distance on the score scale from Q_1 to the median is greater than the distance from the median to Q_3. This will, in general, be true of negatively skewed distributions, but it is not necessarily true of all such distributions. Similarly, for a positively skewed distribution, the distance from the median to Q_3 will, in general, be greater than the distance from Q_1 to the median, but this statement also is not necessarily true for all such distributions.

3.6 Obtaining Centiles from a Cumulative-Proportion Graph

In the cumulative-proportion graph of Figure 3.5, we see that the value of the median or 50th centile is approximately 60. The value of Q_1, the 25th centile, is approximately 54, and the value of Q_3, the 75th centile, is approximately 65. Approximate values of other centiles could be obtained by finding the points on the score axis corresponding to the centiles, as we have done for the 25th, 50th, and 75th centiles. For example, the score corresponding to the 97th centile is approximately 71. With a larger graph, the approximate values of the centiles can be found quite accurately and with relatively little labor.

There is still an additional bit of information to be gained from a study of Figure 3.5. Note that centile distances do not correspond to equal distances on the score continuum. Perpendiculars, corresponding to the centiles, dropped from the graph onto the score continuum would fall close together in the middle of the distribution, but would be farther apart toward both extremes of the distribution. The centile distances, in other words, do not correspond to equal distances on the score continuum. This means that the actual difference in value between two scores falling at the 45th and 55th centiles, for example, is not as great as the difference in value between two scores falling at the 85th and 95th centiles or between two scores falling at the 5th and 15th centiles. This can easily be seen by dropping perpendiculars corresponding to these centiles onto the score continuum and comparing the score differences.

The practical implication of the above discussion is that individual differences in scores falling toward the center of the distribution will tend to be exaggerated when expressed in centiles in comparison with individual differences in scores falling toward either extreme. A three-point increase or decrease in score toward the middle of the distribution, for example, may result in a rather large centile change as compared with a three-point increase or decrease in a score falling at either extreme of the distribution. The typical distributions obtained with educational and psychological tests are characterized by a single mode and some degree of negative or positive skewness. For all such distributions, the statements made concerning the relationship between centile distances and score distances will be true.

Consider, however, a distribution of scores in which each class interval has the same frequency. The histogram for this distribution would be a series of columns equal in height. If the cumulative-proportion graph were constructed for such a distribution, the result would be a straight line. In this instance, the centile distances would have to correspond to equal distances on the score axis. The score distance between the 95th and 96th centiles would be exactly equal to the score distance between any other two adjacent centiles. A *rectangular* distribution of scores is the only type of distribution in which the centiles will be equally spaced along the score continuum.

3.7   The Normal Distribution

The normal distribution is represented by a bell-shaped, symmetrical *curve* such that the total area under the curve is equal to 1. This theoretical curve has some important properties with which you should be familiar. Because the normal distribution curve is symmetrical, the mean and median will coincide and have exactly the same value. Fifty percent of the total area under the curve will therefore fall on each side of the mean. We know also that for any normal distribution, .3413 of the total area will fall between an ordinate at the mean and an ordinate at a distance 1 standard deviation above the mean. This means that the 84th centile will correspond to that value of X that is approximately 1 standard deviation above the mean. Similarly, .3413 of the total area will fall between an ordinate at the mean and an ordinate 1 standard deviation below the mean. Because .3413 + .5000 of the total area will fall above this point, a score that is 1 standard deviation below the mean will correspond approximately to the 16th centile.

Above the ordinate that is 1 standard deviation above the mean will fall .1587 of the area under the curve, and similarly, .1587 of the total area will fall to the left of the ordinate located at 1 standard deviation below the mean. When we go out 1.65 standard deviations from the mean, in each direction, we find that approximately .0500 of the total area will fall to the right of the ordinate located at 1.65 standard deviations above the mean and also that .0500 of the area will fall to the left of the ordinate located at 1.65 standard deviations below the mean. A distance 1.96 standard deviations above the mean will leave .0250 of the area falling to the right of the ordinate at this point. Similarly, .0250 of the total area will fall below or to the left of the ordinate that is 1.96 standard deviations below the mean. Finally, .0050 of the area will fall above the point set by an ordinate which is 2.58 standard

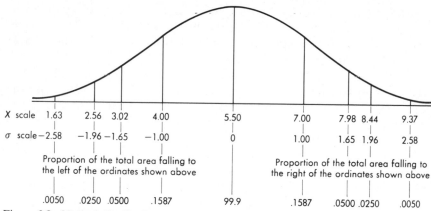

| X scale | 1.63 | 2.56 3.02 | 4.00 | 5.50 | 7.00 | 7.98 8.44 | 9.37 |
| σ scale | −2.58 | −1.96 −1.65 | −1.00 | 0 | 1.00 | 1.65 1.96 | 2.58 |

Proportion of the total area falling to the left of the ordinates shown above

Proportion of the total area falling to the right of the ordinates shown above

| .0050 | .0250 .0500 | .1587 | 99.9 | .1587 | .0500 .0250 | .0050 |

Figure **3.8**—Normal distribution curve with mean μ equal to 5.5 and standard deviation σ equal to 1.5.

deviations above the mean and .0050 of the area will fall below the point that is 2.58 standard deviations below the mean.

The important relations concerning the area of the normal curve and ordinates at points 1.00, 1.65, 1.96, and 2.58 standard deviations above and below the mean are illustrated in Figure 3.8. For this normal curve, the mean has been made equal to 5.5, and the standard deviation has been made equal to 1.5.

In Table 3.2 we give the frequency distribution of a discrete variable that is reasonably normal in form. This distribution also has a mean of 5.5 and a standard deviation of 1.5. The mean and standard deviation of this distribu-

Table 3.2—Frequency distribution of a discrete variable with mean equal to 5.5 and standard deviation equal to 1.5

(1) X	(2) f	(3) cf	(4) cp	(5) Upper limits of intervals
10	1	512	1.00	10.5
9	9	511	.998	9.5
8	36	502	.98	8.5
7	84	466	.91	7.5
6	126	382	.75	6.5
5	126	256	.50	5.5
4	84	130	.25	4.5
3	36	46	.09	3.5
2	9	10	.02	2.5
1	1	1	.002	1.5

tion thus correspond exactly to the mean and standard deviation of the normal curve shown in Figure 3.8. If the distribution of Table 3.2 is reasonably normal in form, then the relationships shown in Figure 3.8 should hold reasonably true for the data of the table.

We have said that in a normal distribution, the 16th centile will fall at a distance approximately 1 standard deviation below the mean. Because the mean of the distribution in Table 3.2 is 5.5 and the standard deviation is 1.5, the 16th centile should fall at the point $5.5 - 1.5 = 4.0$ on the score continuum. Similarly, we have said that the 84th centile should fall approximately 1 standard deviation above the mean and this would correspond to a point $5.5 + 1.5 = 7.0$ on the score continuum.

In each tail of the distribution, 1.65 standard deviations above the mean

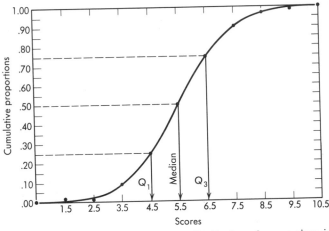

Figure **3.9**—Cumulative-proportion graph for the distribution of scores given in Table 3.2.

and 1.65 standard deviations below the mean, we should have approximately 5 percent of the total number of observations. On the score continuum, these two points would be $5.5 + (1.65)(1.5) = 7.98$ and $5.5 - (1.65)(1.5) = 3.02$, respectively. In the same manner, we may expect $5.5 + (1.96)(1.5) = 8.44$ and $5.5 - (1.96)(1.5) = 2.56$ to represent points on the score continuum above which and below which, respectively, 2.5 percent of the total number of observations fall.

The cumulative-proportion graph for the distribution given in Table 3.2 is shown in Figure 3.9. We can observe that the 16th and 84th centiles correspond approximately to the score values of 4.0 and 7.0, respectively.

The 5th and 95th centiles appear to be close to the values 3.02 and 7.98, respectively. We cannot judge too accurately from the graph the points on the score continuum above which and below which exactly 2.5 percent of the observations will fall. But columns (4) and (5) of Table 3.2 show that 2 percent will fall below the point 2.5 and that 2 percent will fall above 8.5 on the score continuum. It seems reasonably accurate to guess, therefore, that the exact values would not be too far away from the values of 2.56 and 8.44 of the theoretical normal curve.

Note also in Figure 3.9 that if we take two centiles that are the same distance from the mean, but in opposite directions, say the 40th and 60th centiles, the scores corresponding to these centiles will also be equally distant from the mean, but in opposite directions. Any distribution for which this is true is said to be *symmetrical*.

Imagine the graph in Figure 3.9 as being plotted on a rubber sheet that can be stretched. We now pull the sheet at the top and bottom in such a way as to stretch out the distances between centiles on the Y axis at the two extremes of the distribution, until the graph becomes a straight line instead of S-shaped. If we plot a cumulative-proportion distribution on a special kind of paper, called *normal-probability paper*, the effect is much like plotting the distribution on a rubber sheet that has been pulled in the manner described. The resulting graph will be a straight line, if the distribution is normal. Plotting a cumulative-proportion graph on normal-probability paper is an extremely simple and useful way of seeing how closely a given distribution approximates the ideal normal distribution.

In Figure 3.10 we show the cumulative-proportion distribution of Table 3.2 plotted on normal-probability paper. It can readily be observed that the plotted points, in general, fall along a straight line. Only a slight departure from linearity is present at the two extremes.

Take a pencil and fit by inspection a straight line through the points in Figure 3.10. Now drop perpendiculars to the score axis from the straight line corresponding to the centiles discussed above. You will see that the score values corresponding to these centiles are approximately the same as those for a theoretical normal distribution with mean equal to 5.5 and standard deviation equal to 1.5.

3.8 Comparing Different Distributions Graphically

In a study undertaken by Thurstone for the Quartermaster Corps, one of the factors investigated was the food preferences of enlisted men. The details of the study need not concern us, but in Table 3.3 we show the distributions of ratings for two desserts, "vanilla ice cream" and "Roquefort cheese." A high rating indicates that the dessert was liked and a low rating indicates that it was disliked. For purposes of illustration, we have intentionally reduced the total number of ratings made for Roquefort cheese, but without distorting greatly the relative frequencies of the original data.

If we wanted to compare these distributions of ratings graphically, it would not do to plot the frequency polygons or histograms for the frequen-

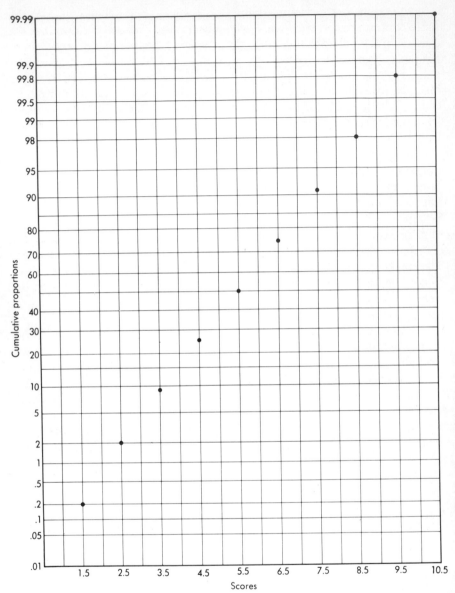

Figure **3.10**—Cumulative-proportion graph for the distribution of scores given in Table 3.2 plotted on normal-probability paper.

cies as given. The reason for this is that we have a difference in the total number of judgments for the two desserts. The areas under the frequency polygons or histograms would therefore not be equal, and the graphs would not be directly comparable. We can, however, express the frequencies as proportions of the total number of judgments for each distribution separately. We have done this for each distribution, and the proportions are shown in columns (3) and (7) of Table 3.3.

If we now plot the frequency polygons (or histograms) for the two distributions, we know from our earlier discussion that the areas of the two distributions will be equal and the two graphs may be compared directly. These frequency polygons are shown in Figure 3.11. This method of comparing two frequency distributions, when they are based upon an unequal number of observations or measurements, is also an extremely useful graphical device. We might, for example, wish to compare graphically the distributions of scores on some test for grades or classes with differing numbers of students.

Table 3.3—Frequency distributions of ratings of two desserts on a 10-point scale ranging from dislike to like*

	Vanilla ice cream ($n = 140$)					Roquefort cheese ($n = 257$)			
(1) X	(2) f	(3) p	(4) cf	(5) cp		(6) f	(7) p	(8) cf	(9) cp
10	3	.02	140	1.00		3	.01	257	1.00
9	10	.07	137	.98		16	.06	254	.99
8	25	.18	127	.91		36	.14	238	.93
7	50	.36	102	.73		43	.17	202	.79
6	30	.21	52	.37		54	.21	159	.62
5	14	.10	22	.16		26	.10	105	.41
4	4	.03	8	.06		26	.10	79	.31
3	2	.01	4	.03		16	.06	53	.21
2	1	.01	2	.01		20	.08	37	.14
1	1	.01	1	.01		17	.07	17	.07

* Data modified from Edwards and Thurstone (1952).

By expressing the frequencies as proportions of the total number of scores for each class separately and then plotting the frequency polygons, we may show the extent to which the various distributions overlap, which one is most variable, and which has the higher central tendency.

It is perfectly obvious, for example, that the median rating for vanilla ice cream in Figure 3.11 falls higher on the scale than the median rating for Roquefort cheese. Furthermore, it is apparent that the distribution of ratings for vanilla ice cream is much more symmetrical about the median or mode than is the distribution of ratings for Roquefort cheese.

Another method of comparing two or more distributions based upon unequal numbers of observations is shown in Figure 3.12. There we have

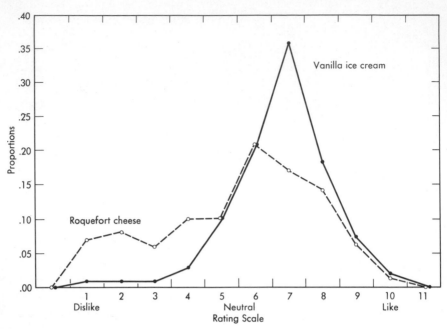

Figure **3.11**—Frequency polygons for the distributions of ratings given in Table 3.3.

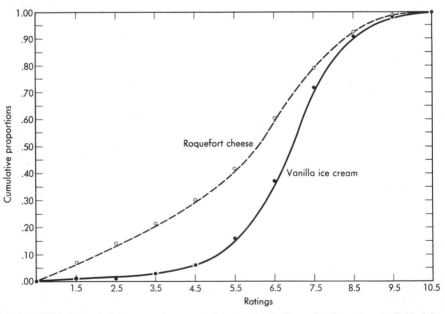

Figure **3.12**—Cumulative-proportion graphs for the distributions of ratings given in Table 3.3.

plotted the cumulative-proportion distributions for each of the desserts.[3] If we apply the information gained earlier in this chapter, then this graph also tells us that the median rating for vanilla ice cream is higher than the median rating for Roquefort cheese. Furthermore, the much steeper rise in the graph for vanilla ice cream, compared with the rise in the graph for Roquefort cheese, tells us that the variability of the ratings for vanilla ice cream is less than the variability of the ratings for Roquefort cheese. The more nearly S-shaped graph for vanilla ice cream, as compared with the graph for Roquefort cheese, also indicates the greater symmetry of the distribution of ice cream ratings. The negative skewness of both distributions is clearly shown by the relatively long tails and less rapid acceleration of the graphs at the low end of the scale.

EXAMPLES

3.1—Sketch the following graphs:

(a)   A cumulative-proportion graph for a negatively skewed distribution.
(b)   A cumulative-proportion graph for a positively skewed distribution.
(c)   A cumulative-proportion graph for a rectangular distribution.

3.2—Construct a histogram for the following distribution of scores and on the same figure draw the frequency polygon.

Scores	f
55–59	1
50–54	2
45–49	7
40–44	12
35–39	16
30–34	23
25–29	15
20–24	12
15–19	7
10–14	3
5–9	2

3.3—The distributions of scores for two categories of Veterans Administration trainees in clinical psychology on the Miller Analogies Test are

---

[3] The cumulative proportions given in columns (5) and (9) of Table 3.3 were obtained by multiplying the cumulative frequencies in columns (4) and (8) by the reciprocals of the n's of the two distributions, that is, by 1/140 and 1/257, respectively. If the proportions given in columns (3) and (7) are added to obtain the cumulative proportions, some of these values will differ slightly from those shown in columns (5) and (9) as a result of rounding errors.

given below. Compare the cumulative-proportion graphs for the two groups. Data are from Kelly and Fiske (1950).

Scores	Ph.D. Granted	Dismissals
	f	f
95–99	1	
90–94	1	1
85–89	6	0
80–84	11	2
75–79	6	4
70–74	9	6
65–69	3	8
60–64	2	3
55–59	1	2
50–54		6
45–49		2
40–44		3
35–39		1
30–34		1

3.4—The following scores were obtained from 301 new employees in an industrial concern on the Junior Calculating Test. Draw a histogram for the distribution and on the same graph draw the frequency polygon. Data are from Selover and Vogel (1948).

Scores	f
9	11
8	20
7	38
6	46
5	72
4	44
3	36
2	22
1	12

3.5—Plot the cumulative-proportion graph for the distribution of scores in Example 3.2.

3.6—Construct a histogram for the data of Example 2.6.

3.7—Calculate the median, Q_1, and Q_3 for the frequency distribution of Example 3.2. For the same example, make a cumulative-proportion graph. Use the graph to estimate the values of the median, Q_1, and Q_3 and compare these values with those you calculated.

3.8—We have a frequency distribution in which the lowest class interval is 30–34 and the highest class interval is 80–84.

(a) If you plot a histogram for this distribution, what would the values on abscissa represent? What would the ordinates show?
(b) If you plot a cumulative proportion graph for the distribution, what would the values on the abscissa represent? What would the ordinates show?

3.9—Suppose that X is a normally distributed variable with mean equal to 50.0 and standard deviation equal to 10.0, and that we have 10,000 observations. Find the values of X rounded to the nearest integer for each of the following:

(a) Approximately .05 of the observations will have values of $X \geq$ _____.
(b) Approximately .68 of the observations will have values between $50.0 \pm$ _____.
(c) Approximately .84 of the observations will have values of $X \leq$ _____.
(d) Approximately .975 of the observations will have values of $X \geq$ _____.

3.10—Give a one-sentence definition of each of the following terms or concepts:

abscissa	cumulative-proportion graph
ordinate	skewed distribution
coordinates of a point	symmetrical distribution
histogram	rectangular distribution

CHAPTER 4

Standard Scores and Normalizing Distributions

4.1 Standard Scores

A particular kind of score that plays a very important role in statistical analysis is called a *standard score*. It is defined as

$$z = \frac{X - \overline{X}}{s} = \frac{x}{s} \qquad (4.1)$$

where X = an original measurement
$\overline{X}$ = the mean of the distribution
s = the standard deviation of the distribution

In order to translate a set of n measures into standard scores, we first express each value as a deviation from the mean of the distribution and then divide each resulting deviation by the standard deviation of the distribution. Some of the z scores will, of course, be negative in sign, because some of the scores or measures will be smaller than the mean. In general, if n is large a distribution of z scores for a variable X that is normally distributed will range in size from about -3.00 to 3.00. When n is small, the range of z scores will not be as great as that observed for distributions based upon larger n's. Table 4.1 shows the approximate range in standard scores to be expected for varying values of n, when samples have been drawn from distributions that are normal in form.

For the distribution of scores in Table 3.2 in the last chapter, we had an n equal to 512. The mean of this distribution was 5.5, and the standard deviation was 1.5. The highest observed value was 10, and the lowest score in the distribution was 1. The standard score corresponding to the highest value in the distribution would therefore be

Table 4.1—Average range of standard scores in samples of varying sizes drawn from a normally distributed population*

n	R	n	R
5	2.3	65	4.7
6	2.5	85	4.9
7	2.7	100	5.0
8	2.8	125	5.2
9	3.0	150	5.3
10	3.1	175	5.4
15	3.5	200	5.5
20	3.7	250	5.6
25	3.9	300	5.8
30	4.1	400	5.9
40	4.3	500	6.1
50	4.5	1000	6.5

* Reproduced from L. H. C. Tippett. On the extreme in individuals and the range of a sample from a normal population. *Biometrika*, **17** (1925), 386, by permission of *Biometrika* and the author.

$$z = \frac{10.0 - 5.5}{1.5} = 3.0$$

and similarly the standard score for the lowest value in the distribution would be

$$z = \frac{1.0 - 5.5}{1.5} = -3.0$$

Our observed range of standard scores is from -3.0 to 3.0 or 6.0, and this range corresponds very well with the expected range of 6.1 for samples based upon an n of 500 cases as given in Table 4.1.

Any set of measures transformed to standard scores will have the following properties: (1) the mean of the transformed distribution, that is, of the standard scores, will be equal to zero, and (2) the variance will be equal to one. Because the standard deviation is the square root of the variance, the standard deviation of a set of standard scores will also be equal to one.

That the mean of a distribution of standard scores will be equal to zero can be proved very easily, because by definition the mean of a set of scores is the sum of the scores divided by n. Thus

$$\bar{z} = \frac{\sum z}{n} = \frac{1}{n} \sum \frac{(X - \bar{X})}{s}$$

or

$$\bar{z} = 0 \tag{4.2}$$

Because the mean of a set of standard scores is zero, as shown above, the variance will simply be the sum of the squared z scores, divided by $n - 1$. Then

$$s_z^2 = \frac{\sum z^2}{n - 1} = \frac{\sum (X - \bar{X})^2}{(n - 1)s^2}$$

or

$$s_z^2 = 1 \tag{4.3}$$

The fact that the mean of any distribution of standard scores will always be equal to zero and the fact that the variance and standard deviation will always be equal to one have some very useful applications in statistical analysis. Standard scores, for example, derived from one distribution may be compared directly with standard scores of another distribution of *comparable* form.

4.2   Combining Scores from Different Tests

Suppose that we wish to find an average of an individual's scores on a history test and on an English test. The history test is scored in terms of the number of right answers and shows a range of scores from 10 to 190 with a mean of 95. The English test, however, is scored in terms of the number of right answers minus the number of wrong answers, and the range of scores is from 50 to 70 with a mean of 59. Obviously, we cannot compare directly the standing of our subject on one test with his standing on the other. We could not find his average standing on both tests by adding his score on the history test and his score on the English examination and dividing by two. This average would have no meaning, for we would be combining different units from different scales. It is as though we added together an individual's height, measured in inches, and his weight, measured in pounds, and divided the sum by two to get an average. Suppose we were foolish enough to do so and found that this average was 110—but 110 what? Inches? Pounds? Surely not either of these, nor would such an average have any other meaning.

If we wish to compare measurements from various distributions of comparable form, we must first reduce the measurements of each distribution to a common scale. By translating the original measures into standard scores for each distribution, we accomplish this end. The standard scores thus obtained are in comparable units.

There may be occasions when it seems legitimate to average original measures from several distributions without first transforming the measures into standard scores or in other ways obtaining a common scale. Suppose, for example, an instructor has given five examinations during the course of a quarter and each examination is scored in terms of the number of correct responses. You may feel that it is reasonable to average the scores from the separate examinations. This may be so, but it should be emphasized that if the distributions of scores on the various examinations have different standard deviations, an average score based upon all the examinations will not give equal weight to each examination.

In general, the scores obtained from the distributions with large standard deviations will have more influence upon the average than scores obtained from distributions with small standard deviations. Only in the exceptional case in which all distributions have comparable standard deviations will the separate scores be weighted equally in determining an average score. If we want each examination to be weighted equally with the others, and if the standard deviations are different, we can accomplish this by first translating the scores from each distribution into standard scores and then averaging the standard scores, under the assumption that all of the distributions are of approximately the same form.

We may illustrate the point made above with the data of Table 4.2. We see that the total number of points on five examinations is 517 for David and 635 for Steven. If we depend upon the raw scores only, Steven would receive a higher grade in the course than would David. Now let us express the scores on the examinations in the form of standard scores. These are obtained by subtracting the means of the examinations from the scores in columns (4) and (5), dividing the resulting deviations by the standard deviations. The means and standard deviations are given in columns (2) and (3), and the resulting standard scores are shown in columns (6) and (7).

Table 4.2—X Scores and z scores of two individuals on five examinations

(1) Examination	(2) $\overline{X}$	(3) s	(4) David's X	(5) Steven's X	(6) David's z	(7) Steven's z
1	120	20	140	160	1.00	2.00
2	80	10	75	60	−.50	−2.00
3	42	8	66	44	3.00	.25
4	68	12	86	71	1.50	.25
5	200	50	150	300	−1.00	2.00
Σ			517	635	4.00	2.50

If we sum the standard scores, we see that David's total is 4.00 and Steven's is 2.50. Because the standard scores reduce the scores from each examination to a common scale, the sum of the standard scores gives each examination equal weight. When this is done, David has a higher standing than Steven on the five examinations. If we sum the original scores, Steven has a higher standing than David, primarily because Steven's best scores are on the examinations with the larger standard deviations (examinations 1 and 5), and these scores are weighted more heavily in determining the sum of the original scores. David's best work, however, is on the examinations with the smaller standard deviations (examinations 3 and 4), and in summing the original scores these examinations contribute less than the examinations with the larger standard deviations.

If we desire to do so, we can, of course, weight the standard scores of the different examinations so that some of the examinations contribute more to the total than others. Suppose, for example, that the last examination is a final one and that the instructor feels that this examination should carry more weight than any of the others. This examination can be given additional weight by simply multiplying the standard scores on it with the desired weight. If the instructor wants the examination to count twice as much as any one of the others, then the total score for each student would be given by

$$z_1 + z_2 + z_3 + z_4 + (2)(z_5) = \text{total score}$$

If the scores are to be averaged, then the divisor would be six instead of five. However, because the divisor would be a constant for all students, the relative standings of the students given by the total scores would be the same as the relative standings given by the averages, and this additional computation would not be necessary for grading purposes.

The advantage of the procedure described is that the instructor would at least know what weights are being assigned to the examinations. By averaging the original scores, the unwary instructor may, in his ignorance, be assigning undue weights to minor examinations. With standard scores he can either weight the examinations equally or weight the individual examinations in terms of the judged importance of the material covered by each.

4.3   Transformed Standard Scores

Because standard scores, as defined by (4.1), take negative as well as positive values, it may sometimes be judged desirable to shift the origin of the distribution in such a way as to make all scores positive in sign. As we have shown in an earlier chapter, adding a constant to each score will have no effect upon the standard deviation of a distribution, but will merely have the result of increasing the mean by the amount of the constant that is added to each score. Thus, if 50 points are added to each of the standard scores obtained by means of formula (4.1), the mean of this new distribution will be 50 instead of zero, but the standard deviation will still be equal to 1. If we wish to increase the standard deviation by any given amount, we multiply the standard scores obtained by (4.1) by an appropriate constant.

We may define a new score with mean equal to a and standard deviation equal to b as

$$Y = a + b\left(\frac{X - \overline{X}}{s}\right) \qquad (4.4)$$

where b = an arbitrary constant by which $z = (X - \overline{X})/s$ is multiplied
$\quad a$ = an arbitrary constant to be added to the product

In (4.1), b is equal to 1 and a is equal to zero, and the distribution of such a set of standard scores, as we already know, has a standard deviation of 1 and a mean of zero.

Suppose we now let a equal 50 and b equal 15, so that (4.4) becomes

$$Y = 50 + 15\left(\frac{X - \overline{X}}{s}\right)$$

This distribution of scores will have a mean equal to a or 50 and a standard deviation equal to b or 15. For a large number of observations, we may expect this transformation to give us a range of scores from approximately -3.00 to 3.00 standard deviations. Because the standard deviation is 15, our expected range will be from 5 to 95. The transformed scores thus have a convenient scale from approximately zero to 100 with a mean equal to 50.

No matter what values we substitute for a and b in (4.4), the resulting mean and standard deviation of the transformed distribution will be equal to a and b, respectively.

4.4   Normalizing a Distribution of Scores

It may be emphasized that changing a set of scores to standard scores does nothing to alter the shape of the original distribution. The only change is to shift the mean to zero and the standard deviation to unity. The form of the distribution remains exactly the same. Students sometimes get the mistaken notion that when scores are changed to standard scores, the distribution of scores is therefore somehow normalized, that is, changed to a normal distribution. This is not the case. If the original score distribution is normal in form, the standard score distribution will also be normal. But if the original distribution is skewed, the standard score distribution will also be skewed.

In Table 4.3 we repeat the distribution of scores on the Minnesota Psycho-Analogies Test for 158 students. The mean of the original distribution, as we mentioned earlier, is 59.3, and the standard deviation is 8.1. In column (3) we give the mid-points of each class interval. You may recall that our assumption is that all of the scores within a given interval can be repre-

Table 4.3—Transforming the scores of Table 3.1 to standard scores, normalized standard scores, and T scores*

(1) X	(2) f	(3) Mid-points of intervals	(4) Ob-served z	(5) Upper Limit cf	(6) Mid-point cf	(7) Mid-point cp	(8) Normal z	(9) T scores
72–74	4	73	1.69	158	156.0	.987	2.23	72.3
69–71	15	70	1.32	154	146.5	.927	1.45	64.5
66–68	21	67	.95	139	128.5	.813	.89	58.9
63–65	21	64	.58	118	107.5	.680	.47	54.7
60–62	24	61	.21	97	85.0	.538	.10	51.0
57–59	16	58	−.16	73	65.0	.411	−.22	47.8
54–56	23	55	−.53	57	45.5	.288	−.56	44.4
51–53	15	52	−.90	34	26.5	.168	−.96	40.4
48–50	7	49	−1.27	19	15.5	.098	−1.29	37.1
45–47	3	46	−1.64	12	10.5	.066	−1.51	34.9
42–44	4	43	−2.01	9	7.0	.044	−1.71	32.9
39–41	1	40	−2.38	5	4.5	.028	−1.91	30.9
36–38	3	37	−2.75	4	2.5	.016	−2.14	28.6
33–35	1	34	−3.12	1	.5	.003	−2.75	22.5
Σ	158							

* Data from Levine (1950).

sented by the mid-point of the interval. Thus the four scores within the class interval 72–74 are all assumed to be represented by 73. In column (4) we show the standard scores, obtained by formula (4.1), corresponding to the mid-points of the intervals. For example, the standard score corresponding to the mid-point of the class interval 72–74 was obtained by

$$z = \frac{73.0 - 59.3}{8.1} = 1.69$$

Direct calculation verifies that the mean of this distribution of z scores is equal to zero and that the standard deviation is equal to 1, within errors of rounding. The form of the distribution remains unchanged by this transformation.

Suppose, however, that we wish to alter the scale of scores in such a way that the transformed distribution will be normal in form. A simple method of doing this is shown in Table 4.3. We first find the cumulative frequencies as shown in column (5). These cumulative frequencies correspond to the upper limits of the class intervals. For our purpose, however, we need the cumulative frequencies up to the mid-points of the class intervals. If we assume that the frequencies within each interval are uniformly distributed throughout the interval, then the cumulative frequency to a given mid-point will be equal to the sum of all of the frequencies below that mid-point plus one half the frequency within the interval in which the mid-point is located. For example, the cumulative frequency falling below the mid-point 49, of the class interval 48–50, is found by adding 12, the sum of the frequencies falling below the interval 48–50, and one half of 7, the frequency within the interval 48–50. We thus have $12 + 7/2 = 15.5$ for the desired cumulative frequency up to the mid-point of the interval. The cumulative frequencies up to the mid-points of each of the other intervals are found in the same manner. These values are entered in column (6) of Table 4.3.

In column (7) the cumulative frequencies of column (6) are expressed as cumulative proportions by dividing each one by 158, the total number of observations. We again use the reciprocal of 158 or $1/158 = .00633$ to multiply the cumulative frequencies rather than the equivalent operation of dividing them by 158 in finding the cumulative proportions entered in column (7).

We shall not discuss the equation of the standard normal curve at this time, other than to state that the total area under this curve is equal to 1.00 and that the curve gives the distribution of a standard normal variable.[1] Any normally distributed variable X with mean μ_X and standard deviation σ_X can be transformed into a standard normal variable by means of[2]

$$z = \frac{X - \mu_X}{\sigma_X}$$

We have proved that if $z = (X - \overline{X})/s_X$, then $\overline{z} = 0$ and $s_z = 1$. We shall prove later[3] that if we replace $\overline{X}$ by μ_X and s_X by σ_X, then $z = (X - \mu_X)/\sigma_X$ will have a mean μ_z equal to zero and a standard deviation σ_z equal to 1. Thus a standard normal variable is a normally distributed variable with mean equal to zero and standard deviation equal to 1. The central ordinate of the standard normal curve corresponds to $\mu_z = 0$ and distances along the base line of the curve are given in terms of $z = (X - \mu_X)/\sigma_X$.

Table III in Appendix B is a table of the standard normal curve. The first column gives values of z as defined above. For example, if you look down the first column until you come to 1.00, this value represents a distance that is one standard deviation above the mean. The second column gives the proportion of the total area falling between an ordinate at the mean and an

---

[1] The equation of the standard normal curve is discussed in Chapter 9.

[2] We use $\overline{X}$ and s to represent the mean and standard deviation of a sample and μ and σ to represent the mean and standard deviation of a population or of a probability distribution. The standard normal curve gives the probability distribution of any normally distributed variable with mean equal to zero and standard deviation equal to 1, as we shall see in Chapter 9.

[3] The proof is given in Chapter 9.

ordinate at the corresponding point given by the value in the first column. For example, in column (2) you will find .3413 tabled opposite the entry $z = 1.00$ in the first column. This tells you that .3413 of the total area under the curve falls between $z = .00$ and $z = 1.00$.

The third column of the table gives the area of the curve falling below the value of z given in the first column or the area in the larger portion of the curve as it is sectioned by the ordinate at z. For example, opposite the z value of 1.00 in the first column, you will find the entry .8413 in the third column. This tells you that .8413 of the total area falls *below* $z = 1.00$.

The fourth column of the table gives the area of the curve above z or in the smaller portion of the curve as sectioned by the ordinate at z. The entry in the fourth column opposite the z value of 1.00 in the first column is .1587. This entry is .1587 because the area in the smaller portion of the curve, .1587, plus the area in the larger portion of the curve, .8413, must equal unity, the total area under the curve.

Because the normal curve is symmetrical, the tabled values are given for only one half of the curve, that is, only for positive values of z. Negative values of z would have exactly the same entries tabled as those for positive values of z. Hence the table may be entered with negative as well as with positive values of z. For $z = -1.00$, column (2) tells us that the area between the ordinates corresponding to $z = -1.00$ and $z = .00$ is .3413. Column (3) tells us that .8413 of the area will fall above $z = -1.00$, and column (4) tells us that .1587 of the area will fall below the ordinate at $z = -1.00$.

We can now complete the project we started, namely, normalizing the distribution of scores in Table 4.3. The entries in column (7) show the proportion of the total number of cases falling below the mid-points of the class intervals. For example, .003 of the total of 158 cases fall below 34, the mid-point of the first interval. We have already shown, in column (4), that the z or standard-score value corresponding to this mid-point for our *observed distribution* of scores is -3.12. What we want to know now, however, is the z or standard-score value corresponding to this mid-point in a *standard normal distribution*. We can find this value from Table III in Appendix B.

We look at Table III to find the value of z below which .003 of the area will fall. Because .500 of the total area in a standard normal distribution will fall below $z = .00$, or the mean of the distribution, any point below which less than .500 of the total area falls must correspond to a negative value of z. If we find the value of z such that .003 of the area of the curve falls to the left of the ordinate at z and such that .997 of the area falls to the right, this will be the value we want. We look in column (4), headed "Area in Smaller Portion," to find .003. We then read the corresponding z value from column (1) and find it to be 2.75. We attach a negative sign to this value (the z is below the mean) and enter -2.75 in column (8) of Table 4.3.

Let us find one more entry in column (8) to make sure that the procedure described is clear. We see that in our observed distribution, .538 of the cases fall below the mid-point 61 of the class interval 60–62. We want to find the z value in a standard normal distribution below which .538 of the total area will fall. Because this proportion is greater than .500, the z value must be to the right of the mean or positive in sign. We now look in Table III, column (3), headed "Area in Larger Portion," to find .538. Our closest approximation to this value is given by .5398; consequently we take the z value corresponding to this entry. It is .10 and this is the value we have entered in column (8) opposite .538 in Table 4.3. You should check several of the other entries in column (8).

The standard scores we have just obtained are normalized standard scores. You would find upon calculation that the mean of this distribution of scores is zero and that the standard deviation is equal to 1. But the distribution will no longer have the same form as the original distribution. We have stretched the score scale in such a way as to normalize the distribution. If, for example, you plot the cumulative proportions against the normalized standard scores in column (8) of Table 4.3 on normal-probability paper, you will find that the graph is a straight line. This will not be true of the original distribution.

4.5   *T* Scores

In column (9) of Table 4.3 we give a particular kind of normalized score that has come to be known as a *T score*. *T* scores are frequently used in constructing norms for standardized psychological and educational tests. The values of the *T* scores are obtained directly from the normalized standard scores of column (8). We have simply multiplied each entry in column (8) by 10 and added 50 to the product. For example, the normalized standard score of 2.23 becomes $(10)(2.23) + 50 = 72.3$ when translated into a *T* score. The figure after the decimal place is usually dropped, and the *T* score is rounded to two digits.

The two constants, 50 and 10, correspond to the a and b constants of formula (4.4). You should know, therefore, that the mean of a distribution of *T* scores will be 50 and that the standard deviation will be equal to 10. Furthermore, the distribution of *T* scores will be normal in form. That this is true is shown in Figure 4.1 where we have plotted on normal-probability paper the cumulative proportions against the corresponding *T* scores. It is apparent that the graph is linear.

T scores are obtained directly from normalized standard scores, and these in turn are related to the proportion of the total area falling below a given value of z in a standard normal distribution. We may thus table, once and for all, the *T* scores corresponding to these proportions. This has been done in Table XI, in Appendix B. If we enter Table XI with the proportions

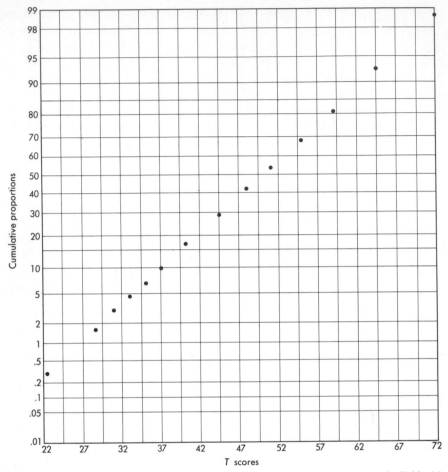

Figure **4.1**—Cumulative-proportion graph for the distribution of T scores given in Table 4.1 plotted on normal-probability paper.

of column (7) of Table 4.3, we can obtain the corresponding T scores without further computations. Table XI may be used to transform the scores in any distribution to T scores. We simply find the proportion of the total number of observations falling below the mid-point of a given score or interval. We then enter Table XI with these proportions to find the corresponding T scores.

4.6 Normalizing Ranked Data

In some cases it may not be possible for us to measure the variable in which we are interested, but it may be possible for us to obtain judgments of the degree to which each person or object possesses the variable. A convenient technique for obtaining such judgments is the *method of rank order*. A judge, for example, might be asked to arrange a series of 10 pictures from the one most liked to the one least liked. After the task is completed, the pictures will be arranged in serial order, and we assign the number 1 to the picture liked most, the number 2 to the next most-liked picture, and so on. Individuals or objects arranged in this way are said to be ranked. The rank itself refers to the relative position of an object or individual in a group of objects or individuals.

It is important in dealing with ranks that we know the total number of objects ranked. A rank of 11, for example, would mean something quite different in a set of 21 ranks than it would if the set of ranks consisted of only 11 objects. In the first instance the rank of 11 is the mean of the set of ranks, and in the second instance it is the lowest rank in the series. Furthermore, we should note that ranks do not tell us anything about the relative distances between the objects, with respect to the variable ranked, in the way in which measurements do. For example, we might rank a group of individuals with respect to their heights and we might also have available measurements of the heights of each individual. The measurements would tell us *how much* taller or shorter one individual was compared with another, whereas the ranks would only tell us whether one individual was taller or shorter than another.

Having obtained a set of ranks, we may make the assumption that the variable that was ranked is approximately normally distributed. We could then use the procedures previously described for normalizing a distribution of observations to normalize the set of ranks. We could thus transform the ranks into T scores or any other form of normalized scores.

Table XII, in Appendix B, enables us to obtain directly the T scores for any set of ranks from 5 to 45. As indicated in the table, the mean of these transformed scores will be 50 and the standard deviation will be 10.

EXAMPLES

4.1—Prove that the mean of a set of standard scores is equal to zero.

4.2—Prove that the variance and standard deviation of a set of standard scores is equal to 1.00.

4.3—Prove that, if we multiply each value in a set of standard scores by a constant b and then add a constant a to the product, the mean of this new distribution will be equal to a and the variance will be equal to b^2.

4.4—If we have a normal distribution, then the centiles corresponding to various standard scores may be obtained from the table of the normal curve. Find the centiles for the following standard scores from Table III, in Appendix B.

(a)	$z = .00$		(e)	$z = -1.00$
(b)	$z = .74$		(f)	$z = 1.04$
(c)	$z = -.67$		(g)	$z = 1.23$
(d)	$z = -.44$		(h)	$z = 2.33$

4.5—Table XII in Appendix B gives the T scores for sets of ranks from 5 to 45. Verify these T scores for the ranks 1 to 10, using the method for normalizing a distribution described in the chapter.

4.6—Plot the cumulative-proportion graph for the T scores of Example 4.5 on normal-probability paper.

4.7—Given a normal distribution of scores with mean equal to 50, standard deviation equal to 10, and n equal to 500:

(a) What is the estimated range of scores?
(b) What score will correspond to Q_1?
(c) What proportion of the scores will fall between 40 and 60?
(d) What score will correspond to the median?

4.8—Using Table XI, in Appendix B, find the T scores for the midpoints of the following class intervals.

Scores	f
55–59	1
50–54	2
45–49	7
40–44	12
35–39	16
30–34	23
25–29	15
20–24	12
15–19	7
10–14	3
5– 9	2

4.9—Sketch the cumulative-proportion graph for a normally distributed variable X with mean equal to 50 and standard deviation equal to 10. On the same figure, sketch the cumulative-proportion graph for a normally distributed variable Y with mean equal to 50 and standard deviation equal to 4. Use the table of the standard normal curve to find selected values of the cumulative proportions corresponding to given values of X and Y as an aid in making your graphs.

4.10—If X is normally distributed with mean equal to 40 and standard deviation equal to 10, then:

(a) What value of X will correspond to the 84th centile?
(b) What value of X will correspond to the 16th centile?
(c) What value of X will correspond to the 95th centile?

4.11—If X is normally distributed with mean equal to 70 and standard deviation equal to 10, and if we have $n = 10,000$ observation of X, then:

(a) How many observations will have values of X between 70 and 80?
(b) How many observations will have $X \geq 80$?
(c) How many observations will have $X \leq 70$?
(d) How many observations will have $X \geq 90$?
(c) How many observations will have $X \leq 40$?
(f) How many observations will have values of X between 50 and 80?

4.12—If X is normally distributed and the cumulative-proportion distribution is plotted on normal-probability paper, what will the graph look like?

4.13—If X is normally distributed and the cumulative-proportion graph is plotted on ordinary coordinate paper, what will the graph look like?

4.14—If X is a normally distributed variable with mean equal to 30.0 and standard deviation equal to 5.0, what would you do to transform X into a standard normal variable?

4.15—What is the area under the standard normal curve equal to?

4.16—If $\overline{X} = 22.0$ and $s_X = 4.0$, and if $Y = 10 + 12(X - \overline{X})/s_X$, then to what will $\overline{Y}$ and s_Y be equal?

4.17—Give a one-sentence definition of each of the following terms or concepts:

standard score	standard normal variable
T score	standard normal curve

CHAPTER 5

Linear Regression

5.1 Introduction

Many psychological research problems are concerned with the relationship between two or more variables. In this chapter we shall discuss methods of determining an equation that will relate values of an observed *dependent* variable Y to values of a second *independent* variable X. We shall assume that the values of the independent variable have been *selected* by the experimenter. These X values may represent number of trials, varying levels of illumination, varying amounts of practice, varying dosages of a drug, intensities of electric shock, or any other independent variable of experimental interest.

For each X value, the experimenter subsequently obtains a corresponding observation of the dependent variable Y. We wish to determine whether these Y values are related to the X values. We shall be concerned primarily with the case of *linear* relationships. By a linear relationship, we mean that if the Y values are plotted against the X values in a graph, the resulting trend of the plotted points can be represented by a straight line. Our problem is to determine an equation for the straight line which represents the trend. We may regard this empirical equation as a rule that relates values of Y to those of X.

5.2 Equation of a Straight Line

Consider the values of X and Y in Table 5.1. What is the rule that relates Y to X? Examination of the pairs of values will show that each value of Y is exactly .5 of the corresponding value of X. We may express this rule in the following way

$$Y = bX \tag{5.1}$$

Table 5.1—Value of $Y = .5X$ for given values of X

X	Y
8	4.0
5	2.5
6	3.0
2	1.0
10	5.0
12	6.0
7	3.5
4	2.0
3	1.5

where $b = .5$ is a constant that multiplies each value of X. If each value of Y in Table 5.1 was exactly equal to the corresponding value of X, then the value of b would have to be equal to 1. If each value of Y was equal to X, but opposite in sign, then the value of b would be equal to -1.

Now examine the values of X and Y in Table 5.2. The rule or equation relating values of Y to X may not be quite so obvious here. Its general form is as follows

$$Y = a + bX \tag{5.2}$$

where b is again a constant that multiplies each value of X, and a is a constant that is added to each of the products. For the data of Table 5.2 the value of b is .5 and the value of a is 4. Thus when $X = 6$, $Y = 4 + (.5)(6) = 7$.

We note that (5.1) and (5.2) are both equations for a straight line. For example, we could take any arbitrary constants for a and b. Then for any

Table 5.2—Values of $Y = 4 + .5X$ for given values of X

X	Y
4	6.0
9	8.5
14	11.0
6	7.0
16	12.0
5	6.5
8	8.0
7	7.5
11	9.5
10	9.0

given set of X values we could substitute in (5.2) and obtain a set of Y values. If these obtained values of Y were plotted against the corresponding X values, the set of plotted points would fall on a straight line.

5.3   The Graph of $Y = a + bX$

Let us plot the values of Y given in Table 5.2 against the corresponding values of X. The graph will give us some additional insight into the nature of the constant b that multiplies each X and also the constant a that is added to the product. In making the graph, we set up two axes at right angles to each other. It is customary to let the horizontal axis represent the independent

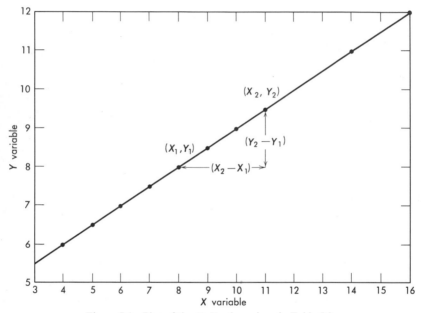

Figure **5.1**—Plot of the X, Y values given in Table 5.2.

or X variable and the vertical axis represent the dependent or Y variable. We need not begin our scale on the X and Y axes at zero. We may begin with any convenient values that permit us to plot the lowest values of X and Y. In Figure 5.1, for example, we begin the X scale with 3 and the Y scale with 5. Nor is it necessary that the X and Y scales be expressed in the same units. You will note in Figure 5.1, for example, that a 1-point increase in X is represented by a distance on the X axis that is only 3/4 the distance corresponding to a 1-point increase on the Y axis.

You will recall that the two values (X, Y) give the coordinates of a point. To find the point on the graph corresponding to (11, 9.5) we go out the X axis to 11 and *imagine* a line perpendicular to the X axis erected at this point.

We now go up the Y axis to 9.5 and *imagine* another line perpendicular to the Y axis erected at this point. The intersection of the two perpendiculars will be the point (11, 9.5) on the graph. It is obviously not necessary to draw the perpendiculars in order to plot a set of points.

5.4 The Slope and Intercept of the Line

It is clear that the points plotted in Figure 5.1 fall along a straight line. We already know that the equation of this line as given by (5.2) is

$$Y = 4 + .5X$$

What is the nature of the multiplying constant $b = .5$? Note, for example, that as we move from 10 to 11 on the X scale, the corresponding increase on the Y scale is from 9 to 9.5. An increase of 1 unit in X, in other words, results in only .5 of a unit increase in Y. Similarly, if we move from 10 to 15 on the X scale, a distance of 5 units, the corresponding increase on the Y scale is from 9 to 11.5, a distance of 2.5 units. It seems apparent, then, that b gives the *rate* at which Y changes with change in X.

The value of b can be determined directly from the graph in Figure 5.1. For example, if we take any two points on the line, with coordinates (X_1, Y_1) and (X_2, Y_2), then

$$b = \frac{Y_2 - Y_1}{X_2 - X_1} \tag{5.3}$$

Substituting in (5.3) with the coordinates (8, 8.0) and (11, 9.5), we have

$$b = \frac{9.5 - 8.0}{11 - 8} = \frac{1.5}{3} = .5$$

In geometry (5.3) is known as a particular form of the equation of a straight line, and the value of b is called the *slope* of the straight line.

The nature of the additive constant a in (5.2) can be readily determined by setting X equal to zero. The value of a must then be the value of Y when X is equal to zero. If the X axis is extended to the left and the Y axis is extended downward in Figure 5.1, you will see that the graph of the straight line will pass through the point (0, a). The number a is called the *Y-intercept* of the line. We already know that a is equal to 4. If the line passed through the point (0, 0), then a would be equal to zero, and the equation of the line would be $Y = bX$.

5.5 Positive and Negative Relationships

We may conclude that if the relationship between two variables is linear, then the values of a and b can be determined by plotting the values and finding the Y-intercept and the slope of the line, respectively. A single equation may then be written that will express the nature of the relationship. When the value of b is positive in sign, the relationship is also described as positive; that is, an increase in X is accompanied by an increase in Y and a decrease in X is accompanied by a decrease in Y. When the value of b is negative, the relationship is also described as negative. A negative relationship means that an increase in X is accompanied by a decrease in Y, and a decrease in X is accompanied by an increase in Y. When two variables are positively related, the line representing this relationship will extend from the lower left of the graph to the upper right and the slope of the line is said to be positive. When the relationship is negative, the line will extend from the upper left of the graph to the lower right and the slope of the line is said to be negative.

When a set of plotted points corresponding to values of an X variable and a Y variable fall precisely on a straight line such that no single point deviates from the line, the relationship between the two variables is said to be perfect. This means that every observed value of Y will be given exactly by $Y = a + bX$. With empirical data we do not expect to find perfect relationships. Errors of measurement may be involved along with other sources of variation. The trend of the plotted points may be linear, but the plotted points will not fall precisely on any line that we might draw.

5.6   Finding a Line of Best Fit

Our problem with empirical data is to find the *line of best fit* that relates Y to X. This line is called the *regression line of Y on X*, and the equation for the line is called a *regression equation*. The value of b in the regression equation is called a *regression coefficient*.

Table 5.3—Finding the line of best fit for $\tilde{Y} = a + bX$

(1) X	(2) Y	(3) X^2	(4) Y^2	(5) XY	(6) $\tilde{Y}$	(7) $(Y - \tilde{Y})$	(8) $(Y - \tilde{Y})^2$
6	6	36	36	36	5.84	.16	.0256
5	4	25	16	20	4.73	− .73	.5329
4	5	16	25	20	3.62	1.38	1.9044
3	3	9	9	9	2.51	.49	.2401
2	1	4	1	2	1.40	− .40	.1600
1	−1	1	1	−1	.29	−1.29	1.6641
−1	−2	1	4	2	−1.93	− .07	.0049
−2	−4	4	16	8	−3.04	− .96	.9216
−3	−3	9	9	9	−4.15	1.15	1.3225
−4	−5	16	25	20	−5.26	.26	.0676
Σ 11	4	121	142	125	4.01	− .01	6.8437

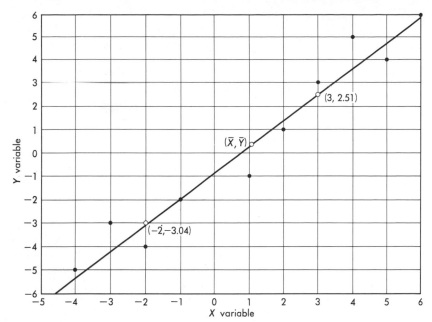

Figure **5.2**—Plot of the X, Y values given in Table 5.3 and the line of best fit.

The notion of a best-fitting line requires some discussion. What does "best fit" mean? A set of empirical values may assist us in understanding this concept. Examine the data in Table 5.3 and the corresponding plotted points in Figure 5.2. It is obvious that the trend of the points can be described by a straight line. If we desire to represent the relationship by means of a *single* straight line, how shall we draw the line, and what will be the resulting values of a and b in the equation for the line?

The line might be drawn by inspection, and sometimes this will prove to be a satisfactory procedure. But if we have a large number of plotted points, drawing the line by inspection will be more difficult. If several different individuals draw what they believe is the line representing the trend, we may have several different lines with corresponding differences in the values of a and b. How shall we select a single line from among the several possible? Which will give the best fit?

Inspectional procedures can never be as satisfactory as those involving analytical methods. If we can determine the line by algebraic operations upon the data, in terms of a criterion of best fit, we may expect agreement among different observers. Furthermore, we shall have a uniquely determined line to represent the trend.

Since we are no longer dealing with a perfect relationship between X and Y, let us make a slight change in notation and write

$$\tilde{Y} = a + bX \tag{5.4}$$

where $\tilde{Y}$ indicates a value falling on the line given by the regression equation. $\tilde{Y}$ as given by (5.4) will no longer necessarily be equal to the observed value of Y corresponding to the observed value of X. The values of $\tilde{Y}$ represent *predicted* values of Y for each given value of X. Then an error of prediction will be given by

$$Y - \tilde{Y} = Y - (a + bX) \tag{5.5}$$

5.7 Method of Least Squares

We shall find the line of best fit by the *method of least squares*. This criterion of best fit demands that the values of a and b be determined in such a way that

$$\sum (Y - \tilde{Y})^2 = \sum [Y - (a + bX)]^2 \tag{5.6}$$

will be a minimum, that is, the sum of squares of our errors of prediction will be less than it would be for any other values of a and b which might be selected. It can be shown that the values of a and b which will make the residual sum of squares $\sum (Y - \tilde{Y})^2$ a minimum must satisfy the following equations[1]

$$\sum Y = na + b \sum X \tag{5.7}$$

and

$$\sum XY = a \sum X + b \sum X^2 \tag{5.8}$$

If we divide both sides of (5.7) by n and solve for a, we have

$$a = \bar{Y} - b\bar{X} \tag{5.9}$$

If we now substitute $\bar{Y} - b\bar{X}$ for a in (5.8) we have

$$\sum XY = (\bar{Y} - b\bar{X}) \sum X + b \sum X^2$$

and solving for b, we obtain

$$b = \frac{\sum XY - \dfrac{(\sum X)(\sum Y)}{n}}{\sum X^2 - \dfrac{(\sum X)^2}{n}} \tag{5.10}$$

The necessary values for computing b are given in Table 5.3. Substituting these values in (5.10), we have

---

[1] The proof requires a knowledge of the rules of differentiation as taught in the first course in the calculus. The solution is obtained by expanding the right-hand side of (5.6). This expression is then differentiated with respect to a and then with respect to b. Setting the derivatives equal to zero. we obtain (5.7) and (5.8).

$$b = \frac{125 - \dfrac{(11)(4)}{10}}{121 - \dfrac{(11)^2}{10}} = \frac{120.6}{108.9} = 1.11$$

Because $\overline{X} = 11/10 = 1.10$ and $\overline{Y} = 4/10 = .40$, and we have just found that $b = 1.11$, we may substitute in (5.9) and find

$$
\begin{aligned}
a &= \quad .40 - (1.11)(1.10) \\
&= -.82
\end{aligned}
$$

The regression equation, given by (5.4), then becomes

$$\tilde{Y} = -.82 + 1.11X$$

Note now that if we predict a value of Y corresponding to the mean of the X distribution, we obtain

$$
\begin{aligned}
\tilde{Y} &= -.82 + (1.11)(1.10) \\
&= -.82 + 1.22 \\
&= \quad .40
\end{aligned}
$$

which is equal to the mean of the Y distribution. The regression line will therefore pass through the point established by the means of the X and Y distributions or, in other words, the point with coordinates $(\overline{X}, \overline{Y})$. This will always be true of any linear regression line fitted by the method of least squares.

The predicted value of Y when X is equal to 3 will be

$$
\begin{aligned}
\tilde{Y} &= -.82 + (1.11)(3) \\
&= \quad 2.51
\end{aligned}
$$

and when X is equal to -2, the predicted value of Y will be

$$
\begin{aligned}
\tilde{Y} &= -.82 + (1.11)(-2) \\
&= -3.04
\end{aligned}
$$

The regression line will therefore pass through the points with coordinates $(3, 2.51)$ and $(-2, -3.04)$. These points are shown in Figure 5.2. If we draw a line through them, this will be the regression line of Y on X.

5.8   The Sum of Products

The denominator of (5.10) we recognize as the sum of squared deviations of X from the mean $\overline{X}$, because, as we have shown earlier,

$$
\begin{aligned}
\sum x^2 &= \sum (X - \overline{X})^2 \\
&= \sum X^2 - \frac{(\sum X)^2}{n}
\end{aligned}
$$

The numerator of (5.10) is equal to the sum of the products of the deviations of X and Y from their respective means. We note, for example, that

$$\sum xy = \sum (X - \bar{X})(Y - \bar{Y})$$
$$= \sum XY - \bar{Y}\sum X - \bar{X}\sum Y + n\bar{X}\bar{Y}$$
$$= \sum XY - \frac{(\sum X)(\sum Y)}{n} \tag{5.11}$$

and (5.10) will be identical with

$$b = \frac{\sum xy}{\sum x^2} \tag{5.12}$$

The *sum of products*, $\sum xy$, is a basic quantity in statistical analysis, and we shall have occasion to refer to it again. You may recall that the sum of squares, $\sum x^2$ or $\sum y^2$, when divided by $n - 1$, gives a measure of variability that we have called the variance. The sum of products, when divided by $n - 1$, gives a similar measure that is called the *covariance* of X and Y. If the numerator and denominator of (5.12) were both divided by $n - 1$, it would be clear that the regression coefficient b is the ratio of the covariance of the two variables to the variance of the independent variable.

5.9   The Residual Sum of Squares

The residual sum of squares or errors of prediction as given by (5.6) is a measure of the variation of the Y values about the regression line. Let us see if we can gain some additional insight into the nature of this sum of squares. By definition

$$\tilde{Y} = a + bX$$

and we have found that $a = \bar{Y} - b\bar{X}$. Then

$$\tilde{Y} = \bar{Y} - b\bar{X} + bX$$

Summing, we have

$$\sum \tilde{Y} = n\bar{Y} - nb\bar{X} + b\sum X$$

but $nb\bar{X} = b\sum X$ and therefore

$$\sum \tilde{Y} = n\bar{Y} \tag{5.13}$$

The sum of the predicted values $\sum \tilde{Y}$ is therefore equal to the sum of the observed values $\sum Y$, and the mean of the predicted values must therefore be equal to the mean of the observed values. We see that this is true, within rounding errors, for the data of Table 5.3, where $\sum \tilde{Y} = 4.01$ and $\sum Y = 4.00$. It also follows that the algebraic sum of the deviations of the observed values from the predicted values must equal zero. Thus

$$\sum (Y - \tilde{Y}) = \sum Y - \sum \tilde{Y} = 0 \qquad (5.14)$$

because we have just shown that $\sum \tilde{Y}$ equals $\sum Y$.

In the development above we showed that a predicted value $\tilde{Y}$ could be written $\tilde{Y} = \overline{Y} - b\overline{X} + bX$. Rearranging the last two terms, we have

$$\begin{aligned}
\tilde{Y} &= \overline{Y} + bX - b\overline{X} \\
&= \overline{Y} + b(X - \overline{X}) \\
&= \overline{Y} + bx
\end{aligned}$$

and subtracting $\overline{Y}$ from both sides we obtain

$$\tilde{Y} - \overline{Y} = bx$$

If we let $\tilde{y} = \tilde{Y} - \overline{Y}$, then we may write

$$\tilde{y} = bx \qquad (5.15)$$

where $\tilde{y}$ = a predicted value of Y expressed in terms of its deviation from the mean of the Y distribution

x = a deviation of X from the mean of the X distribution

b = the regression coefficient

An error of prediction will now be given by the discrepancy between the observed deviation $y = Y - \overline{Y}$ and the predicted deviation $\tilde{y} = \tilde{Y} - \overline{Y}$. Then

$$y - \tilde{y} = y - bx$$

and

$$\sum (y - \tilde{y})^2 = \sum y^2 - 2b \sum xy + b^2 \sum x^2$$

We have $b = \sum xy / \sum x^2$ and substituting in the above expression we obtain

$$\begin{aligned}
\sum (y - \tilde{y})^2 &= \sum y^2 - 2 \frac{(\sum xy)^2}{\sum x^2} + \frac{(\sum xy)^2}{\sum x^2} \\
&= \sum y^2 - \frac{(\sum xy)^2}{\sum x^2} \qquad (5.16)
\end{aligned}$$

Table 5.3 shows that $\sum Y^2 = 142$ and that $\sum Y = 4$. Then

$$\sum y^2 = 142 - \frac{(4)^2}{10} = 140.4$$

We have already found that $\sum xy = 120.6$ and that $\sum x^2 = 108.9$. Then the residual sum of squares, as given by (5.16), will be

$$\sum (y - \tilde{y})^2 = 140.4 - \frac{(120.6)^2}{108.9} = 6.84$$

The value just obtained should check, and does within rounding errors, with the value of $\Sigma (Y - \tilde{Y})^2 = 6.8437$ shown in Table 5.3. We know that $\Sigma (y - \tilde{y})^2$ will equal $\Sigma (Y - \tilde{Y})^2$ because $\tilde{y} = \tilde{Y} - \overline{Y}$ and $y = Y - \overline{Y}$. Thus $y - \tilde{y} = (Y - \overline{Y}) - (\tilde{Y} - \overline{Y}) = Y - \tilde{Y}$.

Now, because Σy^2 measures the variation of the values of Y about the mean of the Y distribution, it is obvious that the residual sum of squares $\Sigma (y - \tilde{y})^2$ can be equal to $\Sigma y^2 = \Sigma (Y - \overline{Y})^2$ only if the regression coefficient is equal to zero. In that case we would know that there is no tendency for Y to change with change in X or, in other words, that the two variables are unrelated. Saying the same thing in a slightly different way, if the sum of products, $\Sigma xy = \Sigma (X - \overline{X})(Y - \overline{Y})$, is zero, then the X and Y variables are unrelated.

On the other hand, if a relationship between X and Y does exist, regardless of whether it is positive or negative, the value of $\Sigma (y - \tilde{y})^2$ will be smaller than Σy^2. When the relationship is negative, as we have pointed out earlier, the sum of products, and consequently the regression coefficient, will be negative in sign. But because the product sum is squared in (5.16), the numerator of the last term will always be positive in sign, and the denominator, the sum of squares, is, of course, always positive. Consequently, a negative relationship will also serve to reduce the residual sum of squares.

When the relationship between two variables is perfect, either positive or negative, the residual sum of squares will be equal to zero, and there will be no errors of prediction. If there is no relationship at all between X and Y, the residual sum of squares will be exactly equal to the sum of squares of the Y values from the mean of the Y distribution. In this instance, the best prediction that we could make for each Y value would be the mean of the Y distribution, for this would minimize the sum of squares of our errors of prediction. We have already shown, for example, that the sum of squared deviations from the mean is less than it would be from any single value not equal to the mean.

By taking into account the relationship between Y and X, when one exists, we reduce the errors of prediction $\Sigma (Y - \overline{Y})^2$ by an amount equal to $(\Sigma xy)^2/\Sigma x^2$. The residual sum of squares measures the remaining variation in Y that cannot be accounted for by the relationship. Instead of measuring the variation of the Y values in terms of their deviations from the mean of the Y distribution, the residual sum of squares measures the variation of each Y value from its corresponding predicted value given by the regression equation, (5.4).

5.10   The Residual Variance and Standard Error of Estimate

If we divide the residual sum of squares by $n - 2$, we obtain a measure known as the *residual variance*. Thus

$$s_{Y \cdot x}^2 = \frac{\sum (y - \tilde{y})^2}{n - 2} \qquad (5.17)$$

and for the data of Table 5.3, we have

$$s_{Y \cdot x}^2 = \frac{6.84}{10 - 2} = .855$$

The residual variance is a measure of the variation of the Y measures about the line of regression. The "dot" separating the Y and X subscripts serves to indicate that the regression line involved is that of Y on X, that is, that we are predicting Y values from corresponding X values.

The square root of the residual variance is called the *standard error of estimate*. Thus

$$s_{Y \cdot x} = \sqrt{\frac{\sum (y - \tilde{y})^2}{n - 2}} \qquad (5.18)$$

and for the data of Table 5.3, we have

$$s_{Y \cdot x} = \sqrt{\frac{6.84}{10 - 2}}$$
$$= \sqrt{.855}$$
$$= .92$$

The residual variance and its square root, the standard error of estimate, are both important in correlation analysis, which we shall take up in detail in the next chapter.

5.11   The Power Curve

So far we have considered only relationships between X and Y that are linear. In other cases the plot of the Y values against the X values may indicate that the trend cannot be represented adequately by a straight line; that is, the relationship may be *curvilinear*. We again would like to find the equation of the curve representing the trend.

Sometimes, a transformation of the X scale, the Y scale, or both the X and Y scales into a logarithmic scale will result in a linear relationship between $\log X$ and Y, or X and $\log Y$, or $\log X$ and $\log Y$. For example, a plot of the observed Y values against the X values may result in a curve for which the general equation is

$$Y = aX^b \qquad (5.19)$$

Equation (5.19) defines a curve in which the Y values are related to some power of the X values, and the curve is called a *power curve*. If b is negative, the curve will extend downward from upper left to lower right. If b is positive, the curve will extend upward from the lower left to the upper right. In the examples at the end of the chapter, we let b take various values from -2 to 2. If you plot the values of Y obtained against the given X values, in these examples, you will gain an understanding of the form of the curve when b is integral or fractional and positive or negative.

If we take logarithms[2] of both sides of (5.19), we obtain

$$\log Y = \log a + b \log X \qquad (5.20)$$

which is a linear relationship in log Y and log X. This will be apparent if (5.20) is compared with (5.2), which we have already shown is the equation of a straight line. Consequently, we may expect the plot of the log Y values

Table 5.4—Finding the line of best fit for log $\tilde{Y} = \log a + b \log X$

(1) X	(2) Y	(3) $\log X$	(4) $\log Y$	(5) $(\log X)^2$	(6) $(\log X)(\log Y)$
80.0	29.0	1.9031	1.4624	3.6218	2.7831
50.0	20.0	1.6990	1.3010	2.8866	2.2104
25.0	15.0	1.3979	1.1761	1.9541	1.6441
20.0	12.0	1.3010	1.0792	1.6926	1.4040
10.0	8.0	1.0000	.9031	1.0000	.9031
7.0	6.0	.8451	.7782	.7142	.6577
4.0	5.0	.6021	.6990	.3625	.4209
2.5	3.2	.3979	.5051	.1583	.2010
1.6	2.8	.2041	.4472	.0417	.0913
1.2	2.1	.0792	.3222	.0063	.0255
Σ		9.4294	8.6735	12.4381	10.3411

against the log X values to be a straight line with slope equal to b and Y intercept equal to log a.

It is not actually necessary to find the logarithms of the Y and X values and to make the plot of these logarithms to determine whether the trend seems to be linear. Instead, we may plot the original values of Y and X on *logarithmic paper*. This paper is ruled in such a way that both the X and Y axes are logarithmic scales. Plotting the original Y and X values on logarithmic paper will be the same as if we found the logarithms of Y and X and plotted the logarithms on ordinary graph paper.

---

[2] Unless otherwise specified all logarithms are *common logarithms* for which the base is 10. Table IX in Appendix D is a table of common logarithms. If you do not remember the algebra of logarithms or how to use a table of logarithms, then you need to review the section on logarithms in Appendix A.

In Table 5.4 we have a set of X values recorded in column (1) and the corresponding values of Y in column (2). The plot of the Y values against the X values on ordinary graph paper is shown in Figure 5.3. We now plot the Y values against the X values on logarithmic paper and this plot is shown in Figure 5.4. It sccms apparent from this graph that log Y is linearly related to log X.

We may now, if we so desire, find the values of log a and the slope of the line b for the line of best fit relating the logarithmic values. Applying the method of least squares to the logarithms of Y and X will give us the line of best fit for the logarithmic relation of (5.20). In column (3) of Table 5.4 we give the values of log X, and in column (4) the values of log Y. Column (5) gives the values of $(\log X)^2$, and column (6) the values of $(\log X)(\log Y)$. The

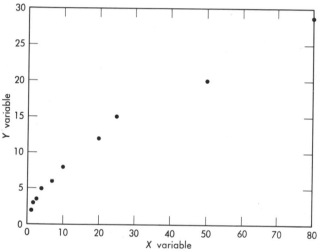

Figure **5.3**—Plot of the X, Y values given in Table 5.4 on ordinary coordinate paper.

sums of these columns will give us the necessary values to substitute in (5.9) to find the value of a and in (5.10) to find the value of b. All that we need to remember is that log X and log Y will now correspond to the X and Y of these formulas.

Taking the appropriate values from Table 5.4, and substituting in (5.10) we find

$$b = \frac{10.3411 - \dfrac{(9.4294)(8.6735)}{10}}{12.4381 - \dfrac{(9.4294)^2}{10}} = \frac{2.1625}{3.5467} = .6097$$

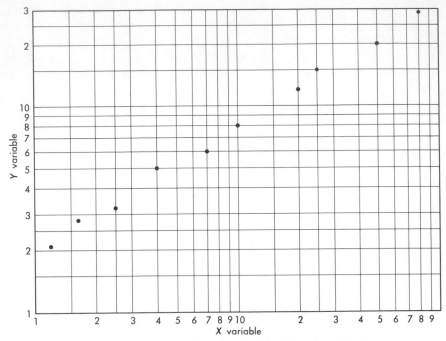

Figure **5.4**—Plot of the X, Y values given in Table 5.4 on logarithmic paper.

We can now solve for log a by means of (5.9). Thus

$$\log a = .8674 - (.6097)(.9429) = .2925$$

The values of a and b determined above will minimize the sum of squared deviations of the observed log Y values from the predicted log Y values of (5.20). We may write the equation for the predicted log Y values as

$$\log \tilde{Y} = .2925 + (.6097)(\log X)$$

Since log $a = .2925$, the value of a may be found by taking the anti-logarithm of .2925. This is equal to 1.961, and consequently we may now express the relationship between Y and X in terms of (5.19) or

$$\tilde{Y} = 1.961 X^{.6097}$$

5.12   The Exponential Curve

The trend of a set of plotted points may be represented by a curve for which the general equation is

$$Y = a10^{bX} \tag{5.21}$$

In (5.21) the independent variable appears as an exponent and the resulting

Table 5.5—Finding the line of best fit for log $\tilde{Y} = \log a + bX$

(1) X	(2) Y	(3) log Y	(4) X^2	(5) (X)(log Y)
7.5	1.2	.0792	56.25	.5940
7.0	1.5	.1761	49.00	1.2327
5.8	2.0	.3010	33.64	1.7458
5.0	2.8	.4472	25.00	2.2360
4.5	3.5	.5441	20.25	2.4484
3.5	4.2	.6232	12.25	2.1812
3.0	5.0	.6990	9.00	2.0970
2.0	7.2	.8573	4.00	1.7146
1.5	8.8	.9445	2.25	1.4168
1.1	9.5	.9777	1.21	1.0755
Σ 40.9	45.7	5.6493	212.85	16.7420

curve is called an *exponential curve*.[3] If we take logarithms of both sides of (5.21) we have

$$\log Y = \log a + bX \qquad (5.22)$$

which is a linear equation in log Y and the original values of X.

It is easy to determine whether or not the trend of a set of plotted points can be represented by a curve of the kind given by (5.21). If we plot the logarithms of Y against the values of X on ordinary rectangular graph paper, we should obtain a straight line. It is simpler, however, to plot the original values of X and Y on *semilogarithmic paper*. This paper has the usual linear scale on one axis, but a logarithmic scale on the other axis. Thus, if the data can be represented by an exponential curve, plotting the original X values on the linear scale and the Y values on the logarithmic scale should result in a straight line. This procedure is much simpler than plotting X and log Y on ordinary coordinate paper.

In Table 5.5, we give values of X in column (1) and values of Y in column (2). The plot of these values on ordinary coordinate paper is shown in Figure 5.5. Figure 5.6 gives the plot of the same values on semilogarithmic paper and it is apparent that the trend is linear. We may obtain the line of best fit

---

[3] The equation may be in the form $Y = ae^{bX}$ in which e is the base of the system of *natural logarithms* and is approximately equal to 2.7183. If we take logarithms to base e of both sides of this equation, we have $\log_e Y = \log_e a + bX$, which is a linear equation in $\log_e Y$ and X. Since we have not included a table of natural logarithms in the appendix, we may take logarithms to base 10 of both sides of the equation and obtain $\log Y = \log a + .4343bX$. This is possible because the logarithm of e to base 10 is approximately .4343. Whenever logarithms are written without a subscript, they usually refer to common logarithms.

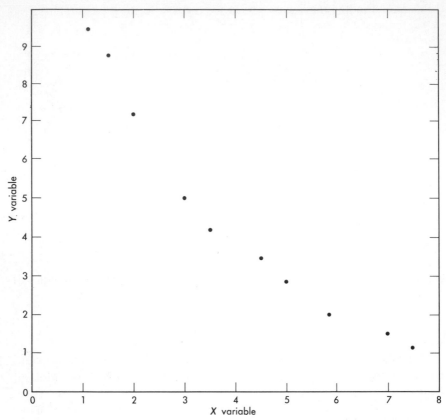

Figure **5.5**—Plot of the X, Y values given in Table 5.5 on ordinary coordinate paper.

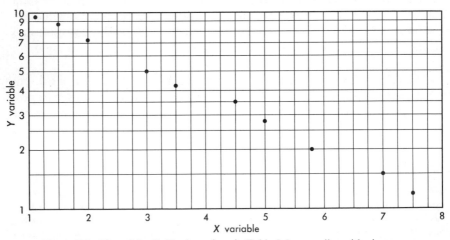

Figure **5.6**—Plot of the X, Y values given in Table 5.5 on semilogarithmic paper.

by the method of least squares. This will be the line of best fit relating the logarithms of Y to the original values of X.

In column (3) of Table 5.5 we give the log Y values. Column (4) gives the values of X^2 and in column (5) we give the values of $(X)(\log Y)$. The sums of the columns in the table enable us to solve for b by means of (5.10). All that we need to remember is that now log Y will correspond to Y. Substituting the appropriate values from Table 5.5 in (5.10), we obtain

$$b = \frac{16.7420 - \dfrac{(40.9)(5.6493)}{10}}{212.85 - \dfrac{(40.9)^2}{10}} = -.1396$$

The value of b is negative in sign. This is to be expected if we look at Figure 5.6 in which the trend of the points is downward from upper left to lower right in the figure. The line, in other words, has a negative slope.

Substituting in (5.9) we obtain the value of log a, the Y intercept. Thus

$$\log a = .5649 - (-.1396)(4.09) = 1.1359$$

Then we may write our prediction equation given by (5.22) as

$$\log \tilde{Y} = 1.1359 + (-.1396)X$$

and, since the antilogarithm of 1.1359 is 13.67, we may write (5.21) as

$$\tilde{Y} = (13.67)(10)^{-.1396X}$$

5.13   The Logarithmic Curve

We may consider one further case, in which the dependent variable Y may appear as an exponent. For example, Y may be related to X in such a way that

$$Y = a + b \log X \qquad\qquad (5.23)$$

which is a linear equation in Y and log X. Consequently, if this relation holds and we plot Y against log X on ordinary coordinate paper the graph should be a straight line. It is again simpler, however, to plot the original values of X and Y on semilogarithmic paper. In this case, we use the logarithmic scale for the X axis and the linear scale for the Y axis.

In Table 5.6 we give values of X in column (1) and in column (2) values of Y. The plot of Y against X on ordinary graph paper is shown in Figure 5.7. The plot of Y against X on semilogarithmic paper is shown in Figure 5.8. The trend can apparently be represented by a straight line, and we may assume that Y values are linearly related to the logarithms of X.

Table 5.6—Finding the line of best fit for $\tilde{Y} = a + b \log X$

(1) X	(2) Y	(3) log X	(4) (log X)²	(5) (log X)(Y)
1.1	9	.0414	.0017	.3726
1.5	12	.1761	.0310	2.1132
1.9	14	.2788	.0777	3.9032
2.2	17	.3424	.1172	5.8208
3.0	18	.4771	.2276	8.5878
3.5	20	.5441	.2960	10.8820
5.0	23	.6990	.4886	16.0770
6.0	25	.7782	.6056	19.4550
7.0	26	.8451	.7142	21.9726
9.9	29	.9956	.9912	28.8724
Σ 41.1	193	5.1778	3.5508	118.0566

The line of best fit may be found by the method of least squares. This will be the line of best fit relating the values of Y to the logarithms of X, and the intercept of this line will be a and the slope will be b. In column (3) of Table 5.6 we give the values of $\log X$ and in column (4) we give values of $(\log X)^2$. Column (5) gives the values of $(\log X)(Y)$. For the sums of the columns of Table 5.6 we obtain the necessary values to substitute in (5.10) to find the value of b. All that we need to remember is that $\log X$ will now correspond to X. Thus

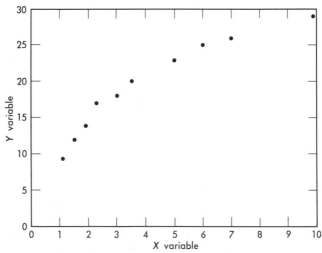

Figure **5.7**—Plot of the X, Y values given in Table 5.6 on ordinary coordinate paper.

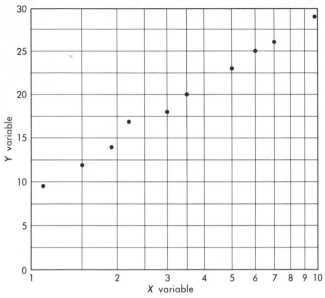

Figure **5.8**—Plot of the X, Y values given in Table 5.6 on semilogarithmic paper.

$$b = \dfrac{118.0566 - \dfrac{(5.1778)(193)}{10}}{3.5508 - \dfrac{(5.1778)^2}{10}} = 20.8382$$

Then substituting in (5.9) we obtain

$$a = 19.3 - (20.8382)(.5178) = 8.51$$

and our prediction equation then becomes

$$\tilde{Y} = 8.51 + 20.84 \log X$$

EXAMPLES

5.1—Prove that $\Sigma\, xy = \Sigma\, (X - \bar{X})(Y - \bar{Y}) = \Sigma\, XY - [(\Sigma\, X)(\Sigma\, Y)]/n$.

5.2—Solve for a, if $\Sigma\, Y = na + b\Sigma\, X$.

5.3—Substitute the value of a found in Example 5.2 in the following expression and solve for b: $\Sigma\, XY = a\Sigma\, X + b\Sigma\, X^2$.

5.4—If $\tilde{Y} = a + bX$, and $a = \bar{Y} - b\bar{X}$, then prove that $\Sigma\, \tilde{Y} = \Sigma\, Y$.

5.5—If $\tilde{y} = bx$, and $b = \Sigma\, xy/\Sigma\, x^2$, then prove that

$$\Sigma\,(y - \tilde{y})^2 = \Sigma\, y^2 - \frac{(\Sigma\, xy)^2}{\Sigma\, x^2}$$

5.6—Find the value of a and b for the equation $Y = a + bX$ for the following data.

X	Y
20	0
16	2
10	5
6	7
0	10

5.7—Using the method of least squares, find the value of a and b for the equation $\tilde{Y} = a + bX$ for the data given below. Plot the points on co-ordinate paper and show the point with coordinates $(\overline{X}, \overline{Y})$. Draw the regression line of Y on X.

X	Y	X	Y
2	3	8	5
2	6	8	8
4	2	8	10
4	4	10	8
4	8	10	12
6	5	12	5
6	7	12	9
6	10	12	11

5.8—Six colors were scaled for their affectivity. Taking all possible pairs gives 15 pairs for which the distance between the pairs is known on the affectivity scale. The reaction time of subjects was measured in choosing a member of each pair. The reaction times have been converted to a percentage of the mean reaction time. It can be hypothesized that reaction time will be faster for pairs separated by greater affective distances than for pairs separated by shorter affective distances. Plot the points and see whether the relationship between Y and X appears to be linear. Data are from Shipley, Coffin, and Hadsell (1945).

X Scale distance	Y Mean reaction time
2.31	83
1.75	91
1.69	91
1.36	87
1.29	93
1.13	93
1.02	96
.95	107

.74	100
.73	104
.62	97
.56	118
.40	113
.39	122
.34	107
.00	116

5.9—Assume that $Y = aX^b$, where $a = 2$ and $b = 2$.

(a)   For the values of X given below find the values of Y.
(b)   Plot the Y values against the X values on ordinary coordinate paper.
(c)   Plot the points on semilogarithmic paper.

Values of X: 1.0, 1.2, 1.4, 1.6, 1.8, 2.0.

5.10—Assume that $Y = aX^b$, where $a = 2$ and $b = -.5$.

(a)   For the values of X given below find the values of Y.
(b)   Plot the Y values against the X values on ordinary coordinate paper.
(c)   Plot the points on semilogarithmic paper.

Values of X: 1, 4, 9, 16, 25, 36.

5.11—Assume that $Y = aX^b$, where $a = 2$ and $b = .5$.

(a)   For the values of X given below find the values of Y.
(b)   Plot the Y values against the X values on ordinary coordinate paper.
(c)   Plot the points on semilogarithmic paper.

Values of X: 1, 4, 9, 16, 25, 36.

5.12—Assume that $Y = aX^b$, where $a = 2$ and $b = -2$.

(a)   For the values of X given below find the values of Y.
(b)   Plot the Y values against the X values on ordinary coordinate paper.
(c)   Plot the points on semilogarithmic paper.

Values of X: 1.0, 1.2, 1.4, 1.6, 1.8, 2.0.

5.13—See if a curve of the form $Y = a10^{bX}$ will fit the following data.

X	Y
1.0	2.5
1.3	2.8
1.5	3.0
1.8	3.7
2.1	4.1
2.3	4.9
2.5	5.0
2.8	6.5
3.1	7.8
3.4	9.2

5.14—See if a curve of the form $Y = aX^b$ will fit the following data.

X	Y
1.5	7.0
2.5	6.0
4.0	4.1
6.0	3.8
15.0	2.6
30.0	2.0
50.0	1.5
70.0	1.4

5.15—See if a curve of the form $Y = a + b \log X$ will fit the following data.

X	Y
1.2	2.2
1.5	2.4
1.7	2.6
2.0	2.6
3.0	3.2
4.4	3.6
7.0	4.2
10.0	4.4

5.16—Under what conditions will $\Sigma (Y - \tilde{Y})^2 = \Sigma (Y - \bar{Y})^2$?

5.17—Give a one-sentence definition of each of the following terms or concepts:

linear relationship	regression coefficient
dependent variable	regression equation
independent variable	covariance
slope of a line	residual variance
Y-intercept of a line	standard error of estimate
positive relationship	power curve
negative relationship	exponential curve
regression line	logarithmic curve

CHAPTER 6

The Product-Moment Correlation Coefficient

6.1 Introduction

In the discussion of linear regression in the last chapter it was assumed that we had some basis for designating one of the two variables investigated as the dependent variable Y and the other as the independent variable X. For example, if we had measures of vocabulary at various age levels, it would seem logical to designate the vocabulary measures as the dependent variable and the age levels as the independent variable. Vocabulary may depend upon age, but it is rather difficult to imagine age as depending upon vocabulary. Or suppose that one of our variables is the number of trials in a learning experiment and the other variable is the amount learned per trial. Again it seems more reasonable to regard the amount learned as depending upon the number of trials rather than the number of trials as depending upon the amount learned. If one of our variables is amount remembered and the other is time elapsed, it would seem more logical to regard the amount remembered as depending upon the passage of time rather than the other way around. In problems of the kind just described, the experimenter would select certain values of the independent variable X for investigation and then subsequently observe the values of the dependent variable Y. His interest would then be in relating the values of the dependent variable Y to those of the independent variable X.

In many problems, however, involving the relationship between two variables, there is no clear-cut basis for designating one of the variables as the independent variable and the other as the dependent variable. If we have measured the heights of husbands and also of their wives, which set of measurements shall we designate the dependent variable? If we have scores on a test of submissiveness and also on a test of aggressiveness, shall we consider the measure of submissiveness or the measure of aggressiveness as the dependent variable?

In problems of the kind described above, it is a more or less arbitrary matter which variable we choose to designate as the dependent variable and which we choose to call the independent variable. If we arbitrarily designate one of the variables as Y and the other as X, then we may consider not only the prediction of Y values from X values, but also the prediction of X values from Y values. In other words, we may reverse the roles of our variables, considering first Y as a dependent variable with X as the independent variable and then considering X as a dependent variable with Y as the independent variable.

In the problems discussed in this chapter, therefore, we shall assume that we are dealing with a population of *paired* (X, Y) *values* and that we have a sample from this population.[1] There is no question here of observing Y values for only certain selected values of X, as in our previous discussion of regression. Under these circumstances we shall have, ordinarily, not one but two regression lines. One will be for the regression of Y on X and the other for the regression of X on Y. We shall thus have two regression equations, one for each line, and also two regression coefficients. Furthermore, we shall have two residual variances and two standard errors of estimate. There is, however, one statistic involving both variables for which we shall have only a single value. That statistic is the *product-moment correlation coefficient*.

6.2   The Correlation Coefficient

In discussing the correlation coefficient, we shall again restrict ourselves to the case of linear relationships. For convenience, we shall assume that one of our variables, Y, is a dependent variable and that the other variable, X, is an independent variable, so that we shall be concerned with the regression of Y on X. Then later we may reverse the roles of our variables, taking X as the dependent variable and Y as the independent variable.

In the case of variables that are linearly related, the correlation coefficient is a measure of the degree of relationship present. Consider first a perfect positive relationship between two variables as shown in Figure 6.1. In this instance, the correlation coefficient will be equal to 1. If we have a perfect negative relationship, as shown in Figure 6.2, the correlation coefficient will be equal to -1. In Figure 6.3, we have a positive relationship between X and Y, but it is not perfect, and the correlation coefficient for these measures is .74. Figure 6.4 shows the plot of a set of X and Y values for which the correlation coefficient is $-.73$. In Figure 6.5, the correlation coefficient is $-.12$.

---

[1] As an example of a population of paired (X, Y) values, consider all male students enrolled at a given university as the population of interest and let X be the height and Y be the weight of a student. For a sample of n students, we would then have n ordered pairs of (X, Y) values.

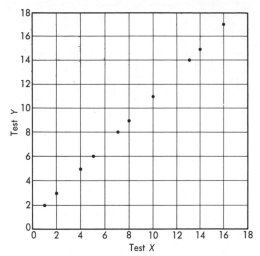

Figure **6.1**—Plot of X and Y values for which the correlation coefficient is equal to 1.00.

Examination of these figures should indicate that the numerical value of the correlation coefficient is related to the scatter of the plotted points about the line representing their trend. The points in Figure 6.5, for example, would show the greatest scatter about the line representing their trend and, in this instance, the correlation coefficient is $-.12$. When the plotted points fall precisely on a straight line, as in Figure 6.1 and Figure 6.2, the correlation coefficient is equal to 1 and -1, respectively. We have, in the last chapter,

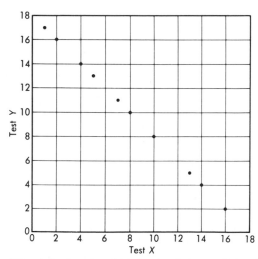

Figure **6.2**—Plot of X and Y values for which the correlation coefficient is equal to -1.00.

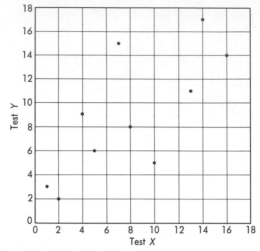

Fig. **6.3**—Plot of X and Y values for which the correlation coefficient is equal to .74.

discussed a measure of the scatter of a set of plotted points about the regression line which we called the residual variance. You may suspect, therefore, that the numerical value of the correlation coefficient is in some way related to the amount of scatter about the regression line, and that is true. We shall show the nature of this relationship later.

The sign of the correlation coefficient is apparently related to the slope of the regression line, because in those instances in which the slope is nega-

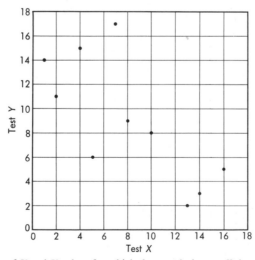

Figure **6.4**—Plot of X and Y values for which the correlation coefficient is equal to $-.73$.

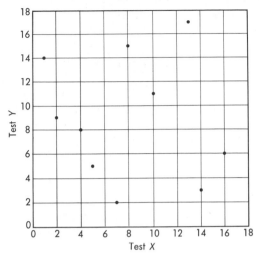

Figure **6.5**—Plot of X and Y values for which the correlation coefficient is equal to $-.12$.

tive, that is, downward from upper left to lower right, the correlation coefficient is negative in sign. When the trend of the plotted points is upward from lower left to upper right, so that the slope of the line is positive, the correlation coefficient is also positive in sign.

The correlation coefficient may range in value from -1 to 1. A correlation coefficient of 1 indicates a perfect positive relationship between two variables; a correlation of zero indicates no relationship whatsoever between the two variables; and a correlation coefficient of -1 indicates a perfect negative relationship. Values between zero and 1 or -1 indicate varying degrees of relationship. It is very seldom, if at all, that perfect relationships are found in the biological and social sciences, in part because of the limitations of our measuring instruments and also because of the difficulties of controlling all possible factors that may influence the two variables being studied. Correlation coefficients representing the relationship between performance on an academic-aptitude test and grades earned in college, for example, typically range from .40 to .60. The correlation coefficient between measures of intelligence on identical twins is substantially higher, being about .90. An examination of the research literature in a given field will reveal the typical values found for the correlation coefficient when various variables are considered.

6.3   Formulas for the Correlation Coefficient

The correlation coefficient may be defined as the ratio between the covariance and the geometric mean of the variance of X and the variance of Y. The geometric mean of two numbers is the square root of their product. Thus

$$r = \frac{\dfrac{\sum xy}{n-1}}{\sqrt{\left(\dfrac{\sum x^2}{n-1}\right)\left(\dfrac{\sum y^2}{n-1}\right)}} \tag{6.1}$$

where r is the correlation coefficient between X and Y. We do not need any subscripts for the correlation coefficient because r_{XY} is identical with r_{YX}.

We note that the denominator of (6.1) is equal to the product of the standard deviation of the X variable and the standard deviation of the Y variable. Then we also have

$$r = \frac{\sum xy}{(n-1)s_X s_Y} \tag{6.2}$$

We have defined a standard score as $z = (X - \bar{X})/s_X$ or x/s_X. Then (6.2) can be written as

$$r = \frac{1}{n-1}\sum \left(\frac{x}{s_X}\right)\left(\frac{y}{s_Y}\right)$$

or

$$r = \frac{\sum z_X z_Y}{n-1} \tag{6.3}$$

If we multiply both the numerator and denominator of (6.1) by $n - 1$, we obtain another commonly used expression for the correlation coefficient. Thus

$$r = \frac{\sum xy}{\sqrt{\sum x^2 \sum y^2}} \tag{6.4}$$

We have already developed methods for calculating the numerator and denominator of (6.4) in terms of the original values of X and Y. Thus we also have

$$r = \frac{\sum XY - \dfrac{(\sum X)(\sum Y)}{n}}{\sqrt{\left(\sum X^2 - \dfrac{(\sum X)^2}{n}\right)\left(\sum Y^2 - \dfrac{(\sum Y)^2}{n}\right)}} \tag{6.5}$$

Multiplying both sides of (6.4) by $\sqrt{\sum x^2 \sum y^2}$, we have

$$r\sqrt{\sum x^2 \sum y^2} = \sum xy \tag{6.6}$$

Thus for the product sum $\Sigma\, xy$ we have the identity $r\sqrt{\Sigma\, x^2\, \Sigma\, y^2}$. If we multiply both sides of (6.2) by $s_X s_Y$, we have an important identity for the covariance. Thus

$$\frac{\Sigma\, xy}{n-1} = r s_X s_Y \tag{6.7}$$

We shall have occasion to use both of these identities in later developments
Substituting the appropriate values from Table 6.1 in (6.5), we have

$$r = \frac{1881 - \dfrac{(146)(99)}{10}}{\sqrt{\left(2868 - \dfrac{(146)^2}{10}\right)\left(1309 - \dfrac{(99)^2}{10}\right)}}$$

$$= \frac{435.6}{\sqrt{(736.4)(328.9)}}$$

$$= .89$$

for this set of $n = 10$ paired (X, Y) values.

Table 6.1—A set of $n = 10$ paired (X, Y) values

X	Y	X^2	Y^2	XY
7	3	49	9	21
13	6	169	36	78
2	2	4	4	4
4	5	16	25	20
15	14	225	196	210
10	10	100	100	100
19	8	361	64	152
28	19	784	361	532
26	15	676	225	390
22	17	484	289	374
Σ 146	99	2868	1309	1881

6.4   The Regression of Y on X

We have previously defined the regression coefficient as the ratio of the covariance of two variables to the variance of the independent variable. Thus, when Y was considered to be the dependent variable and X the independent variable, we had

$$b_Y = \frac{\dfrac{\sum xy}{n-1}}{\dfrac{\sum x^2}{n-1}} = \frac{\sum xy}{\sum x^2}$$

where we have used the subscript Y to indicate that the regression coefficient is for Y on X. In our previous discussion of regression we were concerned only with the regression of Y on X, and the subscript was not necessary.

We have already found that $\sum xy = 435.6$ and that $\sum x^2 = 736.4$ for the data of Table 6.1. The regression coefficient b_Y will therefore be

$$b_Y = \frac{435.6}{736.4} = .59$$

For the same data, we have

$$\overline{Y} = \frac{99}{10} = 9.9$$

and

$$\overline{X} = \frac{146}{10} = 14.6$$

Then the regression equation for predicting Y values from X values will be

$$\tilde{Y} = a + b_Y X$$

where $b_Y = .59$ and $a = \overline{Y} - b_Y\overline{X} = 9.9 - (.59)(14.6) = 1.29$. Substituting in the regression equation with $a = 1.29$ and $b_Y = .59$, we have

$$\tilde{Y} = 1.29 + .59X$$

for the data of Table 6.1.

6.5 The Standard Error of Estimate: $s_{Y \cdot X}$

The residual sum of squares will be given by

$$\sum (y - \tilde{y})^2 = \sum y^2 - \frac{(\sum xy)^2}{\sum x^2}$$

$$= 328.9 - \frac{(435.6)^2}{736.4}$$

$$= 71.23$$

and dividing by $n - 2$, we obtain the residual variance

$$s_{Y \cdot X}^2 = \frac{71.23}{10 - 2} = 8.90$$

If we now take the square root of the residual variance, we obtain the standard error of estimate. Thus

$$s_{Y \cdot X} = \sqrt{8.90} = 2.98$$

The standard error of estimate, as we have pointed out previously, is a measure of the variability of the Y values about the regression line of Y on X. The standard deviation of the Y distribution, on the other hand, is a measure of the variation of the Y values about the mean of the Y distribution. In the present problem, the standard deviation of the Y measures is

$$s_Y = \sqrt{\frac{328.9}{10 - 1}} = 6.04$$

In the absence of any knowledge about the relationship between X and Y, the predicted value of Y for any given value of X would, of course, be the mean of the Y distribution, and the extent of our errors of prediction would be the standard deviation of the Y distribution. If you look for a moment at Figure 6.6, where we have drawn the regression line of Y on X, you may be able to see more clearly just what influence correlation will have in reducing our errors of prediction.

If we draw a horizontal line through the mean of the Y distribution, then the vertical deviation of each plotted point from this line would represent the deviation of $Y - \bar{Y}$, and the sum of these squared deviations would be $\Sigma (Y - \bar{Y})^2$. If the horizontal line through the mean of the Y distribution is now rotated counterclockwise about the point B, where the mean of the X and the mean of the Y distribution fall, then the sum of squared deviations from the line becomes smaller and smaller until the line coincides with the

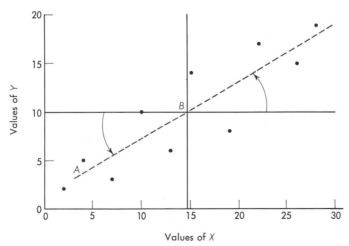

Figure **6.6**—The regression line of Y on X for the data of Table 6.1.

regression line—line AB in Figure 6.6. The sum of squared deviations from this line would now be $\Sigma (Y - \tilde{Y})^2$ and $\Sigma (Y - \tilde{Y})^2$ will be smaller than $\Sigma (Y - \overline{Y})^2$, if there is any relationship between X and Y. In the present example, we have $\Sigma (Y - \overline{Y})^2 = 328.9$, whereas $\Sigma (Y - \tilde{Y})^2 = 71.23$. We see that $\Sigma (Y - \tilde{Y})^2$ represents a considerable reduction in the sum of squared errors of prediction relative to $\Sigma (Y - \overline{Y})^2$.

It is the second variable, X, which makes the regression line and $\Sigma (Y - \tilde{Y})^2$ meaningful. As long as the Y measures are considered alone, the best predicted value of Y for any single X measure would be the horizontal line, or the mean of the Y distribution. But when there is regression of Y on X, we find that different values of Y are associated with different values of X. These associated values become our predictions when we have knowledge of the relationship between the two variables.

Assume that the Y values for any fixed X value are normally distributed about their mean with a variance that is the same for each fixed X value. If Y is related to X and we take a sample of paired (X, Y) values, holding X constant, then it should be clear that the mean Y value for such a sample will depend upon the particular value of X selected and held constant. It should also be clear that the Y values for such a sample will not vary as much as the Y values we would obtain if no restriction were placed upon X and if the X values were also allowed to vary. Then, as our estimate of the variance of these Y values for a constant value of X, we may use the residual variance $s_{Y \cdot X}^2$. This estimate will be useful in later discussions.

6.6   The Regression of X on Y

If we now consider X as the dependent variable and Y as the independent variable, we will have

$$b_X = \frac{\dfrac{\Sigma xy}{n - 1}}{\dfrac{\Sigma y^2}{n - 1}} = \frac{\Sigma xy}{\Sigma y^2} \tag{6.8}$$

where the subscript X indicates that we are now concerned with the regression of X on Y.

The regression equation for predicting X values from Y values will thus be

$$\tilde{X} = a + b_X Y \tag{6.9}$$

where

$$a = \overline{X} - b_X \overline{Y} \tag{6.10}$$

The residual sum of squares $\Sigma (x - \tilde{x})^2 = \Sigma (X - \tilde{X})^2$ in predicting X from Y will be

$$\Sigma (x - \tilde{x})^2 = \Sigma x^2 - \frac{(\Sigma xy)^2}{\Sigma y^2} \tag{6.11}$$

and the residual variance will be

$$s_{X \cdot Y}^2 = \frac{\Sigma (x - \tilde{x})^2}{n - 2} \tag{6.12}$$

The standard error of estimate will be the square root of (6.12) or

$$s_{X \cdot Y} = \sqrt{\frac{\Sigma (x - \tilde{x})^2}{n - 2}} \tag{6.13}$$

6.7 Correlation and Regression Coefficients

We see that if we consider the regression of X on Y, instead of the regression of Y on X, we shall have corresponding formulas for the regression coefficient, the regression line, the residual variance, and the standard error of estimate. Although these formulas correspond in appearance, we should not expect them to yield identical numerical values. The only way in which these formulas could all yield identical pairs of values would be if the means and standard deviations of both the X and Y distributions were identical. Let us see why this is so.

Consider the value of the regression coefficient for Y on X as given by

$$b_Y = \frac{\Sigma xy}{\Sigma x^2}$$

Then multiplying both numerator and denominator of the right-hand side by the same value we have

$$b_Y = \left(\frac{\Sigma xy}{\Sigma x^2} \right) \left(\frac{\sqrt{\Sigma x^2 \Sigma y^2}}{\sqrt{\Sigma x^2 \Sigma y^2}} \right)$$

$$= \left(\frac{\Sigma xy}{\sqrt{\Sigma x^2 \Sigma y^2}} \right) \left(\frac{\sqrt{\Sigma x^2 \Sigma y^2}}{\Sigma x^2} \right)$$

or

$$b_Y = r \frac{\sqrt{\Sigma x^2 \Sigma y^2}}{\Sigma x^2}$$

Dividing both numerator and denominator of the right-hand side by $n - 1$

and substituting identities, we have

$$b_Y = r \frac{s_X s_Y}{s_X^2}$$

We thus have another commonly used expression for the regression coefficient

$$b_Y = r \frac{s_Y}{s_X} \qquad (6.14)$$

And the corresponding expression for the regression coefficient of X on Y would be

$$b_X = r \frac{s_X}{s_Y} \qquad (6.15)$$

It is now readily apparent that if the standard deviation of the Y distribution is exactly equal to the standard deviation of the X distribution, then the two regression coefficients will also be identical and equal to the value of the correlation coefficient. For example, both the X and Y values might be expressed in the form of standard scores with $z_X = (X - \bar{X})/s_X$ and $z_Y = (Y - \bar{Y})/s_Y$. Then, since we know that the standard deviation of a set of standard scores is equal to 1, for these two sets of standard scores the two regression coefficients would be equal and identical with the correlation coefficient.

If we multiply the regression coefficients of (6.14) and (6.15), we obtain

$$\left(r \frac{s_Y}{s_X} \right) \left(r \frac{s_X}{s_Y} \right) = b_Y b_X$$

or

$$r^2 = b_Y b_X$$

and

$$\pm \sqrt{r^2} = \pm \sqrt{b_Y b_X} \qquad (6.16)$$

and we see that the correlation coefficient is the geometric mean of the regression coefficients. Because r may be either plus or minus in sign, we say that $\sqrt{r^2} = r$ if the b's are positive in sign, but $\sqrt{r^2} = -r$ if the b's are negative in sign.[2]

---

[2] It is obvious from (6.14) and (6.15) that if r is negative, then both b_Y and b_X will be negative, whereas if r is positive, then both b_Y and b_X will be positive.

6.8   The Residual Sum of Squares

In the chapter on regression we showed that $\Sigma (y - \tilde{y})^2 = \Sigma y^2 - (\Sigma xy)^2/\Sigma x^2$ where $y - \tilde{y}$ was an error of prediction resulting from the discrepancy between y and $\tilde{y}$ as predicted by the regression equation. If we multiply both $(\Sigma xy)^2$ and Σx^2 by Σy^2, we obtain

$$\Sigma (y - \tilde{y})^2 = \Sigma y^2 - \frac{(\Sigma xy)^2 \Sigma y^2}{\Sigma x^2 \Sigma y^2}$$

From (6.4) we see that

$$r^2 = \frac{(\Sigma xy)^2}{\Sigma x^2 \Sigma y^2}$$

and substituting this identity in the above equation, we get

$$\Sigma (y - \tilde{y})^2 = \Sigma y^2 - r^2 \Sigma y^2 \tag{6.17}$$

Then, solving for r^2, in (6.17), we obtain

$$r^2 = \frac{\Sigma y^2 - \Sigma (y - \tilde{y})^2}{\Sigma y^2} \tag{6.18}$$

or

$$r^2 = 1 - \frac{\Sigma (y - \tilde{y})^2}{\Sigma y^2} \tag{6.19}$$

We shall have occasion to refer to (6.19) in later discussions.

We note that (6.17) tells us that we may express the residual sum of squares in terms of Σy^2 and the correlation coefficient. Thus

$$\Sigma (y - \tilde{y})^2 = \Sigma y^2 (1 - r^2) \tag{6.20}$$

The residual variance can be easily obtained from (6.20) by dividing both sides by $n - 2$. Then

$$s_{Y \cdot X}^2 = \frac{\Sigma y^2 (1 - r^2)}{n - 2} \tag{6.21}$$

and the square root of (6.21) will give the standard error of estimate. Similar expressions for $\Sigma (x - \tilde{x})^2$ and $s_{X \cdot Y}^2$ can be obtained by substituting Σx^2 for Σy^2 in (6.20) and (6.21). Thus

$$\Sigma (x - \tilde{x})^2 = \Sigma x^2 (1 - r^2) \tag{6.22}$$

and

$$s_{X \cdot Y}^2 = \frac{\sum x^2 (1 - r^2)}{n - 2} \tag{6.23}$$

6.9 Coefficients of Determination and Nondetermination

In (6.17) for the residual sum of squares, we showed that $\sum (y - \bar{y})^2 = \sum y^2 - r^2 \sum y^2$. Rearranging these terms, we have

$$\sum y^2 = \sum (y - \bar{y})^2 + r^2 \sum y^2$$

and substituting an identity from (6.20) for $\sum (y - \bar{y})^2$, we obtain

$$\sum y^2 = \sum y^2 (1 - r^2) + r^2 \sum y^2 \tag{6.24}$$

We may now divide both sides of the above expression by $\sum y^2$. In this way we shall express the two terms on the right-hand side as proportions of the sum of squares. Thus

$$1.00 = (1 - r^2) + r^2 \tag{6.25}$$

and we see that the sum of squared deviations about the mean of the Y distribution can be expressed as the sum of two proportions. The proportion given by $(1 - r^2)$ represents the variation, as we know, about the regression line. Apparently, then, this is the proportion of the variation in Y that is independent of the variation in X. The value $(1 - r^2)$ is called the *coefficient of nondetermination* and indicates the proportion of $\sum y^2$ that is independent of the regression of Y on X. The second term of (6.25), represented by r^2, is called the *coefficient of determination*. This coefficient represents the proportion of $\sum y^2$ that is associated with variation in X.

When r is equal to 1, then the coefficient of determination is equal to 1 and we can account for all of the variation represented by $\sum y^2$ in terms of the regression of Y on X. When r is equal to .80, we can account for .64 of the variation represented by $\sum y^2$ in terms of the regression of Y on X. This leaves $1 - r^2 = .36$ as the proportion of $\sum y^2$ that is independent of the variation in X.

We may prefer to think of r^2 and $(1 - r^2)$ in terms of the variance s_Y^2 of the Y distribution rather than in terms of the sum of squares $\sum y^2$. We can do this by dividing both sides of (6.24) by $n - 1$, to obtain

$$\frac{\sum y^2}{n - 1} = (1 - r^2) \frac{\sum y^2}{n - 1} + r^2 \frac{\sum y^2}{n - 1}$$

and then

$$s_Y^2 = (1 - r^2) s_Y^2 + r^2 s_Y^2 \tag{6.26}$$

From (6.26) we see that the proportion of the total variance s_Y^2 associated with variation in X is equal to r^2 and that the proportion of the total variance that is independent of variation in X is $(1 - r^2)$. Do not, however, make the mistake of regarding $(1 - r^2)s_Y^2$ as equal to the residual variance $s_{Y \cdot X}^2$. In (6.26), for example, $(1 - r^2)\Sigma y^2$ has been divided by $n - 1$ and not by $n - 2$ as required by (6.21) for the residual variance.

It can be shown, for example, that $s_{Y \cdot X}^2$ as defined by (6.21) is an unbiased estimate of the population value $\sigma_{Y \cdot X}^2$ whereas $(1 - r^2)s_Y^2$ is a biased estimate of this parameter. The nature of the bias may be indicated if we multiply both the numerator and denominator of the right-hand side of (6.21) by $n - 1$. Then

$$s_{Y \cdot X}^2 = \frac{n - 1}{n - 2} s_Y^2 (1 - r^2)$$

It is apparent, therefore, that $s_Y^2(1 - r^2)$ will, in general, underestimate $\sigma_{Y \cdot X}^2$ and that this bias is most pronounced when n is small. As n becomes very large, the fraction $(n - 1)/(n - 2)$ will approach 1 as a limit, and the bias of $s_Y^2(1 - r^2)$ as an estimate of $\sigma_{Y \cdot X}^2$ becomes less serious.

6.10 The Difference Formula for r

Suppose that we have given a test X and a test Y to a group of subjects and that scores on the two tests are expressed in terms of deviations from the respective means. Then we may define a difference score as

$$d = (X - \overline{X}) - (Y - \overline{Y})$$

or

$$d = x - y \tag{6.27}$$

The variance of the distribution of measures defined by (6.27) will be of interest in later discussions, and this variance is also related to the correlation coefficient between X and Y. Let us see why this is so. By definition

$$d = x - y$$

Then

$$\sum d^2 = \sum x^2 + \sum y^2 - 2 \sum xy$$

We have shown that $\sum xy = r\sqrt{\sum x^2 \sum y^2}$ and therefore

$$\sum d^2 = \sum x^2 + \sum y^2 - 2r\sqrt{\sum x^2 \sum y^2}$$

and

$$\frac{\sum d^2}{n - 1} = \frac{\sum x^2}{n - 1} + \frac{\sum y^2}{n - 1} - 2r\sqrt{\left(\frac{\sum x^2}{n - 1}\right)\left(\frac{\sum y^2}{n - 1}\right)}$$

or

$$s_D^2 = s_X^2 + s_Y^2 - 2rs_Xs_Y \qquad (6.28)$$

If X and Y are uncorrelated, that is, if $r = 0$, then (6.28) tells us that the variance of the differences will be equal to the variance of X plus the variance of Y. On the other hand, if the correlation between X and Y is positive, the variance of the differences will be less than the corresponding variance for the same measures with zero correlation. If the correlation is negative, then the variance of the differences will be greater than the corresponding variance for uncorrelated measures.

From (6.28) we may also obtain an expression for the correlation coefficient in terms of the variance of X, the variance of Y, and the variance of the differences. Thus, solving for r, we have

$$r = \frac{s_X^2 + s_Y^2 - s_D^2}{2s_Xs_Y} \qquad (6.29)$$

The calculation of the rank correlation coefficient, discussed in the next chapter, is based upon r as defined by (6.29).

6.11   Calculation of r When n Is Large

If n is large or if the values of X and Y are large, then the calculation of the sum of products

$$\sum xy = \sum XY - \frac{(\sum X)(\sum Y)}{n}$$

without the aid of a desk calculator is quite tedious. The calculations can be simplified considerably if we code both the X and the Y values in the manner described in Chapter 2. Let

$$X' = \frac{X - m_X}{i_X}$$

where m_X = the mid-point of the lowest class interval for the X distribution
  i_X = the size of the class interval for the X distribution
and let

$$Y' = \frac{Y - m_Y}{i_Y}$$

where m_Y = the mid-point of the lowest class interval for the Y distribution
  i_Y = the size of the class interval for the Y distribution

In Table 6.2 we have $n = 32$ paired (X, Y) values. Suppose that for the data in this table we decide to use a class interval $i_X = 3$ for the X values and a

Table 6.2—Scores on the Stanford-Binet (X) and scores on a Hypnotic Susceptibility Scale (Y) for $n = 32$ subjects*

Subject	X	Y	Subject	X	Y
MJ	136	22	TF	101	0
DJR	106	6	AEH	128	22
HIR	116	20	RR	122	16
SRB	139	8	JM	111	13
IC	103	0	SN	129	7
JDC	126	17	WP	117	10
MC	131	21	FW	116	6
JLF	137	13	SR	129	16
BHH	144	14	HF	109	13
MEG	130	5	CEF	103	0
DC	133	6	MM	104	0
SS	123	4	HMD	111	0
GG	134	9	JMD	131	12
FES	132	8	GA	112	4
MNS	117	6	GH	134	12
MLC	128	0	TF	101	0

* Data from Curtis (1943).

class interval $i_Y = 2$ for the Y values. If, as we suggested in Chapter 2, we begin the lowest class interval with some multiple of the size of the interval, the lowest class interval for the X values will be 99–101 and the lowest class interval for the Y values will be 0 1. Then, following the procedure described in Section 2.20, the X' and Y' values for each of the paired (X, Y) values can easily be determined.

For each pair of (X, Y) values, write the corresponding X' and Y' values on a 3×5 card. For example, for the first pair of (X, Y) values, those for subject MJ, we have $X = 136$ and $Y = 22$. Then, for this subject, as can easily be verified, we would have a 3×5 card with $X' = 12$ and $Y' = 11$. When we have the X' and Y' values for each of the $n = 32$ subjects recorded on separate cards, we then sort the cards according to their Y' values. The frequency with which each Y' value occurs is shown in column (2) of Table 6.3. Columns (4) and (5) give the products fY' and fY'^2, respectively. Column (6) gives the sum of the X' values for all observations that have the same Y' value. The "dot" in $\Sigma X'._{Y'}$ means that we are summing X' values for a constant value of Y'. For example, there are two cards or observations with a Y' value of 11. One of these has an X' value of 9 and the other an X' value of 12. Then, for the two cards with $Y' = 11$, we have $\Sigma X'._{Y'} = 9 + 12 = 21$. The other entries in column (6) were obtained in the same manner. The entries in column (7) were obtained by multiplying the entries in column (6) by the

Table 6.3—The frequency distribution of the Y values of Table 6.2 with a class interval $i_Y = 2$

(1)	(2)	(3)	(4)	(5)	(6)	(7)
Interval	f	Y'	fY'	fY'^2	$\Sigma X'._{Y'}$	$Y' \Sigma X'._{Y'}$
22–23	2	11	22	242	21	231
20–21	2	10	20	200	15	150
18–19	0	9	0	0	0	0
16–17	3	8	24	192	26	208
14–15	1	7	7	49	15	105
12–13	5	6	30	180	40	240
10–11	1	5	5	25	6	30
8– 9	3	4	12	48	35	140
6– 7	5	3	15	45	34	102
4– 5	3	2	6	12	22	44
2– 3	0	1	0	0	0	0
0– 1	7	0	0	0	16	0
Σ	32		141	993	230	1250

Y' values in column (3) to obtain $Y'\Sigma X'._{Y'}$. The sum of column (7) is 1250 and is equal to $\Sigma X'Y'$. Note that the sum of column (4) is 141 and this is equal to $\Sigma Y'$. Similarly, the sum of column (6) is 230 and this is equal to $\Sigma X'$. Then

$$\Sigma xy = \left(\Sigma X'Y' - \frac{(\Sigma X')(\Sigma Y')}{n} \right) i_X i_Y \qquad (6.30)$$

and, for this example

$$\Sigma xy = \left(1250 - \frac{(230)(141)}{32} \right)(3)(2)$$
$$= (236.56)(6)$$
$$= 1419.36$$

As a check upon the accuracy of our calculations, we can now sort the cards according to their X' values and repeat the procedure described above. The result is shown in Table 6.4.

Substituting with the appropriate values from Table 6.4 in (2.8) we have

$$\Sigma x^2 = \left(2208 - \frac{(230)^2}{32} \right)(3)^2 = (554.88)(9) = 4993.92$$

and, similarly, using the appropriate values from Table 6.3 we have

$$\Sigma y^2 = \left(993 - \frac{(141)^2}{32}\right)(2)^2 = (371.72)(4) = 1486.88$$

Then, the correlation coefficient will be

$$r = \frac{\Sigma xy}{\sqrt{\Sigma x^2 \Sigma y^2}}$$

$$= \frac{1419.36}{\sqrt{(4993.92)(1486.88)}}$$

$$= .52$$

Table 6.4—The frequency distribution of the X values of Table 6.2 with a class interval $i_X = 3$

(1) Intervals	(2) f	(3) X'	(4) fX'	(5) fX'^2	(6) $\Sigma Y'._{X'}$	(7) $X' \Sigma Y'._{X'}$
144–146	1	15	15	225	7	105
141–143	0	14	0	0	0	0
138–140	1	· 13	13	169	4	52
135–137	2	12	24	288	17	204
132–134	4	11	44	484	17	187
129–131	5	10	50	500	29	290
126–128	3	9	27	243	19	171
123–125	1	8	8	64	2	16
120–122	1	7	7	49	8	50
117–119	2	6	12	72	8	48
114–116	2	5	10	50	13	65
111–113	3	4	12	48	8	32
108–110	1	3	3	9	6	18
105–107	1	2	2	4	3	6
102–104	3	1	3	3	0	0
99–101	2	0	0	0	0	0
	32		230	2208	141	1250

We note that the coding constants, $i_X = 3$, and $i_Y = 2$, are involved in finding $\Sigma\ xy$ and that $\sqrt{i_X^2}$ and $\sqrt{i_Y^2}$ are involved in finding $\sqrt{\Sigma x^2 \Sigma y^2}$. The coding constants thus are present in both the numerator and the denominator of the formula for r. It is not necessary therefore to multiply the numerator and denominator by the coding constants in order to calculate r. We see, for example, that

$$r = \frac{\sum X'Y' - \frac{(\sum X')(\sum Y')}{n}}{\sqrt{\left(\sum X'^2 - \frac{(\sum X')^2}{n}\right)\left(\sum Y'^2 - \frac{(\sum Y')^2}{n}\right)}}$$

$$= \frac{1250 - \frac{(230)(141)}{32}}{\sqrt{\left(2208 - \frac{(230)^2}{32}\right)\left(993 - \frac{(141)^2}{32}\right)}}$$

$$= \frac{236.56}{\sqrt{(544.88)(371.72)}}$$

$$= .52$$

and this is the same value that we obtained before.

EXAMPLES

6.1—Subtract 24 from each of the X values given below and 14 from each of the Y values. Find the correlation coefficient.

X	Y
36	26
34	27
33	23
32	21
31	22
30	19
28	17
27	14
25	16
24	15

6.2—Calculate the correlation coefficient for the data below.

Y scores	X scores						
	0–2	3–5	6–8	9–11	12–14	15–17	18–20
95–99						1	1
90–94				1		2	
85–89			1	2	1	1	
80–84		2	3	2	4		
75–79		1	3				
70–74	1	1	1	1			
65–69			1				

6.3—The following table shows the relationship between reported weekly wages and verified weekly wages for 61 female workers on jobs held from zero to 12 months prior to the time of the interviews. The interviews were made in 1940–1942 with unemployed persons in St. Paul, Minnesota. Find the correlation coefficient. Data are from Keating, Paterson, and Stone (1950).

Reported weekly wage	Verified weekly wage					
	0–4	5–9	10–14	15–19	20–24	25–29
25–29						2
20–24					3	
15–19			4	19		
10–14			24	3		
5– 9		3	1			
0– 4	2					

6.4—Find the correlation coefficient for Example 5.8, in which mean reaction times were plotted against affective distances for various colors.

6.5—Find the correlation coefficient for the following data.

X	Y
12	12
10	13
9	9
8	8
7	5
6	6
4	0
2	2
1	1
0	3

6.6—Plot the data of Example 6.5 on coordinate paper. Show the point with coordinates $(\bar{X}, \bar{Y})$. Draw the regression line of Y on X and the regression line of X on Y.

6.7—Twenty-five items in an attitude test were rated on a nine-point scale ranging from extremely unfavorable to extremely favorable. The ratings were made independently by two groups of subjects. The scale values of the items were found for each group of subjects. The correlation between the two sets of scale values may be taken as an indication of the reliability of the scale values. Find the value of the correlation coefficient.

Scale values Group 1	Scale values Group 2
8.2	8.9
7.7	8.6
7.3	7.5
7.0	7.3
6.7	7.4
2.7	1.9
2.0	1.2
3.1	3.1
1.8	1.6
1.0	1.0
3.7	3.0
8.4	8.9
4.8	4.5
4.6	4.0
3.2	2.8
6.2	6.3
6.0	6.2
5.1	5.5
4.1	3.4
6.4	6.9

6.8—A class in applied psychology was given Shaffer's (1936) S-scale and C-scale. Shaffer states that there is little relationship between scores on these two scales. Find the value of the correlation coefficient without grouping the scores. On the basis of the correlation coefficient obtained would you agree with Shaffer's conclusion?

C	S	C	S	C	S	C	S	C	S
5	10	15	7	14	10	9	10	18	9
19	9	11	6	13	7	6	19	14	14
17	10	18	11	19	8	8	8	13	6
14	6	13	11	11	11	18	9	18	8
13	10	14	4	18	8	16	6	18	7
7	12	13	8	5	6	5	7	8	4
13	14	13	6	18	13	14	8	19	12
8	10	4	7	17	6	15	7	22	17
6	17	8	9	23	18	18	12		

6.9—The data below are scores on two tests given to an introductory class in general psychology. One test was designed to measure the student's general understanding of the subject matter of the course. We shall call this variable X. The Y variable consists of scores on a vocabulary test of psychological terms. Let $i = 5$ on both variables, and find the correlation coefficient. Begin the first class intervals with a multiple of the size of the interval.

X	Y	X	Y	X	Y	X	Y	X	Y	X	Y	X	Y	X	Y	X	Y	X	Y
55	71	50	57	49	53	58	65	76	65	74	65	74	75	72	71	57	63	96	80
60	59	67	64	53	46	67	67	58	55	68	71	55	65	59	66	63	75	74	76
56	48	69	70	61	65	59	51	53	61	87	78	68	72	74	61	79	71	91	95
56	60	59	68	60	62	63	66	60	59	61	56	55	61	59	52	49	51	82	66
57	67	59	70	45	54	58	61	65	67	66	70	61	63	60	62	58	71	63	74
55	53	56	67	71	61	73	61	74	63	58	72	48	58	73	78	82	80	96	85
61	60	66	58	71	63	48	62	73	73	58	55	69	58	57	62	97	84	90	89
54	63	49	47	67	57	50	68	67	64	45	55	77	63	71	66	82	75	86	75
57	61	60	61	52	52	55	59	55	60	76	68	78	78	74	81	79	76	82	85
58	68	45	57	60	60	61	40	48	66	50	63	86	82	55	62	90	73	97	86

6.10—For the data of Example 6.9, find the regression coefficient b_Y. Using the regression equation $\tilde{Y} = a + b_Y X$, find the predicted score on Y for the following scores on X.

(a) If $X = 48$, then $\tilde{Y} =$
(b) If $X = 55$, then $\tilde{Y} =$
(c) If $X = 73$, then $\tilde{Y} =$
(d) If $X = 82$, then $\tilde{Y} =$
(e) If $X = 90$, then $\tilde{Y} =$

6.11—For the data of Example 6.9, find the regression coefficient b_X. Using the regression equation $\tilde{X} = a + b_X Y$, find the predicted score on X for the following scores on Y.

(a) If $Y = 58$, then $\tilde{X} =$
(b) If $Y = 71$, then $\tilde{X} =$
(c) If $Y = 76$, then $\tilde{X} =$
(d) If $Y = 80$, then $\tilde{X} =$
(e) If $Y = 95$, then $\tilde{X} =$

6.12—Find the standard errors of estimate $s_{Y \cdot X}$ and $s_{X \cdot Y}$ for the data of Example 6.9.

6.13—Prove that if $d = x - y$, then $s_D{}^2 = s_X{}^2 + s_Y{}^2 - 2rs_X s_Y$.

6.14—Prove that $b_Y = r[(s_Y)/(s_X)]$.

6.15—Prove that

$$r^2 = 1 - \frac{\Sigma (y - \tilde{y})^2}{\Sigma y^2}$$

6.16—Prove that $\Sigma y^2 = \Sigma y^2 (1 - r^2) + r^2 \Sigma y^2$.

6.17—Find the correlation coefficient for the following pairs of X and Y

values. Let $i_X = 3$ and let $i_Y = 5$. Begin the first intervals with a multiple of the size of the intervals.

X	Y	X	Y	X	Y	X	Y	X	Y
4	77	25	53	20	67	14	61	31	49
18	37	9	46	27	38	21	52	16	57
24	38	20	52	11	66	29	58	23	62
6	55	25	53	21	37	14	71	31	54
18	42	9	51	27	43	22	52	16	57
24	38	20	57	11	71	29	58	23	67
6	60	25	58	21	42	14	71	33	39
19	42	10	51	27	43	22	52	16	57
24	43	20	57	12	46	29	63	23	67
7	65	25	58	21	42	15	42	33	44
19	47	10	56	27	48	22	52	16	62
24	48	20	57	12	56	30	39	23	72
7	65	26	63	21	42	15	47	34	44
19	47	10	62	28	53	22	57	17	62
24	48	20	62	13	56	30	44	34	49
7	70	26	63	21	47	16	47	17	67
19	47	11	62	28	53	22	57	36	34
24	53	20	62	13	56	31	44	17	67
8	75	26	73	21	47	16	52	36	39
19	52	11	66	28	53	23	62	17	77

6.18—Prove that

$$\frac{\sum xy}{\sqrt{\sum x^2 \sum y^2}} = \frac{\sum z_X z_Y}{n-1}$$

6.19—Prove that $r^2 = b_Y b_X$.

6.20—Prove that $s_Y^2 = (1 - r^2)s_Y^2 + r^2 s_Y^2$.

6.21—Prove that the errors of prediction, $y - \tilde{y}$, are uncorrelated with the values of $X - \overline{X}$. Hint: It is sufficient to show that the numerator of the correlation coefficient is equal to zero.

6.22—Prove $-1.0 \le r \le 1.0$. Hint: Find $\sum (z_X - z_Y)^2/(n-1)$ and $\sum (z_X + z_Y)^2/(n-1)$.

6.23—If $b_Y = .15$ and $b_X = .60$, then what is the value of the correlation coefficient?

6.24—If $r = .60$, $s_Y = 8.0$, and $s_X = 10.0$, then what is the value of b_X?

6.25—Under what conditions will $r = b_Y$?

6.26—If $r = -1.00$, what is the value of $\sum (Y - \tilde{Y})^2$?

6.27—If $r = 1.00$, what is the value of $s_{Y \cdot X}$?

6.28—If $D = X - Y$, then under what conditions will $s_D^2 = s_X^2 + s_Y^2$?

6.29—If $D = X - Y$, and if $r = 1.00$, $s_X = 2.0$, and $s_Y = 3.0$, what will be the value of s_D^2?

6.30—Give a one-sentence definition of each of the following terms or concepts:

correlation coefficient   coefficient of nondetermination
coefficient of determination

CHAPTER 7

Point Coefficients and Other Measures of Association

7.1 Introduction

There are times when an investigator is faced with this situation: he wants to find the relationship between two variables, but the data for one variable are expressed in terms of a dichotomy. By a dichotomy we mean that only two categories or classes of the variable are available. For example, the response of a subject to an item on a test may be scored "right" or "wrong," and we may arbitrarily assign a value of 1 to the right response and a value of zero to the wrong response. If we consider the response to the item a variable, then the variable can take only the two values, 1 or zero. Can we find a measure of the extent to which this variable, response to the item, is related to another variable that can take any one of a number of different values within a given range?

Or suppose that we have a group of male subjects and we wish to determine whether there is any relationship between their marital status and scores on a personality test. Our subjects can be classified as "single" or "married," and we wish to see whether this classification is related to scores on the test. Again, one of our variables is dichotomous, has only two classes, and again we might arbitrarily assign a value of 1 to one of the classes and a value of zero to the other.

Other examples of a dichotomous variable might be subjects who are employed and those who are unemployed; individuals who are Democrats and those who are Republicans; animals that survive and those that die after an injection of a drug; subjects who are male and those who are female; subjects who respond in a particular way in an experimental situation and those who respond in some other fashion. This list could be extended, but the examples cited should be sufficient to indicate the nature of a variable for which we may have only two classes or categories. We shall refer to such variables as *dichotomous variables*.[1] We shall also assume that the observations in one of the two classes or categories are assigned a value of 1 and the observations in the other class or category are assigned a value of zero.

7.2   The Point Biserial Coefficient of Correlation: r_{pb}

Suppose that we have given an intelligence test to a group of subjects and that we also have observed their response in a discrimination experiment. The subjects either make the correct response in the discrimination experiment or they fail to make the correct response. If the subjects make the correct response they are given a score of 1, and if they make the incorrect response they are given a score of zero. We wish to relate the scores on this dichotomous variable, which we shall call the X variable, to the scores on the intelligence test, which we shall call the Y variable.

If we have a variable X such that X can take only the values $X = 1$ or $X = 0$, then ΣX will obviously be just the number of observations for which $X = 1$. For example, if we have $n = 5$ observations with values: 1, 1, 1, 0, and 0, then $\Sigma X = 1 + 1 + 1 + 0 + 0 = 3$. For this same set of observations we have $\Sigma X^2 = 1^2 + 1^2 + 1^2 + 0^2 + 0^2 = 3$, and ΣX^2 will also always be equal to the number of observations for which $X = 1$.

In general, we let n_1 be the number of observations with $X = 1$ and n_0 be the number of observations with $X = 0$ with $n_0 + n_1 = n$. Then for the sum of squared deviations from the mean, we have

$$\Sigma x^2 = \Sigma (X - \bar{X})^2$$

$$= \Sigma X^2 - \frac{(\Sigma X)^2}{n}$$

$$= n_1 - \frac{(n_1)^2}{n} \tag{7.1}$$

or

$$\Sigma x^2 = \frac{n_1 n_0}{n} \tag{7.2}$$

Now suppose that with each of the above X values we have a paired Y value such that Y can take any one of a number of possible values. The exact values of Y do not matter and for convenience we can assume that they are: 1, 2, 3, 4, 5. Then for the set of $n = 5$ paired (X, Y) values we have: (1, 1), (1, 2), (1, 3), (0, 4), and (0, 5). Obviously, all products, XY, of the form $(0, Y)$ will be equal to zero and all products of the form $(1, Y)$ will be equal to

---

[1] Dichotomous variables are also referred to as *binary* variables and *binomial* variables.

Y. Then ΣXY will be just the sum of the n_1 Y values for which $X = 1$ or

$$\Sigma XY = \Sigma Y_1$$

where ΣY_1 is the sum of the Y values for those n_1 observations for which $X = 1$.

We have, as one of the previously developed formulas for the correlation coefficient,

$$r = \frac{\Sigma XY - \frac{(\Sigma X)(\Sigma Y)}{n}}{\sqrt{\left(\Sigma X^2 - \frac{(\Sigma X)^2}{n}\right)\left(\Sigma Y^2 - \frac{(\Sigma Y)^2}{n}\right)}} \qquad (7.3)$$

and, if X can take only values of 1 or zero, then

$$r_{pb} = \frac{\Sigma Y_1 - \frac{n_1 \Sigma Y}{n}}{\sqrt{\frac{n_1 n_0}{n}\left(\Sigma Y^2 - \frac{(\Sigma Y)^2}{n}\right)}} \qquad (7.4)$$

where r_{pb} = the point biserial coefficient of correlation
ΣY_1 = the sum of Y values for the n_1 observations with $X = 1$
ΣY = the sum of the Y values for all n observations
n_1 = the number of observations with $X = 1$
n_0 = the number of observations with $X = 0$
n = the total number of observations

The correlation coefficient given by (7.4) is obviously a special case of the product-moment correlation coefficient given by (7.3).

Table 7.1 gives the paired (X, Y) values for a set of $n = 66$ observations of which $n_0 = 24$ have X values of zero and $n_1 = 42$ have X values of 1. By comparing this table with Tables 6.3 and 6.4 in the previous chapter, you will see that the top half of Table 7.1 is comparable to Table 6.3 and the bottom half is comparable to Table 6.4. The columns at the right are used to find $\Sigma Y, \Sigma Y^2$, and ΣXY. We note, however, that, in addition to giving the total frequency (f) for each Y value, we have also shown how many (f_0) of the Y values have $X = 0$ and how many (f_1) have $X = 1$. For example, we have 18 values of Y equal to 4. Of these 18 Y values, 8 have X values of zero and 10 have X values of 1. Then, we have $\Sigma f_0 = n_0$, the total number of observations with $X = 0$, and $\Sigma f_1 = n_1$, the total number of observations with $X = 1$. It is easy to verify from the data given in the table that:

$$\sum XY = \sum Y_1$$
$$\sum X = n_1$$
$$\sum X^2 = n_1$$

Table 7.1—Calculation of the point biserial coefficient of correlation

Y	X Categories		(1) f	(2) Y	(3) fY	(4) fY^2	(5) $\Sigma X._Y$	(6) $Y\Sigma X._Y$
	f_0	f_1						
9	0	2	2	9	18	162	2	18
8	0	3	3	8	24	192	3	24
7	1	5	6	7	42	294	5	35
6	4	7	11	6	66	396	7	42
5	3	4	7	5	35	175	4	20
4	8	10	18	4	72	288	10	40
3	5	9	14	3	42	126	9	27
2	0	1	1	2	2	4	1	2
1	2	0	2	1	2	2	0	0
0	1	1	2	0	0	0	1	0
(1) f	24	42	66		303	1639	42	208
(2) X	0	1			ΣY	ΣY^2		ΣXY
(3) fX	0	42	42	ΣX				
(4) fX^2	0	42	42	ΣX^2				
(5) $\Sigma Y._X$	95	208	303					
(6) $X\Sigma Y._X$	0	208	208	ΣXY				

for the paired X and Y values in this table.

Substituting with the appropriate values from Table 7.1 in (7.4), we have

$$r_{pb} = \frac{208 - \dfrac{(42)(303)}{66}}{\sqrt{\dfrac{(42)(24)}{66}\left(1639 - \dfrac{(303)^2}{66}\right)}}$$

$$= \frac{15.18}{\sqrt{(15.27)(247.95)}}$$

$$= .25$$

Various alternative but algebraically equivalent expressions for the point biserial coefficient, as defined by (7.4), can be derived. For example, the calculations are somewhat simplified if we multiply both the numerator and denominator of (7.4) by n. Then we have

$$r_{pb} = \frac{n \sum Y_1 - n_1 \sum Y}{\sqrt{n_1 n_0 [n \sum Y^2 - (\sum Y)^2]}} \tag{7.5}$$

Substituting in (7.5) with the appropriate values from Table 7.1, we have

$$r_{pb} = \frac{(66)(208) - (42)(303)}{\sqrt{(42)(24)[(66)(1639) - (303)^2]}}$$

$$= \frac{1002}{\sqrt{(1008)(16,365)}}$$

$$= .25$$

as before.

The sign of the point biserial coefficient of correlation will depend upon whether the mean score on the Y variable is larger or smaller for the n_1 subjects than it is for the n_0 subjects. For the data of Table 7.1 there was a logical basis for assigning a value of $X = 1$ to the subjects making the correct response on the dichotomous variable. Thus the fact that the point biserial correlation coefficient was, in this instance, positive in sign, means that the subjects making the correct response in the discrimination experiment have a higher mean score on the intelligence test than the subjects making the incorrect response.

In many cases, however, we shall have no logical basis for assigning the zero and 1 values for the dichotomous variables. For example, if our dichotomous variable was sex, should we give the males or the females a score of 1? If our dichotomous variable consists of Democrats and Republicans, shall we give the Democrats or the Republicans the score of 1? It should be clear that in such cases the sign of the point biserial coefficient of correlation will be an arbitrary matter.

7.3   The Phi Coefficient: r_ϕ

Suppose that both X and Y are dichotomous variables and can take only the values 1 or zero. In this case, we have the following possible paired (X, Y) values: $(0, 1)$, $(1, 1)$, $(0, 0)$, and $(1, 0)$. The paired values are shown at the left of Table 7.2 and at the right of the table we let the cell entries a, b, c, and d correspond to the *number* of times each of the paired values occurs in a set of n observations. Then, obviously

$$\sum XY = b$$
$$\sum X = \sum X^2 = b + d$$
$$\sum Y = \sum Y^2 = a + b$$

Substituting in (7.3), with the above identities, we have

$$r_\phi = \frac{b - \dfrac{(b + d)(a + b)}{n}}{\sqrt{\left[(b + d) - \dfrac{(b + d)^2}{n}\right]\left[(a + b) - \dfrac{(a + b)^2}{n}\right]}} \qquad (7.6)$$

Table 7.2—The table on the left shows the paired (X, Y) values for two dichotomous variables that can take only the values of 0 or 1. In the table on the right the letters in the cells of the table correspond to the number of times each of the paired values occurs in a sample of n

		X	
		0	1
Y	1	(0, 1)	(1, 1)
	0	(0, 0)	(1, 0)

		X		
		0	1	
Y	1	a	b	$a + b$
	0	c	d	$c + d$
		$a + c$	$b + d$	n

The correlation coefficient defined by (7.6) is called the *fourfold point coefficient* or the *phi coefficient*. Again, it is obvious that the phi coefficient is a special case of the product-moment correlation coefficient given by (7.3).

In Table 7.3 we have the paired responses of 200 subjects to two items in a test. We let X be the response to the first item with $X = 1$ if the response is correct and $X = 0$ otherwise. Similarly, we let Y be the response to the second item with $Y = 1$ if the response is correct and $Y = 0$ otherwise. For the data in this table, we have

$$\sum XY = 45$$
$$\sum X = \sum X^2 = 75$$
$$\sum Y = \sum Y^2 = 90$$

Then substituting in (7.6) with these values, we have

$$r_\phi = \frac{45 - \dfrac{(75)(90)}{200}}{\sqrt{\left(75 - \dfrac{(75)^2}{200}\right)\left(90 - \dfrac{(90)^2}{200}\right)}}$$

$$= \frac{45 - 33.75}{\sqrt{(46.88)(49.50)}}$$

$$= .23$$

Table 7.3—Calculation of the phi coefficient

Y Item 2	Item 1 Incorrect	Item 1 Correct	(1) f	(2) Y	(3) fY	(4) fY^2	(5) $\Sigma X_{.Y}$	(6) $Y\Sigma X_{.Y}$
Correct	45	45	90	1	90	90	45	45
Incorrect	80	30	110	0	0	0	30	0
(1) f	125	75	200		90	90	75	45
(2) X	0	1			ΣY	ΣY^2		ΣXY
(3) fX	0	75	75	ΣX				
(4) fX^2	0	75	75	ΣX^2				
(5) $\Sigma Y_{.X}$	45	45	90					
(6) $X\Sigma Y_{.X}$	0	45	45	ΣXY				

If we multiply out the terms in the numerator and denominator of (7.6) and substitute $a + b + c + d$ for n, then we obtain the following simplified expression for the phi coefficient

$$r_\phi = \frac{bc - ad}{\sqrt{(a + b)(c + d)(a + c)(b + d)}} \tag{7.7}$$

Substituting with the appropriate values of a, b, c, and d, from Table 7.3 in (7.7), we have

$$r_\phi = \frac{(45)(80) - (45)(30)}{\sqrt{(90)(110)(125)(75)}} = .23$$

as before.

As in the case of the point biserial coefficient of correlation, the sign of the phi coefficient depends upon the arrangement of the dichotomous variables in the 2×2 table. In the example of Table 7.3 we had some basis for assigning the value of one to the correct response to the two items and the value of zero to the incorrect response. In many cases, however, assigning the values of zero and one will be an arbitrary matter. The direction of the relationship must, in these cases, be determined from inspection of the arrangement of the dichotomous variables in the table.

7.4   The Biserial Coefficient of Correlation: r_b

The formula for the point biserial coefficient of correlation measures the degree of relationship between a dichotomous variable and a variable that can take more than two possible values within a given range. Under some circumstances, we may make the assumption that the dichotomous variable is essentially continuous and normally distributed. The coefficient used to measure the relationship when this assumption can be made is the *biserial coefficient of correlation* r_b rather than the point biserial coefficient.

The assumption that the dichotomous variable is normally distributed is most likely to be valid when we have artificially dichotomized a variable. For example, we may arbitrarily divide the scores on a test or some other variable into those that are above the mean and those that are below the mean, or into those that are above the median and those that are below the median. In this instance we might assume that the scores are approximately normally distributed. Although the recorded values of the scores will be discrete, we may also assume that the variable or trait that the scores supposedly measure is essentially continuous and that the discrete nature of the scores merely reflects a limitation imposed by our measuring instrument.

A convenient formula for the biserial coefficient of correlation may be obtained by multiplying (7.4) by $\sqrt{pq}/y_p$. Then

$$r_b = \frac{n \sum Y_1 - n_1 \sum Y}{\sqrt{(n_1 n_0)[n \sum Y^2 - (\sum Y)^2]}} \left(\frac{\sqrt{pq}}{y_p}\right) \tag{7.8}$$

where p is the proportion of the total number of subjects in the one category of the dichotomous variable, that is, $p = n_1/n$, and q is the proportion of the total number of subjects in the zero category, that is, $q = n_0/n = 1 - p$. We use y_p to represent the ordinate of the standard normal curve at the point of division of the two groups on the dichotomous variable. We find the value of y_p from Table III, in Appendix B. We enter Table III with $p = n_1/n$ and look down column (3) or column (4) of the table until we find the value most closely approximating p. We then read the corresponding value of y_p from the last column of the table. For example, if p is .488, the value of y_p would be equal to .3988. If p is equal to .591, then we find that y_p would be equal to .3885.

We may simplify the computations involved in (7.8) by substituting n_1/n for p and n_0/n for q. Then

$$r_b = \frac{\left(n \sum Y_1 - n_1 \sum Y\right)\sqrt{\dfrac{n_1 n_0}{n^2}}}{y_p\sqrt{(n_1 n_0)[n \sum Y^2 - (\sum Y)^2]}}$$

or

$$r_b = \frac{\sum Y_1 - \dfrac{n_1}{n} \sum Y}{y_p\sqrt{n \sum Y^2 - (\sum Y)^2}} \tag{7.9}$$

We now obtain the biserial coefficient of correlation for the data shown in Table 7.4. In the table we have calculated the values to be substituted in (7.9). From Table III we find that $y_p = .394$ when p is equal to $.5625$. Substituting in (7.9), we get

$$
\begin{aligned}
r_b &= \frac{172 - (.5625)(281)}{.394\sqrt{(80)(1209) - (281)^2}} \\
&= \frac{172 - 158.06}{.394\sqrt{17,759}} \\
&= \frac{13.94}{52.51} \\
&= .27
\end{aligned}
$$

Table 7.4—Calculation of the biserial coefficient of correlation

	(1) f_0	(2) f_1	(3) f	(4) Y	(5) $f_1 Y$	(6) fY	(7) fY^2
Y							
8	0	2	2	8	16	16	128
7	1	2	3	7	14	21	147
6	2	3	5	6	18	30	180
5	3	7	10	5	35	50	250
4	4	11	15	4	44	60	240
3	12	8	20	3	24	60	180
2	10	10	20	2	20	40	80
1	3	1	4	1	1	4	4
0	0	1	1	0	0	0	0
Σ	35	45	80 ·		172	281	1209
					ΣY_1	ΣY	ΣY^2

If we have dichotomized a variable that is continuous and normally distributed and then found the biserial coefficient of correlation for this dichotomous variable and another variable, the resulting coefficient is an estimate of the corresponding product-moment coefficient that we would have obtained if we had not dichotomized one of the variables. This estimate will be best when we have a large n and when the point of division on the continuous variable that is reduced to a dichotomy is made near the median. This will mean that we shall have approximately the same number of subjects in each of the two categories. We assume, also, of course, that the scores or measures on the dichotomized variable are normally distributed. This assumption is involved when we enter the table of the standard normal curve to obtain the value of the ordinate y_p for the corresponding value of p.

7.5   The Tetrachoric Correlation Coefficient: r_t

In the case of two dichotomous variables where we have used the phi coffi-cient to measure the degree of relationship present, we may, under certain circumstances, assume that both variables are essentially continuous and normally distributed. If we can make this assumption about both of the di-chotomous variables, then the coefficient used to measure the relationship is the *tetrachoric coefficient of correlation*, r_t, rather than the phi coefficient.

The tetrachoric coefficient of correlation could properly be applied, for example, if we have artificially dichotomized two variables, X and Y, that are normally distributed. We may, for example, divide the scores on a test into

Table 7.5—Relationship between success as a salesman and social adjust-ment*

	Unsuccessful	Successful	Totals
Adjusted	*a* 25	*b* 35	60
Maladjusted	*c* 30	*d* 10	40
Totals	55	45	100

* Data from Garrett (1937).

those that are above the median and those that are below the median. We may make a similar division for a second test or variable. If we now assign a score of one to those subjects who are above the median and a score of zero to those who are below, we have the following possible pairs of scores on the two tests.

Above the median on both tests:	$X = 1$ and $Y = 1$
Above median on Test 1, below on Test 2:	$X = 1$ and $Y = 0$
Below median on Test 1, above on Test 2:	$X = 0$ and $Y = 1$
Below the median on both tests:	$X = 0$ and $Y = 0$

We may make a 2×2 correlation table for these pairs of scores as we did in the case of the phi coefficient. Such a table is shown in Table 7.5 where we have also assigned letters to represent the corresponding cell entries. We could now develop an approximation formula for tetrachoric r which would involve the solution of a quadratic equation. We shall instead give a much easier method for estimating tetrachoric r.

We calculate the products ad and bc corresponding to the products of the cell entries in Table 7.5. We then find the ratio $k = bc/ad$ or its reciprocal, whichever is the larger. Thus, if bc is greater than ad, we find

$$k = \frac{bc}{ad} \tag{7.10}$$

and, if ad is greater than bc, we find

$$\frac{1}{k} = \frac{1}{bc/ad} = \frac{ad}{bc} \tag{7.11}$$

In essence, then we put either bc or ad, whichever is the larger, in the numerator and divide by the other product.

We then enter Table X, in Appendix B, with this ratio and read the corresponding value of the tetrachoric coefficient of correlation in the column headed r_t. The values of r_t in Table X are based upon one of the formulas developed by Pearson (1901) to estimate the tetrachoric coefficient of correlation.[2]

In Table 7.5 we report data for which the tetrachoric r as obtained by direct calculation from one of the formulas for the coefficient is .53. We illustrate the use of Table X for the same data. Thus

$$ad = (25)(10) = 250$$
$$bc = (35)(30) = 1050$$

Putting bc in the numerator, because it is larger than ad, we obtain

$$\frac{bc}{ad} = \frac{1050}{250} = 4.2$$

Entering Table X with 4.2 we find that the corresponding estimate of the tetrachoric r is .51. The ease with which this estimate is obtained more than justifies the slight discrepancy between its value and that obtained by direct calculation. In general, the estimates of tetrachoric r obtained from Table X will agree quite well with estimates obtained from other methods of determining the coefficient.[3]

---

[2] Computing diagrams for the tetrachoric coefficient of correlation have been prepared by Chesire, Saffir, and Thurstone (1933). To use these diagrams, the points of division on the variables must be taken into consideration. Table X, prepared by Davidoff and Goheen (1953), does not involve the points of division on the two variables and therefore is extremely convenient to use.

It should be emphasized, however, that Table X provides estimates of r_t that are most accurate when the points of division on the two variables are close to the medians. A table similar to Table X, but with correction graphs for nonmedian dichotomization, has been prepared by Perry, Kettner, Hertzka, and Bouvier (1953).

[3] It should be pointed out that the formulas usually quoted and actually used in calculating r_t are themselves approximations in which terms involving the powers of r_t greater than the second are ignored.

7.6 The Rank Correlation Coefficient: r'

If we have a set of n objects or individuals arranged in order according to the degree of some characteristic that they possess, the individuals or objects are said to be *ranked*. After the individuals are arranged in order, we may then assign the number 1 to the first individual, 2 to the second, 3 to the third, and so on, with the number n corresponding to the nth or last individual. We thus have a series or set of ranks in which X_1, X_2, X_3, $\cdots$, $X_n = 1, 2, 3, \cdots, n$. It can be shown[4] that the sum of the n terms in this series will be given by

$$\sum X = \frac{n(n + 1)}{2} \tag{7.12}$$

and that the sum of the squares of the n terms in the series will be given by

$$\sum X^2 = \frac{n(n + 1)(2n + 1)}{6} \tag{7.13}$$

We have previously shown that the sum of squared deviations from the mean will be given by

$$\sum x^2 = \sum X^2 - \frac{(\sum X)^2}{n}$$

Then, substituting from (7.12) and (7.13) in the above expression, we obtain for the set of ranks

$$\sum x^2 = \frac{n(n + 1)(2n + 1)}{6} - \frac{\left(\dfrac{n(n + 1)}{2}\right)^2}{n}$$

$$= \frac{n^3 - n}{12} \tag{7.14}$$

The mean of the set of ranks may be obtained by dividing both sides of (7.12) by n. Thus

$$\overline{X} = \frac{n + 1}{2} \tag{7.15}$$

When we have available two sets of ranks, X and Y, for the same objects or individuals, we may then wish to determine the degree of relationship between the two sets of ranks. The product-moment correlation coefficient

---

[4] A proof of (7.12) and (7.13) can be found in Edwards (1964).

obtained from two sets of ranks is called a *rank correlation coefficient*, and we shall designate this coefficient by r'.

We have shown earlier that if we let $d = x - y$, then

$$\sum d^2 = \sum x^2 + \sum y^2 - 2r\sqrt{\sum x^2 \sum y^2}$$

We can then express the correlation coefficient as

$$r = \frac{\sum x^2 + \sum y^2 - \sum d^2}{2\sqrt{\sum x^2 \sum y^2}} \tag{7.16}$$

But, if X and Y consist of two sets of n ranks each, $\sum x^2$ will be given by (7.14) as will also $\sum y^2$. Thus, using r' to indicate the rank correlation coefficient and substituting from (7.14) in (7.16), we obtain

$$r' = \frac{\dfrac{n^3 - n}{12} + \dfrac{n^3 - n}{12} - \sum d^2}{2\sqrt{\left(\dfrac{n^3 - n}{12}\right)\left(\dfrac{n^3 - n}{12}\right)}}$$

$$= \frac{2\left(\dfrac{n^3 - n}{12}\right) - \sum d^2}{2\left(\dfrac{n^3 - n}{12}\right)}$$

$$= 1 - \frac{6\sum d^2}{n^3 - n} \tag{7.17}$$

We have $\sum d^2 = \sum (x - y)^2$, and we now show that $\sum d^2 = \sum (X - Y)^2$. Thus, if we let $d = x - y$ and $D = X - Y$, then

$$d = x - y$$
$$= (X - \bar{X}) - (Y - \bar{Y})$$

But, if X and Y are two sets of n ranks each, then $\bar{X}$ will be equal to $\bar{Y}$, and consequently

$$d = X - Y = D \tag{7.18}$$

Then, substituting D for d in (7.17), the rank correlation coefficient may be computed by means of the following formula

$$r' = 1 - \frac{6\sum D^2}{n^3 - n} \tag{7.19}$$

In Table 7.6 we give the ranks assigned to eight morale items by a group of employers and a group of employees. Substituting the appropriate values from the table in (7.19) we obtain

$$r' = 1 - \frac{6(92)}{8^3 - 8} = -.10$$

which indicates that there is a very slight tendency for the ranks assigned by the two groups to the eight morale items to be negatively related.

Table 7.6—Ranks assigned to various morale items by employers and employees*

Item	Employer ranking	Employee ranking	Difference	Difference squared
1. Credit for work done	1	7	−6	36
2. Interesting work	2	3	−1	1
3. Fair pay	3	1	2	4
4. Understanding and appreciation	4	5	−1	1
5. Counsel on personal problems	5	8	−3	9
6. Promotion on merit	6	4	2	4
7. Good physical working conditions	7	6	1	1
8. Job security	8	2	6	36
				92

* Data from Fosdick (1939).

If you apply any of the formulas previously given for the product-moment coefficient of correlation to the ranks of Table 7.6, you will find that the value obtained is identical with that given by (7.19). The rank correlation coefficient, in other words, is the product-moment correlation coefficient applied to two sets of integral ranks.

Sometimes, in obtaining ranks, it may be difficult to distinguish between two of the individuals or objects being ranked. What happens, for example, if two objects seem to be tied for the same rank? If judgments of equality are to be permitted, we might assign an average rank to those objects that are judged equal. For example, if no choice can be made between two objects when we come to, let us say, the assignment of rank 4, then we might assign the average of ranks 4 and 5, or 4.5 to each of these objects. If no choice can be made between three objects, then we might assign the average of ranks 4, 5, and 6, or 5 to each of these objects. In other words, when apparent ties for a given rank are present, we give each of the tied objects the average of the ranks they would ordinarily occupy.

If judgments of equality are permitted so that we have tied ranks, the rank correlation coefficient as given by (7.19) will no longer be identical with the value obtained by applying to the same data one of the other formulas for the correlation coefficient. Formula (7.19) is equivalent to the product-moment coefficient only when the ranks for each variable are integral. Formula (7.19) may still be used, however, to determine the relationship between two sets of ranks, even though tied ranks are present in the data, provided the number of ties is not large. If the number of ties is large, however, then (7.19) should not be used. Instead a correction factor, described in Chapter 17, should be used in connection with (7.17) to find the rank correlation coefficient.

7.7   The Correlation Ratio: η_{YX}

In Table 7.7 we give the values of a variable Y associated with the values of a variable X for $n = 129$ paired (X, Y) values. An examination of Table 7.7 indicates that the Y values at first tend to increase with an increase in X from zero to 5 and then tend to decrease. We wish to determine the relationship between the Y and X values.

Table 7.7—Calculation of the correlation ratio of Y on X

Values of Y	Values of X									f	Y	fY	fY^2
	0	1	2	3	4	5	6	7	8				
8			1	1	1	2				5	8	40	320
7		1	1	1	4	5	4	2		18	7	126	882
6		4	3	1	6	3	2	6	2	27	6	162	972
5		3	2		2	2	1	3		13	5	65	325
4	4	3	2					3	3	15	4	60	240
3	8	6			1				5	20	3	60	180
2	6								9	15	2	30	60
1	3								11	14	1	14	14
0	1								1	2	0	0	0
n	22	17	9	3	14	12	7	14	31	129		557	2993
X	0	1	2	3	4	5	6	7	8			ΣY	ΣY^2
$\sum_{1}^{n} Y_{kn}$	55	76	51	21	85	79	45	77	68	557			

Column	n	$\displaystyle\sum_1^n Y_{kn}$	$\displaystyle\left(\sum_1^n Y_{kn}\right)^2$	$\displaystyle\frac{\left(\sum_1^n Y_{kn}\right)^2}{n}$
0	22	55	3025	137.50
1	17	76	5776	339.76
2	9	51	2601	289.00
3	3	21	441	147.00
4	14	85	7225	516.07
5	12	79	6241	520.08
6	7	45	2025	289.29
7	14	77	5929	423.50
8	31	68	4624	149.16
$\sum$	129	557		2811.36

Let Y_{kn} be the nth observation in the kth column with $k = 1, 2, 3, \cdots, k$ and $n = 1, 2, 3, \cdots, n$. Then let $\overline{Y}_{k\cdot}$ be the mean of the kth column. For example, for the data of Table 7.7 we have

$$\overline{Y}_{1\cdot} = \frac{55}{22} = 2.50$$

We also let $\overline{Y}_{\cdot\cdot}$ be the mean of all of the Y values and, for the data of Table 7.7, we have

$$\overline{Y}_{\cdot\cdot} = \frac{557}{129} = 4.32$$

Then we can write the following identity

$$Y_{kn} - \overline{Y}_{\cdot\cdot} = (Y_{kn} - \overline{Y}_{k\cdot}) + (\overline{Y}_{k\cdot} - \overline{Y}_{\cdot\cdot}) \tag{7.20}$$

If we square (7.20) and sum over the n observations in a given column, the cross product term on the right will be

$$2(\overline{Y}_{k\cdot} - \overline{Y}_{\cdot\cdot})\sum_1^n (Y_{kn} - \overline{Y}_{k\cdot}) = 0$$

Because the cross product term disappears when we sum over the n observations in a given column, we have, summing over all observations,

$$\sum_1^k \sum_1^n (Y_{kn} - \overline{Y}_{\cdot\cdot})^2 = \sum_1^k \sum_1^n (Y_{kn} - \overline{Y}_{k\cdot})^2 + \sum_1^k n(\overline{Y}_{k\cdot} - \overline{Y}_{\cdot\cdot})^2 \tag{7.21}$$

The term on the left in the above expression is the sum of squared deviations of the Y values from the mean of the entire Y distribution. This sum of squares is often referred to as the *total sum of squares*. The two terms on the right tell us that the total sum of squares has been analyzed into two component parts. The first term on the right is based upon the deviations of the individual Y values in each column from the mean of the column. The double summation sign indicates that we sum the n squared deviations within each column and then sum over all k columns. This sum of squares is often called the *sum of squares within columns*. The second term on the right is a sum of squares based upon the deviations of the means of the k columns from the mean of the entire Y distribution. These deviations are squared and then multiplied by the corresponding value of n. The summation sign indicates that we sum these values over the k columns of the table. We shall refer to this sum of squares as the *sum of squares between columns*. As a matter of convenience, we indicate these three sums of squares as follows:

$$\text{Total} \quad = \sum_1^k \sum_1^n (Y_{kn} - \overline{Y}..)^2 \quad = \sum y_t^2$$

$$\text{Within} \quad = \sum_1^k \sum_1^n (Y_{kn} - \overline{Y}_k.)^2 \quad = \sum y_w^2$$

$$\text{Between} \quad = \sum_1^k n(\overline{Y}_k. - \overline{Y}..)^2 \quad = \sum y_b^2$$

The correlation ratio squared may now be defined as

$$\eta_{YX}^2 = \frac{\sum y_b^2}{\sum y_t^2} \tag{7.22}$$

If we take the square root of (7.22), then we have the correlation ratio or

$$\eta_{YX} = \sqrt{\frac{\sum y_b^2}{\sum y_t^2}} \tag{7.23}$$

The total sum of squares can be obtained conveniently from the columns at the right side of Table 7.7. Thus, we have

$$\sum y_t^2 = \sum f Y^2 - \frac{(\sum f Y)^2}{\sum n}$$

where $\sum n$ is the total number of observations. Then, for the present problem

$$\sum y_t^2 = 2993 - \frac{(557)^2}{129}$$

$$= 587.97$$

To calculate the sum of squares between columns, we note that

$$\sum_1^k n(\bar{Y}_{k\cdot} - \bar{Y}_{\cdot\cdot})^2 = \sum_1^k n(\bar{Y}_{k\cdot}^2 - 2\bar{Y}_{k\cdot}\bar{Y}_{\cdot\cdot} + \bar{Y}_{\cdot\cdot}^2)$$

$$= \sum_1^k (n\bar{Y}_{k\cdot}^2 - 2n\bar{Y}_{k\cdot}\bar{Y}_{\cdot\cdot} + n\bar{Y}_{\cdot\cdot}^2)$$

$$= \sum_1^k \frac{\left(\sum_1^n Y_{k\cdot}\right)^2}{n} - \frac{\left(\sum_1^k \sum_1^n Y_{kn}\right)^2}{\sum n} \tag{7.24}$$

where $\sum n$ is the total number of observations.

Thus, for the present problem, we have

$$\sum y_b^2 = \frac{(55)^2}{22} + \frac{(76)^2}{17} + \frac{(51)^2}{9} + \cdots + \frac{(68)^2}{31} - \frac{(557)^2}{129}$$

$$= 2811.36 - \frac{(557)^2}{129}$$

$$= 406.33$$

Then

$$\eta_{YX}^2 = \frac{406.33}{587.97} = .6911$$

and

$$\eta_{YX} = \sqrt{.6911} = .83$$

as the value of the correlation ratio.

7.8   Properties of the Correlation Ratio

We can determine some of the properties of the correlation ratio if we express it in a somewhat different form. From (7.21), we see that the sum of squares between columns will be equal to the total sum of squares minus the sum of squares within columns or

$$\sum y_b^2 = \sum y_t^2 - \sum y_w^2 \tag{7.25}$$

Then the correlation ratio squared of (7.22) may be written

$$\eta_{YX}^2 = \frac{\sum y_t^2 - \sum y_w^2}{\sum y_t^2}$$

$$= 1 - \frac{\sum y_w^2}{\sum y_t^2} \tag{7.26}$$

Now Σy_w^2 can be equal to Σy_t^2 only in the case that Σy_b^2 is equal to zero. In this instance the correlation ratio would also be equal to zero. But in order that Σy_b^2 be equal to zero, each column mean would have to equal the mean of the entire Y distribution, as (7.21) will show. In other words, the correlation ratio will be zero only when each column mean is equal to the mean of the entire Y distribution. Under this condition there will be no change in the average Y values with change in X, and we say that Y is unrelated to X.

The correlation ratio can be equal to 1 only when the variation within columns as measured by Σy_w^2 is zero. In this instance, each individual observation in a given column would correspond exactly to the mean of the column, and the variation in the means of the columns, as measured by Σy_b^2, would be as great as the total variation measured by Σy_t^2.

The sum of squares within columns, in a very real sense, represents the errors made in predicting Y values from X values. If the means of the columns differ, then our best prediction of the Y values in a given column is the mean of the column. An error of prediction will be given by $Y_{kn} - \overline{Y}_{k.}$, and these errors squared and summed over all columns are equal to Σy_w^2. If the means of the columns do not vary from the mean of the entire Y distribution, then our best prediction for each Y value will be $\overline{Y}..$, regardless of the particular column in which it falls and the sum of squares of our errors will be given by

$$\sum_1^k \sum_1^n (Y_{kn} - \overline{Y}..)^2 = \sum y_t^2$$

A measure of the errors of prediction, corresponding to the standard error of estimate for linear relations, may be obtained by first finding

$$s_w^2 = \frac{\sum y_w^2}{\sum n - k} \tag{7.27}$$

where $s_w^2 =$ the variance within columns
  $\Sigma y_w^2 =$ the sum of squares within columns
  $\Sigma n =$ the total number of observations
  $k =$ the number of columns in the correlation table
  Then the square root of (7.27) will be

$$s_w = \sqrt{\frac{\sum y_w^2}{\sum n - k}} \tag{7.28}$$

and s_w may be regarded as the standard error of estimate when predictions of Y values for given values of X are made in terms of the column means.

7.9   The Correlation Ratio and Correlation Coefficient

If the correlation ratio and the correlation coefficient are both computed for the same set of data, then, in general, the correlation ratio will be larger than the correlation coefficient. This may be made clear by a comparison of one of the formulas we developed in Chapter 6 for the correlation coefficient squared with (7.26) for the correlation ratio squared. Thus

$$r^2 = 1 - \frac{\sum (y - \tilde{y})^2}{\sum y^2}$$

and

$$\eta_{YX}{}^2 = 1 - \frac{\sum y_w{}^2}{\sum y_t{}^2}$$

where $\sum y^2 = \sum y_t{}^2$.

In the formula for the product-moment correlation coefficient, the errors of prediction are measured from the linear regression line of Y on X. Only in the case that the means of the columns, such as in Table 7.7, fall precisely on this line will $\sum (y - \tilde{y})^2$ be equal to $\sum y_w{}^2$. If the means of the columns deviate at all from the linear regression line, then $\sum (y - \tilde{y})^2$ will be greater than $\sum y_w{}^2$, and consequently, the correlation ratio will be larger than the correlation coefficient, because $\sum y_t{}^2 = \sum y^2$. If the column means fall precisely on the linear regression line, then the correlation coefficient will be equal to the correlation ratio.[5] In the formula for the correlation ratio, we no longer place the restriction upon the data that the column means must be fitted by a *straight line*.

It should be pointed out that the correlation ratio is extremely sensitive to small numbers of observations in the columns of a table such as Table 7.7. Obviously, if only a single observation were present in each column $\sum y_b{}^2$ would be equal to $\sum y_t{}^2$ and the correlation ratio would be equal to 1. Therefore, in computing a correlation ratio we should make sure that we have a sufficient number of observations in each of the columns of the table. In

---

[5] The sum of squared deviations of a set of n observations is at a minimum when the deviations are taken from the mean of the set, as we have shown previously. Thus

$$\sum_1^k \sum_1^n (Y_{kn} - \bar{Y}_{k\cdot})^2 = \sum y_w{}^2$$

being based upon the deviation of the n observations within each column from the column mean, will be less than the corresponding sum of squared deviations $\sum (y - \tilde{y})^2$ from the linear regression line, if the linear regression line does not pass through the column means.

some cases this may mean that we shall have to use fairly wide intervals on the X axis.

We may also emphasize that in the case of the correlation coefficient r_{XY} is equal to r_{YX} and we have no need for subscripts. But it should be clear from (7.23) that η_{YX} will not, in general, be equal to η_{XY}. The subscripts, therefore, are important in that they let us know whether we are concerned with the relation of Y to X as measured by η_{YX} or the relation of X to Y measured by η_{XY}.

If we desire to find η_{XY} it is only necessary to remember that we are dealing with *rows* instead of columns in the correlation table. Any of the formulas presented for η_{YX} may be used to find η_{XY} by replacing the sums of squares for the Y variable by the corresponding sums of squares for the X variable and substituting the word *rows* for columns in the formulas. For example, we may rewrite (7.22) and obtain

$$\eta_{XY}^2 = \frac{\sum x_b^2}{\sum x_t^2} \tag{7.29}$$

where η_{XY}^2 = the square of the correlation ratio of X on Y
$\sum x_b^2$ = the sum of squares between rows for the X variable
$\sum x_t^2$ = the total sum of squares for the X variable

EXAMPLES

7.1—The data given below show the scores on a test of 40 subjects who were below average on Test X and 30 subjects who were above average in their performance. The distributions of scores of these two groups on a second test Y are given below. Find the biserial coefficient of correlation.

Scores	Below average	Above average
27–29	3	2
24–26	4	4
21–23	5	8
18–20	6	12
15–17	11	2
12–14	6	1
9–11	2	1
6– 8	2	0
3– 5	1	0

7.2—Two judges each ranked a set of pictures from the most liked to the least liked. Find the rank correlation coefficient for the two sets of ranks.

Pictures	Judge 1	Judge 2
A	1	6
B	3	5
C	2	2
D	6	1
E	4	8
F	5	3
G	9	4
H	8	7
I	7	9

7.3—Find the phi coefficient for the 2 × 2 table given below.

Response to item	Sex	
	Women	Men
Pass	10	30
Fail	40	20

7.4—A group of employees who had been rated as above average in the performance of their jobs and a group of employees who had been rated as below average were given a test. There were 121 employees in the above-average group and 79 employees in the below-average group. The value of $\sqrt{\Sigma\, y^2/n}$ on the test for the combined groups was 11.00. The mean score on the test for the combined groups was 82.05. For the above-average group, the mean score was 81.45. Assume that the distribution of ratings was approximately normal and that the dichotomous classification has been imposed upon the data. Find the biserial coefficient of correlation.

7.5—Mangus (1936) had 591 women describe the interests of their fathers and of their ideal husbands in science and religion. Find the phi coefficient for the data reported below.

Father	Ideal husband	
	More interested in religion than in science	More interested in science than in religion
More interested in science than in religion	63	326
More interested in religion than in science	68	134

7.6—Find the correlation ratio, η_{YX}, for the data given below.

Y Distribution	X Distribution					
	3	4	5	6	7	8
4	2	2				
3	2	3	3	1	2	1
2	1	2	3	2	1	1
1		2	1	1		

7.7—Compute the correlation ratio of Y on X for the following data.

Vocabulary test scores	Chronological age								
	15	16	17	18	19	20	21	22	23
150–159					3	1	2	1	2
140–149				2	2	4	4	3	1
130–139			3	1	2	5	5	2	1
120–129		1	2	2	1	4	1	3	4
110–119		3	1	3	3	2			2
100–109	1	1	1						
90– 99		2		1					
80– 89	1								
70– 79	2	2							
60– 69	4								

7.8—Peters and Van Voorhis (1940) report a tetrachoric r of .57 for the data given below. What is the value of tetrachoric r as estimated by the

Number of hours of pedagogy	Teacher classification	
	Unsuccessful teachers	Successful teachers
Six hours or more	20	80
Less than six hours	70	55

method described in the chapter? Do these data meet the assumptions required by tetrachoric r? Would it be better to use the phi coefficient in this instance?

7.9—Lindquist (1940) reports a tetrachoric r of .35 for the following data on responses of 150 students to two test items. What is the value of tetrachoric r as estimated by the method described in the chapter? Can you justify the calculation of tetrachoric r for these data? Would the phi coefficient be a more appropriate measure of association?

Response to item 2	Response to item 1	
	Wrong	Right
Right	24	56
Wrong	36	34

7.10—Assign ranks to the scores listed below and find the rank correlation coefficient.

Subject	X	Y
1	8	4
2	13	14
3	13	6
4	18	13
5	14	8
6	19	12
7	8	10
8	4	7
9	17	6
10	15	7
11	22	17
12	6	17
13	18	9
14	8	9
15	12	4

7.11—A group of men and women were polled to determine whether they liked or disliked a particular radio commentator. The results are shown below. Find the value of the phi coefficient.

	Like	Dislike
Men	55	45
Women	10	60

7.12—Kelly and Fiske (1950) give the following distributions of scores on the Miller Analogies Test for two categories of Veterans Administration trainees in clinical psychology. Find the value of the point biserial coefficient of correlation.

Scores	VA trainees	
	Dismissals	Ph.D. granted
95–99		1
90–94	1	1
85–89	0	6
80–84	2	11
75–79	4	6
70–74	6	9
65–69	8	3
60–64	3	2
55–59	2	1
50–54	6	
45–49	2	
40–44	3	
35–39	1	
30–34	1	

7.13—The following data were obtained from a class in social psychology on a final examination. Find the value of the point biserial coefficient of correlation.

Total scores	Response to item 22	
	Incorrect	Correct
80–84		2
75–79		3
70–74	1	5
65–69	4	7
60–64	3	4
55–59	8	10
50–54	5	9
45–49		1
40–44	2	
35–39	1	1

7.14—Kellar (1934) reports the following data concerning Q and S values of items in an attitude scale. Find the value of η_{YX}.

					X: Scale values of items					
Y: Q Values	1	2	3	4	5	6	7	8	9	10
2.1–2.3		5	9	6	4		5	3		
1.8–2.0		3	3	2	1	2	5	2	7	
1.5–1.7	1			2	1	2		1	4	
1.2–1.4	3								1	8
.9–1.1						1				1
.6– .8	4									3
.3– .5						1				

7.15—A study of 100 women who thought their marriage was successful and 100 women who thought their marriage was unsuccessful revealed a differential in response to the question: Did you have a happy childhood? Find the value of the phi coefficient.

Childhood status	Marital status	
	Unsuccessful marriage	Successful marriage
Happy	40	70
Unhappy	60	30

7.16—Dorcus (1944) had an industrial concern select two extreme groups of workers, a "satisfactory group" and an "unsatisfactory group." Each member of both groups was then given the Humm-Wadsworth Scale, and on the basis of the scores on the scale predictions were made of the group in which the individual belonged. Find the value of the phi coefficient.

Humm-Wadsworth Scale	Company ratings	
	Unsatisfactory	Satisfactory
Satisfactory	6	18
Unsatisfactory	16	8

7.17—Let $p = n_1/n$ and $q = 1 - p$ or n_0/n. Given these definitions of p and q, prove that r_{pb} as defined by (7.5), is also equal to

$$\frac{\overline{Y}_1 - \overline{Y}}{\sqrt{\dfrac{\sum y^2}{n}}} \left(\frac{\sqrt{p}}{\sqrt{q}} \right)$$

and that r_b, as defined by (7.9), is also equal to

$$\frac{\overline{Y}_1 - \overline{Y}}{\sqrt{\dfrac{\sum y^2}{n}}} \left(\frac{p}{y_p} \right)$$

7.18—We have 15 observations that have been assigned the ranks 1 to 15.

(a) What is the mean of the set of ranks?
(b) What is the value of $\Sigma (X - \overline{X})^2$?

7.19—State the conditions and the nature of the variables for which each of the following would be an appropriate measure of relationship:

point-biserial coefficient   tetrachoric correlation coefficient
phi coefficient   rank correlation coefficient
biserial coefficient   correlation ratio

CHAPTER 8

Sets, Sample Spaces, and Random Variables

8.1 Introduction

We have observed that individual members of a group differ from one another in terms of almost any measurement we might care to make on the members of the group. We have also found that the standard deviation provides us with a measure of the degree of variability present in a given set of measurements. Individual measurements differ not only with respect to each other; they also differ from themselves if we repeat the measurements a second time. An individual's height, for example, may be different in the morning upon arising and at night before retiring. One's weight increases with a heavy meal. Individuals tend to perform better on motor tests when not fatigued. Because measurements on the same individual made at different times may vary and because measurements of different individuals made at the same time may vary, we may also expect statistics derived from samples of individual measurements to vary.

The mean score on a motor test for a randomly selected sample of n students tested this morning may not be precisely the same as the mean score obtained when the same students are tested tomorrow morning. Nor would we expect another random sample of n students, drawn from the same larger group or population as the first sample, to have precisely the same mean score as the first sample.

In an experiment described earlier, we had one group of students study with and another without knowledge of results. The mean score on an achievement test was 11.0 for the experimental group, the group that studied with knowledge of results and the mean score on the same test was 14.0 for the control group, the group that studied without knowledge of results. The difference between the two means was therefore 3 points in favor of the control group. If the observed difference between the means was only .5 of a point, we might believe that this small a difference could easily result from the fact that sample means are themselves subject to sampling variability. For example, if the experiment were repeated with two other groups of students, we might now find that the difference between the means favors the experimental group and this could also occur as a result of the fact that means of samples are known to vary from sample to sample.

Because the observed difference between the two means was 3 points in favor of the control group and not .5 of a point, we might feel that this difference is sufficiently large that it could not be attributed to the fact that the means of samples show random variation. How confident can we be that this conclusion is correct? If the same experiment were repeated an indefinitely large number of times, then we should expect the long-run average difference between the two means to be zero, if it is true that students learn just as well without as with knowledge of results. If the long-run average difference between the two means is in fact zero, then how frequently might we expect to obtain a difference of 3 points in favor of the control group as a result of random variation?

To take another example: Suppose that we assume that the chance that a rat will turn to the right at a choice-point in a maze is equal to the chance that the rat will turn to the left. If we really believe this to be the case and if a rat is randomly selected from our rat colony and tested in the maze, then we should be willing to bet a dollar against someone else's dollar that the rat will turn to the right. And we should be just as willing to bet a dollar against another dollar that the rat will turn to the left.

If the chance of a right turn is equal to the chance of a left turn and if we observe the individual behavior of each of 30 randomly selected rats at the choice-point, what would we expect? It seems reasonable to expect that approximately half or 15 of the rats will turn left and approximately 15 will turn right. What if we observed that 20 of the rats turned left and 10 right? This finding would appear to offer some evidence against the notion that right and left turns are equally likely. But the number of left turns is a measure based on a sample of n observations and we may expect this measure to vary from sample to sample. Again, it would be of value to know something about the degree to which the number of left turns can be expected to vary in repeated sampling when it is, in fact, true that left and right turns are equally likely.

We shall use the term *random variation* to describe the variability in measurements of the same individual on different occasions but under the same conditions of measurement. To say that the variability of repeated measurements of the same individual on the same variable is random is more or less to say that the precise value of any single measurement is unpredictable. Similarly, we shall describe the variability in means based on different random samples from the same population and tested under the same conditions as random variation. To say that the means of randomly selected samples from a common population show random variation is also to more or less say that the precise value of the mean for any single random sample is unpredictable.

To describe variability in the measurements of individuals or in statistics based upon randomly selected samples from the same population as random variability is similar to what some individuals would describe as chance variability. We may flip a fair or unbiased coin five times and count the number of H's. If we repeat this process an indefinitely large number of times, we may on some occasions observe five H's, on others four H's, and on still others, three, two, one, or zero H's. The variation in the number of heads obtained when a coin is tossed five times we may describe as being the result of chance. This is what we mean by random variation. The exact number of H's obtained is unpredictable. On any given set of five tosses, we may obtain five, four, three, two, one, or zero H's.

The questions raised above bring us to our next problem in statistical analysis: the problem of how much confidence we have in an observed outcome of an experiment when the outcome is expressed in terms of a sample mean, or a difference between two means, or some other statistic. The statistical methods used in investigating this problem are known as tests of significance and they enable us to determine, among other things, whether an observed difference between two means is sufficiently large that we choose to reject the hypothesis that the average long-run difference between the means is zero.

In this chapter we introduce the concept of a set and of a particular kind of set called the sample space of an experiment. We also illustrate, by means of a simple example, the probability distribution of a discrete random variable and of certain functions of discrete random variables. We shall see, in later developments, that the problem of finding an appropriate probability distribution for the possible outcomes of an experiment is basic in the evaluation of a given outcome of the experiment.

8.2   Sets and Operations on Sets

A *set* is any well-defined collection of objects, things, or symbols. The things that make up a set are called the *elements* of the set. Most of the sets we shall be concerned with consist of numbers and we may define the set either by listing the numbers that belong to the set or by stating a rule that permits us to determine whether or not a given number is a member of the set. For example, suppose that we have a variable X that can take only the values 1, 2, 3, 4, or 5. Then the set S of possible values of X could be indicated by listing the elements within braces as shown below:

$$S = \{1, 2, 3, 4, 5\} \qquad (8.1)$$

or by the following rule

$$S = \{X: X \text{ is an integer and } 1 \leq X \leq 5\} \qquad (8.2)$$

The colon ":" is read "such that."

On any given set S, we may define various subsets. We say that A is a *subset* of S if every element of A is also an element of S. Thus $A = \{1, 2, 3\}$ is a subset of S as defined in (8.1) and so also is $B = \{2, 3, 4\}$ and $C = \{3, 4, 5\}$. If we have a number of different subsets of S, then we can perform operations on them that will result in additional subsets. We define these operations as union, intersection, and complementation, and we illustrate these operations with the set S as defined by (8.1) and the subsets A, B, and C, as defined above, that is

$$A = \{1, 2, 3\} \qquad B = \{2, 3, 4\} \qquad C = \{3, 4, 5\}$$

The *union* of A and B is the set of all elements of S that are members of either A or B or of both A and B. We use $A \cup B$ to indicate the set formed by the union of A and B and we note that

$$A \cup B = \{1, 2, 3, 4\}$$

Similarly, the union of A and C is the set of all elements of S that are members of either A or C or of both A and C. We note that, in our example,

$$A \cup C = \{1, 2, 3, 4, 5\} = S$$

If A and B are both subsets of S, then the *intersection* of A and B is the set of all elements of S that are members of both A and B. We use $A \cap B$ to indicate the set formed by the intersection of A and B. We note that there are two elements that are members of both A and B and these two elements are the integers 2 and 3. Thus

$$A \cap B = \{2, 3\}$$

Similarly, we note that A and C have only one element in common and that element is the integer 3. Thus

$$A \cap C = \{3\}$$

If A is a subset of S, then the *complement* of A, which we designate by $\bar{A}$, is the set of all elements in S that are *not* in A. In the example under consideration we have $A = \{1, 2, 3\}$ and $S = \{1, 2, 3, 4, 5\}$. Then $\bar{A} = \{4, 5\}$. Similarly, the complement of B is $\bar{B} = \{1, 5\}$ and the complement of C is $\bar{C} = \{1, 2\}$.

Suppose we have two or more subsets defined on a set S such that no element of any of the subsets is an element of another subset. For example, suppose we have three subsets, A, B, and C, defined on S such that no element of any one of these three subsets is an element of the other two. Then if,

$$A \cup B \cup C = S$$

the subsets are said to be *mutually exclusive* and *exhaustive*. The subsets, in this instance, are also described as providing a *partition* of the set S.

It is obvious that a subset A and its complement $\bar{A}$ always provide a partition of S into two subsets, because A and $\bar{A}$ have no elements in common and because $A \cup \bar{A} = S$. In our example we have $A = \{1, 2\}$ and $\bar{A} = \{3, 4, 5\}$ so that $A \cup \bar{A} = S = \{1, 2, 3, 4, 5\}$.

The *empty* set, designated as $\emptyset$, is a set with no elements. The empty set is regarded as a subset of every set S. A subset of S has been defined as a set in which every element of the subset is also an element of S. The empty set $\emptyset$ has no elements and thus does not contradict the definition of a subset. The set S is also a subset of itself. Obviously, all of the elements in the subset S are also elements of S and thus to regard S as a subset of itself is consistent with the definition of a subset.

If a set S has n elements, then the total number of different subsets that can be defined on S is 2^n. For example, if $S = \{1, 2, 3\}$, then we have $2^3 = 8$ different subsets that can be defined on S. In addition to S and $\emptyset$, the empty set, we have the subsets shown below:

$$A = \{1\} \qquad D = \{1, 2\}$$
$$B = \{2\} \qquad E = \{1, 3\}$$
$$C = \{3\} \qquad F = \{2, 3\}$$

8.3 Sample Spaces, Probability, and Events

We shall be primarily interested in a particular kind of set: the set of all possible outcomes of an experiment, which is called the *sample space* of the experiment. In order to have a sample space S for an experiment, each possible outcome of the experiment must correspond to exactly one element of S. The elements of a sample space are called *sample points*. For example, suppose that an experiment consists of tossing a coin three times. On each toss the coin may fall H or T and if the outcome of interest is the ordered sequence of H's and T's, then

$$S = \{HHH, HHT, HTH, THH, TTT, TTH, THT, HTT\} \qquad (8.3)$$

and the sample space will consist of eight sample points. We note that, in this instance, every possible outcome of the experiment corresponds to exactly one sample point.

Suppose, however, that the outcome of interest is the number of H's obtained in three tosses of the coin. Then the possible outcomes of the experiment are the integers 3, 2, 1, and 0 and, in this instance, the sample space would have only four sample points. Thus, we would have

$$S = \{3, 2, 1, 0\} \tag{8.4}$$

Note also that each ordered sequence in the first sample space, defined by (8.3), corresponds to exactly one of the numbers, 3, 2, 1, or 0, in the second sample space defined by (8.4).

To each sample point in a sample space we want to assign a number P that provides a measure called the *probability* of the outcome of the experiment represented by the sample point. In order for the numbers P to be called probabilities, they must meet the requirements of the following axioms:[1]

1. The values of P assigned to each sample point must be equal to or greater than zero and equal to or less than 1, that is, $0 \le P \le 1$.
2. The sum of the values of P assigned to the sample points must be equal to 1, that is, we must have $\Sigma\ P = 1$.
3. If n subsets, $A_1, A_2, A_3, \cdots, A_n$, are defined on the sample space and if the n subsets are mutually exclusive and exhaustive, that is, if they provide a partition of the sample space, then we must also have

$$P(A_1) + P(A_2) + P(A_3) + \cdots + P(A_n) = 1$$

Consider the sample space defined by (8.3) that consists of eight sample points. If the coin is a fair or unbiased coin, then, to many individuals, it would seem reasonable to assign a probability of 1/8 to each sample point and we shall do so.

Let E be an event defined on the sample space S of an experiment. By an *event*, we shall mean any subset of S. Then the probability of the event E, which we write $P(E)$, will be equal to the sum of the probabilities of the sample points in the subset E. We consider the following examples with respect to the sample space defined in (8.3) where

$$S = \{HHH, HHT, HTH, THH, TTT, TTH, THT, HTT\}$$

1. We have said that the empty set $\emptyset$ is a subset of S. But $\emptyset$ has no sample points and therefore corresponds to an impossible outcome of the coin tossing experiment. Let E be the event four or more H's. Then $P(E) = 0$.

2. Let E be the event that we have exactly two H's. Then we see that E contains three sample points, HHT, HTH, THH, each with probability of 1/8 so that $P(E) = 3/8$.

---

[1] Note that we have an axiomatic model and that the model does not tell us how to determine what numbers to assign to each sample point, but only the conditions that these numbers must satisfy if they are to be called *probabilities*. As long as the numbers meet the requirements of the axioms, all deductions and derivations based upon the axioms will be mathematically true. In the discussion that follows, we shall consider some examples in which, prior to the experiment itself, we have an intuitive but reasonable basis for assigning probabilities to the sample points.

3. Let E_0 be the event zero H's, E_1 be the event one H, E_2 be the event two H's, and E_3 be the event three H's. We note that E_0, E_1, E_2, E_3 are mutually exclusive and exhaustive and therefore provide a partition of the sample space. For these subsets we have as elements in the sample space of (8.3)

$$E_0 = \{TTT\}$$
$$E_1 = \{TTH, THT, HTT\}$$
$$E_2 = \{HHT, HTH, THH\}$$
$$E_3 = \{HHH\}$$

and we note that

$$P(E_0 \cup E_1 \cup E_2 \cup E_3) = P(E_0) + P(E_1) + P(E_2) + P(E_3) = P(S)$$
$$= \frac{1}{8} + \frac{3}{8} + \frac{3}{8} + \frac{1}{8} \qquad = 1$$

8.4   The Probability of $E_1 \cup E_2$ When $E_1 \cap E_2 = \emptyset$

Let $S = \{e_1, e_2, e_3, e_4, e_5, e_6\}$ and assume that the probability of each sample point is 1/6. Let $E_1 = \{e_1, e_2\}$ and $E_2 = \{e_4, e_5\}$. Then E_1 and E_2 are mutually exclusive, that is, they have no sample points in common, or in other words, $E_1 \cap E_2 = \emptyset$. When two events are mutually exclusive, then

$$P(E_1 \cup E_2) = P(E_1) + P(E_2) \tag{8.5}$$

and, for the present example, we have

$$P(E_1 \cup E_2) = \frac{2}{6} + \frac{2}{6} = \frac{4}{6}$$

It is possible to generalize (8.5) to the case of any number of mutually exclusive events defined on a given sample space. Thus, if E_1, E_2, $E_3, \cdots, E_k$ are mutually exclusive events, then

$$P(E_1 \cup E_2 \cup E_3 \cup \cdots \cup E_k) = P(E_1) + P(E_2) + P(E_3) + \cdots + P(E_k) \tag{8.6}$$

8.5   The Probability of $E_1 \cup E_2$ When $E_1 \cap E_2 \neq \emptyset$

Two events E_1 and E_2 are *not* mutually exclusive if they have one or more sample points in common, that is, if $E_1 \cap E_2 \neq \emptyset$. Let $S = \{e_1, e_2, e_3, e_4, e_5, e_6\}$ and let $E_1 = \{e_1, e_2, e_3\}$ and $E_2 = \{e_2, e_3, e_4, e_5\}$. Then $E_1 \cap E_2 = \{e_2, e_3\}$ and $P(E_1 \cap E_2) = 2/6$, assuming that each sample point has equal probability. We note that if we count the number of sample points that are in E_1 and then count those that are in E_2, then the number of sample points that are in *both* E_1 and E_2 will be counted twice. Thus, if

$E_1 \cap E_2 \neq \emptyset$, we have

$$P(E_1 \cup E_2) = P(E_1) + P(E_2) - P(E_1 \cap E_2) \qquad (8.7)$$

and, for the example under discussion, we have

$$P(E_1 \cup E_2) = \frac{3}{6} + \frac{4}{6} - \frac{2}{6} = \frac{5}{6}$$

Failure to recognize that when events are not mutually exclusive $P(E_1 \cup E_2) \neq P(E_1) + P(E_2)$ can lead to absurd results. Note, that in the example under discussion, $P(E_1) + P(E_2) = 7/6$ and that this is an impossible value for a probability.

8.6   Independent Events

Suppose that a fair coin is tossed twice. Let E_1 be the event heads on the first toss and E_2 be the event heads on the second toss. If the coin is fair, then it seems reasonable to assign a probability of $1/2$ to heads on each toss. Furthermore, it seems reasonable to believe that if heads is obtained on the first toss, this event will in no way change the probability of heads on the second toss. We define two events as *independent* if

$$P(E_1 \cap E_2) = P(E_1)P(E_2) \qquad (8.8)$$

that is, if the probability that both E_1 and E_2 occur is equal to the product of their separate probabilities. In our example, then, if the two tosses of the coin are independent, we would have as the probability of heads on both tosses

$$P(E_1 \cap E_2) = \frac{1}{2} \times \frac{1}{2} = \frac{1}{4}$$

Consider another example. A fair die is rolled three times. Let E_1 be the event 1 on the first roll, E_2 be the event 2 on the second roll, and E_3 be the event 3 on the third roll. If the die is fair, then it seems reasonable to assign a probability of $1/6$ to each of the six possible points that may be face up when the die is rolled. It also seems reasonable to believe that the three rolls are mutually independent. If this is the case, then

$$P(E_1 \cap E_2 \cap E_3) = P(E_1)P(E_2)P(E_3) \qquad (8.9)$$

or, in our example,

$$P(E_1 \cap E_2 \cap E_3) = \frac{1}{6} \times \frac{1}{6} \times \frac{1}{6} = \frac{1}{216}$$

8.7   Nonindependent Events: Conditional Probabilities

Suppose that A and B are two events defined on a sample space and that A and B are *not* independent. We define the *conditional probability* of an event A, given that another event B has occurred, as

$$P(A|B) = \frac{P(A \cap B)}{P(B)} \tag{8.10}$$

where $P(B) \neq 0$, and A, B, and $A \cap B$ are events in a sample space. We note that

$$P(B)P(A|B) = P(A \cap B) \tag{8.11}$$

Similarly, the conditional probability of B, given that A has occurred, is

$$P(B|A) = \frac{P(B \cap A)}{P(A)} \tag{8.12}$$

and we also have

$$P(A)P(B|A) = P(B \cap A) \tag{8.13}$$

Because $A \cap B = B \cap A$, (8.11) and (8.13) are equal. Thus

$$P(A \cap B) = P(B)P(A|B) = P(A)P(B|A) = P(B \cap A) \tag{8.14}$$

We consider two examples involving conditional probabilities.

Example 1. In the game of odd man, three individuals each toss a coin. If two of the coins have the same face and the other is different, then the individual with the different coin is the loser. Let L be the event that there is a loser and H be the event that at least one of the coins is heads. We want to find the conditional probability of a loser, L, given that at least one of the coins is heads.

As a sample space for this experiment, we have

$$S = \{HHH, HHT, HTH, THH, TTH, THT, HTT, TTT\}$$

We assume that $P(H) = P(T) = 1/2$ and that the three tosses are independent. If this is the case, then each sample point in S will have a probability of 1/8.

For the event at least one heads, H, we have

$$H = \{HHH, HHT, HTH, THH, TTH, THT, HTT\}$$

and $P(H) = 7/8$.

For the event a loser, L, we have

$$L = \{HHT, HTH, THH, TTH, THT, HTT\}$$

and $P(L) = 6/8$.

Then, $L \cap H$ will be the number of sample points in both L and H or

$$L \cap H = \{HHT, HTH, THH, TTH, THT, HTT\}$$

and $P(L \cap H) = 6/8$.

Using the probabilities we have just obtained, that is, $P(L \cap H)$ and $P(H)$, then

$$P(L|H) = \frac{P(L \cap H)}{P(H)} = \frac{6/8}{7/8} = \frac{6}{7}$$

We note that if we do not know that one of the coins is heads, our best guess as to the probability of a loser is 6/8. However, given the information that one of the coins is heads, our best guess as to the probability of a loser is 6/7. The event L, in other words, is not independent of the event H. We see that this is so because

$$P(L \cap H) \neq P(L)P(H)$$

or

$$\frac{6}{7} \neq \frac{6}{8} \times \frac{7}{8}$$

Example 2. We have two boxes, B_1 and B_2. B_1 contains one red and one white marble. B_2 contains three red marbles and one white marble. A box is selected by the toss of a fair coin and one marble is then drawn at random from the box selected. Given that a red marble is obtained, what is the probability that the marble was drawn from B_1? In other words, we wish to find

$$P(B_1|R) = \frac{P(B_1 \cap R)}{P(R)}$$

We assume that $P(B_1) = P(B_2) = 1/2, P(R|B_1) = 1/2$, and $P(R|B_2) = 3/4$. Then, we have

$$P(R \cap B_1) = P(B_1)P(R|B_1) = \frac{1}{2} \times \frac{1}{2} = \frac{1}{4}$$

and

$$P(R \cap B_2) = P(B_2)P(R|B_2) = \frac{1}{2} \times \frac{3}{4} = \frac{3}{8}$$

Because R must occur either with B_1 or B_2 and cannot occur simultaneously with both, we have

$$P(R) = P(R \cap B_1) + P(R \cap B_2)$$

$$= \frac{1}{4} + \frac{3}{8}$$

$$= \frac{5}{8}$$

We have found that $P(R \cap B_1) = P(B_1 \cap R) = 1/4$ and that $P(R) = 5/8$. Then

$$P(B_1|R) = \frac{P(B_1 \cap R)}{P(R)} = \frac{1/4}{5/8} = \frac{2}{5}$$

and similarly

$$P(B_2|R) = \frac{P(B_2 \cap R)}{P(R)} = \frac{3/8}{5/8} = \frac{3}{5}$$

If you read once again the discussion of this example and relate the discussion to the tables given below, it will help you to gain a better understanding of how we determined the two probabilities: $P(B_1|R)$ and $P(B_2|R)$.

	R	$\bar{R}$			R	$\bar{R}$	
B_1	$P(B_1 \cap R)$	$P(B_1 \cap \bar{R})$	$P(B_1)$	B_1	1/4	1/4	1/2
B_2	$P(B_2 \cap R)$	$P(B_2 \cap \bar{R})$	$P(B_2)$	B_2	3/8	1/8	1/2
	$P(R)$	$P(\bar{R})$			5/8	3/8	1

8.8 Bayes' Theorem[2]

Let H_1, H_2, $\cdots$, H_k be mutually exclusive and exhaustive events defined on a sample space of an experiment so that $P(H_1) + P(H_2) + \cdots + P(H_k) = 1.0$. Thus, every sample point in the experiment is associated with one and only one of the H_k's. Let E be another event defined on the same sample space with $P(E) \neq 0$. Then, given that E has occurred, we have

$$P(H_1|E) = \frac{P(H_1 \cap E)}{P(H_1 \cap E) + P(H_2 \cap E) + \cdots + P(H_k \cap E)}$$

$$= \frac{P(H_1 \cap E)}{P(E)} \tag{8.15}$$

---

[2] For a detailed discussion of Bayes' theorem in psychological research, see the article by Edwards, Lindman, and Savage (1963).

Similarly, for each H we have

$$P(H_k|E) = \frac{P(H_k \cap E)}{P(E)} \qquad (8.16)$$

We note that (8.16) can also be expressed as

$$P(H_k|E) = \frac{P(H_k)P(E|H_k)}{P(E)} \qquad (8.17)$$

and (8.17) is commonly referred to as Bayes' rule or theorem.

In the two-box problem, B_1 and B_2 correspond to H_1 and H_2 and $P(H_1 \cup H_2) = 1.0$. The probabilities of 1/2 initially assigned to H_1 and H_2 are called *prior* probabilities. The observed event E was the selection of a red marble. Before observing this event, we assigned prior probabilities of 1/2 to both H_1 and H_2 because the box to be selected was to be determined by the toss of a fair coin. We then used the fact that E occurred to modify the prior probabilities assigned to H_1 and H_2. The conditional probabilities, $P(H_1|E)$ and $P(H_2|E)$ were found to be 2/5 and 3/5, respectively, and these probabilities are often referred to as *posterior* probabilities.

Given the event E, a red marble selected, the posterior probabilities are considerably different from the prior probabilities. In other words, if we were betting on which box has been selected, we would be more likely to win if we placed our bet on the second box rather than on the first box, provided, of course, that we know that the marble selected is red, that is, that E did occur.

8.9   Mean and Variance of a Discrete Random Variable

Suppose we have 10 disks lettered, $A, B, C, \cdots, J$. We select at random from a box one of the disks and record the letter. Then a sample space for this experiment would be

$$S = \{A, B, C, D, E, F, G, H, I, J\} \qquad (8.18)$$

If the sampling is random, then we may also assume that the probability of each disk being selected is 1/10 or .1 and to each sample point in (8.18) we would assign $P = .1$. Suppose now that on the opposite side of the disks, we record numbers as follows:

$$
\begin{array}{cccccccccc}
A & B & C & D & E & F & G & H & I & J \\
1 & 2 & 2 & 3 & 3 & 3 & 3 & 4 & 4 & 5
\end{array}
$$

We select a disk at random from the box and record the number that appears on the disk. As a sample space for this experiment we have

$$S = \{1, 2, 3, 4, 5\} \qquad (8.19)$$

The possible outcomes of this experiment are values of a variable X that can take only the values 1, 2, 3, 4, or 5. Then we have

$$
\begin{aligned}
P(X = 1) &= P(A) &&= .1 \\
P(X = 2) &= P(B) + P(C) &&= .2 \\
P(X = 3) &= P(D) + P(E) + P(F) + P(G) &&= .4 \\
P(X = 4) &= P(H) + P(I) &&= .2 \\
P(X = 5) &= P(J) &&= .1
\end{aligned}
$$

To find the probability that $X \geq 4$, we have $P(X = 4) + P(X = 5) = .2 + .1 = .3$. Similarly, $P(2 \leq X \leq 4) = P(X = 2) + P(X = 3) + P(X = 4) = .2 + .4 + .2 = .8$.

Any variable X such that X can take only a finite number of possible values is called a *discrete* variable. For a discrete variable X, let P_i be the probability that X takes the value X_i, with $0 \leq P_i \leq 1$, and such that $\Sigma P_i = 1$. When these conditions are satisfied, then X is called a *discrete random variable*. It is obvious, in the example described above, that X is a discrete random variable.

The set of ordered pairs (X_i, P_i) is called the *probability function* or *probability distribution* of X. The sum of the products $P_i X_i$ over all possible values of the variable is defined as

$$\mu = \sum P_i X_i \tag{8.20}$$

or the *mean* of the probability distribution. For the example cited, we have

$$\mu = (.1)(1) + (.2)(2) + (.4)(3) + (.2)(4) + (.1)(5) = 3$$

Suppose the experiment of drawing a disk at random from the box is repeated an indefinitely large number of times with replacement of the disk after each draw. On each draw we record the value of X. Then the long run average value of X is called the *expectation* of X and is written $E(X)$. We define

$$E(X) = \sum P_i X_i = \mu \tag{8.21}$$

as the average value of X that we would expect to obtain in the long run, that is, with an indefinitely large number of draws with replacement after each draw.

We also define

$$E(X^2) = \sum P_i X_i^2 \tag{8.22}$$

as the long-run average value of X^2. Then the *variance* of X may be defined as

$$
\begin{aligned}
\sigma^2 &= \sum P_i (X_i - \mu)^2 \\
&= \sum P_i X_i^2 - 2\mu \sum P_i X_i + \mu^2 \sum P_i \\
&= E(X^2) - \mu^2
\end{aligned}
\tag{8.23}
$$

or, alternatively, as

$$\sigma^2 = E(X - \mu)^2 \tag{8.24}$$

By expanding the right side of (8.24) and then taking the expectation, it can easily be shown that (8.24) is equal to the right side of (8.23).

In the example cited, we have

$$E(X^2) = (.1)(1) + (.2)(4) + (.4)(9) + (.2)(16) + (.1)(25) = 10.2$$

and substituting in (8.23) we have

$$\sigma^2 = E(X^2) - \mu^2$$
$$= 10.2 - 9$$
$$= 1.2$$

8.10   Independent Random Variables

From a box with the same contents as that described above, suppose we select a disk at random and record the value of the variable. We replace the disk and make a second draw and record the value of the variable. To distinguish between these two draws, we let X_1 correspond to the first draw and X_2 to the second. Then a sample space for this experiment will consist of the set of all ordered pairs (X_1, X_2) such that X_1 can take values of 1, 2, 3, 4, or 5, and X_2 can take values of 1, 2, 3, 4, or 5. The sample space for this experiment is shown in Table 8.1 where we have let the rows correspond to X_1 and the columns correspond to X_2.

Table 8.1—The possible outcomes of an experiment in which $n = 2$ observations are randomly selected with replacement after the first draw. The entries in the cells of the table are the values of the ordered pairs (X_1, X_2) where X_1 and X_2 can take only the values of 1, 2, 3, 4, or 5

X_1 \ X_2	1	2	3	4	5	$P(X_1)$
5	(5, 1)	(5, 2)	(5, 3)	(5, 4)	(5, 5)	.1
4	(4, 1)	(4, 2)	(4, 3)	(4, 4)	(4, 5)	.2
3	(3, 1)	(3, 2)	(3, 3)	(3, 4)	(3, 5)	.4
2	(2, 1)	(2, 2)	(2, 3)	(2, 4)	(2, 5)	.2
1	(1, 1)	(1, 2)	(1, 3)	(1, 4)	(1, 5)	.1
$P(X_2)$	.1	.2	.4	.2	.1	1.0

Let E_1 be an event defined on a sample space and let E_2 be another event defined on the same sample space. Then, as we have pointed out before, if

$$P(E_1 \cap E_2) = P(E_1)P(E_2) \tag{8.25}$$

the two events are said to be *independent*. Alternatively, we say that two events are independent if $P(E_2|E_1) = P(E_2)$. We read "$P(E_2|E_1)$" as "the conditional probability of E_2 given that E_1 has occurred." Thus, if the fact that E_1 has occurred does nothing to alter or change the probability that E_2 will occur, E_1 and E_2 are independent.

Let E_1 be the event $X_1 = 1$ and E_2 be the event $X_2 = 3$. Because we replaced the disk in the box after recording the value of X_1 on the first draw, the probability of obtaining $X_2 = 3$ on the second draw should be unchanged and equal to .4, regardless of the particular value of X obtained on the first draw. Then the probability of the ordered pair (1, 3) should be

$$P(E_1 \cap E_2) = P(X_1 = 1) \, P(X_2 = 3) = (.1)(.4) = .04$$

In the same manner we may argue that all of the ordered (X_1, X_2) pairs are independent. When two discrete random variables are independent, then we use the notation

$$P_i(X_1 = X_i)P_j(X_2 = X_j) = P_iP_j = P_{ij} \tag{8.26}$$

The probabilities P_{ij} associated with each of the 25 sample points in Table 8.1 are given in Table 8.2. The probabilities were calculated using (8.26).

Table 8.2—Probabilities associated with each of the possible outcomes of the experiment described in Table 8.1. Each cell entry in the table gives the probability of the outcome of the corresponding cell entry of Table 8.1

X_1 \ X_2	1	2	3	4	5	$P(X_1)$
5	.01	.02	.04	.02	.01	.1
4	.02	.04	.08	.04	.02	.2
3	.04	.08	.16	.08	.04	.4
2	.02	.04	.08	.04	.02	.2
1	.01	.02	.04	.02	.01	.1
$P(X_2)$	.1	.2	.4	.2	.1	1.0

8.11   The Covariance

Let the outcome of the experiment be the product, $X_1 X_2$, of each of the ordered (X_1, X_2) pairs. If we multiply the values of (X_1, X_2) in Table 8.1, then we see that the possible outcomes of the experiment are 1, 2, 3, 4, 5, 6, 8, 9, 10, 12, 15, 16, 20, 25. Table 8.3 gives the values of these outcomes.

Table 8.3—The probability distribution of the product $X_1 X_2$ for the experiment described in Table 8.1

(1) $X_{1i}X_{2j}$	(2) P_{ij}	(3) $P_{ij}X_{1i}X_{2j}$
25	.01	.25
20	.04	.80
16	.04	.64
15	.08	1.20
12	.16	1.92
10	.04	.40
9	.16	1.44
8	.08	.64
6	.16	.96
5	.02	.10
4	.08	.32
3	.08	.24
2	.04	.08
1	.01	.01
Σ	1.00	9.00

The probabilities associated with each outcome are given in column (2) of the table and were obtained from Table 8.2 by summing the probabilities of the sample points corresponding to each possible value of the product $X_1 X_2$. For example, we have three sample points (4, 1) (1, 4), and (2, 2) for which $X_1 X_2 = 4$. The probabilities of these three sample points are .02, .02, and .04, respectively. Then $P(X_1 X_2 = 4) = .02 + .02 + .04 = .08$ and this value has been recorded in column (2) in Table 8.3 opposite $X_1 X_2 = 4$. Then for the expected value of $X_1 X_2$ we have

$$E(X_1 X_2) = \sum P_{ij} X_{1i} X_{2j} = 9$$

The covariance of X_1 and X_2, which we designate by $C_{X_1 X_2}$, is defined as

$$C_{X_1 X_2} = E(X_1 X_2) - E(X_1)E(X_2) = E(X_1 X_2) - \mu_{X_1}\mu_{X_2} \qquad (8.27)$$

We have previously shown that $E(X_1) = 3$ and, because the probability distribution of X_2 is identical with that of X_1, we also have $E(X_2) = 3$. Thus, for this particular example, we have

$$
\begin{aligned}
C_{X_1X_2} &= E(X_1X_2) - E(X_1)E(X_2) \\
&= 9 - (3)(3) \\
&= 0
\end{aligned}
$$

The reason why the covariance is zero, for this particular example, is because X_1 and X_2 are independent random variables. For any two independent random variables the covariance will always be equal to zero. Thus if

$$E(X_1X_2) - \mu_{X_1}\mu_{X_2} = 0$$

then X_1 and X_2 are independent random variables.

8.12 The Sum of n Random Variables

Let the outcome of the experiment of drawing two disks from the box, with replacement after the first draw, be the sum of the values of X_1 and X_2, that is, let the outcome of interest be $T = X_1 + X_2$. Then the possible outcomes are 2, 3, 4, $\cdots$, 10 and a sample space for this experiment would be

$$S = \{2, 3, 4, 5, 6, 7, 8, 9, 10\} \tag{8.28}$$

We may regard the values of T as events or subsets defined on the sample space as given in Table 8.1. We note that the events, values of T, are mutually exclusive and exhaustive and therefore they provide a partition of S as defined by Table 8.1. Then the probabilities associated with the various values of T can be easily obtained by summing the probabilities of the sample points in the subsets represented by each value of T. For example, for $T = 6$, we have the sample points (5, 1), (4, 2), (3, 3), (2, 4), and (1, 5) with corresponding probabilities of .01, .04, .16, .04, and .01. The sum of these probabilities is .26 and, therefore, $P(T = 6) = .26$. The probabilities associated with each of the values of T are given in column (2) of Table 8.4.

From Table 8.4 we have

$$E(T) = \sum P_iT_i = \mu_T = 6$$

We have previously shown that $E(X_1) = 3$ and, because the probability distribution of X_2 is identical with that of X_1, we also have $E(X_2) = 3$. We have $T = X_1 + X_2$, and we note that

$$E(T) = E(X_1) + E(X_2)$$

or

$$\mu_T = \mu_{X_1} + \mu_{X_2} \tag{8.29}$$

It is the case that (8.29) is true, regardless of whether X_1 and X_2 are independent or not. Furthermore, (8.29) generalizes to the expected value of the sum of any number of random variables. For example, if $X_1, X_2, X_3, \cdots, X_n$ are n random variables and if

$$T = X_1 + X_2 + X_3 + \cdots + X_n$$

then

$$E(T) = E(X_1) + E(X_2) + E(X_3) + \cdots + E(X_n)$$

or

$$\mu_T = \mu_{X_1} + \mu_{X_2} + \mu_{X_3} + \cdots + \mu_{X_n} \tag{8.30}$$

Of particular interest is the case where $X_1, X_2, X_3, \cdots, X_n$ have the same expected values. If this is the case, then

$$\mu_{X_1} = \mu_{X_2} = \mu_{X_3} = \cdots = \mu_{X_n} = \mu$$

and

$$E(T) = E\left(\sum_1^n X\right) = n\mu \tag{8.31}$$

Column (4) of Table 8.4 gives the values of $P_i T_i^2$ and we have $E(T^2) = \Sigma P_i T_i^2 = 38.4$. Then, the variance of T will be given by

$$\sigma_T^2 = E(T^2) - \mu_T^2 \tag{8.32}$$

Table 8.4—The probability distribution of the sum, $T = X_1 + X_2$, for the experiment described in Table 8.1

(1) T_i	(2) P_i	(3) $P_i T_i$	(4) $P_i T_i^2$
10	.01	.10	1.00
9	.04	.36	3.24
8	.12	.96	7.68
7	.20	1.40	9.80
6	.26	1.56	9.36
5	.20	1.00	5.00
4	.12	.48	1.92
3	.04	.12	.36
2	.01	.02	.04
Σ	1.00	6.00	38.40

or, for the example under consideration,

$$\sigma_T^2 = 38.4 - (6)^2$$
$$= 2.4$$

We have previously shown that $\sigma_{X_1}^2 = 1.2$ and, because the probability distribution of X_2 is identical with that of X_1, we also have $\sigma_{X_2}^2 = 1.2$. We note, for this particular example, it is also true that

$$\sigma_T^2 = \sigma_{X_1}^2 + \sigma_{X_2}^2 \tag{8.33}$$

or, for the example under consideration

$$\sigma_T^2 = 1.2 + 1.2$$
$$= 2.4$$

It is only if T is the sum of two *independent* random variables that (8.33) is true. For example, if X_1 and X_2 were not independent random variables, then the variance of T would not be equal to the sum of the variance of X_1 and the variance of X_2.

We can generalize (8.33) to the case of n independent random variables. Let $X_1, X_2, X_3, \cdots, X_n$ be independent random variables. Then, the variance of the sum T of these independent random variables will be

$$\sigma_T^2 = \sigma_{X_1}^2 + \sigma_{X_2}^2 + \cdots + \sigma_{X_n}^2 \tag{8.34}$$

If the variables have equal variances so that $\sigma_{X_1}^2 = \sigma_{X_2}^2 = \sigma_{X_3}^2 = \cdots = \sigma_{X_n}^2 = \sigma^2$, then it is obvious that the variance of the sum will be

$$\sigma_T^2 = n\sigma^2 \tag{8.35}$$

8.13   The Difference between Two Random Variables

We now let the outcome of the experiment of interest be $D = X_1 - X_2$ or the difference between the value of the first and second draw. Then a sample space for this experiment will be

$$S = \{-4, -3, -2, -1, 0, 1, 2, 3, 4\} \tag{8.36}$$

The values of D are events, subsets, defined on the sample space given in Table 8.1. They are mutually exclusive and exhaustive and provide a partition of the sample space of Table 8.1. Column (2) of Table 8.5 gives the probabilities associated with each value of D. We have

$$E(D) = \sum P_i D_i = \mu_D = 0$$

and we note that

$$E(D) = E(X_1 - X_2) = E(X_1) - E(X_2) \tag{8.37}$$

For this particular example, we have $E(D) = 0$, but this, of course, will not be true for any case where $E(X_1) \neq E(X_2)$ or $\mu_{X_1} \neq \mu_{X_2}$.

To find the variance of D, we have

$$\sigma_D^2 = E(D^2) - \mu_D^2 \tag{8.38}$$

Column (4) of Table 8.5 gives the values of $P_i D_i^2$ and we see that $E(D^2) = \Sigma P_i D_i^2 = 2.4$, and $\sigma_D^2 = 2.4$ because $\mu_D = 0$.

Table 8.5—The probability distribution of the difference, $D = X_1 - X_2$, for the experiment described in Table 8.1

(1) D_i	(2) P_i	(3) $P_i D_i$	(4) $P_i D_i^2$
4	.01	.04	.16
3	.04	.12	.36
2	.12	.24	.48
1	.20	.20	.20
0	.26	.00	.00
−1	.20	−.20	.20
−2	.12	−.24	.48
−3	.04	−.12	.36
−4	.01	−.04	.16
Σ	1.00	.00	2.40

We have previously shown that $\sigma_{X_1}^2 = 1.2$ and, because the probability distribution of X_2 is identical with that of X_1, we also have $\sigma_{X_2}^2 = 1.2$. We note, for this particular example, it is true that

$$\sigma_D^2 = \sigma_{X_1}^2 + \sigma_{X_2}^2 \tag{8.39}$$

or

$$\sigma_D^2 = 1.2 + 1.2$$
$$= 2.4$$

We emphasize that (8.39) is true if and only if X_1 and X_2 are *independent* random variables. If they are not independent, then the variance of the difference will not be equal to the sum of the two variances.

8.14   The Mean of n Random Variables

We consider one final case. Let the outcome of the experiment be the mean of the paired values or $(X_1 + X_2)/2$. We have $\Sigma X = T = X_1 + X_2$ and $\bar{X} = \Sigma X/n = (X_1 + X_2)/2$. The possible outcomes of the experiment are now 1.0, 1.5, 2.0, 2.5, $\cdots$, 5.0. The probabilities associated with these sample points will be exactly the same as those associated with the sample points corresponding to values of $T = \Sigma X$. For example, only values of $T = 4$ can result in values of $\overline{X} = 2$, and the subset corresponding to $T = 4$ is $\{(3, 1), (2, 2), (1, 3)\}$.

The probability distribution of $\overline{X}$ is shown in Table 8.6. Column (2) gives the values of P_i and column (3) gives the products $P_i \overline{X}_i$ and we see that $\Sigma P_i \overline{X}_i = 3.0$. Then

$$E(\overline{X}) = E\left(\frac{X_1 + X_2}{2}\right) = \frac{1}{2}[E(X_1) + E(X_2)] = \frac{1}{2}(\mu_{X_1} + \mu_{X_2}) \quad (8.40)$$

We see that $\overline{X}$, as given by (8.40), is a mean based upon a random sample of $n = 2$ observations. If we had drawn $n = 3$ observations in the manner described, and found $\overline{X} = (X_1 + X_2 + X_3)/3$, then, in this instance, we would have

$$E(\overline{X}) = \frac{1}{3}(\mu_{X_1} + \mu_{X_2} + \mu_{X_3})$$

Consider the case of $X_1, X_2, X_3, \cdots, X_n$ random variables such that

$$E(X_1) = E(X_2) = E(X_3) = \cdots = E(X_n) = \mu$$

Then, in this instance, the expected value of

$$\sum_{1}^{n} X = T$$

will be

$$E\left(\sum_{1}^{n} X\right) = n\mu$$

and

$$E\left(\frac{\sum_{1}^{n} X}{n}\right) = E(\overline{X}) = \frac{1}{n}n\mu = \mu \quad (8.41)$$

Formula (8.41) tells us that if we have a random sample of n observations from the same distribution or from distributions with the same mean, then the long-run average value of the sample mean based upon the n observations will be equal to the mean of the distribution.

Column (4) of Table 8.6 gives the values of $P_i \overline{X}_i^2$. Then the variance of the mean will be given by

$$\sigma_{\overline{X}}^2 = E(\overline{X} - \mu_X)^2 \quad (8.42)$$

Table 8.6—The probability distribution of the mean, $\overline{X} = (X_1 + X_2)/2$, for the experiment described in Table 8.1

(1) $\overline{X}_i$	(2) P_i	(3) $P_i\overline{X}_i$	(4) $P_i\overline{X}_i^2$
5.0	.01	.05	.25
4.5	.04	.18	.81
4.0	.12	.48	1.92
3.5	.20	.70	2.45
3.0	.26	.78	2.34
2.5	.20	.50	1.25
2.0	.12	.24	.48
1.5	.04	.06	.09
1.0	.01	.01	.01
Σ	1.00	3.00	9.60

or

$$\sigma_{\overline{X}}^2 = E(\overline{X}^2) - \mu_X^2 \tag{8.43}$$

We have $E(\overline{X}^2) = \Sigma\, P_i\overline{X}_i^2 = 9.60$ and $\mu_X = 3$. Then

$$\sigma_{\overline{X}}^2 = 9.6 - (3)^2$$
$$= .6$$

Let $X_1, X_2, X_3, \cdots, X_n$ be n independent random variables with equal variances. Then (8.35) tells us that the variance of the sum, $T = X_1 + X_2 + X_3 + \cdots + X_n$, will be

$$\sigma_T^2 = n\sigma^2$$

But the mean is obtained by dividing the sum by n and we have previously shown that if we divide a variable by a constant, the variance is divided by the square of the constant. Thus, if $T = X_1 + X_2 + X_3 + \cdots + X_n$ is divided by n, we have

$$\sigma_{T/n}^2 = \frac{1}{n^2}\, n\sigma^2$$

or

$$\sigma_{\overline{X}}^2 = \frac{\sigma^2}{n} \tag{8.44}$$

In the present example we have $n = 2$ independent random variables with $\sigma_{X_1}^2 = \sigma_{X_2}^2 = \sigma^2 = 1.2$ and

$$\sigma_{\bar{X}}^2 = \frac{1.2}{2} = .6$$

as before.

EXAMPLES

8.1—Given a sample space consisting of four sample points, that is, $S = \{e_1, e_2, e_3, e_4\}$. List the 16 different subsets that can be defined on this sample space.

8.2—We have the set $S = \{1, 2, 3, 4, 5, 6, 7, 8, 9\}$, and the following subsets:

$$A = \{1, 2, 3\}$$
$$B = \{3, 4, 5, 6\}$$
$$C = \{1, 3, 5, 6, 7, 8\}$$
$$D = \{8, 9\}$$

List the numbers in each of the following subsets:

(a) $A \cup B$ (g) $B \cup C$ (m) $A \cup B \cup C$
(b) $A \cup C$ (h) $B \cup D$ (n) $B \cup C \cup D$
(c) $A \cup D$ (i) $C \cup D$ (o) $A \cap (B \cup C)$
(d) $A \cap B$ (j) $B \cap C$ (p) $A \cup (B \cap C)$
(e) $A \cap C$ (k) $B \cap D$ (q) $(A \cup B) \cap (A \cap C)$
(f) $A \cap D$ (l) $C \cap D$

8.3—A fair (unbiased) die is rolled twice. Let X_1 be the number of points on the first roll and X_2 the number of points on the second roll. Find the probability of each of the following events:

(a) $P(X_1 \neq X_2)$ (e) $P(X_1 + X_2 < 5)$
(b) $P(X_1 = 2X_2)$ (f) $P(X_1 + X_2 > 10)$
(c) $P(X_1 \leq 3 \text{ and } X_2 > 3)$ (g) $P(X_1 = X_2)$
(d) $P(X_1 + X_2 = 7)$ (h) $P(X_1 + X_2 \neq 11)$

8.4—Suppose we have two independent random variables, X and Y, such that the possible values of both variables are zero and 1. Let $P(X = 1)$ be .5 and $P(X = 0)$ be .5. For Y, let $P(Y = 1)$ be .7 and $P(Y = 0)$ be .3.

(a) Calculate $\mu_X = E(X)$ and $\sigma_X^2 = E(X^2) - \mu_X^2$.
(b) Calculate $\mu_Y = E(Y)$ and $\sigma_Y^2 = E(Y^2) - \mu_Y^2$.
(c) A value of X is selected at random and also a value of Y. Let T be the

sum of the values of X and Y. Calculate $\mu_T = E(T)$ and note that $E(T) = E(X) + E(Y)$.

(d) Calculate $\sigma_T^2 = E(T^2) - \mu_T^2$ and note that $\sigma_T^2 = \sigma_X^2 + \sigma_Y^2$.

(e) Let $D = X - Y$. Calculate $\mu_D = E(D)$ and note that $E(D) = E(X) - E(Y)$.

(f) Calculate $\sigma_D^2 = E(D^2) - \mu_D^2$ and note that $\sigma_D^2 = \sigma_X^2 + \sigma_Y^2$.

(g) Find the probability distribution of the product XY and show that $E(XY) = E(X)E(Y)$.

8.5—A fair coin is tossed in a game until a tail appears or until five heads in a row occur.

(a) What are the possible outcomes of this experiment and what are the probabilities associated with each outcome?

(b) Let X be the number of tosses required to end the game. Calculate $\mu_X = E(X)$ and $\sigma_X^2 = E(X^2) - \mu_X^2$.

8.6—A clinical psychologist is given three test profiles and is told that one is a profile obtained from a schizophrenic (S) patient, one is a profile obtained from a depressed (D) patient, and another is the profile of a paranoid (P) patient. The task of the clinical psychologist is to match the diagnostic labels with the test profiles.

Let X be the number of correct matches. Find $\mu_X = E(X)$ and $\sigma_X^2 = E(X^2) - \mu_X^2$.

8.7—If A and B are independent events, then prove that A and $\bar{B}$, $\bar{A}$ and B, and $\bar{A}$ and $\bar{B}$ are also independent. Hint: Set up a 2×2 table with rows corresponding to A and $\bar{A}$ and columns corresponding to B and $\bar{B}$. Note that we are given that $P(A \cap B) = P(A)P(B)$.

8.8—Consider only those families with exactly three children. We assume that $P(B)$ is equal to $P(G)$ and that these are independent events. Find the probabilities associated with each of the following:

(a) Exactly two boys.
(b) At least one girl.
(c) More girls than boys.
(d) At least one girl and one boy.
(e) The oldest child is a boy.
(f) The second child is a boy.
(g) The youngest child is a boy and the oldest child is a girl.
(h) No girl is younger than a boy, if there is at least one boy and one girl.

8.9—Prove that $E(X - \mu)^2 = E(X^2) - \mu^2$.

8.10—At a small college six males and four females have fellowship status in an academic organization. They elect three females and two males as associate members. From the total of 15 members one individual is selected at random. Let E_1 be the event that the individual selected is a male and E_2 be the event that the individual selected has fellowship status in the organization. Find:

(a) $P(E_1)$ (d) $P(E_1|E_2)$
(b) $P(E_2)$ (e) $P(E_2|E_1)$
(c) $P(E_1 \cap E_2)$

8.11—A card is selected at random from a bridge deck of 52 cards. Find the probability of each of the following events:

(a) the card is the jack of hearts
(b) the card is a heart
(c) the card is a jack
(d) the card is a heart, given that it is a jack
(e) the card is a jack, given that it is a heart
(f) the card is a red card
(g) the card is a 10
(h) the card is a red card, given that it is a 10
(i) the card is a 10, given that it is a red card

8.12—We have three boxes. Each box contains two colored marbles. Box 1 contains two red marbles, Box 2 contains one red and one white marble, and Box 3 contains two white marbles. A box is selected at random and a marble is then selected at random from the box.

(a) Make a table showing the possible outcomes of this experiment and the probability associated with each possible outcome.
(b) What is the probability that the marble selected is red?
     Given that a red marble is drawn, find the conditional probabilities:
(c) $P(B_1|R)$
(d) $P(B_2|R)$
(e) $P(B_3|R)$

8.13—In a university course, 100 students are enrolled. There are 50 males (M) and 50 females (F) in the class. Of the 100 students, 60 are undergraduates (U) and 40 are graduate (G) students. Of the 100 students, 40 are both F and U, that is $F \cap U$ contains 40 students. A student is selected at random from the class. Find the following probabilities:

(a) $P(F \cap G)$ (e) $P(M|U)$
(b) $P(M \cap U)$ (f) $P(U|F)$
(c) $P(M \cap G)$ (g) $P(G|M)$
(d) $P(F|G)$

8.14—Each of 100 students responds either True (T) or False (F) to each of two questions. The number of students responding T to the first questions is 60 and the number responding T to the second question is 70. A total of 60 students give *at least* one F response to the two questions. Let E_1 be the event a T response to the first question and E_2 be the event a T response to the second question. Find the probability of each of the following events.

(a) $P(\bar{E}_1 \cap \bar{E}_2)$ (d) $P(\bar{E}_1 \cap E_2)$

(b) $P(\bar{E}_1 \cup E_2)$ (e) $P(\bar{E}_1 \cup \bar{E}_2)$

(c) $P(E_1 \cap E_2)$

8.15—Give a one-sentence definition of each of the following terms or concepts:

set	partition of a sample space
subset	empty set
$A \cup B$	sample space
$A \cap B$	sample point
complement of a set	independent events
conditional probability	mutually exclusive events
prior probabilities	discrete random variable
posterior probabilities	probability function or distribution
expectation	independent random variables

CHAPTER 9

The Binomial Probability Distribution

9.1 Introduction

A psychologist in conversation with a psychiatrist states that he has developed a new personality scale that provides a measure of psychopathology. He also states that the items in the scale are of such a subtle nature that it would be impossible for the psychiatrist to judge whether the True or False response to each item is the keyed response. By *keyed response*, the psychologist means the response to the item that is regarded as a sign of psychopathology. The psychiatrist is skeptical. He tells the psychologist that he believes he would be able to judge whether the keyed response to an item in the scale is either True or False. The psychologist, however, is also skeptical of the psychiatrist's claim. He is not convinced that the psychiatrist could judge accurately whether the items in the scale are keyed True or False. The psychologist spends a sleepless night thinking about the psychiatrist's claim. The next morning he decides upon a plan that he believes will test how well the psychiatrist can judge the keying of the items in the scale. Having decided upon the plan, he calls the psychiatrist and makes an appointment to have lunch with him.

At their luncheon meeting the psychologist asks the psychiatrist to participate in a friendly game. The psychologist will give the psychiatrist two cards. On one of the cards is printed an item that is keyed True and on the other card is printed an item that is keyed False. He wants the psychiatrist to select the item keyed True. He will then give him another pair of items, one of which is keyed True and one of which is keyed False, and ask him to select the item keyed True. In all, the psychologist proposes to present the psychiatrist with n pairs of items. We shall use this game to illustrate some of the principles of a binomial experiment.

9.2   The Nature of Binomial Experiments

Each presentation of a pair of cards is called a *trial*. On each trial there are only two possible outcomes: either the correct card is selected or it is not. The variable X of interest is the number of correct responses and, on a single trial, X can take only the value of one or zero. Experiments that consist of a set of n independent trials such that on each trial there are only two possible outcomes are called *binomial experiments* and, in such cases,

Table 9.1—Sample space for a binomial experiment with $n = 5$ independent trials

Outcome	Value of T	Outcome	Value of T
11111	5	11000	2
11110	4	10100	2
11101	4	10010	2
11011	4	10001	2
10111	4	01100	2
01111	4	01010	2
11100	3	01001	2
11010	3	00110	2
11001	3	00101	2
10101	3	00011	2
10011	3	10000	1
10110	3	01000	1
01110	3	00100	1
01101	3	00010	1
01011	3	00001	1
00111	3	00000	0

the *binomial probability distribution* provides a basis for evaluating the outcome of the experiment.

Suppose that we have $n = 5$ trials for the experiment described. If the items are in fact subtle so that it is impossible for the psychiatrist to determine which of the two items in each trial is the True-keyed item, then, from the psychologist's point of view, the psychiatrist will merely be giving an educated guess. If the psychiatrist is in fact guessing on each trial, then it seems reasonable to believe that on each trial he is just as likely to be wrong as right. We, therefore, assign a probability of $P = 1/2$ to a correct response ($X = 1$) on each trial. It is convenient to let $Q = 1 - P$ represent the probability of an incorrect response ($X = 0$) on each trial.

Table 9.1 gives a sample space for the experiment with $n = 5$ trials. If the trials are independent and if $P(X = 1)$ is 1/2 on each trial, then each of the $2^5 = 32$ outcomes or sample points listed in the table has probability of 1/32. We let T be the sum of the values of X or the total number of correct responses in 5 trials. We note that each T is a subset of S, as defined in Table 9.1, and that the values of T are mutually exclusive and exhaustive and therefore provide a partition of the sample space of Table 9.1. If the outcome of interest is T, then we have

$$S = \{5, 4, 3, 2, 1, 0\} \tag{9.1}$$

and the probabilities associated with each element of S can be determined by simple addition of the probabilities of the sample points in Table 9.1 corresponding to each value of T.

T is a discrete random variable and the probability distribution of T is shown in Table 9.2. Under the assumptions we used in deriving the probability distribution of T, we see that if the psychiatrist makes five correct responses, that is, if $T = 5$, then this outcome has a probability of approximately .03. This is to say, if the experiment involving $n = 5$ trials were repeated an indefinitely large number of times, and if it is the case that the probability of a correct response on each trial is 1/2, then in the long run 1/32 or approximately .03 of the total number of experiments performed would result in $T = 5$.

If the psychiatrist actually makes five correct responses, then this outcome of the experiment would appear to offer evidence against the hypothesis that he is responding by chance in deciding how the items are keyed. We say it appears to offer evidence against this hypothesis because, if the hypothesis is true, then we have an event, an outcome $T = 5$, that we may regard as relatively improbable.

In more general terms, the hypothesis that an experiment is designed to test is called a *null hypothesis*, which we designate by H_0. In the experiment described, the null hypothesis is

$$H_0 : P(X = 1) \leq 1/2$$

If we decide that the probability of a correct response upon the part of the psychiatrist on each trial is greater than 1/2, then we must obviously believe that he is not responding by chance.

Suppose in the experiment we observed $T = 4$. In evaluating this outcome we should take into account not only the probability of $T = 4$, but also the probability of $T = 5$. We are not interested in the probability of exactly four correct responses, but in the probability of this outcome and all other outcomes more extreme that would also offer evidence against H_0. Table 9.2 shows that in the long run we could expect $1/32 + 5/32 = 6/32$ or approximately .187 of the experiments to result in $T \geq 4$, when H_0 is true, simply as a result of random variation.

Table 9.2—Probability distribution of the sum T for a binomial experiment with $P = 1/2$ and $n = 5$ trials

T_i	P_i
5	1/32
4	5/32
3	10/32
2	10/32
1	5/32
0	1/32

In random experiments, that is, experiments in which the outcomes are subject to random variation, we suggest that it is, in general, wise not to regard the outcome of a single small experiment as necessarily conclusive. It is well known that an improbable outcome will occur with a specified probability as a result of random variation, even when H_0 is true. With a single experiment there is no way of knowing whether or not the outcome happens to be one of these improbable outcomes. If the experiment with the psychiatrist were repeated 100 times, for example, then we may expect approximately three of the experiments to result in $T = 5$ as a result of random variation. In a single experiment, how can we know that an outcome of $T = 5$ is not one of these three? Our confidence in a decision about H_0 is increased when, in a number of different repetitions of the experiment under the same conditions, we obtain consistent results or outcomes.[1]

With $n = 10$ trials, we have $2^{10} = 1024$ possible outcomes of a binomial experiment. To attempt to list these 1024 outcomes would be complex and tedious. But, if the outcome of interest is T, the number of correct responses, then there is no need to list the separate 1024 outcomes. What is needed are methods for determining how many of the 1024 sample points correspond to each possible value of T. In a binomial experiment with $P(X = 1) = 1/2$, each sample point will have probability $1/2^n$, where n is the number of trials. If we can find out how many sample points correspond to each possible value of T, we can also easily determine the probability of each value of T.

---

[1] It should be clear that the outcome of a single experiment cannot provide conclusive proof about H_0 when the outcomes of the experiment are subject to random variation. Improbable events can and will occur as a result of random variation with a specified relative frequency, however surprised we may be that they occur in our experiments.

The following quotation from Fisher (1942, pp. 13–14) is relevant: "In order to assert that a natural phenomenon is experimentally demonstrable we need, not an isolated record, but a reliable method of procedure. In relation to the test of significance, we may say that a phenomenon is experimentally demonstrable when we know how to conduct an experiment which will rarely fail to give us a statistically significant result."

In this case, all that we need to do is to multiply $1/2^n$ by the number of sample points corresponding to any given value of T. To count the number of sample points corresponding to any given value of T, we need to understand permutations and combinations.

9.3 The Number of Permutations of n Objects Taken n at a Time

Suppose we have n different objects and we want to find the number of different *ordered sequences* in which the objects can be arranged. Consider the case of $n = 3$ letters: A, B, and C. We could obviously select any one of the three letters for the first position, then select any one of the two remaining letters for the second position, and then fill the third position with the one remaining letter. Then the $n = 3$ letters can be arranged in

$$3 \times 2 \times 1 = 6$$

different ordered sequences, as shown below:

$$ABC \qquad BAC \qquad CAB$$
$$ACB \qquad BCA \qquad CBA$$

Any given ordered sequence of n objects taken all together is called a *permutation* of the n objects and total number of such permutations is given by

$$_nP_n = n!　\tag{9.2}$$

where $_nP_n$ designates the number of permutations of n objects taken all together and $n!$, called n *factorial*, is the product of all of the integers from n to 1, or

$$n! = n(n - 1)(n - 2) \cdots \times 3 \times 2 \times 1 \tag{9.3}$$

9.4 The Number of Permutations of n Objects Taken r at a Time

The number of permutations of n objects taken r at a time, with $r < n$, is designated by $_nP_r$. For example, suppose we have $n = 4$ letters, A, B, C, and D, and we take the letters $r = 2$ at a time. The first position could be filled by any one of the four letters and the second position by any one of the remaining three letters. We should have, therefore,

$$4 \times 3 = 12$$

permutations of $n = 4$ objects taken $r = 2$ at a time. For the letters A, B, C, and D, the 12 permutations are shown below:

AB	BA	CA	DA
AC	BC	CB	DB
AD	BD	CD	DC

In general, for any n and any r, we can fill the first position in n ways, the second in $n - 1$ ways, the third in $n - 2$ ways, and so on. When we come to the last or rth position, we will have used $r - 1$ of the n objects and will have $n - (r - 1) = n - r + 1$ objects left with which to fill the last position. Thus

$$_nP_r = n(n - 1)(n - 2) \cdots (n - r + 1) \tag{9.4}$$

gives the number of permutations of n different objects taken r at a time.

Multiplying both numerator and denominator of (9.4) by $(n - r)!$, we have

$$_nP_r = \frac{n(n - 1)(n - 2) \cdots (n - r + 1)(n - r)!}{(n - r)!} = \frac{n!}{(n - r)!} \tag{9.5}$$

For the $n = 4$ different letters taken $r = 2$ at a time, we have

$$\frac{4 \times 3 \times 2 \times 1}{(4 - 2)!} = 12$$

permutations. We note that if $r = n$, then $(n - r)! = 0$ and, by convention, we define $0! = 1$. Thus if $r = n$, then $_nP_r = {}_nP_n = n!$, as before.

9.5 The Number of Permutations of n Objects When Some of the Objects Are Alike

Suppose we have n objects such that they can be divided into k subsets. Each subset contains objects that are alike but the objects in any given subset are different from the objects in the other subsets. We let r_1 be the number of objects that are alike of one kind, r_2 be the number of objects that are alike of another kind, and so on for the k subsets, with $r_1 + r_2 + \cdots + r_k = n$.

We consider a simple example of $n = 5$ letters of which $r_1 = 3$ are A's and $r_2 = 2$ are B's. We are interested in the number of permutations of these five letters. If the five letters were all different, that is, if we had the letters $A, B, C, D,$ and E, then we know that we would have $5! = 120$ permutations of the letters. It may seem intuitively reasonable that if the five letters are not all different, then we will have fewer than 120 permutations. Let us see if this is actually the case. We let $_nP_{r_1,r_2} = {}_5P_{3,2}$ be the unknown number of permutations of $n = 5$ objects of which $r_1 = 3$ are alike and $r_2 = 2$ are alike. We wish to find the value of $_5P_{3,\,2}$.

Suppose that we have five cells in a row numbered 1, 2, 3, 4, and 5. If we choose two of the cells in which to place the 2 B's, then the remaining three cells can be filled with the 3 A's. For the two cells that the 2 B's are to occupy, we have the following possibilities: Cells 1 and 2, 1 and 3, 1 and 4, 1 and 5, 2 and 3, 2 and 4, 2 and 5, 3 and 4, 3 and 5, and 4 and 5. Thus we have

$BBAAA$	$BAABA$	$ABBAA$	$ABAAB$	$AABAB$
$BABAA$	$BAAAB$	$ABABA$	$AABBA$	$AAABB$

and these are the possible permutations of $n = 5$ objects of which $r_1 = 3$ and $r_2 = 2$ are alike. In this example, then, we have $_5P_{3,2} = 10$ permutations.

Now suppose that we make the 3 A's different by identifying them by the subscripts 1, 2, and 3. Then, for any one of the above permutations we could permute the 3 A's giving rise to $3! = 6$ permutations. For example, for $BBAAA$, and would have

$$BBA_1A_2A_3 \qquad BBA_2A_1A_3 \qquad BBA_3A_1A_2$$

$$BBA_1A_3A_2 \qquad BBA_2A_3A_1 \qquad BBA_3A_2A_1$$

We see that if the 3 A's were different we would have a total of $3!10 = 60$ permutations.

Now, obviously, if we make the 2 B's different by identifying them by the subscripts 1 and 2, then the 2 B's in each of the 10 original permutations could be permuted in $2!$ ways, independently of the $3!$ ways in which the 3 A's can be permuted. Thus, each of the original 10 permutations would result in $3!2! = 12$ permutations. Then the total number permutations, if all five objects were different would be

$$3!2!10 = 5!$$

We note that $3! = r_1!$, $2! = r_2!$, $10 = {}_5P_{3,2}$, and $5! = n!$ Then, in general,

$$r_1!r_2!{}_nP_{r_1,r_2} = n!$$

and solving for $_nP_{r_1,r_2}$ we have

$$_nP_{r_1,r_2} = \frac{n!}{r_1!r_2!}$$

as the number of permutations of n objects of which r_1 are alike and r_2 are alike.

By the same principles used in developing the above expression for the number of permutations of n objects of which r_1 are alike and r_2 are alike, we could show that the number of permutations of n objects of which r_1 are alike, r_2 are alike, and so on for k subsets, with $r_1 + r_2 + \cdots + r_k = n$, is given by

$$_nP_{r_1,r_2,\cdots,r_k} = \frac{n!}{r_1!r_2!\cdots r_k!} \qquad (9.6)$$

Let $r_1 = 2, r_2 = 1, r_3 = 1,$ and $r_4 = 1.$ Then

$$_5P_{2, 1, 1, 1} = \frac{5!}{2!1!1!1!} = 60$$

and, as we showed earlier, this is the number of permutations of two letters that are alike and three other letters that are all different.

9.6   The Number of Combinations of n Objects Taken r at a Time

In many cases we may not be interested in the number of ordered sequences or permutations of n objects taken r at a time, but instead we may be interested in the number of different sets of r objects that can be selected from n when the order is ignored. For example, suppose we select a sample of $r = 2$ letters from the set, A, B, C, and D, without replacement. These ordered samples have been listed earlier in the chapter. But suppose we are not interested in the order of the letters, but want to know the number of *different unordered* samples of $r = 2$ that can be selected from a set of $n = 4$ different letters. We note that any given sequence of r ordered objects can itself be permuted in $r!$ ways. Then, if order is to be ignored, we have

$$\frac{_4P_2}{_2P_2} = \frac{4!/(4 - 2)!}{2!} = 6$$

unordered samples of $r = 2$ selected from $n = 4$ different objects.

In general, for any n and any $r \leq n$, we have

$$_nC_r = \frac{_nP_r}{_rP_r} = \frac{n!/(n - r)!}{r!} = \frac{n!}{r!(n - r)!} \tag{9.7}$$

where $_nC_r$ refers to the number of combinations of n objects taken r at a time.[2] By *combination* is meant that the ordered sequence of the r objects is ignored. All permutations of n objects taken r at a time with exactly the same r objects represent the same combination.

If we let $r = 2$ and have $n = 3$ letters, A, B, and C, then we have the $3 \times 2 = 6$ permutations shown below:

$$\begin{array}{ccc} AB & AC & BC \\ BA & CA & CB \end{array}$$

---

[2] The number of combinations of n things taken r at a time is also often indicated by

$$\binom{n}{r}$$

in other texts.

But AB and BA represent the same combination as do also AC and CA and BC and CB. Thus we have only three combinations of $n = 3$ objects taken $r = 2$ at a time.

If we let $r = n = 3$, then for the same three letters, A, B, and C, we have six permutations: ABC, ACB, BCA, BAC, CAB, and CBA, but we have only one combination of these three letters.

9.7 A Binomial Experiment with $n = 10$ Trials and with $P = 1/2$

We now apply some of the principles developed in the previous sections to the experiment involving the psychiatrist. Suppose that the psychologist gives the psychiatrist $n = 10$ trials. On the first trial we may have $X = 1$, if the psychiatrist's response is correct, or $X = 0$ if it is not. Independently of what happens on the first trial, we may have $X = 1$ or $X = 0$ on the second trial, and so on, for each of the $n = 10$ trials. Then we have $2^{10} = 1024$ possible outcomes or sample points and, under the conditions of the experiment, we assume that each of these sample points has equal probability of $1/1024$. Let T be the number of correct responses in a set of $n = 10$ trials. Then, T can take values of $10, 9, 8, \cdots, 3, 2, 1,$ or 0. The values of T are mutually exclusive and exhaustive and provide a partition of the sample space of 1024 sample points. It is obvious that there can be only one sample point corresponding to $T = 10$ because, in this case, we would have to have 1111111111 and there is only one way in which this outcome could occur, that is, the psychiatrist would have to give the correct response on each trial.

For the sample point corresponding to the outcome 1111111110, we have $T = 9$. But we can permute the zero and the nine 1's in

$$\frac{10!}{9!1!} = 10$$

ways. Then there must be 10 sample points for which $T = 9$, each with probability $1/1024$, and the probability of $T = 9$ will be the sum of the probabilities of the 10 sample points or $10/1024$. Similarly, the number of sample points with eight 1's and two 0's will be given by

$$\frac{10!}{8!2!} = 45$$

and the probability of $T = 8$ will be $45/1024$. In the same manner, we can find the probabilities associated with each of the other possible values of T. These are given in Table 9.3. If we observe the outcome $T = 8$, then we have

$$P(T \geq 8) = \frac{1}{1024} + \frac{10}{1024} + \frac{45}{1024} = \frac{56}{1024} = .055$$

Table 9.3—Probability distribution of the sum T for a binomial experiment with $P = 1/2$ and $n = 10$ trials

T_i	P_i
10	1/1024
9	10/1024
8	45/1024
7	120/1024
6	210/1024
5	252/1024
4	210/1024
3	120/1024
2	45/1024
1	10/1024
0	1/1024

and we may decide that this outcome offers significant evidence against H_0. Even more improbable, under H_0, would be the outcome $T = 9$ or $T = 10$. If the psychiatrist makes $T = 10$ correct responses, this is an outcome that could be expected to occur as a result of random variation, when H_0 is true, only about 1 time in 1000.

9.8   Type I and Type II Errors and the Power of a Test

Suppose that we decide to reject H_0 if the outcome of the experiment, with $n = 10$ trials, is $T \geq 8$. Now suppose also that H_0 is true and we obtain $T \geq 8$. If we reject H_0 we will be in error. The error made in rejecting H_0 when H_0 is true is called a *Type I error*. In this experiment the probability of a Type I error is .055. The probability of a Type I error is called the *significance level*[3] of a test and is designated by α. If it is true that $P = 1/2$ and if the experiment described were repeated an indefinitely large number of times and if we always rejected H_0 when the outcome was $T \geq 8$, then we would be in error in about .055 of our decisions. In the long run, in other

---

[3] It would appear, judging from published research, that almost all, if not all, research workers use a significance level of .05 in evaluating the results of their experiments, that is, they reject H_0 when the outcome of the experiment has a probability equal to or less than .05, when H_0 is true. Outcomes or results of experiments with $P \leq .05$, when H_0 is true, are, therefore, conventionally referred to as *significant*. We shall, in general, accept this conventional significance level simply because it is convenient to have *some* standard for describing outcomes of experiments as "significant" or "nonsignificant." Thus, if we refer to an outcome of an experiment as significant, we will, in general, mean that the probability of the outcome is equal to or less than .05, when H_0 is true. In this example, we depart from convention in that we regard an outcome with $P \leq .055$, when H_0 is true, as being a significant outcome.

words, about .055 of our decisions that H_0 is false would be in error. We could, of course, decrease the probability of a Type I error by deciding to reject H_0 only if the outcome of the experiment was $T = 10$. In this case, the probability of a Type I error would be approximately .001.

We should be concerned, however, not only with the probability of a Type I error but also with the probability of a Type II error. A *Type II error* occurs if we fail to reject H_0 when H_0 is in fact false and should be rejected. Suppose, for example, that $H_0: P \leq 1/2$ is false and that $H_1: P = 3/5$ is true. Then if H_1 is true, we have $P(T \geq 8) = .167$. Thus the probability of obtaining a *significant* outcome, an outcome that would result in the rejection of H_0, is only about .167, if it is true that $P = 3/5$. In this case, the probability of a Type II error will be $1 - .167 = .833$.

The *power* of a statistical test is defined as the probability of rejecting H_0 when H_0 is false and should be rejected. An equivalent definition of the power of the test is $1 - P(\text{Type II error})$. The power of a test depends on, among other things, the particular alternative H_1 that is true. In a binomial experiment, the other things include the number of trials n, and the significance level α of the test of significance.

If we hold n, the number of trials, constant and equal to 10, and reject H_0 if $T \geq 8$, then we know that the probability of a Type I error will be .055. Figure 9.1[4] shows the power of our test for each of a selected number of values of $P > 1/2$. The graph in Figure 9.1 is called the *power function* of the binomial test for $n = 10$ trials when H_0 is $P = 1/2$ and the probability of a Type I error has been set at .055. Because we are interested only in those alternatives H_1 such that $P > 1/2$, the power function is for a *one-sided* test. We note that our test is not very sensitive to alternatives to H_0 such that P is only slightly greater than 1/2. If $P = .75$, then we have a somewhat better than a 50–50 chance of rejecting H_0. And if it is true that $P = .95$, then in about 99 experiments in 100 we would expect the outcome of the experiment to result in the rejection of H_0.

Suppose we modify the experiment with the psychiatrist by having him presented with three items. He is told that on each trial two of the items will be keyed False and the other True and the task set for him is to select the item keyed True. If he cannot successfully discriminate the True-keyed item from the False-keyed items and responds by chance, we might assume that the probability of a correct response will be 1/3. Then we have a random variable that can take the value $X = 1$, if a correct response is made, or $X = 0$ otherwise, with corresponding probabilities of $P = 1/3$ and $Q = 2/3$. We assume that $P(X = 1) = 1/3$ remains constant for each of the n trials and we propose to use $n = 15$ trials. In this experiment, we will have $2^{15} = 32,768$

---

[4] The probabilities plotted in Figure 9.1 were obtained by finding the probability of $T \geq 8$ correct responses in $n = 10$ trials for each of the values of P given on the base line.

possible outcomes or sample points but the probabilities associated with the sample points will not be equal.[5]

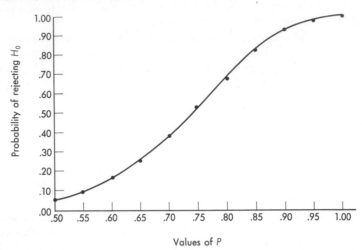

Figure **9.1**—Power function of the one-sided binomial test of the null hypothesis $P = 1/2$ for $n = 10$ trials.

Again, we let T be the number of correct responses in the $n = 15$ trials and T can take values of 15, 14, 13, $\cdots$, 3, 2, 1, or 0. There will be only one sample point corresponding to $T = 15$ and this will be the outcome represented by 111111111111111. Because we assume $P(X = 1) = 1/3$ on each trial and because we assume the n trials are independent, the probability of this outcome will be $P^{15} = (1/3)^{15}$ or, approximately, .00000007. For $T = 14$, we must have 14 values of $X = 1$ and one value of $X = 0$, and the probability of the specific *ordered* outcome 111111111111110 will be $P^{14}Q = (1/3)^{14}(2/3)$ and we note that the probability of this sample point is not the same as the probability associated with the single sample point corresponding to $T = 15$. There will be more than one sample point corresponding to $T = 14$ and the total number will be given by the number of ways in which the 14 values of $X = 1$ and the one value of $X = 0$ can be permuted or

$$\frac{15!}{14!1!} = 15$$

and each of these 15 sample points will involve the product of 14 P's and 1 Q and each will have the same probability $P^{14}Q = (1/3)^{14}(2/3)$. Thus, the probability of $T = 14$ will be equal to

---

[5] It is only in the case of a binomial experiment in which $P(X = 1) = 1/2$ that each of the 2^n sample points will have equal probabilities.

$$P(T = 14) = 15P^{14}Q = 15(1/3)^{14}(2/3)$$

or approximately .00000210.

Similarly, the probability of $T = 13$ will be the sum of the probabilities associated with each of the sample points for which we have 13 values of $X = 1$ and 2 values of $X = 0$. Each of these sample points will involve the product of 13 P's and 2 Q's and each will therefore have probability of $P^{13}Q^2 = (1/3)^{13}(2/3)^2$. The total number of sample points for which we have 13 values of $X = 1$ and 2 values of $X = 0$ will be given by

$$\frac{15!}{13!2!} = 105$$

and the probability of $T = 13$ will be

$$P(T = 13) = 105(1/3)^{13}(2/3)^2$$

or approximately .00002940.

In the same manner, we could find the probabilities associated with each of the other possible values of T. For this experiment we would find that $P(T \geq 9)$ is approximately .03 and $P(T \geq 8)$ is approximately .09. If the observed outcome of the experiment is $T = 9$, then we might decide that this outcome is relatively improbable because only about 3 experiments in 100 would result in $T \geq 9$, as a result of random variation, when the true value of $P = 1/3$. The null hypothesis H_0, that we have tested, is that $P \leq 1/3$ and if we reject H_0, then we are left with the alternative hypothesis H_1 that $P > 1/3$. But if we believe $P > 1/3$, then we must also believe that the psychiatrist is responding to the items on a better than chance basis.

9.9   The Binomial Expansion

You may have noticed that the value of $_nC_r$ gives the coefficient of the $n - r + 1$ term in the binomial expansion of $(P + Q)^n$; that is, $_{10}C_7$, for example, gives the coefficient of the $10 - 7 + 1$ or fourth term of $(P + Q)^{10}$. Expanding we would get

$$(P + Q)^{10} = P^{10} + 10P^9Q + 45P^8Q^2 + 120P^7Q^3 + 210P^6Q^4 + 252P^5Q^5$$
$$+ 210P^4Q^6 + 120P^3Q^7 + 45P^2Q^8 + 10PQ^9 + Q^{10}$$

and

$$_{10}C_7 = \frac{10!}{7!3!} = 120$$

is the coefficient of P^7Q^3.

The exponent of P in each of the terms of the binomial expansion gives the number of correct responses ($X = 1$) and the exponent of Q gives the number of incorrect responses ($X = 0$) and $_nC_r$ gives the number of different arrangements of exactly r values of $X = 1$ and $n - r$ values of $X = 0$. Thus

$$_nC_rP^rQ^{n-r} \tag{9.8}$$

gives the probability of exactly r correct responses and $n - r$ incorrect responses in n binomial trials.[6]

The rules for expanding the binomial $(P + Q)^n$ are summarized below:

1. Each term in the binomial consists of the product of a coefficient and a power of P and a power of Q.

2. The first term always has a coefficient of one which is understood and therefore is not written; the power of P in the first term is always n, and

Table 9.4—The binomial coefficients of $(P + Q)^n$

n	Binomial coefficients										
1						1		1			
2					1		2		1		
3				1		3		3		1	
4			1		4		6		4		1
5		1		5		10		10		5		1
6		1	6		15		20		15		6	1
7	1		7	21		35		35		21	7	1
8	1	8		28	56		70		56	28	8	1
9	1	9	36		84	126		126	84	36	9	1
10	1	10	45	120		210	252	210	120	45	10	1

the power of Q is zero, and Q therefore does not appear; thus the first term is always P^n.

3. In each succeeding term, the power of P decreases by one in regular order, while the power of Q increases by one in regular order, until the final term, Q^n, is reached.

4. The product of the coefficient and the power of P in any given term, divided by one plus the power of Q in that term, will give the coefficient of the term that follows. For example, the coefficient 120, of the fourth term, is obtained by multiplying the coefficient of the third term by its power of P and then dividing by one more than the power of Q. Thus

$$\frac{(45)(8)}{2 + 1} = \frac{360}{3} = 120$$

---

[6] The outcome of any binomial experiment will consist of r values of $X = 1$ and $n - r$ values of $X = 0$. For all such experiments $_nC_r$ is equal to the number of permutations of n objects of which r are alike and $n - r$ are alike, because, in this case, $_nP_{r,(n-r)} = n!/r!(n - r)! = {}_nC_r$.

If you have difficulty in remembering the rules for the binomial expansion, you will find the coefficients for n up to 10 given in Table 9.4. Note that any entry in a given row consists of the sum of the coefficients to the right and left of the entry in the row directly above. Thus the entries for $n = 11$ could be obtained from the entries for $n = 10$. They would be 1, 11, 55, 165, 330, 462, 462, 330, 165, 55, 11, and 1. In this way you can extend Table 9.4 to obtain the binomial coefficients for values of n greater than those given in the table.

The evaluation of the outcomes of binomial experiments by the methods described becomes exceedingly tedious when n is large. There are tables of the binomial probability distribution available for various values of P and for various values of n, but these tables are not always immediately or conveniently available. Fortunately, under certain conditions, which we will discuss later, the binomial probability distribution can be quite satisfactorily approximated by the normal probability distribution.

9.10   The Standard Normal Curve

Any variable that is continuous and normally distributed with $\mu = 0$ and $\sigma = 1$ is called a *standard normal variable*. The distribution of the standard normal variable is given by the equation for the standard normal curve

$$y = \frac{1}{\sqrt{2\pi}} e^{-(1/2)z^2} \tag{9.9}$$

where $y = $ the ordinate of the curve at any given value of z

$\pi = 3.1416$ (rounded), the ratio of the circumference of a circle to its diameter

$e = 2.7183$ (rounded), the base of the system of natural logarithms

$z = $ a continuous variable with $\mu = 0$ and $\sigma = 1$

A variable X with mean equal to μ_X and standard deviation equal to σ_X can be transformed into a new variable z by means of

$$z = \frac{X - \mu_X}{\sigma_X}$$

We have previously shown that $E(X) = \mu_X$ and therefore $E(z) = \mu_z = 0$. Then $\sigma_z^2 = E(z - \mu_z)^2 = E(z^2) = (1/\sigma_X^2)E(X - \mu_X)^2 = \sigma_X^2/\sigma_X^2 = 1$. Furthermore, if X is normally distributed, then z will also be normally distributed and the distribution of z will be given by (9.9).

If $z = (X - \mu_X)/\sigma_X = 0$, then the exponent of e in (9.9) will be equal to zero and we know that any number raised to the zero power is equal to 1. Thus, if we let y_0 be the ordinate of the standard normal curve when $z = 0$, we have

$$y_0 = \frac{1}{\sqrt{2\pi}} = \frac{1}{\sqrt{(2)(3.1416)}} = .3989$$

Now, if you look in the table of the standard normal curve—Table III in Appendix B—to find the value of y tabled there when $z = .00$, you will find that this value is .3989, the value we obtained above. The other entries in the y column of this table may be obtained in exactly the same way by substitution in (9.9) with any given value of z.

Suppose we see what the value of y will be when $z = (X - \mu_X)/\sigma_X = 1.00$. This will correspond to a value of X that is one standard deviation above the mean of X. We know that any number raised to the $-1/2$ power is equal to the reciprocal of the square root of the number. Thus, if we let y_1 be the ordinate corresponding to $z = 1.00$, we have

$$y_1 = \frac{1}{\sqrt{2\pi}} e^{-1/2} = \frac{1}{\sqrt{e}\sqrt{2\pi}} = \frac{1}{\sqrt{2.7183}\sqrt{2(3.1416)}} = .2420$$

Again, if we enter the table of the standard normal distribution with $z = 1.00$, we find .2420 tabled in the y column opposite this value. The value .2420 is the ordinate of the standard normal curve at a distance one standard deviation above the mean. From the equation of the curve, it is obvious that, because z is squared, we shall also obtain a value of y equal to .2420 when $z = -1.00$. The curve, as we now can see, must be symmetrical, because the ordinate of any given negative value of z will be exactly equal to the ordinate for the corresponding positive value of z.

It is not obvious but it is true that the area under the curve defined by (9.9) is equal to 1. Because the area under the curve is equal to 1, the area between any two ordinates corresponding to any two values of z will be a proportion of the total area. Similarly, the area falling to the right of an ordinate corresponding to any given value of z will be a proportion of the total area. And, the area falling to the left of an ordinate corresponding to any value of z will also be a proportion of the total area.

As we have pointed out before, column (1) of Table III gives values of z to two decimal places in units of .01. Column (2) gives the proportion of the total area between the mean $\mu_z = 0$, and a given value of z. Column (3) gives the proportion of the total area in the larger segment of the curve when the curve is divided at the ordinate corresponding to a given value of z, and column (4) gives the proportion of the total area in the smaller segment. Column (5) gives the values of the ordinates of the curve at the corresponding values of z.

9.11   Continuous Variables and Probabilities

Suppose that in an experiment the dependent variable is the time required by an individual to make a response when presented with a given stimulus. Time is generally regarded as a continuous variable but, as we have pointed out previously, all recorded or observed measurements of continuous variables are, in fact, discrete. We shall regard all measurements of continuous variables, therefore, as representing intervals ranging from one-half unit below up to one-half unit above the recorded value. If observed values of time are in terms of seconds, then a given value such as 5 seconds will be regarded as representing an interval ranging from 4.5 seconds up to 5.5 seconds. If our measurements are in terms of tenths of a second, then an observed value of 5.1 seconds will be regarded as representing an interval ranging from 5.05 seconds up to 5.15 seconds.

In assigning probabilities to values of a variable that is continuous, we shall assign the probabilities to the intervals represented by the observed discrete values. Thus, if X is the random variable time recorded in terms of seconds, we shall regard such probabilities as $P(4.5 \leq X < 5.5)$, and $P(X \geq 4.5)$ or $P(X < 4.5)$ as meaningful.

If all observed values of continuous variables are, in fact, discrete, then why should we be concerned with continuous variables? One reason is that if X is a continuous and normally distributed random variable, then we can conveniently and quickly determine such probabilities as: $P(X \geq 4.5)$, $P(X < 4.5)$, or $P(4.5 \leq X < 5.5)$ from a table of the standard normal curve, even though our observed values are discrete. The reason why we can do this is that the area under the standard normal curve is equal to 1. Thus the area under the standard normal curve corresponds to a sample space S for a discrete variable for which $P(S) = 1$ also. If X is a random normal variable, with known standard deviation σ_X and mean μ_X, then the $P(X \geq 4.5)$ will be given by the area falling to the right of

$$z = \frac{4.5 - \mu_X}{\sigma_X}$$

in the standard normal curve.

Furthermore, the probability distributions of certain functions of variables that are known, in fact, to be discrete can in many cases be *approximated* quite satisfactorily by means of the table of the standard normal curve. For example, although it is not too tedious to calculate the probability distribution of T, the number of correct responses in a set of $n = 10$ binomial trials with $P = 1/2$, it would certainly be tedious to do so if the number of trials were increased to $n = 100$. Yet, in this instance, the probability distribution of T can be approximated very well by means of the standard normal curve.

9.12   The Mean and Variance of the Binomial Distribution and of T

If X is a discrete random variable that can take the value of $X = 1$ with probability P and the value of $X = 0$ with probability $Q = 1 - P$, then

$$E(X) = P(1) + Q(0)$$
$$= P \qquad (9.10)$$

or

$$\mu_X = P$$

We also have

$$E(X^2) = P(1^2) + Q(0^2) = P$$

Then

$$\sigma_X{}^2 = E(X^2) - \mu_X{}^2$$
$$= P - P^2$$

or

$$\sigma_X{}^2 = PQ \qquad (9.11)$$

Let T be the sum of $X_1 + X_2 + X_3 + \cdots + X_n$ independent random variables, each with the same mean $\mu_X = P$, and the same variance $\sigma_X{}^2 = PQ$. Then we have

$$E(T) = E(X_1 + X_2 + X_3 + \cdots + X_n)$$

or

$$\mu_T = nP \qquad (9.12)$$

The variance $\sigma_T{}^2$ of a sum of n independent random variables, each with the same variance $\sigma_X{}^2$, will be

$$\sigma_T{}^2 = n\sigma_X{}^2$$

In the present case we have $\sigma_X{}^2 = PQ$, so that

$$\sigma_T{}^2 = nPQ$$

and

$$\sigma_T = \sqrt{nPQ} \qquad (9.13)$$

If T is approximately normally distributed, then

$$z = \frac{T - \mu_T}{\sigma_T}$$

will also be approximately normally distributed. We note that

$$E(z) = \mu_z = \frac{1}{\sigma_T} E(T - \mu_T) = 0$$

and

$$\sigma_z^2 = E(z - \mu_z)^2$$
$$= E(z^2)$$
$$= \frac{1}{\sigma_T^2} E(T - \mu_T)^2$$

But, $E(T - \mu_T)^2 = \sigma_T^2$ and therefore

$$\sigma_z^2 = 1 \quad \text{and} \quad \sigma_z = 1$$

9.13   The Normal Approximation of the Probability Distribution of T

We have said previously that the probability distributions of discrete random variables can, in many cases, be approximated by means of the normal probability distribution. We consider first the experiment in which the psychiatrist was given $n = 10$ trials and in which we assumed the probability of a correct response on each trial was $P = 1/2$.

Figure 9.2 is a histogram for the probability distribution of T. We have used a unit interval on the base line because, although the values of T are discrete, we may assume that $T = 8$, for example, represents an interval ranging from 7.5 up to 8.4999 $\cdots$ which is approximately equal to an interval of unity. The ordinates in Figure 9.2 correspond to the probabilities associated with each value of T. For example, we previously found that $P(T = 8)$ was approximately .044. Then the area of the rectangle corresponding to $T = 8$ will be approximately $1 \times .044 = .044$. Similarly, the areas of each of the other rectangles correspond approximately to the probabilities of each of the other values of T and the total area of the histogram will be approximately 1. Then $P(T \geq 8)$ will be given by the sum of the areas to the right of 7.5 or the sum of the areas of the last three rectangles in the histogram. We have previously found $P(T \geq 8)$ to be approximately .055 and that is the area under the histogram to the right of 7.5 on the base line.

For the distribution of T with $n = 10$ and $P = 1/2$ we have

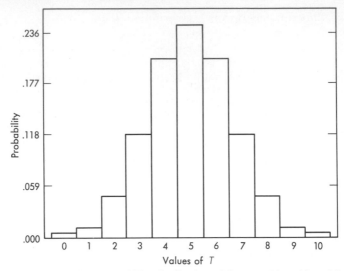

Figure **9.2**—Histogram of the probability distribution of the sum T for a binomial experiment with $P = 1/2$ and $n = 10$ trials.

$$\mu_T = nP = 10(1/2) = 5$$

and

$$\sigma_T = \sqrt{nPQ} = \sqrt{10(1/2)(1/2)} = 1.581$$

Suppose now that a continuous normal distribution with the same mean, $\mu = 5$, and the same standard deviation, $\sigma = 1.581$, were imposed over the histogram of Figure 9.2. For this continuous normal distribution suppose we want to find the probability of the interval 7.5 up to 8.5. To do this we need to know the area under the normal curve corresponding to this interval. To make use of the table of the standard normal curve, we transform 7.5 and 8.5 into standard normal deviates. Thus

$$z = \frac{7.5 - 5.0}{1.581} = 1.58$$

and

$$z = \frac{8.5 - 5.0}{1.581} = 2.21$$

Entering the table of the standard normal curve with $z = 1.58$, we find that .0571 of the total area falls to the right of this value and similarly we find that .0136 falls to the right of $z = 2.21$. Then the proportion of the total area corresponding to the interval 7.5 to 8.5 will be $.0571 - .0136 = .0435$. We note that the probability of this interval, obtained from the standard normal curve, is .0435 and is a quite accurate approximation of the probability .044 of the discrete value of $T = 8$ obtained from the binomial probability distribution.

Similarly we note that the proportion of the total area falling to the right of 7.5 in a normal curve with $\mu = 5$ and $\sigma = 1.581$ is the area to the right of $z = 1.581$ and this is equal to .0571. We have already observed that the proportion of the total area to the right of 7.5 in the histogram of Figure 9.1 is .055. Again, we find that the normal approximation of this area is fairly satisfactory.

In the second experiment with the psychiatrist, we had $n = 15$ trials, with $P = 1/3$. Using the binomial probability distribution, we would find that $P(T \geq 9)$ is approximately .031. Let us see how well we can approximate this probability in terms of a normal distribution with the same mean and standard deviation as the distribution of T. For the T distribution, we have

$$\mu_T = nP = 15(1/3) = 5$$

and

$$\sigma_T = \sqrt{nPQ} = \sqrt{15(1/3)(2/3)} = 1.826$$

The lower limit of $T = 9$ is 8.5 and we want to find the proportion of the total area in the normal distribution falling to the right of 8.5. Then

$$z = \frac{8.5 - 5.0}{1.826} = 1.92$$

From the table of the standard normal curve we find that .027 of the total area is to the right of $z = 1.92$. Thus, the standard normal curve gives .027 as an estimate of $P(T \geq 9)$, whereas the corresponding estimate obtained from the binomial distribution is .031. We see in this case that the normal approximation of the binomial probability is also not too inaccurate.

In general, if nP and nQ are both equal to or greater than 5, then the probabilities obtained from the standard normal distribution will approximate those of the binomial distribution fairly well. This rule should be regarded as setting a *minimum* value for n. If we require that nP and nQ both be equal to or greater than 10, then the approximation of the binomial probabilities by means of the standard normal distribution will be better than if we require that both nP and nQ be equal to or greater than 5.

EXAMPLES

9.1—A student claims that he can detect a difference in taste between two brands of a popular drink. This claim is put to test by presenting him with two cups, one cup containing Brand A, the other Brand B. The student is asked to tell which of the two cups contains Brand A. Care is taken to control various factors other than taste that might influence his choice. The student is given $n = 12$ trials. Assume that the probability of a correct choice is $1/2$ on each trial. Use the binomial distribution to find:

(a) The probability of exactly 12 correct choices.
(b) The probability of exactly 9 correct choices.
(c) The probability of 9 or more correct choices.

9.2—Note that both nP and nQ are greater than 5 in Example 9.1. For Example 9.1, use the table of the standard normal curve to find:

(a) The probability of 12 correct choices.
(b) The probability of 9 correct choices.
(c) The probability of 9 or more correct choices.
(d) Compare the probabilities obtained from the standard normal distribution with those obtained from the binomial distribution.

9.3—In a taste discrimination problem, pats of margarine and butter are presented in pairs to a subject. The subject is asked to taste both and then to decide which is butter. Care is taken to control various factors other than taste that might influence the subject's choice. The subject is given $n = 16$ trials. Assume that the probability of a correct choice on each trial is $1/2$. Use the table of the standard normal curve to find the probability of 12 or more correct choices.

9.4—In an experiment similar to the one described in Example 9.3, a subject is presented with frozen orange juice, fresh orange juice, and canned orange juice. The subject is asked to judge which of the three is fresh orange juice. We shall assume that factors other than taste are controlled and that the probability of a correct choice is $1/3$ on each trial.

(a) What is the *minimum* number of trials we should use if the table of the standard normal curve is to be used in evaluating the outcome of the experiment?
(b) If $n = 18$ trials are given, what is the probability of 10 or more correct choices?
(c) In how many ways can the subject make 16 correct choices in $n = 18$ trials?
(d) Without actually doing the calculations, write the term in the binomial expansion that would give the probability of exactly 14 correct choices in $n = 18$ trials.

9.5—Five unbiased coins are tossed. We assume that for each coin the probability of heads is $1/2$.

(a)   What is the probability that at least two (there may be more than two) of the coins will show heads?
(b)   What is the probability that exactly two of them will show heads?

9.6—A student takes a multiple-choice test of six items. Each item has four alternatives.

(a)   What is the probability that he will get a score of six correct, if he has to guess on each item?
(b)   What is the probability that he will get a score of five or higher, if he has to guess on each item?

9.7—Suppose that a student takes a True-False test consisting of eight items and that he answers each item by flipping an unbiased coin, that is, by chance.

(a)   What is the probability of his getting a score of eight correct?
(b)   What is the probability of his getting a score of six or more correct?

9.8—Six men and three women volunteer to serve in an experiment.

(a)   In how many ways can a group of three be chosen from the group of nine?
(b)   In how many ways can a group of three be chosen from the group of six men?
(c)   What is the probability that, if three are selected at random from the group of nine, the three selected will all be men?

9.9—We have a set of five pictures of children who are superior in intelligence and a set of five pictures of children who are inferior in intelligence. The children are all males, of the same age, and dressed in the same clothes.

(a)   In how many ways can a set of five pictures be selected from the group of 10?
(b)   If a judge is asked to select the five pictures of children with superior intelligence, what is the probability of five correct selections on the basis of chance alone?

9.10—We have a binomial experiment with $P = 1/2$ and with $n = 100$ trials. We let T be the number of correct responses in the set of 100 trials. Find the value of μ_T and $\sigma_T{}^2$.

9.11—Three different cola drinks were presented to each of 105 subjects. The subjects were asked to identify Brand A in the set of three brands presented. The complete study is described by Pronko and Herman (1950). Assume that the probability of a correct identification for each student is 1/3.

(a) How many of the 105 subjects would we expect to make a correct identification on the basis of chance alone?
(b) It was found that 57 subjects correctly identified Brand A. Is this number significantly greater than chance would indicate? Use the table of the standard normal curve in determining your answer.

9.12—Locke and Grimm (1949) gave 69 subjects perfumer's blotters saturated with a standard strength of perfume solution. Some of the perfumes tested were expensive and others were inexpensive. The subjects were asked to judge whether the blotters were saturated with an expensive or inexpensive brand. In one of the tests an expensive brand was classified correctly by 43 subjects and incorrectly by 26 subjects. Assume that the probability of a correct identification for each subject is 1/2.

(a) For the group tested, what is the expected number (T) of subjects making a correct identification?
(b) What is the value of $\sigma_T{}^2$?
(c) What is the probability of 43 or more subjects making a correct identification on the basis of chance alone? Use the table of the standard normal curve in determining your answer.

9.13—It is found that of 30 rats tested at a choice-point in a T maze that 20 turn right and 10 turn left. If we assume that right and left turns are equally probable, what is the probability of 20 or more rats turning right? Use the table of the standard normal curve in determining your answer.
9.14—Expand the binomial $(1/3 + 2/3)^5$.
9.15—Suppose we have a null hypothesis H_0 that $P = 1/2$ and an alternative hypothesis H_1 that $P = 3/4$, and that we plan to make $n = 25$ independent trials.

(a) Let T_0 be the smallest number of correct discriminations that will result in $z \geq 1.645$. Taking into account the fact that T is discrete, what is the value of T_0?
(b) If we test H_0 and if H_1 is, in fact, true, what is the probability of obtaining T equal to or greater than T_0?

9.16—There are two paths, P_1 and P_2, that a rat may use in going from a starting box to a goal box. Assume that each path has equal probability of being chosen. If 10 rats are run in the maze, find the probability that eight of the rats use one of the two paths and that two rats use the other path.
9.17—A fair die is rolled for 12 times. Let T be the number of 5's obtained in a set of 12 rolls. Find $E(T)$ and $E(T - \mu_T)^2$.

9.18—A fair die is rolled three times. Let T be the sum of the points obtained on the three rolls.

(a) Find the exact probability of $T = 15$. Hint: In how many ways can $T = 15$ occur and what is the probability of each way?
(b) Using the same methods find the probability of $T \geq 15$.
(c) Assume that T is approximately normally distributed. Use the table of the standard normal curve to find $P(T = 15)$.
(d) Find the probability of $T \geq 15$ using the table of the standard normal curve.
(e) Compare the exact probabilities and those obtained from the table of the standard normal curve.

9.19—A random sample of $n = 3$ is selected from A, B, C, D, and E, without replacement.

(a) What is the probability that the sample includes A?
(b) What is the probability that the sample includes both A and B?
(c) What is the probability that the sample includes either A or B or both A and B?

9.20—Prove that if a random sample of n elements is selected without replacement from a set of N elements, that n/N is the probability that a given element will be included in the sample.

9.21—A random sample of $n = 3$ is selected from a group of four girls and six boys. Let X be the number of girls in the sample. Find $E(X)$ and $E(X - \mu_X)^2$.

9.22—Let X be a continuous and normally distributed variable with $\mu_X = 0$ and $\sigma_X = 1.0$. Use the table of the standard normal curve to find:

(a) $P(0 \leq X \leq 1)$
(b) $P(-1 \leq X \leq 1)$
(c) $P(|X| \geq 1.645)$
(d) $P(-3.0 \leq X \leq -2.2)$
(e) $P(|X| \geq 1.96)$

(f) $P(|X| \geq 2.58)$
(g) $P(-2.0 \leq X \leq 2.0)$
(h) $P(-2.2 \leq X \leq -1.2)$
(i) $P(.6 \leq X \leq 1.8)$

9.23—Three vending machines, A, B, and C, are placed next to each other. Five individuals each make a purchase from the machines. Assume that each machine has equal probability of being selected. Find the probability that two coins are placed in each of two machines and one coin in the other.

9.24—A box contains three red and two black marbles. Five players, A, B, C, D, and E draw a marble from the box in turn and without replacement. If a player draws a red marble he wins a prize. If the draws are random, show that each player has equal probability of winning a prize.

CHAPTER 10

The t Test for Means

10.1 Selecting a Random Sample

In an introductory psychology course at a university, 100 students are enrolled. For each student we have available a score, X, on a mid-term test. We shall regard these 100 scores as a population.[1] A teaching assistant has scored the test papers and calculated the population mean μ and the population standard deviation σ. He has not, however, made these scores available to us and in fact we do not know the value of any one of the 100 observations of X. To identify the 100 observations, the teaching assistant has arranged them in order of value from highest to lowest and then assigned the numbers 00, 01, 02, $\cdots$, 99 to the observations. The fact that the highest score has been assigned the identifying number 99, the next highest 98, and so on, is unimportant, and furthermore is unknown to us. The teaching assistant could have just as well arranged the test papers alphabetically and then assigned the identifying numbers. Or he could have assigned the identifying numbers in any other manner just so long as each observation is identified by a two-digit number that is different from the numbers assigned to any other observation.

From the population of $N = 100$ observations, we propose to select a sample of $n = 25$. In doing so, we have our choice between two methods of sampling. We might, for example, select the sample of n without replacement. In this method of sampling, the finite population of N would be exhausted if we selected a sample of $n = N$ observations. We choose, however, to sample with replacement. This is to say that after the selection of the first observation it is replaced and the second selection is made from the complete

---

[1] The values of the 100 scores are given in Example 10.13 at the end of the chapter.

set of 100. Similarly, we replace the second observation before selecting the third, and so on. This method of sampling is called *sampling with replacement* and simulates sampling from an infinite population. Because we replace the observation after each draw, we can never exhaust the population no matter how large a sample of n we choose to draw.

If we select a sample of $n = 25$ from $N = 100$ with replacement, we have the possibility of obtaining any one of 100^{25} samples because on each of the 25 draws we may obtain any one of the 100 observations. We want to draw the sample in such a way that each observation, not value of X, has equal probability of being selected. One way in which we might do this would be to have the teaching assistant put the identifying numbers $00, 01, 02, \cdots, 99$ on disks and then to place the 100 disks in a box. We shake the box thoroughly, select a disk, and record the identifying number. We replace the disk, shake the box, select a second disk, and record the identifying number. We continue in this way until we have selected a sample of $n = 25$. We assume that with this method of sampling each of the 100 observations has probability of $1/N$ or $1/100$ of being selected on each draw.

The probability that a specified observation will *not* be selected on a given draw will be 99/100. If a specified observation is *not included in the sample*, then it will have to be *not selected* on each of the $n = 25$ draws. Because the selections are independent, the probability of not obtaining a specified observation on any one of the 25 draws will be $(99/100)^{25}$ and this is the probability that the specified observation will not be included in the sample. Therefore, the *probability that the sample includes the specified observation* will be

$$1 - (99/100)^{25}$$

Instead of recording the 100 identifying numbers on disks and drawing the sample in the manner described above, we can accomplish the same objective by making use of a table of random numbers. Tables of random numbers are generated by a random process that we have reason to believe assigns equal probabilities of $1/10$ to the selection of the digits, $0, 1, 2, 3, \cdots, 9$. Table I in Appendix B is a table of random numbers arranged in five blocks of 25 rows and 40 columns each. Because all of the numbers in this table were generated by a random process, any two digits, $00, 01, 02, 03, \cdots, 99$, in a column or row correspond to two-digit random numbers with equal probabilities of $1/100$. To make use of the table of random numbers, we need to select a block at random, a row at random, and a column at random. This can be accomplished by taking 40 cards from a bridge deck and numbering the cards $00, 01, 02, 03, \cdots, 39$. We shuffle the deck and then turn the cards face up until we obtain one of the two-digit numbers $01, 02, 03, 04,$ or 05. The first one of these numbers to appear will give us the block to enter. We can repeat the process to obtain a two-digit number to give the row of the block and then again to obtain a two-digit number for the column. By means of this process, we obtained 03 for the block, 02 for the row, and 20 for the column. Because we need two-digit numbers we read down columns 20–21, starting in row 02, of the third block of numbers. The first 25 random numbers obtained from the table are recorded in Table 10.1. You will note that two of the observations, 27 and 72, were each selected twice in the sample of $n = 25$. If we had been sampling without replacement, we would have ignored or skipped 27 or 72 the second time they appeared in the table of random numbers and

Table 10.1—The first 25 random numbers obtained reading down in block 03, row 02, and columns 20–21 of Table I, in Appendix B, and the values of X for the observations with these numbers

Random numbers	Values of X	Random numbers	Values of X
40	59	72	65
54	60	89	73
24	54	03	38
80	68	98	85
43	59	78	67
58	61	60	62
27	55	18	52
38	58	72	65
68	64	06	45
82	69	96	78
36	58	27	55
87	71	01	35
16	51		

continued reading in the table until we obtained 25 different two-digit numbers.

10.2   The Standard Error of the Mean of a Random Sample

Having selected our 25 observations, we now ask the teaching assistant to give us the values of X for the 25 observations. These values are also given in Table 10.1. For our sample, we then calculate the sample mean and the sum of the squared deviations from the mean. We have

$$\sum X = 59 + 60 + 54 + \cdots + 35 = 1507$$

and

$$\sum X^2 = (59)^2 + (60)^2 + (54)^2 + \cdots + (35)^2 = 93,919$$

Then

$$\bar{X} = \frac{\sum X}{n} = \frac{1507}{25} = 60.28$$

and

$$\sum (X - \bar{X})^2 = \sum X^2 - \frac{(\sum X)^2}{n}$$

$$= 93,919 - \frac{(1507)^2}{25}$$

$$= 3077.04$$

Then the sample variance will be

$$s^2 = \frac{\sum (X - \bar{X})^2}{n - 1} = \frac{3077.04}{25 - 1} = 128.21$$

and for the sample standard deviation we have $s = \sqrt{128.21} = 11.32$.

If the experiment described were repeated a large number of times, say k times, then for each of the k experiments, we could calculate the sample mean. We know that these k means will be subject to random variation. We could find the mean of all of the k sample means and then find the deviation of each of the sample means from this value. If we squared these deviations and divided the sum of the squared deviations by $k - 1$, we would have a measure of the variability of means, called the *variance of the mean*. The square root of the variance of the mean would be the standard deviation of the mean and this standard deviation is called the standard error of the mean. The *standard error of the mean* measures the variation in a distribution of means and can be interpreted in the same manner as the standard deviation of the individual values of X.

We have not repeated the experiment a large number of times. We can, however, use our single sample to obtain an estimate of the standard error of the mean. For a single random sample, the variance of the mean is estimated by

$$s_{\bar{X}}^2 = \frac{s^2}{n} \tag{10.1}$$

and the standard error of the mean by

$$s_{\bar{X}} = \frac{s}{\sqrt{n}} \tag{10.2}$$

where s is the sample standard deviation and n is the number of observations in the sample. For the experiment under discussion, we have $s = 11.32$, $n = 25$, and therefore

$$s_{\bar{X}} = \frac{11.32}{\sqrt{25}} = 2.264$$

It is obvious from (10.2) that the standard error of the mean can be made smaller by increasing n. For example, if we had selected a sample of $n = 100$ observations and if for this sample $s = 11.32$, then the standard error of the mean would be $s_{\bar{X}} = 11.32/\sqrt{100} = 1.132$ or one half the value obtained with a sample of $n = 25$ observations.

10.3   Unbiased Estimates of μ, σ^2, and $\sigma_{\bar{X}}^2$

Before considering a sample space for the experiment described, we first show that the sample values $\bar{X}$, s^2, and $s_{\bar{X}}^2$ are unbiased estimates of the corresponding population parameters, μ, σ^2, and $\sigma_{\bar{X}}^2$.

We have previously shown that if we draw a random sample of n from a common population, then

$$E\left(\frac{\sum_{1}^{n} X}{n}\right) = \frac{1}{n} E(X_1 + X_2 + \cdots + X_n)$$

$$= \mu$$

so that the mean, $\bar{X} = 60.28$, of our sample is an unbiased estimate of μ.

We have also shown that

$$E(X^2) - \mu^2 = \sigma^2$$

so that

$$E(X^2) = \sigma^2 + \mu^2$$

If we have n random variables each with the same mean μ and the same variance σ^2, then

$$E\left(\sum_{1}^{n} X^2\right) = E(X_1^2 + X_2^2 + \cdots + X_n^2) \qquad (10.3)$$

$$= n(\sigma^2 + \mu^2)$$

Now consider the expected value of the square of the sum of these n random variables or

$$E\left[\left(\sum_{1}^{n} X\right)^2\right] = E[(X_1 + X_2 + \cdots + X_n)^2]$$

and we note that $(X_1 + X_2 + \cdots + X_n)^2$ expanded will result in n^2 terms of which there will be n terms corresponding to $X_1^2, X_2^2, \cdots, X_n^2$ and the expected value of each of these terms will be $\sigma^2 + \mu^2$. We will also have $n^2 - n = n(n - 1)$ cross product terms of $X_i X_j$ where $i \neq j$. We assume that the n random variables are independent and we have previously shown that if this is the case then

$$E(X_i X_j) = \mu_i \mu_j$$

But we have $\mu_i = \mu_j$ so that each of the $n(n - 1)$ values of $X_i X_j$ has expectation μ^2. Thus

$$E\left[\left(\sum_1^n X\right)^2\right] = n(\sigma^2 + \mu^2) + n(n - 1)\mu^2 \tag{10.4}$$

From (10.4) we can obtain the expected value of the correction term. Thus

$$E\left[\frac{\left(\sum_1^n X\right)^2}{n}\right] = \frac{1}{n} E\left[\left(\sum_1^n X\right)^2\right]$$
$$= \sigma^2 + \mu^2 + (n - 1)\mu^2$$
$$= \sigma^2 + n\mu^2 \tag{10.5}$$

Then

$$E\left[\sum_1^n X^2 - \frac{\left(\sum_1^n X\right)^2}{n}\right] = n(\sigma^2 + \mu^2) - (\sigma^2 + n\mu^2)$$

or

$$E\left[\sum_1^n (X - \bar{X})^2\right] = (n - 1)\sigma^2 \tag{10.6}$$

Now if we divide the left side of (10.6) by $n - 1$, before taking the expectation, we see that

$$E\left[\frac{\sum_1^n (X - \bar{X})^2}{n - 1}\right] = \sigma^2 \tag{10.7}$$

and the long-run average value of the sample variance s^2 will be equal to σ^2. Similarly, we have

$$E(s_{\bar{X}}^2) = E\left(\frac{s^2}{n}\right) = \frac{1}{n} E(s^2) = \frac{\sigma^2}{n} = \sigma_{\bar{X}}^2 \tag{10.8}$$

and the long-run average value of $s_{\bar{X}}^2$ will be equal to $\sigma_{\bar{X}}^2$.

For any single random sample of n independent observations of a variable X, the sample mean $\overline{X}$ is said to be an unbiased estimate of μ. The sample estimate is described as *unbiased* because in the long run the average value of the estimate $\overline{X}$ will be equal to μ. We have also seen that the sample variance s^2 is an unbiased estimate of σ^2 and that $s_{\overline{X}}^2$ is an unbiased estimate of $\sigma_{\overline{X}}^2$.

10.4   The t Distribution

If our method of sampling is random and if we sample with replacement, then the sample space for our experiment will consist of 100^{25} sample points, each with probability of $1/100^{25}$. We cannot list these sample points but we shall assume that the outcome of the experiment of interest is $\overline{X}$ and that the distribution of $\overline{X}$ is approximately that of a random normal variable. If σ were known, then $\sigma_{\overline{X}} = \sigma/n$ would also be known. If we also knew the value of μ, then we could obtain

$$z = \frac{\overline{X} - \mu}{\sigma_{\overline{X}}} \qquad (10.9)$$

and z would be a standard normal variable. We could then use the table of the standard normal curve to find such probabilities as: $P(\overline{X} \geq 60)$, $P(\overline{X} \leq 50)$, and $P(50 \leq \overline{X} \leq 60)$.

Although $\sigma_{\overline{X}}$ is not known, we do have $s_{\overline{X}}$ as an estimate of $\sigma_{\overline{X}}$. We define

$$t = \frac{\overline{X} - \mu}{s_{\overline{X}}} \qquad (10.10)$$

The distribution of t is also given by a curve and the area under the curve is equal to 1. The difference between t as defined by (10.10) and z as defined by (10.9) is that z involves a known parameter σ whereas the distribution of t involves a sample estimate s of σ.

As n increases, the limiting form of the t distribution is that of the standard normal distribution. For the standard normal curve the ordinate at $z = 1.96$ will cut off .025 of the total area in the right tail. To cut off .025 of the total area under the t curve in the right tail, when we have $n = 10$ observations, we must have $t = 2.262$. With $n = 25$ observations, the ordinate at $t = 2.064$ will cut off .025 of the total area in the right tail. With $n = 400$, the ordinate at $t = 1.966$ will cut off .025 of the total area in the right tail. With large samples of $n \geq 500$, the distribution of t may be assumed to be approximately that of z.

To make use of the table of t, Table V in Appendix B, we need to know the number of *degrees of freedom* (d.f.) associated with t. The t of (10.10) has $n - 1$ d.f. or one less than the total number of observations. The number of degrees of freedom for t are given by the denominator of $\Sigma (X - \overline{X})^2/(n - 1)$. Because $\Sigma (X - \overline{X}) = 0$, only $n - 1$ of the deviations are free to vary and therefore $\Sigma (X - \overline{X})^2$ has only $n - 1$ d.f. If μ were known, then we could calculate $\Sigma (X - \mu)^2/n$ as an estimate of σ^2. For any set of n observations, we know that $\Sigma (X - \overline{X})^2$ is at a minimum and therefore will be smaller than $\Sigma (X - \mu)^2$ except in the unusual case when a given sample happens to result in $\overline{X} = \mu$. Division of $\Sigma (X - \overline{X})^2$ by n, therefore, would, in general, provide a biased *underestimate* of σ^2. By dividing the sum of squared deviations from the sample mean by its degrees of freedom, $n - 1$, we have seen that we obtain an unbiased estimate of σ^2.

We can substitute in (10.10) with the observed value of a sample mean $\overline{X}$, the observed value of the standard error of the mean $s_{\overline{X}}$, and with any value we choose for μ. Then t will provide a test of the null hypothesis that μ is equal to the value we substituted. If the null hypothesis is true, then the long-run average or expected value of t will be zero and the distribution of t will be symmetrical about this value. Thus the table of t can be used to find the probability of t equal to or greater than the observed value or equal to or less than the observed value, when the null hypothesis is true. For example, suppose we test the null hypothesis $H_0: \mu = 50$. Then for the sample of $n = 25$ with $\overline{X} = 60.28$ and $s_{\overline{X}} = 2.264$, we have

$$t = \frac{60.28 - 50}{2.264} = 4.54.$$

with $n - 1$ or 24 d.f. Entering the table of t with 24 d.f., we find that $P(t \geq 4.54)$ is less than .005, because $t = 2.797$ will cut off .005 of the total area in the right tail when the null hypothesis is true. It would appear highly improbable, therefore, that $\mu = 50$ because if this were the true population mean, then we would obtain samples with $\overline{X} \geq 60.28$ very infrequently as a result of random variation.

10.5   Confidence Interval for the Mean

Instead of testing any number of different null hypotheses about μ and finding out whether or not each one is tenable, we make use of an *interval estimate*. Let us set up the inequality

$$-t \leq \frac{\overline{X} - \mu}{s_{\overline{X}}} \leq t \tag{10.11}$$

where $-t$ is the tabled value that will cut off .025 of the area in the left tail and t is the value that will cut off .025 of the area in the right tail for a specified number of degrees of freedom. Entering the table of t with 24 d.f., we find that these two values are -2.064 and 2.064 because, as we have pointed out previously, the distribution of t is symmetrical. Then from (10.11) we obtain

$$\overline{X} + ts_{\overline{x}} \geq \mu \geq \overline{X} - ts_{\overline{x}} \tag{10.12}$$

and substituting $\overline{X} = 60.28$, $s_{\overline{x}} = 2.264$, and $t = 2.064$, we have

$$60.28 + (2.064)(2.264) \geq \mu \geq 60.28 - (2.064)(2.264)$$
$$64.95 \geq \mu \geq 55.61$$

The interval 55.61 to 64.95 that we have just found is called a *confidence interval* and the limits of the interval are called *confidence limits*. In our example, we have found a 95 percent confidence interval. How do we interpret this interval? Suppose we make the statement that μ falls within the interval.[2] If the interval contains μ, then the statement is certainly correct. On the other hand, if the interval does not contain μ, then the statement is

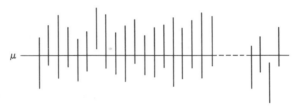

Figure **10.1**—Illustration of the 95 percent confidence limits. The horizontal line represents the fixed value of the population mean μ. Varying values of the lower confidence limit and the upper confidence limit, in successive random samples, are represented by the lower and upper end points, respectively, of the vertical lines. It is assumed that in the long run, 95 percent of the vertical lines will contain the parameter μ.

certainly wrong. In this instance, we can find out whether the statement is right or wrong because the teaching assistant knows the value of μ. In general, however, we do not know the value of μ.

Confidence intervals are statistics and like all other statistics are subject to random variation. If the experiment is repeated a second time, we may have a different value for $\overline{X}$ and a different value for $s_{\overline{x}}$ as a result of random variation and consequently a different 95 percent confidence interval. If for this second experiment we make the statement that the 95 percent confidence interval contains μ, this particular statement will also be either right or wrong. If the experiment were repeated an indefinitely large number of times, then in the long run we would expect .95 of all such statements to be correct and .05 to be incorrect.

The kind of inference we may make in terms of confidence intervals is illustrated in Figure 10.1. We regard the population mean as having a fixed value equal to μ. This value is represented by the horizontal line in the figure. We draw a random sample from the population and calculate a 95 percent confidence interval. The confidence intervals established by successive ran-

---

[2] If you calculate the mean for the 100 scores in Example 10.13, you will find that it does fall within the confidence interval.

dom samples are indicated by the vertical lines in the figure. The end points of these lines represent the lower and upper confidence limits of the various confidence intervals as established from the data of each of the various random samples. We may note that a majority of the confidence intervals contain μ, that is, the population mean is within the limits of the interval. If we had a large number of samples, each with its own 95 percent confidence limits, then our expectation is that .95 of these intervals would contain μ and .05 would not.

Suppose we want more than .95 of our statements about μ to be correct. For example, suppose we want .99 of our statements about μ to be correct in the long run. Then we may establish a 99 percent confidence interval. From the table of *t* we find that .005 of the area will fall to the left of $t = -2.797$ and .005 to the right of $t = 2.797$, when we have 24 d.f. Then we have

$$60.28 + (2.797)(2.264) \geq \mu \geq 60.28 - (2.797)(2.264)$$
$$66.61 \geq \mu \geq 53.95$$

as the limits of our 99 percent confidence interval. In the long run we may expect .99 of our statements about μ, based upon a 99 percent confidence interval, to be correct.

10.6   The *t* Test for the Difference between Two Means

Suppose that there is another class of 100 students enrolled in the same course at the same university and that these students have been given the same test as the first class. We shall also regard these 100 observations of X for the second class as a population. The teaching assistant has scored the test and he knows for this population the values of μ and σ, but we do not. He, not we, now selects two random samples in the manner described previously and gives us the values of X for each of the $n = 25$ observations in each sample. He tells us that he has either: (1) selected two random samples from the first population; (2) selected two random samples from the second population; or (3) selected one random sample from the first population and the other from the second population. Our task is to decide on the basis of the evidence from the two samples whether they have been drawn from the same or from different populations.

We shall assume that one of the samples has the same value of $\bar{X} = 60.28$, $\Sigma (X - \bar{X})^2 = 3077.04$, and $s^2 = 128.21$. For the other sample we find that $\bar{X} = 51.12$, $\Sigma (X - \bar{X})^2 = 2986.96$, and therefore $s^2 = 124.46$. To distinguish between the two samples, we use subscripts. For example, we let $\bar{X}_1$ indicate the mean of the first sample and $\bar{X}_2$ the mean of the second sample. For the moment we shall assume that the difference between $s_1^2 = 128.21$ and $s_2^2 = 124.46$ is sufficiently small that it can be attributed to random variation in sampling from the same population or from two populations with different means but with the same variance σ^2. Later we shall discuss a test of significance of this hypothesis and show that it is tenable.

Assuming that s_1^2 and s_2^2 are both estimates of the same population variance σ^2, our best single estimate of σ^2 will be[3]

$$s^2 = \frac{(n_1 - 1)s_1^2 + (n_2 - 1)s_2^2}{(n_1 - 1) + (n_2 - 1)}$$

$$= \frac{\sum x_1^2 + \sum x_2^2}{n_1 + n_2 - 2} \tag{10.13}$$

where $\sum x_1^2$ is the sum of the n_1 squared deviations in Sample 1 about the mean of Sample 1 and $\sum x_2^2$ is the sum of the n_2 squared deviations in Sample 2 about the mean of Sample 2. For reasons discussed previously, this estimate of σ^2 will have $n_1 + n_2 - 2$ d.f. For the two samples under consideration, we have

$$s^2 = \frac{3077.04 + 2986.96}{25 + 25 - 2} = 126.33$$

We need, first, to obtain an estimate of the variability of the difference between the means of two independent random samples. We have previously shown that the variance of the difference between two independent variables is given by

$$\sigma_{X_1 - X_2}^2 = \sigma_1^2 + \sigma_2^2$$

and if $\sigma_1^2 = \sigma_2^2 = \sigma^2$, then $\sigma_{X_1 - X_2}^2 = 2\sigma^2$. Similarly, if $\overline{X}_1$ and $\overline{X}_2$ are the means of two independent random samples, then the variance of the difference between the means will be given by

$$\sigma_{\overline{X}_1 - \overline{X}_2}^2 = \sigma_{\overline{X}_1}^2 + \sigma_{\overline{X}_2}^2$$

$$= \frac{\sigma_1^2}{n_2} + \frac{\sigma_2^2}{n_2} \tag{10.14}$$

and, if $\sigma_1^2 = \sigma_2^2 = \sigma^2$, then

$$\sigma_{\overline{X}_1 - \overline{X}_2}^2 = \frac{2\sigma^2}{n} \tag{10.15}$$

where $n = n_1 = n_2$.

We do not know the value of σ^2, but under the assumption that s_1^2 and s_2^2 do not differ significantly, our best estimate of σ^2 is given by (10.13).

---

[3] To see that (10.13) is an unbiased estimate of σ^2, we have

$$E(s^2) = \frac{(n_1 - 1)\sigma^2 + (n_2 - 1)\sigma^2}{n_1 + n_2 - 2} = \sigma^2$$

Then we have as an estimate of the variance of the difference between the means of two independent random samples, with $n_1 = n_2 = n$,

$$s_{\overline{X}_1 - \overline{X}_2}^2 = \frac{2s^2}{n} \qquad (10.16)$$

where s^2 is given by (10.13). The standard error of the difference between the means will then be[4]

$$s_{\overline{X}_1 - \overline{X}_2} = \sqrt{\frac{2s^2}{n}} \qquad (10.17)$$

For the two samples under consideration we have $s^2 = 126.33$ and $n_1 = n_2 = n = 25$. Substituting with these values in (10.17), we have

$$s_{\overline{X}_1 - \overline{X}_2} = \sqrt{\frac{2(126.33)}{25}} = 3.17$$

We now define

$$t = \frac{(\overline{X}_1 - \overline{X}_2) - (\mu_1 - \mu_2)}{s_{\overline{X}_1 - \overline{X}_2}} \qquad (10.18)$$

and t as defined by (10.18) will have the same number of degrees of freedom as s^2, that is, $n_1 + n_2 - 2$ d.f.

The null hypothesis we propose to test is that $\mu_1 = \mu_2$. If H_0 is true, then $\mu_1 - \mu_2 = 0$ and, in this case, the expected value of t will also be zero. For our two samples, we have

$$t = \frac{60.28 - 51.12}{3.17} = 2.89$$

with $n_1 + n_2 - 2 = 48$ d.f. If H_0 is false, then we either have $\mu_1 > \mu_2$ or $\mu_1 < \mu_2$ and we are interested in both of these possibilities. From the table of t, we see that $P(t \geq 2.681) = .005$ and $P(t \leq -2.681) = .005$ and therefore $P(2.681 \leq t \leq -2.681) = .01$.[5] Our observed value of t is 2.89 and thus has a probability of less than .01. In other words, if the null hypothesis is true, we would expect to obtain values of t equal to or less than -2.89 or

---

[4] Note that if $n_1 \neq n_2$, then the variance of the difference between the means of two independent random samples will be given by $s^2(1/n_1 + 1/n_2)$ and the standard error of the difference between the means will be given by

$$\sqrt{s^2(1/n_1 + 1/n_2)}$$

[5] If you draw two independent random samples of $n = 25$ observations each from the population of 100 scores in Example 10.13 and test the significance of the difference between the two means, then in the long run you should expect to find that approximately .01 of your tests of significance result in $t \geq 2.681$ or $t \leq -2.681$.

equal to or greater than 2.89, as a result of random variation, in fewer than .01 of a large number of replications of the same experiment. Because the outcome of this particular experiment has a very small probability of occurring when H_0 is true, we may choose to reject H_0 and thus to decide that the two samples were drawn from populations with different population means.

10.7 Confidence Interval for the Difference between Two Means

The test of significance given by (10.18) may result in our rejecting or not rejecting H_0, but regardless of which decision we make, the test itself does not indicate anything about the possible magnitude of the difference between μ_1 and μ_2. We can, however, establish a confidence interval for $\mu_1 - \mu_2$ in the same manner in which we did this for the mean of a single sample. With 48 d.f., we have $t = -2.681$ and $t = 2.681$ cutting off .005 of the total area in each tail of the t distribution. Then the 99 percent confidence limits with $\overline{X}_1 = 60.28, \overline{X}_2 = 51.12$, and $s_{\overline{X}_1 - \overline{X}_2} = 3.17$, will be

$$-2.681 \leq \frac{(60.28 - 51.12) - (\mu_1 - \mu_2)}{3.17} \leq 2.681$$

or

$$9.16 + (3.17)(2.681) \geq \mu_1 - \mu_2 \geq 9.16 - (3.17)(2.681)$$
$$17.66 \geq \mu_1 - \mu_2 \geq .66$$

On the basis of these confidence limits, we may be extremely confident that $\mu_1 - \mu_2 > 0$ and quite confident that $\mu_1 - \mu_2 < 17.66$.

10.8 Failure to Reject a Given Null Hypothesis

In discussing the test of the null hypothesis, $\mu_1 = \mu_2$, we have had occasion to point out that on the basis of an observed value of t, we may choose not to reject a null hypothesis. It is worth stressing that failure to reject a null hypothesis does not, in turn, prove the null hypothesis to be true. If a null hypothesis is not rejected, this means only that the outcome of the experiment is such that it does not fall within the class of those outcomes we choose to regard as improbable when the null hypothesis is true. For example, if we test a null hypothesis $\mu_1 - \mu_2 = 0$ and decide on the basis of the observed t not to reject the null hypothesis, this means only that we consider the hypothesis to be tenable, that is, it is a hypothesis that might be defended insofar as the available data offer what we consider to be insufficient evidence against it. But this particular null hypothesis is only one of many possible hypotheses that would also be regarded as tenable. If we obtain a nonsignificant value of t when we test the hypothesis $\mu_1 - \mu_2 = 0$, then we might also obtain a nonsignificant value if we tested the hypothesis that the difference between μ_1 and μ_2 was .01, or .001, or any one of many other small possible values for the difference between μ_1 and μ_2. Failure to reject a given null hypothesis, in other words, means only that the hypothesis is tenable—along with other hypotheses that might be formulated—and not that it is necessarily true.

10.9 Homogeneity of Two Variances

In evaluating the difference between two means with the t test, we assumed that the two sample variances s_1^2 and s_2^2 were estimates of the same population variance σ^2. This assumption is often referred to as the assumption of *homogeneity of variance*. We assumed homogeneity of variance when we pooled the data from the two samples to obtain a single estimate s^2 of σ^2.

For our two samples we had two independent estimates, $s_1^2 = 128.21$ and $s_2^2 = 124.46$, of the assumed common population variance σ^2. If we wish to test the null hypothesis that $\sigma_1^2 = \sigma_2^2$ and the alternative of interest is that $\sigma_1^2 \neq \sigma_2^2$, then for the test of this null hypothesis we define F as

$$F = \frac{s_1^2}{s_2^2} \quad \text{or} \quad F = \frac{s_2^2}{s_1^2} \tag{10.19}$$

where we put s_1^2 or s_2^2, whichever is the larger, in the numerator and the smaller value in the denominator so that we always have $F \geq 1$.

The F distribution is given by a curve such that the total area under the curve is equal to 1. Table VIII in Appendix B gives the values of $F > 1$ that cut off .05 and .01 of the total area in the *right tail* of the F curve when the null hypothesis is true, that is, when $\sigma_1^2 = \sigma_2^2$. Because we are interested in the alternatives $\sigma_1^2 < \sigma_2^2$ and $\sigma_1^2 > \sigma_2^2$, we want the probabilities for a two-sided test. For a two-sided test, the probabilities of .05 and .01 are doubled. Thus, if we wish to test the null hypothesis $\sigma_1^2 = \sigma_2^2$ with the alternative being $\sigma_1^2 \neq \sigma_2^2$, and if we calculate F, as defined by (10.19), so that the observed value is always greater than one, then for the test of this null hypothesis the tabled values of F have probabilities of .10 and .02 instead of .05 and .01.

For our example, we have

$$F = \frac{s_2^2}{s_1^2} = \frac{128.21}{124.46} = 1.03$$

To evaluate $F \geq 1.03$, we enter the column of the table of F, Table VIII in Appendix B, with the degrees of freedom associated with the numerator of the F ratio and follow this column down to the row entry corresponding to the degrees of freedom associated with the denominator. The value given in lightface type in the body of the table is the value of F with probability .05

and the value in boldface type is the value of F with probability .01 for a *one-sided* test. We have 24 d.f. for the numerator and 24 d.f. for the denominator and the tabled values are 1.98 and 2.66. For a two-sided test, these values have probabilities of .10 and .02, respectively. Because our observed value of $F = 1.03$ is less than 1.98, we know that the probability associated with our test of significance is greater than .10. We may thus decide that the null hypothesis is tenable.

10.10   Violations of Assumptions of the t Test

The t test described is appropriate for evaluating the difference between the means of two independent random samples. For example, we may have a total of n subjects and these subjects may be divided at random into two equal groups of n_1 and n_2 subjects. One of the groups may then be assigned to a given treatment or experimental condition and the other to another treatment or experimental condition. For each group of subjects we obtain measures on a dependent variable X of interest and we want to know whether the two treatment means differ significantly. The t test for the difference between the two means enables us to find the probability of obtaining a difference as large as or larger than the one observed when the null hypothesis $H_0: \mu_1 = \mu_2$ is true. If the outcome of the experiment is such that it is regarded as improbable when the null hypothesis is true, we reject the null hypothesis and conclude that $\mu_1 \neq \mu_2$.

The most important assumption of the t test, as described, is that we have two *independent random* samples. The conditions of independence and randomness are met if we do in fact assign subjects at random to two groups of n_1 and n_2 subjects. This can be done using a table of random numbers.

The various other assumptions of the t test are concerned with the population distribution of the X variable. It is assumed that both samples are from populations in which X is normally distributed and that $\sigma_1^2 = \sigma_2^2$. There is considerable evidence to indicate that departures from normality are relatively unimportant provided that X has approximately the same distribution in the two populations from which the two samples were selected. For example, if X has the same degree and direction of skewness in both populations or if X is rectangularly distributed in both populations, the t test may still be used to evaluate the difference between the two sample means.

There is also considerable evidence to indicate that the assumption of equal population variances is relatively unimportant provided that we have an equal number of observations in each sample,[6] that is, provided $n_1 = n_2$.

---

[6] This is one reason why we have emphasized having $n_1 = n_2$. The t test can, of course, be used when $n_1 \neq n_2$. It can be shown, however, that the standard error of the difference between two means is *minimized*, assuming homogeneity of variance, when $n_1 = n_2$. See the proof asked for in Example 10.14.

Both departures from normality and heterogeneity of variance become less important as the number of observations in the two samples increases.

In summary, we can say, on the basis of the available evidence, that if we have two independent random samples and if $n_1 = n_2 \geq 25$, then it has been found that the *t* test is relatively insensitive to rather drastic violations of assumptions about normality of distribution and heterogeneity of variance. What this general statement means is that any experimenter who randomly assigns subjects to two treatments and who takes care to use at least $n = 25$ subjects in each group need not spend a sleepless night worrying about such assumptions as homogeneity of variance and normality of distribution. The *t* test, as Box (1953) pointed out some years ago is a *robust* test. A robust test of significance is one that is relatively insensitive to the violations of its mathematical assumptions.[7]

10.11 The *t* Test for Paired Observations

In the first chapter we described an experiment in which subjects were paired on the basis of their scores on an aptitude test. Within each pair, one subject was assigned at random to a control group, the group that studied without knowledge of results, and the other to an experimental group, the group that studied with knowledge of results. Because the subjects in each pair were comparable with respect to aptitude and because one subject in each pair was assigned to the control and the other to the experimental group, the mean aptitude test scores for the two groups should also be comparable. Thus, if we should obtain a difference between the means of the two groups on the dependent variable, score on the criterion test, we would not expect this difference merely to reflect a possible difference between the two groups in average ability or aptitude. We note, however, that this objective could also have been attained if we had simply randomly assigned 20 subjects to the control and 20 subjects to the experimental group. With random assignment of the subjects to the two groups, we would also expect any difference between the means of the two groups with respect to aptitude to represent merely random variation and not a source of systematic bias.

More importantly, the major reason for pairing the subjects on the basis of their aptitude test scores was that we believed aptitude score would be positively correlated with performance on the criterion test. If we are correct in this belief, then a pair of subjects with high scores on the aptitude test

---

[7] Boneau (1960) reports the results of an empirical investigation of the distribution of *t* when the two samples have been drawn from nonnormal populations, from populations with different variances, and when $n_1 = n_2$, and $n_1 \neq n_2$, and for various combinations of these conditions. The results he obtained show that the *t* test is robust in all cases, provided that a two-sided test of significance is made, that $n_1 = n_2$, and that both samples have 25 or more observations.

should also have relatively high scores on the criterion test. Similarly, a pair of subjects with low scores on the aptitude test might both be expected to have relatively low scores on the criterion test. Thus, if we correlate the paired scores of the subjects on the criterion test we should find some degree of positive correlation. In this case, the paired scores of the subjects on the criterion test would not be independent variables but instead *correlated* or *nonindependent* variables.

We have previously shown that if we have paired (X_1, X_2) values of a variable and if $D = X_1 - X_2$ or the difference between each of the paired values, then

$$\sum (D - \bar{D})^2 = \sum x_1{}^2 + \sum x_2{}^2 - 2\sum x_1 x_2$$

and dividing by $n - 1$, where n is the number of differences or paired (X_1, X_2) values, we have

$$s_D{}^2 = s_{X_1}{}^2 + s_{X_2}{}^2 - 2r_{X_1 X_2} s_{X_1} s_{X_2}$$

where $s_D{}^2 = s_{X_1 - X_2}{}^2$ is the variance of the distribution of differences. If X_1 and X_2 are nonindependent and linearly related variables, then $r_{X_1 X_2} \neq 0$ and must be considered in estimating the variance of the difference, $D = X_1 - X_2$. The variance of $\bar{D} = \bar{X}_1 - \bar{X}_2$ will be $1/n$th the variance of $D = X_1 - X_2$ or

$$
\begin{aligned}
s_{\bar{D}}{}^2 &= \frac{s_{X_1}{}^2}{n} + \frac{s_{X_2}{}^2}{n} - 2r_{X_1 X_2} \frac{s_{X_1} s_{X_2}}{\sqrt{n}\sqrt{n}} \\
&= s_{\bar{X}_1}{}^2 + s_{\bar{X}_2}{}^2 - 2r_{X_1 X_2} s_{\bar{X}_1} s_{\bar{X}_2}
\end{aligned}
\tag{10.20}
$$

and the standard error of $\bar{D}$ will then be

$$s_D = \sqrt{s_{\bar{X}_1}{}^2 + s_{\bar{X}_2}{}^2 - 2r_{X_1 X_2} s_{\bar{X}_1} s_{\bar{X}_2}} \tag{10.21}$$

If X_1 and X_2 are independent variables, then $r_{X_1 X_2} = 0$, and the last term would be equal to zero. On the other hand, if X_1 and X_2 are correlated variables and if the correlation is *positive*, then the standard error of the difference between the means will be reduced by an amount depending upon the value of $r_{X_1 X_2}$. The greater the degree of positive correlation between the paired observations, the smaller the standard error of the difference between the means.

Table 10.2 gives the scores of the paired subjects on the criterion test as taken from Table 1.1. We could calculate the correlation between the paired criterion scores and use (10.21) to find the standard error of the difference between the means. This, however, is not necessary because we note that

$$\sum (D - \bar{D})^2 = \sum x_1{}^2 + \sum x_2{}^2 - 2 \sum x_1 x_2$$

$$= \sum D^2 - \frac{(\sum D)^2}{n}$$

where n is the number of values of D.

Using the values of D given in Table 10.2, we have

$$\sum D = -4 - 4 + 5 + \cdots + 1 = 60$$

and

$$\sum D^2 = (-4)^2 + (-4)^2 + (5)^2 + \cdots + (1)^2 = 566$$

Then

$$\sum (D - \bar{D})^2 = 566 - \frac{(60)^2}{20} = 386$$

and

$$s_{\bar{D}}{}^2 = \frac{\sum (D - \bar{D})^2}{n(n - 1)} \qquad (10.22)$$

and

$$s_{\bar{D}} = \sqrt{\frac{\sum (D - \bar{D})^2}{n(n - 1)}} \qquad (10.23)$$

Substituting in (10.23) we have for the standard error of the mean difference,

$$s_{\bar{D}} = \sqrt{\frac{386}{20(20 - 1)}} = 1.008$$

To test the null hypothesis that $\mu_D = \mu_1 - \mu_2 = 0$, we have

$$t = \frac{\bar{X}_1 - \bar{X}_2}{s_{\bar{D}}} \qquad (10.24)$$

and t, as defined by (10.24) will have $n - 1$ d.f. where n is the number of differences or paired (X_1, X_2) values. In the present example, we have

$$t = \frac{14 - 11}{1.008} = 2.98$$

with $n - 1 = 19$ d.f. With a two-sided test we find from the table of t that $t = -2.86$ and $t = 2.86$ will cut off .005 of the total area in the left and right tails of the t distribution. Because our observed value of t is equal to 2.98, we may regard it as a relatively improbable value, if the null hypothesis

Table 10.2—Scores on an achievement test for paired subjects in the control and in the experimental group and differences, $X_1 - X_2$, between the paired scores

Paired subjects	Control X_1	Experimental X_2	Difference $X_1 - X_2$
1	14	18	−4
2	8	12	−4
3	15	10	5
4	16	9	7
5	8	14	−6
6	15	10	5
7	15	9	6
8	17	11	6
9	18	13	5
10	13	6	7
11	10	16	−6
12	19	14	5
13	20	16	4
14	17	8	9
15	14	8	6
16	10	8	2
17	14	9	5
18	15	10	5
19	13	11	2
20	9	8	1
Σ	280	220	60

is in fact true. Rejecting the null hypothesis, we conclude that $\mu_1 \neq \mu_2$ and we may, in the manner described previously, establish a 95 or 99 percent confidence for the difference between the means.

We pointed out earlier that the major reason for pairing the subjects on the basis of their aptitude test scores was that we believed we would then find a substantial positive correlation between the scores of the paired subjects on the criterion test. If this had turned out to be the case, we would expect to have a smaller standard error for our test of significance than we would have obtained if subjects had been assigned completely at random to the two groups. Our initial assumption, however, was in error. The correlation between the scores of the paired subjects on the criterion test is not very high. We note, for example, that if we assume X_1 and X_2 are independent variables then, for an estimate of the common population variance σ^2 we have

$$s^2 = \frac{\sum x_1^2 + \sum x_2^2}{n_1 + n_2 - 2}$$

$$= \frac{234 + 198}{20 + 20 - 2}$$

$$= 11.3684$$

Then the standard error of the difference between the two means would be

$$s_{\bar{X}_1 - \bar{X}_2} = \sqrt{\frac{2s^2}{n}}$$

$$= \sqrt{\frac{2(11.3684)}{20}}$$

$$= 1.065$$

Thus, we see that pairing our subjects initially on the basis of their aptitude test scores contributed very little to the reduction in the standard error. For example, the standard error obtained above, assuming $r_{X_1X_2} = 0$, is 1.065 and that obtained by taking into account the correlation between the paired scores is 1.008. This example serves to emphasize that it is advantageous to pair subjects only if the correlation between the paired subjects on the dependent variable is positive and substantial.

For example, assuming homogeneity of variance and with $n_1 = n_2$, as would have to be the case if we have paired observations, $s_{\bar{X}_1} = s_{\bar{X}_2} = s_{\bar{X}}$. Then (10.21) becomes

$$s_{\bar{X}_1 - \bar{X}_2} = \sqrt{2s_{\bar{X}}^2(1 - r_{X_1X_2})}$$

$$= 1.414 s_{\bar{X}} \sqrt{1 - r_{X_1X_2}} \tag{10.25}$$

We note that (10.25) differs from the standard error formula for independent observations only by the factor $\sqrt{1 - r_{X_1X_2}}$. Thus if $r_{X_1X_2} = .50$, we have $\sqrt{1 - .50} = .71$ and the standard error based upon the paired observations will be approximately .7 as large as that based upon independent observations. If $r_{X_1X_2} = .75$, then $\sqrt{1 - .75} = .5$ and the standard error based upon paired observations will be .5 as large as that based upon independent observations.

Another factor should also be considered in comparing experimental designs involving paired observations with those involving independent observations. If we have $n = 40$ subjects and if the subjects are arranged in 20 pairs, then the appropriate t test of significance, as defined by (10.24), will have degrees of freedom equal to one less than the number of pairs or, in this case, 19 d.f. On the other hand, if the subjects are not paired, then the appropriate *t* test of significance, as defined by (10.18), will have degrees of freedom equal to $n_1 + n_2 - 2$, or, in this case 38 d.f. We know that as the degrees of freedom increase, smaller values of *t* are required for significance at a given significance level. Thus for any fixed number of subjects, if the subjects are paired a larger value of *t* will be required for significance with $\alpha = .05$, say, than would be the case if the subjects are not paired but instead assigned completely at random to the two treatments.

EXAMPLES

10.1—Two groups of rats were tested under different experimental conditions. The measures of performance consist of the speed in feet per second during critical test trials for each rat. Data are from Crespi (1942).

(a)   Test the hypothesis that $\sigma_1^2 = \sigma_2^2$.
(b)   Test the hypothesis that $\mu_1 = \mu_2$.

Group 1	Group 2
1.90	3.08
1.87	2.62
1.41	2.58
1.37	2.44
1.13	2.32
.64	1.84
.46	1.44

10.2—The Miller Analogies Test was given to VA trainees in clinical psychology. A group of 40 trainees was granted the Ph.D. degree and another group of 39 trainees was dismissed from the program. Data are from Kelly and Fiske (1950).

(a)   Test the null hypothesis that $\sigma_1^2 = \sigma_2^2$.
(b)   Test the null hypothesis that $\mu_1 = \mu_2$.

	Ph.D. granted	Dismissed
$\overline{X}$	77.6	62.4
s	8.4	13.7
n	40	39

10.3—A test of musical meaning was given to a group of eighth-grade and a group of tenth-grade students. Data are from Watson (1942).

(a) Test the hypothesis that $\sigma_1^2 = \sigma_2^2$.
(b) Test the null hypothesis that $\mu_1 = \mu_2$.

	Eighth grade	Tenth grade
X	90.76	99.32
s	19.32	18.36
n	200	200

10.4—The performance of a control and an experimental group is to be compared. Performance scores of the subjects are given below. Test the null hypothesis that $\mu_1 = \mu_2$.

Control	Experimental
10	7
5	3
6	5
7	7
10	8
6	4
7	5
8	6
6	3
5	2

10.5—Thirty subjects are divided at random into a control group of $n = 10$ subjects and an experimental group of $n = 20$ subjects.

(a) Test the null hypothesis that $\sigma_1^2 = \sigma_2^2$.
(b) Test the null hypothesis that $\mu_1 = \mu_2$.

	Control	Experimental
$\overline{X}$	29.66	26.14
$\sum x^2$	14.50	76.80
n	10	20

10.6—A random sample of 25 subjects yields a mean of 22.4. The estimate of the population standard deviation is 10.0.

(a) Find the 95 percent confidence limits for μ.
(b) Assume that the estimates of σ and μ remain the same, but that the sample size is increased to 100. What would the 95 percent confidence limits now be?

10.7—Forty subjects are divided at random into two groups of 20 subjects each. One group is then assigned to the experimental condition, and the other to the control condition.

(a) Test the null hypothesis that $\sigma_1{}^2 = \sigma_2{}^2$.
(b) Test the null hypothesis that $\mu_1 = \mu_2$.

Control		Experimental	
7	13	2	5
17	7	9	13
14	8	11	10
11	13	9	10
8	11	7	15
11	17	9	10
13	14	10	12
12	15	10	1
10	10	11	10
14	15	4	12

10.8—Individuals are paired on the basis of their performance on a variable that the experimenter believes is correlated with performance on a dependent variable of interest. One member of each pair is then assigned at random to a control group and the other to an experimental group. Values on the dependent variable X are given below for each pair. Test the null hypothesis that $\mu_1 = \mu_2$.

Pair	Experimental X_1	Control X_2
1	2	1
2	5	2
3	2	4
4	3	3
5	7	4
6	3	2
7	5	6
8	4	3
9	5	4
10	4	1

10.9—One of the experiments in a series by Ansbacher (1944) was concerned with judgments of apparent movement. The same subjects judged the apparent length of a 13-centimeter arc at various speeds of rotation. The data given below are judgments of apparent length at zero speed and at one revolution per second. Note that the data are for paired and *not* independent observations. Test the significance of the difference between the two means.

Subjects	Rotation speeds in revolutions per second	
	0	1
1	10.0	9.3
2	12.3	9.1
3	11.3	8.7
4	10.3	8.1
5	8.9	6.7
6	10.0	7.7
7	9.9	8.4
8	10.5	8.4

10.10—In an experiment subjects were given an attitude test before and after viewing a motion picture designed to influence their attitudes. Attitude scores of the subjects on the pretest and posttest are given below. Note that the data are for *paired* observations. Test the significance of the difference between the two means.

Subjects	Pretest	Posttest
1	2.6	2.5
2	4.6	5.7
3	8.9	9.3
4	5.5	6.7
5	1.9	1.5
6	6.2	7.8
7	4.6	4.7
8	5.6	5.9
9	6.9	7.3
10	6.6	7.0

10.11—A study by Bugelski (1942) was concerned with interference of recall of responses to stimuli after learning of new responses. The data given are for the percent of the original trials required for relearning where interference was expected to be present and where it was not. Note that the data are *paired* observations, that is, the same subjects were tested twice, once under a control condition and once under an interference condition. Test the significance of the difference between the two means.

Subjects	Control	Interference
1	.706	.744
2	.862	.585
3	.711	.704
4	.554	.850
5	.556	.591
6	.553	.750
7	.700	1.000
8	1.323	1.345
9	.848	1.250
10	.967	1.000
11	.900	.711
12	.576	1.000
13	.750	1.154
14	.512	.778
15	.950	1.190
16	1.100	.689
17	.950	.895
18	.622	1.379
19	.679	.816
20	.759	.723

10.12—The reaction time of mental patients to verbal questions was studied before and after the patients had received electroshock treatments. The data are from Janis and Astrachan (1951). Note that we have *paired* observations. Test the difference between the means for significance.

Patients	Before shock	After shock
1	12.75	23.71
2	8.24	7.50
3	3.26	12.95
4	9.07	12.56
5	6.22	14.14
6	8.20	9.90
7	7.11	8.95
8	4.52	6.32
9	6.12	5.42

10.13—Given below are the scores of the 100 students on the mid-term test. In the discussion in the chapter, we regarded these 100 scores as a population and we drew a random sample of $n = 25$ from the population using a table of random numbers.

(a) Following the same procedures described in the text, use the table of random numbers to select a sample of 30 observations with replacement after each selection. Let the first 15 observations selected be Sample 1 and the second 15 be Sample 2.

(b) Test the significance of the difference between the two sample means and the two sample variances.

(c) If the two sample means do not differ significantly, combine the data from the two samples and find the 95 percent confidence interval for the mean. Does the population mean, that is, the mean of all 100 observations fall within the 95 percent confidence interval?

87	76	73	70	67	66	64	63	61	60
85	75	72	69	67	65	64	62	61	60
82	74	71	69	67	65	63	62	61	60
78	74	71	68	66	65	63	62	61	60
77	74	70	68	66	64	63	62	61	60

60	59	58	57	56	54	52	50	46	43
60	59	58	57	55	54	52	49	46	42
60	59	58	57	55	53	51	49	46	38
60	59	58	56	55	53	51	48	45	35
60	59	57	56	54	53	50	47	44	33

10.14—Suppose we have n subjects and we want to assign n_1 subjects to Treatment 1 and n_2 subjects to Treatment 2, subject to the restriction that $n_1 + n_2 = n$. Assuming homogeneity of variance, the standard error of the difference between the two treatment means will be

$$s_{\bar{X}_1 - \bar{X}_2} = \sqrt{s^2 \left(\frac{1}{n_1} + \frac{1}{n_2} \right)}$$

Prove that $s_{\bar{X}_1 - \bar{X}_2}$ takes its minimum value when $n_1 = n_2$. Hint: Expand $(n_1 + n_2)^2$ and note that $1/n_1 + 1/n_2 = n/n_1 n_2$.

10.15—Give a one-sentence definition of each of the following terms or concepts:

sampling with replacement   unbiased estimate
sampling without replacement   confidence interval
standard error of the mean   homogeneity of variance
robust test

CHAPTER 11

One-Sided and Two-Sided Tests and the Power of Tests

11.1 The Two-Sided Test: $\mu_1 = \mu_2$

In any well-planned experiment, prior to the experiment itself, a decision is made about the nature of the particular null hypothesis to be tested. We shall consider three possibilities with respect to experiments designed to test the difference between the means of two random samples. In the first case, we consider an experiment in which the experimenter is interested in both the possibility that $\mu_1 > \mu_2$ and the possibility that $\mu_1 < \mu_2$. The experimenter, in this instance, is interested in any difference observed between the two means, regardless of the sign of the difference. The appropriate null hypothesis for this case is $H_0: \mu_1 = \mu_2$. If a test of significance results in the rejection of H_0, then the experimenter is prepared to accept the alternative hypothesis that $\mu_1 \neq \mu_2$.

The experimenter usually specifies the risk he wishes to take in making a Type I error. Let us assume, in the present instance, that the test of significance is to be made in such a way that the probability of a Type I error is set at .05. If the null hypothesis is true, then the expected or long-run average value of $\overline{X}_1 - \overline{X}_2$ will be zero and the expected or long-run average of t will also be zero. For any given sample, however, t will be positive if $\overline{X}_1$ is greater than $\overline{X}_2$ and negative if $\overline{X}_1$ is less than $\overline{X}_2$. We are prepared to reject H_0 if the value of t we obtain from (10.18) is either positive or negative and falls within a *selected* class or subset of values that would occur with probability of .05 when the null hypothesis is true.

Suppose that we have two independent random samples with $n_1 = n_2 = n = 10$ observations each. Let the sample space of the experiment be the set of all possible values of t as given by (10.18). On the sample space we define three events or subsets:

$$E_1 = \{t: t \geq 2.101\}$$
$$E_2 = \{t: t \leq -2.101\}$$
$$E_3 = \{t: -2.101 < t < 2.101\}$$

It is obvious that these three events are mutually exclusive and exhaustive and therefore provide a partition of the sample space. Furthermore, if it is true that $\mu_1 = \mu_2$ and if the t's have a t distribution with $n_1 + n_2 - 2 = 10 + 10 - 2 = 18$ d.f., then, as we can determine from the table of t, $P(E_1) = .025$, $P(E_2) = .025$, $P(E_3) = .95$ and $P(E_1 \cup E_2) = P(E_1) + P(E_2) = .05$.

The nature of the test of significance is illustrated in Figure 11.1. The shaded areas in the two tails of the t distribution correspond to the events

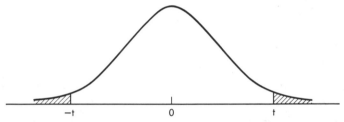

Figure **11.1**—The two-sided test of the null hypothesis $\mu_1 - \mu_2 = 0$. The null hypothesis is rejected if t falls in either of the two shaded areas.

E_1 and E_2. The null hypothesis is rejected if the observed value of t, as given by (10.18) falls in either of the shaded areas. Because the rejection areas are based upon both tails of the distribution of t, this test of significance is often referred to as a two-tailed or *two-sided test of significance*.

11.2   One-Sided Tests: $\mu_1 \leq \mu_2$ and $\mu_1 \geq \mu_2$

In some cases an experimenter may, in advance of the experiment itself, have a *practical* reason for deciding that he is interested only in the alternative $\mu_1 > \mu_2$. For example, suppose that we own a desk calculator that we will identify as Machine 1. We are happy with Machine 1 until a salesman appears on the scene and wants us to purchase a new calculator that we identify as Machine 2. He claims that the average time μ_2 to perform calculations on his machine is considerably less than the average time μ_1 required with the machine we now own. In other words, his claim is that $\mu_1 > \mu_2$.

If the salesman's hypothesis is true, then we may consider the purchase of a new machine. On the other hand, if his hypothesis is false and if it is true that $\mu_1 \leq \mu_2$, we shall keep the machine we have and avoid the expense of purchasing a new one. In this case then, we may decide to test the null hypothesis that $\mu_1 \leq \mu_2$, because the only alternative of practical interest to us is $\mu_1 > \mu_2$. Now the outcome of any experiment in which $\overline{X}_1 - \overline{X}_2 \leq 0$

so that we also have $t \leq 0$ is consistent with the null hypothesis. Only out-comes such that $\bar{X}_1 - \bar{X}_2 > 0$ so that we have $t > 0$ will offer evidence against the null hypothesis.

Again we consider an experiment in which we have two independent random samples of $n_1 = n_2 = n = 10$ observations. We assume that each observation is the time required to perform a given set of calculations on a given machine. From the table of t, we find that with $n_1 + n_2 - 2 = 18$ d.f., a value of $t = 1.734$ will cut off .05 of the total area in the right tail, if it is true that $\mu_1 = \mu_2$. If $\mu_1 < \mu_2$ then the probability of obtaining $t \geq 1.734$ will be less than .05. Thus if we reject the null hypothesis only if we have an observed value of $t \geq 1.734$, the probability of a Type I error will not exceed .05. The worst that could happen to us, as far as a Type I error is concerned, would be if $\mu_1 = \mu_2$ in which case the maximum probability of a Type I error will be .05. We therefore consider two events:

$$E_1 = \{t : t \geq 1.734\}$$
$$E_2 = \{t : t < 1.734\}$$

These two events are mutually exclusive and exhaustive and provide a parti-tion of the sample space consisting of all possible values of t resulting from an experiment designed to test the difference between the means of two in-dependent random samples of $n = 10$ observations each. If the null hypothe-sis is true, then $P(E_1) = .05$ and $P(E_2) = .95$ and we decide to reject the null hypothesis only if E_1 occurs.

The nature of the test of significance for the null hypothesis $\mu_1 \leq \mu_2$ is shown in Figure 11.2. The shaded area in the right tail of the distribution represents .05 of the total area, when the expected or long-run average value of t is zero. In the present problem we reject the null hypothesis only if t is positive and falls within the region represented by the shaded area. If we reject the null hypothesis, we shall accept the alternative hypothesis that $\mu_1 - \mu_2 > 0$ or that $\mu_1 > \mu_2$. Because the region of rejection consists of only one tail of the t distribution, the test of significance is often described as a one-tailed or *one-sided test of significance*.

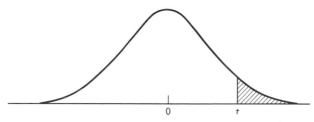

Figure **11.2**—The one-sided test of the null hypothesis $\mu_1 \leq \mu_2$. The null hypothesis is rejected if t falls in the shaded area at the right.

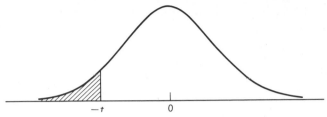

Figure **11.3**—The one-sided test of the null hypothesis $\mu_1 \geq \mu_2$. The null hypothesis is rejected if t falls in the shaded area at the left.

Figure 11.3 illustrates a test of the null hypothesis that $\mu_1 \geq \mu_2$. The alternative to this null hypothesis is $\mu_1 < \mu_2$. The region of rejection is the shaded area in the left tail of the distribution. The test on the left tail of the t distribution is appropriate for those cases where the only alternative to the null hypothesis that is of interest to us is $\mu_1 < \mu_2$.

11.3   The Power of the Two-Sided Test: $\mu_1 = \mu_2$

In our discussion of one- and two-sided tests of significance we have been primarily concerned with the probability of making a Type I error, that is, of rejecting the null hypothesis when it is true. We shall now give some attention to the probability of making a Type II error, that is, of failing to reject the null hypothesis when it is false.

As a matter of convenience and simplicity in presentation, we shall assume that we have two independent random samples drawn from two normal populations with equal and known variances. We shall, therefore, not have to be concerned about degrees of freedom and the table of t, but instead we may use the table of the standard normal curve. The table of the standard normal curve is much more complete than the table of t, and this fact will prove useful in our discussion. The argument presented, the procedure described, and the general conclusions we arrive at will, however, be much the same as if we had used the t distribution. The major difference is that we shall be using the areas or probabilities of the standard normal distribution rather than those of the t distribution.

Let us assume that we have two samples, each with $n_1 = n_2 = n = 10$ observations. We assume that the populations from which the samples were drawn are normally distributed and that the variances of the two populations are the same and known to be equal to $\sigma^2 = 5$. We do not, however, know anything about the two population means. The standard error of the difference between the means will be given by

$$\sigma_{\bar{X}_1 - \bar{X}_2}{}^2 = \sqrt{\frac{2\sigma^2}{n}} = \sqrt{\frac{(2)(5)}{10}} = 1.00$$

Suppose we wish to test the null hypothesis $\mu_1 = \mu_2$, with the probability of a Type I error being set at .05. Our test statistic will be the z ratio with

$$z = \frac{\overline{X}_1 - \overline{X}_2}{\sigma_{\overline{X}_1 - \overline{X}_2}}$$

From the table of the standard normal curve, we find that $z = 1.96$ will cut off .025 of the total area in the right tail and $z = -1.96$ will cut off .025 of the total area in the left tail. For the two-sided test, then, we will reject the null hypothesis if the obtained value of z is equal to or greater than 1.96 or equal to or less than -1.96. If the null hypothesis is true, then for this test, the probability of a Type I error will be equal to .05.

We may note that because $\sigma_{\overline{X}_1 - \overline{X}_2} = 1.00$ we have

$$z = \overline{X}_1 - \overline{X}_2$$

and, for the conditions described, we may say that we will reject the null hypothesis if $\overline{X}_1 - \overline{X}_2 \geq 1.96$ or if $\overline{X}_1 - \overline{X}_2 \leq -1.96$. The frequency with which we shall obtain values of $\overline{X}_1 - \overline{X}_2 \geq 1.96$ or of $\overline{X}_1 - \overline{X}_2 \leq -1.96$ will depend upon the unknown true population mean difference $\mu_1 - \mu_2$.

Let us designate the null hypothesis $\mu_1 = \mu_2$ or, in other words, $\mu_1 - \mu_2 = 0$, as H_0. Then one general class of alternatives to the null hypothesis would be all possible values of $\mu_1 > \mu_2$ so that $\mu_1 - \mu_2 > 0$. Let us designate all members of this class as H_1. Another general class of alternatives, which we may designate as H_2, would be all possible values of $\mu_1 < \mu_2$ so that $\mu_1 - \mu_2 < 0$. From the class of H_1 and H_2 alternatives we may select various values of $\mu_1 - \mu_2$ and determine, if a particular alternative is true, how frequently we would obtain values of $\overline{X}_1 - \overline{X}_2 \geq 1.96$ and $\overline{X}_1 - \overline{X}_2 \leq -1.96$.

Suppose, for example, it is true that $\mu_1 - \mu_2 = 1.00$. Then the sampling distribution of $\overline{X}_1 - \overline{X}_2$ will be normally distributed about the population mean difference $\mu_1 - \mu_2 = 1.00$ and we would have

$$z = \frac{(\overline{X}_1 - \overline{X}_2) - (\mu_1 - \mu_2)}{\sigma_{\overline{X}_1 - \overline{X}_2}}$$
$$= \frac{(1.96) - (1.00)}{1.00}$$
$$= .96$$

and the expected frequency of $\overline{X}_1 - \overline{X}_2 \geq 1.96$ would be the area to the right of $z = .96$ in the standard normal curve. This area is .168. We would also have

$$z = \frac{(-1.96) - (1.00)}{1.00}$$
$$= -2.96$$

and the expected frequency of $\overline{X}_1 - \overline{X}_2 \leq -1.96$ would be the area to the left of $z = -2.96$ in the standard normal curve. This area is .002. Then, if we reject the null hypothesis $\mu_1 - \mu_2 = 0$ whenever $\overline{X}_1 - \overline{X}_2 \geq 1.96$ or whenever $\overline{X}_1 - \overline{X}_2 \leq -1.96$, we shall do so with a theoretical relative frequency of .168 + .002 = .170, if it is true that $\mu_1 - \mu_2 = 1.00$.

Table 11.1—Probability of rejecting and failing to reject the null hypothesis $\mu_1 - \mu_2 = 0$ when $\sigma_{\overline{X}_1 - \overline{X}_2} = 1.00$ and the various values of $\mu_1 - \mu_2$ shown in the table are true. The hypothesis is rejected if $z = \overline{X}_1 - \overline{X}_2 \geq 1.96$ or $z = \overline{X}_1 - \overline{X}_2 \leq -1.96$

(1) Values of $\mu_1 - \mu_2$	(2) Probability of $\overline{X}_1 - \overline{X}_2$ ≥ 1.96	(3) Probability of $\overline{X}_1 - \overline{X}_2$ ≤ -1.96	(4) Probability of rejecting $\mu_1 - \mu_2 = 0$	(5) Probability of not rejecting $\mu_1 - \mu_2 = 0$
4.0	.979	.000	.979	.021
3.5	.938	.000	.938	.062
3.0	.851	.000	.851	.149
2.5	.705	.000	.705	.295
2.0	.516	.000	.516	.484
1.5	.323	.000	.323	.677
1.0	.168	.002	.170	.830
.5	.072	.007	.079	.921
.0	.025	.025	.050	.950
− .5	.007	.072	.079	.921
−1.0	.002	.168	.170	.830
−1.5	.000	.323	.323	.677
−2.0	.000	.516	.516	.484
−2.5	.000	.705	.705	.295
−3.0	.000	.851	.851	.149
−3.5	.000	.938	.938	.062
−4.0	.000	.979	.979	.021

Following the procedure just described, we can determine how frequently the null hypothesis would be rejected when other specific alternatives of the class H_1 and H_2 are true. We have done this for the selected values of $\mu_1 - \mu_2$ shown in column (1) of Table 11.1. The probability of obtaining values of $\overline{X}_1 - \overline{X}_2 \geq 1.96$ for each of these alternatives is shown in column (2) of the table. In column (3) we have the probability of obtaining values of $\overline{X}_1 - \overline{X}_2 \leq -1.96$ for each alternative. The sums of these two probabilities are given in column (4), and these are the probabilities of rejecting the null hypothesis for each of the corresponding alternatives given in column (1).

The only way in which we can make a Type I error is if it is true that $\mu_1 - \mu_2 = 0$ and we reject the null hypothesis. This probability is .05, as column (4) shows. A Type II error will occur, however, whenever the null hypothesis $\mu_1 - \mu_2 = 0$ is false, but we fail to reject it. Since we know the probability of rejecting the null hypothesis for each of the alternatives given in column (1) of Table 11.1, the probability of not rejecting will be equal to one minus the probability of rejecting the null hypothesis. These probabilities are given in column (5) of Table 11.1. Because it is obvious that we cannot make a Type II error if it is true that $\mu_1 - \mu_2 = 0$, all of the probabilities given in column (5) of the table except the one in the row $\mu_1 - \mu_2 = 0$ are the probabilities of making a Type II error for each of the alternatives given in column (1).

We have previously defined the power of a test as $1 - P(\text{Type II error})$. In terms of this definition, the power of a test depends upon the probability of making a Type II error. If this probability is small for a given test of significance, the test has greater power than one for which the probability of a Type II error is larger, assuming that both tests have equal probabilities of making a Type I error.

We have noted before that an equivalent definition of the power of a test is the probability of rejecting the null hypothesis when it is false. The graph of these probabilities for various alternatives to $\mu_1 - \mu_2 = 0$ is shown in Figure 11.4. This graph is called the *power function* of the test of significance. From Figure 11.4 it is obvious that the two-sided test of significance has power against both groups of alternatives H_1 and H_2. Let us now see what happens when we make a one-sided test of significance.

11.4   Power of the One-Sided Test of $\mu_1 \geq \mu_2$

If we test the null hypothesis $\mu_1 \geq \mu_2$, we shall use the left tail of the standard normal curve, just as we used the left tail of the t distribution in testing this hypothesis. From the table of the standard normal curve we find that $z = -1.645$ will cut off .05 of the area in the left tail, and, if we reject the null hypothesis whenever z falls in this region, the probability of a Type I error will not exceed .05. We have only one general class of alternatives to the null hypothesis $\mu_1 \geq \mu_2$, namely, H_2 or all possible values of $\mu_1 < \mu_2$ so that $\mu_1 - \mu_2 < 0$.

We may observe that since we have $\sigma_{\overline{X}_1 - \overline{X}_2} = 1.00$, we have $z = \overline{X}_1 - \overline{X}_2$, as before, and we will reject the null hypothesis if $\overline{X}_1 - \overline{X}_2 \leq -1.645$. The frequency with which we will obtain values of $\overline{X}_1 - \overline{X}_2 \leq -1.645$ will depend upon the unknown true population difference between the means $\mu_1 - \mu_2$. Suppose, for example, that it is true that $\mu_1 - \mu_2 = 1.00$. This is consistent with the null hypothesis $\mu_1 - \mu_2 \geq 0$, and we shall see that the

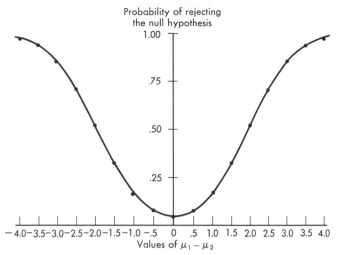

Figure 11.4—The power function of the two-sided test of the null hypothesis $\mu_1 - \mu_2 = 0$ when $\sigma_{\bar{X}_1 - \bar{X}_2} = 1.00$ and the probability of a Type I error is equal to .05.

probability of rejecting the null hypothesis, if this alternative is true, that is, the probability of making a Type I error, will be less than .05.

If it is true that $\mu_1 - \mu_2 = 1.00$, then $\bar{X}_1 - \bar{X}_2$ will be normally distributed about the population mean difference $\mu_1 - \mu_2 = 1.00$ and we have

$$z = \frac{(\bar{X}_1 - \bar{X}_2) - (\mu_1 - \mu_2)}{\sigma_{\bar{X}_1 - \bar{X}_2}}$$

$$= \frac{(-1.645) - (1.00)}{1.00}$$

$$= -2.645$$

and the expected frequency of $\bar{X}_1 - \bar{X}_2 \leq -1.645$ will be given by the area of the standard normal distribution that falls to the left of $z = -2.645$. This area is .004 and corresponds to the probability of rejecting the null hypothesis $\mu_1 \geq \mu_2$ when it is true that $\mu_1 > \mu_2$ and $\mu_1 - \mu_2 = 1.00$.

Suppose, however, that the alternative $\mu_1 - \mu_2 = -1.00$ is true and that we test the null hypothesis $\mu_1 \geq \mu_2$ as before, using the left tail of the standard normal curve. Then

$$z = \frac{(\bar{X}_1 - \bar{X}_2) - (\mu_1 - \mu_2)}{\sigma_{\bar{X}_1 - \bar{X}_2}}$$

$$= \frac{(-1.645) - (-1.00)}{1.00}$$

$$= -.645$$

and the expected relative frequency of $\bar{X}_1 - \bar{X}_2 \leq -1.645$ will be given by the area in the standard normal curve falling to the left of $z = -.645$. This area is .259 and corresponds to the probability of rejecting the null hypothesis $\mu_1 \geq \mu_2$ when it is true that $\mu_1 < \mu_2$ and $\mu_1 - \mu_2 = -1.00$.

In the manner described above, we have determined the probability of rejecting the null hypothesis $\mu_1 \geq \mu_2$ for the various other selected values of $\mu_1 - \mu_2$ shown in column (1) of Table 11.2. These probabilities are given in column (2) of the table. In testing the null hypothesis $\mu_1 \geq \mu_2$, a Type I error will occur whenever this hypothesis is true, but our test of significance rejects the hypothesis. Thus a Type I error can occur only if one of the alternatives $\mu_1 \geq \mu_2$ shown in column (1) of Table 11.2 is true and the null hypothesis is rejected. It can be seen in column (2) of the table that this probability will be .05, if $\mu_1 = \mu_2$. If μ_1 is greater than μ_2, the probability of rejecting the null hypothesis, that is, the probability of making a Type I error, will be less than .05.

Table 11.2—Probability of rejecting and failing to reject the null hypothesis $\mu_1 \geq \mu_2$ when $\sigma_{\bar{X}_1 - \bar{X}_2} = 1.00$ and the various values of $\mu_1 - \mu_2$ shown in the table are true. The hypothesis is rejected if $z = \bar{X}_1 - \bar{X}_2 \leq -1.645$

(1) Values of $\mu_1 - \mu_2$	(2) Probability of rejecting $\mu_1 \geq \mu_2$	(3) Probability of not rejecting $\mu_1 \geq \mu_2$
4.0	.000	1.000
3.5	.000	1.000
3.0	.000	1.000
2.5	.000	1.000
2.0	.000	1.000
1.5	.001	.999
1.0	.004	.996
.5	.016	.984
.0	.050	.950
− .5	.126	.874
−1.0	.259	.741
−1.5	.442	.558
−2.0	.639	.361
−2.5	.804	.196
−3.0	.912	.088
−3.5	.968	.032
−4.0	.991	.009

A Type II error will be made whenever it is true that $\mu_1 < \mu_2$ and we fail to reject the null hypothesis. Thus a Type II error can only be made for those alternatives shown in column (1) of Table 11.3 where $\mu_1 < \mu_2$. Since column (2) gives the probability of rejecting the null hypothesis when the various alternatives shown in column (1) are true, the probability of not rejecting the null hypothesis will be one minus the probability of rejecting. These probabilities are given in column (3) of Table 11.3. For all of the alternatives $\mu_1 < \mu_2$, the probabilities given in column (3) correspond to the probability of making a Type II error, that is, of failing to reject the null

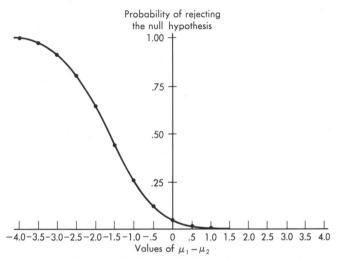

Figure **11.5**—The power function of the one-sided test of the null hypothesis $\mu_1 \geq \mu_2$ when $\sigma_{\bar{X}_1 - \bar{X}_2} = 1.00$ and the probability of a Type I error is not to exceed .05.

hypothesis when it is false. Figure 11.5 shows the power function of the one-sided test of the null hypothesis $\mu_1 \geq \mu_2$.

11.5   Power of the One-Sided Test of $\mu_1 \leq \mu_2$

In Table 11.3 we have followed the procedures described above for the one-sided test of the null hypothesis $\mu_1 \leq \mu_2$. Column (1) of Table 11.3 gives selected values of $\mu_1 - \mu_2$. Column (2) gives the probability of rejecting the null hypothesis for each of the alternatives shown in column (1). For this one-sided test, a Type I error can occur only if one of the alternatives $\mu_1 \leq \mu_2$ is true and we reject the null hypothesis. Column (2) shows that the probability of a Type I error will be .05, if it is true that $\mu_1 = \mu_2$. If $\mu_1 < \mu_2$, the probability of a Type I error will be less than .05.

A Type II error will occur when it is true that $\mu_1 > \mu_2$, but our test fails

Table 11.3—Probability of rejecting and failing to reject the null hypothesis $\mu_1 \leq \mu_2$ when $\sigma_{\overline{X}_1 - \overline{X}_2} = 1.00$ and the various values of $\mu_1 - \mu_2$ shown in the table are true. The hypothesis is rejected if $z = \overline{X}_1 - \overline{X}_2 \geq 1.645$

(1) Values of $\mu_1 - \mu_2$	(2) Probability of rejecting $\mu_1 \leq \mu_2$	(3) Probability of not rejecting $\mu_1 \leq \mu_2$
4.0	.991	.009
3.5	.968	.032
3.0	.912	.088
2.5	.804	.196
2.0	.639	.361
1.5	.442	.558
1.0	.259	.741
.5	.126	.874
.0	.050	.950
− .5	.016	.984
−1.0	.004	.996
−1.5	.001	.999
−2.0	.000	1.000
−2.5	.000	1.000
−3.0	.000	1.000
−3.5	.000	1.000
−4.0	.000	1.000

to reject the null hypothesis. Again, since we know the probability of rejecting the null hypothesis for the various alternatives shown in column (1) of Table 11.3, we can find the probability of failing to reject the null hypothesis for these alternatives. The probability for any given alternative in column (1) will be one minus the corresponding probability of rejecting the null hypothesis. These probabilities are given in column (3) of Table 11.3. Figure 11.6 shows the power function for the one-sided test of the null hypothesis $\mu_1 \leq \mu_2$.

11.6 A Comparison of a One- and a Two-Sided Test When $\mu_1 > \mu_2$

Consider only the one-sided test of the null hypothesis $\mu_1 \leq \mu_2$ and the two-sided test of the null hypothesis $\mu_1 = \mu_2$, when one of the alternatives, $\mu_1 > \mu_2$, is true. In Figure 11.7 we have graphed the power functions of (a) the two-sided test of the null hypothesis $\mu_1 = \mu_2$ and of (b) the one-sided test of the null hypothesis $\mu_1 \leq \mu_2$. It will be clear from an examination of

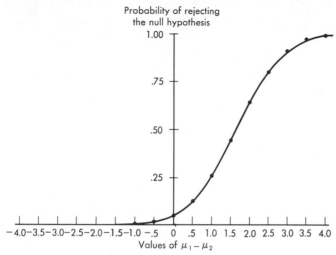

Figure **11.6**—The power function of the one-sided test of the null hypothesis $\mu_1 \leq \mu_2$ when $\sigma_{\bar{x}_1 - \bar{x}_2} = 1.00$ and the probability of a Type I error is not to exceed .05.

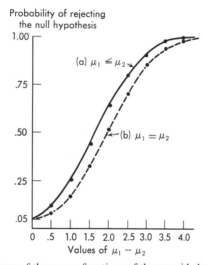

Figure **11.7**—A comparison of the power functions of the one-sided test of the null hypothesis $\mu_1 \leq \mu_2$ and of the two-sided test of the null hypothesis $\mu_1 = \mu_2$ for the class of alternatives $\mu_1 > \mu_2$.

Figure 11.7 that both tests have less power, that is, they are less likely to reject the null hypothesis when it is false—when $\mu_1 > \mu_2$, and $\mu_1 - \mu_2$ is close to zero. The power of both tests increases as μ_1 becomes greater than μ_2. The power of the one-sided test is greater than that of the two-sided test, but both approach maximum power of 1.00 as μ_1 becomes greater than μ_2.

The power of both the one- and two-sided test can be increased by increasing the number of observations in the two treatment groups. As n increases, the standard error of the difference between the two means will decrease, and the power functions of the two tests will show a much more rapid rise than those shown in Figure 11.7. This means that if it is true that $\mu_1 > \mu_2$, then both the one- and the two-sided tests are more likely to detect small positive values of $\mu_1 - \mu_2$ when n is large than when n is small. Similar considerations apply to the one-sided test $\mu_1 \geq \mu_2$ and the two-sided test $\mu_1 = \mu_2$ when it is in fact true that $\mu_1 < \mu_2$.

The probability of making a Type II error will depend upon the true, but unknown, difference between μ_1 and μ_2, and whether we make a one-sided or a two-sided test of significance. In making a two-sided test of the null hypothesis $\mu_1 = \mu_2$, the experimenter is expressing his interest in a difference between $\overline{X}_1$ and $\overline{X}_2$ regardless of the direction of this difference. The two-sided test thus guards against both groups of alternatives H_1 and H_2, that is, $\mu_1 > \mu_2$ and $\mu_1 < \mu_2$. In making a one-sided test of the null hypothesis $\mu_1 \geq \mu_2$, the experimenter is saying that he is willing to accept all values of $\overline{X}_1 - \overline{X}_2 \geq 0$ as compatible with the null hypothesis, regardless of their magnitude, and that he wishes to guard only against the alternatives H_2, that is, of making a Type II error when it is true that $\mu_1 < \mu_2$. Similarly, in making a one-sided test of the null hypothesis $\mu_1 \leq \mu_2$, the experimenter is saying that he is willing to regard all possible values of $\overline{X}_1 - \overline{X}_2 \leq 0$ as compatible with the null hypothesis, regardless of their magnitude, and that he wishes only to guard against the alternatives H_1, that is, of making a Type II error when it is true that $\mu_1 > \mu_2$.

11.7   One- and Two-Sided Tests: General Considerations

In some discrimination experiments, we may be interested only in those outcomes that indicate that a subject has performed better than chance and in other discrimination experiments we may be interested only in those outcomes that indicate that a subject has performed worse than chance. Suppose, for example, that an individual claims to have the power of extrasensory perception. We design a binomial experiment in such a way that if he does not have extrasensory perception, then the probability of a correct response on each trial is $P = 1/2$. In this case, only those outcomes of the experiment better than chance would offer evidence to support his claim. If his performance is significantly worse than chance, this outcome is of no more interest than one that might be obtained from a subject who does not claim to have extrasensory perception and who may do significantly worse than chance as a result of random variation.

On the other hand, if we were testing a subject for deafness in an auditory discrimination experiment, we might be very much concerned with outcomes worse than chance, but not with those that are significantly better than chance. For example, suppose that we have designed a binomial experiment such that for individuals with normal hearing we assume that the probability of a correct response on each trial is $P = .8$. With $n = 100$ trials, we would then be interested in a subject's performance only if he makes fewer than 80 correct responses. If his performance is significantly worse than chance, then, upon further investigation, we may recommend that he consider the possibility of purchasing a hearing aid. But if his performance is significantly better than chance, it would seem reasonable to assume that he has at least normal hearing and is not in need of a hearing aid.

In the above cases, we note that there is a *degree of practicality* involved in deciding to make a one-sided test rather than a two-sided test. In testing the difference between the means of two groups, we may also, at times, be interested only in outcomes in a given direction, because of practical considerations, and thus decide upon a one-sided test.

We take the position, however, that in scientific research that is not primarily concerned with practical decisions, *two-sided tests are most often appropriate*. Theoretical considerations may lead us to expect a difference in only one direction, but we should not blind ourselves to the possibility that we may be wrong. A two-sided test provides power against both the possibility that $\mu_1 > \mu_2$ and the possibility that $\mu_1 < \mu_2$ and, in general, we suggest that we should be concerned about both possibilities.

11.8   Estimating the Number of Observations Needed in an Experiment

It is unfortunately the case that many experiments in the behavioral sciences are concerned primarily with Type I errors and not with Type II errors. In experiments involving a treatment and a control group or two treatment groups, it is almost certain that every null hypothesis of the form $H_0: \mu_1 = \mu_2$, with the alternative being $H_1: \mu_1 \neq \mu_2$, is false and should be rejected. If this is the case, then it is almost certain that when an experimenter makes a two-sided test and fails to reject H_0, he is making a Type II error.

If we are reasonably certain that the two-sided test of H_0, as stated above, is false, then why do we bother with an experiment to test this null hypothesis? There are a number of reasons. We do not necessarily know whether it is true that $\mu_1 > \mu_2$ or whether it is true that $\mu_1 < \mu_2$. The outcome of an experiment provides evidence concerning the sign or direction of the difference between μ_1 and μ_2. Furthermore, we would like to know not only the sign or direction of the difference, but also something about the magnitude of the difference between μ_1 and μ_2. By finding the 95 or 99 percent confidence intervals for the difference between μ_1 and μ_2, based upon the outcome of an experiment, we obtain reasonable information about the limits of the difference between the two means.

In some cases, even though $\mu_1 \neq \mu_2$, the difference between the two means may be so small as to have either no theoretical or no practical significance. For example, if μ_1, the mean burning time for Brand 1 light bulbs, differs from μ_2, the mean burning time for Brand 2 light bulbs, by only a few seconds or even a few minutes, the difference between μ_1 and μ_2 may be judged to have little practical significance even though the difference may be of statistical significance. If the cost of the two bulbs is the same, surely you would not go out of your way to purchase the brand that will, on the average, give you only a few more minutes of burning time. On the other hand a large difference in burning time between the two bulbs may be of practical significance to you in that knowledge of this fact might determine which brand you purchase.

Very small differences between μ_1 and μ_2 may also, under certain circumstances, be of great importance. Suppose that two new drugs are discovered and both are believed to be of value in treating a fatal disease. If it should in fact be the case that the mean recovery rate for patients treated with one drug is $\mu_1 = .61$ and the mean recovery rate for patients treated with the other drug is $\mu_2 = .63$, then for patients suffering from the disease, it may be very important indeed that they receive the drug with the higher recovery rate.

For reasons pointed out above, it would seem reasonable that in planning an experiment some consideration should be given to the magnitude of the difference between μ_1 and μ_2 that would be judged to be of *either* practical *or* theoretical significance. For example, an experimenter might decide that if $H_1 : \mu_1 - \mu_2$ is at least equal to $|\delta|$, where $|\delta|$ is the minimum absolute value of the difference between μ_1 and μ_2, this difference would have either practical or theoretical significance. Assume that it is the case that H_1 is true. If H_1 is true, then the experimenter decides that he wants the probability of a Type II error to be no greater than β. On the other hand, if H_0 is true, he wants the probability of a Type I error to be α. Now, if in addition to these decisions, the experimenter has some estimate of the variance to be expected on the dependent variable under the conditions of the experiment, then it is possible to estimate the number of observations[1] needed for each of the two groups involved in the experiment, in order to meet the requirements for both the probability he has set for a Type I and a Type II error.

We consider the case where it is decided that we want β, the probability of a Type II error, not to exceed .16. We set α, the probability of a Type I error at .05. At the left in Figure 11.8, we have the distribution of $\overline{X}_1 - \overline{X}_2$ when H_0 is true, that is, when $\mu_1 - \mu_2 = 0$. The ordinate at c cuts off .025 of the area in the right tail of this distribution. We let z_0 be the distance from

---

[1] Cohen (1962) has reviewed experiments reported in the *Journal of Abnormal and Social Psychology* and concludes that in many of these investigations the number of observations was so small that the tests of significance could be expected to have relatively little power even if the difference between μ_1 and μ_2 was, in fact, moderately large.

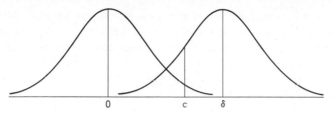

Figure **11.8**—The distribution of $\bar{X}_1 - \bar{X}_2$ when H_0 is true, that is, when $\mu_1 - \mu_2 = 0$, is shown at the left. The ordinate at c cuts off .025 of the total area in the right tail of this distribution. The curve at the right shows the distribution of $\bar{X}_1 - \bar{X}_2$ when H_0 is false and $\mu_1 - \mu_2 = \delta$. The ordinate at c cuts off .16 of the total area in the left tail of this distribution.

zero to c in the standard normal curve and from the table of the standard normal distribution we find that $z_0 = 1.96$ will cut off .025 of the total area in the *right* tail. Thus, if H_0 is true, the probability of $z_0 \geq 1.96$ is .025. The curve at the right in Figure 11.8 shows the distribution of $\bar{X}_1 - \bar{X}_2$ when $\mu_1 - \mu_2 = \delta$. The ordinate at c cuts off .16 of the total area in the *left* tail of this distribution. We let z_1 be the distance from δ to c in the standard normal curve and from the table of the standard normal distribution we find that $z_1 = -1.00$ will cut off .16 of the area in the left tail. Thus, if $\mu_1 - \mu_2 = \delta$, the probability of $z_1 \leq -1.00$ will be .16.

We have

$$z_0 = \frac{c - 0}{\sqrt{\dfrac{2\sigma^2}{n}}} = 1.96 \quad \text{and} \quad z_1 = \frac{c - \delta}{\sqrt{\dfrac{2\sigma^2}{n}}} = -1.00$$

Using the two equations above we have

$$c = 1.96\sqrt{\frac{2\sigma^2}{n}} \quad \text{and} \quad c = \delta - \sqrt{\frac{2\sigma^2}{n}}$$

Then

$$\delta = 1.96\sqrt{\frac{2\sigma^2}{n}} + \sqrt{\frac{2\sigma^2}{n}}$$

$$= \sqrt{\frac{2\sigma^2}{n}}(1.96 + 1.00)$$

and[2]

$$n = \frac{2\sigma^2}{\delta^2}(1.96 + 1.00)^2 \tag{11.1}$$

---

[2] It will make relatively little difference if we substitute 2.00 for 1.96 in (11.1) and by doing so we obtain an easily remembered expression. Thus, $n = 18\sigma^2/\delta^2$.

Now suppose on the basis of previous experiments we can assume that $\sigma = 5$ and that we have decided that if the absolute difference between μ_1 and μ_2 is at least 3 this would be of interest. Then substituting in (11.1) we have

$$n = \frac{2(5)^2}{(3)^2}(2.96)^2 = 48.7$$

and we find that $n_1 = n_2 = n = 49$ is the minimum number of observations we should have in each of our two groups.[3]

If the various assumptions we have made are correct, then, for the two-sided test, the probability of a Type I error will be .05 and the probability of a Type II error will be .16 if $\mu_1 - \mu_2 = 3$ or if $\mu_1 - \mu_2 = -3$. Of course, if the absolute difference between μ_1 and μ_2 is greater than 3, the probability of a Type II error will be less than .16.

In the discussion above, we have considered δ as some absolute difference between μ_1 and μ_2. It is obvious, however, that δ can also be expressed in terms of σ. If we let $\Delta = \delta/\sigma$, then we have

$$\delta = \Delta\sigma \tag{11.2}$$

and substituting $\Delta\sigma$ for δ in (11.1), we obtain

$$n = \frac{2\sigma^2}{\Delta^2\sigma^2}(1.96 + 1.00)^2$$

$$= \frac{2}{\Delta^2}(2.96)^2 \tag{11.3}$$

Table 11.4—The number of observations required in each of two groups for a two-sided test with $\alpha = .05$ and $\beta = .16$ for various values of Δ

Δ	n	Δ	n
.10	1752	.60	49
.15	779	.65	42
.20	438	.70	36
.25	281	.75	31
.30	195	.80	28
.35	143	.85	25
.40	110	.90	22
.45	87	.95	20
.50	70	1.00	18
.55	58		

[3] We have taken $\mu_1 - \mu_2 = \delta$ in finding n. We would obtain the same result by taking $\mu_1 - \mu_2 = -\delta$.

Using (11.3) it is possible to find the number of observations required in each of two groups for a two-sided test with $\alpha = .05$ and $\beta = .16$ for any difference between μ_1 and μ_2 that is expressed in terms of σ. Table 11.4 gives the approximate value of n for various values of Δ. We note that if $\delta = \mu_1 - \mu_2 = .25\sigma$, then approximately 281 observations are needed for each group, regardless of the value of σ. Similarly, if $\delta = \mu_1 - \mu_2 = .50\sigma$, then approximately 70 observations are needed in each group and when $\delta = \mu_1 - \mu_2 = 1.00\sigma$, approximately 18 observations are needed in each group.

EXAMPLES

11.1—In a pilot experiment, with $n_1 = n_2 = 10$ subjects randomly assigned to each of two treatments, the standard error of the difference between the two means was equal to 3.0. Assume that in a repetition of the experiment the estimate of the population variance remains the same. How many subjects will the experimenter have to use in each of his two groups in order to reduce the standard error of the difference between the two means to 1.0?

11.2—An experimenter has reason to believe that $\sigma = 5.0$ for a dependent variable of interest. He plans to assign the same number of subjects to each of two treatments and to make a two-sided test of the null hypothesis $\mu_1 = \mu_2$. He sets α, the probability of a Type I error, at .05. If the true difference between μ_1 and μ_2 is at least 2 or -2, he wants the probability of not rejecting the null hypothesis to be no greater than .16. How many subjects should he use in each of his two groups? Use the table of the standard normal curve in determining your answer.

11.3—In an experiment the standard error of the difference between two means was 1.42 with $n_1 = n_2 = 10$ subjects in each treatment group. A repetition of the experiment is planned and the experimenter wishes to be able to reject the null hypothesis $\mu_1 = \mu_2$ if the absolute difference between μ_1 and μ_2 is 2.56 or greater. Use the table of the standard normal curve in determining your answers.

(a) Find the value of s^2 and assume that $s^2 = \sigma^2$.
(b) How many subjects should the experimenter use in each group, if $\alpha = .05$ and if the probability of a Type II error is to be no greater than .16?
(c) How many subjects should the experimenter use in each group, if $\alpha = .10$ and if the probability of a Type II error is to be no greater than .50?

11.4—Assume that $\sigma_{\bar{X}_1 - \bar{X}_2} = 2.0$. Use the table of the standard normal curve in determining your answers.

(a) What are the values of $\overline{X}_1 - \overline{X}_2$, for a two-sided test, that will result in $z = 1.96$ and $z = -1.96$?

(b) Using the results obtained in (a), find the probability of rejecting the null hypothesis, if $\mu_1 - \mu_2 = 3.0$.

(c) In the same manner find the probability of rejecting the null hypothesis $\mu_1 = \mu_2$, if various other alternatives to the null hypothesis are true. Plot the power function of the test of significance for these alternatives on graph paper.

(d) Suppose that the number of subjects is increased in each treatment group so that $\sigma_{\overline{X}_1 - \overline{X}_2} = 1.0$. Find the power function of the test of significance for various alternatives to the null hypothesis and plot this function on the same graph with that of (c).

(e) What conclusions can you draw from a comparison of the two power functions?

11.5—Find a journal article in which a nonsignificant value of t is reported.

(a) Assume that the value of s^2 reported in the experiment is equal to σ^2.

(b) Let $\alpha = .05$ for a two-sided test of the null hypothesis $\mu_1 = \mu_2$. Assume that the experiment is to be repeated and that, if it is true that $\mu_1 - \mu_2$ is equal to the reported value of $\overline{X}_1 - \overline{X}_2$, you want the probability of a Type II error to be no greater than .16. How many subjects should you use in each treatment group? Use the table of the standard normal curve in determining your answer.

11.6—Explain why, other things being equal, the power of a test increases as n increases.

11.7—If $n_1 = n_2 = n$, then the standard error of the difference between two means is given by $\sqrt{2\sigma^2/n}$ where σ^2 is the population variance. Let $\sigma^2 = 50.0$. Plot the value of the standard error of the difference between two treatment means as a function of n.

11.8—Give a one-sentence definition of each of the following terms or concepts:

one-sided test	Type II error
two-sided test	power of a test
Type I error	

CHAPTER 12

Significance Tests for Correlation and Regression Coefficients

12.1 Introduction

Suppose that there exists a population of paired (X, Y) values and that for this population the correlation coefficient is equal to ρ. If random samples of n are drawn from this population, each of the n observations will consist of an ordered pair (X, Y) of values and for each random sample it will be possible to calculate the sample correlation coefficient r. If ρ is close to zero, then the sampling distribution of r will be approximately normal in form, provided n is not too small. However, if ρ is not close to zero and if n is small, then the sampling distribution of r will not be normal in form but instead skewed. For example, if $\rho = .80$, and $n = 8$, the sample values will tend to cluster about .80, but there will be a tail to the left, that is, the distribution will be left skewed as shown in Figure 12.1.

In this chapter we discuss methods of testing the significance of correlation and regression coefficients and of the difference between two correlation coefficients or two regression coefficients. If we have a single random sample and wish to test the null hypothesis that $\rho = 0$, this test can be made in terms of the t distribution because, if the null hypothesis is true, the sampling distribution of r is approximately normal in form. But, if we wish to test the null hypothesis that $\rho = .80$, then, as Figure 12.1 shows, the sampling distribution of r for small samples will not be normal. Similarly, if we have two small samples drawn from the same population in which $\rho = .80$, the sampling distribution of the difference between the two r's will not be normal in form. We shall see, however, that it is possible to transform r into a new variable z' that is approximately normally distributed. Tests of significance can then be made with respect to the transformed variable z'.

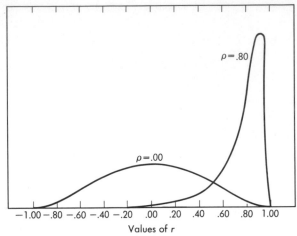

Figure **12.1**—The distribution of the correlation coefficient for random samples of $n = 8$ paired values when the samples are drawn from populations having the indicated values of ρ.

12.2   Testing the Null Hypothesis that $\rho = 0$

In Table 12.1 we give the values of X and Y for two independent random samples. For the first sample we have $n_1 = 15$ observations and for the second sample we have $n_2 = 10$ observations. For the combined sample of $n = 25$ observations, we have

$$r = \frac{837 - \dfrac{(105)(161)}{25}}{\sqrt{\left(609 - \dfrac{(105)^2}{25}\right)\left(1263 - \dfrac{(161)^2}{25}\right)}}$$

$$= \frac{160.8}{\sqrt{(168.00)(226.16)}}$$

$$= .825$$

To test the null hypothesis that ρ, the population correlation, is equal to zero, we find

$$t = \frac{r}{\sqrt{1 - r^2}} \sqrt{n - 2} \tag{12.1}$$

Then t as defined by (12.1) will be distributed in accordance with the tabled values of t with degrees of freedom equal to $n - 2$, when the null hypothesis that the population correlation is zero is true. For our example, we have

$$t = \frac{.825}{\sqrt{1 - (.825)^2}} \sqrt{25 - 2} = 7.00$$

Table 12.1—Values of a dependent variable X and an independent variable Y for two independent random samples of $n = 15$ and $n = 10$ observations

		Sample 1: $n = 15$		
(1) X_1	(2) Y_1	(3) X_1^2	(4) Y_1^2	(5) $X_1 Y_1$
6	10	36	100	60
1	6	1	36	6
1	3	1	9	3
1	4	1	16	4
6	9	36	81	54
7	10	49	100	70
2	3	4	9	6
4	8	16	64	32
8	11	64	121	88
8	11	64	121	88
1	6	1	36	6
5	10	25	100	50
7	10	49	100	70
3	5	9	25	15
3	4	9	16	12
$\sum$ 63	110	365	934	564

		Sample 2: $n = 10$		
X_2	Y_2	X_2^2	Y_2^2	$X_2 Y_2$
3	2	9	4	6
1	4	1	16	4
1	2	1	4	2
7	7	49	49	49
6	6	36	36	36
3	2	9	4	6
1	4	1	16	4
5	6	25	36	30
8	10	64	100	80
7	8	49	64	56
$\sum$ 42	51	244	329	273
$\sum$ 105	161	609	1263	837

Entering the table of t with 23 d.f., we find that the probability of $t \geq 2.807$ or $t \leq -2.807$ is .01, when the null hypothesis is true. Thus, if it is true that $\rho = 0$, then the probability of $t \geq 7.00$ is much smaller than .01 and we may decide to reject the null hypothesis.

It is possible to substitute in (12.1) with various values of n and with the tabled values of t and to solve for the values of r that would be required for significance. This has been done and the resulting values of r are given in Table VI in Appendix B. The values of r given in Table VI are those that would be regarded as significant with probabilities given by the column headings, if one-sided tests are made. For a two-sided test, the probabilities given by the column headings should be doubled.

Table VI is entered with degrees of freedom equal to $n - 2$, where n is the number of paired (X, Y) values. If we enter the table with the $n - 2 = 23$ d.f., we find that $r \geq .505$ or $r \leq -.505$ would be significant with probability of .01 for a two-sided test of the null hypothesis that $\rho = 0$.

It is evident from Table VI that a relatively large observed value of r may not be significant when based upon a small number of observations. On the other hand, as n increases, relatively small values of r will result in the rejection of the null hypothesis. For example, if a correlation coefficient is based upon $n = 1000$ observations, then values of r equal to or greater than .06 or equal to or less than $-.06$ have a probability of approximately .05, when the null hypothesis is true. We have found that similar considerations apply to other tests of significance, as, for example in testing the significance of the difference between two means. Other things being equal, very small differences between two sample means will meet the requirements of statistical significance, if we have a sufficiently large number of observations.

12.3   The z' Transformation for r

Any value of r may be transformed to a new variable z', defined as

$$z' = \frac{1}{2} [\log_e (1 + r) - \log_e (1 - r)] \tag{12.2}$$

where r is the observed value of the correlation coefficient. In order to make the z' values of (12.2) available without the need of a table of natural logarithms, values of r were substituted in (12.2) and the corresponding values of z' were obtained. These z' values are given in Table VII in Appendix B. For our example, we have $r = .825$ and from Table VII we find that the corresponding value of $z' = 1.172$. The z' distribution is symmetrical about zero and if a correlation has a minus sign, then so also will the corresponding value of z'. For example, if we have $r = -.825$, then $z' = -1.172$.

Fisher (1921) has shown that the distribution of z' is approximately normal in form and that for all practical purposes the distribution is independent of the population correlation ρ and the sample size n. This means that the distribution of z' remains approximately normal in form even when samples are drawn from a population in which ρ is large and when n is small. Furthermore, the standard error of z' is related in a very simple way to n and is given by

$$\sigma_{z'} = \frac{1}{\sqrt{n-3}} \qquad (12.3)$$

where n is the number of observations on which r is based. For our example we have $n = 25$ observations and

$$\sigma_{z'} = \frac{1}{\sqrt{25-3}} = .21$$

Now, if z' is approximately normally distributed, then

$$z = \frac{z' - z_\rho'}{\sigma_{z'}} \qquad (12.4)$$

will have a distribution that is approximately that of a standard normal variable with $\mu = 0$ and $\sigma = 1$ and can be evaluated in terms of the table of the standard normal curve. In (12.4) z' is the z' value corresponding to an observed value of r and z_ρ' is the z' value corresponding to ρ.

We can use (12.4) to establish a 95 or 99 percent confidence interval for z_ρ'. For a 99 percent confidence interval we would have

$$-2.58 \leq \frac{z' - z_\rho'}{\sigma_{z'}} \leq 2.58 \qquad (12.5)$$

In our example, we have $r = .825$ and $z' = 1.172$ with $\sigma_{z'} = 1/\sqrt{25-3} = .21$. Then, for a 99 percent confidence interval, we have

$$-2.58 \leq \frac{1.172 - z_\rho'}{.21} \leq 2.58$$

or

$$1.172 + (.21)(2.58) \geq z_\rho' \geq 1.172 - (.21)(2.58)$$
$$1.714 \geq z_\rho' \geq .630$$

as the 99 percent confidence interval for z_ρ'. From the table of z' we find that the r's corresponding to the two z' values are approximately .94 and .56. Thus we may be reasonably confident that $.56 < \rho < .94$.

We may note that the confidence limits, .56 and .94, are not equally distant from the observed value of $r = .825$. The lower confidence limit deviates .265 from the observed value of r and the upper confidence limit deviates .115 from r. However, as n increases, the upper and lower confidence limits on the r scale will become more symmetrical about the observed value of r. For example, if $r = .825$ was based upon $n = 403$ observations, then $\sigma_{z'} = 1/\sqrt{403 - 3} = .05$. If we now find the 99 percent confidence interval, we will observe that the lower limit on the r scale is approximately .78 and the upper limit is approximately .86. These two values, based upon a sample of $n = 403$ observations, are more symmetrical about the observed value of $r = .825$ than the two values based upon a sample of $n = 25$ observations. What this indicates, of course, is that as n increases the skewness of the sampling distribution of r decreases.

12.4   The Significance of the Difference between Two r's

One of the advantages of the z' transformation for r is that it also permits us to test the significance of the difference between two values of r obtained from two independent random samples. To illustrate the test of significance, we use the data given in Table 12.1 for two samples. We show the calculation of r_1 and r_2 in some detail because we want to make use of certain components of the calculations later on in the chapter. For r_1 we have

$$r_1 = \frac{564 - \dfrac{(63)(110)}{15}}{\sqrt{\left(365 - \dfrac{(63)^2}{15}\right)\left(934 - \dfrac{(110)^2}{15}\right)}}$$

$$= \frac{102}{\sqrt{(100.40)(127.33)}}$$

$$= .90$$

and for r_2 we have

$$r_2 = \frac{273 - \dfrac{(42)(51)}{10}}{\sqrt{\left(244 - \dfrac{(42)^2}{10}\right)\left(329 - \dfrac{(51)^2}{10}\right)}}$$

$$= \frac{58.8}{\sqrt{(67.6)(68.9)}}$$

$$= .86$$

The two values, $r_1 = .90$ and $r_2 = .86$, are not equal and we ask whether it is reasonable to believe that the two samples are from a common population so that $\rho_1 = \rho_2$? If we reject this null hypothesis, we will conclude that $\rho_1 \neq \rho_2$ or, in other words, that the difference between $r_1 = .90$ and $r_2 = .86$ is sufficiently great that we do not believe they are both estimates of the same population value ρ.

To make the test of significance, we transform both r_1 and r_2 into z' values. The standard error of the difference between two independent values of z' will be given by the usual formula for the standard error of the difference between two independent variables or, in the case of two z' values,

$$\sigma_{z_1'-z_2'} = \sqrt{\sigma_{z_1'}{}^2 + \sigma_{z_2'}{}^2}$$

$$= \sqrt{\frac{1}{n_1 - 3} + \frac{1}{n_2 - 3}} \tag{12.6}$$

In our example, we have $n_1 = 15$ and $n_2 = 10$ and therefore

$$\sigma_{z_1'-z_2'} = \sqrt{\frac{1}{15 - 3} + \frac{1}{10 - 3}} = .48$$

Then, the difference between z_1' and z_2' divided by the standard error of the difference results in

$$z = \frac{z_1' - z_2'}{\sigma_{z_1'-z_2'}} \tag{12.7}$$

If the null hypothesis $\rho_1 = \rho_2$ is true, then z will have a distribution that is approximately that of a standard normal variable with $\mu = 0$ and $\sigma = 1$ and can be evaluated in terms of the table of the standard normal curve.

In our example, we have $r_1 = .90$ with $z_1' = 1.472$ and $r_2 = .86$ with $z_2' = 1.293$. Then substituting in (12.7) with these two values of z' and with $\sigma_{z_1'-z_2'} = .48$, we have

$$z = \frac{1.472 - 1.293}{.48} = .37$$

For a two-sided test, using the table of the standard normal curve, we find that the probability of $z \geq .37$ or $z \leq -.37$ is about .71, when the null hypothesis that $\rho_1 = \rho_2$ is true. We may regard the null hypothesis as tenable and conclude that the difference between the two correlation coefficients is not sufficiently great to cause us to believe that they may not both be estimates of the same population value ρ.

12.5   Testing the Null Hypothesis that $\beta_Y = 0$

We have previously found that for the combined group of $n = 25$ observations of Table 12.1 that $\Sigma\, xy = 160.8$ and that $\Sigma\, x^2 = 168.0$. Then, the regression coefficient of Y on X will be

$$b_Y = \frac{\Sigma\, xy}{\Sigma\, x^2} = \frac{160.8}{168.0} = .957$$

The standard error of b_Y will be given by

$$s_{b_Y} = \frac{s_{Y\cdot X}}{\sqrt{\Sigma\, x^2}} \qquad (12.8)$$

where $s_{Y\cdot X}$ is the standard error of estimate. For the combined set of $n = 25$ observations of Table 21.1 we have $\Sigma\, y^2 = 226.16$ and

$$s_{Y\cdot X} = \sqrt{\frac{\Sigma\, y^2 - \dfrac{(\Sigma\, xy)^2}{\Sigma\, x^2}}{n - 2}}$$

$$= \sqrt{\frac{226.16 - \dfrac{(160.8)^2}{168.0}}{25 - 2}}$$

$$= 1.772$$

Then

$$s_{b_Y} = \frac{1.772}{\sqrt{168}} = .137$$

To test the null hypothesis that the population regression coefficient, which we designate by β_Y, is equal to zero, we define

$$t = \frac{b_Y - \beta_Y}{s_{b_Y}} \qquad (12.9)$$

and, for our example, we have

$$t = \frac{.957 - 0}{.137} = 6.99$$

with $n - 2$ d.f.

Entering the table of t with $n - 2 = 23$ d.f., we find that for a two-sided test $t \geq 2.807$ or $t \leq -2.807$ has probability of .01, when the null hypothesis is true. The probability associated with our observed value of $t = 6.99$ is, therefore, much less than .01, if the null hypothesis is true, and we may decide to reject the null hypothesis.

When we tested the null hypothesis that $\rho = 0$ for the same data, we had t, as defined by (12.1), equal to 7.00. In testing the null hypothesis that $\beta_Y = 0$, we have t, as defined by (12.9), equal to 6.99. As a matter of fact, the test of the null hypothesis that $\rho = 0$ is identical with the test of the null hypothesis that $\beta_Y = 0$ and 7.00 and 6.99 differ only as a result of rounding errors. We leave the proof that (12.1) and (12.9) are algebraically identical as an exercise.

12.6   The Significance of the Difference between Two Regression Coefficients

For the data of Table 12.1 we may calculate two regression coefficients, one for the sample of $n_1 = 15$ observations and the other for the sample of $n_2 = 10$ observations. We have already calculated Σxy and Σx^2 for each of these two samples in the process of finding the values of r for each sample. Using the results of these calculations, we have

$$b_{Y_1} = \frac{102.0}{100.4} = 1.02$$

and

$$b_{Y_2} = \frac{58.8}{67.6} = .87$$

These two regression coefficients are not equal and to determine whether they differ significantly, we may test the null hypothesis that $\beta_{Y_1} = \beta_{Y_2}$.

We assume that the residual variances for the samples are homogeneous. With this assumption an estimate of the common residual variance will be given by

$$s_{Y \cdot x}^2 = \frac{\left(\Sigma y_1^2 - \frac{(\Sigma x_1 y_1)^2}{\Sigma x_1^2}\right) + \left(\Sigma y_2^2 - \frac{(\Sigma x_2 y_2)^2}{\Sigma x_2^2}\right)}{n_1 + n_2 - 4} \qquad (12.10)$$

Substituting in (12.10) with the results of previous calculations, we have

$$s_{Y \cdot X}^2 = \frac{\left(127.33 - \frac{(102.0)^2}{100.4}\right) + \left(68.90 - \frac{(58.8)^2}{67.6}\right)}{15 + 10 - 4}$$

$$= \frac{23.70 + 17.75}{21}$$

$$= 1.9738$$

The standard error of the difference between b_{Y_1} and b_{Y_2} will then be given by

$$s_{b_{Y_1} - b_{Y_2}} = \sqrt{\frac{s_{Y \cdot X}^2}{\sum x_1^2} + \frac{s_{Y \cdot X}^2}{\sum x_2^2}}$$

$$= \sqrt{s_{Y \cdot X}^2 \left(\frac{1}{\sum x_1^2} + \frac{1}{\sum x_2^2}\right)} \qquad (12.11)$$

where $s_{Y \cdot X}^2$ is defined by (12.10) and, for our example, is equal to 1.9738. Then, substituting in (12.11) with $\sum x_1^2 = 100.4$ and $\sum x_2^2 = 67.6$, we have

$$s_{b_{Y_1} - b_{Y_2}} = \sqrt{1.9738 \left(\frac{1}{100.4} + \frac{1}{67.6}\right)} = .22$$

As a test of significance of the difference between b_{Y_1} and b_{Y_2}, we define

$$t = \frac{(b_{Y_1} - b_{Y_2}) - (\beta_{Y_1} - \beta_{Y_2})}{s_{b_{Y_1} - b_{Y_2}}} \qquad (12.12)$$

with $n_1 + n_2 - 4$ d.f. If the null hypothesis that $\beta_{Y_1} = \beta_{Y_2}$ is true, then the t of (12.12) will be distributed as t with $n_1 + n_2 - 4$ d.f. and can be evaluated in terms of the table of t. For our example, we have $b_{Y_1} = 1.02$ and $b_{Y_2} = .87$, with

$$s_{b_{Y_1} - b_{Y_2}} = .22$$

Substituting in (12.12) with these values we have

$$t = \frac{1.02 - .87}{.22} = .68$$

From the table of t, we find that for 21 d.f. with a two-sided test, $t \leq -2.080$ or $t \geq 2.080$ will be significant with $\alpha = .05$ when the null hypothesis is true. Because our observed value of $t = .68$, we may regard the null hypothesis $\beta_{Y_1} = \beta_{Y_2}$ as tenable.

EXAMPLES

12.1—We have values of X and Y available for a group of $n_1 = 15$ subjects and another group of $n_2 = 10$ subjects.

Group 1		Group 2	
X	Y	X	Y
10	12	14	16
10	13	15	18
14	18	12	14
12	18	8	12
8	14	10	10
15	19	13	14
15	19	13	14
11	17	8	10
9	11	9	12
14	18	9	10
13	17		
8	12		
8	11		
10	14		
11	18		

(a) Find the value for r for the combined group of $n_1 + n_2 = n$ subjects. Find the 95 percent confidence interval for ρ.

(b) Find the values of r for the two groups and test the null hypothesis that $\rho_1 = \rho_2$.

(c) Find the value of b_Y for the combined group of $n_1 + n_2$ subjects and test the null hypothesis that $\beta_Y = 0$.

(d) Find the values of b_{Y_1} and b_{Y_2} for the two groups and test the null hypothesis that $\beta_{Y_1} = \beta_{Y_2}$.

12.2—An investigator reports that $r = .88$ for $n = 10$ pairs of observations. Test the null hypothesis that $\rho = 0$.

12.3—Would a value of $r = .33$ result in the rejection of the null hypothesis that $\rho = 0$, if based upon $n = 10$ pairs of observations and with $\alpha = .05$?

12.4—What value of r would be required in order to reject the null hypothesis that $\rho = 0$ for a sample of $n = 50$ paired observations, if $\alpha = .05$?

12.5—Prove that t as defined by (12.9) is equal to t as defined by (12.1).

12.6—For two independent samples, we have the following data:

	Sample 1	Sample 2
	$r_1 =$ .80	$r_2 =$ .60
	$s_Y =$ 5.0	$s_Y =$ 4.0
	$s_X =$ 10.0	$s_X =$ 8.0
	$n =$ 31	$n =$ 21

(a) Is r_1 significantly different from zero?
(b) Is r_2 significantly different from zero?
(c) Test the difference between r_1 and r_2 for significance.
(d) Find b_{Y_1} and b_{Y_2} and test the significance of the difference between these two regression coefficients.

12.7—Leahy (1935) reports a correlation coefficient of .20 between the intelligence test scores of fathers and their children based upon a sample of 186 cases. Leahy reports that in another sample of 255 cases a correlation of .28 was obtained between the intelligence test scores of fathers and their children. Can we conclude that these two correlation coefficients differ significantly?

12.8—The correlation between scores on a standardized arithmetic test and grades on a final examination for one section of elementary statistics consisting of 48 students was .56. For another section of 44 students, the correlation between the same two variables was .45. Test the significance of the difference between these two correlation coefficients.

12.9—If two correlation coefficients do not differ significantly so that each one may be assumed to be an estimate of the same population value ρ, then we may obtain a weighted average value of z' given by

$$\bar{z}' = \frac{(n_1 - 3)z_1' + (n_2 - 3)z_2'}{(n_1 - 3) + (n_2 - 3)}$$

where z_1' and z_2' correspond to the two sample values r_1 and r_2 and n_1 and n_2 to the size of the two samples. Then the value of r corresponding to the weighted average is an estimate of the population value ρ.

(a) If the two correlation coefficients in Example 12.6 do not differ significantly, find the value of r corresponding to $\bar{z}'$.
(b) If the two correlation coefficients in Example 12.7 do not differ significantly, find the value of r corresponding to $\bar{z}'$.
(c) If the two correlation coefficients in Example 12.8 do not differ significantly, find the value of r corresponding to $\bar{z}'$.

CHAPTER 13

The Analysis of Variance: Randomized Group Design

13.1 Introduction

Assume that we are interested in k different experimental conditions or treatments and that we randomly assign n subjects to each treatment. For each subject in each group or treatment we obtain a measure on a dependent variable X of interest. We assume that the population distribution of X is approximately normal with mean μ and variance σ^2.

Suppose now that the effect of one treatment is to increase the values of X for that treatment. The effect of another treatment may also systematically increase the values of X for that treatment but perhaps not to the same degree as the first treatment. Still another treatment may have the effect of decreasing the values of X for that treatment. Whenever one or more treatments operate differentially so as to result in systematic differences in the treatment means, we describe this as a treatment effect. More precisely, we say that we have a *treatment effect* if the average long-run values of the k treatment means are not all equal to the same value μ. On the other hand, if the average long-run values of the k sample means are such that $\mu_1 = \mu_2 = \cdots = \mu_k = \mu$, then we have no treatment effects. This is the null hypothesis we wish to test.

We know that even in the absence of treatment effects, the observed values of the k sample means will not all be equal to one another because in any given experiment the k means may still vary as a result of random variation. We shall show, however, that treatment effects serve to increase the variability of the k sample means. Thus, if we conclude that the variability in the k treatment means is greater than the variability to be expected in the absence of treatment effects, we shall, in essence, be saying that we have one or more treatment effects. To conclude that we have one or more treatment effects is not to say that every treatment mean differs significantly from every other treatment mean but only that the k means are sufficiently heterogeneous that we do not believe they are all estimates of the same value μ.

The method of data analysis we use in testing the null hypothesis is known as the *analysis of variance*. In this chapter we illustrate the analysis of variance for an experimental design called a randomized group design. In a *randomized group* design we have a total of kn subjects. The kn subjects are randomly assigned to each of k treatments in such a way that for each treatment we have n subjects.[1] Random assignment of the subjects to the k treatments offers assurance that we have independent observations and that the k samples are also independent random samples.

Table 13.1—Values of X and X^2 for $n = 5$ subjects assigned at random to each of $k = 3$ treatments

	Treatment 1		Treatment 2		Treatment 3	
	X	X^2	X	X^2	X	X^2
	10	100	10	100	2	4
	13	169	8	64	3	9
	14	196	7	49	7	49
	13	169	5	25	2	4
	15	225	10	100	6	36
$\sum$	65	859	40	338	20	102

13.2   Sums of Squares and Mean Squares

For simplicity assume that we have $k = 3$ treatments and that $n = 5$ subjects have been randomly assigned to each treatment. Table 13.1 gives the values of the dependent variable X for each subject in each treatment group. We let X_{kn} identify a given observation with the first subscript k designating the treatment group and the second subscript n the number of the observation in the group. In the present example, k can take values of 1, 2, or 3. Because we have $n = 5$ observations for each group, n can take values of 1, 2, 3, 4, or 5. Table 13.2 illustrates the notation for our example of $k = 3$ treatments with $n = 5$ observations for each treatment.

---

[1] A randomized group design does not require that we have an equal number of subjects in each treatment group. But with equal n's the F test is relatively insensitive to heterogeneity of variance. Furthermore, if we wish to make comparisons on the k treatment means, as we ordinarily would, the comparisons are considerably simplified in the case of equal n's, as will be shown in Section 13.7. Comparisons involving unequal n's are discussed in Edwards (1960).

We let $\Sigma\, X..$ be the sum and $\overline{X}..$ be the mean of all kn observations, that is,

$$\sum X.. = \sum_1^{kn} X_{kn} \quad \text{and} \quad \overline{X}.. = \sum X../kn$$

Similarly, we let $\Sigma\, X_k.$ be the sum for the kth treatment and $\overline{X}_k.$ be the mean for the kth treatment, that is,

$$\sum X_k. = \sum_1^n X_{kn} \quad \text{and} \quad \overline{X}_k. = \sum X_k./n$$

Table 13.2—Notation for $k = 3$ groups with $n = 5$ subjects in each group

Treatment 1	Treatment 2	Treatment 3
X_{11}	X_{21}	X_{31}
X_{12}	X_{22}	X_{32}
X_{13}	X_{23}	X_{33}
X_{14}	X_{24}	X_{34}
X_{15}	X_{25}	X_{35}
$\sum X_1.$	$\sum X_2.$	$\sum X_3.$
$\overline{X}_1.$	$\overline{X}_2.$	$\overline{X}_3.$

We may now write the following identity

$$X_{kn} - \overline{X}.. = (X_{kn} - \overline{X}_k.) + (\overline{X}_k. - \overline{X}..) \tag{13.1}$$

and, as we pointed out previously in our discussion of the correlation ratio, if we square (13.1) and sum over all kn observations the cross product term on the right disappears. Thus, we have

$$\sum_1^{kn} (X_{kn} - \overline{X}..)^2 = \sum_1^k \sum_1^n (X_{kn} - \overline{X}_k.)^2 + n\sum_1^k (\overline{X}_k. - \overline{X}..)^2 \tag{13.2}$$

We designate the term on the left as the *total sum of squares*, the first term on the right as the *within treatment* sum of squares, and the second term on the right as the *treatment sum of squares*.

The total sum of squares will be given by

$$\sum_1^{kn} (X_{kn} - \overline{X}..)^2 = \sum_1^{kn} X_{kn}^2 - \frac{(\sum X..)^2}{kn} \tag{13.3}$$

and for the data of Table 13.1, we have

$$\sum_{1}^{kn} (X_{kn} - \bar{X}..)^2 = 1299 - \frac{(125)^2}{15} = 257.33$$

The sum of squares within the first treatment group will be given by

$$\sum_{1}^{n} (X_{1n} - \bar{X}_1.)^2 = \sum_{1}^{n} X_{1n}^2 - \frac{(\sum X_1.)^2}{n}$$

and for the data of Table 13.1, we have

$$\sum_{1}^{n} (X_{1n} - \bar{X}_1.)^2 = 859 - \frac{(65)^2}{5} = 14$$

Similarly, for the other two treatment groups, we have

$$\sum_{1}^{n} (X_{2n} - \bar{X}_2.)^2 = 338 - \frac{(40)^2}{5} = 18$$

and

$$\sum_{1}^{n} (X_{3n} - \bar{X}_3.)^2 = 102 - \frac{(20)^2}{5} = 22$$

Then summing these three sums of squares, we have

$$\text{Within} = 14 + 18 + 22 = 54$$

For the treatment sum of squares, we use the identity developed previously, that is,

$$n \sum_{1}^{k} (\bar{X}_k. - \bar{X}..)^2 = \sum_{1}^{k} \frac{(\sum X_k.)^2}{n} - \frac{(\sum X..)^2}{kn} \qquad (13.4)$$

Thus, for the treatment sum of squares we have

$$\text{Treatments} = \frac{(65)^2}{5} + \frac{(40)^2}{5} + \frac{(20)^2}{5} - \frac{(125)^2}{15} = 203.33$$

and we note that

$$\text{Total} = \text{Within} + \text{Treatments} \qquad (13.5)$$

or, for our example,

$$257.33 = 54.00 + 203.33$$

Each of the above three sums of squares has associated with it a specified number of degrees of freedom. For the total sum of squares we have $kn - 1$

d.f. The within treatment sum of squares for each treatment has $n - 1$ d.f. and because we have k such sums of squares the within treatment sum of squares will have $k(n - 1)$ d.f. The treatment sum of squares has $k - 1$ d.f.

Let us assume that our k samples are random samples of n observations each of a common normally distributed variable X with mean μ and variance σ^2. We do not know the value of σ^2, but under the assumption stated an unbiased estimate of this variance is given by

$$s^2 = \frac{\sum x_1^2 + \sum x_2^2 + \sum x_3^2 + \cdots + \sum x_k^2}{k(n - 1)} \tag{13.6}$$

where $\sum x_1^2$, $\sum x_2^2$, $\sum x_3^2$, $\cdots$, $\sum x_k^2$ are the individual within treatment sums of squares for each of the k treatments. As we have shown previously, each of the terms in the numerator of (13.6) has expectation $(n - 1)\sigma^2$ where σ^2 is the common population variance. Therefore

$$E(s^2) = \frac{k(n - 1)\sigma^2}{k(n - 1)} = \sigma^2$$

It will be noted that the numerator of (13.6) is the within treatment sum of squares and that the denominator is the degrees of freedom associated with this sum of squares. The variance estimate given by (13.6) is commonly referred to as the *mean square within treatments* and may be designated as MS_W. We observe also that the only difference between (13.6) and (10.13) developed earlier in connection with the t test is that we now have $k > 2$ samples instead of $k = 2$ samples. For the example under consideration, we have

$$MS_W = s^2$$
$$= \frac{14 + 18 + 22}{3(5 - 1)}$$
$$= 4.5$$

If we divide the treatment sum of squares by its degrees of freedom, we obtain the *mean square* between treatments or

$$MS_T = \frac{n \sum_{1}^{k} (\bar{X}_{k\cdot} - \bar{X}_{\cdot\cdot})^2}{k - 1} \tag{13.7}$$

and, for our example, we have

$$MS_T = \frac{203.33}{3 - 1} = 101.67$$

The results of our calculations are summarized in Table 13.3.

Table 13.3—Analysis of variance for the data of Table 13.1

Source of variation	Sum of squares	d.f.	Mean square	F
Treatments	203.33	2	101.66	22.59
Within treatments	54.00	12	4.50	
Total	257.33	14		

13.3   Expected Value of MS_T with No Treatment Effects

Let us assume that we have no treatment effects. In this case the long-run average values of the k treatment means will all be equal to the same value μ. In addition, we assume that the average long-run values of the k sample variances are also equal to the same value σ^2. In essence, then, in the absence of any treatment effects, we assume that we have k independent random samples of the same normally distributed variable X with mean μ and variance σ^2. We now show that if this hypothesis is true, then the mean square between treatments is also an unbiased estimate of σ^2.

Consider the sum, $\Sigma X_1.$, of the n observations for Treatment 1. We have previously shown[2] that if we have n independent random values of a variable X, then

$$E\left[\frac{(\Sigma X_1.)^2}{n}\right] = \sigma^2 + n\mu^2 \tag{13.8}$$

and each of the squares of the k treatment sums divided by n has the same expectation as (13.8). Thus

$$E\left[\sum_1^k \frac{(\Sigma X_k.)^2}{n}\right] = k\sigma^2 + kn\mu^2 \tag{13.9}$$

Similarly, we have, as the expectation of the square of the sum of all kn observations divided by kn,

$$E\left[\frac{(\Sigma X..)^2}{kn}\right] = \sigma^2 + kn\mu^2 \tag{13.10}$$

Subtracting (13.10) from (13.9), we have

$$E\left[\sum_1^k \frac{(\Sigma X_k.)^2}{n} - \frac{(\Sigma X..)^2}{kn}\right] = (k\sigma^2 + kn\mu^2) - (\sigma^2 + kn\mu^2)$$

$$= \sigma^2(k - 1) \tag{13.11}$$

---

[2] See Section 10.3.

The right side of (13.11) is the expected value of the treatment sum of squares. The treatment sum of squares, divided by its degrees of freedom, $k - 1$, is the treatment mean square MS_T and we see that

$$E(MS_T) = \sigma^2 \tag{13.12}$$

Thus, if the null hypothesis is true, then the expected value of the treatment mean square MS_T will be exactly the same as the expected value of the within treatment mean square MS_W.

13.4   Expected Value of MS_T with Treatment Effects

Assume that we have k treatments with one or more treatment effects so that $\mu_1, \mu_2, \cdots, \mu_k$ are not all equal to the same value μ. We let

$$\mu = (\mu_1 + \mu_2 + \cdots + \mu_k)/k \tag{13.13}$$

and

$$t_1 = \mu_1 - \mu, t_2 = \mu_2 - \mu, \cdots, t_k = \mu_k - \mu \tag{13.14}$$

so that

$$\sum_1^k t_k = 0 \tag{13.15}$$

The t_k's correspond to treatment effects and in the absence of any treatment effect, the t_k's would all be equal to zero.

Suppose we have assigned n subjects at random to each of the treatment conditions. Then, in general, for a given observation we have

$$\begin{aligned} X_{kn} &= \mu + (\mu_k - \mu) + e_{kn} \\ &= \mu + t_k + e_{kn} \end{aligned} \tag{13.16}$$

where e_{kn} is an independent random error associated with each of the kn observations with $E(e_{kn}) = 0$ and therefore $E(e_{kn}{}^2) = \sigma^2$. Consider, specifically, the n observations for Treatment 1. Then

$$E\left[\frac{(\sum X_1.)^2}{n}\right] = \frac{1}{n}E\left(n\mu + nt_1 + \sum_1^n e_{1n}\right)^2$$
$$= n\mu^2 + nt_1{}^2 + 2n\mu t_1 + \sigma^2 \tag{13.17}$$

and we have a similar expression for each of the k treatments. We note that (13.17) is the same as (13.8) except for the term $nt_1{}^2$ and the cross product term $2n\mu t_1$. However, when we sum (13.17) over the k treatments, the cross product term will be

$$2n\mu \sum_1^k t_k$$

and disappears because $\sum_1^k t_k = 0$. Thus,

$$E\left[\sum_1^k \frac{(\sum X_{k\cdot})^2}{n}\right] = kn\mu^2 + n\sum_1^k t_k^2 + k\sigma^2 \tag{13.18}$$

The expected value of the correction term will be

$$E\left[\frac{(\sum X_{\cdot\cdot})^2}{kn}\right] = \frac{1}{kn} E\left(kn\mu + n\sum_1^k t_k + \sum_1^{kn} e_{kn}\right)^2 \tag{13.19}$$

$$= kn\mu^2 + \sigma^2$$

and subtracting (13.19) from (13.18) we have the expected value of the treatment sum of squares. Thus

$$E\left[\sum_1^k \frac{(\sum X_{k\cdot})^2}{n} - \frac{(\sum X_{\cdot\cdot})^2}{kn}\right] = \sigma^2(k-1) + n\sum_1^k t_k^2 \tag{13.20}$$

and for the expected value of the treatment mean square, we have

$$E(MS_T) = \sigma^2 + \frac{n\sum_1^k t_k^2}{k-1} \tag{13.21}$$

13.5 The Test of Significance

As a test of significance we have

$$F = \frac{MS_T}{MS_W} \tag{13.22}$$

with $k-1$ d.f. for the numerator and $k(n-1)$ d.f. for the denominator. We have defined F in (13.22) as the mean square between treatments divided by the mean square within treatments. The null hypothesis that we are testing is that the samples are random samples drawn from the same normally distributed population with mean μ. If this hypothesis is true, the treatment mean square estimates the same variance as the mean square within treatments and the two mean squares should differ only as a result of random variation.

Our primary interest is in the possibility that the sample means differ or vary to a degree that cannot be reasonably attributed to random variation when the null hypothesis is true. Thus, only if the treatment mean square is larger than the within treatment mean square will the outcome of the experiment offer evidence against the hypothesis that the average long-run values of the treatment means are all equal. That is why the treatment mean square is in the numerator of the F ratio and the within treatment mean square is in the denominator and the test of significance is made using the right tail of the F distribution. Only values of $F > 1$ will provide evidence against the null hypothesis of interest.

If the null hypothesis is false, then

$$F = \frac{MS_T}{MS_W} = \frac{\sigma^2 + \dfrac{n \sum\limits_{1}^{k} t_k^2}{k - 1}}{\sigma^2} \tag{13.23}$$

On the other hand, if the null hypothesis is true, then we have no treatment effects and each of the t_k's would also be equal to zero. If F is significantly greater than 1, then we regard this outcome as indicating that the average long-run values of the treatment means are not all equal to a common value μ.

For our example, we have, as shown in Table 13.3,

$$F = \frac{101.67}{4.50} = 22.59$$

with $k - 1 = 2$ d.f. for the numerator and $k(n - 1) = 12$ d.f. for the denominator. To determine whether the numerator is significantly larger than the denominator, we enter the column of the table of F, Table VIII in Appendix B, with the degrees of freedom of the numerator, 2, and run down this column until we find the row entry corresponding to the degrees of freedom of the denominator, 12. For 2 and 12 d.f., we find that $F \geq 6.93$ has probability .01, when the null hypothesis is true. We know, therefore, that the probability of $F \geq 22.59$ must be considerably smaller than .01. It would appear then that our sample means vary more than can reasonably be attributed to the kind of random variation to be expected in sample means when the samples are all measures of the same normally distributed variable with the same mean μ.

13.6 The *S*-Method for Testing the Difference between Any Two Means

The F test of the mean square between treatments is a general test and by itself, if significant, provides no information about possible differences between a given pair of the treatment means. With k treatment means, we have $k(k - 1)/2$ possible t tests that might be made if we compared each treatment mean with every other treatment mean. We describe the S-method, suggested by Scheffé (1953), for making these tests.

If $n_1 = n_2 = \cdots = n_k = n$, the standard error of the difference between two treatment means will be

$$s_{\overline{X}_1 - \overline{X}_2} = \sqrt{\frac{2s^2}{n}} \qquad (13.24)$$

where s^2 is the mean square within treatments MS_W. For our example we have $s^2 = MS_W = 4.5$ and $n = 5$ and

$$s_{\overline{X}_1 - \overline{X}_2} = \sqrt{\frac{2(4.5)}{5}} = 1.34$$

We define

$$t' = \sqrt{(k-1)F} \qquad (13.25)$$

where F is the tabled value for $k - 1$ d.f. in the numerator and $k(n-1)$ d.f. in the denominator. For our example we have $k = 3$ and $n = 5$ and the tabled value with probability of .05 for 2 and 12 d.f. is 3.88. Then

$$t' = \sqrt{(3-1)3.88} = 2.79$$

We use t' as defined above as the standard against which we shall evaluate the t tests for the difference between any pair of our $k = 3$ means. Any observed t such that $|t| \geq t'$ will be regarded as significant. Our observed sample means are $\overline{X}_1. = 13$, $\overline{X}_2. = 8$, and $\overline{X}_3. = 4$. Then for the t tests of the differences between every possible pair of the $k = 3$ means, we have

$$t = \frac{\overline{X}_1. - \overline{X}_2.}{s_{\overline{X}_1 - \overline{X}_2}} = \frac{13 - 8}{1.34} = 3.73$$

$$t = \frac{\overline{X}_1. - \overline{X}_3.}{s_{\overline{X}_1 - \overline{X}_3}} = \frac{13 - 4}{1.34} = 6.72$$

$$t = \frac{\overline{X}_2. - \overline{X}_3.}{s_{\overline{X}_2 - \overline{X}_3}} = \frac{8 - 4}{1.34} = 2.99$$

All three of the observed t's are greater than $t' = 2.79$ and we may conclude that $\mu_1 \neq \mu_2$, $\mu_1 \neq \mu_3$, and $\mu_2 \neq \mu_3$.

For any of the differences between the means we may establish a 95 (or 99) percent confidence interval. For example, for the difference between $\overline{X}_1.$ and $\overline{X}_2.$ we have

$$-t' \leq \frac{\overline{X}_1. - \overline{X}_2. - (\mu_1 - \mu_2)}{s_{\overline{X}_1 - \overline{X}_2}} \leq t' \qquad (13.26)$$

Substituting in (13.26) with $t' = 2.79$, $\overline{X}_1. - \overline{X}_2. = 5$, and $s_{\overline{X}_1 - \overline{X}_2} = 1.34$, we have

$$-2.79 \leq \frac{5 - (\mu_1 - \mu_2)}{1.34} \leq 2.79$$

or

$$5 + (1.34)(2.79) \geq \mu_1 - \mu_2 \geq 5 - (1.34)(2.79)$$
$$8.74 \geq \mu_1 - \mu_2 \geq 1.26$$

as the 95 percent confidence limits for the difference between μ_1 and μ_2.

13.7 Comparisons on a Set of k Means

The S-method was developed by Scheffé (1953) for testing any and all possible comparisons on a set of k treatment means. Let $a_{1i}, a_{2i}, \cdots, a_{ki}$ be coefficients by which the treatment means are multiplied. Then

$$d_i = a_{1i}\bar{X}_1. + a_{2i}\bar{X}_2. + \cdots + a_{ki}\bar{X}_k. \tag{13.27}$$

is a *comparison* of the k treatment means provided that

$$\sum_1^k a_{\cdot i} = 0$$

that is, if the sum of the coefficients is equal to zero. In our example, we have already tested the difference between all possible pairs of the treatment means or three comparisons on the set of $k = 3$ means. These three comparisons are given by

$$d_1 = (1)\bar{X}_1. + (-1)\bar{X}_2. + (\quad 0)\bar{X}_3. = \bar{X}_1. - \bar{X}_2.$$
$$d_2 = (1)\bar{X}_1. + (\quad 0)\bar{X}_2. + (-1)\bar{X}_3. = \bar{X}_1. - \bar{X}_3.$$
$$d_3 = (0)\bar{X}_1. + (\quad 1)\bar{X}_2. + (-1)\bar{X}_3. = \bar{X}_2. - \bar{X}_3.$$

and we see that the coefficients for d_1 are 1, -1, and 0, and that the sum of the coefficients for this comparison is equal to zero. The coefficients for comparisons d_2 and d_3 also sum to zero.

With the S-method we are not limited to testing the significance of comparisons involving the difference between two means. We can also test such comparisons as

$$d_4 = (1/2)\bar{X}_1. + (1/2)\bar{X}_2. + (-1)\bar{X}_3. = (1/2)(\bar{X}_1. + \bar{X}_2.) - \bar{X}_3.$$

If d_4 is significant, then this comparison would tell us that the average of the means for Treatments 1 and 2 differs significantly from the mean for Treatment 3.

Similarly, we might test the comparison

$$d_5 = (1)\bar{X}_1. + (-1/2)\bar{X}_2. + (-1/2)\bar{X}_3. = \bar{X}_1. - (1/2)(\bar{X}_2. + \bar{X}_3.)$$

If d_5 is significant, then this would tell us that the mean for Treatment 1 differs significantly from the average of the means for Treatments 2 and 3.

We note that the sum of the coefficients for d_4 and d_5 are equal to zero. Thus d_4 and d_5 both meet the requirement stated previously for a comparison on the set of k treatment means.

13.8   The Standard Error of a Comparison

We have previously shown that if

$$T = X_1 + X_2 + \cdots + X_n$$

is the sum of n independent variables, then the variance of T will be

$$\sigma_T^2 = \sigma_1^2 + \sigma_2^2 + \cdots + \sigma_n^2$$

We have also proved that if a variable is multiplied by a constant, then the variance is multiplied by the square of the constant. Now consider the comparison d_4. We assume that each of the means $\overline{X}_{k.}$ has variance equal to s^2/n, where s^2 is the within treatment mean square and is an estimate of σ^2 and n is the number of observations on which the treatment means are based. Then the variance of d_4 will be estimated by

$$s_{d_4}^2 = (1/2)^2 \frac{s^2}{n} + (1/2)^2 \frac{s^2}{n} + (-1)^2 \frac{s^2}{n}$$

$$= \frac{s^2}{n} (3/2)$$

and the standard error for comparison d_4 will be

$$s_{d_4} = \sqrt{\frac{s^2}{n} (3/2)}$$

To test d_4 for significance, we would have

$$t = \frac{\frac{1}{2} (\overline{X}_{1.} + \overline{X}_{2.}) - \overline{X}_{3.}}{\sqrt{\frac{s^2}{n} (3/2)}}$$

and the observed value of t can be evaluated in terms of t' as given by (13.25).

In general, for any comparison on a set of k treatment means, the standard error of the comparison will be given by

$$s_{d_i} = \sqrt{\frac{s^2}{n} \sum_1^k a_{.i}^2} \qquad (13.28)$$

We note that for comparisons involving the difference between any *two* means, $\Sigma_1^k a._i^2 = (1)^2 + (-1)^2 = 2$ and that (13.28) will be equal to

$$s_{\overline{X}_1 - \overline{X}_2} = \sqrt{\frac{2s^2}{n}}$$

The S-method permits what Scheffé has described as "data snooping," that is, we may examine the data and test any or all comparisons that appear to be of interest. To use the S-method in testing comparisons, we must have a significant value of $F = MS_T/MS_W$. If F is significant, then at least one of the possible comparisons on the treatment means will be significant. There may, of course, be more than one significant comparison.

With $k = 4$ treatment means it can be shown that there are 25 different possible comparisons that can be made on the treatment means. Not all of the possible comparisons on a set of k means may be of interest, but the S-method does have the advantage of permitting us to explore our data in any way that we may desire. We may make a test of significance of any comparisons that are suggested by the data, with the realization that if the S-method is used to test every possible comparison, then the probability is $1 - \alpha$ that all statements of significance are correct.

If we do not wish to "snoop our data" so thoroughly, then there are other methods of testing a limited set of selected comparisons that we planned to make prior to the experiment itself. One of these methods will be described in the next chapter.[3]

13.9   The Case of $k = 2$ Treatments

If we have $k = 2$ means the numerator of the F ratio of (13.22) will have 1 d.f. When this is the case, then the tabled values of F are those for the corresponding values of t^2. Consider the case where we have F with 1 and 30 d.f. Then, from the table of F we find that $P(F \geq 4.17) = .05$. From the table of t we find that $t = -2.042$ will cut off .025 of the total area in the left tail and $t = 2.042$ will cut off .025 of the total area in the right tail when t has 30 d.f. For both $t = -2.042$ and $t = 2.042$, we have $t^2 = 4.17$. Thus, the probability of $t^2 \geq 4.17$ will be .05, and this is also the probability of $F \geq 4.17$.

In any case where we have $k = 2$ treatments, we may test the difference between the two means by either the t test or by the F test. The value of F will always be equal, within rounding errors, to the value of t^2. For example, suppose we had only the first two treatments of Table 13.1. Then, for these two treatments we have

---

[3] Other methods for making multiple comparisons are discussed in Edwards (1960).

$$s^2 = MS_W = \frac{14 + 18}{2(5 - 1)} = 4.0$$

and

$$MS_T = \frac{(65)^2}{5} + \frac{(40)^2}{5} - \frac{(105)^2}{10} = 62.5$$

Then

$$F = \frac{MS_T}{MS_W} = \frac{62.5}{4.0} = 15.62$$

For the t test of the difference between the two means we have

$$t = \frac{13 - 8}{\sqrt{\dfrac{2(4.0)}{5}}}$$

Then

$$t^2 = \frac{25}{8.0/5} = 15.62$$

and we see that $t^2 = F$.

13.10   Violations of the Assumptions of the F Test

The F test of the analysis of variance is, like the t test, a robust test. It is robust, in that it is relatively insensitive to violations of the assumption of normality of distribution and equal variances, provided that we have an equal number of observations for each treatment and provided that n is not too small. With random assignment of n subjects to each treatment and with $n \geq 25$, the experimenter need not be overly concerned about normality of distribution and equal variances. Of course, if these assumptions are tenable, then we may safely use the F test with a much smaller number of observations for each treatment.[4]

---

[4] As in the case of the t test, we should be concerned about the power of the F test when the number of observations assigned to the treatment groups is small. For a discussion of the power of the F test, see Mosteller and Bush (1954) and Overall and Dalal (1965). In general, other things being equal, the larger the number of observations we have for the k treatment groups, the greater the power of the F test.

As a rough guide for estimating the number of observations for each of the k treatment groups, let δ be the smallest difference between any two of the treatment means that would be regarded as having practical or theoretical importance. Then, if an estimate of σ^2, the variance of the measures on the dependent variable, is available from a pilot experiment or from other published research, use (11.1) to obtain an estimate of the number of observations for each treatment group.

EXAMPLES

13.1—Five subjects are randomly assigned to each of five treatments.

(a) Use the analysis of variance to determine whether the treatment mean square is significant.
(b) From each value of X subtract 60. Are the sums of squares in the analysis of variance changed by the subtraction of this constant?

Treatments

1	2	3	4	5
68	49	64	67	61
55	59	63	55	59
60	61	54	65	70
67	60	52	64	69
60	61	62	59	61

13.2—Eight subjects are randomly assigned to each of five treatments. Use the analysis of variance to determine whether the treatment mean square is significant.

Treatments

1	2	3	4	5
18	18	4	7	9
13	9	13	3	16
21	15	11	11	26
14	25	11	11	21
25	14	15	7	18
14	6	15	13	11
7	12	11	10	14
20	9	12	10	13

13.3—Ten subjects are randomly assigned to a control group and 10 to an experimental group.

(a) Use the t test to determine whether the means for the two groups differ significantly.
(b) Use the analysis of variance to determine whether the treatment mean square is significant. Compare the value of F obtained here with the value of t^2 for the same data.

Experimental	Control
21	9
19	10
18	20
13	14
15	18
20	5
22	8
25	11
17	12
10	13

13.4—Forty subjects are divided at random into four groups of ten subjects each. Each group receives a different treatment. The measures on the dependent variable of interest are given below. Use the analysis of variance to determine whether the treatment mean square is significant.

Treatments

1	2	3	4
8	9	5	6
5	4	3	1
6	8	7	1
8	4	5	6
9	3	3	5
10	6	1	4
9	7	5	3
7	6	4	6
8	7	3	4
10	6	4	4

13.5—The analysis of variance summary table for a randomized group experiment with $n = 10$ subjects assigned at random to each of $k = 4$ treatments is given below.

Source of variation	Sum of squares	d.f.	Mean square	F
Treatments	83.50	3	27.83	9.09
Within treatments	110.16	36	3.06	
Total	193.66	39		

The values of the four treatment means in the experiment were: $\overline{X}_1. = 17.2$, $\overline{X}_2. = 19.4$, $\overline{X}_3. = 15.8$, and $\overline{X}_4. = 19.0$.

(a) Use Scheffé's test to determine whether there are significant differences between any two treatment means. *Hint:* Test the largest difference first.
(b) Does the mean for Treatment 3 differ significantly from the average of the means for Treatments 2 and 4?

13.6—Prove that

$$\sum_1^k n(\bar{X}_{k\cdot} - \bar{X}_{\cdot\cdot})^2 = \sum_1^k \frac{(\sum X_{k\cdot})^2}{n} - \frac{(\sum X_{\cdot\cdot})^2}{kn}$$

13.7—Prove that if we have $k = 2$ treatments with $n_1 = n_2 = n$, then

$$\sum_1^k n(\bar{X}_{k\cdot} - \bar{X}_{\cdot\cdot})^2 = \frac{(\sum X_{1\cdot} - \sum X_{2\cdot})^2}{2n}$$

13.8—Use the result obtained in Example 13.7 to prove that

$$t^2 = \frac{(\bar{X}_{1\cdot} - \bar{X}_{2\cdot})^2}{\dfrac{2s^2}{n}} = \frac{MS_T}{MS_W} = F$$

13.9—What is the null hypothesis tested by $F = MS_T/MS_W$?

13.10—Give a one-sentence definition of each of the following terms or concepts:

treatment effect	within treatment sum of squares
randomized group design	S-method
treatment sum of squares	comparison

CHAPTER 14

Two-Factor Experiments

14.1 Introduction

In some experiments we may have two or more independent variables each of which is varied in two or more ways. The independent variables are commonly referred to as *factors* and the number of ways in which each factor is varied is referred to as the number of *levels* of the factor. For simplicity, we consider an experiment in which we have two factors, A and B, with each factor varied in two ways. We can designate the two levels of A as A_1 and A_2 and the two levels of B as B_1 and B_2. Now suppose that a given treatment in the experiment consists of one level of A paired with one level of B, for example, A_1B_1. If each level of A is paired with each level of B, then we have $k = ab$ possible treatment combinations, where a is the number of levels of A and b is the number of levels of B. In our example, we have $a = 2$ levels of A and $b = 2$ levels of B. We therefore have $k = 2 \times 2 = 4$ possible treatment combinations or A_1B_1, A_1B_2, A_2B_1, and A_2B_2. If all possible treatment combinations are included in the experiment, then the experiment is said to be a *complete factorial experiment*.

Assume that we have randomly assigned $n = 5$ subjects to each of the k treatment combinations.[1] For each subject we have a measure on a dependent

---

[1] The methods of analysis and tests of significance described in this chapter are applicable to the case where each treatment combination has the same number of observations. For procedures that may be used in the case of unequal n's, see Snedecor (1956) and Scheffé (1959). For reasons discussed previously, having an equal number of observations for each treatment combination is desirable in the case of heterogeneity of variance. Furthermore, the analysis of variance and tests of significance are considerably simplified in the case of equal n's.

We emphasize that in experiments designed to compare differences between the means of treatment groups there is, in general, no good reason for having unequal n's and there are a number of good reasons for having equal n's. One exception is the case where we are only interested in testing the difference between the mean of a control group and the mean of each of a number of treatment groups. For a discussion of this case, see Dunnett (1955) or Edwards (1960).

variable X of interest. Table 14.1 gives the values of X for the $n = 5$ subjects assigned to each treatment.

In the previous chapter a randomized group design was defined as an experiment in which we randomly assigned n subjects to each of k treatments. We also showed that for a randomized group design it is possible to partition the total sum of squares into two parts: the sum of squares within treatments with $k(n - 1)$ d.f. and the sum of squares for treatments with $k - 1$ d.f. It

Table 14.1—Measures on a dependent variable X for a 2×2 factorial experiment with $n = 5$ observations for each treatment combination

	Treatment combinations			
	A_1B_1	A_1B_2	A_2B_1	A_2B_2
	2	8	10	10
	7	11	8	15
	3	11	5	12
	2	10	5	13
	6	15	7	10
$\sum X$	20	55	35	60
$\sum X^2$	102	631	263	738
$\sum x^2$	22	26	18	18

is obvious that in the example under discussion we also have a randomized group design and our first step in analyzing the data of Table 14.1 will be to partition the total sum of squares into the sum of squares within treatments and the sum of squares for treatments.

14.2   Notation for a Two-Factor Experiment

It will be convenient to identify each observation by three ordered subscripts abn. The first subscript a refers to the level of A and, in our example, a can take values of 1 or 2 corresponding to the two levels of A. Similarly, the second subscript b refers to the level of B and b can take values of 1 or 2 corresponding to the two levels of B. The third subscript n identifies a given observation in a given treatment and n can take values of 1, 2, 3, 4, or 5. Table 14.2 illustrates the notation for the data of Table 14.1, with $a = 2$ levels of A, $b = 2$ levels of B, and $n = 5$ observations for each treatment combination.

When we replace a subscript by a "dot," this means that we have summed over the values of the subscript replaced by the dot. Thus

$$\sum X... = \sum_1^{abn} X_{abn}$$

is the sum of all $abn = 20$ observations and, in our example,

$$\sum X... = 2 + 7 + 3 + \cdots + 10 = 170 \text{ and } \bar{X}... = 170/20 = 8.5$$

The sum of the $n = 5$ observations for Treatment A_1B_1 is

$$\sum X_{11.} = 2 + 7 + 3 + 2 + 6 = 20 \text{ and } \bar{X}_{11.} = 20/5 = 4.0$$

and similarly

$$\sum X_{12.} = 8 + 11 + 11 + 10 + 15 = 55 \text{ and } \bar{X}_{12.} = 55/5 = 11.0$$

Then the sum of the bn observations obtained under A_1 will be

$$\sum X_{1..} = \sum X_{11.} + \sum X_{12.}$$
$$= 20 + 55$$
$$= 75$$

and

$$\bar{X}_{1..} = 75/10 = 7.5$$

is the mean for all observations obtained under A_1.

Table 14.2—Notation for a 2×2 factorial experiment with $n = 5$ observations for each treatment combination

Treatment combinations			
A_1B_1	A_1B_2	A_2B_1	A_2B_2
X_{111}	X_{121}	X_{211}	X_{221}
X_{112}	X_{122}	X_{212}	X_{222}
X_{113}	X_{123}	X_{213}	X_{223}
X_{114}	X_{124}	X_{214}	X_{224}
X_{115}	X_{125}	X_{215}	X_{225}
$\sum X_{11.}$	$\sum X_{12.}$	$\sum X_{21.}$	$\sum X_{22.}$
$\bar{X}_{11.}$	$\bar{X}_{12.}$	$\bar{X}_{21.}$	$\bar{X}_{22.}$

14.3 The Analysis of Variance for a Two-Factor Experiment

For the data of Table 14.1 we have found that $\Sigma X... = 170$ and the correction term will therefore be

$$\frac{(\Sigma X...)^2}{kn} = \frac{(170)^2}{20} = 1445$$

We also have

$$\sum_{1}^{abn} X_{abn}{}^2 = (2)^2 + (7)^2 + (3)^2 + \cdots + (10)^2 = 1734$$

Then for the total sum of squares we have

$$\sum_{1}^{abn} (X_{abn} - \overline{X}...)^2 = \sum_{1}^{abn} X_{abn}{}^2 - \frac{(\Sigma X...)^2}{kn}$$
$$= 1734 - 1445$$
$$= 289$$

To obtain the treatment sum of squares, we first find

$$\sum_{1}^{ab} \frac{(\Sigma X_{ab\cdot})^2}{n} = \frac{(20)^2}{5} + \frac{(55)^2}{5} + \frac{(35)^2}{5} + \frac{(60)^2}{5} = 1650$$

Then, for the treatment sum of squares we have

$$\sum_{1}^{ab} n(\overline{X}_{ab\cdot} - \overline{X}...)^2 = \sum_{1}^{ab} \frac{(\Sigma X_{ab\cdot})^2}{n} - \frac{(\Sigma X...)^2}{kn}$$
$$= 1650 - 1445$$
$$= 205$$

Assuming that our calculations of the total sum of squares and the treatment sum of squares are correct, the within treatment sum of squares can be obtained by subtraction. Thus

$$\text{Within} = \text{Total} - \text{Treatment}$$
$$= 289 - 205$$
$$= 84$$

Table 14.3 summarizes the results of our calculations. We have $F = MS_T/MS_W = 68.33/5.25 = 13.02$. From the table of F, we find that with 3 and 16 d.f., the probability of $F \geq 5.29$ is .01, if the null hypothesis is true. We know, therefore, that if the null hypothesis is true, the probability of $F \geq 13.02$ is much less than .01. Thus we may chose to regard the outcome of this experiment as relatively improbable under the null hypothesis that $\mu_{11}, \mu_{12}, \mu_{21},$ and μ_{22} are all estimates of the same value μ.

Table 14.3—Analysis of variance for the data of Table 14.1

Source of variation	Sum of squares	d.f.	Mean square	F
Treatments	205.0	3	68.33	13.02
Within treatments	84.0	16	5.25	
Total	289.0	19		

We might now, if we so desire, use the S-method to "snoop the data," testing any or all comparisons on the set of treatment means. With $k = 4$ treatment means there are 25 possible different comparisons and if all of these comparisons were tested for significance by the S-method, the probability will be $1 - \alpha$ that all statements of significance are correct.

14.4 Comparisons on the Treatment Sums

In the present experiment, however, we shall assume that the experimenter decided prior to the collection of the data that he was interested only in a *selected* set of comparisons, the actual number being $k - 1$, the number of degrees of freedom associated with the treatment sum of squares. Instead of making the comparisons on the treatment means, we shall make them on the treatment sums. In doing so we shall see that the calculations are somewhat simpler and that a comparison on the treatment sums results in a sum of squares with 1 d.f. Then the F test for the comparison will have 1 d.f. in the numerator and, as we shall prove later, the value of F obtained in the test of significance will be exactly equal to the value of t^2 obtained if the same comparison is made on the treatment means.

In the previous chapter we defined

$$d_i = a_{1i}\bar{X}_1. + a_{2i}\bar{X}_2. + \cdots + a_{ki}\bar{X}_k.$$

as a comparison on k treatment means, provided that $\Sigma_1^k a_{\cdot i} = 0$. Similarly, we define

$$D_i = a_{1i}\sum X_1. + a_{2i}\sum X_2. + \cdots + a_{ki}\sum X_k. \qquad (14.1)$$

as a comparison on the treatment sums, provided that $\Sigma_1^k a_{\cdot i} = 0$. We note that

$$d_i = D_i/n \tag{14.2}$$

and we shall use this identity later to prove that $t^2 = F$.

In Table 14.4 we show a set of $k - 1 = 3$ comparisons on the treatment sums. We observe that the sum of the coefficients in each row of the table is equal to zero so that D_1, D_2, and D_3 are in fact comparisons. D_1 is obviously a comparison of the difference between the sum for Treatments A_1B_1 and A_1B_2 and the sum for Treatments A_2B_1 and A_2B_2 or a comparison of the difference between the sum for A_1 and A_2. Thus

$$D_1 = \left(\sum X_{11.} + \sum X_{12.} \right) - \left(\sum X_{21.} + \sum X_{22.} \right)$$
$$= \sum X_{1..} - \sum X_{2..}$$
$$= \sum A_1 - \sum A_2$$

In our example we have

$$D_1 = (20 + 55) - (35 + 60) = -20$$

Table 14.4—A set of three mutually orthogonal comparisons on the treatment sums of Table 14.1

	Treatment sums			
Comparison	A_1B_1	A_1B_2	A_2B_1	A_2B_2
	20	55	35	60
D_1	1	1	-1	-1
D_2	1	-1	1	-1
D_3	1	-1	-1	1

When we made a comparison on the treatment means, we ended up with a difference d_i that we could then test for significance by a t test. When we make a comparison on the treatment sums, we also end up with a difference D_i. This difference can be used to obtain a mean square with 1 d.f. that we can then test for significance with an F test. As we have pointed out previously, the t and F tests for the same comparisons are equivalent in that t^2 will be exactly equal to F and we shall prove this later. The mean square MS_{D_i} for any comparison D_i will be given by

$$MS_{D_i} = \frac{D_i{}^2}{n \sum\limits_1^k a_{.i}{}^2} \tag{14.3}$$

where n is the number of observations for each of the treatment sums and $\Sigma_1^k a_{.i}^2$ is the sum of the squares of the coefficients for the comparison D_i. In our example we have $D_1 = -20$, $n = 5$, and $\Sigma_1^k a_{.1}^2 = 4$ and substituting in (14.3) we have

$$MS_{D_1} = \frac{(-20)^2}{(5)(4)} = 20$$

As a test significance for any comparison D_i we have

$$F = \frac{MS_{D_i}}{MS_W} \tag{14.4}$$

with 1 d.f. in the numerator and with degrees of freedom associated with the mean square within treatments MS_W in the denominator. In our example we have $MS_W = 5.25$ and therefore for the test of significance of D_1 we have

$$F = \frac{20.00}{5.25} = 3.81$$

with 1 and 16 d.f.

From the Table of F we find that with 1 and 16 d.f. the probability of $F \geq 4.49$ is .05 when the null hypothesis is true. Because our observed value of F is less than 4.49, we decide that the outcome of this experiment does not offer significant evidence against the null hypothesis. In other words, we may conclude that the means for A_1 and A_2 do not differ significantly.

We note that

$$\begin{aligned} D_2 &= \left(\sum X_{11.} + \sum X_{21.}\right) - \left(\sum X_{12.} + \sum X_{22.}\right) \\ &= \sum X_{.1.} - \sum X_{.2.} \\ &= \sum B_1 - \sum B_2 \end{aligned}$$

is a comparison of the difference between the sums for B_1 and B_2. We have

$$D_2 = (20 + 35) - (55 + 60) = -60$$

and

$$MS_{D_2} = \frac{(-60)^2}{(5)(4)} = 180$$

Then

$$F = \frac{MS_{D_2}}{MS_W} = \frac{180}{5.25} = 34.29$$

with 1 and 16 d.f. and this is a highly significant value.

For the third comparison, we have

$$D_3 = (20 + 60) - (55 + 35) = -10$$

and

$$MS_{D_3} = \frac{(-10)^2}{(5)(4)} = 5$$

Then

$$F = \frac{5.00}{5.25} < 1$$

and it is obvious that the F test of D_3 cannot be significant because $F < 1$. The meaning of the comparison D_3 is not as obvious as the meaning of comparisons D_1 and D_2 and, for the time being, we shall not attempt to clarify the nature of D_3 other than to say that it corresponds to the interaction effect $A \times B$. We shall discuss the meaning of an interaction effect later.

14.5 Orthogonal Comparisons

If we multiply the coefficients for comparisons D_1 and D_2 in Table 14.4 we observe that the sum of the products of the coefficients for these two comparisons is equal to zero. That is,

$$(1)(1) + (1)(-1) + (-1)(1) + (-1)(-1) = 0$$

Any two comparisons on a set of k treatment means or sums such that the sum of the products of the coefficients for the two comparisons is equal to zero are said to be *orthogonal* or *independent*. If you find the sum of the products of the coefficients for comparisons D_1 and D_3 and for D_2 and D_3 you will observe that they also sum to zero. These three comparisons are thus *mutually orthogonal*. For any mutually orthogonal set of $k - 1$ comparisons on a set of k treatments sums, the sum of the sums of squares for the comparisons will be equal to the treatment sum of squares. We note that this is true for our example, because

$$20 + 180 + 5 = 205$$

and 205 is the sum of squares between treatments.

14.6 Comparisons on the Treatment Means

Let us now make the same set of orthogonal comparisons on the treatment means that we have made on the treatment sums. Multiplying the treatment means by the coefficients for the comparisons, we have

$$d_1 = (4 + 11) - (7 + 12) = -4$$
$$d_2 = (4 + 7) - (11 + 12) = -12$$
$$d_3 = (4 + 12) - (11 + 7) = -2$$

Because the sum of the squares of the coefficients for each of these comparisons is equal to 4, each comparison will have the same standard error, equal to

$$s_{d_i} = \sqrt{\frac{5.25}{5}(4)} = 2.05$$

Then for the first comparison, we have

$$t = \frac{d_1}{s_{d_1}} = \frac{-4}{2.05} = -1.951$$

and we note that $t^2 = (-1.951)^2 = 3.81 = F$ for the same comparison on the treatment sums. Similar calculations will show that the squared values of t for the comparisons d_2 and d_3 on the treatment means are also equal to the corresponding values of F for comparisons D_2 and D_3 on the treatment sums.

14.7   Proof that $t^2 = F$

We now prove that the value of t^2 for any comparison on the treatment means is exactly equal to the corresponding value of F when the same comparison is made on the treatment sums. From (14.2) we note that $d_i = D_i/n$ and $d_i^2 = D_i^2/n^2$. Then

$$t^2 = \frac{d_i^2}{\dfrac{s^2}{n}\sum_1^k a_{.i}^2} = \frac{D_i^2/n^2}{\dfrac{s^2}{n}\sum_1^k a_{.i}^2} = \frac{D_i^2/n\sum_1^k a_{.i}^2}{s^2} = \frac{MS_{D_i}}{MS_W} = F \quad (14.5)$$

Thus it does not matter whether we make a comparison on the treatment means and evaluate the comparison by a t test or whether we make the same comparison on the treatment sums and evaluate the comparison by the F test.

14.8   The Meaning of a Two-Factor Interaction Effect

We stated earlier that the comparison D_3 on the treatment sums or its equivalent d_3 on the treatment means corresponds to the $A \times B$ interaction effect. If the null hypothesis for d_3 is true, then

$$E(d_3) = (\mu_{11} + \mu_{22}) - (\mu_{12} + \mu_{21}) = 0 \qquad (14.6)$$

and it must also be true that

$$\mu_{11} - \mu_{12} = \mu_{21} - \mu_{22} \qquad (14.7)$$

We note that the left side of (14.7) is the difference between the population means of B_1 and B_2 under A_1 and the right side is the difference between the population means of B_1 and B_2 under A_2. If the null hypothesis is true, then these two differences must be equal.

We have sample means that are estimates of the two differences. For the difference between the means of B_1 and B_2 under A_1, we have $\overline{X}_{11.} - \overline{X}_{12.}$ $= 4 - 11 = -7$ and for the difference between the means of B_1 and B_2

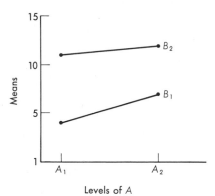

Figure **14.1**—Means for the levels of B_1 and B_2 for each level of A for the data of Table 14.1.

under A_2, we have $\overline{X}_{21.} - \overline{X}_{22.} = 7 - 12 = -5$. If we have a significant $A \times B$ interaction effect then -7 and -5 must differ significantly. But

$$t = \frac{d_3}{\sqrt{\dfrac{s^2}{n} \sum_1^k a_{.3}^2}} = \frac{-2}{\sqrt{\dfrac{5.25}{5}(4)}} = -.976$$

is not a significant value and therefore we conclude that the $A \times B$ interaction is not significant.

We can gain a somewhat clearer notion of the nature of an $A \times B$ interaction effect if we plot the means for B_1 and B_2 for each level of A as we have done in Figure 14.1. If the two lines shown in the figure were perfectly parallel, then both d_3 and D_3 would obviously be equal to zero. Another way of describing a significant $A \times B$ interaction effect is to say that the two lines in Figure 14.1 are not parallel within the limits of random sampling.

The $A \times B$ interaction effect is symmetrical with respect to both A and B. In the above discussion, we considered the difference between the means of B_1 and B_2 under A_1 and under A_2, that is, with the level of A held constant. But we note that if the null hypothesis with respect to d_3 is true, then it will also be true that

$$\mu_{11} - \mu_{21} = \mu_{12} - \mu_{22} \qquad (14.8)$$

In other words, if the null hypothesis is true, then the difference between the population means of A_1 and A_2 under B_1 must be equal to the difference between the population means of A_1 and A_2 under B_2. For our example, the estimates of these two differences are $\overline{X}_{11.} - \overline{X}_{21.} = 4 - 7 = -3$ and $\overline{X}_{12.} - \overline{X}_{22.} = 11 - 12 = -1$ and again the difference between these two differences is -2 which, as we have shown, is not significant.

14.9   Orthogonal Comparisons: A Specific Example

We have intentionally considered in the previous discussion an abstract example in which the two factors A and B and the two levels of the factors were not identified. We now consider, for the same example, a concrete case in which we identify A and B and the levels of A and B as variables of possible experimental interest. Let A correspond to type of drive and assume that A_1 = thirst and A_2 = hunger. Let B be the number of hours of deprivation of water or food with B_1 = 12 hours of deprivation and B_2 = 24 hours of deprivation. We also assume that we have n = 5 rats assigned to each treatment combination. Then, the means for each treatment combination will correspond to:

$$A_1B_1 = T_{12} \qquad A_2B_1 = H_{12}$$
$$A_1B_2 = T_{24} \qquad A_2B_2 = H_{24}$$

The three planned orthogonal comparisons described previously would now correspond to:

$$D_1 = (T_{12} + T_{24}) - (H_{12} + H_{24})$$
$$D_2 = (T_{12} + H_{12}) - (T_{24} + H_{24})$$
$$D_3 = (T_{12} - T_{24}) - (H_{12} - H_{24})$$

It seems obvious that each of these three comparisons would be of experimental interest. We note that D_3, the comparison of the interaction effect, is also given by

$$D_3 = (T_{12} - H_{12}) - (T_{24} - H_{24})$$

14.10   Additional Sets of Mutually Orthogonal Comparisons

For the experiment described, there are other sets of mutually orthogonal comparisons that could have been planned prior to the experiment itself. Table 14.5 shows the original set of orthogonal comparisons, and two additional sets of orthogonal comparisons. If you calculate the sums of squares for the comparisons D_4, D_5, and D_6 you will find that they sum to 205 and this sum is equal to the sum of squares for treatments. Similarly, if you calculate

Table 14.5—Three different sets of mutually orthogonal comparisons on $k = 4$ treatment sums

Sets of comparisons		Treatment sums				Nature of the comparisons
		T_{12}	T_{24}	H_{12}	H_{24}	
		20	55	35	60	
	D_1	1	1	−1	−1	T vs H
Set 1	D_2	1	−1	1	−1	12 vs 24
	D_3	1	−1	−1	1	$D_1 \times D_2$
	D_4	1	−1	0	0	T_{12} vs T_{24}
Set 2	D_5	0	0	1	−1	H_{12} vs H_{24}
	D_6	1	1	−1	−1	T vs H
	D_7	1	0	−1	0	T_{12} vs H_{12}
Set 3	D_8	0	1	0	−1	T_{24} vs H_{24}
	D_9	1	−1	1	−1	12 vs 24

the sums of squares for comparisons D_7, D_8, and D_9 you will find that they also sum to 205, the treatment sum of squares.

We note that one of our original comparisons, D_1, is the same as D_6 and that another, D_2, is the same as D_9. But the other four comparisons, D_4, D_5, D_7, and D_8, are new. If the factors and levels of the factors are as we have identified them, then it would seem that these four comparisons would also be of experimental interest. If we wish to test all seven comparisons, the three original comparisons and the four new ones, then we should use the S-method described previously. The methods of significance testing described in this chapter should be used only when we have planned comparisons that are mutually orthogonal and equal to or less in number than $k - 1$, the degrees of freedom associated with the treatment sum of squares.[2]

---

[2] Note that we evaluated the three mutually orthogonal comparisons in this experiment in terms of the tabled value of F with 1 and $k(n - 1)$ d.f. For 1 and 16 d.f., the tabled value with probability of .05 is $F = 4.49$. If we were to use the S-method to evaluate the same comparisons, then we would have $F' = (k - 1)F$, where F is the tabled value with $k - 1$ and $k(n - 1)$ d.f. For the present example, we have $k - 1 = 3$ and $k(n - 1) = 16$ d.f. and the tabled value of F with probability of .05 is 3.24. Then $F' = (4 - 1)(3.24) = 9.72$ is the standard in terms of which we would evaluate the same comparisons using the S-method.

In the present experiment, we would arrive at the same conclusions regarding the significance of the comparisons using either the S-method or the method described in the chapter. It is obvious, however, that the S-method requires a larger value of F for significance than does the method described in the chapter. Thus, using the S-method, a comparison may not be judged

14.11   General Equations for the Sums of Squares in a Two-Factor Experiment

For any experiment involving two factors A and B, with n observations for each treatment combination, we can write the following identity

$$\overline{X}_{ab\cdot} - \overline{X}... = (\overline{X}_{a}.. - \overline{X}...) + (\overline{X}_{\cdot b\cdot} - \overline{X}...)$$
$$+ (\overline{X}_{ab\cdot} - \overline{X}_{a}.. - \overline{X}_{\cdot b\cdot} + \overline{X}...) \quad (14.9)$$

If we square (14.9) and sum over all abn observations, all cross product terms on the right disappear. Thus

$$\sum_{1}^{ab} n(\overline{X}_{ab\cdot} - \overline{X}...)^2 = \sum_{1}^{a} bn(\overline{X}_{a}.. - \overline{X}...)^2 + \sum_{1}^{b} an(\overline{X}_{\cdot b\cdot} - \overline{X}...)^2$$
$$+ \sum_{1}^{ab} n(\overline{X}_{ab\cdot} - \overline{X}_{a}.. - \overline{X}_{\cdot b\cdot} + \overline{X}...)^2 \quad (14.10)$$

The term on the left of (14.10) is the treatment sum of squares. The first term on the right is the A sum of squares and the second term is the B sum of squares. The last term on the right is the $A \times B$ interaction sum of squares.

Although we have considered a numerical example in which A and B have only two levels each, it is obvious from (14.10) that we are not restricted to this case. We may have any number of levels for A and any number for B. Let a be the number of levels of A and b be the number of levels of B. Then the treatment sum of squares will have $ab - 1$ d.f., the A sum of squares will have $a - 1$ d.f., the B sum of squares will have $b - 1$ d.f., and the $A \times B$ interaction sum of squares will have $(a - 1)(b - 1)$ d.f.

To illustate the calculations for experiments in which the two factors have more than two levels, we give in Table 14.6 the results of an experiment in which A and B each have three levels and in which $n = 5$ subjects were randomly assigned to each of the nine treatment combinations. For the total sum of squares, we have

$$\text{Total} = (7)^2 + (10)^2 + (10)^2 + \cdots + (10)^2 - \frac{(340)^2}{45} = 369.11$$

---

significant, whereas using the method described in the chapter the same comparison may be declared significant.

Of course, there is nothing sacred about a .01 or a .05 probability of a Type I error and, as Scheffé has suggested, one might consider using the S-method with $\alpha = .10$ rather than $\alpha = .05$. Values of F with probability of .10 under the null hypothesis have been tabled by Merrington and Thompson (1943). The Merrington and Thompson tables are reproduced in Edwards (1960).

To calculate the treatment sum of squares, we have

$$\text{Treatment} = \frac{(50)^2}{5} + \frac{(40)^2}{5} + \frac{(25)^2}{5} + \cdots + \frac{(45)^2}{5} - \frac{(340)^2}{45} = 201.11$$

Table 14.6—Measures on a dependent variable X for a 3×3 factorial experiment with $n = 5$ observations for each treatment combination

	A_1			A_2			A_3		
	B_1	B_2	B_3	B_1	B_2	B_3	B_1	B_2	B_3
	7	6	3	4	10	4	2	5	7
	10	5	3	6	10	6	2	4	9
	10	8	4	7	11	7	3	7	9
	11	9	8	9	11	8	7	8	10
	12	12	7	9	13	10	6	11	10
$\sum$	50	40	25	35	55	35	20	35	45

Assuming that the total and treatment sums of squares are calculated correctly, the within treatment sum of squares can be obtained by subtraction. Thus

$$\text{Within} = 369.11 - 201.11 = 168.00$$

Table 14.7 summarizes the analysis of variance. As a test of significance of the mean square for treatments, we have $F = 5.38$ with 8 and 36 d.f. From the table of F, Table VIII in Appendix B, we see that $F \geq 3.04$ has probability of .01 under the null hypothesis. Because our obtained value of F exceeds 3.04, we may conclude that the variation in the treatment means is greater than that to be expected as a result of random sampling from a common population.

We now proceed to analyze the treatment sum of squares into a sum of

Table 14.7—Analysis of variance for the data of Table 14.6. The total sum of squares has been partitioned into the treatment sum of squares and the within treatment sum of squares

Source of variation	Sum of squares	d.f.	Mean square	F
Treatments	201.11	8	25.14	5.38
Within treatments	168.00	36	4.67	
Total	369.11	44		

squares for A, a sum of squares for B, and the $A \times B$ interaction sum of squares. For the A sum of squares, we have

$$A = \frac{(115)^2}{15} + \frac{(125)^2}{15} + \frac{(100)^2}{15} - \frac{(340)^2}{45} = 21.11$$

Similarly, for the B sum of squares, we have

$$B = \frac{(105)^2}{15} + \frac{(130)^2}{15} + \frac{(105)^2}{15} - \frac{(340)^2}{45} = 27.78$$

Then, the $A \times B$ sum of squares can be obtained by subtraction. Thus

$$A \times B = \text{Treatments} - A - B$$

or, for our example

$$A \times B = 201.11 - 21.11 - 27.78 = 152.22$$

Note that if we set up a two-way table with the rows corresponding to the levels of one factor and columns corresponding to the levels of the other factor and if the cell entries are the sums for the treatment combinations, as in Table 14.8, then the sum of squares between cells of the table corresponds to the sum of squares for treatment combinations, the row sum of squares corresponds to the sum of squares for one factor and the column sum of squares corresponds to the sum of squares for the other factor. Thus, in more general terms, the two-factor interaction sum of squares is the row $\times$ column interaction sum of squares for the two-way table or

$$R \times C = \text{Cells} - \text{Rows} - \text{Columns}$$

Table 14.9 summarizes the analysis of variance of the experiment. With $\alpha = .05$, a value of $F \geq 3.26$ is required for significance with 2 and 36 d.f. Thus we may conclude that the differences among the three means for the levels of A are not significant and also that the differences among the means

Table 14.8—Sums for the treatment combinations of the 3×3 factorial experiment. Original data given in Table 14.6

	B_1	B_2	B_3	Σ
A_1	50	40	25	115
A_2	35	55	35	125
A_3	20	35	45	100
Σ	105	130	105	340

Table 14.9—Analysis of variance for the data of Table 14.6. The treatment sum of squares has been partitioned into the sum of squares for the A effect, the B effect, and the $A \times B$ interaction sum of squares

Source of variation	Sum of squares	d.f.	Mean square	F
A	21.11	2	10.56	2.26
B	27.78	2	13.89	2.97
$A \times B$	152.22	4	38.06	8.15
Within treatments	168.00	36	4.67	
Total	369.11	44		

for the three levels of B are not significant. With 4 and 36 d.f., $F \geq 3.89$ has probability of .01 and our observed $F = 8.15$ for the $A \times B$ interaction effect is highly significant.

We can gain some information concerning the nature of the $A \times B$ inter-action from Figure 14.2. At the left in the figure, the means for each level of B have been plotted for the three levels of A and at the right the means for each level of A have been plotted for the three levels of B. We note that under A_1 the mean for B_1 is larger than the mean for B_3, but that the direction of this difference is reversed under A_3. Under A_2, the means for B_1 and B_3 are equal and the mean for B_2 exceeds both.

Assuming that the experimenter introduced the levels of A and B because he had some hypotheses about the possible differences in the means for a given level of one factor when paired with levels of the other factor, further exploration of the data with the S-method would seem to be a reasonable procedure. Because the treatment mean square is significant, we know that

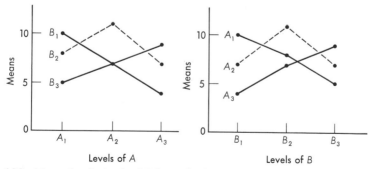

Figure **14.2**—Means for the levels of B for each of the three levels of A at the left and means for the levels of A for each of the three levels of B at the right. Original data given in Table 14.6.

there is at least one significant comparison on the treatment means for the treatment combinations and, of course, there may be more.

It is also possible to analyze the treatment sum of squares with 8 d.f. into a set of eight mutually orthogonal comparisons, each with 1 d.f. One such set of mutually orthogonal comparisons is shown in one of the examples at the end of the chapter. Whether a given set of *meaningful* and mutually orthogonal comparisons could have been planned prior to the experiment itself is another matter. The S-method, as we have pointed out before, is a convenient method for testing not only planned comparisons, but also those that are suggested by the data.

EXAMPLES

14.1—In a two-factor experiment with two levels of A and two levels of B, $n = 5$ subjects were assigned at random to each of the treatment combinations. Complete the analysis of variance.

	A_1		A_2	
B_1	B_2	B_1	B_2
2	9	8	10
3	7	11	14
5	6	10	7
7	5	5	8
6	4	6	11

14.2—We have a two-factor experiment with two levels for each factor, and with $n = 10$ subjects assigned at random to each treatment combination. Complete the analysis of variance.

	A_1		A_2	
B_1	B_2	B_1	B_2
11	5	10	8
11	10	11	7
12	10	10	9
13	8	5	2
12	8	7	1
12	4	6	1
8	3	7	0
8	5	12	5
7	1	6	2
13	7	3	5

14.3—We have a two-factor experiment with three levels for each factor and with $n = 10$ subjects assigned at random to each treatment combination. Complete the analysis of variance.

A_1			A_2			A_3		
B_1	B_2	B_3	B_1	B_2	B_3	B_1	B_2	B_3
8	9	5	6	6	9	7	7	5
5	4	3	1	5	8	3	5	9
6	8	7	1	9	9	6	8	8
8	4	5	6	7	11	2	5	7
9	3	3	5	5	8	3	5	7
10	6	1	4	6	11	5	8	8
9	7	5	3	6	10	3	6	6
7	6	4	6	5	7	3	6	8
8	7	3	4	4	8	4	6	5
10	6	4	4	7	9	4	4	7

14.4—Below we have coefficients by which the treatment sums are to be multiplied in a 3×3 factorial experiment.

Comparison	A_1			A_2			A_3		
	B_1	B_2	B_3	B_1	B_2	B_3	B_1	B_2	B_3
1	1	1	1	1	1	1	-2	-2	-2
2	1	1	1	-1	-1	-1	0	0	0
3	-1	-1	2	-1	-1	2	-1	-1	2
4	-1	1	0	-1	1	0	-1	1	0
5	-1	-1	2	-1	-1	2	2	2	-4
6	-1	1	0	-1	1	0	2	-2	0
7	-1	-1	2	1	1	-2	0	0	0
8	-1	1	0	1	-1	0	0	0	0

(a) Does each row of the table, in fact, represent a comparison on the treatment sums? Why?

(b) Are the comparisons mutually orthogonal? Why?

14.5—Make the comparisons given in Example 14.4 on the treatment sums of Example 14.3.

(a) What comparisons, if any, are significant?

(b) The A sum of squares has 2 d.f. This sum of squares has been partitioned into two orthogonal comparisons each with 1 d.f. What are these two comparisons?

(c) The B sum of squares has 2 d.f. This sum of squares has also been partitioned into two orthogonal comparisons each with 1 d.f. What are these two comparisons?

(d)   What are the four comparisons into which the $A \times B$ sum of squares has been partitioned?

14.6—Assume in Example 14.4, that A_1 = Thirst, A_2 = Hunger, and A_3 = Sex and that B_1, B_2, and B_3 correspond to 0, 24, and 48 hours of deprivation of each of these drives.

(a)   Which, if any, of the comparisons make experimental sense in this context?
(b)   Can you find a more meaningful set of mutually orthogonal comparisons?

14.7—In Table 14.6 in the text we have the results on another two-factor experiment with three levels for each factor. Make the comparisons given in Example 14.4 on the treatment sums of Table 14.6.

(a)   What comparisons, if any, are significant?
(b)   Use the S-method to test the significance of the same comparisons.

14.8—For purposes of illustration, consider a two-factor experiment with $n = 2$ subjects assigned at random to each treatment combination.

A_1		A_2	
B_1	B_2	B_1	B_2
2	9	8	10
3	7	11	14

Note that (14.9) is an equation involving three terms on the right side. Write out the numerical values of (14.9) for the data given above. Note that when (14.9) is squared and summed all cross product terms on the right sum to zero.

14.9—Give a one-sentence definition of each of the following terms or concepts:

factor	orthogonal comparisons
two-factor experiment	two-factor interaction effect
level of a factor	

CHAPTER 15

Experiments Concerned with Change in Performance Over Trials

15.1 Introduction

Many experiments in psychology are concerned with change in performance over a series of trials. For example, a hungry rat may be placed in the starting box of a maze and we may measure the time required by the rat to run from the starting box to the goal box containing food. Each run is called a trial. Or a subject may be presented with a list of words that are paired with numbers. The words are presented one at a time and the task set for the subject is to learn to anticipate the number that follows each word. One run through the complete list is called a trial and on each trial we may count either the number of correct responses or the number of errors made by the subject. As still another example, a subject may be required to track a moving target on a screen with a light beam which he can manipulate. His performance may be observed for a period of three minutes. Each three-minute period for which his performance is observed is called a trial.

The dependent variable in experiments such as those described above is often the number of errors made on each trial, the number of correct responses on each trial, or the time required to complete a trial. Of experimental interest is the change in performance over the trials or the trend of the trial means for a group of subjects.

15.2 The Analysis of Variance with $s = 5$ Subjects and $t = 3$ Trials

For simplicity we consider an example in which $s = 5$ subjects are given $t = 3$ trials. For each subject we have a measure of performance on each trial and these measures are given in Table 15.1. We note that the row means are a measure of the average performance of each subject over the $t = 3$ trials. The

Table 15.1—Measures on a dependent variable X for $s = 5$ subjects tested on $t = 3$ trials

S's	Trials			Sum	Mean
	T_1	T_2	T_3		
1	2	4	7	13	4.33
2	2	6	10	18	6.00
3	3	7	10	20	6.67
4	7	9	11	27	9.00
5	6	9	12	27	9.00
Sum	20	35	50	105	7.00
Mean	4.0	7.0	10.0		

column means are a measure of the average performance of the $s = 5$ subjects on each trial. We may identify each observation by two ordered subscripts ts, where t refers to the trial and s refers to the subject. The notation we shall use is illustrated in Table 15.2 for our example where we have $t = 3$ trials and $s = 5$ subjects.

Table 15.2—Notation for an experiment in which $s = 5$ subjects are tested on $t = 3$ trials

Subjects	Trials			Sum	Mean
	T_1	T_2	T_3		
1	X_{11}	X_{21}	X_{31}	$\Sigma X_{.1}$	$\bar{X}_{.1}$
2	X_{12}	X_{22}	X_{32}	$\Sigma X_{.2}$	$\bar{X}_{.2}$
3	X_{13}	X_{23}	X_{33}	$\Sigma X_{.3}$	$\bar{X}_{.3}$
4	X_{14}	X_{24}	X_{34}	$\Sigma X_{.4}$	$\bar{X}_{.4}$
5	X_{15}	X_{25}	X_{35}	$\Sigma X_{.5}$	$\bar{X}_{.5}$
Sum	$\Sigma X_{1.}$	$\Sigma X_{2.}$	$\Sigma X_{3.}$	$\Sigma X_{..}$	$\bar{X}_{..}$
Mean	$\bar{X}_{1.}$	$\bar{X}_{2.}$	$\bar{X}_{3.}$		

We may, in the usual manner, find the total sum of squares for the data of Table 15.1. Thus

$$\text{Total} = (2)^2 + (2)^2 + (3)^2 + \cdots + (12)^2 - \frac{(105)^2}{15}$$

$$= 879 - 735$$

$$= 144$$

and the total sum of squares will have $ts - 1 = 15 - 1 = 14$ d.f.
 The sum of squares for trials (columns) will be given by

$$\text{Trials} = \frac{(20)^2}{5} + \frac{(35)^2}{5} + \frac{(50)^2}{5} - \frac{(105)^2}{15}$$

$$= 825 - 735$$

$$= 90$$

and the trial sum of squares will have $t - 1 = 3 - 1 = 2$ d.f. It is obvious that the sum of squares for trials measures the variation in the trial means.

Similarly, if we calculate the sum of squares for subjects (rows), this sum of squares will measure the variation in the subject means. The sum of squares for subjects will be given by

$$\text{Subjects} = \frac{(13)^2}{3} + \frac{(18)^2}{3} + \cdots + \frac{(27)^2}{3} - \frac{(105)^2}{15}$$

$$= 783.67 - 735.00$$

$$= 48.67$$

If we now subtract the trial and subject sums of squares from the total sum of squares, we obtain a residual sum of squares that is called the Subjects × Trials or S's × T sum of squares. Thus

$$S\text{'s} \times T = \text{Total} - \text{Trials} - \text{Subjects} \qquad (15.1)$$

and, for our example, we have

$$S\text{'s} \times T = 144.00 - 90.00 - 48.67 = 5.33$$

and this sum of squares will have degrees of freedom equal to $(s - 1)(t - 1) = (5 - 1)(3 - 1) = 8$.

Table 15.3—Analysis of variance for the data of Table 15.1

Source of variation	Sum of squares	d.f.	Mean square	F
Trials	90.00	2	45.00	67.2
Subjects	48.67	4	12.17	
S's × T	5.33	8	.67	
Total	144.00	14		

Table 15.3 summarizes the analysis of variance. As an estimate of experimental error for testing the significance of the mean square for trials, MS_T, we use the S's $\times T$ mean square, MS_{ST}. For the test of significance, we define

$$F = \frac{MS_T}{MS_{ST}} \tag{15.2}$$

and, in our example, we have

$$F = \frac{45.00}{.67} = 67.2$$

a highly significant value for 2 and 8 d.f. We may conclude that there are significant differences among the trial means.

15.3 Sums of Squares and Mean Squares in the Analysis of Variance

In this experiment we had $s = 5$ independent subjects with $t = 3$ repeated measurements on each subject. We may assume that measurements obtained from different subjects are independent, but that the repeated measurements on the same subject are not independent. We have previously shown that the expected value of a covariance, $C_{X_i X_j}$, is equal to zero, provided that X_i and X_j are independent. Thus, we may assume that

$$E(C_{X_{ts} X_{ts}}) = 0, \text{ if } t = t \text{ and } s \neq s \tag{15.3}$$

because, in this case, the observations are obtained from different subjects. On the other hand,

$$E(C_{X_{ts} X_{ts}}) \neq 0, \text{ if } t \neq t \text{ and } s = s \tag{15.4}$$

because, in this case, we have measurements on the same subject and, in general, measurements obtained from the same subject are not independent.

We can gain an understanding of the implications of (15.3) and (15.4) if we examine Table 15.4. In this table we have expressed the values of X_{ts} as deviations from the corresponding trial means $\bar{X}_t$. The entries in the table, therefore, correspond to

$$x_{ts} = X_{ts} - \bar{X}_t. \tag{15.5}$$

It is obvious that the sum of the squared deviations *within* each trial (column) involves a sum of squared values in which $t = t$ and $s \neq s$. For example, for Trial 1, we have

Table 15.4—Values of $X_{ts} - \bar{X}_t$. for the data of Table 15.1

Subjects	Trials			Σ
	T_1	T_2	T_3	
1	-2	-3	-3	-8
2	-2	-1	0	-3
3	-1	0	0	-1
4	3	2	1	6
5	2	2	2	6
Σ	0	0	0	0

$$\sum x_1.^2 = x_{11}^2 + x_{12}^2 + x_{13}^2 + x_{14}^2 + x_{15}^2$$

and this sum of squares is based upon $s = 5$ independent subjects. Similar considerations apply to the sum of squares within Trial 2 and within Trial 3. Squaring and summing the values of Table 15.4, we have the sum of squares within trials, which we designate by $\sum x_W^2$. Thus

$$\sum x_W^2 = \sum x_1.^2 + \sum x_2.^2 + \sum x_3.^2 \tag{15.6}$$

or, in our example,

$$\sum x_W^2 = 22 + 18 + 14 = 54$$

We note that the sum of squares within trials corresponds to the sum of squares within treatments in a randomized group design. It is obvious, from (15.1), that the $S\text{'s} \times T$ sum of squares is also given by

$$S\text{'s} \times T = \text{Within trials} - \text{Subjects} \tag{15.7}$$

or, in our example,

$$S\text{'s} \times T = 54.00 - 48.67 = 5.33$$

as before.

If we sum the entries in each row of Table 15.4, we have a sum of $t = 3$ measures for each subject. For example, for the first subject we have

$$\sum x._1 = x_{11} + x_{21} + x_{31} \tag{15.8}$$

Then

$$\left(\sum x._1\right)^2 = x_{11}^2 + x_{21}^2 + x_{31}^2 + 2(x_{11}x_{21} + x_{11}x_{31} + x_{21}x_{31}) \tag{15.9}$$

and, in this case, we have $t \neq t$ but $s = s$, and (15.4) is applicable. We show in detail in Table 15.5 the numerical values of (15.9) for each of the $s = 5$

Table 15.5—Values of $(\Sigma x._s)^2$ for the data of Table 15.4

$(\Sigma x._1)^2 = (-2)^2 + (-3)^2 + (-3)^2 + 2[(-2)(-3) + (-2)(-3) + (-3)(-3)]$

$(\Sigma x._2)^2 = (-2)^2 + (-1)^2 + \quad (0)^2 + 2[(-2)(-1) + (-2) \; (0) + (-1) \; (0)]$

$(\Sigma x._3)^2 = (-1)^2 + \quad (0)^2 + \quad (0)^2 + 2[(-1) \; (0) + (-1) \; (0) + \quad (0) \; (0)]$

$(\Sigma x._4)^2 = \quad (3)^2 + \quad (2)^2 + \quad (1)^2 + 2[\; (3) \; (2) + \quad (3) \; (1) + \quad (2) \; (1)]$

$(\Sigma x._5)^2 = \quad (2)^2 + \quad (2)^2 + \quad (2)^2 + 2[\; (2) \; (2) + \quad (2) \; (2) + \quad (2) \; (2)]$

$\displaystyle\sum_1^s (\Sigma x._s)^2 = \quad 22 \quad + \quad 18 \quad + \quad 14 \quad + 2(\quad 18 \quad + \quad 13 \quad + \quad 15 \quad)$

---

subjects. At the bottom of the table we give the sums for each term in (15.9), where the summation is over the $s = 5$ subjects.

We note that $22 + 18 + 14 = 54 = \Sigma x_W^2$, the sum of squares within trials or columns, and that $2(18 + 13 + 15) = 92$ is the sum of the $t(t - 1)$ cross product sums, $\Sigma x_{ts}x_{ts}$, where $t \neq t$ but $s = s$. We indicate the mean of the cross product sums by

$$\overline{\Sigma x_{ts}x_{ts}} = \overline{\Sigma x_{is}x_{js}} \tag{15.10}$$

where the subscripts i and j serve to remind us that $t \neq t$. Then, for our example we have

$$\overline{\Sigma x_{is}x_{js}} = \frac{2(46)}{t(t-1)} = \frac{92}{6} = 15.33$$

and the sum of the $t(t - 1)$ cross product sums will, of course, be $t(t - 1)\overline{\Sigma x_{is}x_{js}}$.

For the sum of all ts observations in Table 15.4, we have $\Sigma x.. = 0$ and, therefore, the correction term will also be equal to zero. Then the sum of squares for subjects, which we designate by Σx_S^2, will be given by

$$\Sigma x_S^2 = \sum_1^s \frac{(\Sigma x._s)^2}{t} = \frac{\Sigma x_W^2}{t} + \frac{t(t-1)\overline{\Sigma x_{is}x_{js}}}{t} \tag{15.11}$$

and, in our example, we have

$$\Sigma x_S^2 = \frac{146}{3} = \frac{54}{3} + \frac{6(15.33)}{3} = 48.67$$

as before.

Now let us examine the nature of the S's $\times T$ sum of squares. From (15.7) we see that the S's $\times T$ sum of squares is equal to the within trials sum of squares, Σx_W^2, minus the subject sum of squares or

$$S\text{'s} \times T = \sum x_W^2 - \sum x_S^2 \tag{15.12}$$

Substituting in (15.12) with the identity for Σx_S^2, given by (15.11), we have

$$S\text{'s} \times T = \sum x_W^2 - \left(\frac{\sum x_W^2}{t} + \frac{t(t-1)\overline{\sum x_{is}x_{js}}}{t} \right) \tag{15.13}$$

The S's $\times T$ sum of squares has degrees of freedom equal to $(s-1)(t-1)$ and dividing both sides of (15.13) by $(s-1)(t-1)$ we have the S's $\times T$ mean square, which we designate by MS_{ST}. Then

$$MS_{ST} = \frac{\sum x_W^2(t-1)}{t(s-1)(t-1)} - \frac{(t-1)\overline{\sum x_{is}x_{js}}}{(s-1)(t-1)} \tag{15.14}$$

or

$$MS_{ST} = MS_W - \frac{\overline{\sum x_{is}x_{js}}}{s-1} \tag{15.15}$$

where MS_W is the mean square within trials.

The second term on the right of (15.15) is the mean of the $t(t-1)$ *covariances* and we have previously shown that the covariance, $\Sigma x_i x_j/(n-1)$, is equal to $r_{ij}s_i s_j$. Then, we also have

$$\frac{\overline{\sum x_{is}x_{js}}}{s-1} = \overline{r_{ij}s_i s_j} \tag{15.16}$$

and therefore

$$MS_{ST} = MS_W - \overline{r_{ij}s_i s_j} \tag{15.17}$$

As before, we assume that $E(MS_W) = \sigma^2$. If we can also assume that the expected values of each of the correlations r_{ij} are equal to the same value ρ and that $E(s_i) = E(s_j) = \sigma$, then

$$E\,(\overline{r_{ij}s_i s_j}) = \rho\sigma^2 \tag{15.18}$$

and

$$E(MS_{ST}) = \sigma^2(1 - \rho) \tag{15.19}$$

Under the assumptions we have made, it can also be shown that if there are trial effects, that is, if the average long-run values of the trial means are not all equal to the same value μ, then the expected value of the mean square for trials will be[1]

$$E(MS_T) = \sigma^2(1 - \rho) + \frac{s \sum\limits_{1}^{t} T_t^2}{t - 1} \tag{15.20}$$

where T_t is a trial effect and corresponds to t_k, a treatment effect, in a randomized group design. We now note that

$$F = \frac{MS_T}{MS_{ST}} = \frac{\sigma^2(1 - \rho) + \dfrac{s \sum\limits_{1}^{t} T_t^2}{t - 1}}{\sigma^2(1 - \rho)} \tag{15.21}$$

and the F of (15.21) is a test of the null hypothesis that there are no trial effects, that is,

$$\sum\limits_{1}^{t} T_t^2 = 0$$

It is obvious from (15.21) that if $\rho = 0$, then the F test of the trial mean square is essentially the same as the F test of the treatment mean square in a randomized group design. For the randomized group design, we had independent observations and for independent observations we have $E(r_{ij}) = 0$. It is also obvious from (15.21) that if ρ is positive, then for any fixed treatment effects, T_t, the value of F will increase as the value of ρ increases. The sensitivity of the F test of (15.21), in other words, depends upon the value of ρ.

15.4   Assumptions Involved in the Test of Significance

The validity of the F test of (15.21) depends upon the validity of the assumptions we have made concerning the r_{ij}'s and the variances. In addition to assuming that the variances of the $s = 5$ observations for each trial are homogeneous, that is, that the variances within trials have the same expected values, we have also assumed that the covariances between trials are homogeneous. This second assumption, in the case of equal variances, is equivalent to assuming that the $t(t - 1)$ correlation coefficients are homogeneous in the sense that the expected values of the correlation coefficients are all equal to the same value ρ.

In a later section of this chapter, we shall discuss a conservative test that may prove to be useful when the assumption of equal variances and correlations is not tenable.

---

[1] A proof is given in Edwards (1964).

15.5   Linear and Quadratic Components of the Trial Sum of Squares

In experiments designed to measure change in performance over a series of trials, our primary interest is usually in the trend of the trial means. If the experiment is a learning experiment and if the measures obtained on each trial represent amount learned or accuracy of performance, then, in general, we would expect the trial means to increase from trial to trial. If we plot the trial means against trials, the trend of the plotted points may be fairly accurately described by a straight line fitted through the points as in Figure 15.1, provided that the increase from trial to trial is relatively constant. In this case the trend of the trial means would be described as linear.

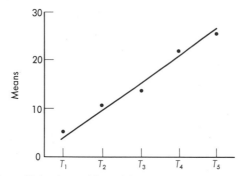

Figure **15.1**—A set of five trial means with a linear trend.

Because the slope of the line is positive, the linear trend is also described as positive.

In some cases, the differences in the trial means may not be relatively constant from trial to trial. For example, the differences in the trial means may be relatively large on the early trials, whereas on later trials the differences may tend to become smaller. In this case, a plot of the trial means against the trials would show that there is a curvature in the trend of the means as in Figure 15.2.

For any set of $t \geq 3$ trial means it is possible to make a comparison D_1 on the trial sums (or means) that provides information concerning the linear trend of the means. The linear comparison, if significant, tells us that all or a significant part of the variation in the trial means can be accounted for by the linear trend of the means. If the means fall precisely on a straight line and the trend is either upward or downward, the sum of squares for the linear comparison, with 1 d.f., will be exactly equal to the sum of squares for trials. The sum of squares for the linear comparison is generally referred to as the *linear component* of the trial sum of squares.

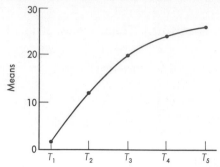

Figure **15.2**—A set of five trial means with some degree of curvature in the trend.

If there is an apparent curvature in the trend of the trial means, as in Figure 15.2, we may make a second comparison D_2 on the trial sums (or means) that is orthogonal to the linear comparison. The sum of squares for D_2 will also have 1 d.f. This second comparison provides information concerning the curvature in the trend of the means. If D_2 is significant, for example, this tells us that there is a significant curvature in the trend of the means. The sum of squares for D_2 is generally referred to as the *quadratic component* of the trial sum of squares.[2]

Table 15.6 gives the coefficients of the linear and quadratic comparisons for experiments in which we have from $t = 3$ to $t = 9$ trial means.[3]

15.6 Significance of the Linear Component for the Data of Table 15.1

For the data of Table 15.1, we have $t = 3$ trial means and the coefficients for the linear comparison D_1 are $-1, 0$, and 1. Then, making this comparison on the trial sums for this example, we have

$$D_1 = (-1)(20) + (0)(35) + (1)(50) = 30$$

Because D_1 has 1 d.f., the mean square for D_1 will be equal to the sum of squares for D_1 and, in our example, we have

---

[2] With t trial means it is possible to make $t - 1$ orthogonal comparisons concerning the trend of the means. For example, with $t = 5$ trials, in addition to the linear and quadratic components, we may obtain the cubic and quartic components of the trial sum of squares. Coefficients for the cubic and higher degree comparisons can be found in Fisher and Yates (1949).

[3] The coefficients given in Table 15.6 are based upon the assumption that the trials are equally spaced and that the same number of observations are available for each trial. If the trials are not equally spaced or if, for some reason, the number of observations varies from trial to trial, the coefficients given in Table 15.6 should not be used. For methods of dealing with unequal intervals and unequal n's, see Gaito (1965). Robson (1959) and Grandage (1958) also describe methods for obtaining coefficients for unequal intervals.

Table 15.6—Coefficients for linear and quadratic comparisons on a set of t trial sums or means

Comparison	Number of trials 1	2	3	4	5	6	7	8	9	Σa_i^2
Linear	−1	0	1							2
Quadratic	1	−2	1							6
Linear	−3	−1	1	3						20
Quadratic	1	−1	−1	1						4
Linear	−2	−1	0	1	2					10
Quadratic	2	−1	−2	−1	2					14
Linear	−5	−3	−1	1	3	5				70
Quadratic	5	−1	−4	−4	−1	5				84
Linear	−3	−2	−1	0	1	2	3			28
Quadratic	5	0	−3	−4	−3	0	5			84
Linear	−7	−5	−3	−1	1	3	5	7		168
Quadratic	7	1	−3	−5	−5	−3	1	7		168
Linear	−4	−3	−2	−1	0	1	2	3	4	60
Quadratic	28	7	−8	−17	−20	−17	−8	7	28	2772

$$MS_{D_1} = \frac{D_1^2}{s\sum_{1}^{t} a_{\cdot 1}^2} = \frac{(30)^2}{(5)(2)} = 90$$

We note that the sum of squares for $D_1 = 90$ and that this is exactly equal to the trial sum of squares, as it must be if the trial means fall precisely on a straight line as they do in this example. The linear component of the trial sum of squares, in other words, accounts for all of the variation in the trial means in this example.

To test the significance of D_1, we have

$$F = \frac{MS_{D_1}}{MS_{ST}} = \frac{90.00}{.67} = 134.33$$

a highly significant value for 1 and 8 d.f.

15.7   An Example with $s = 10$ Subjects and $t = 4$ Trials

Consider the example shown in Figure 15.3 and assume that each trial sum is based upon $s = 10$ observations. We have $t = 4$ trials and the sum of squares for trials will be

$$\text{Trials} = \frac{(5)^2}{10} + \frac{(20)^2}{10} + \frac{(25)^2}{10} + \frac{(30)^2}{10} - \frac{(80)^2}{40}$$

$$= 195 - 160$$

$$= 35$$

and for the trial mean square we have

$$MS_T = \frac{35}{4 - 1} = 11.67$$

Let us assume that MS_{ST}, for this example, is equal to 4.00. Then we have

$$F = \frac{MS_T}{MS_{ST}} = \frac{11.67}{4.00} = 2.92$$

a nonsignificant value ($P > .05$) with 3 and 27 d.f. If we were to make a decision on the basis of this test alone, we would conclude that there are no significant differences in the trial means. But assume that we had planned to make a test of the linear component prior to the experiment itself. Then for the linear comparison we have

$$D_1 = (-3)(5) + (-1)(20) + (1)(25) + (3)(30) = 80$$

and

$$MS_{D_1} = \frac{D_1{}^2}{s \sum_1^t a_{.1}{}^2} = \frac{(80)^2}{(10)(20)} = 32$$

with 1 d.f. We note that almost all of the variation in the trial means, represented by the trial sum of squares, which is equal to 35, is accounted for by the linear component, which is equal to 32.

As a test of significance of MS_{D_1} with $MS_{ST} = 4.0$ we have

$$F = \frac{MS_{D_1}}{MS_{ST}} = \frac{32.0}{4.0} = 8$$

a significant value ($P < .01$) with 1 and 27 d.f. This example illustrates that it is possible for the linear component of the trial sum of squares to be significant even though the mean square for trials is not significant. In this example, almost all of the variation in the trial means is accounted for by

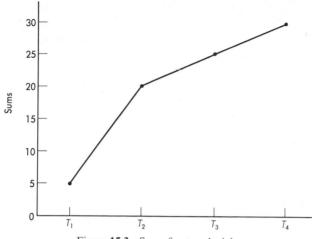

Figure **15.3**—Sums for $t = 4$ trials.

the linear component. Because the linear component has but 1 d.f., whereas the trial sum of squares has $t - 1$ d.f., it is possible for MS_{D_1} to be large, even though MS_T may be relatively small.

For the quadratic component, we have

$$D_2 = (1)(5) + (-1)(20) + (-1)(25) + (1)(30) = -10$$

and

$$MS_{D_2} = \frac{D_2^{\,2}}{s \sum_1^t a_{\cdot 2}^{\,2}} = \frac{(-10)^2}{(10)(4)} = 2.5$$

with 1 d.f. As a test of significance of D_2 we have

$$F = \frac{MS_{D_2}}{MS_{ST}} = \frac{2.5}{4.0} < 1$$

and this is obviously a nonsignificant value because $F < 1$.

15.8   Test of Significance of Deviations from Linear Regression

Instead of making the comparison D_2, we may choose to subtract the sum of squares for the linear comparison with 1 d.f. from the trial sum of squares with $t - 1$ d.f. to obtain

$$\text{Deviations from linear regression} = \text{Trials} - \text{Linear} \qquad (15.22)$$

The sum of squares defined by (15.22) will have $t - 2$ d.f. and measures the deviation of the trial means from linear regression. To determine whether the trend of the trial means deviates significantly from linearity, in our example, we have

$$F = \frac{(35 - 32)/2}{4.0} < 1$$

a nonsignificant value because $F < 1$. We may conclude that the trend of the means is essentially linear because we do not have a significant value of F in the test for deviations from linear regression.

15.9   Another Example with $s = 10$ Subjects and $t = 4$ Trials

Consider now the plot of the trial sums in Figure 15.4. In this case there is apparently a greater curvature in the trend of the trial means than in Figure 15.3. With $s = 10$ observations for each trial, the sum of squares for trials will be

$$\text{Trials} = \frac{(5)^2}{10} + \frac{(25)^2}{10} + \frac{(30)^2}{10} + \frac{(25)^2}{10} - \frac{(85)^2}{40}$$

$$= 217.50 - 180.62$$

$$= 36.88$$

and the mean square for trials will be

$$MS_T = \frac{36.88}{4 - 1} = 12.29$$

Again, we assume that $MS_{ST} = 4.0$ and, as a test of significance of the trial mean square, we have

$$F = \frac{MS_T}{MS_{ST}} = \frac{12.29}{4.00} = 3.07$$

a significant value ($P < .05$) with 3 and 27 d.f.

For the linear comparison of the trend, we have

$$D_1 = (-3)(5) + (-1)(25) + (1)(30) + (3)(25) = 65$$

and

$$MS_{D_1} = \frac{D_1{}^2}{s \sum_1^t a_{.1}{}^2} = \frac{(65)^2}{(10)(20)} = 21.12$$

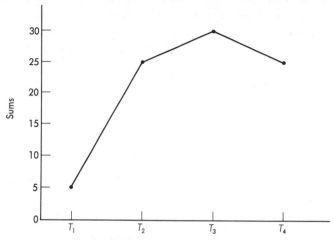

Figure **15.4**—Sums for $t = 4$ trials.

As a test of significance of D_1 we have,

$$F = \frac{MS_{D_1}}{MS_{ST}} = \frac{21.12}{4.00} = 5.28$$

a significant value ($P < .05$) with 1 and 27 d.f. and we may conclude that the linear component of the trial sum of squares is significant.

For the quadratic comparison, we have

$$D_2 = (1)(5) + (-1)(25) + (-1)(30) + (1)(25) = -25$$

and

$$MS_{D_2} = \frac{D_2{}^2}{s\sum_1^t a_{\cdot 2}{}^2} = \frac{(-25)^2}{(10)(4)} = 15.62$$

Then, as a test of the significance of D_2, we have

$$F = \frac{MS_{D_2}}{MS_{ST}} = \frac{15.62}{4.00} = 3.90$$

From the table of F, we find that with 1 and 27 d.f. $F \geq 4.21$ has probability of .05 when the null hypothesis is true. Because our observed value of $F = 3.90$ is close to the value required for significance with $\alpha = .05$, we may, in this instance, decide that the outcome of the test of significance is sufficiently inconclusive that it would be better to withhold judgment about the curvature in the trend until we have more conclusive evidence based upon the results of subsequent experiments.

We may note, however, that in this example, we have as the sum of squares for deviations from linear regression, as given by (15.22),

Deviations from linear regression $= 36.88 - 21.12 = 15.76$

and that, as an F test of the significance of deviations from linear regression, we have

$$F = \frac{15.76/2}{4.0} = 1.97$$

a nonsignificant value with 2 and 27 d.f. The results of this test indicate that the trial means do not deviate significantly from linearity.

15.10   An Experiment Involving a Treatment Factor

In the previous sections, we discussed experiments involving change in performance over a series of trials. In these experiments all subjects were tested under the same conditions and our primary interest was in the trend of the trial means. We now consider experiments in which we have a treatment factor A that is varied in two or more ways. For simplicity we shall assume that A is varied in only two ways. Subjects are randomly assigned to the two levels of A so that we have $s = 5$ subjects for each level. Each subject is then given $t = 3$ trials and on each trial we have a measure X of performance on a dependent variable of interest. The measures of X for each subject on each trial for each level of A are given in Table 15.7. In this experiment, our primary interest is in the possible differences in the trends of the trial means for the subjects in Treatment A_1 and Treatment A_2.

For the total sum of squares, we have

$$\text{Total} = (2)^2 + (2)^2 + (3)^2 + \cdots + (7)^2 - \frac{(180)^2}{30}$$

$$= 1312 - 1080$$

$$= 232$$

Now consider only the row sums of Table 15.7, that is, the sums for each of the 10 subjects. We note that we have $s = 5$ subjects that have been assigned at random to A_1 and also $s = 5$ subjects that have been assigned at random to A_2. Other than the fact that we have a sum of $t = 3$ observations for each subject, the row measures are comparable to those obtained with a randomized group design in which $n = s$ subjects are assigned at random to each of two treatments. We may, therefore, partition the row sum of squares into two parts: a sum of squares measuring the variation between A_1 and A_2, and a pooled sum of squares measuring the variation between S's in A_1

Table 15.7—Values of a dependent variable X for an experiment in which $s = 5$ subjects were assigned at random to each of two experimental conditions, A_1 and A_2, and in which each subject was tested on $t = 3$ trials

Treatments	S's	Trials			Σ
		T_1	T_2	T_3	
	1	2	4	7	13
	2	2	6	10	18
A_1	3	3	7	10	20
	4	7	9	11	27
	5	6	9	12	27
	Σ	20	35	50	105
	1	2	2	4	8
	2	2	4	6	12
A_2	3	3	5	6	14
	4	7	6	7	20
	5	6	8	7	21
	Σ	20	25	30	75

and the variation between S's in A_2. For the row or subject sum of squares, we have

$$\text{Subjects} = \frac{(13)^2}{3} + \frac{(18)^2}{3} + \frac{(20)^2}{3} + \cdots + \frac{(21)^2}{3} - \frac{(180)^2}{30}$$
$$= 1198.67 - 1080.00$$
$$= 118.67$$

and for the sum of squares for A, we have

$$A = \frac{(105)^2}{15} + \frac{(75)^2}{15} - \frac{(180)^2}{30}$$
$$= 1110 - 1080$$
$$= 30$$

Subtracting the sum of squares for A from the sum of squares for subjects, we obtain

$$S\text{'s}(A) = \text{Subjects} - A \tag{15.23}$$

or, in our example,

$$S's(A) = 118.67 - 30.00 = 88.67$$

The notation $S's(A)$ indicates that this source of variation is the variation between S's *within* the different levels of A. The sum of squares for $S's(A)$ corresponds to a within treatment sum of squares in a randomized group design and this sum of squares divided by its degrees of freedom we shall designate as $MS_{S(A)}$. $MS_{S(A)}$ is the appropriate error mean square for testing the significance of the A mean square.

It is also possible to calculate the $S's(A)$ sum of squares directly. For example, the sum of squares between S's in A_1 will be given by

$$S's(A_1) = \frac{(13)^2}{3} + \frac{(18)^2}{3} + \cdots + \frac{(27)^2}{3} - \frac{(105)^2}{15}$$

$$= 783.67 - 735.00$$

$$= 48.67$$

and this sum of squares will have $s - 1 = 5 - 1 = 4$ d.f. Similarly, the sum of squares between S's in A_2 will be given by

$$S's(A_2) = \frac{(8)^2}{3} + \frac{(12)^2}{3} + \cdots + \frac{(21)^2}{3} - \frac{(75)^2}{15}$$

$$= 415 - 375$$

$$= 40$$

and this sum of squares will also have $s - 1 = 5 - 1 = 4$ d.f.

Then the pooled sum of squares between S's in A_1 and between S's in A_2 will be

$$S's(A) = S's(A_1) + S's(A_2) \tag{15.24}$$

or

$$S's(A) = 48.67 + 40.00 = 88.67$$

which is equal to the value we obtained by subtraction in (15.23). The $S's(A)$ sum of squares will have $a(s - 1) = 2(5 - 1) = 8$ d.f.

For the trial sum of squares, we obtain

$$\text{Trials} = \frac{(40)^2}{10} + \frac{(60)^2}{10} + \frac{(80)^2}{10} - \frac{(180)^2}{30}$$

$$= 1160 - 1080$$

$$= 80$$

and this sum of squares will have $t - 1 = 3 - 1 = 2$ d.f.

Subtracting the sums of squares for trials and subjects from the total sum of squares, we have the S's $\times T$ sum of squares or

$$S\text{'s} \times T = \text{Total} - \text{Trials} - \text{Subjects} \qquad (15.25)$$

and in our example

$$S\text{'s} \times T = 232.00 - 80.00 - 118.67 = 33.33$$

In Table 15.8 we give the trial sums for each level of A. We may regard these sums as corresponding to those in a two-factor experiment in which one factor A is varied in two ways and the other factor T is varied in three ways. Then the sum of squares between treatment combinations or the cells of Table 15.8 will be

$$\text{Treatment combinations} = \frac{(20)^2}{5} + \frac{(35)^2}{5} + \cdots + \frac{(30)^2}{5} - \frac{(180)^2}{30}$$

$$= 1210 - 1080$$

$$= 130$$

Table 15.8—Trial sums for each level of A for the data of Table 15.7

Levels of A	Trials			Σ
	T_1	T_2	T_3	
A_1	20	35	50	105
A_2	20	25	30	75
Σ	40	60	80	180

We have already found that the A sum of squares is equal to 30.0 and that the T sum of squares is equal to 80.0. Subtracting these two sums of squares from the sum of squares for treatment combinations, we obtain the $A \times T$ interaction sum of squares. Thus

$$A \times T = 130 - 30 - 80 = 20$$

and this sum of squares will have $(a - 1)(t - 1) = (2 - 1)(3 - 1) = 2$ d.f. Subtracting the $A \times T$ sum of squares from the S's $\times T$ sum of squares we obtain

$$S\text{'s}(A) \times T = S\text{'s} \times T - A \times T \qquad (15.26)$$

or, in our example,

$$S\text{'s}(A) \times T = 33.33 - 20.00 = 13.33$$

The notation $S\text{'s}(A) \times T$ indicates that this source of variation is the $S\text{'s} \times T$ interaction *within* the different levels of A. For example, for A_1, the first level of A, we have

$$S\text{'s}(A_1) \times T = \text{Total}(A_1) - \text{Trials}(A_1) - S\text{'s}(A_1)$$
$$= 144.00 - 90.00 - 48.67$$
$$= 5.33$$

and similarly for those observations obtained under A_2, we have

$$S\text{'s}(A_2) \times T = \text{Total}(A_2) - \text{Trials}(A_2) - S\text{'s}(A_2)$$
$$= 58 - 10 - 40$$
$$= 8$$

and we note that

$$S\text{'s}(A) \times T = S\text{'s}(A_1) \times T + S\text{'s}(A_2) \times T \qquad (15.27)$$

or, in our example

$$S\text{'s}(A) \times T = 5.33 + 8.00$$
$$= 13.33$$

which is the same value we obtained by subtraction in (15.26). The $S\text{'s}(A) \times T$ sum of squares will have $a(s - 1)(t - 1) = 2(5 - 1)(3 - 1) = 16$ d.f.

In the experiments described earlier in the chapter, we did not have an A factor and consequently we had but one sum of squares for $S\text{'s} \times T$. The mean square for $S\text{'s} \times T$ was then used as an error mean square in testing the significance of the mean square for trials. However, if we have a treatment factor A with two or more levels, then we can obtain an $S\text{'s} \times T$ sum of squares for each level of A. We assume that each of the corresponding mean squares are estimates of the same error mean square and consequently the $S\text{'s} \times T$ sums of squares for the various levels of A may be pooled to obtain the $S\text{'s}(A) \times T$ sum of squares. This pooled sum of squares divided by its degrees of freedom provides an estimate of experimental error that we designate as $MS_{S(A)T}$. $MS_{S(A)T}$ corresponds to MS_{ST} in experiments in which we do not have a

Table 15.9—Analysis of variance for the data of Table 15.7

Source of variation	Sum of squares	d.f.	Mean square	F
A	30.00	1	30.00	2.71
$S\text{'s}\,(A)$	88.67	8	11.08	
Trials	80.00	2	40.00	48.19
$A \times T$	20.00	2	10.00	12.05
$S\text{'s}\,(A) \times T$	13.33	16	.83	
Total	232.00	29		

treatment factor A and is used to test the significance of the mean square for trials and the $A \times T$ mean square.

Table 15.9 summarizes the analysis of variance. We have $F = 2.71$ with 1 and 8 d.f. for the test of significance of the A mean square and this is not a significant value. From the table of F, we find that $F \geq 6.23$ has probability of .01 when we have 2 and 16 d.f. and thus both the $A \times T$ mean square and the mean square for trials are highly significant.

15.11   The Significance of the Linear Component of the Trial Sum of Squares

Figure 15.5 shows the trial sums for the combined levels of A. It is obvious that the trial means fall precisely on a straight line and we should find that the sum of squares for the linear component of the trend is exactly equal to the trial sum of squares. For the linear comparison, we have

$$D_1 = (-1)(40) + (0)(60) + (1)(80) = 40$$

and

$$MS_{D_1} = \frac{(40)^2}{(10)(2)} = 80$$

and we note that the linear component of the trend accounts for all of the variation in the trial sum of squares. In the denominator of MS_{D_1} we have $10 = (2)(5)$, the number of observations for each trial sum, and $2 = \Sigma_1^t a_{.1}{}^2$, the sum of squares of the coefficients for the comparison D_1. As a test of significance of D_1, we have

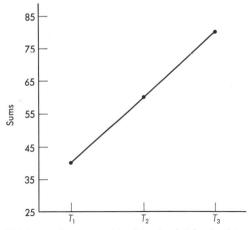

Figure **15.5**—Trial sums for the combined levels of A for the data of Table 15.7.

$$F = \frac{MS_{D_1}}{MS_{S(A)T}} = \frac{80.00}{.83} = 96.39$$

with 1 and 16 d.f. and this is a highly significant value.

We emphasize again that it is entirely possible in a given experiment for the linear component D_1 to be significant despite the fact that the trial mean square may not be significant. The reason for this is that if the trend of the trial means is quite linear, but if the differences between the means are small, the sum of squares for D_1 will be almost as large as the sum of squares for trials. But D_1 has only 1 d.f., whereas the trial sum of squares has $t - 1$ d.f. Thus, if most of the variation in the trial means can be attributed to the linear trend of the means, MS_{D_1} may be quite large and MS_T may be relatively small because the two sums of squares have different degrees of freedom.

15.12   The Test of Significance of the Linear Component of the $A \times T$ Sum of Squares

In Figure 15.6 we have plotted the trial sums for each level of A. The fact that the $A \times T$ mean square is significant is another way of stating that the two lines in the figure are not parallel within the limits of random sampling. We note, however, that the trend of the trial means for both A_1 and A_2 is linear, but that the slope of the trend for A_1 is steeper than the slope of the trend for A_2. Let us find the sum of squares for the linear component for each level of A. For A_1 we have

$$D_1(A_1) = (-1)(20) + (0)(35) + (1)(50) = 30$$

and

$$MS_{D_1(A_1)} = \frac{(30)^2}{(5)(2)} = 90$$

In the denominator of $MS_{D_1(A_1)}$ we have $s = 5$, the number of observations for each trial sum for A_1, and $\Sigma_1^t a_{.1}^2 = 2$, the sum of squares of the coefficients for the comparison $D_1(A_1)$. Similarly, for the linear component of the trend of the trial means for A_2, we have

$$D_1(A_2) = (-1)(20) + (0)(25) + (1)(30) = 10$$

and

$$MS_{D_1(A_2)} = \frac{(10)^2}{(5)(2)} = 10$$

Each of the above two mean squares is also a sum of squares because each has 1 d.f. We note that $MS_{D_1(A)}$, the mean square for the linear component of the trial sum of squares for the combined levels of A_1 and A_2 is also a sum of squares because it too has 1 d.f. Then we may define the *sum of squares*

$$D_1(A \times T) = [MS_{D_1(A_1)} + MS_{D_1(A_2)}] - MS_{D_1(A)} \qquad (15.28)$$

The sum of squares defined by (15.28) is the linear component of the $A \times T$ sum of squares. The first two terms on the right are sums of squares each with 1 d.f. and their sum has 2 d.f. The last term on the right is also a sum of squares with 1 d.f. Then $D_1(A \times T)$, in our example, will have $1 + 1 - 1 = 1$ d.f.

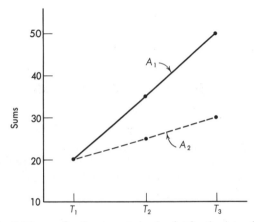

Figure **15.6**—Trial sums for the separate levels of A for the data of Table 15.7.

For the general case, the degrees of freedom for $D_1(A \times T)$ will be given by $a - 1$, where a is the number of levels of the treatment factor A. For example, if we have an experiment with $a = 3$ levels of A, then

$$D_1(A \times T) = [MS_{D_1(A_1)} + MS_{D_1(A_2)} + MS_{D_1(A_3)}] - MS_{D_1(A)}$$

and, in this case, $D_1(A \times T)$ will obviously have $1 + 1 + 1 - 1 = 3 - 1 = a - 1$ d.f. In general, then, $MS_{D_1(A \times T)} = D_1(A \times T)/(a - 1)$.
    In our example, we have

$$D_1(A \times T) = \frac{(30)^2}{(5)(2)} + \frac{(10)^2}{(5)(2)} - \frac{(40)^2}{(10)(2)}$$

$$= 90 + 10 - 80$$

$$= 20$$

and we note that the $D_1(A \times T)$ sum of squares is equal to the $A \times T$ sum of squares for this example. The fact that the linear component of the $A \times T$

sum of squares is equal to the $A \times T$ sum of squares tells us that the only difference between the trends of the trial means for A_1 and A_2 is with respect to the linear components of the trends. To determine whether the two linear components differ significantly, we have

$$F = \frac{MS_{D_1(A \times T)}}{MS_{S(A)T}} \tag{15.29}$$

or, for our example,

$$F = \frac{20.00}{.83} = 24.10$$

a highly significant value with 1 and 16 d.f.

15.13   The Test of Significance of the Quadratic Component of the $A \times T$ Sum of Squares

Suppose that we have an experiment in which the trends of the trial means for A_1 and for A_2 show some degree of curvature. Then, we may wish to determine whether the trends for A_1 and A_2 differ significantly in their curvature. To make this test, we find the quadratic component of the $A \times T$ sum of squares and this will be given by

$$D_2(A \times T) = \left[MS_{D_2(A_1)} + MS_{D_2(A_2)}\right] - MS_{D_2(A)} \tag{15.30}$$

The degrees of freedom for $D_2(A \times T)$ will be equal to the number of terms within the brackets minus 1. Because we will have one term within the brackets for each level of A, the degrees of freedom for $D_2(A \times T)$ will be equal to $a - 1$.

If you calculate $D_2(A \times T)$ for the present example you will find that this sum of squares is equal to zero. In experiments in which $D_2(A \times T)$ is not equal to zero, the mean square will be given by

$$MS_{D_2(A \times T)} = \frac{D_2(A \times T)}{a - 1} \tag{15.31}$$

The test of significance of the differences in the curvatures of the trends of the means for the various levels of A, will then be given by

$$F = \frac{MS_{D_2(A \times T)}}{MS_{S(A)T}} \tag{15.32}$$

with $a - 1$ and $a(s - 1)(t - 1)$ d.f.

15.14   Violations of Assumptions and Conservative F Tests

Because so many experiments in the behavioral sciences involve repeated measurements on the same subjects, we give some consideration at this point to violations of the assumptions of the analysis of variance for these experiments. We have previously emphasized that with an adequate and equal number of subjects assigned at random to each treatment in a randomized group design, the F test of significance of the treatment mean square is robust. This means that the F test in a randomized group design is relatively insensitive to departures from normality of distribution and heterogeneity of variance. Because subjects are randomly assigned to the treatments, all observations in a randomized group design may be assumed to be independent.

In experiments of the kind described in this chapter, however, we have several observations for each subject and, in general, repeated observations on the same subject are *not* independent. The analysis of variance for experiments with repeated measurements of the same subjects, therefore, not only involves the assumption of normality of distribution and equal variances but also the assumption of equal correlations.

If the same subjects are given t trials, then observations obtained on trials that are relatively close together may be more highly correlated than observations on trials that are more widely separated. For example, if subjects are given $t = 6$ trials, then performance on Trials 2 and 3 may be more highly correlated than performance on Trials 2 and 6. If the set of $t(t - 1)$ correlations cannot be assumed to be homogeneous, that is, if the correlations are not all estimates of the same value ρ, then we have a violation of the assumption of equal correlations.

Box (1954b) has considered the effects of inequality of variances and correlations for the case where we have t measurements on each of s subjects. Box was able to show that, under the null hypothesis, the F obtained in the usual test of significance of the trial mean square is not distributed with $t - 1$ and $(s - 1)(t - 1)$ d.f., but instead is approximately distributed as F would be if the degrees of freedom are reduced by a fraction ε. The exact value of ε is a function of the $t \times t$ variance-covariance matrix. If the t variances are equal and the $t(t - 1)$ correlations are equal, then the assumptions of the analysis of variance are met and, in this case, ε takes its maximum value and is equal to 1. In this instance, the degrees of freedom for evaluating F remain unchanged. However, if the assumption of equal variances and correlations is violated, then we should evaluate the observed F by entering the F table with

$$(t - 1)\varepsilon \text{ and } (s - 1)(t - 1)\varepsilon \qquad (15.33)$$

degrees of freedom. It is obvious, from (15.33), that the maximum reduction in the degrees of freedom occurs when ε takes its minimum value.

Geisser and Greenhouse (1958) have shown that the minimum value of $\varepsilon = 1/(t - 1)$. Therefore, if we multiply the degrees of freedom for F by $1/(t - 1)$ and enter the F table with these reduced degrees of freedom, we will have a conservative F test because the minimum value of ε results in a maximum reduction of the degrees of freedom.

Box considered what we shall call Case I: an experiment in which we have s subjects and all subjects are tested under the same condition so that we have t measures for each subject. Geisser and Greenhouse extended Box's results to what we shall call Case II: an experiment in which we have a treatment factor A with s subjects assigned to each level of A and with t measures for each subject. In both cases, conservative F tests may be made such that if the results of the tests are significant, the results of more exact tests would also be significant. We now describe these conservative tests for Case I and Case II.

15.15   A Conservative Test for Case I

In Case I we have s subjects and t measurements for each subject obtained under the same condition. We complete the analysis of variance in the usual way and obtain an analysis of variance summary table such as Table 15.3. In this table we have $s = 5$ subjects and $t = 3$ trials. For the test of significance of the trial mean square we have $F = 67.2$. If we can assume equal variances and equal correlations, then we evaluate $F = 67.2$ in terms of the tabled value with $t - 1$ and $(s - 1)(t - 1)$ or 2 and 8 d.f.

To make a conservative test, we multiply the degrees of freedom of both the numerator and denominator by the minimum value of $\varepsilon = 1/(t - 1)$. Thus we obtain

$$(t - 1)\varepsilon = (t - 1)\frac{1}{t - 1} = 1$$

d.f. for the numerator and

$$(s - 1)(t - 1)\varepsilon = (s - 1)(t - 1)\frac{1}{t - 1} = s - 1 = 4$$

d.f. for the denominator. Entering the table of F with 1 and 4 d.f., we find that $F \geq 21.20$ has a probability of .01 when the null hypothesis is true. Because our observed value of $F = 67.2$ exceeds this value, we may conclude that the trial means differ significantly. Because we have made a conservative F test, we know that a more exact test would also be significant.

15.16   Conservative F Tests for Case II

In Case II we have a treatment factor A with s subjects assigned at random to each level of A. For each subject we have t measurements. We complete the analysis of variance in the usual way and obtain an analysis of variance summary table such as Table 15.9. The F test of the significance of the difference between the levels of A is made and evaluated in the usual way, without reduction in the degrees of freedom, because this F test involves independent observations.

For the test of significance of the trial mean square we have $F = 48.19$ with $t - 1$ and $a(s - 1)(t - 1)$ or 2 and 16 d.f. To make a conservative test of the significance of the trial mean square, we multiply the degrees of freedom for both numerator and denominator by $1/(t - 1)$ and obtain the reduced degree of freedom. This gives us 1 d.f. for the numerator and $a(s - 1)$ $= 8$ d.f. for the denominator. Entering the F table with 1 and 8 d.f. we find that $F \geq 11.26$ has a probability of .01 when the null hypothesis is true. Because our observed value of $F = 48.19$ exceeds the tabled value for 1 and 8 d.f. and because we have made a conservative test, we know that a more exact test would also be significant.

In testing the significance of the $A \times T$ mean square, we have $F = 12.05$ with $(a - 1)(t - 1)$ and $a(s - 1)(t - 1)$ or 2 and 16 d.f. To make a conservative test we multiply the degrees of freedom for both numerator and denominator by $1/(t - 1)$ and obtain $a - 1$ and $a(s - 1)$ or 1 and 8 d.f. We have already found that with 1 and 8 d.f., $F \geq 11.26$ has probability of .01 when the null hypothesis is true. The results of our conservative test are significant and we know that a more exact test would also be significant.

It may happen that the usual F test gives a significant result, but that the conservative test does not. If we have reason to believe that the assumption of equal variances and correlations is violated, then we may resort to an exact test. The calculations for the exact multivariate test are involved and complex without the aid of an electronic computer. Worked examples can be found in Danford, Hughes, and McNee (1960) and in Winer (1962).

EXAMPLES

15.1—Five subjects are tested on three trials.

(a) Complete the analysis of variance.
(b) Find the linear and quadratic components of the trial sum of squares and test these for significance.
(c) Is the sum of the above two components equal to the trial sum of squares?

S's	Trials			Σ
	1	2	3	
1	3	10	7	20
2	7	11	9	27
3	2	7	4	13
4	6	10	6	22
5	2	12	9	23
Σ	20	50	35	105

15.2—Five subjects are tested on four trials.

(a) Complete the analysis of variance.
(b) Find the linear and quadratic components of the trial sum of squares and test these for significance.

S's	Trials				Σ
	1	2	3	4	
1	2	4	5	7	18
2	3	5	6	8	22
3	5	6	8	10	29
4	7	9	11	14	41
5	6	7	10	11	34
Σ	23	31	40	50	144

15.3—Twenty subjects were divided at random into two groups of $n = 10$ subjects. Subjects in Group 1 were rewarded for each correct response made in a learning experiment and subjects in Group 2 were rewarded for each correct response and punished for each wrong response. Each subject was given six trials.

(a) Complete the analysis of variance.
(b) Find the linear and quadratic components of the over-all trial sum of squares and test these for significance.
(c) Is there a significant difference in the linear trends of the trial means for the two groups?
(d) Is there a significant difference in the curvature of the trends of the trial means for the two groups?

	S's			Trials			
		1	2	3	4	5	6
	1	9	3	2	5	10	12
	2	10	7	3	11	11	11
	3	5	6	10	5	8	15
	4	4	11	9	13	5	11
Group	5	8	11	5	13	9	7
1	6	6	3	4	10	10	12
	7	6	2	6	8	9	14
	8	4	4	6	10	14	6
	9	4	10	4	11	5	15
	10	1	6	4	5	11	13
	1	8	9	13	9	18	14
	2	5	10	9	7	10	12
	3	3	4	8	10	11	19
	4	5	8	13	11	15	18
Group	5	1	4	13	14	17	15
2	6	4	8	6	12	9	20
	7	10	7	14	13	9	16
	8	10	9	9	16	9	11
	9	2	9	9	14	12	19
	10	9	10	8	12	16	11

15.4—Under what condition will the linear component of the trial sum of squares be exactly equal to the trial sum of squares?

15.5—Suppose that $n = 10$ subjects have been tested on $t = 3$ trials and that the trial sums are: 100, 200, and 100. Without doing any calculations, what can you say about the linear and quadratic components of the trial sum of squares?

15.6—Suppose that 10 subjects are assigned at random to each of three treatments and that each subject in each treatment group is tested on five trials. Assume that all assumptions of the analysis of variance for this experiment are satisfied.

(a) Show the analysis of variance summary table with the sources of variation and degrees of freedom associated with each.
(b) Show the various F tests you would make and explain what each of these tests would indicate if F is significant.
(c) Find the tabled values of F required for significance with $P = .05$ for each of your F tests.

(d)   Find the values of F required for significance with $P = .05$, if conservative F tests are made.

(e)   How many degrees of freedom will the linear component of the Treatment $\times$ Trial sum of squares have? If the F test of this comparison is significant, what would this indicate?

The χ^2 Test of Significance

16.1 Introduction

Suppose we have a set of c mutually exclusive and exhaustive classes or categories for a variable so that any given observation can be assigned to one and only one of the c classes. We consider some examples.

1. The behavior of each of n rats is observed at the choice point of a T-maze and we observe whether each rat turns left or right. We have a variable with $c = 2$ classes, a right turn or a left turn, and the outcome of the experiment is the number of observations in each class.

2. Subjects are asked to taste four different brands of frozen orange juice and to state which brand they prefer. In this instance, we have $c = 4$ categories and the outcome of the experiment is the number of subjects choosing each of the four brands.

3. Subjects respond to an item in a personality inventory by marking the item True, ?, or False. We have $c = 3$ categories and the outcome of the experiment is the number of subjects making each of the three responses.

4. A coin is tossed n times and we observe on each toss whether the coin falls heads or tails. We have $c = 2$ categories and the outcome of the experiment is the number of times the coin falls heads and the number of times it falls tails.

In all of the examples cited above, the outcome of the experiment consists of the number of observations in each of a set of c mutually exclusive and exhaustive categories. We designate the *observed number* of observations in the respective categories as $f_1, f_2, \cdots, f_i, \cdots, f_c$. We may then test any null hypothesis that gives the probability P_i of an observation in the ith class, provided $\Sigma P_i = 1.00$. Then, for a sample of n observations, the *expected num-*

ber, F_i, in the ith category will be

$$F_i = nP_i \tag{16.1}$$

and it is obvious that, because $\Sigma\, P_i = 1.00$,

$$\sum F_i = n \sum P_i = n$$

In other words, the sum of the expected numbers F_i must be equal to the sum of the observed numbers. If the null hypothesis is true, then the observed numbers in the c categories should not differ from the expected numbers except as a result of random variation.

16.2   The χ^2 Test with $c = 2$ Categories

As a test of the null hypothesis, we define

$$\chi^2 = \sum_{i=1}^{c} \frac{(f_i - F_i)^2}{F_i} \tag{16.2}$$

If the null hypothesis is true, then χ^2, as defined by (16.2) will have a distribution that is approximately that of χ^2 with $c - 1$ d.f. We consider an example with $c = 2$ categories.

We observe a sample of $n = 50$ rats at the choice point in a T-maze. We find that $f_1 = 30$ rats turn left and $f_2 = 20$ rats turn right. We are interested in testing the null hypothesis that right and left turns are equally probable, so that $P_1 = 1/2$ and $P_2 = 1 - P_1 = Q = 1/2$. Then, if the null hypothesis is true, the expected number of rats turning left and right will be

$$F_1 = 50(1/2) = 25 \quad \text{and} \quad F_2 = 50(1/2) = 25$$

and

$$\chi^2 = \frac{(30 - 25)^2}{25} + \frac{(20 - 25)^2}{25} = 2.0$$

Table IV, in Appendix B, is a table of χ^2. To evaluate $\chi^2 = 2.0$, we enter the row of the table of χ^2 with $c - 1 = 1$ d.f. The column headings of the table give the proportion of the total area in the χ^2 distribution falling to the right of ordinates erected at the tabled entries. Note that the tabled values in each row are different because the distribution of χ^2 is different for different degrees of freedom. For 1 d.f., we find that $\chi^2 \geq 2.706$ has probability of .10 when the null hypothesis is true. Thus, the probability of $\chi^2 \geq 2.0$ is greater than .10 and we may decide that the outcome of the experiment offers insufficient evidence to reject the null hypothesis.

16.3 The Relationship between z^2 and χ^2 with 1 Degree of Freedom

If we have $c = 2$ categories and if P is the probability of an observation falling in one category, then $Q = 1 - P$ will be the probability of an observation falling in the other category. The outcome of an experiment involving n observations may also be evaluated in terms of the binomial distribution

$$(P + Q)^n$$

We have suggested previously that if both nP and nQ are equal to or greater than 5, then the probabilities of the binomial distribution may be approximated by those of the standard normal distribution. Thus, we may also use

$$z = \frac{f_1 - nP_1}{\sqrt{nP_1(1 - P_1)}} \tag{16.3}$$

to evaluate the outcome of an experiment with $c = 2$ categories.

For the present example, we would have

$$z = \frac{30 - 25}{\sqrt{50(1/2)(1/2)}} = 1.414$$

and we note that $z^2 = (1.414)^2 = 2.0$. From the table of the standard normal curve we find that the probability of z equal to or greater than 1.414 is .08 and that the probability of z equal to or less than -1.414 is also .08. Thus the probability of $z^2 \geq 2.0$ is approximately .16 and this is also the probability of $\chi^2 \geq 2.0$ with 1 d.f.

We now prove that χ^2, as defined by (16.2) with 1 d.f., is equal to z^2. We have

$$\chi^2 = \frac{(f_1 - F_1)^2}{F_1} + \frac{(f_2 - F_2)^2}{F_2}$$

$$= \frac{(f_1 - nP)^2}{nP} + \frac{(f_2 - nQ)^2}{nQ}$$

$$= \frac{Q(f_1 - nP)^2 + P(f_2 - nQ)^2}{nPQ}$$

We note that

$$(f_2 - nQ)^2 = [f_2 - n(1 - P)]^2 = (-f_1 + nP)^2 = (f_1 - nP)^2$$

and that $P + Q = 1.00$, so that

$$\chi^2 = \frac{(f_1 - nP)^2}{nPQ} = z^2 \tag{16.4}$$

and we note that (16.4) is equal to the square of (16.3).

16.4   The Distribution of χ^2

Assume that X is a normally distributed variable with mean μ and variance σ^2. Then, we may define

$$\chi^2 = \frac{(X - \mu)^2}{\sigma^2} = z^2 \tag{16.5}$$

and (16.5) will have a χ^2 distribution with 1 d.f. We note that the distribution of χ^2, in this instance, will be the same as the distribution of the square of the normal deviate z. We also have

$$E(\chi^2) = \frac{\sigma^2}{\sigma^2} = E(z^2) = 1.0 \tag{16.6}$$

and we see that $E(\chi^2)$, in this instance, is also equal to its degrees of freedom, and this will always be true, that is, $E(\chi^2)$ will always be equal to the degrees of freedom associated with χ^2. Because almost all of the total area of the distribution of z^2 will fall between 0.0 and 9.0 and because the expected value is equal to 1.0, it is obvious that the distribution of χ^2 with 1 d.f. will be skewed to the right.

If we have n independent values of χ^2 as defined by (16.5), then the sum of these χ^2 values will also be a value of χ^2 with n degrees of freedom, that is,

$$\chi^2 = \frac{\sum\limits_{1}^{n} (X - \mu)^2}{\sigma^2} \tag{16.7}$$

will be distributed as χ^2 with n degrees of freedom. We also have

$$E(\chi^2) = \frac{n\sigma^2}{\sigma^2} = n \tag{16.8}$$

and we note that in this case also, we have $E(\chi^2)$ equal to its degrees of freedom.

We may observe, from the table of χ^2, that if we have $n = 19$ d.f., then the median value of $\chi^2 = 18.338$, that is, $P(\chi^2 \geq 18.338) = .50$. In this instance, the median value of χ^2 and the expected value are fairly close together. Furthermore, .90 of the total area falls between $\chi^2 = 10.117$ and

$\chi^2 = 30.144$. Thus, it is clear that as the number of degrees of freedom increases, the distribution of χ^2 tends to become more symmetrical.

Now consider

$$\chi^2 = \frac{\sum\limits_{1}^{n}(X - \bar{X})^2}{\sigma^2} \tag{16.9}$$

where we have replaced the parameter μ by the sample estimate $\bar{X}$. We have shown previously that if $n = 2$, then only one of the two deviations $X - \bar{X}$ is free to vary and $\sum_1^n (X - \bar{X})^2$, in this case, will have 1 d.f. In general we have found that $\sum_1^n (X - \bar{X})^2$ has $n - 1$ d.f. If we take the expectation of (16.9), we have

$$E(\chi^2) = \frac{(n - 1)\sigma^2}{\sigma^2} = n - 1 \tag{16.10}$$

and the χ^2 of (16.9) will be distributed as χ^2 with $n - 1$ d.f.

16.5 The χ^2 Test with $c = 3$ Categories

A multiple-choice item in a test consists of four alternatives, only one of which is correct. One hundred students respond to the item and 40 make the correct response and the remaining 60 students select one of the incorrect alternatives. We are interested only in the responses of the 60 students who selected one of the incorrect alternatives. More specifically, we wish to test the null hypothesis that the incorrect alternatives are equally attractive. If this null hypothesis is true, then the probability that each incorrect alternative will be selected will be $P_1 = P_2 = P_3 = 1/3$. We have $n = 60$ observations. Then the expected numbers for each of the three alternatives will all be equal to

$$F_i = 60(1/3) = 20$$

Table 16.1 gives the observed numbers and the expected numbers under the null hypothesis. We have

$$\chi^2 = \frac{(15 - 20)^2}{20} + \frac{(10 - 20)^2}{20} + \frac{(35 - 20)^2}{20} = 17.5$$

with $c - 1 = 2$ d.f. From the table of χ^2 we find that with 2 d.f. $\chi^2 \geq 9.21$ has probability of .01, when the null hypothesis is true. Then the probability of $\chi^2 \geq 17.5$, under the null hypothesis, is much less than .01 and we may decide to reject the null hypothesis.

Table 16.1—Observed number of subjects choosing each of three incorrect
alternatives on a multiple-choice item. The expected numbers
are based on the assumption that each of the three incorrect
alternatives is equally probable

	Incorrect alternative			Totals
	1	2	3	
Observed number	15	10	35	60
Expected number	20	20	20	60

16.6   The χ^2 Test for an $r \times c$ Contingency Table

In some problems each observation may be classified in terms of a set of
r mutually exclusive and exhaustive categories corresponding to one variable
A and also in terms of another set of c mutually exclusive and exhaustive
categories corresponding to another variable B. The outcomes of such an
experiment can be recorded in terms of an $r \times c$ contingency table where the
rows correspond to the r categories of A and the columns correspond to the c
categories of B. The cell entries of the $r \times c$ table correspond to the number of
observations in the ith category of A and the jth category of B. Table 16.2
illustrates the notation for the $r \times c$ contingency table.

Let P_i be the probability of an observation falling in the ith category of A,
the row variable, and assume that this probability is given by

$$P_i = P(A_i) = \frac{n_{i.}}{n} \tag{16.11}$$

and we note that

$$\sum_{i=1}^{r} P_i = 1.00 \tag{16.12}$$

Similarly, let P_j be the probability of an observation falling in the jth category
of B, the column variable, and assume that this probability is given by

$$P_j = P(B_j) = \frac{n_{.j}}{n} \tag{16.13}$$

and we note that

$$\sum_{j=1}^{c} P_j = 1.00 \tag{16.14}$$

Table 16.2—Notation for an $r \times c$ contingency table with r categories for A and c categories for B

Categories for A	Categories for B						Totals
	B_1	B_2	·	B_j	·	B_c	
A_1	f_{11}	f_{12}	·	f_{1j}	·	f_{1c}	$n_1.$
A_2	f_{21}	f_{22}	·	f_{2j}	·	f_{2c}	$n_2.$
·	·	·	·	·	·	·	·
A_i	f_{i1}	f_{i2}	·	f_{ij}	·	f_{ic}	$n_i.$
·	·	·	·	·	·	·	·
A_r	f_{r1}	f_{r2}	·	f_{rj}	·	f_{rc}	$n_r.$
Totals	$n._1$	$n._2$	·	$n._j$	·	$n._c$	n

We wish to test the null hypothesis that the row (A) and column (B) classifications are statistically independent. Let P_{ij} be the probability of an observation falling in the ith category of A and the jth category of B. Then, if the null hypothesis is true, we have

$$P_{ij} = P_i P_j \tag{16.15}$$

or

$$P_{ij} = P(A_i)P(B_j)$$
$$= \frac{n_i . n._j}{n^2} \tag{16.16}$$

We note that for any given row of the $r \times c$ table, P_i will be constant and that P_j will vary. Then summing (16.15) over the c columns of the ith row, we have

$$\sum_{j=1}^{c} P_{ij} = P_i \sum_{j=1}^{c} P_j = P_i \tag{16.17}$$

and summing (16.17) over the r rows, we have

$$\sum_{i=1}^{r} \sum_{j=1}^{c} P_{ij} = 1.00 \tag{16.18}$$

Multiplying (16.15) by n, we obtain the expected number of observations in the ith category of A and the jth category of B, under the null hypothesis that the row and column classifications are independent. Thus

$$F_{ij} = nP_{ij} \tag{16.19}$$

and

$$\sum_{i=1}^{r} \sum_{j=1}^{c} F_{ij} = n \tag{16.20}$$

If the null hypothesis is true, then

$$\chi^2 = \sum_{i=1}^{r} \sum_{j=1}^{c} \frac{(f_{ij} - F_{ij})^2}{F_{ij}} \tag{16.21}$$

will be approximately distributed as χ^2 with $(r - 1)(c - 1)$ d.f. It is not necessary, however, to actually calculate the values of F_{ij}. Substituting in (16.21) with an identity for F_{ij}, we have

$$\chi^2 = \sum_{i=1}^{r} \sum_{j=1}^{c} \frac{\left(f_{ij} - \dfrac{n_i . n_{.j}}{n}\right)^2}{\dfrac{n_i . n_{.j}}{n}}$$

$$= \frac{1}{n} \sum_{i=1}^{r} \sum_{j=1}^{c} \frac{(nf_{ij} - n_i . n_{.j})^2}{n_i . n_{.j}} \tag{16.22}$$

We consider an example with $r = 3$ categories for A and with $c = 3$ categories for B. Suppose that 250 mental patients can be classified into $r = 3$ mutually exclusive and exhaustive diagnostic categories. Each patient has responded to an item in a personality inventory and we have $c = 3$ categories of response: True, ?, and False. The marginal totals of Table 16.3 give the number of patients in each diagnostic category and the number making each response to the item. The cell entries of the $r \times c$ table give the number of patients in a given category of the row classification and a given category of the column classification.

Although we could use (16.22) to calculate χ^2 and thus avoid the necessity

Table 16.3—An $r \times c$ contingency table for $r = 3$ diagnostic categories and $c = 3$ item response categories

Diagnostic category	Response to item			Totals
	True	?	False	
A_1	10	35	50	95
A_2	20	40	10	70
A_3	35	40	10	85
Totals	65	115	70	250

Table 16.4—Calculation of χ^2 for the data of Table 16.3

f_{ij}	F_{ij}	$f_{ij} - F_{ij}$	$(f_{ij} - F_{ij})^2$	$(f_{ij} - F_{ij})^2/F_{ij}$
10	24.7	-14.7	216.09	8.75
35	43.7	-8.7	75.69	1.73
50	26.6	23.4	547.56	20.58
20	18.2	1.8	3.24	.18
40	32.2	7.8	60.84	1.89
10	19.6	-9.6	92.16	4.70
35	22.1	12.9	166.41	7.53
40	39.1	.9	.81	.02
10	23.8	-13.8	190.44	8.00
				$\chi^2 = 53.38$

of finding the expected numbers, we use (16.21) for purposes of illustration. In Table 16.4 we repeat the observed numbers of the cells of Table 16.3 and also show the expected numbers. For this example, we have $\chi^2 = 53.38$ with $(3 - 1)(3 - 1) = 4$ d.f. From the table of χ^2 we find that with 4 d.f., $\chi^2 \geq 13.277$ has probability of .01, under the null hypothesis that the row and column classifications are independent. Thus, if the null hypothesis is true, the probability of $\chi^2 \geq 53.38$ is much less than .01 and we may decide to reject the null hypothesis.[1]

16.7 The χ^2 Test for the Contingency Coefficient: C

The contingency coefficient C is a measure of association that is sometimes used in conjunction with an $r \times c$ contingency table.[2] The contingency coefficient can take values between zero and 1, but it can reach its maximum value only when the number of categories for both criteria of classification is large. For a 3×3 table, for example, C cannot exceed .816 and for a 10×10 table, the maximum value of C is .949.[3]

The contingency coefficient can be obtained directly from χ^2. Thus

$$C = \sqrt{\frac{\chi^2}{n + \chi^2}} \qquad (16.23)$$

[1] For the $r \times c$ contingency table with more than 1 d.f., it is possible to partition the table in various ways and to make additional tests of significance. See, for example, the articles by Bresnahan and Shapiro (1966), Castellan (1965), Cochran (1954), and Lancaster (1949).

[2] For a discussion of various other measures of association for cross-classifications, see Goodman and Kruskal (1954, 1959).

[3] For a further discussion of the contingency coefficient and its limitations, see Kelley (1923) and Yule and Kendall (1947).

where n is the total number of observations in the contingency table. For the data of Table 16.3, we have $\chi^2 = 53.38$ and $n = 250$. Substituting in (16.23) with these values, we obtain

$$C = \sqrt{\frac{53.38}{250 + 53.38}} = .42$$

As we pointed out previously, χ^2 for the $r \times c$ contingency table provides a test of the null hypothesis that the two criteria of classification are independent. If we obtain a significant value of χ^2, then we also know that C is significantly greater than zero.

16.8   The χ^2 Test for the Phi Coefficient: r_ϕ

In an earlier chapter we discussed the use of the phi coefficient r_ϕ to measure the degree of association or relationship between two variables when each variable could take only one of two possible values. It would also obviously be possible to calculate χ^2 for a 2×2 contingency table and the resulting value of χ^2 provides a test of the null hypothesis that the row and column classifications are independent. Thus, if we obtain a significant value of χ^2 for the 2×2 table, we may also conclude that r_ϕ is significantly greater than zero.

The phi coefficient and χ^2 are related in the following way

$$r_\phi = \sqrt{\frac{\chi^2}{n}} \tag{16.24}$$

and

$$\chi^2 = nr_\phi{}^2 \tag{16.25}$$

where n is the total number of observations in the 2×2 table.

If we have calculated r_ϕ as a measure of association for a 2×2 table and wish to test the null hypothesis that $\rho_\phi = 0$, then we can square the obtained value of r_ϕ and multiply by n to obtain χ^2. Suppose for example that we have $r_\phi = .23$ with $n = 200$ observations. Then

$$\chi^2 = 200(.23)^2 = 10.58$$

with 1 d.f. By reference to the table of χ^2 we find that for 1 d.f. $\chi^2 \geq 6.635$ has probability of .01, when the null hypothesis is true. Consequently, our observed value of $\chi^2 = 10.58$ has probability less than .01 and we may decide to reject the null hypothesis that $\rho_\phi = 0$.

We have previously shown that

$$r_\phi = \frac{bc - ad}{\sqrt{(a + b)(c + d)(a + c)(b + d)}} \tag{16.26}$$

Then squaring (16.26) and multiplying by n, we obtain a convenient method for calculating χ^2 for a 2×2 table. Thus

$$\chi^2 = \frac{n(bc - ad)^2}{(a + b)(c + d)(a + c)(b + d)} \tag{16.27}$$

16.9 Correction for Discontinuity

When we have χ^2, as defined by (16.2) with 1 d.f., then we should also apply a *correction for discontinuity*, suggested by Yates (1934). The correction consists of reducing the absolute values of $f_1 - F_1$ and $f_2 - F_2$ by .5 before squaring. Thus

$$\chi_c^2 = \frac{(|f_1 - F_1| - .5)^2}{F_1} + \frac{(|f_2 - F_2| - .5)^2}{F_2} \tag{16.28}$$

where the subscript c indicates that we have made a correction for discontinuity.

Assume, for example, that we have $f_1 = 18$ and $f_2 = 12$ for $c = 2$ categories and we wish to test the null hypothesis that $P_1 = P_2 = 1/2$. Then the two values of $f_i - F_i$ will be equal to 3 and -3, and χ^2 without a correction for discontinuity will be equal to 1.2. With a correction for discontinuity we have $\chi_c^2 = .83$.

In the case of a 2×2 contingency table, the correction for discontinuity applied to (16.27) results in

$$\chi_c^2 = \frac{n\left(|bc - ad| - \dfrac{n}{2}\right)^2}{(a + b)(c + d)(a + c)(b + d)} \tag{16.29}$$

The reason for applying the correction for discontinuity is that, whereas the observed numbers are discrete, the distribution of χ^2 is continuous. The correction for discontinuity applied to χ^2 with 1 d.f. is comparable to the correction for discontinuity for z when we use the table of the standard normal curve to approximate the probabilities of the binomial distribution.

16.10 Small Expected Numbers

There is some agreement that the χ^2 test of significance should not be applied when any one of the *expected* numbers is less than 5 and χ^2 has but 1 d.f. If we have a single criterion of classification with $c = 2$ categories and if the expected number for either category is less than 5, then we can use the binomial distribution $(P + Q)^n$ to evaluate the outcome of the experiment. If we have a 2 × 2 table and if any expected cell number is less than 5, then an exact test may be applied to evaluate the outcome of the experiment.[4]

For contingency tables with more than 1 d.f., Cochran (1954) suggests that if no more than 20 percent, or 1 out of 5, of the expected numbers are less than 5, then a minimum expected number of 1 is allowable in using the χ^2 test of significance.

Lewontin and Felsenstein (1965) have investigated the distribution of χ^2 for the case of an $r \times c$ contingency table in which either r or c has two categories and the other classification has at least five categories. The results of their investigation show that the χ^2 test of significance is remarkably robust, provided that all of the expected numbers are equal to or greater than 1.

16.11   The Median Test

Suppose that $n = 34$ subjects have been divided at random into two groups of $n_1 = n_2 = 17$ subjects. One group is a control group and the other is an experimental group, assigned to some treatment, and for each subject we have a measure on a dependent variable X of interest. The values of X for the control and experimental groups are given in Table 16.5.

If we combine the two sets of measurements, we obtain the frequency distribution shown in Table 16.6. It can easily be determined that the median of the combined distribution is equal to 6.5. If an observed value of X is above the median we assign it a plus sign and if it is below the median we assign it a minus sign. In Table 16.5 we have indicated whether each value of X is plus or minus for the members of the control and the experimental groups.

For the experimental group we have 12 plus values and 5 minus values, whereas for the control group we have 12 minus values and 5 plus values. We summarize these results in Table 16.7. We note that if we calculate χ^2 for the data of Table 16.7, we will, in essence, be testing the null hypothesis that the row and column classifications are independent. If we have two independent random samples of $n_1 = n_2$ observations from the same population, then the observed number of plus signs and the observed number of minus signs should be equal within the limits of random sampling for both samples, that is, for both the control and experimental groups. A significant value of χ^2, on the other hand, will indicate that the number of plus and minus signs is not

---

[4] The exact test for the 2 × 2 table is described in Edwards (1960), Feller (1957), Fisher (1936), Hays (1963), Hodges and Lehman (1964), Mosteller, Rourke, and Thomas (1961), and various other texts. Tables are also available that make the exact test for the 2 × 2 table relatively simple to apply. See, for example, Finney (1948), Latscha (1953), and Mainland, Herrera, and Sutcliffe (1956).

Table 16.5—Values of X for a control and experimental group. Plus signs have been given to values of $X > 6.5$, the median of the combined distribution, and minus signs to values of $X < 6.5$

Control		Experimental	
X	Sign	X	Sign
10	+	11	+
9	+	11	+
8	+	10	+
7	+	10	+
7	+	9	+
6	−	9	+
5	−	8	+
5	−	8	+
5	−	8	+
4	−	7	+
3	−	7	+
3	−	7	+
3	−	6	−
2	−	4	−
1	−	3	−
1	−	3	−
1	−	2	−

Table 16.6—Frequency distribution for the combined n_1 and n_2 values of X given in Table 16.5. The median of the combined distribution is equal to 6.5

X	f
11	2
10	3
9	3
8	4
7	5
6	2
5	3
4	2
3	5
2	2
1	3

Table 16.7—Number of values of $X > 6.5$ and number of values of $X < 6.5$ for the control and experimental groups. Original data given in Table 16.5

	—	+	Totals
Experimental	5	12	17
Control	12	5	17
Totals	17	17	34

independent of the classification of the subjects as control or experimental. This, in turn, would indicate that the observations for the two samples are not from a common population.

For the χ^2 test, we have, using (16.29)

$$\chi_c^2 = \frac{34\left(\left|(12)(12) - (5)(5)\right| - \dfrac{34}{2}\right)^2}{(17)(17)(17)(17)} = 4.24$$

a significant value ($P < .05$) with 1 d.f.

The median test can be generalized to the case of more than two groups. For example, if we have k groups of observations, we combine the measures for all groups into a single distribution and find the median for the combined distribution. Then we count the number of observations in each group falling above and below the median and calculate χ^2 for the resulting $2 \times k$ table.

In Table 16.8 we give the counts above and below a common median for $k = 4$ groups of 25 observations each. The obtained value of χ^2 for the data of Table 16.8 is 13.28 with 3 d.f. and the probability of obtaining a value of $\chi^2 \geq 13.28$, when the null hypothesis is true, is less than .01.

Table 16.8—Number of observations falling above and below a common median for each of four groups of 25 observations

	Groups				
	A	B	C	D	Total
Above median	8	12	20	10	50
Below median	17	13	5	15	50
Total	25	25	25	25	100

16.12   The Median Test as a Substitute for the t and F Tests

The null hypothesis tested by the median test is a general one, namely, that the k samples are independent samples from a common population. But, in order to apply the median test, we must have available measures of a variable X for each subject so that it is possible to find the median of the combined distribution of X values. Ordinarily, if each observation represents a value of a variable X, we would test the significance of the difference between the k groups of observations using either a t test for the case of two groups or an F test for the case of more than two groups. The median test is thus, in essence, a substitute test for either the t test or the F test.

Why would anyone want to use a substitute test for the t or F tests? The reason that is commonly given is that the median test can be used when the data violate the assumptions of the t and F tests. The median test assumes that the samples are from a common population or from identically distributed populations. The only additional assumption involved in the t or F tests, however, is that the populations are normally distributed. In other words, other than specifying the form of the population distribution, the median and the t and F tests involve the same assumption.

Mood and Graybill (1963, pp. 412–413) point out that the median test is primarily sensitive to differences in location, that is, it is primarily sensitive to whether the populations differ by a translation up or down a common scale, rather than to differences in the shapes of the populations. But this is also true of the t and F tests. We have emphasized in earlier discussions that the t and F tests are robust and primarily sensitive to differences in population means and relatively insensitive to differences in shape or nonnormality of the population distributions, provided the number of observations in each of the samples is not too small. Furthermore, the t and F tests are relatively insensitive to heterogeneity of variance, provided we have the same number of observations in each sample. We would suggest, therefore, that instead of relying on the median test as a substitute for the t and F tests, it is sound experimental procedure to increase sample size and to make the same number of observations for each sample and then to use the usual t and F tests in analyzing the data in cases where we may believe that the data will violate the assumptions involved in the t and F tests.

EXAMPLES

Make a discontinuity correction for all problems involving
1 degree of freedom

16.1—Previous experience with a particular achievement test indicated that for seventh-grade children the ratio of those receiving a passing mark to those failing was 3 to 1. We wish to test whether this hypothesis (3:1) holds also for sixth-grade children. In a sample of 100 students drawn from the sixth grade, we find that 60 pass the test and 40 fail. Is the hypothesis tenable?

16.2—A poll of fraternity men on a university campus showed that the ratio of those on the honor list to those not on the list was 1:4. To find out whether this ratio would hold for sorority members, a sample of 150 sorority members was drawn. Forty of the sorority members were on the honor list and 110 were not. Is the 1:4 hypothesis tenable?

16.3—A chairman of a committee confronted with a choice between the use of two slogans decided to sample a number of individuals to determine which they preferred. In a sample of 80 he found that 50 approved Slogan 1 and 30 approved Slogan 2. Test the hypothesis that the population ratio is 1:1.

16.4—Sixty cases in a mental hospital responded to an item in a personality inventory. For each patient we also have available the psychiatric diagnosis. Test for independence of the two criteria of classification for the data given below.

Psychiatric diagnosis	Response to item		
	Yes	?	No
Schizoid	18	9	3
Manic	6	9	15

16.5—A group of 200 subjects responded to an item in an attitude test. Five categories of response were permitted. We also have available the sex classification of the subjects. Test for the independence of the two criteria of classification for the data given below.

Sex	Response to item				
	Strongly disagree	Disagree	Undecided	Agree	Strongly agree
Men	5	5	12	18	60
Women	25	25	20	20	10

16.6—Kuo (1930) reared kittens under three different conditions: (1) one group of kittens was isolated from all contact with rats except on the experimental test; (2) the kittens in another group were reared with their mothers whom they saw kill a rat or mouse every four days outside the cage; (3) one group lived with a single rodent from age six to eight days onward. The test situation consisted of putting a kitten together with a rat to determine whether or not the kitten would kill. The data are given below. Test for the independence of the two criteria of classification.

Experimental condition	Response to rodent	
	Kills	Does not kill
Reared in isolation	9	11
Reared with mother	18	3
Reared with rodent	3	15

16.7—One hundred and seventy patients in a mental hospital were rated in terms of whether they showed improvement or no improvement after therapy. We also have available information concerning which of two therapeutic procedures was used for each patient. Test for the independence of the two criteria of classification for the data given below.

Method used	Rating after therapy	
	No improvement	Improvement
Procedure 1	10	42
Procedure 2	58	60

16.8—Rosenzweig (1943) has studied the recall of subjects for finished and unfinished tasks when they worked on the tasks under differing sets of instructions. The "informal" group was told that the experimenter was interested in knowing something about the task, that the ability of the subjects was not under investigation. The "formal" group, on the other hand, was under the impression that the tasks were an intelligence test. Test the independence of the two criteria of classification for the data given below.

Test situation	Kind of recall		
	Recalls more finished tasks	Recalls more unfinished tasks	No difference
Informal	7	19	4
Formal	17	8	5

16.9—Sixty subjects were observed leaving a classroom. They could leave through either one of two doors. Thirty-six of the subjects went out through one of the doors and 24 went out through the other. Is the hypothesis that each door is equally likely to be selected tenable?

16.10—An item on an examination was based upon a discussion of a topic that was treated in each of two textbooks. One hundred subjects had read the discussion in one of the books, and 100 subjects had read the discussion in the other textbook. We have available information concerning whether the subjects passed or failed the item on the examination. Test for the independence of the two criteria of classification for the data given below.

Textbook read	Response to item	
	Failed	Passed
Text No. 1	10	90
Text No. 2	30	70

16.11—A group of 100 subjects was asked to choose between the aromas of two pipe tobaccos. We have available information concerning which tobacco was chosen and also the sex classification of the subjects. Test for the independence of the two criteria of classification for the data given below.

Sex	Tobacco chosen	
	Brand 1	Brand 2
Men	10	40
Women	20	30

16.12—A total of 572 members of the Kansas State Alumni Association were sent cards concerning their membership in the association. The subjects were divided in such a way that approximately 1/4 received a white card, 1/4 a yellow card, 1/4 a blue card, and 1/4 a cherry-colored card. We have available information concerning whether the members responded to the card and also concerning the color of the card received. Test for the independence of the two criteria of classification for the data given below. Data are from Dunlap (1950).

Color of card received	Response to card	
	Returned	Not returned
White	60	87
Yellow	73	71
Blue	65	76
Cherry	54	86

16.13—Eight bottles of each of 6 brands of beer were given to each of 20 families for 5 days, and then 12 bottles of each brand were given on the sixth day for use over the week end. No charge was made for the beer. All brands carried the same plain label. We have available the number of bottles consumed for each brand and the number not consumed. Test for the independence of the two criteria of classification for the data given below. Data are from Fleishman (1951).

	Reaction to brand	
Brand	Consumed	Not consumed
A	625	415
B	613	427
C	591	449
D	566	474
E	514	526
F	497	543

16.14—Test the significance of the phi coefficient for the data of Example 7.5.

16.15—Use the median test to compare the two sets of observations given below.

Group 1		Group 2	
14	8	6	3
8	18	14	10
9	15	11	12
14	12	11	10
12	9	16	8
18	12	11	10
15	14	13	11
16	13	2	11
11	11	11	12
16	15	13	5

Rank Order Statistics and Tests of Significance[1]

17.1   Significance of the Rank Correlation: r'

Suppose that we have a set of n objects, things, or stimuli. We assume that the objects differ in terms of the degree to which they possess some common attribute or quality. Two judges are asked to rank the objects with respect to the attribute of interest and, as a result, we obtain two sets of ranks—one from each judge. If we correlate the two sets of ranks, then, as we have previously shown, the rank correlation coefficient r' will provide a measure of the degree of agreement between the ranks of the two judges.[2]

In some cases the rank order for a set of n objects has already been established by an experimenter in terms of some criterion. For example, we may have five solutions that differ only in terms of the amount of sugar that has been added to each. In this case the rank order of the solutions with respect to the amount of sugar each contains is known to the experimenter. The task set for a judge is to duplicate this rank order to the best of his ability. If we then obtain the rank correlation coefficient between the ranks assigned by the judge and the criterion ranks, r' provides a measure of the degree to which the judge can accurately rank the solutions.

In Table 17.1 we give the ranks assigned to 10 objects in terms of an external criterion A. The ranks assigned to these same objects by two judges, B and C, are also given in the table. At the bottom of the table we give the

---

[1] Some of the material in this chapter is based upon a report (Edwards, 1951) prepared for the Instructional Film Research Program. I am indebted to Dr. C. R. Carpenter for permission to quote freely from this report.

[2] The τ coefficient can also be used in place of the rank correlation coefficient. In general, however, it is easier to calculate r' than τ. The relative merits of r' and τ are discussed by Kendall (1948).

Table 17.1—Rank order of 10 objects in terms of a criterion A and ranks assigned by two judges B and C to the 10 objects

	Objects									
	1	2	3	4	5	6	7	8	9	10
Criterion A	1	2	3	4	5	6	7	8	9	10
Judge B	1	2	5	6	4	3	9	10	7	8
Judge C	6	4	5	1	8	10	2	3	9	7

	Values of D^2										ΣD^2
$(A - B)^2$	0	0	4	4	1	9	4	4	4	4	34
$(A - C)^2$	25	4	4	9	9	16	25	25	0	9	126
$(B - C)^2$	25	4	0	25	16	49	49	49	4	1	222

squared differences between the indicated sets of ranks. To find the degree to which Judge B agrees with Judge C, we can calculate r' as defined previously. Thus

$$r_{BC}' = 1 - \frac{6 \sum D^2}{n^3 - n}$$

$$= 1 - \frac{6(222)}{990}$$

$$= -.345$$

The negative value of r' indicates that there is some tendency for one judge to assign high ranks to the objects that are assigned low ranks by the other judge.

Table XIII, in Appendix B, enables us to test the null hypothesis that $\rho' = 0$. The first column gives the value of n, the number of objects ranked, from 4 to 10, and the second column gives selected values of r' for these sets of ranks.[3] The third column gives the probability of obtaining r' equal to or greater than the value given in column (2) when the null hypothesis $\rho' = 0$ is true. The tabled values of r' are thus for a one-sided test. With $n = 10$ ranks, we find that the probability of $r' \leq -.442$ is .1021 under the null hypothesis. Thus the probability of obtaining $r' \leq -.345$ must be greater than .1021, when the null hypothesis is true, and we may decide that our observed value does not offer sufficient evidence against the null hypothesis.

---

[3] Olds (1938) tabled the values of ΣD^2 for n from 2 through 7 in terms of exact frequencies, and for n equal to 8, 9, and 10 by means of an approximation function. We have used his table to compute the corresponding values of r'. These are given in Table XIII in Appendix B.

How well do the two judges agree with the set of ranks established by the experimenter? The rank correlation coefficients for Judge B and Judge C with the experimenter's order A are

$$r_{BA}' = 1 - \frac{6(34)}{990} = .794$$

and

$$r_{CA}' = 1 - \frac{6(126)}{990} = .236$$

From Table XIII, we may conclude that $r' = .794$ is significant ($P < .01$), whereas $r' = .236$ may be regarded as nonsignificant ($P > .10$), under the null hypothesis. Consequently, we may conclude that Judge B is able to rank the objects in an order that is significantly related to that established by the experimenter, whereas Judge C is not. By testing a number of different judges, we could, in this way, select those who show a relatively high degree of accuracy in ranking the objects and eliminate those who do not.

When n is greater than 10, the sampling distribution of r', under the null hypothesis that $\rho' = 0$, may be approximated by the t distribution. Thus

$$t = \frac{r'}{\sqrt{1 - r'}} \sqrt{n - 2}$$

with $n - 2$ d.f. provides a test of the null hypothesis that $\rho' = 0$. It is, however, not necessary to calculate t to determine whether r' is significant. Instead, we may enter Table VI, in Appendix B, with $n - 2$ d.f. and evaluate r' in terms of the tabled values in the same manner in which we used Table VI in evaluating r.

17.2   Kendall's Coefficient of Concordance: W

Just as the rank correlation coefficient is a measure of the degree of agreement between two sets of n ranks, so is Kendall's (1948) coefficient of concordance, W, a measure of the degree of agreement among m sets of n ranks. If we have a group of n objects ranked by each of m judges, W provides information concerning the degree to which the m sets of ranks are in agreement. The coefficient of concordance, unlike the rank correlation coefficient, however, can only be positive in sign and ranges in value from zero to one. If the ranks assigned by each judge to the n objects are the same as those assigned by every other judge, then $W = 1.0$. If there is maximum disagreement among the judges, then $W = 0$.

We emphasize that it is the agreement among the judges that is measured by the coefficient of concordance. The fact that W may be large does not necessarily mean that the order established by the rankings of the judges is correct. Judges may agree with respect to an order that is incorrect in terms of some external criterion. A high value of W may indicate, however, that the judges are applying essentially the same standard to the objects being ranked, regardless of other considerations. Such a finding may be of considerable importance when no external criterion of the order of the objects is available. For example, in investigating the rank order of a set of n objects in terms of some attribute for which we have no direct measure, we are dealing with opinions and value judgments. If an objective ranking were available, we could test the accuracy of the ranks assigned by each judge in terms of the objective ranking by means of the rank correlation coefficient. We would, in this instance, be testing the ability of the judges to rank the objects in

Table 17.2—Notation for an $m \times n$ table of ranks with $m = 3$ judges and $n = 5$ objects

Judges	Objects					Sum	Mean
	1	2	3	4	5		
1	X_{11}	X_{21}	X_{31}	X_{41}	X_{51}	$\Sigma X_{\cdot 1}$	$\overline{X}_{\cdot 1}$
2	X_{12}	X_{22}	X_{32}	X_{42}	X_{52}	$\Sigma X_{\cdot 2}$	$\overline{X}_{\cdot 2}$
3	X_{13}	X_{23}	X_{33}	X_{43}	X_{53}	$\Sigma X_{\cdot 3}$	$\overline{X}_{\cdot 3}$
Sum	$\Sigma X_1 \cdot$	$\Sigma X_2 \cdot$	$\Sigma X_3 \cdot$	$\Sigma X_4 \cdot$	$\Sigma X_5 \cdot$	$\Sigma X_{\cdot\cdot}$	$\overline{X}_{\cdot\cdot}$
Mean	$\overline{X}_1 \cdot$	$\overline{X}_2 \cdot$	$\overline{X}_3 \cdot$	$\overline{X}_4 \cdot$	$\overline{X}_5 \cdot$		

accordance with an objective standard. But in the absence of an objective ordering of the n objects, the community of agreement among judges may be regarded as a means of establishing an ordering of the objects.

If judges cannot agree in their rankings, then it may be because the attribute is poorly or ambiguously defined. Or it may be because the objects do not differ sufficiently in the degree to which they possess the attribute. If the differences in the degree to which the objects possess the attribute are so small that they cannot be reliably discriminated, then we cannot expect judges to agree in their rankings of the objects.

Consider the general case in which we have n objects that have been ranked by each of m judges. The ranks can be arranged in an $m \times n$ table such as Table 17.2, where we have $m = 3$ judges and $n = 5$ objects. Each rank is identified by two ordered subscripts nm, where n corresponds to an object and m to a judge. It is obvious that Table 17.2 is similar to a table that shows the results of an experiment in which s subjects are given t trials. Instead of s subjects, we now have m judges and, instead of t trials, we have n objects. Thus, the same methods of data analysis used previously in analyzing the results of an experiment in which s subjects are given t trials should be applicable to an $m \times n$ table in which the cell entries are ranks.

In experiments in which s subjects were given t trials, we found that the total sum of squares could be analyzed into several parts. Thus

$$\text{Total} = \text{Subjects} + \text{Trials} + \text{Subjects} \times \text{Trials}$$

Substituting "judges" for "subjects" and "objects" for "trials," we have

$$\text{Total} = \text{Judges} + \text{Objects} + \text{Judges} \times \text{Objects}$$

or, more generally

$$\text{Total} = \text{Rows} + \text{Columns} + \text{Rows} \times \text{Columns}$$

We know that the sum of squares within columns is given by

$$\text{Within columns} = \text{Total} - \text{Columns}$$

and it is also obvious that the $R \times C$ sum of squares will be given by

$$R \times C = \text{Total} - (\text{Columns} + \text{Rows})$$

However, if ranks from 1 to n are present in each row of Table 17.2, then the row sums will all be equal and consequently the row means will all be equal. Because the row sum of squares is based upon variation of the row means, then, if each row contains ranks from 1 to n, the row sum of squares will have to be equal to zero. Then, in this case,

$$R \times C = \text{Total} - \text{Columns} \tag{17.1}$$

and because the right side of (17.1) is the within column sum of squares we have

$$R \times C = \text{Within columns} \tag{17.2}$$

if each row contains ranks from 1 to n.

Let us assume that there is perfect agreement among the $m = 3$ judges. If this is true, then each judge must assign the same rank to each given object as every other judge. Then one of the columns of Table 17.2 would contain all 1's, another all 2's, another all 3's, another all 4's and still another all 5's. The column sums would therefore have to be 3, 6, 9, 12, and 15—but not necessarily in this order. Table 17.3 illustrates the case of perfect agreement for $m = 3$ judges and $n = 5$ objects.

Now suppose we find the total sum of squares for the entries in Table 17.3. We could then analyze the total sum of squares into the sum of squares within columns and the sum of squares between columns. It is obvious, however, in the case of perfect agreement, that the within column sum of squares

Table 17.3—A Case of perfect agreement in the ranks assigned to $n = 5$ objects by $m = 3$ judges so that $W = 1.0$

Judges	Objects					$\Sigma X_{.m}$	$\bar{X}_{.m}$
	1	2	3	4	5		
1	3	1	5	2	4	15	3
2	3	1	5	2	4	15	3
3	3	1	5	2	4	15	3
$\Sigma X_{n.}$	9	3	15	6	12	45	3
$\bar{X}_{n.}$	3	1	5	2	4		

must be equal to zero. The reason for this is that the ranks within every column will be exactly equal to the corresponding means of the columns. Consequently, the sum of squares within each column has to be equal to zero. But we know that the within column sum of squares is given by

$$\text{Within columns} = \text{Total} - \text{Columns} \qquad (17.3)$$

and if the left side of (17.3) is equal to zero, then we must also have

$$\text{Total} = \text{Columns} \qquad (17.4)$$

Let us now define W, the coefficient of concordance, as

$$W = \frac{\text{Column sum of squares}}{\text{Total sum of squares}} \qquad (17.5)$$

and, as we have just shown, if there is perfect agreement among the judges, then the column sum of squares will be equal to the total sum of squares and W will be equal to 1.0.

We may note that W, as defined above, is exactly the same as the square of the correlation ratio η_{YX}^2. W is, in other words, the correlation ratio squared for a table of $m \times n$ ranks.

Now consider the case of maximum disagreement among the judges. Again, we let $m = 3$ and $n = 5$. Maximum disagreement will be present among the m judges when the mean ranks for the n objects are all equal. This is true of the ranks assigned to the $n = 5$ objects by the $m = 3$ judges in Table 17.4. We note that for the data in this table the column sum of squares must be equal to zero because the column means are all equal. Thus, in this example, W is equal to zero.

Table 17.4—Ranks assigned by $m = 3$ judges to $n = 5$ objects with $W = 0$

Judges	Objects					$\Sigma X_{\cdot m}$	$\overline{X}_{\cdot m}$
	1	2	3	4	5		
1	3	1	5	2	4	15	3
2	5	4	1	2	3	15	3
3	1	4	3	5	2	15	3
$\Sigma X_{n\cdot}$	9	9	9	9	9	45	3
$\overline{X}_{n\cdot}$	3	3	3	3	3		

17.3   Calculation of the Sums of Squares for an $m \times n$ Table of Ranks

Any of the methods we have described previously for calculating the total sum of squares and the between column sum of squares may be applied to an $m \times n$ table of ranks. However, if the entries in each row of the table are a set of ranks from 1 to n, then the total sum of squares can be obtained quite easily and depends only upon the values of m and n. For example, we have previously shown that the sum of ranks for any one row or judge will be given by

$$\sum_1^n X = \frac{n(n + 1)}{2} \tag{17.6}$$

Because (17.6) is a constant for each row of the $m \times n$ table, the sum of all mn ranks will be

$$\sum_1^m \sum_1^n X_{nm} = \sum X.. = \frac{mn(n + 1)}{2} \tag{17.7}$$

Then, for the correction term, which we shall need later, we have

$$\frac{(\sum X..)^2}{mn} = \frac{mn(n + 1)^2}{4} \tag{17.8}$$

We also know that the sum of squared deviations *within* each row of an $m \times n$ table of ranks is

$$\sum_1^n (X - \overline{X})^2 = \frac{n^3 - n}{12}$$

and because each row mean is equal to the mean $\overline{X}..$ of all mn ranks, we have for the total sum of squares

$$\text{Total} = m \sum_1^n (X - \overline{X}..)^2 = \frac{m(n^3 - n)}{12} \qquad (17.9)$$

The column sum of squares will be given by

$$\text{Columns} = \sum_1^n \frac{(\sum X_{n\cdot})^2}{m} - \frac{(\sum X..)^2}{mn} \qquad (17.10)$$

Substituting in (17.10) with the correction term as given by (17.8), we have

$$\text{Columns} = \sum_1^n \frac{(\sum X_{n\cdot})^2}{m} - \frac{mn(n + 1)^2}{4} \qquad (17.11)$$

To illustrate one application of the coefficient of concordance, we give in Table 17.5 data obtained by the Instructional Film Research Program at

Table 17.5—Ranks assigned to $n = 5$ films by $m = 10$ judges

	Films				
	1	2	3	4	5
1	5	2	1	4	3
2	1	2	3	4	5
3	1	2	4	3	5
4	1	3	2	4	5
5	1	3	2	4	5
6	4	3	1	2	5
7	3	2	1	4	5
8	1	3	4	2	5
9	3	4	2	1	5
10	3	2	1	4	5
$\Sigma X_{n\cdot}$	23	26	21	32	48
$\overline{X}_{n\cdot}$	2.3	2.6	2.1	3.2	4.8

Pennsylvania State University. Five films were shown to a group of 10 film specialists and they were asked to rank the films from best to worst. The rankings were made on the basis of an over-all evaluation of content, production, casting, and so forth. The ranks thus probably represent judgments of a rather complex standard.

For the sum of squares between columns, we have

$$\text{Columns} = \frac{(23)^2}{10} + \frac{(26)^2}{10} + \cdots + \frac{(48)^2}{10} - \frac{10(5)(6)^2}{4} = 47.4$$

and for the total sum of squares, we have, using (17.9),

$$\text{Total} = \frac{10(5^3 - 5)}{12} = 100.0$$

Then, substituting in (17.5) with these two sums of squares, we have

$$W = \frac{47.4}{100.0} = .474$$

17.4   Significance Test of W Corrected for Discontinuity

The sampling distribution of W, under the null hypothesis that the m judges are independent in their rankings or that there is no community of agreement among the judges has been investigated by Kendall (1948), who reports that W may be tested for significance in terms of the F distribution. For small values of m, however, Kendall and Smith (1939b) have shown that the probabilities given by the F distribution show greatest agreement with those of the exact distribution, if a correction is made for discontinuity. W, with a discontinuity correction is given by

$$W' = \frac{\text{Column sum of squares} - (1/m)}{\text{Total sum of squares} + (2/m)} \tag{17.12}$$

where m is the number of judges or sets of ranks. In the example under discussion, we have, with $m = 10$ judges,

$$W' = \frac{47.4 - .1}{100.0 + .2} = .472$$

It is obvious that as m increases, both $1/m$ and $2/m$ decrease. The discontinuity correction thus becomes relatively unimportant when m is large. We note that in our example, with $m = 10$, the value of W' differs only slightly from the value of W.

Table XIV, in Appendix B, gives the values of W' that have probabilities of .05 and .01, when the null hypothesis is true, for values of n from 3 to 7 and for selected values of m from 3 to 20.[4] By reference to Table XIV we find that with $m = 10$ and $n = 5$, $W' \geq .307$ has probability of .01, when the null hypothesis is true. Because our observed value of $W' = .472$ exceeds the tabled value, we may decide to reject the null hypothesis and conclude that the judges show a significantly greater degree of agreement than would be expected on the basis of chance.

---

[4] The F test for W' also involves a correction factor for the degrees of freedom in the numerator and denominator of the F ratio. Instead of giving the formulas for the corrected degrees of freedom, we simplify the test of significance by giving in Table XIV the values of W' that have probabilities of .05 and .01 when the null hypothesis is true. The values of W' in Table XIV are based upon Friedman's (1940) Table II.

17.5   The F Test for W

If m is relatively large, say $m \geq 10$, then

$$F = \frac{\text{Column sum of squares}/(n-1)}{\text{Within column sum of squares}/(m-1)(n-1)}$$

$$= \frac{(m-1)W}{1-W} \tag{17.13}$$

will be approximately distributed as F with $n - 1$ d.f. for the numerator and $(m - 1)(n - 1)$ d.f. for the denominator. In our example, we have

$$F = \frac{(10-1).474}{1-.474} = 8.11$$

From the table of F, we find that with 4 and 36 d.f., $F \geq 3.89$ has probability of .01, when the null hypothesis is true. Our observed value of $F = 8.11$ is, therefore, highly significant.

17.6   The χ^2 Test for W

Friedman (1937, 1940) has shown that if we have a table of $m \times n$ ranks, then as m becomes indefinitely large,

$$\chi_r^2 = \frac{(n-1)\text{ Column sum of squares}}{(n^3-n)/12} \tag{17.14}$$

is approximately distributed as χ^2 with $n - 1$ d.f. under the null hypothesis that the column means are all equal to the same value μ.

Substituting in (17.14) with the data for the 10 film specialists, we obtain

$$\chi_r^2 = \frac{(5-1)47.4}{(5^3-5)/12} = 18.96$$

and from the table of χ^2 we find that with $n - 1 = 4$ d.f., the probability of $\chi^2 \geq 18.96$ is much less than .01, when the null hypothesis is true.

It is evident from the above discussion that χ_r^2 and W are closely related. For example, dividing both sides of (17.14) by $m(n - 1)$, we have

$$\frac{\chi_r^2}{m(n-1)} = W \tag{17.15}$$

and, therefore

$$\chi_r^2 = m(n-1)W \tag{17.16}$$

17.7   The Average Value of the $m(m - 1)$ Values of r'

In some problems it is useful to know the average value $\bar{r}'$ of the $m(m - 1)$ rank correlation coefficients. It would, of course, be possible to calculate r' for each pair of judges and to use these values in obtaining the average value of r'. It is not necessary to do so, however, because the average value can be readily obtained from the coefficient of concordance. Thus

$$\bar{r}' = \frac{mW - 1}{m - 1} \tag{17.17}$$

Substituting in (17.17) with the value of $W = .474$ for the $m = 10$ film specialists we have

$$\bar{r}' = \frac{10(.474) - 1}{10 - 1} = .416$$

17.8   The Reliability of the Average Ranks Assigned to n Objects

For the ranks given to the five films by the $m = 10$ judges, we found that there was a significant degree of agreement among the judges. Each of the 10 sets of ranks provides information about the possible ordering of the five films. We observe that the judges are not in perfect agreement. It is reasonable to believe, however, that the average of the ranks assigned to each of the five films by the $m = 10$ judges may provide a better estimate of the ordering of the films than the ordering based upon the rankings of a single judge.

If we obtain the average rank assigned to each of the n objects, then we may be interested in knowing how reliable are the averages thus obtained. For example, if we had another comparable group of $m = 10$ judges and they also ranked the five films, to what degree would the averages based upon this second group of judges be correlated with the averages obtained from the first group? An estimate of this correlation coefficient can be obtained from the general definition of the reliability coefficient

$$r_{tt} = 1 - \frac{s_e^2}{s_X^2} \tag{17.18}$$

where r_{tt} is the reliability coefficient, s_e^2 is an estimate of the variance of the random errors in a set of measurements, and s_X^2 is the observed variance for the set of measurements. We note that if $s_e^2 = 0$, then $r_{tt} = 1.0$. We are interested in the observed variance based upon the sums (or means) of the ranks assigned to each of the n films and this variance is

$$s_X^2 = \text{Column sum of squares}/(n - 1)$$

As an estimate of the error variance in the $m \times n$ table of ranks, we have

$$s_e^2 = \text{Within column sum of squares}/(m - 1)(n - 1)$$

Then

$$r_{tt} = 1 - \frac{\text{Within column sum of squares}/(m - 1)(n - 1)}{\text{Column sum of squares}/(n - 1)}$$

$$= 1 - \frac{\text{Within column sum of squares}}{(m - 1)\,\text{Column sum of squares}} \qquad (17.19)$$

The sum of squares within columns for the data of Table 17.5 is 52.6 and the sum of squares between columns is 47.4. Then substituting in (17.19) with these values and with $m = 10$, we have

$$r_{tt} = 1 - \frac{52.6}{(10 - 1)(47.4)} = .877$$

as an estimate of the correlation we might obtain between the sums (or means) of the ranks assigned to the $n = 5$ films by two comparable groups of $m = 10$ judges.[5]

It can also be shown that the value of r_{tt} as given by (17.19) is related to $\bar{r}'$, defined by (17.17), in terms of the Spearman-Brown prophecy formula.[6] Thus

$$r_{tt} = \frac{m\bar{r}'}{1 + (m - 1)\bar{r}'} \qquad (17.20)$$

where m is the number of judges or sets of ranks.

For the ranks assigned by the 10 film specialists to the five films, we found that $\bar{r}'$ was equal to .416. Then substituting in (17.20) with this value, we obtain

$$r_{tt} = \frac{10(.416)}{1 + (10 - 1)(.416)} = .877$$

which is the same value we obtained before.

17.9 A Rank Test for the Difference between Two Groups

Suppose we have a group of n_1 observations and another group of n_2 observations and that for each observation we have a value of a variable X of interest. We let $n = n_1 + n_2$, the total number of observations, and we re-

---

[5] It can be shown that (17.19) is a special case of a formula developed by Horst (1949) for the reliability of the mean *ratings* assigned to n objects by m judges. Horst's formula simplifies to (17.19) when each judge's ratings consist of a set of n ranks.

[6] For a general discussion of the Spearman-Brown prophecy formula, see Gulliksen (1950).

place the values of X for the combined set of n observations by the ranks 1, 2, 3, $\cdots$, n. In other words, we substitute for the largest value of X the rank 1, and for the next largest value the rank 2, and so on, with the smallest value of X being assigned the rank n. After we have ranked the $n = n_1 + n_2$ observations, we can then find the sum (or mean) of the ranks for each group.

We now consider a test of significance of the difference between the two groups when we have ranks obtained in the manner described above for the observations in each group. Methods for testing the significance of the difference between the sums of the ranks for the two groups have been investigated by Festinger (1946), Kruskal and Wallis (1952), Mann and Whitney (1947), White (1952), and Wilcoxon (1945, 1947, 1949).

We let n_1 be the number of observations in the group with the smaller number and let T be the sum of the ranks for this group. We also let T' be the *conjugate* total or the sum of ranks for the group with the smaller number of observations when the observation in the set of n with the smallest value of X has been assigned rank 1 and the observation with the largest value of X has been assigned rank n. The conjugate total will be given by

$$T' = n_1(n_1 + n_2 + 1) - T$$
$$= n_1(n + 1) - T \tag{17.21}$$

so that there is no necessity for reranking the observations to obtain the conjugate total. The test of significance will be made using either T or T', whichever is the smaller.

Table XV, in Appendix B, gives the value of T or T', whichever is the smaller, at the .05 and .01 levels of significance. It will be obvious later that, because we enter Table XV with *either T or T'*, whichever is the smaller, the tabled values correspond to a two-sided test of significance. We illustrate the use of Table XV with the data of Wright (1946), cited by White (1952).

The values recorded in Table 17.6 are the survival times in minutes of the peroneal nerve of rabbits and cats under anoxic conditions. We have arranged the observations in order of magnitude. We wish to determine whether the survival times tend to be longer in one of the two species than in the other. We have assigned ranks to the observations in Table 17.6 based upon the combined distribution of $n = 18$ rabbits and cats. We may note that in assigning the ranks, we have given tied values the average of the ranks they would ordinarily occupy. For example, when we come to rank 3, we have two values of 35 minutes. We give these two values the average of ranks 3 and 4, or 3.5.

For the data of Table 17.6, we see that T for the smaller group of $n_1 = 4$ cats is 18. From (17.21), we find that

$$T' = 4(18 + 1) - 18 = 58$$

In this instance, T is smaller than T'. Consequently, we evaluate the rank

Table 17.6—Survival time in minutes of the peroneal nerve under anoxic conditions for 4 cats and 14 rabbits*

| Animal | Survival time | | Cat ranks $n_1 = 4$ | Rabbit ranks $n_2 = 14$ |
	Minutes	Ranks		
Cat	45	1	1	
Cat	43	2	2	
Rabbit	35	3.5		3.5
Rabbit	35	3.5		3.5
Cat	33	5	5	
Rabbit	30	6.5		6.5
Rabbit	30	6.5		6.5
Rabbit	28	8.5		8.5
Rabbit	28	8.5		8.5
Cat	25	10	10	
Rabbit	23	11		11
Rabbit	22	12.5		12.5
Rabbit	22	12.5		12.5
Rabbit	20	14		14
Rabbit	17	15		15
Rabbit	16	16.5		16.5
Rabbit	16	16.5		16.5
Rabbit	15	18		18
Σ			18.0	153.0

* Data from Wright (1946).

total $T = 18$ in terms of the tabled value in Table XV for $n_1 = 4$ and $n_2 = 14$. From Table XV, we find that $T \leq 19$ has probability of .05 when the null hypothesis is true. Because our observed value is *smaller* than the tabled value, we reject the null hypothesis and conclude that the survival times in the two groups do differ.

17.10   Summary of Steps in the Rank Test for the Difference between Two Groups

We may summarize the procedure of applying the rank test in the following steps.

1. Let the group with the smaller number of observations be n_1 and the group with the larger number of observations be n_2. If the number of observations in each group is the same, then one of the groups may be arbitrarily assigned n_1 and the other n_2.

2. Combine the $n_1 + n_2$ observations and rank the observations, with

rank 1 being assigned to the observation with the largest value and rank n to the observation with the smallest value.

3. If ties are present, give the tied observations the average of the ranks they would otherwise occupy.

4. Find the sum of ranks T for the group with the smaller number of observations.

5. Calculate the conjugate total T' as defined by (17.21).

6. Find the tabled value in Table XV for n_1 and n_2 observations. If either T or T' is equal to or less than the tabled values, then the null hypothesis may be rejected with $\alpha = .05$ or $\alpha = .01$ for a two-sided test.

17.11   The Standard Normal Curve Approximation for the Rank Test

Assume that the smaller group of n_1 observations represents a random sample from the set of ranks 1 to n, where n is the total number of observations. We may regard the ranks as a population in which $n = N$. We know that the population mean of the $n = N$ ranks is

$$\mu = \frac{n + 1}{2}$$

If we draw a random sample of n_1 observations from a population with mean μ, then the expected value of the sum T of the n_1 observations will be

$$E(T) = \mu_T = n_1\mu$$

But $\mu = (n + 1)/2$ and, therefore

$$\mu_T = \frac{n_1(n + 1)}{2} \tag{17.22}$$

For our example, then, the expected value of T will be

$$\mu_T = \frac{4(18 + 1)}{2} = 38$$

The variance of the population of $n = N$ ranks, as we have shown before, will be

$$\sigma^2 = \frac{n^2 - 1}{12}$$

The variance of a sum of n_1 independent observations drawn from a common population with variance σ^2 is, of course, equal to $n_1\sigma^2$. However, we do not have n_1 independent observations because the n_1 observations have been drawn without replacement from a finite population of $n = N$ ranks. In this case, the variance of the sum needs to be multiplied by a finite population correction factor that takes into account the fact that we have sampled without replacement.[7] The finite population correction factor is given by

$$\frac{n - n_1}{n - 1} \tag{17.23}$$

Thus, the variance of the sum T of the n_1 ranks will be

$$\sigma_T{}^2 = \frac{n_1(n^2 - 1)}{12}\left(\frac{n - n_1}{n - 1}\right)$$

$$= \frac{n_1 n_2(n + 1)}{12} \tag{17.24}$$

and

$$\sigma_T = \sqrt{\frac{n_1 n_2(n + 1)}{12}} \tag{17.25}$$

In our example, we have $n_1 = 4$, $n_2 = 14$, and $n = 18$. Then

$$\sigma_T = \sqrt{\frac{4(14)(18 + 1)}{12}} = 9.416$$

The distribution of T approaches that of a normal distribution as n_1 and n_2 become large. Thus, if we have values of n_1 and n_2 that exceed those in Table XV, then we may calculate

$$z = \frac{T - \mu_T}{\sigma_T} \tag{17.26}$$

and z will have a distribution which is approximately that of the standard normal distribution and can be evaluated in terms of the table of the standard normal curve.

In our example, we have $T = 18$, $\mu_T = 38$, and $\sigma_T = 9.416$. Then substituting in (17.26) with these values, we obtain

$$z = \frac{18 - 38}{9.416} = -2.124$$

and $z = -2.124$ may be evaluated in terms of the table of the standard normal curve.

We have found that the rank total T for the $n_1 = 4$ observations is 18 and that T' is equal to 58. It is also true that if T had been equal to 58, then the conjugate total T' would have been equal to 18. As we have emphasized,

---

[7] For a derivation of the finite population correction factor, see Edwards (1964).

Table XV is so arranged as to make use of either T or T', whichever is the smaller, with probability .05 and .01 that *either T or T'* is equal to or less than the tabled values. Thus the tabled values correspond to a two-sided test.

We have, as a matter of convenience, defined z in (17.26) only in terms of T, regardless of whether T is larger than or smaller than T'. If T is smaller than T', then the value of z in (17.26) will be negative in sign, whereas if T is larger than T', then the value of z will be positive in sign. Consequently, if we wish to make a two-sided test corresponding to the test of Table XV, with $\alpha = .05$, then we should be prepared to reject the null hypothesis if $z \leq -1.96$ or $z \geq 1.96$. In our example, we have $z = -2.124$ and for a two-sided test this is a significant value with $P < .05$ under the null hypothesis. We may observe that if the value of T' had been equal to 18, then we would have had T equal to 58, and, in this case,

$$z = \frac{58 - 38}{9.416} = 2.124$$

Thus, by considering both positive and negative values of z in the test of significance, we are making a two-sided test that corresponds to the one made in using Table XV.

17.12   Correction for Discontinuity for the Rank Test

It is obvious that the sum of the n_1 ranks T will always be integral, provided that there are no tied ranks,[8] whereas the standard normal distribution is continuous. Therefore, we may make a correction for the discontinuity in T. If T is smaller than μ_T, then we want to find the area in the standard normal distribution falling to the left of T. On the other hand, if T is larger than μ_T, we want to find the area in the standard normal distribution falling to the right of T. The corrections for discontinuity are, therefore,

$$T + .5 - \mu_T$$

if T is smaller than μ_T and

$$T - .5 - \mu_T$$

if T is larger than μ_T. We illustrate these two corrections for our example.

We have $T = 18$ and T is less than $\mu_T = 38$. Thus, z, corrected for discontinuity, will be

$$z_c = \frac{18 + .5 - 38}{9.416} = -2.07$$

---

[8] With ties present, the value of T will either be an integer or a number ending in .5. If T has a decimal of .5, then the correction for discontinuity would be .25 rather than .5.

If T' had been equal to 18, then T would have been equal to 58 and in this case $T > \mu_T$. Therefore, in this instance, we would have

$$z_c = \frac{58 - .5 - 38}{9.416} = 2.07$$

We note that $|z_c| < |z|$ in this example and this will always be the case. Despite the fact the absolute value of z_c is less than z, we still have, in this example, a significant value of z_c for the two-sided test of significance.

17.13   Accuracy of the Standard Normal Curve Approximation

From Table XV we note that the tabled value of T for $n_1 = 4$ and $n_2 = 14$ observations with $\alpha = .05$ is 19. Thus the probability of either $T \leq 19$ or $T' \leq 19$ is .05 under the null hypothesis. With $n_1 = 4$ and $n_2 = 14$ observations, we also have $\mu_T = 38$. Letting $T = 19$ and making a discontinuity correction, we obtain

$$z_c = \frac{19 + .5 - 38}{9.416} = -1.965$$

and from the table of the normal curve we find that the area to the left of $z_c = -1.965$ is approximately .0247. For the two-sided test we consider also the probability of $T' \leq 19$ so that $T = 57$. In this case, we would have $z_c = 1.965$ and the area to the right of this value is also approximately .0247. Thus, for the two-sided test in terms of the standard normal distribution, corresponding to the two-sided test of Table XV, we have $P = .0494$ and this values does not differ greatly from the exact probability of $P = .05$ obtained from Table XV.

17.14   The Kruskal-Wallis H Test for More Than Two Groups

In Table 17.7 we give the values of a dependent variable X for a randomized group design with three treatments and with five subjects assigned to each treatment. If we now arrange the 15 values of X in order of magnitude and then rank them, we obtain the ranks shown in the table alongside of the original values of X. We have given values of X that are tied for a given rank the average of the ranks they would ordinarily occupy.

A test of the null hypothesis that these three samples have been drawn at random from a common population may be made in terms of a statistic developed by Kruskal and Wallis (1952) that they designate as H. This statistic is given by

$$H = \left(\frac{12}{n(n + 1)}\right)\left(\sum_1^k \frac{T_k^2}{n_k}\right) - 3(n + 1) \qquad (17.27)$$

where k = the number of groups
$\quad n_k$ = the number of observations in the kth group
$\quad n$ = the total number of observations or $\Sigma_1^k n_k$
$\quad T_k$ = the sum of ranks or rank total for the kth group

It is obvious from (17.27) that there is no necessity for the number of observations in each of the k groups to be equal, as it happens to be for the example of Table 17.7.

Table 17.7—Scores and ranks for three groups of five subjects each

	Group 1		Group 2		Group 3	
	Score	Rank	Score	Rank	Score	Rank
	7	8	4	12	2	14.5
	10	3.5	6	10.5	2	14.5
	10	3.5	7	8	3	13
	11	2	9	5.5	7	8
	12	1	9	5.5	6	10.5
T		18.0		41.5		60.5
$T^2/5$		64.80		344.45		732.05

It can also be shown that (17.27) is algebraically equal to

$$H = \frac{\text{Column sum of squares}}{(n^3 - n)/12(n - 1)} \qquad (17.28)$$

The proof can be developed by substituting in (17.28) with an identity for the column sum of squares and then simplifying the resulting expression. We leave the proof as an exercise.

In our example, we have

$$\sum_1^k \frac{T_k^2}{n_k} = \frac{(18.0)^2}{5} + \frac{(41.5)^2}{5} + \frac{(60.5)^2}{5} = 1141.3$$

Then, substituting in (17.27) with this value and $n = 15$, we obtain

$$H = \frac{12(1141.3)}{15(15 + 1)} - 3(15 + 1)$$

$$= 9.065$$

Kruskal and Wallis (1952) show that if the null hypothesis is true, and if the number of observations in each group is not too small, then H is approximately distributed as χ^2 with $k - 1$ d.f. For our example, we have $k - 1 = 2$ d.f. and from the table of χ^2, Table IV in Appendix B, we find that with 2 d.f. the probability of $H \geq 9.065$ is less than .02, when the null hypothesis is true.

The null hypothesis tested by H is that the k samples are from the same population or, as we might state, identical populations. If the null hypothesis is rejected, we accept the alternative hypothesis that the populations are not identical. As in the case of the F test, however, experimental interest is usually in means and not in variances or other characteristics of the populations. Kruskal and Wallis offer reasons to believe that the H test may be relatively insensitive to differences in variances. In general, therefore, the test may be useful in testing differences in means, without the necessity of assuming homogeneity of variance. That is, if the null hypothesis is rejected, we shall, in general, be able to conclude that the population means are not all equal.

17.15   The Kruskal-Wallis Test and White's Test for $k = 2$ Groups

We may apply the H test to the data of Table 17.6 where we have $k = 2$ groups of observations. The rank total for the group with 4 observations is 18 and the rank total for the group with 18 observations is 153. Then

$$\sum_1^k \frac{T_k^2}{n_k} = \frac{(18)^2}{4} + \frac{(153)^2}{14} = 1753.071$$

Substituting in (17.27) with this value and with $n = 18$, we have

$$H = \frac{12(1753.071)}{18(18 + 1)} - 3(18 + 1) = 4.511$$

Because we have $k = 2$ groups, we have 1 d.f. and from the table of χ^2 we find that the probability of $H \geq 4.511$ is less than .05, when the null hypothesis is true.

In the discussion of White's rank-order test for the data of Table 17.6, we found that a test of significance based upon the standard normal curve resulted in $z = 2.124$, or $z = -2.124$ and we note that $z^2 = 4.511 = H$. The probability of $z^2 \geq 4.511$ is given by the area in the table of the standard normal curve falling to the left of $z \leq -2.124$ plus the area falling to the right of $z \geq 2.124$. The sum of these two areas is approximately .0338. This is also the probability of $H \geq 4.511$ with $k = 2$ groups.

We see that in the case of $k = 2$ groups, z^2, as defined by (17.26), is identical with H as defined by (17.27) or (17.28).

17.16   The Wilcoxon Test for Paired Observations

Suppose that we have an experiment with two treatments but such that subjects are paired or matched in some way. For example, we might pair subjects on the basis of an aptitude test. One subject in each pair is then assigned at random to Treatment 1 and the other to Treatment 2. In Table 17.8 we give in columns (1) and (2) the values of a dependent variable X for 15 paired subjects. Column 3 gives the difference between each of the paired

Table 17.8—Ranks assigned to the absolute differences $|X_1 - X_2|$ after values of $X_1 - X_2 = 0$ are eliminated

(1) X_1	(2) X_2	(3) $X_1 - X_2$	(4) Ranks	(5) Ranks $(+)$	(6) Ranks $(-)$
4	6	-2	3		3
1	2	-1	1.5		1.5
4	9	-5	11.5		11.5
7	4	3	6	6	
8	8	0			
8	5	3	6	6	
7	7	0			
9	8	1	1.5	1.5	
9	4	5	11.5	11.5	
9	6	3	6	6	
9	5	4	9.5	9.5	
1	4	-3	6		6
7	3	4	9.5	9.5	
1	9	-8	13		13
4	1	3	6	6	
		Σ	91.0	56.0	35.0

values of X. We note that we have two values of $X_1 - X_2 = 0$. We eliminate these two zero differences from consideration as we would also any other values of $X_1 - X_2 = 0$ that we might have obtained.

We now rank the $n = 13$ differences that are not equal to zero in terms of their absolute values, that is, without regard to their signs. These ranks are given in column (4). It is important to note that the ranks in column (4) have been assigned in such a way that *the smallest absolute difference is given the smallest rank and that the largest absolute difference is given the largest rank*. The reason for ranking the differences in this manner is because we want small differences to be given less weight than large differences. In column (5) we have entered the ranks from column (4) corresponding to positive differences and in column (5) the ranks corresponding to negative differences.

We let the sum of ranks corresponding to positive values of $X_1 - X_2$ be T_1 and the sum of ranks corresponding to negative values of $X_1 - X_2$ be T_2. Then it is obvious that

$$T_1 + T_2 = \frac{n(n + 1)}{2} \qquad (17.29)$$

where n is the number of differences that are not equal to zero. Because we eliminated two values of $X_1 - X_2 = 0$, we have $n = 13$.

Let us assume that there is no difference between the two treatments, so that the probability that the difference, $X_1 - X_2$, is positive is equal to the probability that it is negative. Under this assumption, the probability that a given rank has a positive sign will be equal to the probability that it has a negative sign. Thus, if X is a given rank, we have $P(+X) = P(-X) = 1/2$. Then the expected value of both T_1, the sum of the positive ranks, and T_2, the sum of the negative ranks, will be

$$\mu_T = P(X_1 + X_2 + X_3 \cdots + X_n)$$

but $P = 1/2$ and the sum within parentheses is the sum of a set of n ranks and is equal to $n(n + 1)/2$. Thus

$$\mu_T = \frac{n(n + 1)}{4} \qquad (17.30)$$

It can also be shown[9] that the variance of both T_1 and T_2 is equal to

$$\sigma_T{}^2 = \frac{(2n + 1)\mu_T}{6} \qquad (17.31)$$

and, therefore,

$$\sigma_T = \sqrt{\frac{(2n + 1)\mu_T}{6}} \qquad (17.32)$$

Wilcoxon (1947) has pointed out that if the null hypothesis is true and if $n \geq 8$, then the distribution of both T_1 and T_2 is approximately normal. Thus

$$z = \frac{T_1 - \mu_T}{\sigma_T} \quad \text{and} \quad z = \frac{T_2 - \mu_T}{\sigma_T} \qquad (17.33)$$

will have a distribution that is approximately that of a standard normal distribution and z may be evaluated in terms of the standard normal curve.

---

[9] For a proof of (17.31), see Edwards (1964).

For the data of Table 17.8, we have $T_1 = 56.0$ and $T_2 = 35.0$. With $n = 13$ ranks, we also have

$$\mu_T = \frac{13(14)}{4} = 45.5$$

and

$$\sigma_T = \sqrt{\frac{(26 + 1)(45.5)}{6}} = 14.31$$

Substituting in (17.33) with the values we have obtained, we have

$$z = \frac{56.0 - 45.5}{14.31} = .73 \quad \text{and} \quad z = \frac{35.0 - 45.5}{14.31} = -.73$$

For a two-sided test we find from the table of the standard normal curve that if the null hypothesis is true, then the probability of $z \geq .73$ or $z \leq -.73$ is approximately .47 and we may regard the null hypothesis as tenable.

17.17   Corrections for Tied Ranks

We have suggested earlier, in connection with the rank correlation co-efficient, that if observations are tied for a given rank, then they should be assigned the average of the ranks they would ordinarily occupy. We also followed this procedure in applying White's rank-order test and the Kruskal-Wallis H test. Although tied observations did not enter into our discussion of the coefficient of concordance W, we may at this time point out that if tied observations are present in problems involving W, then we would also assign the tied observations the average of the ranks they would ordinarily occupy. As long as the number of ties is not too large, corrections that could be introduced for taking the ties into account will have relatively little influence on the various rank order statistics that we calculate in the usual way ignoring the presence of tied ranks. However, if the number of tied ranks is large, a correction for this condition should be made.

It is obvious that assigning tied observations the average of the ranks they would ordinarily occupy does not in any way change the sum or the mean of the set of n ranks.

If we have a set of n ranks with no ties present, then

$$\sum_1^n X^2 = \frac{n(n + 1)(2n + 1)}{6} \quad \text{and} \quad \sum_1^n (X - \bar{X})^2 = \frac{n^3 - n}{12}$$

However, if we have tied ranks, then

$$\sum_1^n X^2 < \frac{n(n + 1)(2n + 1)}{6} \quad \text{and} \quad \sum_1^n (X - \bar{X})^2 < \frac{n^3 - n}{12}$$

We define a correction factor for each group of tied ranks as

$$C = \frac{k^3 - k}{12} \tag{17.34}$$

where k represents the number of observations in a group tied for a given rank. Thus, if we have two observations tied for a given rank, then $C = (2^3 - 2)/12 = .5$. If we have three observations tied for a given rank, then $C = (3^3 - 3)/12 = 2.0$. Values of C for k up to 15 are given in Table 17.9. It may be noted that Table 17.9 can also be used to obtain the value of $(n^3 - n)/12 = n(n^2 - 1)/12$ for values of n up to 15.

If we have tied ranks, then

$$\sum_1^n X^2 = \frac{n(n + 1)(2n + 1)}{6} - \sum C \tag{17.35}$$

and

$$\sum_1^n (X - \bar{X})^2 = \frac{n^3 - n}{12} - \sum C \tag{17.36}$$

where $\sum C$ indicates that we must sum the correction factor for each group of tied ranks.

We use the subscript c to indicate an adjustment or correction for the presence of tied ranks. Summarized below are the corrections for the various statistics presented earlier in the chapter.

Table 17.9—Values of the correction factor $C = (k^3 - k)/12$ for tied ranks

Number of ties k	Correction $(k^3 - k)/12$ C
2	.5
3	2.0
4	5.0
5	10.0
6	17.5
7	28.0
8	42.0
9	60.0
10	82.5
11	110.0
12	143.0
13	182.0
14	227.5
15	280.0

The rank correlation coefficient. Let Σx_c^2 be the corrected sum of squares for the X variable or

$$\Sigma x_c^2 = \frac{n^3 - n}{12} - \Sigma C$$

and let Σy_c^2 be the corrected sum of squares for the Y variable or

$$\Sigma y_c^2 = \frac{n^3 - n}{12} - \Sigma C$$

Then the rank correlation coefficient corrected for tied ranks will be

$$r_c' = \frac{\Sigma x_c^2 + \Sigma y_c^2 - \Sigma D^2}{2\sqrt{\Sigma x_c^2 \Sigma y_c^2}} \tag{17.37}$$

If there are no tied ranks, then $r_c' = r'$.

The coefficient of concordance. W corrected for tied ranks is given by

$$W_c = \frac{\text{Column sum of squares}}{\dfrac{m(n^3 - n)}{12} - \Sigma C} \tag{17.38}$$

If there are no tied ranks then $W_c = W$.

Because we have already made a correction for tied ranks in W_c, as defined by (17.38), we use this value to obtain

$$\chi_{r_c}^2 = m(n - 1)W_c \tag{17.39}$$

which is identical with

$$\chi_{r_c}^2 = \frac{m(n - 1) \, \text{Column sum of squares}}{\dfrac{m(n^3 - n)}{12} - \Sigma C} \tag{17.40}$$

White's rank order test. If there are tied ranks, calculate

$$\sigma_{T_c} = \sqrt{\frac{n_1 n_2}{n(n - 1)}\left(\frac{n^3 - n}{12} - \Sigma C\right)} \tag{17.41}$$

and use σ_{T_c} in place of σ_T in the test of significance as given by (17.26). If there are no tied ranks, then $\sigma_{T_c} = \sigma_T$.

Kruskal-Wallis test. H, corrected for tied ranks will be given by

$$H_c = \frac{H}{1 - \dfrac{\Sigma C}{(n^3 - n)/12}} \tag{17.42}$$

If there are no tied ranks then $H_c = H$.

Wilcoxon test. For the Wilcoxon test, calculate

$$\sigma_{T_c} = \sqrt{\frac{1}{4}\left(\frac{n(n+1)(2n+1)}{6} - \sum C\right)} \qquad (17.43)$$

and use σ_{T_c} in place of σ_T in the test of significance as given by (17.33). If there are no tied ranks, then $\sigma_{T_c} = \sigma_T$.

EXAMPLES

17.1—At a neuropsychiatric hospital, three psychiatrists were asked to rank seven patients according to the judged severity of the patients' psychological problems. Each psychiatrist made his rankings independently, that is, without knowledge of the ranks assigned to the patients by the other psychiatrists.

(a) Find the value of W and of W'.
(b) Is W' significant?
(c) What is the reliability of the average ranks?

	Patients						
Psychiatrists	A	B	C	D	E	F	G
1	5	2	1	6	3	4	7
2	2	1	3	7	5	4	6
3	5	2	1	4	6	3	7

17.2—Uhrbrock (1948) had 7 interviewers rank 11 applicants for a position. The applicants had been preselected from various colleges on the basis of psychological tests and preliminary interviews.

(a) Find the value of W.
(b) Test W for significance, using χ_r^2.
(c) What is the reliability of the average ranks as given by (17.19).
(d) Find the average intercorrelation of the ranks.
(e) Check the value obtained for r_{tt} in terms of (17.20).

Inter- viewers	Applicants										
	Jn	Wy	De	Sn	Pt	Mc	Le	Bw	Bn	Dy	Ls
1	3	10	9	8	1	6	4	7	11	2	5
2	8	9	7	10	2	1	5	3	11	4	6
3	4	9	5	10	1	2	3	8	11	6	7
4	3	7	4	9	1	2	6	8	11	5	10
5	1	6	8	7	5	4	10	3	9	11	2
6	5	11	8	7	1	10	2	4	9	3	6
7	5	9	4	8	2	1	6	10	11	3	7

17.3—Anderson (1934) had 25 occupations ranked by 673 North Carolina State College students. The occupations were ranked in terms of (A) social contribution, (B) social prestige, and (C) economic return. The ranks based upon the combined judgments of the 673 students are given below.

(a)   Find the three possible rank correlation coefficients.
(b)   Use W to determine how much agreement there is among the three sets of ranks.
(c)   Use χ_r^2 to test the significance of W.
(d)   Average the three coefficients obtained in (a) and see that this average checks with that given by (17.17).

Occupation	A Social contribution	B Social prestige	C Economic return	Σ
Clergyman	1	3	16	20
Physician	2	2	3	7
Professor	3	5	10	18
Banker	4	1	1	6
Schoolteacher	5	11	19	35
Manufacturer	6	6	2	14
Lawyer	7	4	4	15
Farmer	8	14	12	34
Engineer	9	9	5	23
Artist	10	7	8	25
Merchant	11	12	9	32
Factory manager	12	10	6	28
Machinist	13	18	11	42
Carpenter	14	19	17	50
Bookkeeper	15	17	18	50
Insurance agent	16	15	13	44
Salesman	17	16	14	47
Factory operative	18	21	20	59
Barber	19	20	21	60
Blacksmith	20	22	22	64
Baseball player	21	13	7	41
Soldier	22	23	24	69
Chauffeur	23	24	23	70
Man of leisure	24	8	15	47
Ditch digger	25	25	25	75

17.4—Dulsky and Krout (1950) had 14 factory supervisors ranked on promotion potential by three executives who had observed the supervisors at work. Two psychologists also ranked the supervisors on the basis of an information blank and various psychological tests. The ranks are given below.

(a) Calculate the three rank correlation coefficients for the executive rank-ings and also the rank correlation coefficient for the ranks assigned by the two psychologists.
(b) Find the coefficient of concordance using the ranks obtained from all five judges.
(c) Test W for significance using χ_r^2.
(d) Find the reliability of the average ranks.

Supervisor	Rankings by three executives			Rankings by two psychologists		Σ
	1	2	3	4	5	
A	7	4	8	9	8	36
B	2	1	2	3	3	11
C	1	2	1	10	7	21
D	5	3	6	5	5	24
E	4	8	7	4	2	25
F	3	5	5	8	13	34
G	6	6	4	1	1	18
H	9	11	9	6	4	39
I	11	7	10	7	10	45
J	14	10	12	12	14	62
K	10	9	11	14	9	53
L	12	14	13	11	11	61
M	8	12	3	2	6	31
N	13	13	14	13	12	65

17.5—Sixteen graduate students in psychology took the Ph.D. qualify-ing examination in statistics. Their papers were read and graded by two examiners. The grades given the papers by each examiner have been trans-lated into ranks and the ranks are given below.

(a) Find the value of r'.
(b) Can we conclude that the agreement between the two examiners is significantly greater than chance?

Students	Examiner		Students	Examiner	
	A	B		A	B
1	1	1	9	3	3
2	2	2	10	10	5.5
3	7	10	11	8.5	11
4	4	5.5	12	12	13.5
5	11	9	13	14.5	15.5
6	5	5.5	14	13	12
7	8.5	5.5	15	16	15.5
8	6	8	16	14.5	13.5

17.6—Schultz (1945) collected data on the socioeconomic level, aptitude level, and college attendance of male high school graduates. Ranks within rows were assigned on the basis of the percent of college attendance for the number of subjects falling in each cell of the row.

(a)   Find the value of the coefficient of concordance.
(b)   Test W for significance using χ_r^2.
(c)   Interpret your results.

Aptitude intervals	Socioeconomic Status					
	0–14	15–18	19–22	23–26	27–30	31 plus
100 plus	6	2	4.5	4.5	3	1
90–99	5	4	2	3	6	1
80–89	6	4	2	3	5	1
70–79	6	4	1	5	3	2
60–69	6	4	5	2	3	1
50–59	5.5	5.5	3	6	4	1
40–49	2	5	3	6	4	1
15–39	4	6	2	5	3	1
Sum	40.5	34.5	21.5	32.5	30.0	9.0

17.7—Weise and Bitterman (1951) tested two groups of 10 rats each under different conditions. Two lamps were located at each choice point. For one group, both lamps were on. For the other group, one lamp at each choice point was on and the other was off. The scores given below are error scores based on 24 days of training.

One lamp	Both lamps
164	69
157	117
123	102
196	39
209	62
188	101
174	54
136	65
117	92
109	86

(a)   Arrange the combined observations in order of magnitude and assign ranks from 1 to 20.
(b)   Use White's test and Table XV to determine whether the two groups differ.

(c) Without making a correction for discontinuity, find the value of z.
(d) Show that the value of z^2 is equal to H.

17.8—Twenty-two subjects were divided at random into two groups of 11 subjects each. One group was then tested under Experimental Condition A and the other under Experimental Condition B. The measures obtained on the dependent variable are given below.

(a) Arrange the combined observations in order of magnitude and assign ranks from 1 to 22.
(b) Use White's test and Table XV to determine whether the two groups differ.

Experimental Condition A	Experimental Condition B
36	33
50	29
100	80
90	62
38	45
95	34
70	43
76	98
79	60
75	40
44	30

17.9—Make a correction for discontinuity and find the value of z for the data of Example 17.8.

17.10—Use the H test to determine whether the hypothesis that the following four sets of observations are from identical populations is tenable.

Group 1	Group 2	Group 3	Group 4
30	19	22	38
28	17	24	45
36	20	32	42
29	20	29	39
36	15	24	36
34	16		32
36	29		
	13		
	27		
	18		
	17		

17.11—Use the H test to determine whether the hypothesis that the following three sets of observations are from identical populations is tenable.

Group A	Group B	Group C
38	22	32
55	24	33
54	42	30
44	41	35
48	31	30
22	32	28

17.12—Eleven patients were rated by four psychiatrists on a diagnostic rating scale. The ratings were then ranked and the tied ratings for each psychiatrist were given the average of the ranks they would ordinarily occupy. Data are from Kogan and Pumroy (1952).

(a) Calculate W with and without a correction for tied ranks and compare the two values.

(b) Test the two values for significance using the χ_r^2 test.

Psychia-trists	\multicolumn{11}{c}{Patients}	Σ
	A	B	C	D	E	F	G	H	I	J	K	
1	7.0	1.5	7.0	7.0	7.0	7.0	7.0	1.5	7.0	7.0	7.0	66.0
2	7.5	2.5	7.5	7.5	1.0	2.5	7.5	7.5	7.5	7.5	7.5	66.0
3	6.5	6.5	6.5	6.5	6.5	6.5	6.5	6.5	6.5	1.0	6.6	66.0
4	6.5	6.5	1.0	6.5	6.5	6.5	6.5	6.5	6.5	6.5	6.5	66.0
Σ	27.5	17.0	22.0	27.5	21.0	22.5	27.5	22.0	27.5	22.0	27.5	264.0

17.13—Scores and ranks on two variables, X and Y, are given below for 10 subjects. Calculate r with and without making a correction for tied ranks and compare the two values.

\multicolumn{2}{c}{Scores}		\multicolumn{2}{c}{Ranks}		Rank difference
X	Y	X	Y	D
32	18	1.0	1.0	.0
20	16	2.5	2.0	.5
20	11	2.5	4.5	−2.0
18	11	4.5	4.5	.0
18	11	4.5	4.5	.0
10	11	6.5	4.5	2.0
10	5	6.5	8.0	−1.5
5	5	8.0	8.0	.0
4	5	9.5	8.0	1.5
2	2	9.5	10.0	− .5

17.14—In Chapter 16, it was stated that the expected value of χ^2 is always equal to its degrees of freedom. Prove that the expected value of χ_r^2 as defined by (17.14) is equal to $n - 1$.

17.15—Using the definition of χ_r^2 as given by (17.14), prove that χ_r^2 is equal to $m(n - 1)W$.

17.16—Prove that the right sides of (17.27) and (17.28) are equal.

17.17—Under what conditions will $W = 1.00$?

References

Anderson, W. W. The occupational attitudes of college men. *Journal of Social Psychology*, 1934, **5**, 435–466.

Ansbacher, H. L. Distortion in the perception of real movement. *Journal of Experimental Psychology*, 1944, **34**, 1–23.

Berkshire, J. R. (Ed.) *Improvement of grading practices for Air Training Command schools.* Air Training Command, Scott Air Force Base, Illinois, ATRC Manual 50-900-9, 1951.

Boneau, C. A. The effects of violations of assumptions underlying the *t* test. *Psychological Bulletin*, 1960, **57**, 49–64.

Box, G. E. P. Non-normality and tests on variances. *Biometrika*, 1953, **40**, 318–335.

Box, G. E. P. Some theorems on quadratic forms applied in the study of analysis of variance problems. I. Effects of inequality of variance in the one-way classification. *Annals of Mathematical Statistics*, 1954a, **25**, 290–302.

Box, G. E. P. Some theorems on quadratic forms applied in the study of analysis of variance problems. II. Effects of inequality of variance and of correlation between errors in the two-way classification. *Annals of Mathematical Statistics*, 1954b, **25**, 484–498.

Bresnahan, Jean L., and M. M. Shapiro. A general equation and technique for the exact partitioning of chi-square contingency tables. *Psychological Bulletin*, 1966, **66**, 252–262.

Bugelski, B. R. Interference with recall of original responses after learning new responses to old stimuli. *Journal of Experimental Psychology*, 1942, **30**, 368–379.

Castellan, N. J., Jr. On the partitioning of contingency tables. *Psychological Bulletin*, 1965, **64**, 330–338.

Chesire, L., M. Saffir, and L. L. Thurstone. *Computing digrams for the tetrachoric correlation coefficient.* Chicago: University of Chicago Bookstore, 1933.

Cochran, W. G. The χ^2 test of goodness-of-fit. *Annals of Mathematical Statistics*, 1952, **23**, 315–345.

Cochran, W. G. Some methods for strengthening the common χ^2 tests. *Biometrics*, 1954, **10**, 417–451.

Cohen, J. The statistical power of abnormal-social psychological research. A review. *Journal of Abnormal and Social Psychology*, 1962, **65**, 145–153.

Crespi, L. P. Quantitative variation of incentive and performance in the white rat. *American Journal of Pscychology*, 1942, **55**, 467–517.

Curtis, J. W. A study of the relationship between hypnotic susceptibility and intelligence. *Journal of Experimental Psychology*, 1943, **33**, 337–339.

Danford, M. B., H. M. Hughes, and R. C. McNee. On the analysis of repeated-measurements experiments. *Biometrics*, 1960, **16,** 547–565.

Davidoff, M. D., and H. W. Goheen. A table for the rapid determination of the tetrachoric correlation coefficient. *Psychometrika*, 1953, **18,** 115–121.

Dorcus, R. M. A brief study of the Humm-Wadsworth Temperament Scale and the Guilford-Martin Personnel Inventory in an industrial situation. *Journal of Applied Psychology*, 1944, **28,** 302–307.

Dulsky, S. G., and M. H. Krout. Predicitng promotion potential on the basis of psychological tests. *Personnel Psychology*, 1950, **3,** 345–351.

Dunlap, J. W. The effect of color in direct mail advertising. *Journal of Applied Psychology*, 1950, **34,** 280–281.

Dunnett, C. W. A multiple comparison procedure for comparing several treatments with a control. *Journal of the American Statistical Association*, 1955, **50,** 1096–1121.

Edwards, A. L. *Applications of ranking in film research and the statistical analysis of ranks.* Instructional Film Research Program. Pennsylvania State University, University Park, 1951.

Edwards, A. L. *Experimental design in psychological research.* (Rev. ed.) New York: Holt, Rinehart and Winston, 1960.

Edwards, A. L. *Expected values of discrete random variables and elementary statistics.* New York: Wiley, 1964.

Edwards, A. L., and L. L. Thurstone. An internal consistency check for scale values determined by the method of successive intervals. *Psyehometrika*, 1952, **17,** 169–180.

Edwards, W., H. Lindman, and L. Savage. Bayesian statistical inference in psychological research. *Psychological Review*, 1963, **70,** 193–242.

Feller, W. *An introduction to probability theory and its applications.* (2d ed.) New York: Wiley, 1957.

Festinger, L. The significance of the difference between means without reference to the frequency distribution function. *Psychometrika*, 1946, **11,** 97–105.

Finney, D. J. The Fisher-Yates test of significance in 2×2 contingency tables. *Biometrika*, 1948, **35,** 145–156.

Fisher, R. A. On the "probable error" of a coefficient of correlation. *Metron*, 1921, **1,** Part 4, 1–32.

Fisher, R. A. *Statistical methods for research workers.* (6th ed.) Edinburgh: Oliver & Boyd, 1936.

Fisher, R. A. *The design of experiments.* (3d ed.) Edinburgh: Oliver & Boyd, 1942.

Fisher, R. A., and F. Yates. *Statistical tables for biological, agricultural, and medical research.* (3d ed.) New York: Hafner, 1949.

Fleishman, E. A. An experimental consumer panel technique. *Journal of Applied Psychology*, 1951, **35,** 133–135.

Fosdick, S. J. Report to the National Retail Dry Goods Association. Quoted In G. W. Hartmann and T. M. Newcomb (Eds.), *Industrial conflict.* New York: Holt, Rinehart and Winston, 1939. P. 119.

Friedman, M. The use of ranks to avoid the assumption of normality implicit in the analysis of variance. *Journal of the American Statistical Association,* 1937, **32,** 675–701.

Friedman, M. A comparison of alternative tests of significance for the problem of *m* rankings. *Annals of Mathematical Statistics,* 1940, **11,** 86–92.

Gaito, J. Unequal intervals and unequal *n* in trend analyses. *Psychological Bulletin,* 1965, **63,** 125–127.

Garrett, H. E. *Statistics in psychology and education.* (2d ed.) New York: David McKay Company, 1937.

Geisser, S., and W. W. Greenhouse. An extension of Box's results on the use of the *F* distribution in multivariate analysis. *Annals of Mathematical Statistics,* 1958, **29,** 885–891.

Goodman, L. A., and W. H. Kruskal. Measures of association for cross classifications. *Journal of the American Statistical Association,* 1954, **49,** 732–764.

Goodman, L. A., and W. H. Kruskal. Measures of association for cross classifications. II: Further discussion and references. *Journal of the American Statistical Association,* 1959, **54,** 123–163.

Grandage, A. Orthogonal coefficients for unequal intervals. *Biometrics,* 1958, **14,** 287–289.

Gulliksen, H. *Theory of mental tests.* New York: Wiley, 1950.

Hays, W. L. *Statistics for psychologists.* New York: Holt, Rinehart and Winston, 1963.

Hodges, J. L., Jr., and E. L. Lehmann. *Basic concepts of probability and statistics.* San Francisco: Holden-Day, 1964.

Horst, P. A generalized expression for the reliability of measures. *Psychometrika,* 1949, **14,** 21–31.

Janis, I. L., and Myrtle A. Astrachan. The effects of electroconvulsive treatment on memory efficiency. *Journal of Abnormal and Social Psychology,* 1951, **46,** 501–511.

Keating, Elizabeth, D. G. Paterson, and C. H. Stone. Validity of work histories obtained by interview. *Journal of Applied Psychology,* 1950, **34,** 6–11.

Kellar, B. The construction and validation of a scale for measuring attitude toward any homemaking activity. In H. H. Remmers (Ed.), *Studies in attitudes: Bulletin of Purdue University,* 1934, **35,** 47–63.

Kelley, T. L. *Statistical method.* New York: Macmillan, 1923.

Kelly, E. L., and D. W. Fiske. The prediction of success in the VA training program in clinical psychology. *American Psychologist,* 1950, **5,** 395–406.

Kendall, M. G. *Rank correlation methods*. London: Griffin, 1948.

Kendall, M. G., and B. B. Smith. Randomness and random sampling numbers. *Journal of the Royal Statistical Society*, 1938, **101**, 147–166.

Kendall, M. G., and B. B. Smith. Second paper on random sampling numbers. *Journal of the Royal Statistical Society Supplement*, 1939a, **6**, 51–61.

Kendall, M. G., and B. B. Smith. The problem of *m* rankings. *Annals of Mathematical Statistics*, 1939b, **10**, 275–287.

Kogan, W. S., and Shirley Pumroy. Unpublished data from a paper presented at the Western Psychological Association meetings, 1952.

Kruskal, W. H., and W. A. Wallis. Use of ranks in one-criterion variance analysis. *Journal of the American Statistical Association*, 1952, **47**, 583–621.

Kuo, Z. Y. The genesis of the cat's response to the rat. *Journal of Comparative Psychology*, 1930, **11**, 1–30.

Lancaster, H. O. The derivation and partition of χ^2 in certain discrete distributions. *Biometrika*, 1949, **36**, 117–129.

Latscha, R. Tests of significance in a 2×2 contingency table. *Biometrika*, 1953, **40**, 74–86.

Leahy, A. M. A study of adopted children as a method of investigating nature-nurture. *Journal of the American Statistical Association*, 1935, **30**, 281–287.

Levine, A. S. Minnesota Psycho-Analogies Test. *Journal of Applied Psychology*, 1950, **34**, 300–305.

Lewontin, R. C., and J. Felsenstein. The robustness of homogeneity tests in $2 \times N$ tables. *Biometrics*, 1965, **21**, 19–33.

Lindquist, E. F. *Statistical analysis in educational research*. Boston: Houghton Mifflin, 1940.

Locke, B., and C. H. Grimm. Odor selection preferences and identification. *Journal of Applied Psychology*, 1949, **33**, 167–174.

Lublin, Shirley Curran. Reinforcement schedules, scholastic aptitude, autonomy need, and achievement in a programed course. *Journal of Educational Psychology*, 1965, **56**, 295–302.

Mainland, D., L. Herrera, and M. I. Sutcliffe. *Tables for use with binomial samples*. New York: New York University College of Medicine, Department of Medical Statistics, 1956.

Mangus, A. R. Relationships between the young woman's conception of her intimate male associates and of her ideal husband. *Journal of Social Psychology*, 1936, **7**, 403–420.

Mann, H. B., and D. R. Whitney. On a test of whether one of two random variables is stochastically larger than the other. *Annals of Mathematical Statistics*, 1947, **18**, 50–60.

Marks, E. S. Standardization of a race attitude test for Negro youth. *Journal of Social Psychology*, 1943, **18**, 245–278.

Merrington, Maxine, and Catherine M. Thompson. Table of percentage points of the inverted beta (F) distribution. *Biometrika*, 1943, **33,** 73–88.

Mood, A. M., and F. A. Graybill. *Introduction to the theory of statistics.* (2d ed.) New York: McGraw-Hill, 1963.

Mosteller, F., and R. R. Bush. Selected quantitative techniques. In G. Lindzey (Ed.), *Handbook of social psychology*, Vol. I. Reading, Mass.: Addison-Wesley, 1954. Pp. 289–334.

Mosteller, F., R. E. K. Rourke, and G. B. Thomas, Jr. *Probability and statistics.* Reading, Mass.: Addison-Wesley, 1961.

Olds, E. G. Distributions of sums of squares of rank differences for small numbers of individuals. *Annals of Mathematical Statistics*, 1938, **9,** 133–148.

Olds, E. G. The 5% significance levels for sums of squares of rank differences and a correction. *Annals of Mathematical Statistics*, 1949, **20,** 117–118.

Overall, J. E., and S. N. Dalal. Design of experiments to maximize power relative to cost. *Psychological Bulletin*, 1965, **64,** 339–350.

Pearson, K. On the correlations of characters not quantitatively measureable. *Philosophical Transactions, Series A*, 1901, **195,** 1–47.

Perry, N. C., N. W. Kettner, A. F. Hertzka, and E. A. Bouvier. Estimating the tetrachoric correlation coefficient via I. A cosine-pi dichotomization. *Studies of aptitudes of high-level personal.* Technical Memorandum No. 2. Los Angeles: University of Southern California, 1953.

Peters, C. C., and W. R. Van Voorhis. *Statistical procedures and their mathematical bases.* New York: McGraw-Hill, 1940.

Pronko, N. H., and D. T. Herman. Identification of cola beverages. IV. Postscript. *Journal of Applied Psychology*, 1950, **34,** 68–69.

Robson, D. S. A simple method for constructing orthogonal polynomials when the independent variable is unequally spaced. *Biometrics*, 1959, **15,** 187–191.

Rosenzweig, S. An experimental study of "repression" with special reference to need-persistive and ego-defensive reactions to frustration. *Journal of Experimental Psychology*, 1943, **32,** 64–74.

Scheffé, H. A method for judging all contrasts in the analysis of variance. *Biometrika*, 1953, **40,** 87–104.

Scheffé, H. *The analysis of variance.* New York: Wiley, 1959.

Schultz, F. G. Recent developments in the statistical analysis of rank data adapted to educational research. *Journal of Experimental Education*, 1945, **13,** 149–152.

Selover, R. B., and J. Vogel. The value of a testing program in a tight labor market. *Personnel Psychology*, 1948, **1,** 447–456.

Shaffer, L. F. *The psychology of adjustment.* Boston: Houghton Mifflin, 1936.

Shipley, W. C., Judith E. Coffin, and Kathryn C. Hadsell. Affective distance and other factors determining reaction time in judgments of color preferences. *Journal of Experimental Psychology* 1945, **34,** 206–215.

Snedecor, G. W. *Statistical methods.* (5th ed.) Ames: Iowa State University Press, 1956.

Tippett, L. H. C. On the extreme individuals and the range of a sample from a normal population. *Biometrika,* 1925, **17,** 364–387.

Uhrbrock, R. S. The personnel interview. *Personnel Psychology,* 1948, **1,** 273–302.

Watson, K. B. The nature and measurement of musical meanings. *Psychological Monographs,* 1942, **54,** No. 224.

Weise, P., and M. E. Bitterman. Response-selection in discriminative learning. *Psychological Review,* 1951, **58,** 185–194.

White, C. The use of ranks in a test of significance for comparing two treatments. *Biometrics,* 1952, **8,** 33–41.

Wilcoxon, F. Individual comparisons by ranking methods. *Biometrics,* 1945, **1,** 80–82.

Wilcoxon, F. Probability tables for individual comparisons by ranking methods. *Biometrics,* 1947, **3,** 119–122.

Wilcoxon, F. *Some rapid approximate statistical procedures.* Stamford, Conn.: American Cyanamid Co., 1949.

Winer, B. J. *Statistical principles in experimental design.* New York: McGraw-Hill, 1962.

Wright, E. B. A comparative study of the effects of oxygen lack on peripheral nerve. *American Journal of Physiology,* 1946, **147,** 78–89.

Yates, F. Contingency tables involving small numbers and the χ^2 test. *Journal of the Royal Statistical Society Supplement,* 1934, **1,** 217–235.

Yule, G. U., and M. G. Kendall. *An introduction to the theory of statistics.* (13th ed.) London: Griffin, 1947.

Glossary

$\neq$	not equal to
$>$	greater than
$<$	less than
$\geq$	equal to or greater than
$\leq$	equal to or less than
$!$	factorial
$\cup$	union
$\cap$	intersect
$\{\ \}$	used to enclose elements of a set
$\emptyset$	empty set
$\lvert x \rvert$	absolute value of x
$E(\ )$	expected value of the term or terms within parentheses
$P(\ )$	probability of the event or events within parentheses
$\sum$	sum of
$\sum(\ )$	sum of the term or terms within parentheses
α	probability of a Type I error
β	probability of a Type II error
β_Y	population regression coefficient
χ^2	a variable with a chi square distribution
δ	difference between two population means; $\mu_1 - \mu_2$
η_{YX}	correlation ratio
ε	correction factor used in reducing degrees of freedom in a repeated measurements design
ρ	population correlation coefficient
σ	population standard deviation
σ^2	population variance; $E(X - \mu)^2$
μ	population mean; $E(X)$
A	a set
$\bar{A}$	set of elements not in set A
AD	average deviation
$A \cup B$	set of elements that are in A or B or in both A and B
$A \cap B$	set of elements that are in both A and B
$A \times B$	interaction of two factors A and B
a_{ki}	coefficients used in making comparisons on a set of means or sums
b_Y	sample regression coefficient
C	contingency coefficient
C_{25}	the 25th centile; Q_1
C_{50}	the 50th centile; Mdn
C_{75}	the 75th centile; Q_3

$C_{X_1 X_2}$	population covariance; $E(X_1 X_2) - \mu_{X_1}\mu_{X_2}$
$_nC_r$	number of combinations of n things taken r at a time
D	difference between two paired values; $X_1 - X_2$ or $X - Y$
$\bar{D}$	mean of a set of differences
D_i	a comparison on a set of treatment sums
d_i	a comparison on a set of treatment means
d.f.	degrees of freedom
E_1	an event
$\bar{E}_1$	not the event E_1
$E(X)$	expected value of X; μ
$E(X - \mu)^2$	expected value of $(X - \mu)^2$; σ^2
F	a variable with an F distribution
F_i	expected number of observations in a given class
f_i	observed number of observations in a given class
H	Kruskal-Wallis test statistic of differences in rank totals
H_0	null hypothesis
H_1	class of alternatives to H_0
H_2	class of alternatives to H_0
i	width or range of a class interval
k	number of samples or treatment groups
l	lower limit of a class interval
Mdn	median; C_{50}
MS	mean square in the analysis of variance
m	mid-point of a class interval
N	number of observations in a population
n	number of observations in a sample; number of trials in a binomial experiment
$n!$	n factorial; product of the integers from n to 1
P	probability
$P(A)$	probability of A
$P(A\|B)$	conditional probability; probability of A given that B has occurred
$P(E_1)$	probability of the event E_1
$P(\bar{E}_1)$	probability of not E_1; $1 - P(E_1)$
$P(E_1 \cup E_2)$	probability of E_1 or E_2 or both E_1 and E_2
$P(E_1 \cap E_2)$	probability that both E_1 and E_2 occur
$_nP_n$	number of permutations of n things taken all together
$_nP_r$	number of permutations of n things taken r at a time
Q	semi-interquartile range
Q_1	the first quartile; C_{25}
Q_3	the third quartile; C_{75}
R	range of the values of a set of measurements
r	sample product-moment correlation coefficient

r^2	coefficient of determination
r_b	biserial coefficient of correlation
r_{pb}	point biserial coefficient of correlation
r_ϕ	phi coefficient
r_t	tetrachoric correlation coefficient
r_{tt}	reliability coefficient
r'	rank correlation coefficient
$r!$	r factorial; product of the integers from r to 1
S	sample space of an experiment; set of all possible outcomes of an experiment
s	sample standard deviation; number of subjects in a repeated measurements design
s^2	sample variance
$s_{\bar{X}}$	standard error of a sample mean
$s_{\bar{X}}^2$	variance of a sample mean
$s_{\bar{X}_1 - \bar{X}_2}$	standard error of the difference between two sample means
$s_{\bar{X}_1 - \bar{X}_2}^2$	variance of the difference between two sample means
$s_{Y \cdot X}$	standard error of estimate
$s_{Y \cdot X}^2$	residual variance
T	a sum or total
t	a variable with a t distribution; number of trials in a repeated measurements design
t_k	a treatment effect
W	coefficient of concordance
X	a variable
X'	a coded variable
$\bar{X}$	mean of a sample
$\tilde{X}$	predicted value of X
x	deviation of a given value of X from the mean $\bar{X}$
$\tilde{x}$	deviation of $\tilde{X}$ from $\bar{X}$
Y	a variable
Y'	a coded variable
$\bar{Y}$	mean of a sample
$\tilde{Y}$	predicted value of Y
y	deviation of given value of Y from the mean $\bar{Y}$
$\tilde{y}$	deviation of $\tilde{Y}$ from $\bar{Y}$
z	a standard score; a standard normal variable
z'	transformed value of the correlation coefficient

A Review of Some Elementary Mathematical Rules and Principles

Order of Operations and Symbols of Grouping

Rule 1.   Numbers in a series involving only the operation of multiplication or the operation of addition may be multiplied or added in any order without changing the answer. Thus

$$\frac{2 \times 3 \times 4}{2 \times 3} = \frac{24}{6} = 4 \qquad \text{and} \qquad \frac{4 \times 2 \times 3}{3 \times 2} = \frac{24}{6} = 4$$

$$\frac{2 + 3 + 4}{5 + 6} = \frac{9}{11} \qquad \text{and} \qquad \frac{4 + 2 + 3}{6 + 5} = \frac{9}{11}$$

Rule 2.   When the operations of division and multiplication are involved along with the operations of subtraction and addition, the multiplication and division should be performed first. Thus

$$2 + 3 \times 8 = 26$$

$$3 \times 2 - 1 = 5$$

$$4 + \frac{4}{2} = 6$$

$$4 + 8 \times 2 - 2 \times 1 = 18$$

Rule 3.   In order to prevent ambiguity in the operations performed and their order, we make use of symbols of grouping. Parentheses and brackets are commonly used symbols. When symbols of grouping are used, the terms within the symbols should be treated as a single number. Thus

$$(2 + 4) + (8 - 3) + 2(4 + 1) = 6 + 5 + 10 = 21$$

$$(2 + 4)/2 = 6/2 = 3$$

$$(5 + 4)/(2 + 1) = 9/3 = 3$$

$$2[(5 + 4)/(2 + 1)] = (2)(9/3) = 6$$

Rule 4.   When numbers or symbols are enclosed in parentheses or brackets without any intervening signs, the operation of multiplication is indicated.

385

$$(2)(4 + 5) = (2)(9) = 18$$

$$\left[\frac{(2)(2)}{4} + 4\right][(3)(6) - 2] = (5)(16) = 80$$

Rule 5. If a minus sign precedes the parentheses and the parentheses are removed, the sign of every term within the parentheses must be changed. Thus

$$(8 + 2 - 1) - (6 + 4 - 3) = 8 + 2 - 1 - 6 - 4 + 3 = 2$$

Operations with Zero

Rule 1. If we add or subtract zero from any number, the result is the number itself. Thus

$$2 + 0 = 2$$

$$8 - 0 = 8$$

Rule 2. The product of zero and any other number or numbers is equal to zero. Thus

$$(8)(0) = 0$$

$$(8)(4)(0)(2)(1) = 0$$

$$(8)(4) - (6)(0) = 32 - 0 = 32$$

Rule 3. If a is not equal to zero, then $0/a$ is equal to zero, regardless of the value of a.

Rule 4. The use of zero as a divisor is an operation that is not permitted.

Operations with Radicals

A radical is any expression such as $c = \sqrt[n]{a}$. The number c is said to be the nth root of a, the symbol $\sqrt{}$ is called a radical sign, and a is called the radicand. The bar used with the radical sign is a symbol of grouping and means that the complete expression under the bar must be treated as a single number. We shall be concerned only with square roots, that is, where n is equal to 2, and it is customary to write the radical sign without the value of n when this is the case.

The expression $c = \sqrt{a}$ implies that $c^2 = a$, and it is obvious that a has two roots, for $(-c)(-c) = c^2$ and $(c)(c) = c^2$. We shall have occasion to deal with only the principal or positive square root of a, unless otherwise noted.

Rule 1. To multiply two radicals, multiply their radicands. To divide one radical by another, divide the radicand of the first by the radicand of the second. Thus

$$\sqrt{a}\,\sqrt{b} = \sqrt{ab}$$

$$\sqrt{5}\,\sqrt{7} = \sqrt{35}$$

$$\frac{\sqrt{a}}{\sqrt{b}} = \sqrt{\frac{a}{b}}$$

$$\frac{\sqrt{7}}{\sqrt{8}} = \sqrt{\frac{7}{8}}$$

Rule 2. To multiply or divide a radical by any number, multiply or divide the radicand by the square of the number. Thus

$$a\sqrt{b - \frac{c}{d}} = \sqrt{a^2\left(b - \frac{c}{d}\right)} = \sqrt{a^2 b - \frac{a^2 c}{d}}$$

$$5\sqrt{3 - \frac{4}{5}} = \sqrt{25\left(3 - \frac{4}{5}\right)} = \sqrt{75 - 20} = \sqrt{55}$$

$$\frac{\sqrt{a}}{c} = \frac{\sqrt{a}}{\sqrt{c^2}} = \sqrt{\frac{a}{c^2}}$$

$$\frac{\sqrt{3}}{2} = \frac{\sqrt{3}}{\sqrt{2^2}} = \sqrt{\frac{3}{4}}$$

Exponents

If we have n factors each equal to a given number a, where a is not equal to zero, then the product

$$a^n$$

is called the nth power of a. The number n is called the *exponent* and the number a is called the *base*. Thus

$$a^5 = (a)(a)(a)(a)(a)$$

Rule 1. Any number a, not equal to zero, but with zero exponent, is defined as

$$a^0 = 1$$

Then any value of a not equal to zero may also be defined as

Rule 2. $a^{-n} = \dfrac{1}{a^n}$

Rule 3. $a^{1/n} = \sqrt[n]{a}$

Rule 4. $a^{-1/n} = \dfrac{1}{\sqrt[n]{a}}$

Letting a equal 10 and n equal 2, we have for the above three expressions:

$$10^{-2} = \frac{1}{10^2}$$

$$10^{1/2} = \sqrt{10}$$

$$10^{-1/2} = \frac{1}{\sqrt{10}}$$

We also have the following rules for exponents:

Rule 5. $(a^m)(a^n) = a^{m+n}$

Rule 6. $(a^m)^n = a^{mn}$

Rule 7. $(ab)^n = (a^n)(b^n)$

Rule 8. $\left(\dfrac{a}{b}\right)^n = \dfrac{a^n}{b^n}$

Letting $a = 10$, $b = 5$, $m = 3$, and $n = 2$, we have for the above four expressions:

$$(10^3)(10^2) = 10^5$$

$$(10^3)^2 = 10^6$$

$$(10 \times 5)^2 = (10^2)(5^2)$$

$$\left(\frac{10}{5}\right)^2 = \frac{10^2}{5^2}$$

Logarithms

If we have

$$n = b^a$$

then

$$\log_b n = a$$

Thus the logarithm of a number n to the base b is the exponent that must be applied to b to obtain n. If base 10 is used, so that

$$100 = 10^{2.0000}$$

then

$$\log_{10} 100 = 2.0000$$

Logarithms to base 10 are called *common logarithms*, and for common logarithms it is customary to omit the base and simply write $\log 100 = 2.0000$.

The common logarithm of any positive number consists of two parts, an integer called the *characteristic* and a decimal fraction called the *mantissa*. The characteristic depends only upon the position of the decimal point in the number, and the mantissa depends only upon the particular sequence of digits in the number. In the example above, for $\log 100 = 2.0000$, 2 is the characteristic and .0000 is the mantissa.

If a number is larger than 1, the characteristic of its logarithm will be positive and 1 less than the number of digits to the left of the decimal point. If the number is positive, but less than 1, then the characteristic of its logarithm will be negative and 1 more than the number of zeros between the decimal point and the first nonzero digit. Thus

Number	Characteristic of logarithm
1000.	3
100.	2
10.	1
1.	0
.1	-1
.01	-2
.001	-3
.0001	-4

The characteristic of the logarithm of a number can be determined, as shown above, by inspection of the position of the decimal point. The mantissa of the logarithm of a number can be found from a table of logarithms. Table IX, in Appendix B, gives the mantissas of the logarithms of any three-digit number. The first two digits of the number are given in the column headed N, the third digit of the number is given at the top of the table. The mantissa is given in the body of the table. To find $\log 27.7$, we first observe that the characteristic is 1. Then from Table IX we find that the mantissa is .4425. Thus

$$\log 27.7 = 1.4425$$

Note also that $\log 277 = 2.4425$, $\log 2.77 = .4425$, $\log .277 = .4425 - 1$, and log .0277 = .4425 − 2. In the case of negative characteristics, the characteristic is written at the right of the mantissa, with a negative sign attached. It is fairly common practice to add *and* subtract a number from the logarithm so that it becomes a positive number minus 10 or some multiple of 10. For example, if we have

$$a - b = a - b$$

then

$$a - b = n + a - b - n$$

and therefore

$$\log .277 \ = .4425 - 1 = 9.4425 - 10$$

$$\log .0277 = .4425 - 2 = 8.4425 - 10$$

It is possible to find the mantissa of the logarithm of any four-digit positive number from Table IX also. The method of doing this is explained at the bottom of Table IX, and we shall not repeat the explanation here.

Given a logarithm, we can find the *antilogarithm* or number corresponding to it by proceeding in the reverse of the way in which we find a logarithm. For example, to find the antilogarithm of 8.4425 − 10, we see from the table of logarithms that the mantissa .4425 corresponds to the sequence of digits 277. Since the characteristic is 8 − 10, or −2, the number is less than unity and will have one zero between the decimal point and the first figure. Thus antilog 8.4425 − 10 = .0277.

Rule 1.   The logarithm of a product is equal to the sum of the logarithms of the numbers multiplied. For example, to find the product of *a* and *b*, we find the logarithm of *a* and the logarithm of *b* and sum the logarithms. The antilogarithm of the sum will be the product. Thus

$$a = bc$$

and

$$\log a = \log b + \log c$$

Letting *b* = 3 and *c* = 4, then

$$a = (3)(4)$$

$$\log a = \log 3 + \log 4$$

$$= .4771 + .6021$$

$$= 1.0792$$

and antilog 1.0792 = 12.

Rule 2.   The logarithm of the quotient of two numbers is equal to the logarithm of the numerator minus the logarithm of the denominator. For example, to divide one number by another, we find the logarithm of the numerator and subtract from this the logarithm of the denominator. The antilogarithm of the remainder will be the quotient. Thus

$$a = \frac{b}{c}$$

and

$$\log a = \log b - \log c$$

Letting $b = 12$ and $c = 3$, then

$$a = \frac{12}{3}$$

$$\log a = \log 12 - \log 3$$

$$= 1.0792 - .4771$$

$$= .6021$$

and antilog $.6021 = 4$.

Rule 3.   The logarithm of the power of a number is equal to the product of the exponent and the logarithm of the number. For example, to find the square of a number, we find the logarithm of the number and multiply this by the exponent 2. Then the antilogarithm of the product will be the square of the number. Thus

$$a = b^n$$

and

$$\log a = n \log b$$

Letting $b = 3$ and $n = 2$, then

$$a = 3^2$$

$$\log a = 2 \log 3$$

$$= 2(.4771)$$

$$= .9542$$

and antilog $.9542 = 9$.

Summation

If we have n values of a variable X, then the sum of the n values is indicated by

$$\sum_1^n X = X_1 + X_2 + X_3 + \cdots + X_n$$

Let $n = 3$ with $X_1 = 4$, $X_2 = 6$, and $X_3 = 5$. Then

$$\sum_1^n X = 4 + 6 + 5 = 15$$

Let X be one variable and Y be another variable such that with each value of X there is a paired value of Y. Then, if we have n such paired values,

$$\sum_1^n (X + Y) = (X_1 + Y_1) + (X_2 + Y_2) + \cdots + (X_n + Y_n)$$

$$= (X_1 + X_2 + \cdots + X_n) + (Y_1 + Y_2 + \cdots + Y_n)$$

$$= \sum_1^n X + \sum_1^n Y$$

With $X_1 = 4$, $X_2 = 6$, $X_3 = 5$, and with $Y_1 = 2$, $Y_2 = 3$, $Y_3 = 7$, we have

$$\sum_1^n (X + Y) = (4 + 2) + (6 + 3) + (5 + 7)$$

$$= (4 + 6 + 5) + (2 + 3 + 7)$$

$$= 15 + 12$$

Similarly,

$$\sum_1^n (X - Y) = \sum_1^n X - \sum_1^n Y$$

or, for the same example,

$$\sum_1^n (X - Y) = (4 - 2) + (6 - 3) + (5 - 7)$$

$$= (4 + 6 + 5) - (2 + 3 + 7)$$

$$= 15 - 12$$

If we replace Y by a constant a that is to be added to each value of X, then, obviously,

$$\sum_1^n (X + a) = \sum_1^n X + na$$

and, similarly,

$$\sum_1^n (X - a) = \sum_1^n X - na$$

For example, if $X_1 = 4$, $X_2 = 6$, and $X_3 = 5$ and if $a = 10$, then

$$\sum_1^n (X + a) = (4 + 10) + (6 + 10) + (5 + 10)$$

$$= (4 + 6 + 5) + (10 + 10 + 10)$$
$$= 15 + 3(10)$$

and

$$\sum_1^n (X - a) = 15 - 3(10)$$

If each value of X is multiplied by a constant a, then

$$\sum_1^n aX = a\sum_1^n X$$

For the same $n = 3$ values of X and with $a = 10$, we have

$$\sum_1^n aX = 10(4) + 10(6) + 10(5)$$

$$= 10(4 + 6 + 5)$$

Similarly,

$$\sum_1^n \frac{X}{a} = \frac{1}{a}\sum_1^n X$$

or, for the same example,

$$\sum_1^n \frac{X}{a} = \frac{4}{10} + \frac{6}{10} + \frac{5}{10}$$

$$= \frac{1}{10}(4 + 6 + 5)$$

Equations

In performing operations upon equations there is one simple rule: whatever is done to one side of the equation must also be done to the other side. If you multiply one side by a number or symbol, then you must also multiply the other side by the same number or symbol. The same rule applies to division, addition, subtraction, squaring, and taking the square root. The following examples illustrate this rule:

1. If $a = bc$ then dividing both sides by b $\dfrac{a}{b} = c$

2. If $a = b + c$ then subtracting b from both sides $a - b = c$

3. If $a = b + c$ then squaring both sides
$$a^2 = (b + c)^2$$
$$= b^2 + 2bc + c^2$$

4. If $a = b - c$.   then squaring both sides
$$a^2 = (b - c)^2$$
$$= b^2 - 2bc + c^2$$

5. If $a = b - c$ then adding c to both sides $a + c = b$

6. If $a = b + c$ then multiplying both sides by d
$$da = d(b + c)$$
$$= db + dc$$

7. If $a^2 = \dfrac{b}{c}$ then taking the square root of both sides $a = \sqrt{\dfrac{b}{c}}$

8. If $a = b + c$ then dividing both side by b
$$\frac{a}{b} = \frac{b + c}{b}$$
$$= \frac{b}{b} + \frac{c}{b}$$
$$= 1 + \frac{c}{b}$$

9. If $a + b = c + d$ then dividing both sides by n $\dfrac{a + b}{n} = \dfrac{c + d}{n}$

10. If $-a - b = c - d$ then multiplying both sides by -1 $a + b = -c + d$

Tables

TABLE I. *Table of Random Numbers**

COLUMN NUMBER

Row	00000 01234	00000 56789	11111 01234	11111 56789	22222 01234	22222 56789	33333 01234	33333 56789
				1st Thousand				
00	23157	54859	01837	25993	76249	70886	95230	36744
01	05545	55043	10537	43508	90611	83744	10962	21343
02	14871	60350	32404	36223	50051	00322	11543	80834
03	38976	74951	94051	75853	78805	90194	32428	71695
04	97312	61718	99755	30870	94251	25841	54882	10513
05	11742	69381	44339	30872	32797	33118	22647	06850
06	43361	28859	11016	45623	93009	00499	43640	74036
07	93806	20478	38268	04491	55751	18932	58475	52571
08	49540	13181	08429	84187	69538	29661	77738	09527
09	36768	72633	37948	21569	41959	68670	45274	83880
10	07092	52392	24627	12067	06558	45344	67338	45320
11	43310	01081	44863	80307	52555	16148	89742	94647
12	61570	06360	06173	63775	63148	95123	35017	46993
13	31352	83799	10779	18941	31579	76448	62584	86919
14	57048	86526	27795	93692	90529	56546	35065	32254
15	09243	44200	68721	07137	30729	75756	09298	27650
16	97957	35018	40894	88329	52230	82521	22532	61587
17	93732	59570	43781	98885	56671	66826	95996	44569
18	72621	11225	00922	68264	35666	59434	71687	58167
19	61020	74418	45371	20794	95917	37866	99536	19378
20	97839	85474	33055	91718	45473	54144	22034	23000
21	89160	97192	22232	90637	35055	45489	88438	16361
22	25966	88220	62871	79265	02823	52862	84919	54883
23	81443	31719	05049	54806	74690	07567	65017	16543
24	11322	54931	42362	34386	08624	97687	46245	23245

* Table I is reproduced from M. G. Kendall and B. B. Smith. Randomness and random sampling numbers. *J. R. statist. Soc.*, **101** (1938), 147–166, by permission of the Royal Statistical Society.

TABLE I. *Table of Random Numbers*—*Continued*

Row	00000 01234	00000 56789	11111 01234	11111 56789	22222 01234	22222 56789	33333 01234	33333 56789
					Column Number			
				2nd Thousand				
00	64755	83885	84122	25920	17696	15655	95045	95947
01	10302	52289	77436	34430	38112	49067	07348	23328
02	71017	98495	51308	50374	66591	02887	53765	69149
03	60012	55605	88410	34879	79655	90169	78800	03366
04	37330	94656	49161	42802	48274	54755	44553	65090
05	47869	87001	31591	12273	60626	12822	34691	61212
06	38040	42737	64167	89578	39323	49324	88434	38706
07	73508	30908	83054	80078	86669	30295	56460	45336
08	32623	46474	84061	04324	20628	37319	32356	43969
09	97591	99549	36630	35106	62069	92975	95320	57734
10	74012	31955	59790	96982	66224	24015	96749	07589
11	56754	26457	13351	05014	90966	33674	69096	33488
12	49800	49908	54831	21998	08528	26372	92923	65026
13	43584	89647	24878	56670	00221	50193	99591	62377
14	16653	79664	60325	71301	35742	83636	73058	87229
15	48502	69055	65322	58748	31446	80237	31252	96367
16	96765	54692	36316	86230	48296	38352	23816	64094
17	38923	61550	80357	81784	23444	12463	33992	28128
18	77958	81694	25225	05587	51073	01070	60218	61961
19	17928	28065	25586	08771	02641	85064	65796	48170
20	94036	85978	02318	04499	41054	10531	87431	21596
21	47460	60479	56230	48417	14372	85167	27558	00368
22	47856	56088	51992	82439	40644	17170	13463	18288
23	57616	34653	92298	62018	10375	76515	62986	90756
24	08300	92704	66752	66610	57188	79107	54222	22013

* Table I is reproduced from M. G. Kendall and B. B. Smith. Randomness and random sampling numbers. *J. R. statist. Soc.*, **101** (1938), 147–166, by permission of the Royal Statistical Society.

TABLE I. Table of Random Numbers*—Continued

COLUMN NUMBER

3rd Thousand

Row	00000 01234	00000 56789	11111 01234	11111 56789	22222 01234	22222 56789	33333 01234	33333 56789
00	89221	02362	65787	74733	51272	30213	92441	39651
01	04005	99818	63918	29032	94012	42363	01261	10650
02	98546	38066	50856	75045	40645	22841	53254	44125
03	41719	84401	59226	01314	54581	40398	49988	65579
04	28733	72489	00785	25843	24613	49797	85567	84471
05	65213	83927	77762	03086	80742	24395	68476	83792
06	65553	12678	90906	90466	43670	26217	69900	31205
07	05668	69080	73029	85746	58332	78231	45986	92998
08	39302	99718	49757	79519	27387	76373	47262	91612
09	64592	32254	45879	29431	38320	05981	18067	87137
10	07513	48792	47314	83660	68907	05336	82579	91582
11	86593	68501	56638	99800	82839	35148	56541	07232
12	83735	22599	97977	81248	36838	99560	32410	67614
13	08595	21826	54655	08204	87990	17033	56258	05384
14	41273	27149	44293	69458	16828	63962	15864	35431
15	00473	75908	56238	12242	72631	76314	47252	06347
16	86131	53789	81383	07868	89132	96182	07009	86432
17	33849	78359	08402	03586	03176	88663	08018	22546
18	61870	41657	07468	08612	98083	97349	20775	45091
19	43898	65923	25078	86129	78491	97653	91500	80786
20	29939	39123	04548	45985	60952	06641	28726	46473
21	38505	85555	14388	55077	18657	94887	67831	70819
22	31824	38431	67125	25511	72044	11562	53279	82268
23	91430	03767	13561	15597	06750	92552	02391	38753
24	38635	68976	25498	97526	96458	03805	04116	63514

* Table I is reproduced from M. G. Kendall and B. B. Smith. Randomness and random sampling numbers. *J. R. statist. Soc.*, **101** (1938), 147–166, by permission of the Royal Statistical Society.

TABLE I. *Table of Random Numbers*—*Continued*

Row	COLUMN NUMBER							
	00000 01234	00000 56789	11111 01234	11111 56789	22222 01234	22222 56789	33333 01234	33333 56789
				4th Thousand				
00	02490	54122	27944	39364	94239	72074	11679	54082
01	11967	36469	60627	83701	09253	30208	01385	37482
02	48256	83465	49699	24079	05403	35154	39613	03136
03	27246	73080	21481	23536	04881	89977	49484	93071
04	32532	77265	72430	70722	86529	18457	92657	10011
05	66757	98955	92375	93431	43204	55825	45443	69265
06	11266	34545	76505	97746	34668	26999	26742	97516
07	17872	39142	45561	80146	93137	48924	64257	59284
08	62561	30365	03408	14754	51798	08133	61010	97730
09	62796	30779	35497	70501	30105	08133	00997	91970
10	75510	21771	04339	33660	42757	62223	87565	48468
11	87439	01691	63517	26590	44437	07217	98706	39032
12	97742	02621	10748	78803	38337	65226	92149	59051
13	98811	06001	21571	02875	21828	83912	85188	61624
14	51264	01852	64607	92553	29004	26695	78583	62998
15	40239	93376	10419	68610	49120	02941	80035	99317
16	26936	59186	51667	27645	46329	44681	94190	66647
17	88502	11716	98299	40974	42394	62200	69094	81646
18	63499	38093	25593	61995	79867	80569	01023	38374
19	36379	81206	03317	78710	73828	31083	60509	44091
20	93801	22322	47479	57017	59334	30647	43061	26660
21	29856	87120	56311	50053	25365	81265	22414	02431
22	97720	87931	88265	13050	71017	15177	06957	92919
23	85237	09105	74601	46377	59938	15647	34177	92753
24	75746	75268	31727	95773	72364	87324	36879	06802

* Table I is reproduced from M. G. Kendall and B. B. Smith. Randomness and random sampling numbers. *J. R. statist. Soc.,* **101** (1938), 147-166, by permission of the Royal Statistical Society.

TABLE I. Table of Random Numbers*—Concluded

COLUMN NUMBER

Row	00000 01234	00000 56789	11111 01234	11111 56789	22222 01234	22222 56789	33333 01234	33333 56789
				5th Thousand				
00	29935	06971	63175	52579	10478	89379	61428	21363
01	15114	07126	51890	77787	75510	13103	42942	48111
02	03870	43225	10589	87629	22039	94124	38127	65022
03	79390	39188	40756	45269	65959	20640	14284	22960
04	30035	06915	79196	54428	64819	52314	48721	81594
05	29039	99861	28759	79802	68531	39198	38137	24373
06	78196	08108	24107	49777	09599	43569	84820	94956
07	15847	85493	91442	91351	80130	73752	21539	10986
08	36614	62248	49194	97209	92587	92053	41021	80064
09	40549	54884	91465	43862	35541	44466	88894	74180
10	40878	08997	14286	09982	90308	78007	51587	16658
11	10229	49282	41173	31468	59455	18756	08908	06660
12	15918	76787	30624	25928	44124	25088	31137	71614
13	13403	18796	49909	94404	64979	41462	18155	98335
14	66523	94596	74908	90271	10009	98648	17640	68909
15	91665	36469	68343	17870	25975	04662	21272	50620
16	67415	87515	08207	73729	73201	57593	96917	69699
17	76527	96996	23724	33448	63392	32394	60887	90617
18	19815	47789	74348	17147	10954	34355	81194	54407
19	25592	53587	76384	72575	84347	68918	05739	57222
20	55902	45539	63646	31609	95999	82887	40666	66692
21	02470	58376	79794	22482	42423	96162	47491	17264
22	18630	53263	13319	97619	35859	12350	14632	87659
23	89673	38230	16063	92007	59503	38402	76450	33333
24	62986	67364	06595	17427	84623	14565	82860	57300

* Table I is reproduced from M. G. Kendall and B. B. Smith. Randomness and random sampling numbers. J. R. statist. Soc., 101 (1938), 147–166, by permission of the Royal Statistical Society.

TABLE II. *Table of Squares, Square Roots, and Reciprocals*
of Numbers from 1 to 1000*

N	N^2	$\sqrt{N}$	$1/N$	N	N^2	$\sqrt{N}$	$1/N$
1	1	1.0000	1.000000	41	1681	6.4031	.024390
2	4	1.4142	.500000	42	1764	6.4807	.023810
3	9	1.7321	.333333	43	1849	6.5574	.023256
4	16	2.0000	.250000	44	1936	6.6332	.022727
5	25	2.2361	.200000	45	2025	6.7082	.022222
6	36	2.4495	.166667	46	2116	6.7823	.021739
7	49	2.6458	.142857	47	2209	6.8557	.021277
8	64	2.8284	.125000	48	2304	6.9282	.020833
9	81	3.0000	.111111	49	2401	7.0000	.020408
10	100	3.1623	.100000	50	2500	7.0711	.020000
11	121	3.3166	.090909	51	2601	7.1414	.019608
12	144	3.4641	.083333	52	2704	7.2111	.019231
13	169	3.6056	.076923	53	2809	7.2801	.018868
14	196	3.7417	.071429	54	2916	7.3485	.018519
15	225	3.8730	.066667	55	3025	7.4162	.018182
16	256	4.0000	.062500	56	3136	7.4833	.017857
17	289	4.1231	.058824	57	3249	7.5498	.017544
18	324	4.2426	.055556	58	3364	7.6158	.017241
19	361	4.3589	.052632	59	3481	7.6811	.016949
20	400	4.4721	.050000	60	3600	7.7460	.016667
21	441	4.5826	.047619	61	3721	7.8102	.016393
22	484	4.6904	.045455	62	3844	7.8740	.016129
23	529	4.7958	.043478	63	3969	7.9373	.015873
24	576	4.8990	.041667	64	4096	8.0000	.015625
25	625	5.0000	.040000	65	4225	8.0623	.015385
26	676	5.0990	.038462	66	4356	8.1240	.015152
27	729	5.1962	.037037	67	4489	8.1854	.014925
28	784	5.2915	.035714	68	4624	8.2462	.014706
29	841	5.3852	.034483	69	4761	8.3066	.014493
30	900	5.4772	.033333	70	4900	8.3666	.014286
31	961	5.5678	.032258	71	5041	8.4261	.014085
32	1024	5.6569	.031250	72	5184	8.4853	.013889
33	1089	5.7446	.030303	73	5329	8.5440	.013699
34	1156	5.8310	.029412	74	5476	8.6023	.013514
35	1225	5.9161	.028571	75	5625	8.6603	.013333
36	1296	6.0000	.027778	76	5776	8.7178	.013158
37	1369	6.0828	.027027	77	5929	8.7750	.012987
38	1444	6.1644	.026316	78	6084	8.8318	.012821
39	1521	6.2450	.025641	79	6241	8.8882	.012658
40	1600	6.3246	.025000	80	6400	8.9443	.012500

* Portions of Table II have been reproduced from J. W. Dunlap and A. K. Kurtz, *Handbook of Statistical Nomographs, Tables, and Formulas*, World Book Company, New York (1932), by permission of the authors and publishers.

TABLE II. *Table of Squares, Square Roots, and Reciprocals*
of Numbers from 1 to 1000—Continued*

N	N^2	$\sqrt{N}$	$1/N$	N	N^2	$\sqrt{N}$	$1/N$
81	6561	9.0000	.012346	121	14641	11.0000	.00826446
82	6724	9.0554	.012195	122	14884	11.0454	.00819672
83	6889	9.1104	.012048	123	15129	11.0905	.00813008
84	7056	9.1652	.011905	124	15376	11.1355	.00806452
85	7225	9.2195	.011765	125	15625	11.1803	.00800000
86	7396	9.2736	.011628	126	15876	11.2250	.00793651
87	7569	9.3274	.011494	127	16129	11.2694	.00787402
88	7744	9.3808	.011364	128	16384	11.3137	.00781250
89	7921	9.4340	.011236	129	16641	11.3578	.00775194
90	8100	9.4868	.011111	130	16900	11.4018	.00769231
91	8281	9.5394	.010989	131	17161	11.4455	.00763359
92	8464	9.5917	.010870	132	17424	11.4891	.00757576
93	8649	9.6437	.010753	133	17689	11.5326	.00751880
94	8836	9.6954	.010638	134	17956	11.5758	.00746269
95	9025	9.7468	.010526	135	18225	11.6190	.00740741
96	9216	9.7980	.010417	136	18496	11.6619	.00735294
97	9409	9.8489	.010309	137	18769	11.7047	.00729927
98	9604	9.8995	.010204	138	19044	11.7473	.00724638
99	9801	9.9499	.010101	139	19321	11.7898	.00719424
100	10000	10.0000	.010000	140	19600	11.8322	.00714286
101	10201	10.0499	.00990099	141	19881	11.8743	.00709220
102	10404	10.0995	.00980392	142	20164	11.9164	.00704225
103	10609	10.1489	.00970874	143	20449	11.9583	.00699301
104	10816	10.1980	.00961538	144	20736	12.0000	.00694444
105	11025	10.2470	.00952381	145	21025	12.0416	.00689655
106	11236	10.2956	.00943396	146	21316	12.0830	.00684932
107	11449	10.3441	.00934579	147	21609	12.1244	.00680272
108	11664	10.3923	.00925926	148	21904	12.1655	.00675676
109	11881	10.4403	.00917431	149	22201	12.2066	.00671141
110	12100	10.4881	.00909091	150	22500	12.2474	.00666667
111	12321	10.5357	.00900901	151	22801	12.2882	.00662252
112	12544	10.5830	.00892857	152	23104	12.3288	.00657895
113	12769	10.6301	.00884956	153	23409	12.3693	.00653595
114	12996	10.6771	.00877193	154	23716	12.4097	.00649351
115	13225	10.7238	.00869565	155	24025	12.4499	.00645161
116	13456	10.7703	.00862069	156	24336	12.4900	.00641026
117	13689	10.8167	.00854701	157	24649	12.5300	.00636943
118	13924	10.8628	.00847458	158	24964	12.5698	.00632911
119	14161	10.9087	.00840336	159	25281	12.6095	.00628931
120	14400	10.9545	.00833333	160	25600	12.6491	.00625000

* Portions of Table II have been reproduced from J. W. Dunlap and A. K. Kurtz. *Handbook of Statistical Nomographs, Tables, and Formulas,* World Book Company, New York (1932), by permission of the authors and publishers.

TABLE II. *Table of Squares, Square Roots, and Reciprocals of Numbers from 1 to 1000*—Continued*

N	N^2	$\sqrt{N}$	$1/N$	N	N^2	$\sqrt{N}$	$1/N$
161	25921	12.6886	.00621118	201	40401	14.1774	.00497512
162	26244	12.7279	.00617284	202	40804	14.2127	.00495050
163	26569	12.7671	.00613497	203	41209	14.2478	.00492611
164	26896	12.8062	.00609756	204	41616	14.2829	.00490196
165	27225	12.8452	.00606061	205	42025	14.3178	.00487805
166	27556	12.8841	.00602410	206	42436	14.3527	.00485437
167	27889	12.9228	.00598802	207	42849	14.3875	.00483092
168	28224	12.9615	.00595238	208	43264	14.4222	.00480769
169	28561	13.0000	.00591716	209	43681	14.4568	.00478469
170	28900	13.0384	.00588235	210	44100	14.4914	.00476190
171	29241	13.0767	.00584795	211	44521	14.5258	.00473934
172	29584	13.1149	.00581395	212	44944	14.5602	.00471698
173	29929	13.1529	.00578035	213	45369	14.5945	.00469484
174	30276	13.1909	.00574713	214	45796	14.6287	.00467290
175	30625	13.2288	.00571429	215	46225	14.6629	.00465116
176	30976	13.2665	.00568182	216	46656	14.6969	.00462963
177	31329	13.3041	.00564972	217	47089	14.7309	.00460829
178	31684	13.3417	.00561798	218	47524	14.7648	.00458716
179	32041	13.3791	.00558659	219	47961	14.7986	.00456621
180	32400	13.4164	.00555556	220	48400	14.8324	.00454545
181	32761	13.4536	.00552486	221	48841	14.8661	.00452489
182	33124	13.4907	.00549451	222	49284	14.8997	.00450450
183	33489	13.5277	.00546448	223	49729	14.9332	.00448430
184	33856	13.5647	.00543478	224	50176	14.9666	.00446429
185	34225	13.6015	.00540541	225	50625	15.0000	.00444444
186	34596	13.6382	.00537634	226	51076	15.0333	.00442478
187	34969	13.6748	.00534759	227	51529	15.0665	.00440529
188	35344	13.7113	.00531915	228	51984	15.0997	.00438596
189	35721	13.7477	.00529101	229	52441	15.1327	.00436681
190	36100	13.7840	.00526316	230	52900	15.1658	.00434783
191	36481	13.8203	.00523560	231	53361	15.1987	.00432900
192	36864	13.8564	.00520833	232	53824	15.2315	.00431034
193	37249	13.8924	.00518135	233	54289	15.2643	.00429185
194	37636	13.9284	.00515464	234	54756	15.2971	.00427350
195	38025	13.9642	.00512821	235	55225	15.3297	.00425532
196	38416	14.0000	.00510204	236	55696	15.3623	.00423729
197	38809	14.0357	.00507614	237	56169	15.3948	.00421941
198	39204	14.0712	.00505051	238	56644	15.4272	.00420168
199	39601	14.1067	.00502513	239	57121	15.4596	.00418410
200	40000	14.1421	.00500000	240	57600	15.4919	.00416667

* Portions of Table II have been reproduced from J. W. Dunlap and A. K. Kurtz. *Handbook of Statistical Nomographs, Tables, and Formulas,* World Book Company, New York (1932), by permission of the authors and publishers.

TABLE II. *Table of Squares, Square Roots, and Reciprocals of Numbers from 1 to 1000*—Continued*

N	N^2	$\sqrt{N}$	$1/N$	N	N^2	$\sqrt{N}$	$1/N$
241	58081	15.5242	.00414938	281	78961	16.7631	.00355872
242	58564	15.5563	.00413223	282	79524	16.7929	.00354610
243	59049	15.5885	.00411523	283	80089	16.8226	.00353357
244	59536	15.6205	.00409836	284	80656	16.8523	.00352113
245	60025	15.6525	.00408163	285	81225	16.8819	.00350877
246	60516	15.6844	.00406504	286	81796	16.9115	.00349650
247	61009	15.7162	.00404858	287	82369	16.9411	.00348432
248	61504	15.7480	.00403226	288	82944	16.9706	.00347222
249	62001	15.7797	.00401606	289	83521	17.0000	.00346021
250	62500	15.8114	.00400000	290	84100	17 0294	.00344828
251	63001	15.8430	.00398406	291	84681	17.0587	.00343643
252	63504	15.8745	.00396825	292	85264	17.0880	.00342466
253	64009	15.9060	.00395257	293	85849	17.1172	.00341297
254	64516	15.9374	.00393701	294	86436	17.1464	.00340136
255	65025	15.9687	.00392157	295	87025	17.1756	.00338983
256	65536	16.0000	.00390625	296	87616	17.2047	.00337838
257	66049	16.0312	.00389105	297	88209	17.2337	.00336700
258	66564	16.0624	.00387597	298	88804	17.2627	.00335570
259	67081	16.0935	.00386100	299	89401	17.2916	.00334448
260	67600	16.1245	.00384615	300	90000	17.3205	.00333333
261	68121	16.1555	.00383142	301	90601	17.3494	.00332226
262	68644	16.1864	.00381679	302	91204	17.3781	.00331126
263	69169	16.2173	.00380228	303	91809	17.4069	.00330033
264	69696	16.2481	.00378788	304	92416	17.4356	.00328947
265	70225	16.2788	.00377358	305	93025	17.4642	.00327869
266	70756	16.3095	.00375940	306	93636	17.4929	.00326797
267	71289	16.3401	.00374532	307	94249	17.5214	.00325733
268	71824	16.3707	.00373134	308	94864	17.5499	.00324675
269	72361	16.4012	.00371747	309	95481	17.5784	.00323625
270	72900	16.4317	.00370370	310	96100	17.6068	.00322581
271	73441	16.4621	.00369004	311	96721	17.6352	.00321543
272	73984	16.4924	.00367647	312	97344	17.6635	.00320513
273	74529	16.5227	.00366300	313	97969	17.6918	.00319489
274	75076	16.5529	.00364964	314	98596	17.7200	.00318471
275	75625	16.5831	.00363636	315	99225	17.7482	.00317460
276	76176	16.6132	.00362319	316	99856	17.7764	.00316456
277	76729	16.6433	.00361011	317	100489	17.8045	.00315457
278	77284	16.6733	.00359712	318	101124	17.8326	.00314465
279	77841	16.7033	.00358423	319	101761	17.8606	.00313480
280	78400	16.7332	.00357143	320	102400	17.8885	.00312500

* Portions of Table II have been reproduced from J. W. Dunlap and A. K. Kurtz. *Handbook of Statistical Nomographs, Tables, and Formulas,* World Book Company, New York (1932), by permission of the authors and publishers.

TABLE II. *Table of Squares, Square Roots, and Reciprocals of Numbers from 1 to 1000*—Continued*

N	N^2	$\sqrt{N}$	$1/N$	N	N^2	$\sqrt{N}$	$1/N$
321	103041	17.9165	.00311526	361	130321	19.0000	.00277008
322	103684	17.9444	.00310559	362	131044	19.0263	.00276243
323	104329	17.9722	.00309598	363	131769	19.0526	.00275482
324	104976	18.0000	.00308642	364	132496	19.0788	.00274725
325	105625	18.0278	.00307692	365	133225	19.1050	.00273973
326	106276	18.0555	.00306748	366	133956	19.1311	.00273224
327	106929	18.0831	.00305810	367	134689	19.1572	.00272480
328	107584	18.1108	.00304878	368	135424	19.1833	.00271739
329	108241	18.1384	.00303951	369	136161	19.2094	.00271003
330	108900	18.1659	.00303030	370	136900	19.2354	.00270270
331	109561	18.1934	.00302115	371	137641	19.2614	.00269542
332	110224	18.2209	.00301205	372	138384	19.2873	.00268817
333	110889	18.2483	.00300300	373	139129	19.3132	.00268097
334	111556	18.2757	.00299401	374	139876	19.3391	.00267380
335	112225	18.3030	.00298507	375	140625	19.3649	.00266667
336	112896	18.3303	.00297619	376	141376	19.3907	.00265957
337	113569	18.3576	.00296736	377	142129	19.4165	.00265252
338	114244	18.3848	.00295858	378	142884	19.4422	.00264550
339	114921	18.4120	.00294985	379	143641	19.4679	.00263852
340	115600	18.4391	.00294118	380	144400	19.4936	.00263158
341	116281	18.4662	.00293255	381	145161	19.5192	.00262467
342	116964	18.4932	.00292398	382	145924	19.5448	.00261780
343	117649	18.5203	.00291545	383	146689	19.5704	.00261097
344	118336	18.5472	.00290698	384	147456	19.5959	.00260417
345	119025	18.5742	.00289855	385	148225	19.6214	.00259740
346	119716	18.6011	.00289017	386	148996	19.6469	.00259067
347	120409	18.6279	.00288184	387	149769	19.6723	.00258398
348	121104	18.6548	.00287356	388	150544	19.6977	.00257732
349	121801	18.6815	.00286533	389	151321	19.7231	.00257069
350	122500	18.7083	.00285714	390	152100	19.7484	.00256410
351	123201	18.7350	.00284900	391	152881	19.7737	.00255754
352	123904	18.7617	.00284091	392	153664	19.7990	.00255102
353	124609	18.7883	.00283286	393	154449	19.8242	.00254453
354	125316	18.8149	.00282486	394	155236	19.8494	.00253807
355	126025	18.8414	.00281690	395	156025	19.8746	.00253165
356	126736	18.8680	.00280899	396	156816	19.8997	.00252525
357	127449	18.8944	.00280112	397	157609	19.9249	.00251889
358	128164	18.9209	.00279330	398	158404	19.9499	.00251256
359	128881	18.9473	.00278552	399	159201	19.9750	.00250627
360	129000	18.9737	.00277778	400	160000	20.0000	.00250000

* Portions of Table II have been reproduced from J. W. Dunlap and A. K. Kurtz. *Handbook of Statistical Nomographs, Tables, and Formulas*, World Book Company, New York (1932), by permission of the authors and publishers.

TABLE II. *Table of Squares, Square Roots, and Reciprocals of Numbers from 1 to 1000*—Continued*

N	N²	√N	1/N	N	N²	√N	1/N
401	160801	20.0250	.00249377	441	194481	21.0000	.00226757
402	161604	20.0499	.00248756	442	195364	21.0238	.00226244
403	162409	20.0749	.00248139	443	196249	21.0476	.00225734
404	163216	20.0998	.00247525	444	197136	21.0713	.00225225
405	164025	20.1246	.00246914	445	198025	21.0950	.00224719
406	164836	20.1494	.00246305	446	198916	21.1187	.00224215
407	165649	20.1742	.00245700	447	199809	21.1424	.00223714
408	166464	20.1990	.00245098	448	200704	21.1660	.00223214
409	167281	20.2237	.00244499	449	201601	21.1896	.00222717
410	168100	20.2485	.00243902	450	202500	21.2132	.00222222
411	168921	20.2731	.00243309	451	203401	21.2368	.00221729
412	169744	20.2978	.00242718	452	204304	21.2603	.00221239
413	170569	20.3224	.00242131	453	205209	21.2838	.00220751
414	171396	20.3470	.00241546	454	206116	21.3073	.00220264
415	172225	20.3715	.00240964	455	207025	21.3307	.00219780
416	173056	20.3961	.00240385	456	207936	21.3542	.00219298
417	173889	20.4206	.00239808	457	208849	21.3776	.00218818
418	174724	20.4450	.00239234	458	209764	21.4009	.00218341
419	175561	20.4695	.00238663	459	210681	21.4243	.00217865
420	176400	20.4939	.00238095	460	211600	21.4476	.00217391
421	177241	20.5183	.00237530	461	212521	21.4709	.00216920
422	178084	20.5426	.00236967	462	213444	21.4942	.00216450
423	178929	20.5670	.00236407	463	214369	21.5174	.00215983
424	179776	20.5913	.00235849	464	215296	21.5407	.00215517
425	180625	20.6155	.00235294	465	216225	21.5639	.00215054
426	181476	20.6398	.00234742	466	217156	21.5870	.00214592
427	182329	20.6640	.00234192	467	218089	21.6102	.00214133
428	183184	20.6882	.00233645	468	219024	21.6333	.00213675
429	184041	20.7123	.00233100	469	219961	21.6564	.00213220
430	184900	20.7364	.00232558	470	220900	21.6795	.00212766
431	185761	20.7605	.00232019	471	221841	21.7025	.00212314
432	186624	20.7846	.00231481	472	222784	21.7256	.00211864
433	187489	20.8087	.00230947	473	223729	21.7486	.00211416
434	188356	20.8327	.00230415	474	224676	21.7715	.00210970
435	189225	20.8567	.00229885	475	225625	21.7945	.00210526
436	190096	20.8806	.00229358	476	226576	21.8174	.00210084
437	190969	20.9045	.00228833	477	227529	21.8403	.00209644
438	191844	20.9284	.00228311	478	228484	21.8632	.00209205
439	192721	20.9523	.00227790	479	229441	21.8861	.00208768
440	193600	20.9762	.00227273	480	230400	21.9089	.00208333

* Portions of Table II have been reproduced from J. W. Dunlap and A. K. Kurtz. *Handbook of Statistical Nomographs, Tables, and Formulas,* World Book Company, New York (1932), by permission of the authors and publishers.

TABLE II. *Table of Squares, Square Roots, and Reciprocals*
of Numbers from 1 to 1000*—Continued

N	N²	√N	1/N	N	N²	√N	1/N
481	231361	21.9317	.00207900	521	271441	22.8254	.00191939
482	232324	21.9545	.00207469	522	272484	22.8473	.00191571
483	233289	21.9773	.00207039	523	273529	22.8692	.00191205
484	234256	22.0000	.00206612	524	274576	22.8910	.00190840
485	235225	22.0227	.00206186	525	275625	22.9129	.00190476
486	236196	22.0454	.00205761	526	276676	22.9347	.00190114
487	237169	22.0681	.00205339	527	277729	22.9565	.00189753
488	238144	22.0907	.00204918	528	278784	22.9783	.00189394
489	239121	22.1133	.00204499	529	279841	23.0000	.00189036
490	240100	22.1359	.00204082	530	280900	23.0217	.00188679
491	241081	22.1585	.00203666	531	281961	23.0434	.00188324
492	242064	22.1811	.00203252	532	283024	23.0651	.00187970
493	243049	22.2036	.00202840	533	284089	23.0868	.00187617
494	244036	22.2261	.00202429	534	285156	23.1084	.00187266
495	245025	22.2486	.00202020	535	286225	23.1301	.00186916
496	246016	22.2711	.00201613	536	287296	23.1517	.00186567
497	247009	22.2935	.00201207	537	288369	23.1733	.00186220
498	248004	22.3159	.00200803	538	289444	23.1948	.00185874
499	249001	22.3383	.00200401	539	290521	23.2164	.00185529
500	250000	22.3607	.00200000	540	291600	23.2379	.00185185
501	251001	22.3830	.00199601	541	292681	23.2594	.00184843
502	252004	22.4054	.00199203	542	293764	23.2809	.00184502
503	253009	22.4277	.00198807	543	294849	23.3024	.00184162
504	254016	22.4499	.00198413	544	295936	23.3238	.00183824
505	255025	22.4722	.00198020	545	297025	23.3452	.00183486
506	256036	22.4944	.00197628	546	298116	23.3666	.00183150
507	257049	22.5167	.00197239	547	299209	23.3880	.00182815
508	258064	22.5389	.00196850	548	300304	23.4094	.00182482
509	259081	22.5610	.00196464	549	301401	23.4307	.00182149
510	260100	22.5832	.00196078	550	302500	23.4521	.00181818
511	261121	22.6053	.00195695	551	303601	23.4734	.00181488
512	262144	22.6274	.00195312	552	304704	23.4947	.00181159
513	263169	22.6495	.00194932	553	305809	23.5160	.00180832
514	264196	22.6716	.00194553	554	306916	23.5372	.00180505
515	265225	22.6936	.00194175	555	308025	23.5584	.00180180
516	266256	22.7156	.00193798	556	309136	23.5797	.00179856
517	267289	22.7376	.00193424	557	310249	23.6008	.00179533
518	268324	22.7596	.00193050	558	311364	23.6220	.00179211
519	269361	22.7816	.00192678	559	312481	23.6432	.00178891
520	270400	22.8035	.00192308	560	313600	23.6643	.00178571

* Portions of Table II have been reproduced from J. W. Dunlap and A. K. Kurtz. *Handbook of Statistical Nomographs, Tables, and Formulas,* World Book Company, New York (1932), by permission of the authors and publishers.

TABLE II. *Table of Squares, Square Roots, and Reciprocals of Numbers from 1 to 1000*—Continued*

N	N^2	$\sqrt{N}$	$1/N$	N	N^2	$\sqrt{N}$	$1/N$
561	314721	23.6854	.00178253	601	361201	24.5153	.00166389
562	315844	23.7065	.00177936	602	362404	24.5357	.00166113
563	316969	23.7276	.00177620	603	363609	24.5561	.00165837
564	318096	23.7487	.00177305	604	364816	24.5764	.00165563
565	319225	23.7697	.00176991	605	366025	24.5967	.00165289
566	320356	23.7908	.00176678	606	367236	24.6171	.00165017
567	321489	23.8118	.00176367	607	368449	24.6374	.00164745
568	322624	23.8328	.00176056	608	369664	24.6577	.00164474
569	323761	23.8537	.00175747	609	370881	24.6779	.00164204
570	324900	23.8747	.00175439	610	372100	24.6982	.00163934
571	326041	23.8956	.00175131	611	373321	24.7184	.00163666
572	327184	23.9165	.00174825	612	374544	24.7386	.00163399
573	328329	23.9374	.00174520	613	375769	24.7588	.00163132
574	329476	23.9583	.00174216	614	376996	24.7790	.00162866
575	330625	23.9792	.00173913	615	378225	24.7992	.00162602
576	331776	24.0000	.00173611	616	379456	24.8193	.00162338
577	332929	24.0208	.00173310	617	380689	24.8395	.00162075
578	334084	24.0416	.00173010	618	381924	24.8596	.00161812
579	335241	24.0624	.00172712	619	383161	24.8797	.00161551
580	336400	24.0832	.00172414	620	384400	24.8998	.00161290
581	337561	24.1039	.00172117	621	385641	24.9199	.00161031
582	338724	24.1247	.00171821	622	386884	24.9399	.00160772
583	339889	24.1454	.00171527	623	388129	24.9600	.00160514
584	341056	24.1661	.00171233	624	389376	24.9800	.00160256
585	342225	24.1868	.00170940	625	390625	25.0000	.00160000
586	343396	24.2074	.00170648	626	391876	25.0200	.00159744
587	344569	24.2281	.00170358	627	393129	25.0400	.00159490
588	345744	24.2487	.00170068	628	394384	25.0599	.00159236
589	346921	24.2693	.00169779	629	395641	25.0799	.00158983
590	348100	24.2899	.00169492	630	396900	25.0998	.00158730
591	349281	24.3105	.00169205	631	398161	25.1197	.00158479
592	350464	24.3311	.00168919	632	399424	25.1396	.00158228
593	351649	24.3516	.00168634	633	400689	25.1595	.00157978
594	352836	24.3721	.00168350	634	401956	25.1794	.00157729
595	354025	24.3926	.00168067	635	403225	25.1992	.00157480
596	355216	24.4131	.00167785	636	404496	25.2190	.00157233
597	356409	24.4336	.00167504	637	405769	25.2389	.00156986
598	357604	24.4540	.00167224	638	407044	25.2587	.00156740
599	358801	24.4745	.00166945	639	408321	25.2784	.00156495
600	360000	24.4949	.00166667	640	409600	25.2982	.00156250

* Portions of Table II have been reproduced from J. W. Dunlap and A. K. Kurtz. *Handbook of Statistical Nomographs, Tables, and Formulas,* World Book Company, New York (1932), by permission of the authors and publishers.

TABLE II. *Table of Squares, Square Roots, and Reciprocals of Numbers from 1 to 1000*—Continued*

N	N²	√N	1/N	N	N²	√N	1/N
641	410881	25.3180	.00156006	681	463761	26.0960	.00146843
642	412164	25.3377	.00155763	682	465124	26.1151	.00146628
643	413449	25.3574	.00155521	683	466489	26.1343	.00146413
644	414736	25.3772	.00155280	684	467856	26.1534	.00146199
645	416025	25.3969	.00155039	685	469225	26.1725	.00145985
646	417316	25.4165	.00154799	686	470596	26.1916	.00145773
647	418609	25.4362	.00154560	687	471969	26.2107	.00145560
648	419904	25.4558	.00154321	688	473344	26.2298	.00145349
649	421201	25.4755	.00154083	689	474721	26.2488	.00145138
650	422500	25.4951	.00153846	690	476100	26.2679	.00144928
651	423801	25.5147	.00153610	691	477481	26.2869	.00144718
652	425104	25.5343	.00153374	692	478864	26.3059	.00144509
653	426409	25.5539	.00153139	693	480249	26.3249	.00144300
654	427716	25.5734	.00152905	694	481636	26.3439	.00144092
655	429025	25.5930	.00152672	695	483025	26.3629	.00143885
656	430336	25.6125	.00152439	696	484416	26.3818	.00143678
657	431649	25.6320	.00152207	697	485809	26.4008	.00143472
658	432964	25.6515	.00151976	698	487204	26.4197	.00143266
659	434281	25.6710	.00151745	699	488601	26.4386	.00143062
660	435600	25.6905	.00151515	700	490000	26.4575	.00142857
661	436921	25.7099	.00151286	701	491401	26.4764	.00142653
662	438244	25.7294	.00151057	702	492804	26.4953	.00142450
663	439569	25.7488	.00150830	703	494209	26.5141	.00142248
664	440896	25.7682	.00150602	704	495616	26.5330	.00142045
665	442225	25.7876	.00150376	705	497025	26.5518	.00141844
666	443556	25.8070	.00150150	706	498436	26.5707	.00141643
667	444889	25.8263	.00149925	707	499849	26.5895	.00141443
668	446224	25.8457	.00149701	708	501264	26.6083	.00141243
669	447561	25.8650	.00149477	709	502681	26.6271	.00141044
670	448900	25.8844	.00149254	710	504100	26.6458	.00140845
671	450241	25.9037	.00149031	711	505521	26.6646	.00140647
672	451584	25.9230	.00148810	712	506944	26.6833	.00140449
673	452929	25.9422	.00148588	713	508369	26.7021	.00140252
674	454276	25.9615	.00148368	714	509796	26.7208	.00140056
675	455625	25.9808	.00148148	715	511225	26.7395	.00139860
676	456976	26.0000	.00147929	716	512656	26.7582	.00139665
677	458329	26.0192	.00147710	717	514089	26.7769	.00139470
678	459684	26.0384	.00147493	718	515524	26.7955	.00139276
679	461041	26.0576	.00147275	719	516961	26.8142	.00139082
680	462400	26.0768	.00147059	720	518400	26.8328	.00138889

* Portions of Table II have been reproduced from J. W. Dunlap and A. K. Kurtz. *Handbook of Statistical Nomographs, Tables, and Formulas*, World Book Company, New York (1932), by permission of the authors and publishers.

TABLE II. *Table of Squares, Square Roots, and Reciprocals of Numbers from 1 to 1000*—Continued*

N	N^2	$\sqrt{N}$	$1/N$	N	N^2	$\sqrt{N}$	$1/N$
721	519841	26.8514	.00138696	761	579121	27.5862	.00131406
722	521284	26.8701	.00138504	762	580644	27.6043	.00131234
723	522729	26.8887	.00138313	763	582169	27.6225	.00131062
724	524176	26.9072	.00138122	764	583696	27.6405	.00130890
725	525625	26.9258	.00137931	765	585225	27.6586	.00130719
726	527076	26.9444	.00137741	766	586756	27.6767	.00130548
727	528529	26.9629	.00137552	767	588289	27.6948	.00130378
728	529984	26.9815	.00137363	768	589824	27.7128	.00130208
729	531441	27.0000	.00137174	769	591361	27.7308	.00130039
730	532900	27.0185	.00136986	770	592900	27.7489	.00129870
731	534361	27.0370	.00136799	771	594441	27.7669	.00129702
732	535824	27.0555	.00136612	772	595984	27.7849	.00129534
733	537289	27.0740	.00136426	773	597529	27.8029	.00129366
734	538756	27.0924	.00136240	774	599076	27.8209	.00129199
735	540225	27.1109	.00136054	775	600625	27.8388	.00129032
736	541696	27.1293	.00135870	776	602176	27.8568	.00128866
737	543169	27.1477	.00135685	777	603729	27.8747	.00128700
738	544644	27.1662	.00135501	778	605284	27.8927	.00128535
739	546121	27.1846	.00135318	779	606841	27.9106	.00128370
740	547600	27.2029	.00135135	780	608400	27.9285	.00128205
741	549081	27.2213	.00134953	781	609961	27.9464	.00128041
742	550564	27.2397	.00134771	782	611524	27.9643	.00127877
743	552049	27.2580	.00134590	783	613089	27.9821	.00127714
744	553536	27.2764	.00134409	784	614656	28.0000	.00127551
745	555025	27.2947	.00134228	785	616225	28.0179	.00127389
746	556516	27.3130	.00134048	786	617796	28.0357	.00127226
747	558009	27.3313	.00133869	787	619369	28.0535	.00127065
748	559504	27.3496	.00133690	788	620944	28.0713	.00126904
749	561001	27.3679	.00133511	789	622521	28.0891	.00126743
750	562500	27.3861	.00133333	790	624100	28.1069	.00126582
751	564001	27.4044	.00133156	791	625681	28.1247	.00126422
752	565504	27.4226	.00132979	792	627264	28.1425	.00126263
753	567009	27.4408	.00132802	793	628849	28.1603	.00126103
754	568516	27.4591	.00132626	794	630436	28.1780	.00125945
755	570025	27.4773	.00132450	795	632025	28.1957	.00125786
756	571536	27.4955	.00132275	796	633616	28.2135	.00125628
757	573049	27.5136	.00132100	797	635209	28.2312	.00125471
758	574564	27.5318	.00131926	798	636804	28.2489	.00125313
759	576081	27.5500	.00131752	799	638401	28.2666	.00125156
760	577600	27.5681	.00131579	800	640000	28.2843	.00125000

* Portions of Table II have been reproduced from J. W. Dunlap and A. K. Kurtz. *Handbook of Statistical Nomographs, Tables, and Formulas,* World Book Company, New York (1932), by permission of the authors and publishers.

TABLE II. *Table of Squares, Square Roots, and Reciprocals of Numbers from 1 to 1000*—Continued*

N	N^2	$\sqrt{N}$	$1/N$	N	N^2	$\sqrt{N}$	$1/N$
801	641601	28.3019	.00124844	841	707281	29.0000	.00118906
802	643204	28.3196	.00124688	842	708964	29.0172	.00118765
803	644809	28.3373	.00124533	843	710649	29.0345	.00118624
804	646416	28.3549	.00124378	844	712336	29.0517	.00118483
805	648025	28.3725	.00124224	845	714025	29.0689	.00118343
806	649636	28.3901	.00124069	846	715716	29.0861	.00118203
807	651249	28.4077	.00123916	847	717409	29.1033	.00118064
808	652864	28.4253	.00123762	848	719104	29.1204	.00117925
809	654481	28.4429	.00123609	849	720801	29.1376	.00117786
810	656100	28.4605	.00123457	850	722500	29.1548	.00117647
811	657721	28.4781	.00123305	851	724201	29.1719	.00117509
812	659344	28.4956	.00123153	852	725904	29.1890	.00117371
813	660969	28.5132	.00123001	853	727609	29.2062	.00117233
814	662596	28.5307	.00122850	854	729316	29.2233	.00117096
815	664225	28.5482	.00122699	855	731025	29.2404	.00116959
816	665856	28.5657	.00122549	856	732736	29.2575	.00116822
817	667489	28.5832	.00122399	857	734449	29.2746	.00116686
818	669124	28.6007	.00122249	858	736164	29.2916	.00116550
819	670761	28.6182	.00122100	859	737881	29.3087	.00116414
820	672400	28.6356	.00121951	860	739600	29.3258	.00116279
821	674041	28.6531	.00121803	861	741321	29.3428	.00116144
822	675684	28.6705	.00121655	862	743044	29.3598	.00116009
823	677329	28.6880	.00121507	863	744769	29.3769	.00115875
824	678976	28.7054	.00121359	864	746496	29.3939	.00115741
825	680625	28.7228	.00121212	865	748225	29.4109	.00115607
826	682276	28.7402	.00121065	866	749956	29.4279	.00115473
827	683929	28.7576	.00120919	867	751689	29.4449	.00115340
828	685584	28.7750	.00120773	868	753424	29.4618	.00115207
829	687241	28.7924	.00120627	869	755161	29.4788	.00115075
830	688900	28.8097	.00120482	870	756900	29.4958	.00114943
831	690561	28.8271	.00120337	871	758641	29.5127	.00114811
832	692224	28.8444	.00120192	872	760384	29.5296	.00114679
833	693889	28.8617	.00120048	873	762129	29.5466	.00114548
834	695556	28.8791	.00119904	874	763876	29.5635	.00114416
835	697225	28.8964	.00119760	875	765625	29.5804	.00114286
836	698896	28.9137	.00119617	876	767376	29.5973	.00114155
837	700569	28.9310	.00119474	877	769129	29.6142	.00114025
838	702244	28.9482	.00119332	878	770884	29.6311	.00113895
839	703921	28.9655	.00119190	879	772641	29.6479	.00113766
840	705600	28.9828	.00119048	880	774400	29.6648	.00113636

* Portions of Table II have been reproduced from J. W. Dunlap and A. K. Kurtz. *Handbook of Statistical Nomographs, Tables, and Formulas,* World Book Company, New York (1932), by permission of the authors and publishers.

TABLE II. *Table of Squares, Square Roots, and Reciprocals of Numbers from 1 to 1000*—Continued*

N	N^2	$\sqrt{N}$	$1/N$	N	N^2	$\sqrt{N}$	$1/N$
881	776161	29.6816	.00113507	921	848241	30.3480	.00108578
882	777924	29.6985	.00113379	922	850084	30.3645	.00108460
883	779689	29.7153	.00113250	923	851929	30.3809	.00108342
884	781456	29.7321	.00113122	924	853776	30.3974	.00108225
885	783225	29.7489	.00112994	925	855625	30.4138	.00108108
886	784996	29.7658	.00112867	926	857476	30.4302	.00107991
887	786769	29.7825	.00112740	927	859329	30.4467	.00107875
888	788544	29.7993	.00112613	928	861184	30.4631	.00107759
889	790321	29.8161	.00112486	929	863041	30.4795	.00107643
890	792100	29.8329	.00112360	930	864900	30.4959	.00107527
891	793881	29.8496	.00112233	931	866761	30.5123	.00107411
892	795664	29.8664	.00112108	932	868624	30.5287	.00107296
893	797449	29.8831	.00111982	933	870489	30.5450	.00107181
894	799236	29.8998	.00111857	934	872356	30.5614	.00107066
895	801025	29.9166	.00111732	935	874225	30.5778	.00106952
896	802816	29.9333	.00111607	936	876096	30.5941	.00106838
897	804609	29.9500	.00111483	937	877969	30.6105	.00106724
898	806404	29.9666	.00111359	938	879844	30.6268	.00106610
899	808201	29.9833	.00111235	939	881721	30.6431	.00106496
900	810000	30.0000	.00111111	940	883600	30.6594	.00106383
901	811801	30.0167	.00110988	941	885481	30.6757	.00106270
902	813604	30.0333	.00110865	942	887364	30.6920	.00106157
903	815409	30.0500	.00110742	943	889249	30.7083	.00106045
904	817216	30.0666	.00110619	944	891136	30.7246	.00105932
905	819025	30.0832	.00110497	945	893025	30.7409	.00105820
906	820836	30.0998	.00110375	946	894916	30.7571	.00105708
907	822649	30.1164	.00110254	947	896809	30.7734	.00105597
908	824464	30.1330	.00110132	948	898704	30.7896	.00105485
909	826281	30.1496	.00110011	949	900601	30.8058	.00105374
910	828100	30.1662	.00109890	950	902500	30.8221	.00105263
911	829921	30.1828	.00109769	951	904401	30.8383	.00105152
912	831744	30.1993	.00109649	952	906304	30.8545	.00105042
913	833569	30.2159	.00109529	953	908209	30.8707	.00104932
914	835396	30.2324	.00109409	954	910116	30.8869	.00104822
915	837225	30.2490	.00109290	955	912025	30.9031	.00104712
916	839056	30.2655	.00109170	956	913936	30.9192	.00104603
917	840889	30.2820	.00109051	957	915849	30.9354	.00104493
918	842724	30.2985	.00108932	958	917764	30.9516	.00104384
919	844561	30.3150	.00108814	959	919681	30.9677	.00104275
920	846400	30.3315	.00108696	960	921600	30.9839	.00104167

* Portions of Table II have been reproduced from J. W. Dunlap and A. K. Kurtz. *Handbook of Statistical Nomographs, Tables, and Formulas,* World Book Company, New York (1932), by permission of the authors and publishers.

TABLE II. *Table of Squares, Square Roots, and Reciprocals of Numbers from 1 to 1000*—Concluded*

N	N^2	$\sqrt{N}$	$1/N$	N	N^2	$\sqrt{N}$	$1/N$
961	923521	31.0000	.00104058	981	962361	31.3209	.00101937
962	925444	31.0161	.00103950	982	964324	31.3369	.00101833
963	927369	31.0322	.00103842	983	966289	31.3528	.00101729
964	929296	31.0483	.00103734	984	968256	31.3688	.00101626
965	931225	31.0644	.00103627	985	970225	31.3847	.00101523
966	933156	31.0805	.00103520	986	972196	31.4006	.00101420
967	935089	31.0966	.00103413	987	974169	31.4166	.00101317
968	937024	31.1127	.00103306	988	976144	31.4325	.00101215
969	938961	31.1288	.00103199	989	978121	31.4484	.00101112
970	940900	31.1448	.00103093	990	980100	31.4643	.00101010
971	942841	31.1609	.00102987	991	982081	31.4802	.00100908
972	944784	31.1769	.00102881	992	984064	31.4960	.00100806
973	946729	31.1929	.00102775	993	986049	31.5119	.00100705
974	948676	31.2090	.00102669	994	988036	31.5278	.00100604
975	950625	31.2250	.00102564	995	990025	31.5436	.00100503
976	952576	31.2410	.00102459	996	992016	31.5595	.00100402
977	954529	31.2570	.00102354	997	994009	31.5753	.00100301
978	956484	31.2730	.00102249	998	996004	31.5911	.00100200
979	958441	31.2890	.00102145	999	998001	31.6070	.00100100
980	960400	31.3050	.00102041	1000	1000000	31.6228	.00100000

* Portions of Table II have been reproduced from J. W. Dunlap and A. K. Kurtz. *Handbook of Statistical Nomographs, Tables, and Formulas*, World Book Company, New York (1932), by permission of the authors and publishers.

TABLE III. *Areas and Ordinates of the Normal Curve in Terms of x/σ*

(1) z STANDARD SCORE $\left(\dfrac{x}{\sigma}\right)$	(2) A AREA FROM MEAN TO $\dfrac{x}{\sigma}$	(3) B AREA IN LARGER PORTION	(4) C AREA IN SMALLER PORTION	(5) y ORDINATE AT $\dfrac{x}{\sigma}$
0.00	.0000	.5000	.5000	.3989
0.01	.0040	.5040	.4960	.3989
0.02	.0080	.5080	.4920	.3989
0.03	.0120	.5120	.4880	.3988
0.04	.0160	.5160	.4840	.3986
0.05	.0199	.5199	.4801	.3984
0.06	.0239	.5239	.4761	.3982
0.07	.0279	.5279	.4721	.3980
0.08	.0319	.5319	.4681	.3977
0.09	.0359	.5359	.4641	.3973
0.10	.0398	.5398	.4602	.3970
0.11	.0438	.5438	.4562	.3965
0.12	.0478	.5478	.4522	.3961
0.13	.0517	.5517	.4483	.3956
0.14	.0557	.5557	.4443	.3951
0.15	.0596	.5596	.4404	.3945
0.16	.0636	.5636	.4364	.3939
0.17	.0675	.5675	.4325	.3932
0.18	.0714	.5714	.4286	.3925
0.19	.0753	.5753	.4247	.3918
0.20	.0793	.5793	.4207	.3910
0.21	.0832	.5832	.4168	.3902
0.22	.0871	.5871	.4129	.3894
0.23	.0910	.5910	.4090	.3885
0.24	.0948	.5948	.4052	.3876
0.25	.0987	.5987	.4013	.3867
0.26	.1026	.6026	.3974	.3857
0.27	.1064	.6064	.3936	.3847
0.28	.1103	.6103	.3897	.3836
0.29	.1141	.6141	.3859	.3825
0.30	.1179	.6179	.3821	.3814
0.31	.1217	.6217	.3783	.3802
0.32	.1255	.6255	.3745	.3790
0.33	.1293	.6293	.3707	.3778
0.34	.1331	.6331	.3669	.3765

TABLE III. *Areas and Ordinates of the Normal Curve in Terms of x/σ—Continued*

(1) z STANDARD SCORE $\left(\dfrac{x}{\sigma}\right)$	(2) A AREA FROM MEAN TO $\dfrac{x}{\sigma}$	(3) B AREA IN LARGER PORTION	(4) C AREA IN SMALLER PORTION	(5) y ORDINATE AT $\dfrac{x}{\sigma}$
0.35	.1368	.6368	.3632	.3752
0.36	.1406	.6406	.3594	.3739
0.37	.1443	.6443	.3557	.3725
0.38	.1480	.6480	.3520	.3712
0.39	.1517	.6517	.3483	.3697
0.40	.1554	.6554	.3446	.3683
0.41	.1591	.6591	.3409	.3668
0.42	.1628	.6628	.3372	.3653
0.43	.1664	.6664	.3336	.3637
0.44	.1700	.6700	.3300	.3621
0.45	.1736	.6736	.3264	.3605
0.46	.1772	.6772	.3228	.3589
0.47	.1808	.6808	.3192	.3572
0.48	.1844	.6844	.3156	.3555
0.49	.1879	.6879	.3121	.3538
0.50	.1915	.6915	.3085	.3521
0.51	.1950	.6950	.3050	.3503
0.52	.1985	.6985	.3015	.3485
0.53	.2019	.7019	.2981	.3467
0.54	.2054	.7054	.2946	.3448
0.55	.2088	.7088	.2912	.3429
0.56	.2123	.7123	.2877	.3410
0.57	.2157	.7157	.2843	.3391
0.58	.2190	.7190	.2810	.3372
0.59	.2224	.7224	.2776	.3352
0.60	.2257	.7257	.2743	.3332
0.61	.2291	.7291	.2709	.3312
0.62	.2324	.7324	.2676	.3292
0.63	.2357	.7357	.2643	.3271
0.64	.2389	.7389	.2611	.3251
0.65	.2422	.7422	.2578	.3230
0.66	.2454	.7454	.2546	.3209
0.67	.2486	.7486	.2514	.3187
0.68	.2517	.7517	.2483	.3166
0.69	.2549	.7549	.2451	.3144

TABLE III. *Areas and Ordinates of the Normal Curve in Terms of x/σ—Continued*

(1) z STANDARD SCORE $\left(\frac{x}{\sigma}\right)$	(2) A AREA FROM MEAN TO $\frac{x}{\sigma}$	(3) B AREA IN LARGER PORTION	(4) C AREA IN SMALLER PORTION	(5) y ORDINATE AT $\frac{x}{\sigma}$
0.70	.2580	.7580	.2420	.3123
0.71	.2611	.7611	.2389	.3101
0.72	.2642	.7642	.2358	.3079
0.73	.2673	.7673	.2327	.3056
0.74	.2704	.7704	.2296	.3034
0.75	.2734	.7734	.2266	.3011
0.76	.2764	.7764	.2236	.2989
0.77	.2794	.7794	.2206	.2966
0.78	.2823	.7823	.2177	.2943
0.79	.2852	.7852	.2148	.2920
0.80	.2881	.7881	.2119	.2897
0.81	.2910	.7910	.2090	.2874
0.82	.2939	.7939	.2061	.2850
0.83	.2967	.7967	.2033	.2827
0.84	.2995	.7995	.2005	.2803
0.85	.3023	.8023	.1977	.2780
0.86	.3051	.8051	.1949	.2756
0.87	.3078	.8078	.1922	.2732
0.88	.3106	.8106	.1894	.2709
0.89	.3133	.8133	.1867	.2685
0.90	.3159	.8159	.1841	.2661
0.91	.3186	.8186	.1814	.2637
0.92	.3212	.8212	.1788	.2613
0.93	.3238	.8238	.1762	.2589
0.94	.3264	.8264	.1736	.2565
0.95	.3289	.8289	.1711	.2541
0.96	.3315	.8315	.1685	.2516
0.97	.3340	.8340	.1660	.2492
0.98	.3365	.8365	.1635	.2468
0.99	.3389	.8389	.1611	.2444
1.00	.3413	.8413	.1587	.2420
1.01	.3438	.8438	.1562	.2396
1.02	.3461	.8461	.1539	.2371
1.03	.3485	.8485	.1515	.2347
1.04	.3508	.8508	.1492	.2323

TABLE III. *Areas and Ordinates of the Normal Curve in Terms of x/σ—Continued*

(1) z STANDARD SCORE $\left(\frac{x}{\sigma}\right)$	(2) A AREA FROM MEAN TO $\frac{x}{\sigma}$	(3) B AREA IN LARGER PORTION	(4) C AREA IN SMALLER PORTION	(5) y ORDINATE AT $\frac{x}{\sigma}$
1.05	.3531	.8531	.1469	.2299
1.06	.3554	.8554	.1446	.2275
1.07	.3577	.8577	.1423	.2251
1.08	.3599	.8599	.1401	.2227
1.09	.3621	.8621	.1379	.2203
1.10	.3643	.8643	.1357	.2179
1.11	.3665	.8665	.1335	.2155
1.12	.3686	.8686	.1314	.2131
1.13	.3708	.8708	.1292	.2107
1.14	.3729	.8729	.1271	.2083
1.15	.3749	.8749	.1251	.2059
1.16	.3770	.8770	.1230	.2036
1.17	.3790	.8790	.1210	.2012
1.18	.3810	.8810	.1190	.1989
1.19	.3830	.8830	.1170	.1965
1.20	.3849	.8849	.1151	.1942
1.21	.3869	.8869	.1131	.1919
1.22	.3888	.8888	.1112	.1895
1.23	.3907	.8907	.1093	.1872
1.24	.3925	.8925	.1075	.1849
1.25	.3944	.8944	.1056	.1826
1.26	.3962	.8962	.1038	.1804
1.27	.3980	.8980	.1020	.1781
1.28	.3997	.8997	.1003	.1758
1.29	.4015	.9015	.0985	.1736
1.30	.4032	.9032	.0968	.1714
1.31	.4049	.9049	.0951	.1691
1.32	.4066	.9066	.0934	.1669
1.33	.4082	.9082	.0918	.1647
1.34	.4099	.9099	.0901	.1626
1.35	.4115	.9115	.0885	.1604
1.36	.4131	.9131	.0869	.1582
1.37	.4147	.9147	.0853	.1561
1.38	.4162	.9162	.0838	.1539
1.39	.4177	.9177	.0823	.1518

TABLE III. *Areas and Ordinates of the Normal Curve in Terms of x/σ—Continued*

(1) z STANDARD SCORE $\left(\dfrac{x}{\sigma}\right)$	(2) A AREA FROM MEAN TO $\dfrac{x}{\sigma}$	(3) B AREA IN LARGER PORTION	(4) C AREA IN SMALLER PORTION	(5) y ORDINATE AT $\dfrac{x}{\sigma}$
1.40	.4192	.9192	.0808	.1497
1.41	.4207	.9207	.0793	.1476
1.42	.4222	.9222	.0778	.1456
1.43	.4236	.9236	.0764	.1435
1.44	.4251	.9251	.0749	.1415
1.45	.4265	.9265	.0735	.1394
1.46	.4279	.9279	.0721	.1374
1.47	.4292	.9292	.0708	.1354
1.48	.4306	.9306	.0694	.1334
1.49	.4319	.9319	.0681	.1315
1.50	.4332	.9332	.0668	.1295
1.51	.4345	.9345	.0655	.1276
1.52	.4357	.9357	.0643	.1257
1.53	.4370	.9370	.0630	.1238
1.54	.4382	.9382	.0618	.1219
1.55	.4394	.9394	.0606	.1200
1.56	.4406	.9406	.0594	.1182
1.57	.4418	.9418	.0582	.1163
1.58	.4429	.9429	.0571	.1145
1.59	.4441	.9441	.0559	.1127
1.60	.4452	.9452	.0548	.1109
1.61	.4463	.9463	.0537	.1092
1.62	.4474	.9474	.0526	.1074
1.63	.4484	.9484	.0516	.1057
1.64	.4495	.9495	.0505	.1040
1.65	.4505	.9505	.0495	.1023
1.66	.4515	.9515	.0485	.1006
1.67	.4525	.9525	.0475	.0989
1.68	.4535	.9535	.0465	.0973
1.69	.4545	.9545	.0455	.0957
1.70	.4554	.9554	.0446	.0940
1.71	.4564	.9564	.0436	.0925
1.72	.4573	.9573	.0427	.0909
1.73	.4582	.9582	.0418	.0893
1.74	.4591	.9591	.0409	.0878

TABLE III. *Areas and Ordinates of the Normal Curve in Terms of x/σ—Continued*

(1) z STANDARD SCORE $\left(\frac{x}{\sigma}\right)$	(2) A AREA FROM MEAN TO $\frac{x}{\sigma}$	(3) B AREA IN LARGER PORTION	(4) C AREA IN SMALLER PORTION	(5) y ORDINATE AT $\frac{x}{\sigma}$
1.75	.4599	.9599	.0401	.0863
1.76	.4608	.9608	.0392	.0848
1.77	.4616	.9616	.0384	.0833
1.78	.4625	.9625	.0375	.0818
1.79	.4633	.9633	.0367	.0804
1.80	.4641	.9641	.0359	.0790
1.81	.4649	.9649	.0351	.0775
1.82	.4656	.9656	.0344	.0761
1.83	.4664	.9664	.0336	.0748
1.84	.4671	.9671	.0329	.0734
1.85	.4678	.9678	.0322	.0721
1.86	.4686	.9686	.0314	.0707
1.87	.4693	.9693	.0307	.0694
1.88	.4699	.9699	.0301	.0681
1.89	.4706	.9706	.0294	.0669
1.90	.4713	.9713	.0287	.0656
1.91	.4719	.9719	.0281	.0644
1.92	.4726	.9726	.0274	.0632
1.93	.4732	.9732	.0268	.0620
1.94	.4738	.9738	.0262	.0608
1.95	.4744	.9744	.0256	.0596
1.96	.4750	.9750	.0250	.0584
1.97	.4756	.9756	.0244	.0573
1.98	.4761	.9761	.0239	.0562
1.99	.4767	.9767	.0233	.0551
2.00	.4772	.9772	.0228	.0540
2.01	.4778	.9778	.0222	.0529
2.02	.4783	.9783	.0217	.0519
2.03	.4788	.9788	.0212	.0508
2.04	.4793	.9793	.0207	.0498
2.05	.4798	.9798	.0202	.0488
2.06	.4803	.9803	.0197	.0478
2.07	.4808	.9808	.0192	.0468
2.08	.4812	.9812	.0188	.0459
2.09	.4817	.9817	.0183	.0449

TABLE III. *Areas and Ordinates of the Normal Curve in Terms of* x/σ—*Continued*

(1) z STANDARD SCORE $\left(\dfrac{x}{\sigma}\right)$	(2) A AREA FROM MEAN TO $\dfrac{x}{\sigma}$	(3) B AREA IN LARGER PORTION	(4) C AREA IN SMALLER PORTION	(5) y ORDINATE AT $\dfrac{x}{\sigma}$
2.10	.4821	.9821	.0179	.0440
2.11	.4826	.9826	.0174	.0431
2.12	.4830	.9830	.0170	.0422
2.13	.4834	.9834	.0166	.0413
2.14	.4838	.9838	.0162	.0404
2.15	.4842	.9842	.0158	.0396
2.16	.4846	.9846	.0154	.0387
2.17	.4850	.9850	.0150	.0379
2.18	.4854	.9854	.0146	.0371
2.19	.4857	.9857	.0143	.0363
2.20	.4861	.9861	.0139	.0355
2.21	.4864	.9864	.0136	.0347
2.22	.4868	.9868	.0132	.0339
2.23	.4871	.9871	.0129	.0332
2.24	.4875	.9875	.0125	.0325
2.25	.4878	.9878	.0122	.0317
2.26	.4881	.9881	.0119	.0310
2.27	.4884	.9884	.0116	.0303
2.28	.4887	.9887	.0113	.0297
2.29	.4890	.9890	.0110	.0290
2.30	.4893	.9893	.0107	.0283
2.31	.4896	.9896	.0104	.0277
2.32	.4898	.9898	.0102	.0270
2.33	.4901	.9901	.0099	.0264
2.34	.4904	.9904	.0096	.0258
2.35	.4906	.9906	.0094	.0252
2.36	.4909	.9909	.0091	.0246
2.37	.4911	.9911	.0089	.0241
2.38	.4913	.9913	.0087	.0235
2.39	.4916	.9916	.0084	.0229
2.40	.4918	.9918	.0082	.0224
2.41	.4920	.9920	.0080	.0219
2.42	.4922	.9922	.0078	.0213
2.43	.4925	.9925	.0075	.0208
2.44	.4927	.9927	.0073	.0203

TABLE III. *Areas and Ordinates of the Normal Curve in Terms of x/σ—Continued*

(1) z STANDARD SCORE $\left(\dfrac{x}{\sigma}\right)$	(2) A AREA FROM MEAN TO $\dfrac{x}{\sigma}$	(3) B AREA IN LARGER PORTION	(4) C AREA IN SMALLER PORTION	(5) y ORDINATE AT $\dfrac{x}{\sigma}$
2.45	.4929	.9929	.0071	.0198
2.46	.4931	.9931	.0069	.0194
2.47	.4932	.9932	.0068	.0189
2.48	.4934	.9934	.0066	.0184
2.49	.4936	.9936	.0064	.0180
2.50	.4938	.9938	.0062	.0175
2.51	.4940	.9940	.0060	.0171
2.52	.4941	.9941	.0059	.0167
2.53	.4943	.9943	.0057	.0163
2.54	.4945	.9945	.0055	.0158
2.55	.4946	.9946	.0054	.0154
2.56	.4948	.9948	.0052	.0151
2.57	.4949	.9949	.0051	.0147
2.58	.4951	.9951	.0049	.0143
2.59	.4952	.9952	.0048	.0139
2.60	.4953	.9953	.0047	.0136
2.61	.4955	.9955	.0045	.0132
2.62	.4956	.9956	.0044	.0129
2.63	.4957	.9957	.0043	.0126
2.64	.4959	.9959	.0041	.0122
2.65	.4960	.9960	.0040	.0119
2.66	.4961	.9961	.0039	.0116
2.67	.4962	.9962	.0038	.0113
2.68	.4963	.9963	.0037	.0110
2.69	.4964	.9964	.0036	.0107
2.70	.4965	.9965	.0035	.0104
2.71	.4966	.9966	.0034	.0101
2.72	.4967	.9967	.0033	.0099
2.73	.4968	.9968	.0032	.0096
2.74	.4969	.9969	.0031	.0093
2.75	.4970	.9970	.0030	.0091
2.76	.4971	.9971	.0029	.0088
2.77	.4972	.9972	.0028	.0086
2.78	.4973	.9973	.0027	.0084
2.79	.4974	.9974	.0026	.0081

TABLE III. *Areas and Ordinates of the Normal Curve in Terms of x/σ—Continued*

(1) z STANDARD SCORE $\left(\dfrac{x}{\sigma}\right)$	(2) A AREA FROM MEAN TO $\dfrac{x}{\sigma}$	(3) B AREA IN LARGER PORTION	(4) C AREA IN SMALLER PORTION	(5) y ORDINATE AT $\dfrac{x}{\sigma}$
2.80	.4974	.9974	.0026	.0079
2.81	.4975	.9975	.0025	.0077
2.82	.4976	.9976	.0024	.0075
2.83	.4977	.9977	.0023	.0073
2.84	.4977	.9977	.0023	.0071
2.85	.4978	.9978	.0022	.0069
2.86	.4979	.9979	.0021	.0067
2.87	.4979	.9979	.0021	.0065
2.88	.4980	.9980	.0020	.0063
2.89	.4981	.9981	.0019	.0061
2.90	.4981	.9981	.0019	.0060
2.91	.4982	.9982	.0018	.0058
2.92	.4982	.9982	.0018	.0056
2.93	.4983	.9983	.0017	.0055
2.94	.4984	.9984	.0016	.0053
2.95	.4984	.9984	.0016	.0051
2.96	.4985	.9985	.0015	.0050
2.97	.4985	.9985	.0015	.0048
2.98	.4986	.9986	.0014	.0047
2.99	.4986	.9986	.0014	.0046
3.00	.4987	.9987	.0013	.0044
3.01	.4987	.9987	.0013	.0043
3.02	.4987	.9987	.0013	.0042
3.03	.4988	.9988	.0012	.0040
3.04	.4988	.9988	.0012	.0039
3.05	.4989	.9989	.0011	.0038
3.06	.4989	.9989	.0011	.0037
3.07	.4989	.9989	.0011	.0036
3.08	.4990	.9990	.0010	.0035
3.09	.4990	.9990	.0010	.0034
3.10	.4990	.9990	.0010	.0033
3.11	.4991	.9991	.0009	.0032
3.12	.4991	.9991	.0009	.0031
3.13	.4991	.9991	.0009	.0030
3.14	.4992	.9992	.0008	.0029

TABLE III. *Areas and Ordinates of the Normal Curve in Terms of x/σ—Concluded*

(1) z STANDARD SCORE $\left(\dfrac{x}{\sigma}\right)$	(2) A AREA FROM MEAN TO $\dfrac{x}{\sigma}$	(3) B AREA IN LARGER PORTION	(4) C AREA IN SMALLER PORTION	(5) y ORDINATE AT $\dfrac{x}{\sigma}$
3.15	.4992	.9992	.0008	.0028
3.16	.4992	.9992	.0008	.0027
3.17	.4992	.9992	.0008	.0026
3.18	.4993	.9993	.0007	.0025
3.19	.4993	.9993	.0007	.0025
3.20	.4993	.9993	.0007	.0024
3.21	.4993	.9993	.0007	.0023
3.22	.4994	.9994	.0006	.0022
3.23	.4994	.9994	.0006	.0022
3.24	.4994	.9994	.0006	.0021
3.30	.4995	.9995	.0005	.0017
3.40	.4997	.9997	.0003	.0012
3.50	.4998	.9998	.0002	.0009
3.60	.4998	.9998	.0002	.0006
3.70	.4999	.9999	.0001	.0004

TABLE IV. *Table of* χ^2*

Degrees of Freedom df	$P = .99$	.98	.95	.90	.80	.70	.50	.30	.20	.10	.05	.02	.01
1	.000157	.000628	.00393	.0158	.0642	.148	.455	1.074	1.642	2.706	3.841	5.412	6.635
2	.0201	.0404	.103	.211	.446	.713	1.386	2.408	3.219	4.605	5.991	7.824	9.210
3	.115	.185	.352	.584	1.005	1.424	2.366	3.665	4.642	6.251	7.815	9.837	11.341
4	.297	.429	.711	1.064	1.649	2.195	3.357	4.878	5.989	7.779	9.488	11.668	13.277
5	.554	.752	1.145	1.610	2.343	3.000	4.351	6.064	7.289	9.236	11.070	13.388	15.086
6	.872	1.134	1.635	2.204	3.070	3.828	5.348	7.231	8.558	10.645	12.592	15.033	16.812
7	1.239	1.564	2.167	2.833	3.822	4.671	6.346	8.383	9.803	12.017	14.067	16.622	18.475
8	1.646	2.032	2.733	3.490	4.594	5.527	7.344	9.524	11.030	13.362	15.507	18.168	20.090
9	2.088	2.532	3.325	4.168	5.380	6.393	8.343	10.656	12.242	14.684	16.919	19.679	21.666
10	2.558	3.059	3.940	4.865	6.179	7.267	9.342	11.781	13.442	15.987	18.307	21.161	23.209
11	3.053	3.609	4.575	5.578	6.989	8.148	10.341	12.899	14.631	17.275	19.675	22.618	24.725
12	3.571	4.178	5.226	6.304	7.807	9.034	11.340	14.011	15.812	18.549	21.026	24.054	26.217
13	4.107	4.765	5.892	7.042	8.634	9.926	12.340	15.119	16.985	19.812	22.362	25.472	27.688
14	4.660	5.368	6.571	7.790	9.467	10.821	13.339	16.222	18.151	21.064	23.685	26.873	29.141
15	5.229	5.985	7.261	8.547	10.307	11.721	14.339	17.322	19.311	22.307	24.996	28.259	30.578
16	5.812	6.614	7.962	9.312	11.152	12.624	15.338	18.418	20.465	23.542	26.296	29.633	32.000
17	6.408	7.255	8.672	10.085	12.002	13.531	16.338	19.511	21.615	24.769	27.587	30.995	33.409
18	7.015	7.906	9.390	10.865	12.857	14.440	17.338	20.601	22.760	25.989	28.869	32.346	34.805
19	7.633	8.567	10.117	11.651	13.716	15.352	18.338	21.689	23.900	27.204	30.144	33.687	36.191
20	8.260	9.237	10.851	12.443	14.578	16.266	19.337	22.775	25.038	28.412	31.410	35.020	37.566
21	8.897	9.915	11.591	13.240	15.445	17.182	20.337	23.858	26.171	29.615	32.671	36.343	38.932
22	9.542	10.600	12.338	14.041	16.314	18.101	21.337	24.939	27.301	30.813	33.924	37.659	40.289
23	10.196	11.293	13.091	14.848	17.187	19.021	22.337	26.018	28.429	32.007	35.172	38.968	41.638
24	10.856	11.992	13.848	15.659	18.062	19.943	23.337	27.096	29.553	33.196	36.415	40.270	42.980
25	11.524	12.697	14.611	16.473	18.940	20.867	24.337	28.172	30.675	34.382	37.652	41.566	44.314
26	12.198	13.409	15.379	17.292	19.820	21.792	25.336	29.246	31.795	35.563	38.885	42.856	45.642
27	12.879	14.125	16.151	18.114	20.703	22.719	26.336	30.319	32.912	36.741	40.113	44.140	46.963
28	13.565	14.847	16.928	18.939	21.588	23.647	27.336	31.391	34.027	37.916	41.337	45.419	48.278
29	14.256	15.574	17.708	19.768	22.475	24.577	28.336	32.461	35.139	39.087	42.557	46.693	49.588
30	14.953	16.306	18.493	20.599	23.364	25.508	29.336	33.530	36.250	40.256	43.773	47.962	50.892

* Table IV is reprinted from Table III of Fisher: *Statistical Methods for Research Workers*, Oliver & Boyd Ltd., Edinburgh, by permission of the author and publishers.

For larger values of df, the expression $\sqrt{2\chi^2} - \sqrt{2(df)} - 1$ may be used as a normal deviate with unit standard error.

TABLE V. *Table of t**

df	P = .450	.400	.350	.300	.250	.200	.150	.100	.050	.025	.010	.005
1	.158	.325	.510	.727	1.000	1.376	1.963	3.078	6.314	12.706	31.821	63.657
2	.142	.289	.445	.617	.816	1.061	1.386	1.886	2.920	4.303	6.965	9.925
3	.137	.277	.424	.584	.765	.978	1.250	1.638	2.353	3.182	4.541	5.841
4	.134	.271	.414	.569	.741	.941	1.190	1.533	2.132	2.776	3.747	4.604
5	.132	.267	.408	.559	.727	.920	1.156	1.476	2.015	2.571	3.365	4.032
6	.131	.265	.404	.553	.718	.906	1.134	1.440	1.943	2.447	3.143	3.707
7	.130	.263	.402	.549	.711	.896	1.119	1.415	1.895	2.365	2.998	3.499
8	.130	.262	.399	.546	.706	.889	1.108	1.397	1.860	2.306	2.896	3.355
9	.129	.261	.398	.543	.703	.883	1.100	1.383	1.833	2.262	2.821	3.250
10	.129	.260	.397	.542	.700	.879	1.093	1.372	1.812	2.228	2.764	3.169
11	.129	.260	.396	.540	.697	.876	1.088	1.363	1.796	2.201	2.718	3.106
12	.128	.259	.395	.539	.695	.873	1.083	1.356	1.782	2.179	2.681	3.055
13	.128	.259	.394	.538	.694	.870	1.079	1.350	1.771	2.160	2.650	3.012
14	.128	.258	.393	.537	.692	.868	1.076	1.345	1.761	2.145	2.624	2.977
15	.128	.258	.393	.536	.691	.866	1.074	1.341	1.753	2.131	2.602	2.947
16	.128	.258	.392	.535	.690	.865	1.071	1.337	1.746	2.120	2.583	2.921
17	.128	.257	.392	.534	.689	.863	1.069	1.333	1.740	2.110	2.567	2.898
18	.127	.257	.392	.534	.688	.862	1.067	1.330	1.734	2.101	2.552	2.878
19	.127	.257	.391	.533	.688	.861	1.066	1.328	1.729	2.093	2.539	2.861
20	.127	.257	.391	.533	.687	.860	1.064	1.325	1.725	2.086	2.528	2.845
21	.127	.257	.391	.532	.686	.859	1.063	1.323	1.721	2.080	2.518	2.831
22	.127	.256	.390	.532	.686	.858	1.061	1.321	1.717	2.074	2.508	2.819
23	.127	.256	.390	.532	.685	.858	1.060	1.319	1.714	2.069	2.500	2.807
24	.127	.256	.390	.531	.685	.857	1.059	1.318	1.711	2.064	2.492	2.797
25	.127	.256	.390	.531	.684	.856	1.058	1.316	1.708	2.060	2.485	2.787
26	.127	.256	.390	.531	.684	.856	1.058	1.315	1.706	2.056	2.479	2.779
27	.127	.256	.389	.531	.684	.855	1.057	1.314	1.703	2.052	2.473	2.771
28	.127	.256	.389	.530	.683	.855	1.056	1.313	1.701	2.048	2.467	2.763
29	.127	.256	.389	.530	.683	.854	1.055	1.311	1.699	2.045	2.462	2.756
30	.127	.256	.389	.530	.683	.854	1.055	1.310	1.697	2.042	2.457	2.750
∞	.12566	.25335	.38532	.52440	.67449	.84162	1.03643	1.28155	1.64485	1.95996	2.32634	2.57582

Additional Values of t at the .025 and .005 Levels of Significance†

df	.025	.005	df	.025	.005	df	.025	.005
32	2.037	2.739	55	2.005	2.668	125	1.979	2.616
34	2.032	2.728	60	2.000	2.660	150	1.976	2.609
36	2.027	2.718	65	1.998	2.653	175	1.974	2.605
38	2.025	2.711	70	1.994	2.648	200	1.972	2.601
40	2.021	2.704	75	1.992	2.643	300	1.968	2.592
42	2.017	2.696	80	1.990	2.638	400	1.966	2.588
44	2.015	2.691	85	1.989	2.635	500	1.965	2.586
46	2.012	2.685	90	1.987	2.632	1000	1.962	2.581
48	2.010	2.681	95	1.986	2.629	∞	1.960	2.576
50	2.008	2.678	100	1.984	2.626			

* Table V is reprinted from Table IV of Fisher: *Statistical Methods for Research Workers*, Oliver & Boyd Ltd., Edinburgh, by permission of the author and publishers.

† Additional entries were taken from Snedecor: *Statistical Methods*, Iowa State College Press, Ames, Iowa, by permission of the author and publisher. Values for 75, 85, 95, and 175 degrees of freedom were obtained by linear interpolation.

The probabilities given are for a one-sided test.

TABLE VI. *Values of the Correlation Coefficient for Various Levels of Significance**

df P =	.050	.025	.010	.005
1	.988	.997	.9995	.9999
2	.900	.950	.980	.990
3	.805	.878	.934	.959
4	.729	.811	.882	.917
5	.669	.754	.833	.874
6	.622	.707	.789	.834
7	.582	.666	.750	.798
8	.549	.632	.716	.765
9	.521	.602	.685	.735
10	.497	.576	.658	.708
11	.476	.553	.634	.684
12	.458	.532	.612	.661
13	.441	.514	.592	.641
14	.426	.497	.574	.623
15	.412	.482	.558	.606
16	.400	.468	.542	.590
17	.389	.456	.528	.575
18	.378	.444	.516	.561
19	.369	.433	.503	.549
20	.360	.423	.492	.537
21	.352	.413	.482	.526
22	.344	.404	.472	.515
23	.337	.396	.462	.505
24	.330	.388	.453	.496
25	.323	.381	.445	.487
26	.317	.374	.437	.479
27	.311	.367	.430	.471
28	.306	.361	.423	.463
29	.301	.355	.416	.456
30	.296	.349	.409	.449
35	.275	.325	.381	.418
40	.257	.304	.358	.393
45	.243	.288	.338	.372
50	.231	.273	.322	.354
60	.211	.250	.295	.325
70	.195	.232	.274	.302
80	.183	.217	.256	.283
90	.173	.205	.242	.267
100	.164	.195	.230	.254

Additional values of r *at the .025 and .005 Levels of Significance*

df	.025	.005	df	.025	.005	df	.025	.005
32	.339	.436	48	.279	.361	150	.159	.208
34	.329	.424	55	.261	.338	175	.148	.193
36	.320	.413	65	.241	.313	200	.138	.181
38	.312	.403	75	.224	.292	300	.113	.148
42	.297	.384	85	.211	.275	400	.098	.128
44	.291	.376	95	.200	.260	500	.088	.115
46	.284	.368	125	.174	.228	1,000	.062	.081

*Table VI is reprinted from Table V.A. of R. A. Fisher, *Statistical Methods for Research Workers*, Oliver & Boyd Ltd., Edinburgh, by permission of the author and publishers.

Additional entries were calculated using the table of *t*.

The probabilities given are for a one-sided test.

TABLE VII. *Table of z' Values for r**

r	z'	r	z'	r	z'	r	z'	r	z'
.000	.000	.200	.203	.400	.424	.600	.693	.800	1.099
.005	.005	.205	.208	.405	.430	.605	.701	.805	1.113
.010	.010	.210	.213	.410	.436	.610	.709	.810	1.127
.015	.015	.215	.218	.415	.442	.615	.717	.815	1.142
.020	.020	.220	.224	.420	.448	.620	.725	.820	1.157
.025	.025	.225	.229	.425	.454	.625	.733	.825	1.172
.030	.030	.230	.234	.430	.460	.630	.741	.830	1.188
.035	.035	.235	.239	.435	.466	.635	.750	.835	1.204
.040	.040	.240	.245	.440	.472	.640	.758	.840	1.221
.045	.045	.245	.250	.445	.478	.645	.767	.845	1.238
.050	.050	.250	.255	.450	.485	.650	.775	.850	1.256
.055	.055	.255	.261	.455	.491	.655	.784	.855	1.274
.060	.060	.260	.266	.460	.497	.660	.793	.860	1.293
.065	.065	.265	.271	.465	.504	.665	.802	.865	1.313
.070	.070	.270	.277	.470	.510	.670	.811	.870	1.333
.075	.075	.275	.282	.475	.517	.675	.820	.875	1.354
.080	.080	.280	.288	.480	.523	.680	.829	.880	1.376
.085	.085	.285	.293	.485	.530	.685	.838	.885	1.398
.090	.090	.290	.299	.490	.536	.690	.848	.890	1.422
.095	.095	.295	.304	.495	.543	.695	.858	.895	1.447
.100	.100	.300	.310	.500	.549	.700	.867	.900	1.472
.105	.105	.305	.315	.505	.556	.705	.877	.905	1.499
.110	.110	.310	.321	.510	.563	.710	.887	.910	1.528
.115	.116	.315	.326	.515	.570	.715	.897	.915	1.557
.120	.121	.320	.332	.520	.576	.720	.908	.920	1.589
.125	.126	.325	.337	.525	.583	.725	.918	.925	1.623
.130	.131	.330	.343	.530	.590	.730	.929	.930	1.658
.135	.136	.335	.348	.535	.597	.735	.940	.935	1.697
.140	.141	.340	.354	.540	.604	.740	.950	.940	1.738
.145	.146	.345	.360	.545	.611	.745	.962	.945	1.783
.150	.151	.350	.365	.550	.618	.750	.973	.950	1.832
.155	.156	.355	.371	.555	.626	.755	.984	.955	1.886
.160	.161	.360	.377	.560	.633	.760	.996	.960	1.946
.165	.167	.365	.383	.565	.640	.765	1.008	.965	2.014
.170	.172	.370	.388	.570	.648	.770	1.020	.970	2.092
.175	.177	.375	.394	.575	.655	.775	1.033	.975	2.185
.180	.182	.380	.400	.580	.662	.780	1.045	.980	2.298
.185	.187	.385	.406	.585	.670	.785	1.058	.985	2.443
.190	.192	.390	.412	.590	.678	.790	1.071	.990	2.647
.195	.198	.395	.418	.595	.685	.795	1.085	.995	2.994

* Table VII was constructed by F. P. Kilpatrick and D. A. Buchanan.

TABLE VIII. *The 5 (Roman Type) and 1 (Boldface Type) Percent Points for the Distribution of* F*

n_1 degrees of freedom (for greater mean square)

n_2	1	2	3	4	5	6	7	8	9	10	11	12	14	16	20	24	30	40	50	75	100	200	500	∞
1	161 / **4,052**	200 / **4,999**	216 / **5,403**	225 / **5,625**	230 / **5,764**	234 / **5,859**	237 / **5,928**	239 / **5,981**	241 / **6,022**	242 / **6,056**	243 / **6,082**	244 / **6,106**	245 / **6,142**	246 / **6,169**	248 / **6,208**	249 / **6,234**	250 / **6,258**	251 / **6,286**	252 / **6,302**	253 / **6,323**	253 / **6,334**	254 / **6,352**	254 / **6,361**	254 / **6,366**
2	18.51 / **98.49**	19.00 / **99.00**	19.16 / **99.17**	19.25 / **99.25**	19.30 / **99.30**	19.33 / **99.33**	19.36 / **99.34**	19.37 / **99.36**	19.38 / **99.38**	19.39 / **99.40**	19.40 / **99.41**	19.41 / **99.42**	19.42 / **99.43**	19.43 / **99.44**	19.44 / **99.45**	19.45 / **99.46**	19.46 / **99.47**	19.47 / **99.48**	19.47 / **99.48**	19.48 / **99.49**	19.49 / **99.49**	19.49 / **99.49**	19.50 / **99.50**	19.50 / **99.50**
3	10.13 / **34.12**	9.55 / **30.82**	9.28 / **29.46**	9.12 / **28.71**	9.01 / **28.24**	8.94 / **27.91**	8.88 / **27.67**	8.84 / **27.49**	8.81 / **27.34**	8.78 / **27.23**	8.76 / **27.13**	8.74 / **27.05**	8.71 / **26.92**	8.69 / **26.83**	8.66 / **26.69**	8.64 / **26.60**	8.62 / **26.50**	8.60 / **26.41**	8.58 / **26.35**	8.57 / **26.27**	8.56 / **26.23**	8.54 / **26.18**	8.54 / **26.14**	8.53 / **26.12**
4	7.71 / **21.20**	6.94 / **18.00**	6.59 / **16.69**	6.39 / **15.98**	6.26 / **15.52**	6.16 / **15.21**	6.09 / **14.98**	6.04 / **14.80**	6.00 / **14.66**	5.96 / **14.54**	5.93 / **14.45**	5.91 / **14.37**	5.87 / **14.24**	5.84 / **14.15**	5.80 / **14.02**	5.77 / **13.93**	5.74 / **13.83**	5.71 / **13.74**	5.70 / **13.69**	5.68 / **13.61**	5.66 / **13.57**	5.65 / **13.52**	5.64 / **13.48**	5.63 / **13.46**
5	6.61 / **16.26**	5.79 / **13.27**	5.41 / **12.06**	5.19 / **11.39**	5.05 / **10.97**	4.95 / **10.67**	4.88 / **10.45**	4.82 / **10.27**	4.78 / **10.15**	4.74 / **10.05**	4.70 / **9.96**	4.68 / **9.89**	4.64 / **9.77**	4.60 / **9.68**	4.56 / **9.55**	4.53 / **9.47**	4.50 / **9.38**	4.46 / **9.29**	4.44 / **9.24**	4.42 / **9.17**	4.40 / **9.13**	4.38 / **9.07**	4.37 / **9.04**	4.36 / **9.02**
6	5.99 / **13.74**	5.14 / **10.92**	4.76 / **9.78**	4.53 / **9.15**	4.39 / **8.75**	4.28 / **8.47**	4.21 / **8.26**	4.15 / **8.10**	4.10 / **7.98**	4.06 / **7.87**	4.03 / **7.79**	4.00 / **7.72**	3.96 / **7.60**	3.92 / **7.52**	3.87 / **7.39**	3.84 / **7.31**	3.81 / **7.23**	3.77 / **7.14**	3.75 / **7.09**	3.72 / **7.02**	3.71 / **6.99**	3.69 / **6.94**	3.68 / **6.90**	3.67 / **6.88**
7	5.59 / **12.25**	4.74 / **9.55**	4.35 / **8.45**	4.12 / **7.85**	3.97 / **7.46**	3.87 / **7.19**	3.79 / **7.00**	3.73 / **6.84**	3.68 / **6.71**	3.63 / **6.62**	3.60 / **6.54**	3.57 / **6.47**	3.52 / **6.35**	3.49 / **6.27**	3.44 / **6.15**	3.41 / **6.07**	3.38 / **5.98**	3.34 / **5.90**	3.32 / **5.85**	3.29 / **5.78**	3.28 / **5.75**	3.25 / **5.70**	3.24 / **5.67**	3.23 / **5.65**
8	5.32 / **11.26**	4.46 / **8.65**	4.07 / **7.59**	3.84 / **7.01**	3.69 / **6.63**	3.58 / **6.37**	3.50 / **6.19**	3.44 / **6.03**	3.39 / **5.91**	3.34 / **5.82**	3.31 / **5.74**	3.28 / **5.67**	3.23 / **5.56**	3.20 / **5.48**	3.15 / **5.36**	3.12 / **5.28**	3.08 / **5.20**	3.05 / **5.11**	3.03 / **5.06**	3.00 / **5.00**	2.98 / **4.96**	2.96 / **4.91**	2.94 / **4.88**	2.93 / **4.86**
9	5.12 / **10.56**	4.26 / **8.02**	3.86 / **6.99**	3.63 / **6.42**	3.48 / **6.06**	3.37 / **5.80**	3.29 / **5.62**	3.23 / **5.47**	3.18 / **5.35**	3.13 / **5.26**	3.10 / **5.18**	3.07 / **5.11**	3.02 / **5.00**	2.98 / **4.92**	2.93 / **4.80**	2.90 / **4.73**	2.86 / **4.64**	2.82 / **4.56**	2.80 / **4.51**	2.77 / **4.45**	2.76 / **4.41**	2.73 / **4.36**	2.72 / **4.33**	2.71 / **4.31**
10	4.96 / **10.04**	4.10 / **7.56**	3.71 / **6.55**	3.48 / **5.99**	3.33 / **5.64**	3.22 / **5.39**	3.14 / **5.21**	3.07 / **5.06**	3.02 / **4.95**	2.97 / **4.85**	2.94 / **4.78**	2.91 / **4.71**	2.86 / **4.60**	2.82 / **4.52**	2.77 / **4.41**	2.74 / **4.33**	2.70 / **4.25**	2.67 / **4.17**	2.64 / **4.12**	2.61 / **4.05**	2.59 / **4.01**	2.56 / **3.96**	2.55 / **3.93**	2.54 / **3.91**
11	4.84 / **9.65**	3.98 / **7.20**	3.59 / **6.22**	3.36 / **5.67**	3.20 / **5.32**	3.09 / **5.07**	3.01 / **4.88**	2.95 / **4.74**	2.90 / **4.63**	2.86 / **4.54**	2.82 / **4.46**	2.79 / **4.40**	2.74 / **4.29**	2.70 / **4.21**	2.65 / **4.10**	2.61 / **4.02**	2.57 / **3.94**	2.53 / **3.86**	2.50 / **3.80**	2.47 / **3.74**	2.45 / **3.70**	2.42 / **3.66**	2.41 / **3.62**	2.40 / **3.60**
12	4.75 / **9.33**	3.88 / **6.93**	3.49 / **5.95**	3.26 / **5.41**	3.11 / **5.06**	3.00 / **4.82**	2.92 / **4.65**	2.85 / **4.50**	2.80 / **4.39**	2.76 / **4.30**	2.72 / **4.22**	2.69 / **4.16**	2.64 / **4.05**	2.60 / **3.98**	2.54 / **3.86**	2.50 / **3.78**	2.46 / **3.70**	2.42 / **3.61**	2.40 / **3.56**	2.36 / **3.49**	2.35 / **3.46**	2.32 / **3.41**	2.31 / **3.38**	2.30 / **3.36**
13	4.67 / **9.07**	3.80 / **6.70**	3.41 / **5.74**	3.18 / **5.20**	3.02 / **4.86**	2.92 / **4.62**	2.84 / **4.44**	2.77 / **4.30**	2.72 / **4.19**	2.67 / **4.10**	2.63 / **4.02**	2.60 / **3.96**	2.55 / **3.85**	2.51 / **3.78**	2.46 / **3.67**	2.42 / **3.59**	2.38 / **3.51**	2.34 / **3.42**	2.32 / **3.37**	2.28 / **3.30**	2.26 / **3.27**	2.24 / **3.21**	2.22 / **3.18**	2.21 / **3.16**

* Table VIII is reproduced from Snedecor: *Statistical Methods*, Iowa State College Press, Ames, Iowa, by permission of the author and publisher.

TABLE VIII. The 5 (Roman Type) and 1 (Boldface Type) Percent Points for the Distribution of F*—Continued

n_1 degrees of freedom (for greater mean square)

n_2	1	2	3	4	5	6	7	8	9	10	11	12	14	16	20	24	30	40	50	75	100	200	500	∞
14	4.60 / **8.86**	3.74 / **6.51**	3.34 / **5.56**	3.11 / **5.03**	2.96 / **4.69**	2.85 / **4.46**	2.77 / **4.28**	2.70 / **4.14**	2.65 / **4.03**	2.60 / **3.94**	2.56 / **3.86**	2.53 / **3.80**	2.48 / **3.70**	2.44 / **3.62**	2.39 / **3.51**	2.35 / **3.43**	2.31 / **3.34**	2.27 / **3.26**	2.24 / **3.21**	2.21 / **3.14**	2.19 / **3.11**	2.16 / **3.06**	2.14 / **3.02**	2.13 / **3.00**
15	4.54 / **8.68**	3.68 / **6.36**	3.29 / **5.42**	3.06 / **4.89**	2.90 / **4.56**	2.79 / **4.32**	2.70 / **4.14**	2.64 / **4.00**	2.59 / **3.89**	2.55 / **3.80**	2.51 / **3.73**	2.48 / **3.67**	2.43 / **3.56**	2.39 / **3.48**	2.33 / **3.36**	2.29 / **3.29**	2.25 / **3.20**	2.21 / **3.12**	2.18 / **3.07**	2.15 / **3.00**	2.12 / **2.97**	2.10 / **2.92**	2.08 / **2.89**	2.07 / **2.87**
16	4.49 / **8.53**	3.63 / **6.23**	3.24 / **5.29**	3.01 / **4.77**	2.85 / **4.44**	2.74 / **4.20**	2.66 / **4.03**	2.59 / **3.89**	2.54 / **3.78**	2.49 / **3.69**	2.45 / **3.61**	2.42 / **3.55**	2.37 / **3.45**	2.33 / **3.37**	2.28 / **3.25**	2.24 / **3.18**	2.20 / **3.10**	2.16 / **3.01**	2.13 / **2.96**	2.09 / **2.89**	2.07 / **2.86**	2.04 / **2.80**	2.02 / **2.77**	2.01 / **2.75**
17	4.45 / **8.40**	3.59 / **6.11**	3.20 / **5.18**	2.96 / **4.67**	2.81 / **4.34**	2.70 / **4.10**	2.62 / **3.93**	2.55 / **3.79**	2.50 / **3.68**	2.45 / **3.59**	2.41 / **3.52**	2.38 / **3.45**	2.33 / **3.35**	2.29 / **3.27**	2.23 / **3.16**	2.19 / **3.08**	2.15 / **3.00**	2.11 / **2.92**	2.08 / **2.86**	2.04 / **2.79**	2.02 / **2.76**	1.99 / **2.70**	1.97 / **2.67**	1.96 / **2.65**
18	4.41 / **8.28**	3.55 / **6.01**	3.16 / **5.09**	2.93 / **4.58**	2.77 / **4.25**	2.66 / **4.01**	2.58 / **3.85**	2.51 / **3.71**	2.46 / **3.60**	2.41 / **3.51**	2.37 / **3.44**	2.34 / **3.37**	2.29 / **3.27**	2.25 / **3.19**	2.19 / **3.07**	2.15 / **3.00**	2.11 / **2.91**	2.07 / **2.83**	2.04 / **2.78**	2.00 / **2.71**	1.98 / **2.68**	1.95 / **2.62**	1.93 / **2.59**	1.92 / **2.57**
19	4.38 / **8.18**	3.52 / **5.93**	3.13 / **5.01**	2.90 / **4.50**	2.74 / **4.17**	2.63 / **3.94**	2.55 / **3.77**	2.48 / **3.63**	2.43 / **3.52**	2.38 / **3.43**	2.34 / **3.36**	2.31 / **3.30**	2.26 / **3.19**	2.21 / **3.12**	2.15 / **3.00**	2.11 / **2.92**	2.07 / **2.84**	2.02 / **2.76**	2.00 / **2.70**	1.96 / **2.63**	1.94 / **2.60**	1.91 / **2.54**	1.90 / **2.51**	1.88 / **2.49**
20	4.35 / **8.10**	3.49 / **5.85**	3.10 / **4.94**	2.87 / **4.43**	2.71 / **4.10**	2.60 / **3.87**	2.52 / **3.71**	2.45 / **3.56**	2.40 / **3.45**	2.35 / **3.37**	2.31 / **3.30**	2.28 / **3.23**	2.23 / **3.13**	2.18 / **3.05**	2.12 / **2.94**	2.08 / **2.86**	2.04 / **2.77**	1.99 / **2.69**	1.96 / **2.63**	1.92 / **2.56**	1.90 / **2.53**	1.87 / **2.47**	1.85 / **2.44**	1.84 / **2.42**
21	4.32 / **8.02**	3.47 / **5.78**	3.07 / **4.87**	2.84 / **4.37**	2.68 / **4.04**	2.57 / **3.81**	2.49 / **3.65**	2.42 / **3.51**	2.37 / **3.40**	2.32 / **3.31**	2.28 / **3.24**	2.25 / **3.17**	2.20 / **3.07**	2.15 / **2.99**	2.09 / **2.88**	2.05 / **2.80**	2.00 / **2.72**	1.96 / **2.63**	1.93 / **2.58**	1.89 / **2.51**	1.87 / **2.47**	1.84 / **2.42**	1.82 / **2.38**	1.81 / **2.36**
22	4.30 / **7.94**	3.44 / **5.72**	3.05 / **4.82**	2.82 / **4.31**	2.66 / **3.99**	2.55 / **3.76**	2.47 / **3.59**	2.40 / **3.45**	2.35 / **3.35**	2.30 / **3.26**	2.26 / **3.18**	2.23 / **3.12**	2.18 / **3.02**	2.13 / **2.94**	2.07 / **2.83**	2.03 / **2.75**	1.98 / **2.67**	1.93 / **2.58**	1.91 / **2.53**	1.87 / **2.46**	1.84 / **2.42**	1.81 / **2.37**	1.80 / **2.33**	1.78 / **2.31**
23	4.28 / **7.88**	3.42 / **5.66**	3.03 / **4.76**	2.80 / **4.26**	2.64 / **3.94**	2.53 / **3.71**	2.45 / **3.54**	2.38 / **3.41**	2.32 / **3.30**	2.28 / **3.21**	2.24 / **3.14**	2.20 / **3.07**	2.14 / **2.97**	2.10 / **2.89**	2.04 / **2.78**	2.00 / **2.70**	1.96 / **2.62**	1.91 / **2.53**	1.88 / **2.48**	1.84 / **2.41**	1.82 / **2.37**	1.79 / **2.32**	1.77 / **2.28**	1.76 / **2.26**
24	4.26 / **7.82**	3.40 / **5.61**	3.01 / **4.72**	2.78 / **4.22**	2.62 / **3.90**	2.51 / **3.67**	2.43 / **3.50**	2.36 / **3.36**	2.30 / **3.25**	2.26 / **3.17**	2.22 / **3.09**	2.18 / **3.03**	2.13 / **2.93**	2.09 / **2.85**	2.02 / **2.74**	1.98 / **2.66**	1.94 / **2.58**	1.89 / **2.49**	1.86 / **2.44**	1.82 / **2.36**	1.80 / **2.33**	1.76 / **2.27**	1.74 / **2.23**	1.73 / **2.21**
25	4.24 / **7.77**	3.38 / **5.57**	2.99 / **4.68**	2.76 / **4.18**	2.60 / **3.86**	2.49 / **3.63**	2.41 / **3.46**	2.34 / **3.32**	2.28 / **3.21**	2.24 / **3.13**	2.20 / **3.05**	2.16 / **2.99**	2.11 / **2.89**	2.06 / **2.81**	2.00 / **2.70**	1.96 / **2.62**	1.92 / **2.54**	1.87 / **2.45**	1.84 / **2.40**	1.80 / **2.32**	1.77 / **2.29**	1.74 / **2.23**	1.72 / **2.19**	1.71 / **2.17**
26	4.22 / **7.72**	3.37 / **5.53**	2.98 / **4.64**	2.74 / **4.14**	2.59 / **3.82**	2.47 / **3.59**	2.39 / **3.42**	2.32 / **3.29**	2.27 / **3.17**	2.22 / **3.09**	2.18 / **3.02**	2.15 / **2.96**	2.10 / **2.86**	2.05 / **2.77**	1.99 / **2.66**	1.95 / **2.58**	1.90 / **2.50**	1.85 / **2.41**	1.82 / **2.36**	1.78 / **2.28**	1.76 / **2.25**	1.72 / **2.19**	1.70 / **2.15**	1.69 / **2.13**

* Table VIII is reproduced from Snedecor: Statistical Methods, Iowa State College Press, Ames, Iowa, by permission of the author and publisher.

TABLE VIII. The 5 (Roman Type) and 1 (Boldface Type) Percent Points for the Distribution of F*—Continued

n_1 degrees of freedom (for greater mean square)

n_2	1	2	3	4	5	6	7	8	9	10	11	12	14	16	20	24	30	40	50	75	100	200	500	∞
27	4.21 **7.68**	3.35 **5.49**	2.96 **4.60**	2.73 **4.11**	2.57 **3.79**	2.46 **3.56**	2.37 **3.39**	2.30 **3.26**	2.25 **3.14**	2.20 **3.06**	2.16 **2.98**	2.13 **2.93**	2.08 **2.83**	2.03 **2.74**	1.97 **2.63**	1.93 **2.55**	1.88 **2.47**	1.84 **2.38**	1.80 **2.33**	1.76 **2.25**	1.74 **2.21**	1.71 **2.16**	1.68 **2.12**	1.67 **2.10**
28	4.20 **7.64**	3.34 **5.45**	2.95 **4.57**	2.71 **4.07**	2.56 **3.76**	2.44 **3.53**	2.36 **3.36**	2.29 **3.23**	2.24 **3.11**	2.19 **3.03**	2.15 **2.95**	2.12 **2.90**	2.06 **2.80**	2.02 **2.71**	1.96 **2.60**	1.91 **2.52**	1.87 **2.44**	1.81 **2.35**	1.78 **2.30**	1.75 **2.22**	1.72 **2.18**	1.69 **2.13**	1.67 **2.09**	1.65 **2.06**
29	4.18 **7.60**	3.33 **5.42**	2.93 **4.54**	2.70 **4.04**	2.54 **3.73**	2.43 **3.50**	2.35 **3.33**	2.28 **3.20**	2.22 **3.08**	2.18 **3.00**	2.14 **2.92**	2.10 **2.87**	2.05 **2.77**	2.00 **2.68**	1.94 **2.57**	1.90 **2.49**	1.85 **2.41**	1.80 **2.32**	1.77 **2.27**	1.73 **2.19**	1.71 **2.15**	1.68 **2.10**	1.65 **2.06**	1.64 **2.03**
30	4.17 **7.56**	3.32 **5.39**	2.92 **4.51**	2.69 **4.02**	2.53 **3.70**	2.42 **3.47**	2.34 **3.30**	2.27 **3.17**	2.21 **3.06**	2.16 **2.98**	2.12 **2.90**	2.09 **2.84**	2.04 **2.74**	1.99 **2.66**	1.93 **2.55**	1.89 **2.47**	1.84 **2.38**	1.79 **2.29**	1.76 **2.24**	1.72 **2.16**	1.69 **2.13**	1.66 **2.07**	1.64 **2.03**	1.62 **2.01**
32	4.15 **7.50**	3.30 **5.34**	2.90 **4.46**	2.67 **3.97**	2.51 **3.66**	2.40 **3.42**	2.32 **3.25**	2.25 **3.12**	2.19 **3.01**	2.14 **2.94**	2.10 **2.86**	2.07 **2.80**	2.02 **2.70**	1.97 **2.62**	1.91 **2.51**	1.86 **2.42**	1.82 **2.34**	1.76 **2.25**	1.74 **2.20**	1.69 **2.12**	1.67 **2.08**	1.64 **2.02**	1.61 **1.98**	1.59 **1.96**
34	4.13 **7.44**	3.28 **5.29**	2.88 **4.42**	2.65 **3.93**	2.49 **3.61**	2.38 **3.38**	2.30 **3.21**	2.23 **3.08**	2.17 **2.97**	2.12 **2.89**	2.08 **2.82**	2.05 **2.76**	2.00 **2.66**	1.95 **2.58**	1.89 **2.47**	1.84 **2.38**	1.80 **2.30**	1.74 **2.21**	1.71 **2.15**	1.67 **2.08**	1.64 **2.04**	1.61 **1.98**	1.59 **1.94**	1.57 **1.91**
36	4.11 **7.39**	3.26 **5.25**	2.86 **4.38**	2.63 **3.89**	2.48 **3.58**	2.36 **3.35**	2.28 **3.18**	2.21 **3.04**	2.15 **2.94**	2.10 **2.86**	2.06 **2.78**	2.03 **2.72**	1.98 **2.62**	1.93 **2.54**	1.87 **2.43**	1.82 **2.35**	1.78 **2.26**	1.72 **2.17**	1.69 **2.12**	1.65 **2.04**	1.62 **2.00**	1.59 **1.94**	1.56 **1.90**	1.55 **1.87**
38	4.10 **7.35**	3.25 **5.21**	2.85 **4.34**	2.62 **3.86**	2.46 **3.54**	2.35 **3.32**	2.26 **3.15**	2.19 **3.02**	2.14 **2.91**	2.09 **2.82**	2.05 **2.75**	2.02 **2.69**	1.96 **2.59**	1.92 **2.51**	1.85 **2.40**	1.80 **2.32**	1.76 **2.22**	1.71 **2.14**	1.67 **2.08**	1.63 **2.00**	1.60 **1.97**	1.57 **1.90**	1.54 **1.86**	1.53 **1.84**
40	4.08 **7.31**	3.23 **5.18**	2.84 **4.31**	2.61 **3.83**	2.45 **3.51**	2.34 **3.29**	2.25 **3.12**	2.18 **2.99**	2.12 **2.88**	2.07 **2.80**	2.04 **2.73**	2.00 **2.66**	1.95 **2.56**	1.90 **2.49**	1.84 **2.37**	1.79 **2.29**	1.74 **2.20**	1.69 **2.11**	1.66 **2.05**	1.61 **1.97**	1.59 **1.94**	1.55 **1.88**	1.53 **1.84**	1.51 **1.81**
42	4.07 **7.27**	3.22 **5.15**	2.83 **4.29**	2.59 **3.80**	2.44 **3.49**	2.32 **3.26**	2.24 **3.10**	2.17 **2.96**	2.11 **2.86**	2.06 **2.77**	2.02 **2.70**	1.99 **2.64**	1.94 **2.54**	1.89 **2.46**	1.82 **2.35**	1.78 **2.26**	1.73 **2.17**	1.68 **2.08**	1.64 **2.02**	1.60 **1.94**	1.57 **1.91**	1.54 **1.85**	1.51 **1.80**	1.49 **1.78**
44	4.06 **7.24**	3.21 **5.12**	2.82 **4.26**	2.58 **3.78**	2.43 **3.46**	2.31 **3.24**	2.23 **3.07**	2.16 **2.94**	2.10 **2.84**	2.05 **2.75**	2.01 **2.68**	1.98 **2.62**	1.92 **2.52**	1.88 **2.44**	1.81 **2.32**	1.76 **2.24**	1.72 **2.15**	1.66 **2.06**	1.63 **2.00**	1.58 **1.92**	1.56 **1.88**	1.52 **1.82**	1.50 **1.78**	1.48 **1.75**
46	4.05 **7.21**	3.20 **5.10**	2.81 **4.24**	2.57 **3.76**	2.42 **3.44**	2.30 **3.22**	2.22 **3.05**	2.14 **2.92**	2.09 **2.82**	2.04 **2.73**	2.00 **2.66**	1.97 **2.60**	1.91 **2.50**	1.87 **2.42**	1.80 **2.30**	1.75 **2.22**	1.71 **2.13**	1.65 **2.04**	1.62 **1.98**	1.57 **1.90**	1.54 **1.86**	1.51 **1.80**	1.48 **1.76**	1.46 **1.72**
48	4.04 **7.19**	3.19 **5.08**	2.80 **4.22**	2.56 **3.74**	2.41 **3.42**	2.30 **3.20**	2.21 **3.04**	2.14 **2.90**	2.08 **2.80**	2.03 **2.71**	1.99 **2.64**	1.96 **2.58**	1.90 **2.48**	1.86 **2.40**	1.79 **2.28**	1.74 **2.20**	1.70 **2.11**	1.64 **2.02**	1.61 **1.96**	1.56 **1.88**	1.53 **1.84**	1.50 **1.78**	1.47 **1.73**	1.45 **1.70**

*Table VIII is reproduced from Snedecor: *Statistical Methods*, Iowa State College Press, Ames, Iowa, by permission of the author and publisher.

TABLE VIII. *The 5 (Roman Type) and 1 (Boldface Type) Percent Points for the Distribution of* F*—Concluded*

n_1 degrees of freedom (for greater mean square)

n_2	1	2	3	4	5	6	7	8	9	10	11	12	14	16	20	24	30	40	50	75	100	200	500	∞
50	4.03 / 7.17	3.18 / 5.06	2.79 / 4.20	2.56 / 3.72	2.40 / 3.41	2.29 / 3.18	2.20 / 3.02	2.13 / 2.88	2.07 / 2.78	2.02 / 2.70	1.98 / 2.62	1.95 / 2.56	1.90 / 2.46	1.85 / 2.39	1.78 / 2.26	1.74 / 2.18	1.69 / 2.10	1.63 / 2.00	1.60 / 1.94	1.55 / 1.86	1.52 / 1.82	1.48 / 1.76	1.46 / 1.71	1.44 / 1.68
55	4.02 / 7.12	3.17 / 5.01	2.78 / 4.16	2.54 / 3.68	2.38 / 3.37	2.27 / 3.15	2.18 / 2.98	2.11 / 2.85	2.05 / 2.75	2.00 / 2.66	1.97 / 2.59	1.93 / 2.53	1.88 / 2.43	1.83 / 2.35	1.76 / 2.23	1.72 / 2.15	1.67 / 2.06	1.61 / 1.96	1.58 / 1.90	1.52 / 1.82	1.50 / 1.78	1.46 / 1.71	1.43 / 1.66	1.41 / 1.64
60	4.00 / 7.08	3.15 / 4.98	2.76 / 4.13	2.52 / 3.65	2.37 / 3.34	2.25 / 3.12	2.17 / 2.95	2.10 / 2.82	2.04 / 2.72	1.99 / 2.63	1.95 / 2.56	1.92 / 2.50	1.86 / 2.40	1.81 / 2.32	1.75 / 2.20	1.70 / 2.12	1.65 / 2.03	1.59 / 1.93	1.56 / 1.87	1.50 / 1.79	1.48 / 1.74	1.44 / 1.68	1.41 / 1.63	1.39 / 1.60
65	3.99 / 7.04	3.14 / 4.95	2.75 / 4.10	2.51 / 3.62	2.36 / 3.31	2.24 / 3.09	2.15 / 2.93	2.08 / 2.79	2.02 / 2.70	1.98 / 2.61	1.94 / 2.54	1.90 / 2.47	1.85 / 2.37	1.80 / 2.30	1.73 / 2.18	1.68 / 2.09	1.63 / 2.00	1.57 / 1.90	1.54 / 1.84	1.49 / 1.76	1.46 / 1.71	1.42 / 1.64	1.39 / 1.60	1.37 / 1.56
70	3.98 / 7.01	3.13 / 4.92	2.74 / 4.08	2.50 / 3.60	2.35 / 3.29	2.23 / 3.07	2.14 / 2.91	2.07 / 2.77	2.01 / 2.67	1.97 / 2.59	1.93 / 2.51	1.89 / 2.45	1.84 / 2.35	1.79 / 2.28	1.72 / 2.15	1.67 / 2.07	1.62 / 1.98	1.56 / 1.88	1.53 / 1.82	1.47 / 1.74	1.45 / 1.69	1.40 / 1.62	1.37 / 1.56	1.35 / 1.53
80	3.96 / 6.96	3.11 / 4.88	2.72 / 4.04	2.48 / 3.56	2.33 / 3.25	2.21 / 3.04	2.12 / 2.87	2.05 / 2.74	1.99 / 2.64	1.95 / 2.55	1.91 / 2.48	1.88 / 2.41	1.82 / 2.32	1.77 / 2.24	1.70 / 2.11	1.65 / 2.03	1.60 / 1.94	1.54 / 1.84	1.51 / 1.78	1.45 / 1.70	1.42 / 1.65	1.38 / 1.57	1.35 / 1.52	1.32 / 1.49
100	3.94 / 6.90	3.09 / 4.82	2.70 / 3.98	2.46 / 3.51	2.30 / 3.20	2.19 / 2.99	2.10 / 2.82	2.03 / 2.69	1.97 / 2.59	1.92 / 2.51	1.88 / 2.43	1.85 / 2.36	1.79 / 2.26	1.75 / 2.19	1.68 / 2.06	1.63 / 1.98	1.57 / 1.89	1.51 / 1.79	1.48 / 1.73	1.42 / 1.64	1.39 / 1.59	1.34 / 1.51	1.30 / 1.46	1.28 / 1.43
125	3.92 / 6.84	3.07 / 4.78	2.68 / 3.94	2.44 / 3.47	2.29 / 3.17	2.17 / 2.95	2.08 / 2.79	2.01 / 2.65	1.95 / 2.56	1.90 / 2.47	1.86 / 2.40	1.83 / 2.33	1.77 / 2.23	1.72 / 2.15	1.65 / 2.03	1.60 / 1.94	1.55 / 1.85	1.49 / 1.75	1.45 / 1.68	1.39 / 1.59	1.36 / 1.54	1.31 / 1.46	1.27 / 1.40	1.25 / 1.37
150	3.91 / 6.81	3.06 / 4.75	2.67 / 3.91	2.43 / 3.44	2.27 / 3.14	2.16 / 2.92	2.07 / 2.76	2.00 / 2.62	1.94 / 2.53	1.89 / 2.44	1.85 / 2.37	1.82 / 2.30	1.76 / 2.20	1.71 / 2.12	1.64 / 2.00	1.59 / 1.91	1.54 / 1.83	1.47 / 1.72	1.44 / 1.66	1.37 / 1.56	1.34 / 1.51	1.29 / 1.43	1.25 / 1.37	1.22 / 1.33
200	3.89 / 6.76	3.04 / 4.71	2.65 / 3.88	2.41 / 3.41	2.26 / 3.11	2.14 / 2.90	2.05 / 2.73	1.98 / 2.60	1.92 / 2.50	1.87 / 2.41	1.83 / 2.34	1.80 / 2.28	1.74 / 2.17	1.69 / 2.09	1.62 / 1.97	1.57 / 1.88	1.52 / 1.79	1.45 / 1.69	1.42 / 1.62	1.35 / 1.53	1.32 / 1.48	1.26 / 1.39	1.22 / 1.33	1.19 / 1.28
400	3.86 / 6.70	3.02 / 4.66	2.62 / 3.83	2.39 / 3.36	2.23 / 3.06	2.12 / 2.85	2.03 / 2.69	1.96 / 2.55	1.90 / 2.46	1.85 / 2.37	1.81 / 2.29	1.78 / 2.23	1.72 / 2.12	1.67 / 2.04	1.60 / 1.92	1.54 / 1.84	1.49 / 1.74	1.42 / 1.64	1.38 / 1.57	1.32 / 1.47	1.28 / 1.42	1.22 / 1.32	1.16 / 1.24	1.13 / 1.19
1000	3.85 / 6.66	3.00 / 4.62	2.61 / 3.80	2.38 / 3.34	2.22 / 3.04	2.10 / 2.82	2.02 / 2.66	1.95 / 2.53	1.89 / 2.43	1.84 / 2.34	1.80 / 2.26	1.76 / 2.20	1.70 / 2.09	1.65 / 2.01	1.58 / 1.89	1.53 / 1.81	1.47 / 1.71	1.41 / 1.61	1.36 / 1.54	1.30 / 1.44	1.26 / 1.38	1.19 / 1.28	1.13 / 1.19	1.08 / 1.11
∞	3.84 / 6.64	2.99 / 4.60	2.60 / 3.78	2.37 / 3.32	2.21 / 3.02	2.09 / 2.80	2.01 / 2.64	1.94 / 2.51	1.88 / 2.41	1.83 / 2.32	1.79 / 2.24	1.75 / 2.18	1.69 / 2.07	1.64 / 1.99	1.57 / 1.87	1.52 / 1.79	1.46 / 1.69	1.40 / 1.59	1.35 / 1.52	1.28 / 1.41	1.24 / 1.36	1.17 / 1.25	1.11 / 1.15	1.00 / 1.00

*Table VIII is reproduced from Snedecor: *Statistical Methods,* Iowa State College Press, Ames, Iowa, by permission of the author and publisher.

TABLE IX. *Table of Four-Place Logarithms**

N	0	1	2	3	4	5	6	7	8	9	1 2 3	4 5 6	7 8 9
1.0	.0000	.0043	.0086	.0128	.0170	.0212	.0253	.0294	.0334	.0374	4 8 12	17 21 25	29 33 37
1.1	.0414	.0453	.0492	.0531	.0569	.0607	.0645	.0682	.0719	.0755	4 8 11	15 19 23	26 30 34
1.2	.0792	.0828	.0864	.0899	.0934	.0969	.1004	.1038	.1072	.1106	3 7 10	14 17 21	24 28 31
1.3	.1139	.1173	.1206	.1239	.1271	.1303	.1335	.1367	.1399	.1430	3 6 10	13 16 19	23 26 29
1.4	.1461	.1492	.1523	.1553	.1584	.1614	.1644	.1673	.1703	.1732	3 6 9	12 15 18	21 24 27
1.5	.1761	.1790	.1818	.1847	.1875	.1903	.1931	.1959	.1987	.2014	3 6 8	11 14 17	20 22 25
1.6	.2041	.2068	.2095	.2122	.2148	.2175	.2201	.2227	.2253	.2279	3 5 8	11 13 16	18 21 24
1.7	.2304	.2330	.2355	.2380	.2405	.2430	.2455	.2480	.2504	.2529	2 5 7	10 12 15	17 20 22
1.8	.2553	.2577	.2601	.2625	.2648	.2672	.2695	.2718	.2742	.2765	2 5 7	9 12 14	16 19 21
1.9	.2788	.2810	.2833	.2856	.2878	.2900	.2923	.2945	.2967	.2989	2 4 7	9 11 13	16 18 20
2.0	.3010	.3032	.3054	.3075	.3096	.3118	.3139	.3160	.3181	.3201	2 4 6	8 11 13	15 17 19
2.1	.3222	.3243	.3263	.3284	.3304	.3324	.3345	.3365	.3385	.3404	2 4 6	8 10 12	14 16 18
2.2	.3424	.3444	.3464	.3483	.3502	.3522	.3541	.3560	.3579	.3598	2 4 6	8 10 12	14 15 17
2.3	.3617	.3636	.3655	.3674	.3692	.3711	.3729	.3747	.3766	.3784	2 4 6	7 9 11	13 15 17
2.4	.3802	.3820	.3838	.3856	.3874	.3892	.3909	.3927	.3945	.3962	2 4 5	7 9 11	12 14 16
2.5	.3979	.3997	.4014	.4031	.4048	.4065	.4082	.4099	.4116	.4133	2 3 5	7 9 10	12 14 15
2.6	.4150	.4166	.4183	.4200	.4216	.4232	.4249	.4265	.4281	.4298	2 3 5	7 8 10	11 13 15
2.7	.4314	.4330	.4346	.4362	.4378	.4393	.4409	.4425	.4440	.4456	2 3 5	6 8 9	11 13 14
2.8	.4472	.4487	.4502	.4518	.4533	.4548	.4564	.4579	.4594	.4609	2 3 5	6 8 9	11 12 14
2.9	.4624	.4639	.4654	.4669	.4683	.4698	.4713	.4728	.4742	.4757	1 3 4	6 7 9	10 12 13
3.0	.4771	.4786	.4800	.4814	.4829	.4843	.4857	.4871	.4886	.4900	1 3 4	6 7 9	10 11 13
3.1	.4914	.4928	.4942	.4955	.4969	.4983	.4997	.5011	.5024	.5038	1 3 4	6 7 8	10 11 12
3.2	.5051	.5065	.5079	.5092	.5105	.5119	.5132	.5145	.5159	.5172	1 3 4	5 7 8	9 11 12
3.3	.5185	.5198	.5211	.5224	.5237	.5250	.5263	.5276	.5289	.5302	1 3 4	5 6 8	9 10 12
3.4	.5315	.5328	.5340	.5353	.5366	.5378	.5391	.5403	.5416	.5428	1 3 4	5 6 8	9 10 11
3.5	.5441	.5453	.5465	.5478	.5490	.5502	.5514	.5527	.5539	.5551	1 2 4	5 6 7	9 10 11
3.6	.5563	.5575	.5587	.5599	.5611	.5623	.5635	.5647	.5658	.5670	1 2 4	5 6 7	8 10 11
3.7	.5682	.5694	.5705	.5717	.5729	.5740	.5752	.5763	.5775	.5786	1 2 3	5 6 7	8 9 10
3.8	.5798	.5809	.5821	.5832	.5843	.5855	.5866	.5877	.5888	.5899	1 2 3	5 6 7	8 9 10
3.9	.5911	.5922	.5933	.5944	.5955	.5966	.5977	.5988	.5999	.6010	1 2 3	4 5 7	8 9 10
4.0	.6021	.6031	.6042	.6053	.6064	.6075	.6085	.6096	.6107	.6117	1 2 3	4 5 6	8 9 10
4.1	.6128	.6138	.6149	.6160	.6170	.6180	.6191	.6201	.6212	.6222	1 2 3	4 5 6	7 8 9
4.2	.6232	.6243	.6253	.6263	.6274	.6284	.6294	.6304	.6314	.6325	1 2 3	4 5 6	7 8 9
4.3	.6335	.6345	.6355	.6365	.6375	.6385	.6395	.6405	.6415	.6425	1 2 3	4 5 6	7 8 9
4.4	.6435	.6444	.6454	.6464	.6474	.6484	.6493	.6503	.6513	.6522	1 2 3	4 5 6	7 8 9
4.5	.6532	.6542	.6551	.6561	.6571	.6580	.6590	.6599	.6609	.6618	1 2 3	4 5 6	7 8 9
4.6	.6628	.6637	.6646	.6656	.6665	.6675	.6684	.6693	.6702	.6712	1 2 3	4 5 6	7 7 8
4.7	.6721	.6730	.6739	.6749	.6758	.6767	.6776	.6785	.6794	.6803	1 2 3	4 5 5	6 7 8
4.8	.6812	.6821	.6830	.6839	.6848	.6857	.6866	.6875	.6884	.6893	1 2 3	4 4 5	6 7 8
4.9	.6902	.6911	.6920	.6928	.6937	.6946	.6955	.6964	.6972	.6981	1 2 3	4 4 5	6 7 8
5.0	.6990	.6998	.7007	.7016	.7024	.7033	.7042	.7050	.7059	.7067	1 2 3	3 4 5	6 7 8
5.1	.7076	.7084	.7093	.7101	.7110	.7118	.7126	.7135	.7143	.7152	1 2 3	3 4 5	6 7 8
5.2	.7160	.7168	.7177	.7185	.7193	.7202	.7210	.7218	.7226	.7235	1 2 2	3 4 5	6 7 7
5.3	.7243	.7251	.7259	.7267	.7275	.7284	.7292	.7300	.7308	.7316	1 2 2	3 4 5	6 6 7
5.4	.7324	.7332	.7340	.7348	.7356	.7364	.7372	.7380	.7388	.7396	1 2 2	3 4 5	6 6 7

* Table IX is reprinted from D. E. Smith, W. D. Reeve, and E. L. Morss: *Elementary Mathematical Tables*, Ginn and Company, by permission of the authors and publishers.

To obtain the mantissa for a four-digit number, find in the body of the table the mantissa for the first three digits and then, neglecting the decimal point temporarily, add the number in the proportional-parts table at the right which is on the same line as the mantissa already obtained and in the column corresponding to the fourth digit.

TABLE IX. *Table of Four-Place Logarithms*—Concluded*

N	0	1	2	3	4	5	6	7	8	9	1 2 3	4 5 6	7 8 9
5.5	.7404	.7412	.7419	.7427	.7435	.7443	.7451	.7459	.7466	.7474	1 2 2	3 4 5	5 6 7
5.6	.7482	.7490	.7497	.7505	.7513	.7520	.7528	.7536	.7543	.7551	1 2 2	3 4 5	5 6 7
5.7	.7559	.7566	.7574	.7582	.7589	.7597	.7604	.7612	.7619	.7627	1 2 2	3 4 5	5 6 7
5.8	.7634	.7642	.7649	.7657	.7664	.7672	.7679	.7686	.7694	.7701	1 1 2	3 4 4	5 6 7
5.9	.7709	.7716	.7723	.7731	.7738	.7745	.7752	.7760	.7767	.7774	1 1 2	3 4 4	5 6 7
6.0	.7782	.7789	.7796	.7803	.7810	.7818	.7825	.7832	.7839	.7846	1 1 2	3 4 4	5 6 6
6.1	.7853	.7860	.7868	.7875	.7882	.7889	.7896	.7903	.7910	.7917	1 1 2	3 4 4	5 6 6
6.2	.7924	.7931	.7938	.7945	.7952	.7959	.7966	.7973	.7980	.7987	1 1 2	3 3 4	5 6 6
6.3	.7993	.8000	.8007	.8014	.8021	.8028	.8035	.8041	.8048	.8055	1 1 2	3 3 4	5 5 6
6.4	.8062	.8069	.8075	.8082	.8089	.8096	.8102	.8109	.8116	.8122	1 1 2	3 3 4	5 5 6
6.5	.8129	.8136	.8142	.8149	.8156	.8162	.8169	.8176	.8182	.8189	1 1 2	3 3 4	5 5 6
6.6	.8195	.8202	.8209	.8215	.8222	.8228	.8235	.8241	.8248	.8254	1 1 2	3 3 4	5 5 6
6.7	.8261	.8267	.8274	.8280	.8287	.8293	.8299	.8306	.8312	.8319	1 1 2	3 3 4	5 5 6
6.8	.8325	.8331	.8338	.8344	.8351	.8357	.8363	.8370	.8376	.8382	1 1 2	3 3 4	4 5 6
6.9	.8388	.8395	.8401	.8407	.8414	.8420	.8426	.8432	.8439	.8445	1 1 2	2 3 4	4 5 6
7.0	.8451	.8457	.8463	.8470	.8476	.8482	.8488	.8494	.8500	.8506	1 1 2	2 3 4	4 5 6
7.1	.8513	.8519	.8525	.8531	.8537	.8543	.8549	.8555	.8561	.8567	1 1 2	2 3 4	4 5 5
7.2	.8573	.8579	.8585	.8591	.8597	.8603	.8609	.8615	.8621	.8627	1 1 2	2 3 4	4 5 5
7.3	.8633	.8639	.8645	.8651	.8657	.8663	.8669	.8675	.8681	.8686	1 1 2	2 3 4	4 5 5
7.4	.8692	.8698	.8704	.8710	.8716	.8722	.8727	.8733	.8739	.8745	1 1 2	2 3 4	4 5 5
7.5	.8751	.8756	.8762	.8768	.8774	.8779	.8785	.8791	.8797	.8802	1 1 2	2 3 3	4 5 5
7.6	.8808	.8814	.8820	.8825	.8831	.8837	.8842	.8848	.8854	.8859	1 1 2	2 3 3	4 5 5
7.7	.8865	.8871	.8876	.8882	.8887	.8893	.8899	.8904	.8910	.8915	1 1 2	2 3 3	4 4 5
7.8	.8921	.8927	.8932	.8938	.8943	.8949	.8954	.8960	.8965	.8971	1 1 2	2 3 3	4 4 5
7.9	.8976	.8982	.8987	.8993	.8998	.9004	.9009	.9015	.9020	.9025	1 1 2	2 3 3	4 4 5
8.0	.9031	.9036	.9042	.9047	.9053	.9058	.9063	.9069	.9074	.9079	1 1 2	2 3 3	4 4 5
8.1	.9085	.9090	.9096	.9101	.9106	.9112	.9117	.9122	.9128	.9133	1 1 2	2 3 3	4 4 5
8.2	.9138	.9143	.9149	.9154	.9159	.9165	.9170	.9175	.9180	.9186	1 1 2	2 3 3	4 4 5
8.3	.9191	.9196	.9201	.9206	.9212	.9217	.9222	.9227	.9232	.9238	1 1 2	2 3 3	4 4 5
8.4	.9243	.9248	.9253	.9258	.9263	.9269	.9274	.9279	.9284	.9289	1 1 2	2 3 3	4 4 5
8.5	.9294	.9299	.9304	.9309	.9315	.9320	.9325	.9330	.9335	.9340	1 1 2	2 3 3	4 4 5
8.6	.9345	.9350	.9355	.9360	.9365	.9370	.9375	.9380	.9385	.9390	1 1 2	2 3 3	4 4 5
8.7	.9395	.9400	.9405	.9410	.9415	.9420	.9425	.9430	.9435	.9440	0 1 1	2 2 3	3 4 4
8.8	.9445	.9450	.9455	.9460	.9465	.9469	.9474	.9479	.9484	.9489	0 1 1	2 2 3	3 4 4
8.9	.9494	.9499	.9504	.9509	.9513	.9518	.9523	.9528	.9533	.9538	0 1 1	2 2 3	3 4 4
9.0	.9542	.9547	.9552	.9557	.9562	.9566	.9571	.9576	.9581	.9586	0 1 1	2 2 3	3 4 4
9.1	.9590	.9595	.9600	.9605	.9609	.9614	.9619	.9624	.9628	.9633	0 1 1	2 2 3	3 4 4
9.2	.9638	.9643	.9647	.9652	.9657	.9661	.9666	.9671	.9675	.9680	0 1 1	2 2 3	3 4 4
9.3	.9685	.9689	.9694	.9699	.9703	.9708	.9713	.9717	.9722	.9727	0 1 1	2 2 3	3 4 4
9.4	.9731	.9736	.9741	.9745	.9750	.9754	.9759	.9763	.9768	.9773	0 1 1	2 2 3	3 4 4
9.5	.9777	.9782	.9786	.9791	.9795	.9800	.9805	.9809	.9814	.9818	0 1 1	2 2 3	3 4 4
9.6	.9823	.9827	.9832	.9836	.9841	.9845	.9850	.9854	.9859	.9863	0 1 1	2 2 3	3 4 4
9.7	.9868	.9872	.9877	.9881	.9886	.9890	.9894	.9899	.9903	.9908	0 1 1	2 2 3	3 4 4
9.8	.9912	.9917	.9921	.9926	.9930	.9934	.9939	.9943	.9948	.9952	0 1 1	2 2 3	3 4 4
9.9	.9956	.9961	.9965	.9969	.9974	.9978	.9983	.9987	.9991	.9996	0 1 1	2 2 3	3 3 4

* Table IX is reprinted from D. E. Smith, W. D. Reeve, and E. L. Morss: *Elementary Mathematical Tables*, Ginn and Company, by permission of the authors and publishers.

To obtain the mantissa for a four-digit number, find in the body of the table the mantissa for the first three digits and then, neglecting the decimal point temporarily, add the number in the proportional-parts table at the right which is on the same line as the mantissa already obtained and in the column corresponding to the fourth digit.

TABLE X.   *Values of Estimated* r_t, *Based upon Pearson's "Cosine Method,"*
for Various Values of $\dfrac{bc^*}{ad}$

r_t	$\dfrac{bc}{ad}$	r_t	$\dfrac{bc}{ad}$	r_t	$\dfrac{bc}{ad}$
.00	0–1.00	.35	2.49–2.55	.70	8.50– 8.90
.01	1.01–1.03	.36	2.56–2.63	.71	8.91– 9.35
.02	1.04–1.06	.37	2.64–2.71	.72	9.36– 9.82
.03	1.07–1.08	.38	2.72–2.79	.73	9.83– 10.33
.04	1.09–1.11	.39	2.80–2.87	.74	10.34– 10.90
.05	1.12–1.14	.40	2.88–2.96	.75	10.91– 11.51
.06	1.15–1.17	.41	2.97–3.05	.76	11.52– 12.16
.07	1.18–1.20	.42	3.06–3.14	.77	12.17– 12.89
.08	1.21–1.23	.43	3.15–3.24	.78	12.90– 13.70
.09	1.24–1.27	.44	3.25–3.34	.79	13.71– 14.58
.10	1.28–1.30	.45	3.35–3.45	.80	14.59– 15.57
.11	1.31–1.33	.46	3.46–3.56	.81	15.58– 16.65
.12	1.34–1.37	.47	3.57–3.68	.82	16.66– 17.88
.13	1.38–1.40	.48	3.69–3.80	.83	17.89– 19.28
.14	1.41–1.44	.49	3.81–3.92	.84	19.29– 20.85
.15	1.45–1.48	.50	3.93–4.06	.85	20.86– 22.68
.16	1.49–1.52	.51	4.07–4.20	.86	22.69– 24.76
.17	1.53–1.56	.52	4.21–4.34	.87	24.77– 27.22
.18	1.57–1.60	.53	4.35–4.49	.88	27.23– 30.09
.19	1.61–1.64	.54	4.50–4.66	.89	30.10– 33.60
.20	1.65–1.69	.55	4.67–4.82	.90	33.61– 37.79
.21	1.70–1.73	.56	4.83–4.99	.91	37.80– 43.06
.22	1.74–1.78	.57	5.00–5.18	.92	43.07– 49.83
.23	1.79–1.83	.58	5.19–5.38	.93	49.84– 58.79
.24	1.84–1.88	.59	5.39–5.59	.94	58.80– 70.95
.25	1.89–1.93	.60	5.60–5.80	.95	70.96– 89.01
.26	1.94–1.98	.61	5.81–6.03	.96	89.02–117.54
.27	1.99–2.04	.62	6.04–6.28	.97	117.55–169.67
.28	2.05–2.10	.63	6.29–6.54	.98	169.68–293.12
.29	2.11–2.15	.64	6.55–6.81	.99	293.13–923.97
.30	2.16–2.22	.65	6.82–7.10	1.00	923.98–
.31	2.23–2.28	.66	7.11–7.42		
.32	2.29–2.34	.67	7.43–7.75		
.33	2.35–2.41	.68	7.76–8.11		
.34	2.42–2.48	.69	8.12–8.49		

* Table X is reprinted from M. D. Davidoff and H. W. Goheen, A table for the rapid determination of the tetrachoric correlation coefficient. *Psychometrika*, 1953, **18,** 115-121, by permission of the authors and the editors of *Psychometrika*.

To use the table, set the data up in a 2 × 2 table as shown in the text, Chap. 7. Enter the table with bc/ad or its reciprocal, whichever is the larger, and read the corresponding value of r_t. The accuracy of the values given for r_t does not extend beyond the second decimal, and interpolation between the values listed for bc/ad is not recommended.

TABLE XI.   *Table of* T *Scores**

PROPORTION	T SCORE	PROPORTION	T SCORE
.001	20	.540	51
.002	21	.579	52
.003	22	.618	53
.004	23	.655	54
.005	24	.692	55
.006	25	.726	56
.008	26	.758	57
.011	27	.788	58
.014	28	.816	59
.018	29	.841	60
.023	30	.864	61
.029	31	.885	62
.036	32	.903	63
.045	33	.919	64
.055	34	.933	65
.067	35	.945	66
.081	36	.955	67
.097	37	.964	68
.115	38	.971	69
.136	39	.977	70
.159	40	.982	71
.184	41	.986	72
.212	42	.989	73
.242	43	.992	74
.274	44	.994	75
.308	45	.995	76
.345	46	.996	77
.382	47	.997	78
.421	48	.998	79
.460	49	.999	80
.500	50		

* Table XI is modified from a table published by the Air Training Command in ATRC Manual 50-900-9 prepared under the direction of J. R. Berkshire.

The proportions refer to the proportion of the total frequency below a given score plus $\frac{1}{2}$ the frequency of that score. *T* scores are read directly from the given proportions.

TABLE XII. T Scores Corresponding to Ranks*

RANK	Number of Persons or Objects Ranked																																									RANK
---	5	6	7	8	9	10	11	12	13	14	15	16	17	18	19	20	21	22	23	24	25	26	27	28	29	30	31	32	33	34	35	36	37	38	39	40	41	42	43	44	45	---
1	63	64	65	65	66	66	67	67	68	68	68	69	69	69	69	70	70	70	70	70	71	71	71	71	71	71	71	72	72	72	72	72	72	72	72	72	72	73	73	73	73	1
2	55	57	58	59	60	60	61	62	62	62	63	63	64	64	64	64	65	65	65	65	66	66	66	66	66	66	67	67	67	67	67	67	67	68	68	68	68	68	68	68	68	2
3	50	52	54	55	56	57	57	58	59	59	60	60	60	61	61	62	62	62	62	63	63	63	63	63	64	64	64	64	64	64	65	65	65	65	65	65	65	66	66	66	66	3
4	45	48	50	52	53	54	55	55	56	57	57	58	58	59	59	59	60	60	60	61	61	61	61	62	62	62	62	62	62	63	63	63	63	63	63	64	64	64	64	64	64	4
5	37	43	46	48	50	51	52	53	54	55	55	56	56	57	57	58	58	58	59	59	59	59	60	60	60	60	61	61	61	61	61	62	62	62	62	62	62	62	63	63	63	5
6		36	42	45	47	49	50	51	52	53	53	54	55	55	56	56	56	57	57	57	58	58	58	59	59	59	59	59	60	60	60	60	60	61	61	61	61	61	61	62	62	6
7			35	41	44	46	48	49	50	51	52	52	53	54	54	55	55	55	56	56	56	57	57	57	58	58	58	58	59	59	59	59	59	60	60	60	60	60	60	60	61	7
8				35	40	43	45	47	48	49	50	51	51	52	53	53	54	54	55	55	55	56	56	56	56	57	57	57	57	58	58	58	58	59	59	59	59	59	59	60	60	8
9					34	40	42	45	46	47	48	49	50	51	51	52	52	53	53	54	54	54	55	55	55	56	56	56	57	57	57	57	57	58	58	58	58	58	58	59	59	9
10						34	39	42	44	45	47	48	49	49	50	51	51	52	52	53	53	53	54	54	54	55	55	55	56	56	56	56	56	57	57	57	57	57	58	58	58	10
11							33	38	41	43	45	46	47	48	49	49	50	51	51	52	52	52	53	53	54	54	54	54	55	55	55	55	56	56	56	56	57	57	57	57	57	11
12								33	38	41	43	44	45	46	47	48	49	49	50	51	51	51	52	52	53	53	53	54	54	54	54	55	55	55	55	56	56	56	56	56	57	12
13									32	38	40	42	44	45	46	47	48	48	49	49	50	50	51	51	52	52	52	53	53	53	54	54	54	54	55	55	55	55	56	56	56	13
14										32	37	40	42	43	44	45	46	47	48	48	49	50	50	50	51	51	52	52	52	53	53	53	53	54	54	54	54	55	55	55	55	14
15											32	37	40	41	43	44	45	46	47	47	48	49	49	50	50	50	51	51	52	52	52	52	53	53	53	54	54	54	54	54	55	15
16												31	36	39	41	42	44	45	45	46	47	48	48	49	49	50	50	50	51	51	51	52	52	52	53	53	53	53	54	54	54	16
17													31	36	39	41	42	43	44	45	46	47	47	48	48	49	49	50	50	50	51	51	51	52	52	52	52	53	53	53	53	17
18														31	36	38	40	42	43	44	45	46	46	47	47	48	48	49	49	50	50	50	51	51	51	52	52	52	52	53	53	18
19															31	36	38	40	41	43	44	44	45	46	46	47	48	48	48	49	49	50	50	50	51	51	51	51	52	52	52	19
20																30	35	38	40	41	42	43	44	45	46	46	47	47	48	48	49	49	49	50	50	50	51	51	51	51	52	20
21																	30	35	38	39	41	42	43	44	45	45	46	46	47	47	48	48	49	49	49	50	50	50	51	51	51	21
22																		30	35	37	39	41	42	43	44	44	45	46	46	47	47	48	48	48	49	49	49	50	50	50	51	22
23																			30	35	37	39	40	41	42	43	44	45	45	46	46	47	47	48	48	48	49	49	49	50	50	23
24																				30	34	37	39	40	41	42	43	44	44	45	46	46	47	47	47	48	48	49	49	49	49	24
25																					29	34	37	38	40	41	42	43	43	44	45	45	46	46	47	47	48	48	48	49	49	25
26																						29	34	37	38	40	41	42	43	43	44	45	45	46	46	46	47	47	48	48	48	26
27																							29	34	36	38	39	41	41	42	43	44	44	45	45	46	46	47	47	47	48	27
28																								29	34	36	38	39	40	41	42	43	43	44	45	45	46	46	46	47	47	28
29																									29	34	36	38	39	40	41	42	43	43	44	44	45	45	46	46	47	29
30																										29	33	36	38	39	40	41	42	42	43	44	44	45	45	46	46	30
31																											29	33	36	37	39	40	41	41	42	43	43	44	44	45	45	31
32																												28	33	36	37	38	40	40	41	42	42	43	43	44	44	32
33																													28	33	35	37	38	39	40	41	42	42	43	44	44	33
34																														28	33	35	37	38	39	40	41	42	42	43	43	34
35																															28	33	35	37	38	39	40	41	42	42	43	35
36																																28	33	35	37	38	39	40	41	41	42	36
37																																	28	32	35	36	38	39	40	40	41	37
38																																		28	32	35	36	38	39	40	40	38
39																																			28	32	35	36	37	38	39	39
40																																				28	32	34	36	37	38	40
41																																					28	32	34	36	37	41
42																																						27	32	34	36	42
43																																							27	32	34	43
44																																								27	32	44
45																																									27	45

This table converts rankings to a normalized standard score scale with a mean of 50 and a standard deviation of 10. To use the table, first determine the number of persons or objects ranked. Then, enter the table with the rank of the individual or object. (A rank of 3 indicates a person who is third from the top.) At the intersection of the row indicating rank, and the column indicating number of persons or objects ranked will be found the standard score. For example, the 4th person in a group of 22 would have a score of 60. While the 17th person in a group of 30 would have a score of 49.

* Table XII is reprinted from a table published by the Air Training Command in ATRC Manual 50-900-9 prepared under the direction of J. R. Berkshire.

TABLE XIII. *Values of the Rank Correlation Coefficient* r′ *at Selected Significance Points**

n	r′	p
4	1.000	.0417
5	1.000	.0083
5	.900	.0417
5	.800	.0667
5	.700	.1167
6	.943	.0083
6	.886	.0167
6	.829	.0292
6	.771	.0514
6	.657	.0875
7	.857	.0119
7	.786	.0240
7	.750	.0331
7	.714	.0440
7	.679	.0548
7	.643	.0694
7	.571	.1000
8	.810	.0108
8	.738	.0224
8	.690	.0331
8	.643	.0469
8	.619	.0550
8	.595	.0639
8	.524	.0956
9	.767	.0106
9	.700	.0210
9	.650	.0323
9	.617	.0417
9	.583	.0528
9	.550	.0656
9	.467	.1058
10	.733	.0100
10	.661	.0210
10	.612	.0324
10	.576	.0432
10	.552	.0515
10	.527	.0609
10	.442	.1021

* Values of r′ were computed from Table IV of E. G. Olds, Distributions of sums of squares of rank differences for small numbers of individuals. *Annals of Mathematical Statistics*, 1938, 9, 133–148, by permission of the author and the editors of the *Annals of Mathematical Statistics*.

The probabilities given are for a one-sided test of significance.

TABLE XIV. *The 5 (Roman Type) and 1 (Boldface Type) Percent Points for the Distribution of* W'*

m	n				
	3	4	5	6	7
3			.689	.645	.615
			.811	**.764**	**.727**
4		.591	.540	.505	.480
		.737	**.669**	**.621**	**.587**
5		.485	.442	.413	.392
		.626	**.563**	**.520**	**.488**
6		.410	.373	.349	.331
		.541	**.484**	**.445**	**.417**
8	.362	.313	.285	.266	.252
	.506	**.424**	**.376**	**.345**	**.323**
10	.292	.253	.230	.214	.203
	.416	**.347**	**.307**	**.281**	**.263**
15	.196	.170	.155	.145	.137
	.288	**.239**	**.211**	**.192**	**.179**
20	.148	.128	.117	.109	.103
	.219	**.181**	**.160**	**.146**	**.136**

* Values of W' were computed from Table II of M. Friedman, A comparison of alternative tests of significance for the problem of m rankings. *Annals of Mathematical Statistics*, 1940, 11, 86–92, by permission of the author and the editors of the *Annals of Mathematical Statistics*.

The probabilities given are for obtaining a value of W' equal to or greater than the tabled value.

For n greater than 7 and for values of m not given, the significance of W may be tested by means of the F distribution or the χ^2 distribution as described in Chap. 17.

TABLE XV. *Values of T or T', Whichever Is the Smaller, Significant at the 5 and 1 Percent Levels**

5 Percent Level

n_2 \ n_1	2	3	4	5	6	7	8	9	10	11	12	13	14	15
4			10											
5		6	11	17										
6		7	12	18	26									
7		7	13	20	27	36								
8	3	8	14	21	29	38	49							
9	3	8	15	22	31	40	51	63						
10	3	9	15	23	32	42	53	65	78					
11	4	9	16	24	34	44	55	68	81	96				
12	4	10	17	26	35	46	58	71	85	99	115			
13	4	10	18	27	37	48	60	73	88	103	119	137		
14	4	11	19	28	38	50	63	76	91	106	123	141	160	
15	4	11	20	29	40	52	65	79	94	110	127	145	164	185
16	4	12	21	31	42	54	67	82	97	114	131	150	169	
17	5	12	21	32	43	56	70	84	100	117	135	154		
18	5	13	22	33	45	58	72	87	103	121	139			
19	5	13	23	34	46	60	74	90	107	124				
20	5	14	24	35	48	62	77	93	110					
21	6	14	25	37	50	64	79	95						
22	6	15	26	38	51	66	82							
23	6	15	27	39	53	68								
24	6	16	28	40	55									
25	6	16	28	42										
26	7	17	29											
27	7	17												
28	7													

1 Percent Level

n_2 \ n_1	2	3	4	5	6	7	8	9	10	11	12	13	14	15
5				15										
6			10	16	23									
7			10	17	24	32								
8			11	17	25	34	43							
9		6	11	18	26	35	45	56						
10		6	12	19	27	37	47	58	71					
11		6	12	20	28	38	49	61	74	87				
12		7	13	21	30	40	51	63	76	90	106			
13		7	14	22	31	41	53	65	79	93	109	125		
14		7	14	22	32	43	54	67	81	96	112	129	147	
15		8	15	23	33	44	56	70	84	99	115	133	151	171
16		8	15	24	34	46	58	72	86	102	119	137	155	
17		8	16	25	36	47	60	74	89	105	122	140		
18		8	16	26	37	49	62	76	92	108	125			
19	3	9	17	27	38	50	64	78	94	111				
20	3	9	18	28	39	52	66	81	97					
21	3	9	18	29	40	53	68	83						
22	3	10	19	29	42	55	70							
23	3	10	19	30	43	57								
24	3	10	20	31	44									
25	3	11	20	32										
26	3	11	21											
27	4	11												
28	4													

* Table XV is reprinted from C. White, The use of ranks in a test of significance for comparing two treatments. *Biometrics*, 1952, 8, 33–41, by permission of the author and editors of *Biometrics*.
n_1 and n_2 are the numbers of cases in the two groups. If the groups are unequal in size, n_1 refers to the smaller.
The probabilities given are for a two-sided test of significance.

APPENDIX C

Answers to the Examples

Chapter 1

1.1 $\bar{X} = 24.0$

1.2

(a)	16.9	(f)	86.0	(j)	38.0		
(b)	17.0	(g)	9.2	(k)	3.64		
(c)	9.0	(h)	158.0	(l)	14.0		
(d)	16.5	(i)	21.25	(m)	5.0		
(e)	31.5						

1.3 $\bar{X} = 20.0$ $s^2 = 10.45$ $s = 3.23$

1.4 $Mdn = 20.12$ $Q_1 = 17.75$ $Q_3 = 22.42$

1.5 $Mdn = 21.5$ $C_{60} = 22.77$ $C_{13} = 13.84$

1.6 (a)

Section 1	Section 2
$\bar{X}_1 = 82.0$	$\bar{X}_2 = 74.0$
$AD_1 = 3.6$	$AD_2 = 5.4$
$s_1^2 = 19.7895$	$s_2^2 = 45.0526$
$s_1 = 4.45$	$s_2 = 6.71$

    (b) Section 1   (c) Section 1   (d) None

1.7
(a) x
(b) $n\bar{X}$ or $X_1 + X_2 + \cdots + X_n$
(c) $(n-1)s^2$ or $\Sigma(X - \bar{X})^2$
(d) $\Sigma X/n$
(e) x^2
(f) $\Sigma x^2/(n-1)$ or $\Sigma(X - \bar{X})^2/(n-1)$
(g) Σx^2 or $\Sigma(X - \bar{X})^2$
(h) $\bar{X}$
(i) $\sqrt{\Sigma x^2/(n-1)}$ or $\sqrt{\Sigma(X - \bar{X})^2/(n-1)}$
(j) ΣX
(k) $X - \bar{X}$
(l) s^2 or $\Sigma(X - \bar{X})^2/(n-1)$
(m) Σx or $\Sigma X - n\bar{X}$ or 0

1.8 See text, Section 1.6

1.9   Given: $D = X_1 - X_2$

Then $\Sigma D = \Sigma X_1 - \Sigma X_2$

$$\frac{\Sigma D}{n} = \frac{\Sigma X_1}{n} - \frac{\Sigma X_2}{n}$$

$$\overline{D} = \overline{X}_1 - \overline{X}_2$$

1.10 $\overline{X} = \dfrac{\Sigma X_1 + \Sigma X_2}{n_1 + n_2} = \dfrac{n_1\overline{X}_1 + n_2\overline{X}_2}{n_1 + n_2}$

1.11   (a) $\Sigma(X - \overline{X})^2 = (n - 1)s^2$

(b) $\Sigma(X - \overline{X}) = 0$

(c) $\Sigma(X - 10)/n = \overline{X} - 10$

(d) $\Sigma(X + 1)^2 = \Sigma X^2 + 2\Sigma X + n$

(e) $(X - \overline{X})^2 = X^2 - 2X\overline{X} + \overline{X}^2$

(f) $\Sigma kX = k\,\Sigma X$

1.12   See text, Section 1.12

1.13 $Mdn = 4.83$ and $s^2 = 20.32$

Chapter 2

2.1   (a) $\overline{X} = 25.0$ $\Sigma(X - \overline{X})^2 = 64.0$

(b) $\overline{X} = 22 + 21/7 = 25.00$ $\Sigma(X - \overline{X})^2 = 127 - (21)^2/7 = 64.0$

(c) $\Sigma(X - \overline{X})^2 = 4439 - (175)^2/7 = 64.0$

2.2   (a) $\overline{X} = 22.17$ and $s = 7.4$

2.3 $\overline{X} = 46.79$ $Mdn = 46.75$ $s = 5.9$

2.4 $\overline{X} = 18.1$ $Mdn = 18.7$ $s = 5.5$

2.5 $\overline{X} = 31.3$ $Mdn = 32.8$ $s = 8.2$ $C_{30} = 26.5$

2.6 $\overline{X} = 7.25$ $s = 3.1$

2.7 $\overline{X} = 72.3$ $s = 12.5$

2.8   See text, Section 2.6

2.9   See text, Section 2.5

2.10   See text, Section 2.6

2.11   See text, Section 2.7

2.12   See text, Section 2.15

2.13   Given: $X' = iX$

Then $\Sigma X' = i\,\Sigma X$

$$\frac{\Sigma X'}{ni} = \overline{X}$$

2.14   Given: $iX = X'$. From 2.13 above, we have $\overline{X}' = \Sigma X'/n = i\overline{X}$.

Then $iX - i\overline{X}$ $= X' - \overline{X}'$

$X - \overline{X}$ $= (1/i)(X' - \overline{X}')$

$\Sigma(X - \overline{X})^2 = (1/i^2)\,\Sigma(X' - \overline{X}')^2$

$= (1/i^2)(\Sigma X'^2 - (\Sigma X')^2/n)$

2.15 $\overline{X} = 3.03$ or $\overline{X} = 3.0$

2.17 (a) $i = 3$ (c)   94   (e)   90–94
      (b)   93–95   (d) $i = 5$ (f)   92

Chapter 3

3.7 $Mdn = 31.89$ $Q_1 = 24.83$ $Q_3 = 38.56$
3.8   (a)   See text, Section 3.2
      (b)   See text, Section 3.4
3.9   (a) $X \geq 66$ rounded   (c) $X \leq 60$ rounded
      (b) 50 ± 10 (d) $X \geq 30$ rounded

Chapter 4

4.1   See text, Section 4.1
4.2   See text, Section 4.1
4.3   Given: $Y = a + bz$
      Then $\Sigma Y = na + b \Sigma z$
         $\overline{Y} = a$
      because we have already proved that $\Sigma z = 0$.
      Then $Y - \overline{Y} = bz$
         $\Sigma (Y - \overline{Y})^2 = b^2 \Sigma z^2$
            $s_Y^2 = b^2$
      because we have already proved that $\Sigma z^2/(n - 1) = 1$.
4.4   (a) C_{50} (c) C_{25} (e) C_{16} (g) C_{89}
      (b) C_{77} (d) C_{33} (f) C_{85} (h) C_{99}
4.7   (a) $R = (6.1)(10) = 61$ (c)   .6826
      (b) $X = 43$ rounded   (d) $X = 50$
4.10 (a) $X = 50$ (b) $X = 30$ (c) $X = 56$ rounded
4.11 (a)   3413   (c)   5000   (e)   13
      (b)   1587   (d)   228   (f)   8185
4.12 See text, Section 4.4
4.13 See text, Section 4.4
4.14 Use $(X - 30)/5$ to transform the X values
4.15 See text, Section 4.4
4.16 $\overline{Y} = 10.0$ and $s_Y = 12.0$

Chapter 5

5.1   See text, Section 5.8
5.2   See text, Section 5.7
5.3   See text, Section 5.7
5.4   See text, Section 5.9
5.5   See text, Section 5.9
5.6 $a = 10$ and $b = -.5$

5.7 $a = 3.62$ and $b = .483$

5.9 $Y = 2X^2$

5.10 $Y = 2\dfrac{1}{\sqrt{X}}$

5.11 $Y = 2\sqrt{X}$

5.12 $Y = 2\dfrac{1}{X^2}$

5.13 If $Y = a10^{bX}$, then $\log Y = \log a + bX$, and the plot of Y against X on semilogarithmic paper should be linear.

5.14 If $Y = aX^b$, then $\log Y = \log a + b \log X$, and the plot of Y against X on logarithmic paper should be linear.

5.15 If $Y = a + b \log X$, then the plot of Y against X on semilogarithmic paper should be linear.

5.16 See text, Section 5.9

Chapter 6

6.1 $r = .94$ **6.4** $r = -.86$ **6.7** $r = .99$

6.2 $r = .71$ **6.5** $r = .89$ **6.8** $r = .12$

6.3 $r = .92$ **6.6** $b_Y = 1.00$ and $b_X = .79$ **6.9** $r = .73$

6.10 $b_Y = .58$ (a) 56   (b) 60   (c) 70   (d) 76   (e) 80

6.11 $b_X = .93$ (a) 58   (b) 70   (c) 75   (d) 78   (e) 92

6.12 $s_{Y \cdot X} = 6.90$ and $s_{X \cdot Y} = 8.75$

6.13 See text, Section 6.10

6.14 See text, Section 6.7

6.15 See text, Section 6.8

6.16 See text, Section 6.9

6.17 $r = -.59$

6.18 See text, Section 6.3

6.19 See text, Section 6.7

6.20 See text, Section 6.9

6.21 Using (6.4), the numerator of the correlation coefficient will be $\Sigma\, x(y - \tilde{y}) = \Sigma\, xy - \Sigma\, x\tilde{y}$. But $\tilde{y} = bx$. Then $\Sigma\, x(y - \tilde{y}) = \Sigma\, xy - b \Sigma\, x^2$. We have $b = \Sigma\, xy/\Sigma\, x^2$. Thus

$$\Sigma\, x(y - \tilde{y}) = \Sigma\, xy - \Sigma\, xy = 0$$

6.22 We have $\Sigma (z_X - z_Y)^2/(n - 1) = 2(1 - r)$. Because $\Sigma (z_X - z_Y)^2/(n - 1) \geq 0$, we must have $r \leq 1.0$. Similarly, $\Sigma (z_X + z_Y)^2/(n - 1) = 2(1 + r)$. Because $\Sigma (z_X + z_Y)^2/(n - 1) \geq 0$, we must have $r \geq -1.0$.

6.23 $r = .30$

6.24 $b_X = .75$

6.25 See text, Section 6.7

6.26 See text, Section 6.8
6.27 See text, Section 6.8
6.28 See text, Section 6.10
6.29 $s_D^2 = 1$

Chapter 7

7.1 $r_b = .36$	**7.5** $r_\phi = .20$	**7.9** $r_t = .34$	**7.13** $r_{pb} = .25$	
7.2 $r' = .13$	**7.6** $\eta_{YX} = .41$	**7.10** $r' = .27$	**7.14** $\eta_{YX} = .83$	
7.3 $r_\phi = .41$	**7.7** $\eta_{YX} = .82$	**7.11** $r_\phi = .41$	**7.15** $r_\phi = .30$	
7.4 $r_b = -.09$	**7.8** $r_t = .57$	**7.12** $r_{pb} = .56$	**7.16** $r_\phi = .42$	

7.17 We are given

$$r_{pb} = \frac{n \sum Y_1 - n_1 \sum Y}{\sqrt{(n_0 n_1)[n \sum Y^2 - (\sum Y)^2]}}$$

Dividing both numerator and denominator by nn_1, we obtain

$$r_{pb} = \frac{\bar{Y}_1 - \bar{Y}}{\sqrt{\dfrac{n_0}{n_1}} \sqrt{\dfrac{\sum y^2}{n}}}$$

Multiplying both numerator and denominator of the above expression by $\sqrt{p} = \sqrt{n_1/n}$, we have

$$r_{pb} = \frac{\bar{Y}_1 - \bar{Y} \sqrt{p}}{\sqrt{\dfrac{\sum y^2}{n}} \sqrt{q}}$$

We know (see Section 7.4) that r_{pb} multiplied by $\sqrt{pq}/y_p$ is equal to r_b. Then, multiplying the above expression for r_{pb} by $\sqrt{pq}/y_p$ gives

$$r_b = \frac{\bar{Y}_1 - \bar{Y}}{\sqrt{\dfrac{\sum y^2}{n}}} \left(\frac{p}{y_p}\right)$$

7.18 (a) $\bar{X} = 8$ (b) $\sum (X - \bar{X})^2 = 280$

Chapter 8

8.1 In addition to S and $\emptyset$, we have

$\{e_1\}$	$\{e_1, e_2\}$	$\{e_1, e_2, e_3\}$
$\{e_2\}$	$\{e_1, e_3\}$	$\{e_1, e_2, e_4\}$
$\{e_3\}$	$\{e_1, e_4\}$	$\{e_1, e_3, e_4\}$
$\{e_4\}$	$\{e_2, e_3\}$	$\{e_2, e_3, e_4\}$
	$\{e_2, e_4\}$	
	$\{e_3, e_4\}$	

8.2   (a) $\{1, 2, 3, 4, 5, 6\}$
    (b) $\{1, 2, 3, 5, 6, 7, 8\}$
    (c) $\{1, 2, 3, 8, 9\}$
    (d) $\{3\}$
    (e) $\{1, 3\}$
    (f) $\{\emptyset\}$
    (g) $\{1, 3, 4, 5, 6, 7, 8\}$
    (h) $\{3, 4, 5, 6, 8, 9\}$
    (i) $\{1, 3, 5, 6, 7, 8, 9\}$

    (j) $\{3, 5, 6\}$
    (k) $\{\emptyset\}$
    (l) $\{8\}$
    (m) $\{1, 2, 3, 4, 5, 6, 7, 8\}$
    (n) $\{1, 3, 4, 5, 6, 7, 8, 9\}$
    (o) $\{1, 3\}$
    (p) $\{1, 2, 3, 5, 6\}$
    (q) $\{1, 3\}$

8.3   (a) $P = 30/36$
    (b) $P = 3/36$
    (c) $P = 9/36$
    (d) $P = 6/36$

    (e) $P = 6/36$
    (f) $P = 3/36$
    (g) $P = 6/36$
    (h) $P = 34/36$

8.4   (a) $\mu_X = .5$ and $\sigma_X^2 = .25$
    (b) $\mu_Y = .7$ and $\sigma_Y^2 = .21$
    (c) $\mu_T = 1.2$
    (d) $\sigma_T^2 = .46$

    (e) $\mu_D = -.2$
    (f) $\sigma_D^2 = .46$
    (g) $E(XY) = .35$

8.5   (a)

Outcomes	P
T	1/2
HT	1/4
HHT	1/8
$HHHT$	1/16
$HHHHT$	1/32
$HHHHH$	1/32

    (b) $\mu_X = 1.9375$ and $\sigma_X^2 = 1.4336$

8.6 $\mu_X = 1.0$ and $\sigma_X^2 = 1.0$

8.7   We have the following 2×2 table:

	B	$\bar{B}$	
A	$P(A \cap B)$	$P(A \cap \bar{B})$	$P(A)$
$\bar{A}$	$P(\bar{A} \cap B)$	$P(\bar{A} \cap \bar{B})$	$P(\bar{A})$
	$P(B)$	$P(\bar{B})$	

We know that $P(A) = P(A \cap B) + P(A \cap \bar{B})$ so that $P(A \cap \bar{B})$ $= P(A) - P(A \cap B)$. Given that $P(A \cap B) = P(A)P(B)$, we have

$$P(A \cap \bar{B}) = P(A) - P(A)P(B)$$
$$= P(A)[1 - P(B)]$$
$$= P(A)P(\bar{B})$$

which proves that A and $\bar{B}$ are independent. We also have

$$P(\bar{A} \cap \bar{B}) = P(\bar{B}) - P(A \cap \bar{B})$$

But we have just proved that $P(A \cap \bar{B}) = P(A)P(\bar{B})$. Thus

$$\begin{aligned} P(\bar{A} \cap \bar{B}) &= P(\bar{B}) - P(A)P(\bar{B}) \\ &= P(\bar{B})[1 - P(A)] \\ &= P(\bar{B})P(\bar{A}) \end{aligned}$$

which proves that $\bar{B}$ and $\bar{A}$ are independent. Similarly, it can be shown that $P(\bar{A} \cap B) = P(\bar{A})P(B)$.

8.8   (a) $P = 3/8$ (e) $P = 4/8$
    (b) $P = 7/8$ (f) $P = 4/8$
    (c) $P = 4/8$ (g) $P = 2/8$
    (d) $P = 6/8$ (h) $P = 2/6$

8.9   We have $E(X - \mu)^2 = E(X^2 - 2\mu X + \mu^2)$
$$\begin{aligned} &= E(X^2) - 2\mu E(X) + \mu^2 \\ &= E(X^2) - \mu^2 \end{aligned}$$

8.10   (a) $P = 8/15$ (d) $P = 3/5$
    (b) $P = 2/3$ (e) $P = 3/4$
    (c) $P = 2/5$

8.11   (a) $P = 1/52$ (d) $P = 1/4$ (g) $P = 1/13$
    (b) $P = 1/4$ (e) $P = 1/13$ (h) $P = 1/2$
    (c) $P = 1/13$ (f) $P = 1/2$ (i) $P = 1/13$

8.12   (b) $P = 1/2$ (d) $P = 1/3$
    (c) $P = 2/3$ (e) $P = 0$

8.13   (a) $P = 1/10$ (e) $P = 1/3$
    (b) $P = 1/5$ (f) $P = 4/5$
    (c) $P = 3/10$ (g) $P = 3/5$
    (d) $P = 1/4$

8.14   (a) $P = 1/10$ (d) $P = 3/10$
    (b) $P = 8/10$ (e) $P = 6/10$
    (c) $P = 4/10$

Chapter 9

9.1   (a) $P = 1/4096 = .0002$
    (b) $P = 220/4096 = .0537$
    (c) $P = 299/4096 = .0730$

9.2   (a) $P = .0007$ (b) $P = .0532$ (c) $P = .0749$

9.3 $P = .0401$

9.4 (a) 15   (c) 153

(b) $P = .0392$

(d) $\dfrac{18!}{4!14!}\left(\dfrac{1}{3}\right)^{14}\left(\dfrac{2}{3}\right)^{4}$

9.5 (a) $P = 26/32 = .8125$ (b) $P = 10/32 = .3125$

9.6 (a) $P = 1/4096 = .0002$ (b) $P = 19/4096 = .0046$

9.7 (a) $P = 1/256 = .0039$ (b) $P = 37/256 = .1445$

9.8 (a) 84   (b) 20   (c) $P = 20/84 = .2381$

9.9 (a) 252   (b) $P = 1/252 = .004$

9.10 $\mu_T = 50$ and $\sigma_T^{2} = 25$

9.11 (a) 35   (b) $z = 4.45, P < .0001$

9.12 (a) 34 rounded   (b) $\sigma_T^{2} = 17.25$ (c) $z = 1.93, P = .0268$

9.13 $z = 1.64, P = .0505$

9.14 $(1/3)^5 + 5(1/3)^4(2/3) + 10(1/3)^3(2/3)^2 + 10(1/3)^2(2/3)^3 + 5(1/3)(2/3)^4$
$+ (2/3)^5$

9.15 (a) $T_0 = 18$ (b) $P = .54$

9.16 $P = 90/1024 = .088$

9.17 $E(T) = 12(1/6) = 2$ and $E(X - \mu_T)^2 = 12(1/6)(5/6) = 5/3$

9.18 (a) $P = 10/216 = .0463$ (c) $P = .0430$

(b) $P = 20/216 = .0926$ (d) $P = .0885$

9.19 (a) $P = 6/10$ (b) $P = 3/10$ (c) $P = 9/10$

9.20 The total number of possible samples is $_NC_n$. If a specified element is in the sample, then the remaining $n - 1$ elements can be selected in $_{N-1}C_{n-1}$ ways. Then, the desired probability is given by

$$\frac{_{N-1}C_{n-1}}{_NC_n} = \frac{n}{N}$$

9.21 $E(X) = 144/120 = 1.2$ and $E(X - \mu_X)^2 = .56$

9.22 (a) $P = .3413$ (d) $P = .0126$ (g) $P = .9544$

(b) $P = .6826$ (e) $P = .0500$ (h) $P = .1012$

(c) $P = .1000$ (f) $P = .0098$ (i) $P = .2384$

9.23 $P = 90/243 = .37$

9.24 $P = 6/10$ for each player.

Chapter 10

10.1 (a) $F = 1.05$, d.f. $= 6$ and 6

(b) $t = 3.60$, d.f. $= 12$

10.2 (a) $F = 2.66$, d.f. $= 38$ and 39

(b) $t = 5.94$, d.f. $= 72$

10.3 (a) $F = 1.11$, d.f. $= 199$ and 199

(b) $t = 4.55$, d.f. $= 398$

10.4 (a) $t = 2.33$, d.f. $= 18$

10.5 (a) $F = 2.51$, d.f. $= 19$ and 9
      (b) $t = 5.03$, d.f. $= 28$
10.6 (a) $18.27 \leq \mu \leq 26.53$
      (b) $20.42 \leq \mu \leq 24.38$
10.7 (a) $F = 1.38$, d.f. $= 19$ and 19
      (b) $t = 2.88$, d.f. $= 38$
10.8 $t = 1.86$, d.f. $= 9$
10.9 $t = 8.10$, d.f. $= 7$
10.10 $t = 2.55$, d.f. $= 9$
10.11 $t = 2.11$, d.f. $= 19$
10.12 $t = 2.72$, d.f. $= 8$
10.14 If $n = n_1 + n_2$, then $1/n_1 + 1/n_2 = n/n_1 n_2$ and the standard error of the difference between the two means will be at a minimum when $n_1 n_2$ is at its maximum. Expansion of $(n_1 - n_2)^2$ shows that $n_1 n_2$ is at its maximum when $n_1 = n_2$.

Chapter 11

11.1 $n = 90$
11.2 $n = 110$
11.3 (a) $\sigma^2 = 10.08$ (b) $n = 27$ (c) $n = 9$
11.4 (a) -3.92 and 3.92 (b) $P = .323$

Chapter 12

12.1 (a) $r = .82$ and $.63 \leq \rho \leq .92$
      (b) $r_1 = .876$ and $r_2 = .899$; $z = .25$
      (c) $b_Y = 1.03$, d.f. $= 23$, $t = 6.9$
      (d) $b_{Y_1} = 1.06$ and $b_{Y_2} = .94$; $s_{Y \cdot X}^2 = 2.03$; $t = .51$, d.f. $= 21$
12.2 From Table VI, $P < .01$
12.3 From Table VI, No
12.4 From Table VI, $r = .28$
12.5 We can write (12.9) as

$$\frac{\sum xy \sqrt{\sum x^2}}{\sum x^2} \bigg/ \sqrt{\left(\sum y^2 - \frac{(\sum xy)^2}{\sum x^2}\right) \bigg/ (n - 2)}$$

but $\sum x^2 = \sqrt{\sum x^2} \sqrt{\sum x^2}$. Substituting with this identity in the above expression and multiplying both numerator and denominator by $1/\sqrt{\sum y^2}$, we obtain (12.1).
12.6 (a) Yes, according to Table VI
      (b) Yes, according to Table VI
      (c) $z = 1.34$
      (d) $t = .95$, d.f. $= 48$

12.7 $z = .88$
12.8 $z = .68$
12.9   (a) $r = .735$ (b) $r = .245$ (c) $r = .510$

Chapter 13

13.1   (a) $F = 1.10$, d.f. $= 4$ and 20 (b) No
13.2 $F = 3.25$, d.f. $= 4$ and 35
13.3   (a) $t = 2.99$ (b) $F = 8.95$
13.4 $F = 11.79$, d.f. $= 3$ and 36
13.5   (a) $\bar{X}_{2\cdot} - \bar{X}_{3\cdot}$, $t = 4.62$
           $\bar{X}_{3\cdot} - \bar{X}_{4\cdot}$, $t = -4.10$
           (b) $t = 5.0$
13.6   See text, Section 7.7
13.7   For the case of two groups, we have

$$\sum_{1}^{k} n(\bar{X}_{k\cdot} - \bar{X}_{\cdot\cdot})^2 = \frac{(\sum X_{1\cdot})^2}{n} + \frac{(\sum X_{2\cdot})^2}{n} - \frac{(\sum X_{1\cdot} + \sum X_{2\cdot})^2}{2n}$$

Multiply the numerator and denominator of the first two terms on the right by 2 so that all terms have a common denominator of $2n$. Expanding the numerator of the last term on the right, we have

$$(\sum X_{1\cdot} + \sum X_{2\cdot})^2 = (\sum X_{1\cdot})^2 + (\sum X_{2\cdot})^2 + 2(\sum X_{1\cdot})(\sum X_{2\cdot})$$

Substituting with this identity and simplifying, we obtain

$$\sum_{1}^{k} n(\bar{X}_{k\cdot} - \bar{X}_{\cdot\cdot})^2 = \frac{(\sum X_{1\cdot})^2 + (\sum X_{2\cdot})^2 - 2(\sum X_{1\cdot})(\sum X_{2\cdot})}{2n}$$

$$= \frac{(\sum X_{1\cdot} - \sum X_{2\cdot})^2}{2n}$$

13.8   We have

$$t^2 = \frac{(\bar{X}_{1\cdot} - \bar{X}_{2\cdot})^2}{\dfrac{2s^2}{n}}$$

$$= \frac{\dfrac{1}{2n}(\sum X_{1\cdot} - \sum X_{2\cdot})^2}{s^2}$$

We proved in Example 13.7 that the numerator of the above expression is the treatment sum of squares with 1 d.f. and the numerator is therefore MS_T. We have previously proved that $s^2 = MS_W$. Therefore $t^2 = MS_T/MS_W = F$.

Chapter 14

14.1

Source of Variation	F	d.f.
A	11.78	1 and 16
B	2.95	1 and 16
A × B	—	1 and 16

14.2

Source of Variation	F	d.f.
A	7.93	1 and 36
B	21.00	1 and 36
A × B	—	1 and 36

14.3

Source of Variation	F	d.f.
A	1.35	2 and 81
B	5.40	2 and 81
A × B	22.94	4 and 81

14.4   (a)   See text, Section 14.4
(b)   See text, Section 14.5

14.5   (a)

Comparison	F	d.f.
1	2.02	1 and 81
2	—	1 and 81
3	8.10	1 and 81
4	2.70	1 and 81
5	4.05	1 and 81
6	5.40	1 and 81
7	66.12	1 and 81
8	16.19	1 and 81

(b)   Comparisons 1 and 2
(c)   Comparisons 3 and 4
(d)   Comparisons 5, 6, 7, and 8

14.7   (a)

Comparison	F	d.f.
1	3.81	1 and 36
2	—	1 and 36
3	1.49	1 and 36
4	4.46	1 and 36
5	20.10	1 and 36
6	1.43	1 and 36
7	1.43	1 and 36
8	9.64	1 and 36

(b)   Using the S-method we have $t' = 4.20$ and therefore $F' = t'^2 = 17.64$. The only comparison for which $F > F'$ is Comparison 5.

Chapter 15

15.1   (a) $F = MS_T/MS_{ST}$ $= 19.31$ d.f. $= 2$ and 8
    (b) $F = MS_{D_1}/MS_{ST}$ $= 9.66$ d.f. $= 1$ and 8
         $F = MS_{D_2}/MS_{ST}$ $= 28.97$ d.f. $= 1$ and 8

15.2   (a) $F = MS_T/MS_{ST}$ $= 98.44$ d.f. $= 3$ and 12
    (b) $F = MS_{D_1}/MS_{ST}$ $= 294.55$ d.f. $= 1$ and 12
         $F = MS_{D_2}/MS_{ST}$ $= -$ d.f. $= 1$ and 12

15.3   (a) $F = MS_A/MS_{S(A)}$ $= 43.35$ d.f. $= 1$ and 18
         $F = MS_T/MS_{S(A)T}$ $= 17.41$ d.f. $= 5$ and 90
         $F = MS_{AT}/MS_{S(A)T}$ $= 1.59$ d.f. $= 5$ and 90
    (b) $F = MS_{D_1}/MS_{S(A)T}$ $= 84.05$ d.f. $= 1$ and 90
         $F = MS_{D_2}/MS_{S(A)T}$ $= -$ d.f. $= 1$ and 90
    (c) $F = MS_{D_1(A \times T)}/MS_{S(A)T}$ $= 3.88$ d.f. $= 1$ and 90
    (d) $F = MS_{D_2(A \times T)}/MS_{S(A)T}$ $= 1.53$ d.f. $= 1$ and 90

15.4   See text, Section 15.5
15.5   Because we have $t - 1 = 2$ d.f., the sum of the linear and quadratic components must be equal to the treatment sum of squares. Because the linear component is obviously equal to zero, the quadratic component must be equal to the treatment sum of squares.

Chapter 16

16.1 $\chi^2 = 11.21$, d.f. $= 1$ **16.5** $\chi^2 = 64.50$, d.f. $= 4$
16.2 $\chi^2 = 3.76$, d.f. $= 1$ **16.6** $\chi^2 = 18.89$, d.f. $= 2$
16.3 $\chi^2 = 4.51$, d.f. $= 1$ **16.7** $\chi^2 = 12.25$, d.f. $= 1$
16.4 $\chi^2 = 14.00$, d.f. $= 2$ **16.8** $\chi^2 = 8.76$, d.f. $= 2$

16.9 $\chi^2 = 2.02$, d.f. $= 1$

16.10 $\chi^2 = 11.28$, d.f. $= 1$

16.11 $\chi^2 = 3.86$, d.f. $= 1$

16.12 $\chi^2 = 5.15$, d.f. $= 3$

16.13 $\chi^2 = 53.38$, d.f. $= 5$

16.14 $\chi^2 = 23.64$, d.f. $= 1$

16.15 $\chi^2 = 4.90$, d.f. $= 1$

Chapter 17

17.1 (a) $W = .762$ and $W' = .752$

(b) From Table XIV, $P < .01$

(c) $r_{tt} = .84$

17.2 (a) $W = .554$

(b) $\chi^2 = 38.81$, d.f. $= 10$

(c) $r_{tt} = .87$ (d) $\bar{r}' = .48$ (e) $r_{tt} = .87$

17.3 (a) $r_{12}' = .81$, $r_{13}' = .65$, $r_{23}' = .82$

(b) $W = .838$

(c) $\chi_r^2 = 60.37$, d.f. $= 24$

(d) $\bar{r}' = .76$

17.4 (a) $r_{12}' = .80$, $r_{13}' = .89$, $r_{23}' = .70$, $r_{45}' = .79$

(b) $W = .696$

(c) $\chi_r^2 = 45.23$, d.f. $= 13$

(d) $r_{tt} = .89$

17.5 (a) $r' = .91$ (b) From Table VI, $P < .01$

17.6 (a) $W = .559$ (b) $\chi_r^2 = 22.36$, d.f. $= 5$

17.7 (b) From Table XV, $P < .01$ for $T = 56.5$

(c) $z = -3.667$

(d) $z^2 = 13.45$ and $H = 13.44$

17.8 (b) From Table XV, $P > .05$ for $T = 99$

17.9 $z = 1.77$

17.10 $H = 21.97$, d.f. $= 3$

17.11 $H = 4.46$, d.f. $= 2$

17.12 (a) $W = .076$ and $W_c = .194$

(b) $\chi_{r_c}^2 = 7.76$, d.f. $= 10$ and $\chi_r^2 = 3.04$, d.f. $= 10$

17.13 $r' = .921$ and $r_c' = .917$

17.14 Let $n = N$ so that $\mu = (n + 1)/2$ and $\sigma^2 = (n^2 - 1)/12$. We have

$$\chi_r^2 = \frac{(n - 1) \text{ Column sum of squares}}{(n^3 - n)/12}$$

$$= \frac{\dfrac{n - 1}{n} \, m \sum_{1}^{n} (\bar{X}_{\cdot n} - \mu)^2}{\sigma^2}$$

and taking the expectation of the above expression, we have

$$E(\chi^2) = \frac{\left(\dfrac{n-1}{n}\right)mn\dfrac{\sigma^2}{m}}{\sigma^2} = n - 1$$

17.15 If both the numerator and denominator of the right side of (17.14) are multiplied by m, then it is obvious that $\chi_r^2 = m(n-1)W$.

17.16 Substituting with an identity in (17.28), we have

$$H = \frac{\displaystyle\sum_1^k \frac{T_k^2}{n_k} - \frac{n(n+1)^2}{4}}{(n^3 - n)/12(n-1)}$$

$$= \frac{12}{n(n+1)}\left(\sum_1^k \frac{T_k^2}{n_k} - \frac{n(n+1)^2}{4}\right)$$

$$= \frac{12}{n(n+1)}\left(\sum_1^k \frac{T_k^2}{n_k}\right) - 3(n+1)$$

which completes the proof.

17.17 See text, Section 17.2

Index of Names

Subject Index

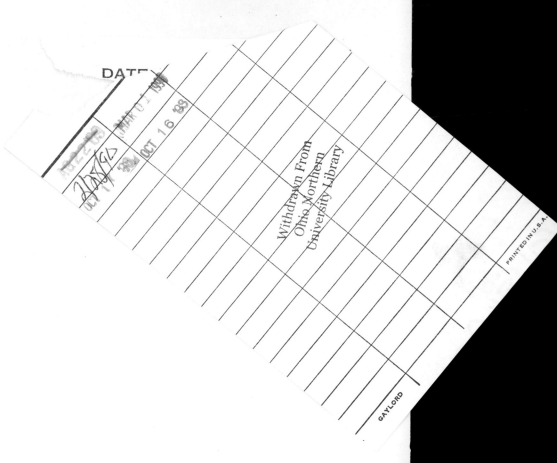